AL STEWART
THE TRUE LIFE ADVENTURES OF
A FOLK ROCK TROUBADOUR

Neville Judd

Helter
Skelter
publishing

Published 2005 by Helter Skelter Publishing,
Southbank House, Black Prince Rd, London SE1 7SJ.
First edition published by Helter Skelter Publishing in 2002.

Copyright © 2002 and 2005 Neville Judd

For copyright of lyrics quoted in the book, see page 363

A CIP record for this book is available from the British Library

ISBN 1-900924-76-5

CONTENTS

Only two albums whose roots lay in the legendary London folk scene of the mid sixties ever made the American Top Thirty.

This is the true story of the person that made them both.

For Poppet

This book could not have been written without the help of many people.

Al, thank you for your time, patience and use of the guestroom!

I would especially like to express my gratitude to –

Jonny and Abi Kremer, whose help and encouragement has meant a great deal to me.
Joan and Basil, who could not have been kinder or more generous with their time
or cups of tea!
Luke O'Reilly, whose precise memory and disarming honesty revolutionised
the project.
Peter White, who never complained, as time after time he was cajoled into "another
Al interview" in houses and hotel rooms around the world.
Steve Chapman, who knows full well how helpful he has been for the past 15 years
and who took the risk of sending me Al's complete cuttings collection.
And Joan, James, JoJo, Percy, Lizzie and Daisy…my American family.

I was also helped very much by –

Ian Anderson
Tori Amos
Randall Armor
Bill Ashton
Basia
Bena
Sean Body
David Bowie
Jo Brooks
Julia Creasey
Chris Desmond
Dave and Jilly
Kim Dyer
Karl Dallas
Linda Fitzgerald Moore
Michael Fagrey
Mike Flicker
Robert Fripp
Colin Harper
Harry and Carol
Mike Heatley
Marie Heldzingen
Maggie Holland
Joan Holliday
Hazel and John
Bert Jansch
Ed de Joy
Krysia
Robin Lamble

Nigel and Angie Lendon
Mandi
Pete Morgan
Ralph McTell
Russ Martin
Dave Nachmanoff
New York City
Yoko Ono
Chris Owen
Dennis Overstreet
Jimmy Page
Alan Parsons
Judith Piepe
Tim Renwick
Right Angle
Pete Smith
Starbucks
Daisy Stewart
Kris Stewart
Violet Stewart
Richard Thompson
Jerry Trehayne
Caroline Walker
Mary Wedgbury
Louis Weiner
Geoff Westwood
Dave Woodfield
Adam Yurman

ABOUT THE AUTHOR

Neville Judd, Union Square, New York City 2005.

Neville Judd has previously contributed to biographies and articles on David Bowie. His influences are Thomas Hardy, Italo Calvino, Stevie Smith and Frasier Crane.

1945

In which Al is born in Glasgow and after a dismal few years at public school finds himself in Bournemouth with his Hofner Colorama guitar in the last days before Beatlemania.

"I was a post-war baby in a small Scots town,
I was three years old, when we moved down south,
Hard times written in my Mother's looks,
With her widow's pension and her ration book."

Al – "This is exactly what happened. I was that small child!"

Hollywood. February 1977. Al is driving down Sunset Strip towards the Rainbow Bar and Grill. It is early afternoon and he is on his way to a breakfast meeting with his manager Luke. He turns on the radio and "Year Of The Cat" is playing. He tunes in to another station and hears the same song. It has been like this for a month now. But it had been a lifetime coming. As the bright LA sun beats down, his mind drifts back to how all of this came to be.

Alastair Ian Stewart was born in the middle of a balmy Scottish night on September 5th 1945 in Glasgow. The small nursing home that would be Al and his mother Joan's home for the next two weeks provided ample time for her to think back over the course of her life so far and the tragic series of events that had left her widowed and living with relatives beside the Clyde. Joan's had been an extraordinary life in many ways. Her own introduction to music had come through her father who had been a professional trumpet player in many of the dance bands of the big band era. He played for Jack Hilton, Jack Payne, Harry Davison and also at the opening of The London Casino giving Joan a true musical lineage.

Joan takes up the story – "I was born in Northamptonshire in a small village called Yardley Hastings near Northampton and at that time my father had just come back from the army in the First World War. He was actually playing at the Opera House in Northampton when I was born and shortly after this we went to Scarborough where we lived for five years. He played in a dance band in the pavilion on the front at Scarborough. That's where I went to school and when the Pavilion was closed down and turned into an ice rink he got a job in Glasgow playing in the Opera House there."

Joan went to school in Glasgow for about eighteen months and then moved from there to London in 1935, living in South Kensington. From here her father went out and played for West End shows, broadcasting and recording with many of the top bands up until the outbreak of the Second World War. The family unit by now included Joan's younger sister Hazel.

Hazel – "We were now living in Chelsea and our father came home one afternoon and said that he'd bought a sweet shop! This sounded fun to the rest of us but really wasn't something that our mother wanted to do but for the next fifteen years she had to run it!"

The small shop, at 58 New Kings Road, was named 'Eve Underwood' after Joan's mother.

Joan – "When we had the Munich Crisis Dad said 'Out of London' because the war was going to be too dangerous. So my sister Hazel and I were sent back to Yardley to stay with an aunt in 1938 whilst Dad stayed behind in London. However the thing that troubled me most was that I wouldn't be able to see my boyfriend of the time because he was staying in London and I would be miles away out in the country!"

Hazel clearly remembers being at their grandparents' house in Yardley Hastings listening to the radio broadcast that announced the outbreak of WW2.

Joan had by now got herself a job in a Northampton hat shop having trained as a milliner in London. By this time her father was living in Liverpool having joined The Liverpool Philharmonic Orchestra and could only occasionally return to London.

Joan – "Because my mother was all alone our father had bought the sweet shop in Fulham just before the war as a hobby for her really. When the war started in 1939 I was in the hat shop and the children were all evacuated from London and my sister Hazel was taken in locally to me as an evacuee. Then my father said he didn't even want my mother in London with a war on and so she too came to live in Yardley Hastings with this aunt and we all lived there for a year or so."

With the outbreak of war and the resulting conscription Joan had to make some big decisions – "Big decisions indeed. I had to join either the army, navy, airforce or the nursing service. Hazel wasn't called up because she was too young. She was at the village school by then. With my mother with us somehow our shop in London was kept going. My father stayed down there and in fact he stayed all through the war and was one of only four trumpeters in London so you can imagine how much work he was offered! He really had a terrific amount to do because all of the others had left town and he was too old to be called up."

When he wasn't doing gigs he was fire watching and although much of the family home above the sweetshop became blitzed he stayed there all through the war.

Joan – "He wouldn't leave his fire watching post. We had an old Scottie dog that Dad ended up living with in one room in this blitzed house – the rest of it was destroyed. To see that happen to our home was truly heartbreaking."

By now Joan had opted for the nursing service.

"I didn't fancy the army, navy or airforce – that didn't seem to be my style at all and so I decided that I would do nursing and had fifteen months intensive training and then we were cast onto the poor, unsuspecting patients."

The training was at The Bromsgrove Emergency Hospital that was attached to a mental unit.

"At night we had to lock ourselves away in case any of the mental patients escaped. One night one of them did while I was on night duty. I had some fun then I can tell you trying to protect the patients from this man that was on the loose!"

In 1941 Joan was transferred to the cottage hospital at Stratford upon Avon which, like all of the hospitals during the war, had a huge emergency wing built on to it. The nurses from Coventry and Warwick who were bombed out of their hospitals were now working there too.

Joan – "They mainly staffed the emergency room but I was a nursing trainee. We had a lot of the crashed air crews, the RAF boys, who used to come in and it was at a time when they'd just started experimenting with skin grafting and we used to have to rebuild their faces. I worked in the theatre there for quite a while."

The distance between Yardley Hastings and Stratford meant that during these early war years the two Underwood sisters saw less of each other than at any other time in their lives.

The long hours worked at the cottage hospital under the shadow of WW2 were something that Joan found hard to wind down from. But the regime there was sufficiently relaxed to allow a piano in the staff quarters and it was to there that Joan would retire at the end of a long day and play topical songs for both herself and colleagues. Some of her happiest moments of WW2 would be spent relaxing with her fellow nurses on dark evenings around that piano in the nursing quarters at Stratford upon Avon. It was now, in the bleak mid-war years of 1942, that Joan's life was about to change forever.

Joan – "Our hospital at Stratford had the most wonderful community spirit and a super matron that we all adored. There were only about sixteen nurses in the cottage hospital and we were all nurses in training. We'd also got to know some of the local airforce boys by then because there was a big airforce station nearby at Wellesbourne."

On Christmas Eve the matron called all of the nurses in and told them: "You girls should entertain your gentlemen friends. I'll open up the office and you can have the use of it for the week and I'll provide food and drink and you can invite your friends in because I would love to meet them."

Joan again – "She was that sort of person – she looked after her girls and they had to have the right sort of friends. So anyway, in came two RAF boys, I didn't know either of them as I hadn't been out with any RAF chaps before. I can remember sitting on the arm of the settee and from then on Alastair would always say 'I can see you now sitting there and swinging your leg, smiling and saying "hello, would you like some trifle?"' Later on he told me 'You didn't know it but trifle was my favourite food and I warmed to you from the first moment.'

We talked for a little while and before he left he told his friend 'That's the girl I'm going to marry.'

We had had our old gramophone going playing Glenn Miller and we entertained them that Christmas Eve and before he left Alastair said to me 'I'd like to see you again, would you like to come to the cinema one night?' The cinema was only about three doors away from the hospital and so I said 'Oh yes that would be fine' but it took him two years to persuade me to marry him! There was a line in a song that was featured in a film we went to see at this time that went 'It can't be wrong, it must be right.' Alastair had kept on singing it to me saying 'You know its right don't you? You know that you've got to marry me, don't you? You know that we're made for each other don't you?' And I'd reply 'Oh no, I don't want to marry anyone, I'm not going to get married, I'm never going to be married, I'm going to be a nurse'."

But after two years Alastair broke down Joan's resistance and they got married.

Joan – "We got married in Greenock, Scotland in the local parish church in a wedding dress I'd made myself and then we went off to Edinburgh on honeymoon."

The wedding itself was, it being the war, a very simple affair. Joan had two bridesmaids, her sister Hazel and best friend Pam.

"All through the war I remained at Stratford Hospital and Alastair was at Wellesbourne, just up the road from us, where he completed two tours of operations which was all that was required of anyone."

Greenock, 1944

Joan and Alastair now settled in Stratford, taking a small house at 4 Narrow Lane as their married home together. Back in London Joan's father was still living a life of constant danger amongst the air raids and explosions as he made his way each day around town. Joan would occasionally visit him there and could inspect the damage for herself.

"There was a hole outside our house that you could get two London buses in. All the gas mains and water mains went. Nothing got repaired properly until after the war, everything was literally falling to bits. Daddy was living in this one back room. I once went back with my husband Alastair to London to see one of Daddy's shows during the war and it was absolutely terrifying. He took us to a restaurant for lunch and there were these doodlebugs coming over. Dad, who was a very calm sort of man, said 'Oh, it will be alright – you don't have to worry until you hear the engine cut out!'

Alastair and I were sitting there in that restaurant absolutely shaking with fright because we weren't used to air raids like that. But my father was so used to them that they weren't bothering him anymore."

Joan's husband had by now risen to the rank of second in command at his R.A.F. Station.

"By the time Alastair went on the last flights, which he should never have gone on, he was doing all the instructing at the base. But a friend of his, Colin, someone whom Alastair had always flown with as a navigator, asked him to fly. This friend was a pilot with him in The Pathfinders, (the group that led all of the other planes to the towns that they were bombing) and he'd explained to Alastair how he wanted to go on 'one last important mission' and how he wouldn't fly with any other navigator other than my husband. So Alastair said he would go back because he'd promised his great friend Colin he would."

Up until this time Alastair and his young wife had believed that they both had a very good chance of getting through the war without injury. They often discussed this as the war turned more and more in the Allies' favour.

"Before we had married he'd said to me that I wasn't to worry because he'd done his whole tour of operations and that he should now get through the war as it was pretty safe. He had had some near misses of course, a bar of chocolate saving him once!"

But their good luck was not to last and tragedy lay in wait for them.

On March 11th 1945 Joan had been spending a rare day with her parents and sister at the house in Narrow Lane. Hazel had taken the branch line train there from nearby Honeybourne where she had been spending the last few months with an aunt. Through much of those war months Joan had been on her own as her husband had been confined to his base and so she looked forward to these times when her family would visit.

Into this world of contented domesticity rode the telegram boy with the news that any family dreaded.

Joan – "Alastair had been killed. He had gone back on what he had promised me would be just one last trip in that March of 1945. In fact we were never told exactly what happened but what we do know is that his plane exploded in mid-air and all ten boys on board were killed."

Alastair was just a few weeks short of his twenty fifth birthday when he died. Three nurses from Joan's hospital were also widowed by the same crash.

"When he died, which was a pretty grim period as you can imagine, I was three months pregnant with Al and it was then that I remembered one of the last things he had said to me which was 'Don't worry, I'm sure I'm going to come through this because there's no danger in this particular tour of Ops and if anything should happen to me my father will look after you.'

So then I had no option but to go up and live with Grandpa Stewart in Greenock because I hadn't got anywhere else to go. If I hadn't been pregnant I would have gone back to the hospital and carried on with my career there because I loved nursing so much. I was dedicated to it but there was no option because in those days if you were married you weren't allowed to work."

It was therefore with an overwhelming sense of loss and bewilderment that Joan made

73, Union Street, Greenock. Al's first home.

plans to leave Stratford.

"I think one of the biggest wrenches was leaving the girls at Stratford hospital because there were only sixteen of us and we were like a family. We had all gone through so much together."

Joan still meets up with many of them once a year.

She spent part of the spring of 1945 back with her parents in London before getting the train up to Glasgow where she was due to have Al.

Soon after she arrived at her new home at 73 Union Street, Greenock the war ended.

In Greenock she lived with her father in law. Grandpa Stewart was a stern and distant man who worked everyday at the Clydesdale and North of Scotland Bank in Glasgow.

Joan – "When I first moved up there he had a housekeeper who'd worked for him since his wife had died tragically in childbirth when my husband Alastair was a young boy and so Grandpa Stewart had lost both his wife and his second son and had really been a widower all of his life. But when I went to live with him he decided that he felt that he didn't really need a housekeeper any more and that we could manage on our own. I was glad of something to do quite honestly. It was a huge house, absolutely enormous and so I took on all of the housekeeping, I did all of the cooking and cleaning. It was rather marvellous really because there I was all alone in the world except for Grandpa Stewart with whom there was both an age and culture gap."

Grandfather Stewart in his office at the Bank

These were difficult times for Joan as she came to terms with the restrictions that life at the Stewart's brought with it. It bears repeating that she was a young woman of only twenty five at the time, recently bereaved after less than a year of marriage and now living apart from most of her family in a house imbued with its extreme sense of Victorian morality.

"Dear old Grandpa, he was a very strict Presbyterian Victorian Scot and he was absolutely rigid in all of his outlook, views and opinions and I didn't really know what I was going into at all. I'd never really met anyone like that before – it was incredible. I committed so many sins unknowingly, for instance talking to anyone of the opposite sex. It was a truly shattering experience to me."

Another example of how controlling Grandpa Stewart was to Joan was demonstrated when one of Alastair's airforce colleagues called on her one day in Greenock unexpectedly and after a brief supper was escorted to the nearest train station in pouring rain by Mr. Stewart! Such claustrophobic control was born out of his belief that the widow of an officer and a gentleman should be seen to have virtually no personal life whatsoever. And so Joan spent the summer of 1945 virtually exiled in Glasgow awaiting her baby's arrival.

"I was in the nursing home for a fortnight before Al was born, in the early hours of the morning on September 5th 1945. I stayed on there for two weeks afterwards because it had been a very difficult birth."

Initially life in Scotland wasn't too bad for Joan and the young Al.

"Living right on the Clyde I used to take my Alastair down to the promenade and although parts of Greenock were industrial where we lived it was very nice, as you could see right across the river to Dunoon. I had this wonderful friend there, who I'm still in touch with, called Irene Gatherer, who used to work in Grandpa's bank. He had introduced me to her thinking that she would be a suitable companion and she remained by my side the whole time and was the most wonderful friend."

It is clear that Joan's time in Greenock would have been all but impossible without her friendship with Irene. With their babies tucked up in prams they did the shopping, visited the doctors' surgery and made the best of those post war years.

Hazel – "We would all escape the house by doing things like riding up and down the Clyde on the McBrains Ferry where we could forget about everything for an afternoon."

Joan now had everything materially that she needed but it had come at a price.

"We certainly weren't poor, as my husband had left me several thousand pounds which is more than most people had. However I can clearly remember one year when Christmas came and I was in the local grocers. In those days everything was rationed but the lady in the store very kindly told me 'We're letting each of our customers have a bottle of whisky this Christmas.' I thought great and took the bottle of whisky home. When Grandpa Stewart saw the bottle of whisky he exploded in an absolute fury saying 'How dare you bring alcohol into this house?'

He informed me in no uncertain terms terms that I had committed what amounted to an unforgiveable sin in his eyes! This iron rule was fast becoming too much for me and I was very glad when my sister came up to Greenock soon afterwards."

By now it was January 1949 and Al was three years old. Joan explained the situation to her sister who had in fact already decided that something had to be done to rescue Joan from this most restricting of domestic situations.

Hazel now took charge of the situation by getting the train up to Greenock and confronting her sister about the role that she had allowed herself to assume in Scotland.

Joan – "To be honest I had been thinking that myself just lately. Although it had of course been kind of Grandpa Stewart to have kept me and not to have been charging me any keep and to have paid for the nursing home and things like that it really was time for me to move on."

Joan was missing England and her family too much to stay on any longer and along with Hazel had decided that it was time for direct action given that it was ridiculous for Grandpa Stewart to expect his daughter-in-law to continue living out a virtually friendless

Al at "Tadpoles Cottage"

and despondent life hundreds of miles from most of her family.

Hazel – "It wasn't until I got up to Greenock that I realised how awful life up there was for my sister. I had visited her there shortly after she had had Al but it wasn't until this later visit that I saw it all for what it was. She was in a terrible state. It was as if she was living in a Jane Austen novel except that it was raining all of the time!"

Joan – "So Hazel virtually told me that I was to go in and tell Grandpa Stewart that I was going back to England and that of course I would be taking Al with me. I went in and I was shaking like a leaf because I really was scared of him but I managed to tell him that I really would like to go back to England. He was quite nice about it actually and he said that he knew I would one day go back and that he quite understood. He even offered to help me to find somewhere to live which surprised me and was very nice of him."

Joan and Al left Scotland shortly after for London and a family home still in ruins in Chelsea's New Kings Road. The house at this stage was virtually derelict as the bomb damage reports had been submitted but the money to finance the rebuilding was yet to come through. The precarious nature of the structure was made all too apparent by what was to happen one evening a few weeks later.

Joan – "One morning I was in the house still sound asleep at 6am when the ceiling came down, smashing all of the furniture in what was a quite old fashioned building with heavy ceilings made of thick plaster. I got up and there was my silhouette left on the bed and so I'd somehow been protected. Luckily Al had been asleep in another room in a cot. If he'd been in the room with me he would definitely have been killed."

Both Joan and Al were much happier in London than they had been in Scotland. The experience of living in Scotland had changed Joan and she was determined to forge a life for herself that for the time being wasn't dependent on anyone else. The house above the shop in Parsons Green wouldn't be her home for long though however. She was more content there than she had been in Glasgow and still remembers much of what went on.

Joan – "At this time the sweetshop was still in the premises below and Al used to run into the shop there and say to my mother 'Granny, can I have some money?' When he was told that she didn't have any to give away he'd say 'Yes you have, there's a drawer full of money!', pointing to the till. He was always full of fun. He was a truly happy little boy!"

Soon after this Joan and Al moved up to Stratford where they stayed with a friend of

Joan

"Tadpoles Cottage" 1949

Joan's in The School House in Church Street, Weston Subedge. After a short time they moved on to Tadpoles Cottage in Chapel Lane, Mickleton which they would now rent for a couple of years. Grandpa Stewart remained unimpressed throughout all this time however, coming down to stay on a couple of occasions and expressing his undiluted horror at the slum that he considered the four hundred years old cottage to be.

Joan – "However I thought it was beautiful, it was all black and white beams and those in the bedroom came right down and you had to duck right under them. It had a wonderful garden too. Grandpa Stewart's idea of a house was a stately home and he used to say that he wasn't going to have his grandson brought up in a cottage!"

Home movie footage of this time shows it to be a beautiful and substantial house with a large garden and stream; clearly not a slum. It's still there today and so Grandpa Stewart's reservations are most easily explained away as being motivated more by prejudice than fact. Joan remembers the time that she and Al spent here with clarity and affection and although bringing up a child on her own in England in the late 1940s wasn't easy their domestic circumstances were most certainly not the hand to mouth existence that they are sometimes portrayed as being.

'Hard times written in my mother's looks, with her widow's pension and her ration books.'

This was Al's revisionist take on his childhood in the 1973 song "Post World War Two Blues" featured on the album *Past, Present And Future*. Joan has always thought this to be too harsh a picture of their life together there however.

Al's first school was a small private establishment in Stratford called The Croft House. He hated it and would regularly return home from the school complaining about the events of the day to his mother.

Joan

Al in London, 1948

Joan – "Al was forever telling me how he felt frustrated there and he did come to hate his teachers with a passion. This was a source of great worry to me naturally enough but yes, from day one, Al hated school."

These teachers would in turn eventually seek Joan out to discuss Al's rebellious and disruptive behaviour that had begun to cause serious problems. Whenever he was told to leave the classroom he would walk up and down the short corridor outside singing at the top of his voice.

The family had by now once again moved house to what would be Al's fifth home in as many years.

Joan – "By this time we were living in a house on the top of a hill at Wilmcote. Here the atmosphere was fresh and pure. Grandpa Stewart liked it because it was somewhere where his grandson could breathe proper air."

But it was not the home that Joan had envisaged for herself.

London, 1949

Wilmcote, 1952

Joan – "Certainly not! My father in law had found this house and decided that it was where I ought to live. But I didn't want to live there. I wanted to live in Stratford because that was where Al's father and I had decided that we were going to have our nice modest little house together. But when I put this to Grandpa Stewart he said that his grandson – '...wasn't going to live in a town and breathe in all of those awful fumes, he's got to live on the top of a hill'.

"This put us five miles out of Stratford which meant that I had to make that journey with Al in and out of school everyday. We would cycle the mile down to the station, get on the train to Stratford and then walk to school at the other end. I would then come home returning to collect Al later on in the afternoon by cycling back up the hill from Wilmcote station with shopping on the front of the bike and Al on the back more often than not moaning about his day at school. But we managed somehow. But that was Grandpa Stewart. If we'd lived in Stratford we could have walked to school and it would have been so much easier for both Al and I."

Following The Croft Al next attended the Berowne prep school on the Birmingham Road in Stratford, a private establishment, somewhat in the mould of his first school. At the end of the day he would return to a home that was more often that not filled with the sound of music.

Joan – "All through this time I continued to play the piano on a daily basis. I would also sing around the house of course. During our time at Wilmcote I also belonged to the local choral society and in fact by the age of two Al had started to hum along to entire sections of Handel's *Messiah* which he would have heard me playing. Once, when he'd heard Caruso singing on one of the choral society's records, he asked me why the man was crying? So he was paying close attention to the music even in those very early days."

These were difficult times for Joan, a single mother, doing her best to provide for the two of them at Wilmcote. Hazel was acutely aware of the financial restraints that her elder sister was under at this time.

Hazel – "Very much so. These were very tough times for Joan. She was finding it very hard buying Wilmcote on her widows pension and Al was a real handful at this time and basically he needed a father around."

It was now, at Wilmcote, that Al first began to read. He also demonstrated that his ability to commit to memory long passages of someone else's work wasn't limited to classical music. He would spend weekends memorising entire passages from children's books and also the poetry of Robert Louis Stevenson.

Joan – "Together Al and I would listen to shows on our radio such as *Educating Archie* and *Take It From Here*. He also really loved *The Goon Show* and *Life With The Lyons*."

Al would also devour comics and whilst he loved *The Dandy* and *The Beano* perhaps his favourite piece of literature was *Thomas The Tank Engine*.

Through all this time though Joan never saw Al demonstrate any particular skills or interest in playing an instrument. It's perfectly clear when she's asked to talk about Al's early musical leanings that there simply were none at this moment in time.

Joan – "I must say that I didn't think at the time there was anything musically special about Al despite the fact that I'd always sung a lot to him. I can't say that he showed any real interest in music at that time. He was just a normal little boy really, quite normal. He didn't keep asking me to teach him how to play the piano or anything like that even though it would have been a perfectly logical thing for him to do given the amount of music that there was around the house."

Al was sent away to boarding school at Wycliffe College which is in Stonehouse, Gloucestershire in 1955. The stories about Al and Wycliffe are numerous and all in various ways misleading. Certainly he was a highly intelligent pupil who for much of the time there worked very hard but the open hostility that he eventually encountered from some of the masters, his almost total lack of interest in the classroom ethic and the sense of rebellion that his later love of skiffle fostered, all conspired to make his years there very difficult. The bleak and troubled life at boarding school that he wrote about in the song "Love Chronicles" barely scratched the surface of what must have seemed like a prison sentence.

Things didn't start too well when he lost a tooth whilst playing ghosts almost straight away!

Someone who was there at boarding school with Al was Jerry Trehayne who remembers much of what actually went on – "There were bits of life at Wycliffe that were actually a lot of fun but much of the tougher side was seen as character building. Much of it was based around the outdoor life and sports, which Al absolutely hated! I remember on Sunday evenings one of the old boys would come and give a lecture on climbing or how to survive an avalanche in the Himalayas or something like that. The Headmaster also gave a talk once about a trip he made with some of the school to Switzerland. He'd show slides and maps. This was all part of the school's ethos. We were all encouraged to explore the local countryside on our bicycles, visiting Roman villas and old churches and having picnics together."

Al has characterised this time in his life as "Prayers, Hymns, Latin and Running!"

Al – "Because that's what it was. I can still now hear all of those hymns spinning around inside my head. Every morning we would have to sing them. I hated it."

It was now in 1956 that Joan married her long time companion Basil, who she had first met in Parsons Green at Hazel's twenty-first birthday party. She sold the house in

Wilmcote and together she and Basil took on the tenancy of an English pub in the small Cotswold village of Beckford. Their life together at The Beckford appears to have been full of incident on a daily basis. Staff, such as a mad, alcoholic, ex-army bar manager and his replacement, straight out of prison, added to the rigours of making a go of things in the tiny village. After a short time they informed Dairs, the brewery, that they were going to move on. After a brief exploration of what premises Bexhill on Sea had to offer they arrived in Bournemouth where they had the pick of over 30 premises through Rumsey & Rumsey agents. They eventually elected to take on a small café opposite a village green called The Buttery, remembered by Al primarily for its freshly baked jam doughnuts and its table tennis table.

Al was a popular pupil at Wycliffe by all accounts, with a highly developed sense of humour and a love of rock 'n' roll that had been sustained by two possessions that he had with him – a small radio on which he would listen to Radio Luxembourg late into the night after lights out and his acoustic guitar which had been branded "an immoral instrument" by the Headmaster long before Al was discovered to own such a thing. It was shortly after the family had moved to Bournemouth that Al bought his first musical instrument and it took a great deal of convincing to get his parents to advance him the fifteen shillings to buy it. The object of such importance was the guitar that he had spotted in Minn's Music Shop in Bournemouth. Within a week he had mastered, on his own, all of the chords to play such classics as Lonnie Donegan's "Rock Island Line". Al became obsessed by skiffle. This resulted in his first ever original composition, a three-chord skiffle tune that he called "Lay Your Bones Down Jones". In fact, such was this passion for skiffle that his parents queued up one evening at the stage door of the Bournemouth Pavilion Theatre to get Lonnie Donegan's autograph for him.

Back at Wycliffe Al would bribe the college matrons into hiding the guitar amongst piles of sheets in the college laundry. Whether it was as a consequence of giving the other boys simple guitar lessons between classes or the occasional clandestine rehearsals of his embryonic first group, The Snowballs, Al's ownership of the said immoral instrument (an *electric guitar* that is) was soon revealed and he was forced to resort to leaving it under the care and protection of Stonehouse Railway Station's left luggage room. There it would stay until it would be liberated by Al for sixpence a day whereupon he would play it for an hour or so in the adjoining fields. It was here, in those Gloucestershire fields, that he polished up his first songs.

Al did in fact also have *acoustic guitar* lessons there at Wycliffe from a master in the evenings. It wasn't part of the curriculum but he was definitely having *special tuition* there. This was because he was the only person in Wycliffe that wanted to learn the guitar, the only one.

In small school exercise books Al had also now begun to write his own nonsense verse. His source of inspiration to do this was primarily the author Edward Lear whose *The Nonsense Omnibus* had fired Al's idling imagination that, up until he discovered Lear, had been all but extinguished at Wycliffe. It was also the source of many of the characters that would crop up in those first fumbling attempts at original prose in his school exercise books. Besides these works of fantasy, Al started keeping what amounted to a journal of criticism of his work in which he would detail thoughts on the way his writing to date was progressing. Looking back over these very early pieces of original verse he took stock of his writing style thus far and on March 14th 1962 he wrote in his journal "Towards the end of 1960 I began, upon impulse, to churn out yards of comic and curious verse, writing it down in a book. The urge to create verse lasted less than a year in that form, mainly because I discovered something else which gave me much more pleasure still. I had always had an interest in music, and so naturally, at the beginning of the year 1961, my musical and versifying ability met. Looking back on the result, 'Lay Your Bones Down Jones', I can't honestly say it is a musical gem but it gave me a lot of pleasure at the time and paved the way for the first stage of my songwritership. During that year I wrote some half-a-dozen other songs, without taking it seriously, and then at the end of that year I entered my second stage, and started turning out many songs each month, largely because of the success of one of my numbers, 'So I Keep Walkin' which was the first of my own songs I had ever performed in public, and which duly won me an encore and a great deal of self confidence at its launching, the 18th of December 1961. Since then I have doubled my number of songs written, and keep adding more all the time. My personal favourite is 'A Tribute to Philip' but the most popular generally seems to be 'Why' and 'Kolei Valley'. I may give up song writing, but this book should prove interesting to look back on, anyway."

On November 30th 1960, in one of the exercise books, Al had written "Awurgle The Ghol".

AWURGLE THE GHOL
As the story tells us,
Awurgle was a ghol.
Softly in the Limpell,
You could hear him troll.
"Wurglie" loved a Grenkleen
Whose hair was sky blue pink:
"She's my Solomoah!"
That's what he said; I think.

Every day at sunset (on Sunday?)
He'd sing a plurrick song,
Underneath the window,
Of her homely Dong
At midnight he would hear her
As she softly spoke:
"Take your R.B. music,
And jump into the lake!"

One day in the street he
Saw her with a poon
Red with rage he gronkled
Like Shillklifs on the moon
He quickly drew his dagger
And with a rumblous sniff
Plunged the dreadful weapon
Into the Poon's midriff

Now in jail he's moaning
For the love he's lost
They're hanging him tomorrow
In the Grellish Grost
The Grenckeen didn't love him
That's a fact that's clear
For while he walked on to his doom,
She got drunk on beer.

The moral of the story
Is look before you leap.
And if you can in future
Liten in your sleep
If you hear a gurgle, A whimper or a moan
It's only poor Awurgle In the ghostly Ghône.

He followed this remarkable piece of comedic verse with a short entry in the style of a journal. "The next poem is not exactly nonsense – in fact it was written in a dark and doomy mood at about the same time as 'Awurgle the Ghol'. It illustrates the horror of blindth, although this may be metaphorical, for most people are really blind to the real beauties and 'exiguities' of life, although their actual vision is not impaired in any way. The poem may be taken metaphorically or 'literally' as I shall not worry anyway."

"Disturbed sheep never count a loss of a Poon".
POONERY
"by me"
From the flickering eastern shores
To the prison's bolted doors
Every man and child alive
Be he three or ninety-five
Has, at some time in his life,
(With his mother, son or wife)
Seen a glitter on the moon,
And thought what on earth's a poon?

A Poon is something creepy,
Which attacks you when you're sleepy.
And is something like a gheik
Which itself is quite a freak
If you meet it in the night
It can give you quite a fright
For it Greckles loud and clear
As it guzzles down its beer

In concluding I must say
Rather quickly, if I may
That to help a weary Poon,
Is a well-deserving boon
And you may find when you wake up
That your mother's special make-up
Has been smeared upon the floor
By someone you never saw
If you do then do not swear
(at least not when granny's there)
But instead cry out like goons
That you love all gheiks and Poons!?

Life was pretty hard on Al even when lessons for the day ended because of his relationship with Mr Payne, his housemaster. Unfortunately for Al the person who hated the guitar more than anyone else in the entire school was Payne who along with his wife and family lived in the same house as Al.

Jerry Trehayne again – "Al was forever being called into Di Payne's study for whatever reason. I don't think anybody else would be able to help with any actual facts because a lot of these battles went on directly between the two of them. It was a head to head situation and I don't think that the rest of us as boys were probably fully aware of what was going on. Al represented everything that Di Payne was against. He wasn't a particularly happy man anyway. He was very bitter about how his sports career as a rugby player had been cut short by him losing a leg in the Second World War and his family life was quite traumatic too, there were always huge domestic rows that we boys could hear coming from the Payne's quarters. He seemed to be losing control of his family and was quite possibly overcompensating with this strict doctrine in his role as Housemaster. Al came to symbolise all that was wrong in this free New World to Di Payne".

Chris Owen – "I was there in *School House* with Al at this time. The whole Wycliffe agenda was based around a pre-War ethos with its feet firmly placed in the days of the British Empire. So for Al to come up against someone like Di Payne, who was very much into early morning runs and also cold showers, it was all very hard. We would all get up at the crack of dawn and the house would go out on these freezing runs across the countryside."

Certainly Di Payne got on much worse with Al than he did with any of the other boys in School House. This was down to the fact that Al and Al alone questioned Payne's authority.

In January '61 Al wrote "At a Lear Party "and "The Wondrous Chase".

AT A "LEAR" PARTY

The Dong was there, the wonderful Dong,
The Dong with the luminous nose
And over in the corner was
The Pobble who has no toes
And all the folk of the Didjery Dee
To the Akond of Swat and the Plum pudding flea
Had come from lands across the sea
To the land where the Bong-tree grows
They'd come from the great Gromboolian plain
And from lands both far and few
To attend a party in Bong-tree Glane
The Quangle-Wangle too
And everyone from the Jumblie race
To the runcible cat with a crimson face
Had come to this weird and wonderful place
To play at Shullie-Dooh

"And Now the time has come," they cried
"To play at everything
Let the Quangle-Wangle play his harp
And the Owl and the pussy-cat sing"
Up stepped the Yonghy-Bonghy-Bo
Who said, "I cannot sing I know,
But I'll conduct this plurrick show
And make the slowe-bells ring"

And so they danced the whole night through
In the land where the Bong tree grows
And everyone was happy except
The Pobble who has no toes
For he said "My Aunt Jobiska thinks
That life's a game of tiddly-winks
And doesn't like the astersphinx
Except upon her nose."

And so as the angry Jamhan howled
He heard the Nimmak hum
And everybody knew at once
The Cummerbund was come
And the Attery Squash and the Bisky Bat
Fled to the Quangle-Wangle's hat,
And the cummerbund said, "Fancy that",
And at them – every one!
Now awful darkness and silence reign
Over the great Gromboolian plain
And Skillklifs scream in terrible pain
The whole of the long night through
And all melodious is the sound
Of the Cummerbund as it turns around
And softly paws the grisly ground
Where the cauliflower once grew.

Al – "I think my aunt Hazel used to like Edward Lear. She was the artistic one in the family. She was forever reading things like that. I liked Lewis Carroll too. I think it might have been as simple as the fact that we had the collective poems of Edward Lear in a great big fat book in the house so that would have been something – it was just there and so you could read the story of the four little children who went round the world or whatever it is. Well Guy Slingsby and Violet of course."

THE WONDROUS CHASE
(THE CHILLINOCK CURSES)
Over the grooby hills and away
The flying Chillinok went
Tearing across the scroobious vale
With its garters buckled and bent.
For leven pobbles and poons by the score
And cummerbunds forever more
And come from the hills of the Chankly Bore
To follow the Chillinok's scent
And on the moon, at the hour of dawn
They started this wondrous chase
But the Chillinok run fast and strong
At a right meloobious pace
And the jam-trees sang in chorus sweet
As the angry chillinok trod on their feet
"See how the Cummerbunds run thro' the wheat
In this hour of dark disgrace"

And all the folk of the Didjery Dee
Had come to watch that day
Dongs and bongs and the plum-pudding flea
And the Churkle who never could stay
And some of the better ones joined in the hunt
And all made their way with a hiss or grunt
To the Poons and the Pobbles and Gheiks up in front
To hear what they had to say.

Said a Poon, "We all know well enough
That the Chillinoks legs are plenty
But when he set off he had twenty-one
And now he has only twenty!
And all the world at once did cry
"We'll catch Mr Chilly and 'till we die,
We'll live forever on Chillinok pie!
Boiled and pickled and scenty!"
And seven times around the world,
The Chillinok was chased,
And when he was caught, everyone said,
"Oh, how nice he will taste. "
"Shall we eat him cooked or raw?
On a plate or off the floor?

And when he's gone shall we ask for more?
Or make some Chillinok paste?
And while they were thinking what to do,
The Chillinok slunk away
And nobody ever saw him again
For a year, and a month, and a day
And as he vanished into the night
The Polbost said with gruncip bright
"If he dies, it will serve him right?!"
So think you what you may (Snarl!))?!!?

The moral of this story is
To beware of the scent of the Bong
For in chasing poor Chillinoks scroobiously
It's certain that you're doing wrong.
So go on your way with a leap and a bound,
And for fear of what's tracking you, never look round
Till you come to the land of the twice gruling sound
Then put back your head and cry "Dong."

Some music was tolerated at Wycliffe though, where the annual production of a Gilbert and Sullivan operetta was one of the highlights of the school year. Put on by the senior school, with costumes and professional lighting, the rest of the school all duly trooped along to the theatre to see it. An early Al appearance on stage there was, however, not in a musical or even a Gilbert and Sullivan show. It was in a school production of *Robin Hood.*

The school magazine *The Star* duly reported – "The production adequately performed by Peter Bagely, Robert Orm, Alastair Stewart and Steven Green."

It was Al's first ever review.

The line in "Love Chronicles" that refers to cross country running is based on fact. The boys would all head out through the farms behind the school and then up a very steep hill called Dove Row, over some sizeable Cotswold stone walls at the top and then back down the side of the hill and across ploughed fields back to Wycliffe. This was in all weathers through the winter and so most of this route would have been an absolute quagmire. Although there wasn't a locked school gate or high walls, going into the village wasn't something that anyone did very much – making life at the school very isolated.

Jerry Trehayne – "You just lived your life on the campus. I remember the house we lived in literally abutted the road through the middle of Stonehouse, if we had our windows open we could hear the conversations of people walking by in the street below. In summer we'd sit with the windows ajar trading insults with the local lads as they passed by – the people out there in the real world! It was quite tough sometimes, once I remember hearing Eden Kane singing "Well I Ask You" booming across the town from the local fun fair which of course was strictly off limits to all of us boys. Music wasn't just important to Al. It was an incredible time for all of us. We were all very aware of who Elvis Presley was and this is a measure of how liberal in many ways the school became that once on one of the Sunday evening film shows there was this huge concession and we were shown *Jailhouse Rock*! Normally we'd had to wait for the long school holidays to see anything like that."

Jerry was in the perfect position to put Al's actions at school into a wider context.

"What it comes down to is that my friend Al was the only one of us that got near to forming a skiffle group there. We certainly did call it 'skiffle' then rather than rock 'n' roll. I used to help Al carry his electric guitar on the Pine Express train from Bournemouth West Station, which was usually full of people from the Midlands as that was where it had originated from. We'd sit there on our trips to and from Stonehouse in train carriages full of holidaymakers. In fact at the bottom of the garden of one of our school houses, The Grove, was a small fence and below that was the railway line and some of us spent quite a lot of time just sitting there collecting train numbers. There sometimes wasn't really that much to do in our spare time."

In many ways it's very easy to understand where the school was coming from. Founded in the early years of this century by the Siblys, a family of staunch Wesleyan Methodists, with close ties to the armed services, the 1950s were still times when such institutions were coming to terms with the challenges the post-war years were throwing up and having a budding Elvis/Lonnie Donegan rebel influencing the other boys was definitely something that they found hard to deal with. The school had grown considerably since it was first acquired as a large country house and the many house blocks where the boys lived were all dotted around the school's substantial grounds. There was an internal school hierarchy with head boys, prefects and head of houses and so discipline was very much in evidence all of the time. Much of the recreation was school organised, there was no television, but radios were tolerated and in the senior schoolhouse there was a record player, which was a real centre for the boys. Situated in a poky little room downstairs it also housed the lockers in which the personal belongings of the pupils, including their 78s, could be secreted away.

It would be another five years before Al discovered Tolkein but the vocabulary and use of metre he now employed in "Far Underground" not only anticipated "The Elf" but also showed the delight that he felt for language was there at age 16 when he was writing purely for his own satisfaction. There is no doubt that this form of escapism was one of his prime preoccupations through 1961 and served him not only as an outlet for a stifled and frustrated imagination but enabled him to carve out a style all of his own during this time at Wycliffe.

On May 3rd '61, when Al wrote "Far Underground", he first made use of that metre which would serve him so well when it came to the composition of his lyrics.

FAR UNDERGROUND
(or a recipe for growing lentil soup)

Far underground the creatures stay
Who never see the light of day
They grin; I hear them grin
Their gobbled feet reflect their mind
Which, looking closely, one may find
Toothlessly within.

Fat black lips with dripping slubber
Rolling eyes in seething blubber
Gush unceasing ooze.
Smooth white bellies, cold and round
Slide about with slopping sound
Full of horrid stews

Grissley Sockets, bare of eyes
Stare ahead in mild surprise
Fearlessly renowned.
Furrowed flesh in crab-like cramp
These, of all things bear the stamp
Of Creatures underground.
(possibly loathsome)

At the back of his mind there was *definitely* a thought that someone else would one day look back over these juvenile sketches as part of a wider review of his work.

Writing in the journal on November 2nd 1961 he declares – "Well, summer's been and gone, and I reckon it must be six months since I last wrote in this book, leastwise my dates tell me so. This next bit, from 'Quentin Crumpleton's Diary', gets away from the sheer, unrestrained adventures into fancy which produced Awurgle, and his companions from the land where the Bong-tree grows, and yet is not quite sane enough to ride with cowboys on 'a hundred years or more'. Quentin, among other things, makes a proposal of marriage to one of his girl friends, and, not surprisingly I suppose, he gets turned down, which is really just what he wants, as it cures him of being a tea-addict! Some people attribute the inspiration for it to Lady Macbeth but I guess it's as genuine 'Stewart' as you're likely to come across."

THE PROPOSAL
From 'The diary of Quentin Crumpleton'
("we don't have that sort of thing here!")

I cannot ride an elephant
Across the Irish Sea
I cannot see a tin-tack
Half a mile away from me
My kitchen door is locked; and now
I've gone and lost the key.
But if you'd say you would,
I'd boil a better cup of tea.

I've got some pink pajamas
That I haven't paid for yet.
I've bought a double-bed; that's
Put me even more in debt.
I'm always short of money,
Even though I never bet.
But if you'd say you would
I'd boil a better cup of tea

I don't get drunk on Sundays, and
I'm only thirty-two
I've got a steady job; though
I don't eat much, it's true.
I'm a little absent-minded, but
Then darling, so are you,
And if you'd say you would
I'd boil a better cup of tea

You've heard all my proposal
So decide I think you should
What's that now? Do I love you?
I suppose you're fairly good
You'll go straight home to mother?
Yes, I rather thought you would,
But it doesn't matter now because
I've given up drinking tea

Al – "These early pieces of nonsense verse and a little later the first songs I wrote would have been written during prep when I was supposed to be working, which was something that I was never very good at."

Chris Owen – "Al would always sit just behind me for these evening prep sessions. Every now and then I would feel a tap on my shoulder and he would pass over a note containing a song or more than likely a poem that he'd just written! These would usually all be in the style of Edward Lear of course. I would then either change a line or two or write out my own reply and back it would go to Al. This happened each evening at Wycliffe. John Wyndham Lewis, who was also slightly mad, was part of all this and he was sat there at the end of my row for prep. So there was a little circle of us there."

Al again – "Mostly what I did was to make lists of fictitious and real songs. For the real ones I used to write down the artist, title, serial number and any other bits of information that I could find on just about every pop single that came out of America. I was a huge fan of anything and everything American. There are many of these serial numbers that I can still repeat today which goes to show just how intense I was about the whole thing. It means that to this day I have an enormous amount of knowledge about the stupidest things."

Jerry Trehayne once again – "We could take records and through that we all slowly started getting the feeling of individual tastes. One of my abiding memories is that we all used to play tag table tennis, you would start with up to seven or eight of you playing but first of all you needed to put on a record such as Little Richard album. We would all run around the table playing a sort of musical chairs around the table tennis table with a distorted version of 'Good Golly Miss Molly' or 'Tutti Fruiti' blaring out."

It was a genuine release from the horrendous and boring day to day tedium going on upstairs. And it was out of this enforced atmosphere of routine and discipline that Al used the slight leverage space, that he'd slowly won by dint of his battles with the school, to form his skiffle group, The Snowballs, along with fellow students Richie Allen, Geoffrey Seys-Llewellyn and Ed Pressdee.

Jerry Trehayne also remembers them all meeting up to practice in one of the music rooms where normally the school's classical musicians would gather to practice.

Chris Owen – "After much hanging around in the music room Al had formed The Snowballs. I played a stand up bass made from an old tea chest and Geoffrey Seys-Llewelyn played piano. He really was the most wonderful pianist and completely instinctive. But we had no back beat. I was forever telling Al that what we really needed was a set of drums and then one day I discovered this local village pub that also had a small stage with a drum kit! Well, after a number of conversations with the landlord of the pub they let us borrow them! So we were ready to roll. We in fact had two drummers, Chris Gray and Ed Pressdee both playing drums at various times for the group."

The Snowballs were the only group at Wycliffe and they only ever played about half a dozen gigs in all their time together. When they were first formed they performed mainly Lonnie Donegan songs.

Another friend of Al's, Phil Davies, remembers seeing Al and The Snowballs perform at an end of term revue show at Wycliffe.

Phil Davies – "They were up on stage playing cover versions of the time by people like The Shadows. They were in some sort of a Revue playing a sleazy band in a nightclub. I remember that they were all smoking which was in defiance of the school rules, but got away from it as artistic licence!"

Chris Owen – "We did a couple of these school, end of term, plays together in fact. They were put together by the Entertainments Organiser, Roger Davis. He was a fellow student and was responsible for producing these Revues. He wrote this play of his own that basically starred The Snowballs after his initial plan for us to do a proper concert was vetoed by the school. It was quite like a Pantomime in many ways. I also played a Welsh waiter in it that was forever throwing instant mashed potato around the stage. It was all pretty basic, a farce really with musical interludes!

There would be a few minutes of all this and then we would play another song."

Al's sense of humour was already well established by this time and at one of these school shows he performed a satirical song that he had composed about the headmaster, George Loosley. The school wasn't really technically equipped however for what were its first ever *skiffle* shows.

Chris Owen – "I invented some primitive lighting effects for a Junior School concert that The Snowballs did. This involved me turning the main stage lighting on and off. It was that basic! I asked someone at the back of the hall afterwards what it had looked like and they said 'Rubbish'. This was hardly Hollywood!"

Al's only previous experience of playing in a group had been as a member of his parents' acoustic trio. He took his music so seriously that he once hit a fellow pupil over the head with a vase when he tried to take Al's copy of the *NME* away from him!

From Wycliffe, Al would sometimes call on the services of his Uncle John, asking him to help transport the group's equipment around the school's scattered campus for those early shows.

Al's love of music by now knew no bounds. He even managed to sneak out of school one evening and stay out overnight attending a Jerry Lee Lewis concert.

Phil Davies again – "There was no-one else going in the same direction at the same time as Al. He was out on his own and through his absolute love of music obviously formed a good following, a growing collection of people who supported him. Of course he was now actually *doing* what the rest of us were all worshipping through records, he was directly putting it in practice. In the end the school had to recognise that this was a force to be reckoned with so the credit for that must certainly go to Al. The school's headmaster had said in the middle of Al's time at Wycliffe that 'The guitar would not lead to you living the sort of life that befitted someone from a school such as ours' and understandably this was something that Al agreed with wholeheartedly."

Chris Owen – "Once Al started to do these school concerts he became very popular amongst the boys. No one else had ever done anything like this there before and it made a huge impact on all of us. He had always been a rebel at Wycliffe and now he had channelled that very rebellion into his music and become a hero. He really had."

Back at Wycliffe after the Christmas break in the January of 1962 his nonsense verses have given way to a style driven more by rhythm than the imagery that personified the earlier work. The pieces have verses, chorus points and guitar chords.

On 10th January 1962 Al composed the sub-Auden song "Kolei Valley", listed as song number 13 in his exercise book.

Al – "Ah, 'Kolei Valley'. Now that's a song that I remember. It may not have been the most accomplished piece of writing but I absolutely loved it at the time. Definitely lyrics rather than nonsense verse!"

KOLEI VALLEY

Verse I
Bones lie buried in the cold damp ground
And late on at night you can hear that sound,
From that dark, gloomy place where the dead dog whines
In Kolei Valley where the sun never shines.

Verse II
It's been like this for a million years
It's the valley of misery, the valley of tears,
And you know that you're close, when the dead dog whines
To Kolei Valley where the sun never shines

Verse III
Now it's full of the bones of the wicked and the cruel
And it's haunted by their sprits all the long night through
If you're looking for peace you won't find any signs
In Kolei Valley where the sun never shines

Verse IV
But you're sure to find trouble and you're sure to find woe
If you take my advice, then you'll never, never go
To that place full of torment where the dead dog whines
In Kolei Valley, where the sun never shines.

Chorus
In Kolei Valley where the birds never sing
They've never head the sound of a single living thing
From the murk and the gloom comes a lonesome cry
Repent, or you'll end up here when you die ....

Verse V
In Kolei Valley where nothing draws breath
The Valley's full of air, and the air's full of death
Now you don't pay taxes and you don't pay fines
In Kolei Valley where the sun never shines

Verse VI
But I'd rather pay a tax and I'd rather pay a fine
Than stay in Kolei Valley 'till the end of time
In that land full of horrors where the dead dog whines
That's Kolei Valley where the sun never shines
CHORUS

Verse VII
Now I've seen a lot of places and I know them all well
But I've never seen a place looking more like hell
It's chock full of devils and Frankenstein
That's Kolei Valley where the sun never shines

Verse VIII
Oh I've given you my warning so you'd better mend your life
If your life's full of torment and trouble and strife
Or you may find yourself where the dead dog whines
In Kolei Valley where the sun never shines
[END]

Al – "Just how many times I played each of the records that I had at Wycliffe I can't remember. It would also be nice to have some of those back! I think that the song I played the most ever was probably 'Donna' by Ritchie Valens. I played it about 130 times, but the Dowland Brothers being a local band from Bournemouth were heavily represented in the top 20. I think 'Break Ups' might have been No. 2 or No. 3. I used to play records all the time basically whenever I wasn't doing anything else! They bought a record player and put it in the games room right before I got there or maybe it was even just after I arrived. The only person who had records in the whole school was me and I had just zillions of them so basically it became my record player. I mean in theory it was communal but nobody else had any records so I basically commandeered it and it became my own personal private property."

In taking charge of the music Al had accidentally adopted the role of school rebel. By so doing he not only earned the respect of his classmates but also the close attention of the teaching staff.

Al – "Well it didn't help I can tell you! I had one album, which was Buddy Holly's greatest hits, and we used to play it all the time. I was a big fan. It was all my music. Basically people made me play the records that they liked but they were my records. Lonnie Donegan had an EP, a live EP on which there is a song called 'Glory' I think, and there was one particular guy who used to play in the school rugby team and he would make me play 'Glory' before every rugby match. So they would come in and it would be ready to go for example. Now they did ban the guitar for a year or so. They said it was this immoral instrument and seeing that the only thing I really enjoyed doing was playing the guitar and listening to records I am surprised they didn't take away the record player at the same time and make my life even worse! It really wasn't going to make me happy."

Life was becoming increasingly tedious for Al at Wycliffe and besides paying little attention to lessons he was becoming ever more frustrated at the waste of his time that it had turned into. He continued to constantly write songs at the school however and in March 1962 composed the instrumental "Kerguelen".

It was a short jazzy piece not dissimilar to "Lullaby of Birdland" and took its name from the island that Captain James Cook had christened 189 years previously on Christmas Day 1776, Kerguelen being the name of the French Sea Captain who, whilst looking for a lost continent in the Southern Ocean in 1773 had been carried hopelessly off course by the Roaring Forties and then literally blown towards the remote island's rocky shores. It is also therefore the first of Al's "sea" songs.

Composing could only allow Al to escape momentarily from life at the school however. One other means of escape was the movies. A little known fact is that Al also ran his own secret cinema at Wycliffe! He used his trust fund allowance to buy a movie projector and films. He found an out-of-the-way room in the Science Block, had leaflets produced and charged everyone to come and watch Charlie Chaplin movies, using the takings to buy more films.

Chris Owen – "It was a huge success. Sometimes we had to have two showings because so many boys wanted to come and see the films."

Al – "But there was nothing I wanted to learn at Wycliffe. They were not teaching me anything useful. I mean bearing in mind that I already knew how to read and write and count when I got there, I can't actually think that there was anything I learnt there that has been of any use to me. I knew what I wanted to do. No one at school knows what they want to do but I wanted to be a rock 'n' roll star. Of course if you have a fully formed plan and you know exactly what you want to be when you grow up school is completely useless. I mean what I wanted to be was out there playing the guitar, as I had to go to Wycliffe I missed some very important times. I was *two years* late for everything. What happened was that the people who would become the stars – The Beatles, the Stones and all the others during '61 and '62 were all playing clubs when I was still learning how to play the guitar! Now admittedly I was a little younger but when you think about Jimmy Page, who is my age, when he was 16 he was out doing session work, playing on P.J. Proby records and the like!"

By the time that Al sat his school examinations he had all but given up his studies and certainly didn't take those examinations seriously.

Chris Owen – "We were doing 'O' level Biology. As part of the exam we were each given two specimens to draw. We got a dead frog and a tomato that had been cut in half. Al then wrote on his exam paper that 'Specimen A has eaten Specimen B and therefore I cannot draw it!' I know that he did this because he showed it to me before he handed it in!"

He failed most of his exams. The tough regime at Wycliffe with the accent on sports, good works and chapel did not however, in Al's opinion, leave any lasting impressions.

Al – "No, absolutely not. I'm actually of the opinion that idealism in any form is to be avoided at all costs, just because I see what happens when idealists get hold of almost anything. The Bolsheviks were all idealists originally, well Stalin probably wasn't but they made a hell of a mess of the Soviet Union. Intellectuals are also very dangerous, especially intellectuals with a chip on their shoulder."

Music was playing a greater and greater role in Al's life now. In April 1962 he wrote a song that was never recorded and seems lost for ever called "Blues Behind Bars" and a short time later, on holiday in Bournemouth, he used money saved from having worked at Fortes restaurant in the town to buy himself a Hofner Colorama guitar.

Al – "I was very pleased about this! It was a very impressive guitar and was my very first solid Hank B. Marvin style instrument and of course it had to be red! This was the guitar that I played in both The Snowballs and their later evolution at Wycliffe as The Sunbeams."

Up until this time Al had led what amounted to a very directionless existence. He was unhappy at school, separated from the evolving world of rock and roll by what he saw as literally an incarceration at Wycliffe and felt completely unfulfilled. However this was about to change. It all started with a bus ride one afternoon into Bournemouth.

BOURNEMOUTH

In which Al joins a succession of Bournemouth beat groups before coming under the spell of Bob Dylan and moving up to London and the Soho folk scene.

Up until this point in his life Al had felt that life had been pretty hard. His time at Wycliffe had been, he felt, a disaster and he was looking for a way out. He was about to find it. On September 6th, the day after Al's seventeenth birthday, fate intervened on his behalf and he met Jonny Kremer.

Jonny Kremer – "We are talking about the Autumn of 1962 and it is just prior to The Beatles. The '60s for us started circa late 1962 with 'Love Me Do', the first *James Bond* film and Carnaby Street, John Stephens shops, Mary Quant etc. Our friendship too started at exactly that point. Al was about to leave school and what we had in common was a basic interest in what was happening in UK pop music then, which was electric guitars and The Shadows who had been holding sway since 1960. Our immediate point of meeting was connected specifically with the fact that Al was already quite an accomplished electric guitarist as a school boy, and I had recently started to attempt to play a few Shadows tunes, taught to me by my Dad. One day in my Dad's small shop, which sold guitars and amplifiers, Al walked in and made an enquiry and that enquiry led to the beginning of our friendship."

From his vantage point on the top deck of the bus from Bournemouth to Wimborne Al had spotted a guitar reverb unit sitting in the front window display of Monty Kremer's shop and had jumped off the bus and run into the shop, greeting a surprised Jonny with the words "How much and what is that?"

They told him that it was a Bird reverberation unit and its price to which Al replied "I'll have to go back home and get my guitar and amplifier and try it."

JK – "So we probably thought that that would be the last we'd see of him and Al got on the next bus back home to Wimborne."

However Jonny and Monty were wrong and several hours later Al was back on their doorstep carrying a guitar and a small amplifier so that he could try out the echo unit.

JK – "I must confess he never actually bought this item and by this time the shop was ready to close and we offered to give Al a lift back home with his equipment. We had already established that we had quite a shared interest in electric guitars. I knew that he was still on holiday and I was hoping that he could maybe teach me some more guitar chords in the time before he returned to Wycliffe!"

Over the next couple of weeks Jonny and Al discovered that they had a great deal in common and spent a good deal of that time shuffling between one another's homes. The author John Wyndham and a mutual passion for rock and roll trivia were initially two of the shared interests that they discovered they had. During long sessions of playing the guitar Jonny introduced Al to a version of "In The Hall Of The Mountain King" that had been a hit for Nero and the Gladiators that he went on to perform later that term at the school concert. Two weeks after meeting Jonny Al caught The Pines Express back to Stonehouse and Wycliffe College for one last tumultuous term.

On his arrival for those final few weeks at public school in Gloucestershire Al found the regime there much as he had found it before. There was by now, a mixture of resignation and tolerance from the staff there towards Al and his music. To many of the boys he was something of a hero for having bucked the system and everyone knew that this was to be his last term. Back at Wycliffe he kept in touch with Jonny by letter.

Writing mainly on Sunday afternoons, it's easy to imagine from these letters back home what was going on in Al's mind. The most obvious point is that music was clearly taking over his life because much of the narrative of these original and illuminating letters was about records and his group The Snowballs who by this time were seen as a legitimate part of college life. In a letter back to Jonny dated October 1st Al talks about a Del Shannon review that he'd seen and that he himself had a gig coming up at college on November 26th that he calls "a really big show" going on to say that due to Jonny's influence "The Hall of the Mountain King" was now going to form part of the performance! He also wrote about how much he liked the new Carole King record "It Might As Well Rain Until September".

These were the last few weeks before The Beatles took the country by storm. On October 5th EMI released their first single, "Love Me Do".

A few weeks later on October 21st Al wrote home to say that there was another concert planned at Wycliffe Junior School on the following Saturday about which he was clearly excited. There were a few lines about The Everly Brothers and news that he'd been to see a football match between a showbiz eleven and The Magpies.

He then included what is quite possibly his earliest set list:

Jet Black – The Shadows
Blue Moon – Instrumental
Grand Coulee Dam – Lonnie Donegan
Guitar Tango – The Shadows
Does Your Chewing Gum Lose Its Flavour On The Bedpost Overnight –
    Lonnie Donegan
Lullaby Of Birdland – George Shearing
Green Leaves of Summer – Kenny Ball
Guest Artist – Piano Pieces
Apache – The Shadows
I Ran All The Way Home – The Impalas
FBI – The Shadows
Toot Toot Tootsie – Featuring Pianist
Drum Boogie – Featuring Drummer
Oh Boy – Buddy Holly

When he got out of college at weekends his Auntie Hazel, who lived not too far away, would take Al to Gloucester where he'd invariably spend some of the time in one of the town's two record shops. It was on one of these trips that he bought a Kenny Ball LP and so he certainly wasn't limited in his musical appreciation at this time to just skiffle or American R&B. In a letter on November 19th, his last one from Wycliffe as it turns out, he mentions the upcoming big school concert and that the School's Musical Director was producing *A Child Of Our Time* at Wycliffe and that the composer, "a bloke called Tippett", was coming too! This of course was the composer Sir Michael Tippett. Al goes on to say that there's also "a one act play… at the end of term and so there's plenty to keep us busy."

From these letters, containing no information about his studies, other friends at Wycliffe or anything other than music, music, music, it's clear to see how things had become impractical there for everyone in as far as it being a good idea for Al to resume his studies after the Christmas Holidays.

And so Al left at the end of the winter term 1962.

Speaking to the British music magazine *Nuggets* at the end of 1976 he had this to say about it all.

"Finally the school and I came to an amicable agreement which was that I should leave, mainly because I had totally abandoned two of my courses and stopped doing any

Live in the Assembly Hall at Wycliffe

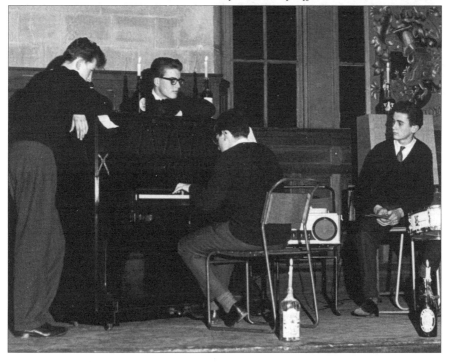

work, but I was giving concerts!"

Wycliffe had served as the one constant that took Al from a small homesick boy to a 17-year old fledgling skiffle star heading down to unsuspecting Bournemouth in those last moments before Beatlemania would sweep all before it.

And so by the start of 1963 Al was out of the confines of a public school and into the life of a teenager living with his parents near to Bournemouth. He had serious regrets about the time that he felt had been wasted at Wycliffe however.

"Because I had to go to that wretched school till I was 17 it meant that I had missed out on being in proper bands and also of course hadn't done things like 6-hour sessions in the Star Club in Hamburg either! By the time I had eventually done all that in order to catch up, which takes a couple of years, it was 1965 and Bob Dylan had come along and the first wave of the British Beat Boom was already over! So in a way if I had got out of school at Christmas term 1960 and then had spent 1961 and 1962 in beat groups, which I would have done probably, I would then have found my way into some equivalent band like The Hollies and I could have become Graham Hicks who people used to say I looked like in the early days!"

By the time he left Wycliffe Joan and Basil were living in the Dorset hamlet of Canford Bottom. During the summer holidays Al had had the short lived job in Fortes Restaurant opposite The Pavilion theatre but now he needed to find a more permanent means of funding his forays into the burgeoning pop scene in Bournemouth, which as one of England's premier sea-side resorts provided an unending supply of visiting bands and girls and was now seeing the formation of its own "scene" with clubs, record shops and local groups. He managed to get a position as a junior sales assistant in the drapery department of Beales department store in the centre of town and although it was a dead end and very boring job it was a means to an end in as far as he was now able to spend much of the time chatting up the girls that came into the store and also now had money to spend on them in the evenings. It was whilst working at Beales that Al went out with Jeanie, of "I missed the bus and walked twelve miles home" fame, from "Love Chronicles". She worked in another department to Al and he really did miss that last bus back home to Canford Bottom.

Al – "But by the time I got out of school in Christmas 1962 I was just too late for that first initial thing. The Beatles were already recording by then and it was on its way to being over by the time I had gone through what you have got to go through which is all the local dance hall gigs. So by 1965 that had gone, Bob Dylan had arrived. It was kind of convenient because although I missed out on what I would have loved to do and therefore never got to be *Al Beatle* I was also too early to become *Al Dylan*. I was behind the bus for one thing and ahead of it for the other!"

There remains, even today, a sense with Al of him having quite possibly missed out on what, musically at least, he feels he could have made the most impact with. The songs of the early '60s retain a magic for him that totally eclipses any other era.

Al spent that first Christmas without the return to school hanging over him with his family in Canford Bottom. To get an accurate picture of Al's rite of passage through the crucial two year period in between Wycliffe and Bunjies coffee bar there's no better guide than Jonny Kremer. This is how he recalls those times.

J.K. – "And amazing times they were too! In England, we were then in the grips of one of the worst winters of the century. It was freezing outside! On Boxing Day of that year, there was a heavy snowfall and for two or three months in some areas the snow didn't clear completely and it was still very heavily covering the ground in the days immediately after Christmas and well into the New Year of 1963. At this precise moment The Beatles released 'Please Please Me' and the Swinging Sixties really started to move."

By February 23rd "Please Please Me" had reached No. 1 in the *Disc* singles charts. In most towns in England at this time kids were buying guitars and forming bands and Bournemouth was no exception. The culture of change that was pushed to the fore by the arrival not only in the pop charts but also the consciousness of the nation by the Beatles' arrival prompted the most sudden changes in street fashion towns like Bournemouth had ever seen. New groups seemed to appear weekly.

That week, on January 15th, Bob Dylan was wandering into Bunjies Coffee Bar in London and along with Richard Fariña played his only set on the same tiny stage that Al would two years later claim for himself. Back in Bournemouth Al and Jonny had other things on their minds however.

J.K. – "Bournemouth was a town where just about everybody seemed to be in a group and there were dozens and dozens of them! Some didn't last long and some were developed from embryonic groups that had already existed but each one caught the lightning and moved into the modern world with Beatle period music. And at this time Andy Summers was already an established guitarist in Bournemouth and Robert Fripp was with a local group called The League of Gentlemen. Both of them were slightly younger than Al. Robert Fripp had given Al those guitar lessons and the connection with Andy Summers really came about a year or so later when Al bought a guitar from him. But the scene in Bournemouth was one in which The Pavilion dance hall, in the centre of town, had a specific group-orientated night, usually a Tuesday, which was given the provocative title of *Big Beat Night* and featured Zoot Money, then the number one name in Bournemouth. His group was later to record under the name of Zoot Money's Big Roll Band and subsequently to that as Dantalions Chariot with Andy Summers as their lead guitarist. In its original incarnation in 1963 it had been called The Sands Combo and they were regulars at The Pavilion."

The support group to The Sands Combo was Tony Blackburn and the Sabres, Tony Blackburn being seriously keen on the idea that he could become Bournemouth's very own Cliff Richard. Al would himself soon progress to becoming an honorary Sabre for a solitary gig and a ten-shilling fee.

J.K. – "In his role as headliner every Tuesday at The Pavilion Zoot Money had managed to become the clown prince of Bournemouth. During his act he would come on and throw pies into the band members and generally create havoc on stage!"

Geoff Westwood – "Bournemouth was full of characters like that. The guy that ran The Pavilion was Jan Ralfini who also had a dance band and Tony Blackburn used to sing with Ralfini's band some nights besides playing with that separate four piece group of his own called The Sabres."

Al's brief life as a Sabre had come about when Tony Blackburn had asked him one night to deputise for his lead guitarist after some problem had arisen. Al was forced to spend the next 30 minutes in the band's dressing room desperately learning their set for that evening's performance.

Al – "The first and very nearly the last time! Tony always used to tell people that I played the electric guitar too loud when I was with him. I can still picture him now, singing

Monty Kremer

Al & Jonny, Bournemouth 1964.
'The men from Rickenbacker'.

his heart out in a gold lamé jacket, rolling around on that stage in Bournemouth in 1963, quite bizarre…"

Al's search for a regular job in a local band was just about to be rewarded however.

Geoff Westwood again – "Now Tony would prowl the stage in the famous glitter jacket and was, in his own mind at least, Cliff Richard. And it was to act as a backing band for this vision in gold that Pete Ballam one morning gathered together a number of musicians, including Al and I."

The Trappers, as they would become, were without doubt the most important of the many groups that Al played lead guitar for during his two years of freedom in Bournemouth. Al became a full time member of The Trappers in the April of 1963.

The rhythm guitarist in The Trappers was 19-year-old Geoff Westwood. Born in the English Midlands industrial town of Sutton Coldfield, he was an ex-grammar school student whose major influences at the time were Elvis Presley and Buddy Holly. Lonnie Donegan also loomed large in his list of heroes and Geoff first started playing guitar at local youth clubs and village halls throughout the time that Al was still only half thinking about forming The Snowballs at Wycliffe. In 1962 Geoff moved down to Bournemouth, where his friends were living and started work at the Cottage Hospital in Poole. Whilst still feeling his way in this new town Geoff would go out and see bands including Zoot Money and The Kapota All Stars whose bass player was one Pete Ballam. Now The Kapota All Stars regularly played a gig at the run-down Beacon Hotel in Bournemouth, which was not the ideal venue but somewhere to perform nonetheless. Around about this time Pete Ballam was at the Beacon Hotel with Tony Blackburn one evening when Tony asked him whether he was interested in getting together a replacement backing band together to back him at The Pavilion. Tony and Pete knew each other because not only had they seen each other's bands but also they both lived in Longfleet Road. They were also both customers, along with virtually every other musician in Bournemouth, of the legendary Don Strike's music shop in Westbourne and whilst not best mates they were certainly aware of one another.

Pete Ballam was also, like Tony Blackburn, one of Bournemouth's more extrovert characters. He would cruise around the town at night in a Ford Capri that he'd customised with a back end that had been kitted out with cocoa tins as rear light mountings!

Geoff Westwood – "It was at Pete's house that Saturday morning that I first met young Al along with the other members of what would soon become The Trappers. Pete had got Al's name from Don Strike because he hadn't played with anyone yet in Bournemouth and had only just left school."

And so on that fateful day, Al, Geoff, Pete and a young drummer named Barry Barnes, all met up for the first time at 97 Longfleet Road for a rehearsal and audition in the front room of Pete's mother's house! In fact prior to playing as The Sabres there had been several other rehearsals at Pete's house, some of which included Tony Blackburn running through songs in that same front room.

Geoff Westwood – "We would sometimes also use The Brewers Arms skittle alley to rehearse in which was great. It was down in Poole and was somewhere that we could really blast it out!"

Al – "And blast it out we did! This was all just great. I was actually in a band!"

J.K. – "Working in The Trappers would take care of Al's Tuesdays. Wednesdays were an even bigger night for him on the Bournemouth scene because a club called Le Disque a Go! Go! had opened and the boom in groups was such in those days that it was not only open seven days a week but on certain nights it would have a double header, in which it would close around midnight and re-open again with a second group."

Al – "Le Disque a Go! Go! became our home from home in many ways. It was one of the places in Bournemouth at that time where just about everybody went, I certainly spent a lot of time there with Jonny."

Le Disque a Go! Go! also hosted groups from outside the area who were on the fringe of the London circuit. On a Wednesday night around about April 1963 they started to have a group called the Mann-Hugg Blues Brothers. Al and Jonny would go there with about twenty to thirty other people, which, within a few months was to become two hundred, totally packing out this small cellar basement club. The group evolved into Manfred Mann and Al and Jonny knew them quite well. They watched their first record come and go and be a flop, and their second record come and go and be a flop, and then a year later, *Ready Steady Go* had as its theme music Manfred's third record "5, 4, 3, 2, 1".

J.K. – "That first single was an instrumental called 'Why Should We Not?'. Al had written some lyrics for it and showed them to Manfred one night at Le Disque, only to be told that they would rather keep it as an instrumental. Al's career as a lyricist failing to get going just yet."

Ironically a couple of decades later Manfred Mann would go on to record Al's "Nostradamus".

It seemed that everyone in Bournemouth between the ages of 16 and 20 was either in or best friends with one of the town's beat groups by now.

J.K. – "It was just the most amazing time to be growing up in. We genuinely felt that we were part of something back then. These were the groups that Al had as competition around town in Bournemouth in '63."

Johnny Quantrose 5	Trendsetters Ltd	The Dictators
The Crescendoes	Sara and The Cinnamon	Zoot Money & Sands Combo
Trackmarks	The Temors	Inner Circle
The Corvettes	Surfing Gremmies	Palmer James
The Black Jacks	Kingpins	Indigos
Initials	Freewheelers	The Valliants
Lisa and The Brethren	The Classics	The Tall Men
Southern Sounds	Thursday's Children	The Bunch
The Mob	Shades of Blue	The G Men
Sound by Five	Impacts	The Interns

Al and Jonny filled their days playing poker and rummy with Jonny's dad, Monty, in the back of his Bournemouth shop. When not playing cards they'd be tearing around Bournemouth, hanging out at the Westover Road Ice Rink, going to the movies and chasing after girls. "Millie Brown", a song written by Al 30 years later, was composed with these early months in Bournemouth in mind.

At this time '60s package tours of groups could do serious business and the Winter Gardens and Gaumont were two places in town where Al would go to catch up on these touring bands.

Then between 19th and 24th August 1963 the Beatles came to Bournemouth playing there for a week.

J.K. – "We managed to get tickets to go and see them play on their first night, which was the Monday. By that time, to put it in context, they'd already made the breakthrough from 'Love Me Do' to 'Please Please Me'. They'd already solidified the position with 'From Me To You' being number one, and everyone was waiting to see what happened next. What happened next was 'She Loves You'. So the whole mania thing was enormous. It just so happened that the week they were in Bournemouth, was the week this single was released and also the week it entered the charts at number one."

It was also the week that Al and Jonny met The Beatles.

Al – "The area around the theatre and the Beatles hotel was just a sea of screaming fans and that's what confronted us when we came out after the gig. We were on a real high by then and decided that we just had to try and get to chat to them somehow which was looking to be impossible really."

J.K. – "The Beatles and other Brian Epstein managed groups, were staying in an hotel very close to the venue, for the obvious reason of limiting the Beatlemania problems. This meant that getting close to them anywhere, was very difficult. We were feeling very exhilarated having just seen them and more or less on the spur of the moment decided we shouldn't let this moment go by. It would be great to say hello, particularly we wanted to talk to John Lennon. It was very guitar-orientated and the guitar John Lennon played was a very unusual one. It was a short scale model and watching them on stage I wasn't sure exactly what it was but Al, who was terrifically good at such things, said 'I think it is a Rickenbacker' and this became a starting point for our scam. I decided we would talk our way, if we could, into meeting them. So when everyone was leaving Al and I went to the theatre manager's office immediately after the gig. In those days, on the package tours, they would perform twice a night, which seems perhaps extraordinary to think that the Beatles would perform once in an evening and two hours later you could go back and see them again, but this was the case. So this was in between performances."

So Jonny leads Al, who was by now having misgivings about the whole thing, into the manager's office, only yards from the Beatles' dressing room.

J.K. – "I said to the manager that we had come down from London, had business with the Beatles' management, but couldn't get access to them backstage because of all these hundreds of screaming teenagers, and what could he do to help? Of course this was total nerve, we were both exactly the same age as those teenagers outside in the street!

I believe he was on his own there, there might have been a secretary around somewhere. He responded immediately to my request by picking up the telephone and calling down to the stage door, checking our names and telling them that a Mr. Kremer and a Mr Stewart would be round shortly. So let us in! I thanked the theatre manager and we left him there in his little office. The stage door entrance was down an alleyway beside the side of the Gaumont Theatre where they were performing. It was jam packed with girls. They were there with their autograph books and they were there to scream if someone even so much as stuck their head out from behind the stage door."

Al and Jonny enlisted the help of some local bobbies to clear a path for them through the fans so that they could get through.

J.K. – "A pathway was made for us, we reached the stage door, the stage door keeper opens the door and admits us, quickly slamming it shut behind Al and I. At this point I remember a number of girls cramming autograph books into our hands and begging us to get autographs for them.

We were back stage and here a slight problem developed because we obviously weren't really from Rickenbacker. Anyway I asked somebody which way to the Beatles' dressing room and we were directed to it. I knocked on the door and Neil Aspinall answered. In those days he was their tour manager having developed out of being a roadie. Now at this point, speaking to Neil Aspinall, we couldn't maintain we were from Rickenbacker any longer and so we came clean and just asked him whether it was possible for us to talk to John Lennon about his Rickenbacker. He paused for a second and told us to wait right there and a short time passes and John Lennon is in front of us."

In the mayhem of that first evening playing in Bournemouth their ruse worked and there was Lennon, complete with the horn-rimmed glasses that he never wore in public, standing in the doorway of the Beatles' dressing room. He went and got the said Rickenbacker and handed it to Jonny Kremer.

J.K. – "I strummed a couple of chords very nervously and quickly passed it to Al who said to Lennon that we were in a local group. He also thought, in the scheme of things, he wouldn't play it for too long, but he played it a bit too, and this was a great thing for us. Al chatted with him about guitar amps and why he used Vox amps for their gigs when they used Fenders on their albums. Lennon explained to us how Brian Epstein wanted them to use Vox, because they had a contract with them but that he didn't think a lot of them; and would throw them off the end of the pier if he had the chance."

Their few minutes with Lennon were filled with a short conversation about the Rolling

Stones who at that time were only just getting known. In the days that followed Al and Jonny, spurred on by the total success of running The Beatles to ground at the Gaumont, kept up their assault on them by hiding on one occasion in the wings during a later Beatles show and also by staking out the band's Bournemouth hotel.

J.K. – "We soon realised they were staying two doors from the theatre concert hall, and managed the second stage of our campaign on the Wednesday by talking our way through Beatles mania and successfully getting into their hotel! By now we'd become friendly with a member of Billy J. Kramer and the Dakotas. They were having a string of hit records in those days, courtesy of Lennon and McCartney songs and they were the support act to the Beatles then."

That member of the Dakotas was Ray Jones and it was Al and Jonny's friendship with him that gave them this partial access to the Fab Four.

J.K. – "There was a great moment when just before the evening's performance was going to start that day, when he was about to join up with the other members of the group and Billy J. Kramer himself in the theatre. The quickest way to do it was to go out of the front of the hotel run the short distance along Westover Road and into the Gaumont through its main entrance. Hundreds of girl fans would sit on the wall opposite the hotel and when we all came out and made this run to the Gaumont Theatre these girls, like a scene out of *A Hard Day's Night*, rushed across screaming and chasing, as we all rushed into the Gaumont. They all ran screaming in after us and the doorman stopped them getting in. I must admit that Al and I thought that this was great. Actually we then wound up on stage where they were rehearsing and sitting strumming a guitar there was Billy J. Kramer, who Al didn't actually recognise and thought was part of the band's road crew! We also managed to get into the Palace Court Hotel and we were in the hotel lounge on the first floor."

It was here that things gathered a momentum of their own and became almost surreal for the two impostors.

J.K. – "We were sitting in the lounge that had been sectioned off for the Beatles with John, George and Ringo. We were sitting next to them at one time while *Beatles Monthly* was interviewing them. And I recall we had this idea to invite them to a party and we thought they would come. We believed anything could happen. We would have it at Le Disque a Go! Go! When we actually asked Ringo Starr he said they would check with Brian Epstein. But of course they weren't going out anywhere as they were staying in the hotel. I remember there was another guy on the tour, an Epstein managed singer called Tommy Quickly, who made a few records, but never had hits, and he was very keen on the idea of the party but none of this ever came to anything."

The famous cover shot for the album *With The Beatles* was taken here in the hotel's dining room by the photographer Robert Freeman on August 22nd.

Al was by this time writing songs on an almost daily basis and Jonny would often be the first person to hear these.

J.K. – "In fact when we first met I remember looking through exercise books full of songs he'd written while at school, and he was constantly telling me he would be making records someday. Unfortunately nobody would listen except for me and this would continue to be the case for many years to come. Al took advantage occasionally when playing throughout 1963 in clubs and with The Trappers to actually perform one or two of his songs solo. He'd have a moment in which he'd just do a song. It wasn't an immediately outrageous success, but it was probably the real beginning of him becoming a singer songwriter. I remember he'd written one particular song called 'So I Kept Walking' which was a Johnny Cash style number and he'd perform that along with the odd guitar instrumental he'd written. He loved guitar instrumentals."

Al had a couple of guitars at the time. He had an acoustic cello style of guitar made by Voss with a Rogers electric pick-up added to it but it wasn't something he actually performed with. For that he mainly played a Hofner solid electric guitar and later on he bought a Fender Stratocaster. But in 1963 he played his beloved Hofner Colorama. Fashion though was something that he had little interest in.

J.K. – "Clothes and Al were never a big thing. I mean his visual sense of things was never the greatest. We had Beatle Boots, I remember I certainly did. But he wasn't fast in terms of combing his hair forward for instance. Eventually he did do that too and he did let me influence a lot of the clothes he wore in those days. The thing was that he wasn't paid very much for playing in The Sabres, I think that Tony Blackburn was given something like £5 to perform at the Pavilion and was asked to pay the group out of it as well. So really there was not a lot of money around but being as it was the early sixties it was not all that necessary".

Another piece of Al's that was to draw on his memories of Bournemouth at this time was the track "Love Chronicles" released in 1969.

This lyric is taken from that song:

"In the halcyon days of my late adolescence my goal seemed clearly in sight / Playing electric guitar in a beat group we set the ballrooms alight / Acting it up for the dyed blonde receptionists who told us we were all right / An ego trip for a teenage superstar on 30 shillings a night."

Throughout their short time with Tony Blackburn as The Sabres none of the band members became particularly close friends with him. He was great mates with Jan Ralfini and it was this friendship that certainly did him no harm at all when it came to getting those shows at The Pavilion. Besides Ralfini there were a number of other minor impresarios in Bournemouth and between them they had the town sewn up. Sid Fay, Bill Collins and Jan Ralfini were old school Mr. Fixits with interests in all of Bournemouth's entertainment venues. And so Tony Blackburn's friendship with Ralfini was very useful for him.

Geoff Westwood – "Very useful indeed. Jan Ralfini was notorious for not paying musicians union rates of pay. The original deal was for us to just back Tony but when we discovered that we weren't getting the fee that we should have for these Pavilion shows we decided to take decisive action! There was a confrontation between the band members, Tony and Jan Ralfini and that was it, we quit."

Those shows at The Pavilion had been very successful however and had got the band noticed. The place would be packed every night and the shows generally went down a storm. The Sabres would come on first – Al on lead guitar, Pete on bass, Geoff on rhythm guitar and Barry on drums, whereupon living out the fantasy of being in a pop band in the early '60s, they'd play a set of some original compositions and a few covers before the besequinned Tony Blackburn would make his grand entrance with the band making fun of him all the while. The band minus Tony would then finish off the evening. During the band's two sets without Tony, Al would usually take the lead on a couple of songs including an original composition here and there.

This short-lived union of The Trappers with Tony Blackburn featured these songs:
End of the World
I'm Walkin'
The Night has a Thousand Eyes
Hully Gully
Spanish Harlem
Dancing Shoes
How Do You Do It

Geoff Westwood – "This was Al's real head start on all of us. He'd got this knack for writing songs and it was obvious right away that he had a natural gift for composition. He was a jolly good guitar player, was supremely confident both as a person and

The Trappers at Bransgore Village Hall in 1963   *Geoff Westwood*

performer and had his own opinions and thoughts on just about everything, even then."

Al's Vox and Geoff's Trix amps were part of a relatively natty back line in those days. The amps and PAs were even built into one colossal white unit by Pete Balham's next door neighbour! And so after having come together as someone's backing band The Sabres or The Trappers, as they now became known, needed to go out and find themselves a new singer to take over from Tony Blackburn. The new Trapper was another Tony, Tony Barrett – a resident of Westbourne.

Geoff Westwood again – "Tony Barrett looked the part alright! He was tall, thin, had a little moustache and for a short period everything was fine."

In the end his liking for slightly more than the odd drink became more than the group could cope with but initially all was hunky dory. In The Trappers Tony Barrett wore an ordinary suit whilst the other four band members went out and bought themselves 'Beatle

Jackets' which were made from a black velvet style material with the trademark round collars, the band's image was completed with narrow grey trousers and a knitted tie each!

Geoff Westwood remembers that Tony's "big hero was Bobby Darin and it certainly showed in his singing style."

Eventually a couple of obscure Bobby Darin numbers were slotted into The Trappers set. One of these, "I Ain't Sharin' Sharon" turned out to be massively successful for them as a live number and would "bring the house down" according to Al.

This is some of the set list that 'The Trappers' with Tony Barrett performed:

Summertime	How Do You Do It?	Walk Right In
You Know What I Mean	That's What Love Will Do	Just a Matter of Time
Don't Ya Think It's Time	I'm Walking	Early In The Morning
From A Jack To A King	Doin' The Hully Gully	End Of The World
The Night Has A Thousand Eyes	When You Ask About Love	Dancing Shoes
My Way	Walking Backwards	Baby My Heart
Got A Funny Feeling	Harvest Of Love	Sweet Nothin's
I Ain't Sharin' Sharon	I Like It	Lucky Lips
Rhythm Of The Rain	Sweets For My Sweet	Brown Eyed Handsome Man
Twist and Shout		

Their gigs soon started getting them noticed. In September 1963 The Trappers got this review in the *Bournemouth Echo* – "Two three fingered, three five fingered musicians and £1000 worth of equipment go to make the sound produced every Tuesday by The Trappers group at Le Disque a Go Go… Up until a short time ago The Trappers were almost unknown. Then, from nowhere, they shot into popularity. This they deserve for, as pure twist groups go, these boys have got what it takes. But, as with most groups, their popularity did not come easily."

The article continued with an amazing piece of information. A few scant facts in a provincial music column that show how, in terms of his craft, Al has always written songs in exactly the same way.

The Bournemouth Echo again – "Al has composed between 40 and 50 numbers which they intend to use in future shows. His particular method of writing songs is first to think of the title, then arrange chord orders, then come the words."

So that's how it's done.

Al – "These gigs were a lot of fun for me and I would often use them to try out songs that I'd just written. So many of those things that have, thankfully, been lost for ever were debuted by me in my little solo spots with The Trappers. One of them was 'Whatever Happened to Baby Jane?' which was a guitar instrumental that I wrote and remember playing at the Ship Inn at Wool. It had tons of reverb I seem to remember and it's one of the very earliest songs of mine that I can still remember to this day."

The Trappers started to both rehearse and perform to paying customers at Bransgore Village Hall. It was here that Al cut his teeth as both a guitarist and songwriter. He would show the new songs that he had written at home to the other band members and together they would work on their arrangements.

Geoff Westwood – "It was our place and we played there all of the time. We could make as much noise as we wanted. It only cost £2 to hire and we would take £15 on the door – or rather my mum and dad would! Al didn't drive back in those days and so one of us would pick him up and drive him to gigs. We played big places and we certainly played small ones. One of the smallest was in the basement of Lolita's Coffee Bar at 64 Charminster Road. Besides ordinary shows we would also enter competitions too. The most infamous one was for the *Best Band in Dorset*, which was staged at a big drill hall in Weymouth in August 1963. We played a great set of three or four numbers but lost out to another group by the name of the Crescendos – unfairly we thought."

In fact a couple of years later they discovered that it had indeed been rigged and that The Trappers had never stood a chance of winning. But it was the shows at Bransgore Village Hall that remained special to the band members.

Geoff Westwood – "Most of the locals would turn out and would be either dancing or sitting around the perimeter of the room on chairs. Those evenings would be just us, no one else, just Al, Pete, Barry, Tony and myself. It was brilliant! We played each other's songs, sharing the lead vocal duties, did instrumentals and cover versions at those shows."

Besides performing in The Trappers Al played some more low-key dates at his local pub as part of a duo with Geoff Westwood. This gig, which was secured via Al's friendship with the landlord's daughter, was unpaid but of huge assistance to the two Trappers. Here, with no pressure (and sometimes no audience), Al and Geoff would play a selection of instrumentals, Buddy Holly covers and "work in progress" numbers on their two electric guitars! Canford Bottom was also used as a rehearsal venue. The summerhouse in the cottage's back garden was used to both write and practise songs by Al and the band through 1963.

The other instrumentals that were Al Stewart originals performed at gigs with The Trappers at this time were "Con Man"And "Hot Ice".

In time the other band members gradually became disenchanted with Tony Barrett when basically he turned out to not be quite the singer that he'd claimed to be. Initially the other band members went out and did some gigs without telling Tony but in the end five officially became four once again.

Some of The Trappers songs were duets featuring various band members. These included: –

Blue Suede Shoes	Some Other Guy
Walk Like A Man	I'll Never Get Over You
From Me To You	We Know
Twist And Shout	Summer Skies and Golden Sands
Bad To Me	Hog For You Baby
She Loves You	Secret Love

The Trappers in 1963 played these instrumentals –

Tonight	Lullaby Of The Leaves
Con Man	Whatever Happened To Baby Jane? (written by Al in September 1963)
High Noon	Eight Million Cossack Melodies
Trappin	Gypsy Pete
Footmash	Czardas
Shazam	Hot Ice
Diamonds	Dance On
Scarlett O'Hara	Grandfather Clock
In The Mood	Cobra
Tonight	Trambone

Geoff Westwood – "We became quite a good group ultimately. I specifically remember the last booking we ever took at Ringwood that was packed. Wall to wall. It turned out to be a very emotional show for us when all is said and done. Al had decided that he was going to leave and because of that Pete was giving up as well."

In fact things ultimately didn't happen quite the way everyone thought they were about to and Geoff continued to work with Pete in The South Coast Five.

Geoff Westwood – "Al had always told us that he would be moving on eventually and how he was absolutely determined to move up to London at the earliest opportunity. In that respect throughout all the time that he was with us in The Trappers he was always totally focused on this dream. He was going to make it and was always convinced of that. The day that Al left The Trappers the band broke up. I held auditions at Le Disque a Go! Go! and along with Pete, who had changed his mind about leaving, formed my new group."

Al – "I've probably played more gigs at Bransgore Village Hall than anywhere else except Bunjies and Les Cousins. I loved playing in The Trappers because it was so much fun. I was 17 and playing in a group and had really started to write songs properly by then."

The list of shows that Al and The Trappers performed in 1963 has survived intact and is reproduced here for the first time.

Tuesday	30th April	Bournemouth Pavilion (with Tony Blackburn) 2 sets
Saturday	18th May	Brangsore Village Hall
		The Bure Club, Christchurch
Friday	21st June	The Ship Inn, Wool
Saturday	29th June	Bransgore Village Hall
Tuesday	2nd July	Le Disque a Go Go
Monday	1st July	Cellar Club Poole
Sunday	7th July	Cellar Club Poole
Saturday	13th July	Bransgore Village Hall
Tuesday	16th July	Le Disque a Go Go
Saturday	20th July	The Ship Inn, Wool
Tuesday	23rd July	Le Disque a Go Go
Friday	26th July	Bransgore Village Hall
Tuesday	30th July	Le Disque a Go Go
Friday	2nd August	Bransgore Village Hall
Tuesday	6th August	Le Disque a Go Go
Wednesday	7th August	Branksome Dene Convalescent Home
Friday	9th August	Bransgore Village Hall
Saturday	10th August	Ship Inn, Wool
Sunday	11th August	Le Disque a Go Go
Tuesday	13th August	Le Disque a Go Go
Friday	16th August	Territorial Army Drill Hall, Weymouth
Saturday	17th August	Club Rondo, Bournemouth
Tuesday	20th August	Le Disque a Go Go
Wednesday	21st August	Branksome Dene Convalescent Home
Saturday	24th August	Cellar Club, Poole
Sunday	25th August	Club Rondo, Bournemouth
Monday	26th August	Swanage Labour Hall
Tuesday	27th August	Le Disque a Go Go
Friday	30th August	Bransgore Village Hall
Tuesday	3rd September	Le Disque a Go Go
Friday	6th September	Bransgore Village Hall
Saturday	7th September	Ship Inn Wool
Sunday	8th September	Le Disque a Go Go
Monday	9th September	Swanage Labour Hall
Tuesday	10th September	Le Disque a Go Go
Wednesday	11th September	Fordingbridge (private party)
Friday	13th September	Bransgore Village Hall
Saturday	14th September	Big Beat Competition Weymouth
Friday	20th September	Bransgore Village Hall
Saturday	21st September	The Wheel House Club Bournemouth
Friday	27th September	Bransgore Village Hall
Saturday	28th September	Ringwood Mink Farm
Friday	11th October	Ringwood Congregational Church Hall

Dave La Kaz and the G Men, 1964. On the beach at Bournemouth.

This was the autumn in which the phrase *Beatlemania* had been coined by the British press. Two days after his last ever gig with The Trappers Al watched, along with half the country, The Beatles show-stopping appearance on Val Parnell's TV show *Sunday Night at the London Palladium*, at home with his parents in Canford Bottom.

It seems that Al had decided to leave The Trappers for another band. This must have happened all very quickly as he wrote to Chris Owen at the beginning of November inviting him to one of his first gigs with them on November 8th in Bath.

The group was Dave La Kaz and the G Men. With Wycliffe now well and truly behind him and some serious experience of playing electric guitar to trade on he had approached Dave La Kaz directly.

Dave Woodfield's route to becoming the singer Dave La Kaz was as colourful as the stage name that he had taken. He had previously been part of the Bournemouth Group The Bluetones before being invited to join The G Men (as in Guitar Men) sometime in 1963. He was initially asked to perform at a show in Swanage, just along the coast from his home, as his audition. The result was that he got the gig, being asked to take over from one Bill Napier on lead vocals, whereupon he changed his surname to La Kaz (Malay for "fast") having spent part of his national service in Malaya during the Korean War. The group thereafter became known as Dave La Kaz and The G Men. They were clearly one of the area's most in-demand groups often performing three or more gigs in a week. The group at this time was Dave La Kaz on lead vocals, Terry Squire on lead guitar, Derek Scammed on drums, Mike Piggott on bass and Bev Strike on rhythm guitar. They performed at places such as the Cellar Club in Poole, the Downstairs Club in Lansdowne Road and had a Friday night residency at Swanage Community Hall, the venue for Dave La Kaz's live audition.

Throughout this time they built up a good reputation as an excellent rock and roll band, playing mostly cover versions of rock standards. Many people followed them from venue to venue and they soon acquired a varied group of fans. One of them was Al. He would often be seen at gigs or backstage and got to know the band quite well during this time. So much so that he used to come down the steps to their somewhat dingy rehearsal room, which at that time was situated in the basement of Bournemouth's Beaucroft Hotel, and ask to sit in on their rehearsals. Here he'd keep in the background as the group worked on

Dave La Kaz and the G Men, 1964

new songs on what was surprisingly good equipment. The reason for this was Bev Strike. Bev's father owned the famous musical equipment shop in the arcade at Westbourne and they thus were all in the perfect position to get their hands on a succession of new and second-hand instruments. One of these even included a double-neck bass guitar, which Bev proudly played when he took over from Mike Piggott upon his departure. This directly contributed to Al joining the band. What they needed was a committed rhythm guitarist to fit seamlessly and immediately into the group. They already knew that Al could play well and so he was offered the gig one afternoon whilst they were all at the rehearsal space. He even fitted into the suit vacated by Mike Piggott. The G Men all wore hand-made dark blue mohair suits and frilly shirts from Burton's in Bournemouth – Dave himself wearing a slightly different jacket from the others. A picture of rebellious sophistication they certainly all were, as photographs of the time show. This was clearly no ordinary semi-pro early sixties group and their dedication and professionalism saw them in good stead with Al in their line-up for over a year.

They had a legitimate management agency looking after them called *Avon Entertainments* working out of a small office at 124 Old Christchurch Road, and the group got paid £25 a night for all of them. This was for gigs that could last for up to four hours, and out of this they had to deduct the cost of the Commer van and petrol. But it was clearly all worth it. Dave Woodfield recalls that a walk through Bournemouth on a Saturday would result in people continually saying "Hi" and "Last week's gig was amazing!" Al was clearly enjoying this first brush with celebrity.

Dave Woodfield – "He loved it. Al was always so full of energy too at this time. When he joined our band we weren't absolutely sure that it was going to work out but it certainly did! He was always coming up with ideas for our act and worked very hard at his playing."

There are many stories surrounding particular shows played by the G Men that could be included here. Here are three of them. On Tuesday 7th January 1964 they played a gig at Willenhall Baths in Birmingham where St Mary's Catholic Social Club had organised a dance at ten shillings a ticket to see the world famous Ted Heath Band supported by The G Men. The group arrived and walked on stage to perform their set which went down spectacularly well – the audience being on their feet throughout.

Dave Woodfield – "We finished our set and returned to the spartan dressing room but thirty minutes later we were back on stage after the Ted Heath Band had been booed off! We basically played our set all over again. It was a real eye-opener and made us all realise that we were well on the way to becoming a pretty good band."

The previous December they were on a bill at Reading Town Hall that featured a local group Kay and the Koronets and the then up-and-coming Rolling Stones. Both Al and Dave remember them as being quite stand-offish, refusing to mix with anyone in the backstage area (having just appeared on the TV show *Ready Steady Go* with their hit "Little Red Rooster" they could be forgiven for feeling a little full of themselves). However Brian Jones came over with his guitar and chatted with the Bournemouth group. Things were very different in those far off days of the early '60s – the concert poster for the evening boasts the legend "Lucky Ticket Prize to be presented by the Rolling Stones"! Dave Woodfield remembers that Al and the rest of them watched the Rolling Stones' set from the wings.

READING TOWN HALL
8 p.m. to 1 a.m.
Friday, 27th December

JOHN MANNING presents
London's answer to The Beatles

THE ROLLING STONES
DIRECT FROM A.T.V. "READY STEADY GO"

also South England's Recording Group

DAVE LA KAZ & THE G MEN

plus Reading's own

KAY & THE KORONETS
(by arrangement with Consort Entertainments Ltd.)

Don't Miss Reading's Last Big Night of 1963
Lucky Ticket Prize to be presented by
The Rolling Stones
LICENSED BAR :: ADMISSION 10/-
TICKETS NOW ON SALE at:— Norman Hackett Ltd., 5 Bristol & West Arcade
(Opposite Town Hall)
The Tudor Press (Phone 56587) Reading

Al wrote to Chris Owen, explaining how he came to be in his new band.

"It just so happened that the bass player left to join The Dowlands. The rhythm player decided he wanted to play bass and me, being short of money, took on the job of rhythm guitarist."

Still writing songs on a daily basis, Al next composed "Forward the Iron March of Time", in February of 1964 at home in Canford Bottom.

Another tale concerns one of the more prestigious shows that they played in London. By now it was Spring 1964 and the ever resourceful Don Strike had supplied the band with a serious piece of keyboard equipment, a Vox Continental organ and Dave started to look around for someone to join the band to play it. His short search had so far proved unsuccessful when he pulled up one afternoon in the Commer van to pick Al up from his house at Canford Bottom. As Dave walked down the drive to the house he could hear great thundering chords of organ music emanating from inside the house and when Al appeared Dave asked him what record it was that had been playing. "Oh, that was me!" Al laughed, too modest to have put himself forward for the position of keyboard player but a job that nonetheless became his as a result of what he'd been playing that afternoon. A short while later they were playing a concert at The Dorchester Hotel in London, supporting Sidney Lipton. After their 90 minute set the main act asked whether the sound of the Vox Continental could be added to their band and so for a few songs Al improvised with the Sidney Lipton band, going down, according to Dave – "like a storm!"

Al was writing his own original material throughout all of his time with Dave La Kaz and the G Men. Song number 42 in his songbook, composed on February 22nd 1964, was this one:

BARKING UP THE WRONG TREE

Verse I

You're barking up the wrong tree,
Tryin' to mess around with me.
I thought I told you once before,
Don't wanna see you at my door.
You should have come a month ago,
That's when I cared about you too;
You weren't there, now I don't care, I can see –
You're barking up the wrong tree

Verse II

You're barking up the wrong tree,
Go away and let me be,
I don't want you comin' round.
I can tell you're just a hound.
You're sorry now but you're too late,
So take your fingers off my gate,
Your poor mind must be blind not to see –
You're barking up the wrong tree.

Chorus

Ain't it a shame, but you're the only one to blame,
Remember telling me to go?
Now I just don't want to know.

Verse III

You're barking up the wrong tree
I've locked my door an' lost the key
It won't pay, go away, let me be
You're barking up the wrong tree
[End]

Whilst the feel and emotional content of the G Men's music was rock 'n' roll (and most of the bills they appeared on reflected this) they would often play with big bands, novelty acts and cabaret stars such as Frankie Howerd and Bruce Forsyth. And so adaptability became their watchword.

Meanwhile, on April 12th, Al's future flat mate Paul Simon was arriving at Heathrow airport on his first trip to England. It would be a year before they first met.

J.K. – "One day in the spring of 1964, Manfred Mann, who by then had left the club scene and were having Top Ten hits, arrived back in town at the Winter Gardens on a tour with Bill Haley and The Comets and Phil Spector's Crystals. That night Al and I went to a private all night party with them at Le Disque after the club had closed. This was not long before the Manfreds started having No. 1 hits in America. I remember us watching, alongside The Crystals, half of Manfred Mann and half of Zoot Money's band plus Alex Harvey, jamming on the club's tiny stage in the small hours of the morning. Not surprisingly Al didn't make it back to Wimborne the next day, but stayed with us."

Al was living quite the life of Riley at this time. He wrote to Chris Owen – "Dear Ghol,

(Hee, Hee), which is how I always feel in the morning when I think of all the other clods at work and me slowly waking up to another delightfully lazy day (well you'd feel like being lazy after being out until 2am every night)."

His late nights were not getting in the way of his song writing however and in May 1964 Al wrote one of his earliest subjective pieces of work, the brooding and bleak song that was "Child Of The Bomb". In the lyrics the narrative is that of a nucleur survivor and it now seem stylistically clichéed:

> "Once there were flowers, once birds used to fly,
> trees whose green branches reached out to the sky,
> for now there is nothing but dark blistered earth,
> blackened and dead since the hour of my birth,
> why have they done this to my world?
> What made them have their weapons heard?
> I will never know how it has come,
> I was born a child of the bomb".

Heady lyrics none the less for someone yet to turn 19. Throughout that Spring Al continued to write songs on an almost daily basis, composing four of the best in just one month! During June 1964 he came up with "Ours Is Not To Reason Why", "New Ambassadors", "Love is an Ageless Thing" and "Dark Haired Girl". This turned out to be one of Al's earliest love songs to be based on fact and its genesis lay in the centre of Bournemouth. The El Cabala coffee shop was a favourite hangout place (a location that gained real notoriety at this time by its patronage by Christine Keeler and Mandy Rice Davies during their exile from London during the Profumo affair, which was later made into the film *Scandal*) and it was from the El Cabala that Al would walk up Old Christchurch Road to visit *Bourne Radio*. The shop was fitted out like most of the record shops of the time with racks of singles, EPs and albums. There were the booths, so fashionable at the time, inside which you could listen to songs before you bought them, or as in the case of many of Bournemouth's teens *instead* of buying them. Over the course of Al's many regular visits into the record department of Bourne Radio he had been introduced for the first time to the music of Bob Dylan. There were Dylan's albums on the walls and the girl running the place, Sandi, seemed to have an almost encyclopaedic knowledge about him, which was something that impressed Al, as hardly anyone at the time knew even his name. He started to strike up a rapport with her and gradually fell completely under her spell which turned out to be something of a disaster as she was already involved with an older man in Bournemouth and to all intents and purposes their relationship (and specifically Al's love for her) went unrequited. The fact that Al perceived her as having everything that he wanted in a girl – she was truly hip, beautiful and intelligent – and that she basically wasn't interested in him at all forced him to take action. He did two things. Firstly he composed the beautiful ballad on his guitar that became "Dark Haired Girl" including among his simple words of loss – "It was all for the love of a dark haired girl"– a song that was plainly written in the style of its successor "Love Chronicles" five years later. Secondly, he decided that he didn't want to be around a town full of memories of her any more and so in June 1964 he caught the train up to London to put some distance between himself and Sandi. Al spent some time in Hounslow, West London and then on June 28th he moved to 98 Philbeach Gardens SW5 from where he wrote back home the next day:

"Everything is quite promising but nothing definite yet. I played The Black Horse Club on Saturday and also in Trafalgar Square."

Al was out and about in the West End of London, on the run from his life at home in Bournemouth and he was seriously looking for work. He remembers feeling a sense of real escape. It was the first time that he had the freedom to do as he wished. In many ways however the trip was a disappointment to him.

Al – "I had always been trying to get up to London, I mean I was 18, who wouldn't have? I remember on that first trip up in 1964 I stayed first of all at a place in Hounslow for about £3 a week which was an outrageous amount and I remember I tried to get myself signed to *Ember Records* and took them my 'Child of the Bomb' 45 and told the woman assistant to the guy that ran it that I was a 'bomb singer' saying 'bet you haven't got one of those on your label'. Well as they were mostly an R&B label of course they didn't!"

Al left Ember the demo and proceeded to hear absolutely nothing from them. Whilst living in Hounslow he was trying to get gigs and managed to get a booking at the Black Horse pub in Fitzrovia.

Al – "The top of the bill was someone called Ian McCann who was a flat picker and a very good bluegrass guitar player and I got up and sang them 'Child of the Bomb' and people laughed, it was that bad! I'd got up thinking I was Bob Dylan, mind you I was playing to a bluegrass audience who would probably have hated Dylan in person but my own effort at being Bob Dylan was so ludicrous that people were actually laughing at me whilst I was singing. So that night was the beginning and end of my career as a bomb singer! I sang a Dylan song too and they didn't like that either. That was a bit of an eye-opener because back in Bournemouth Bob Dylan was the hippest of the hip but when I arrived in London in 1964 I discovered that the folk clubs there were far more traditional and up until then I didn't even know that traditional music existed!"

This would prove to be the catalyst that was to pre-empt Al's early return back home to Bournemouth once again. He recalls it as being a moment of monumental disappointment and left him totally disillusioned and bewildered.

Al – "I thought to myself why are they playing this hillbilly music? London wasn't anything musically like I'd hoped it would be but I thought it can't all be like this and so I went back a while later and stayed. Whilst I was up there on this first trip I met a couple of girls that had met some guys from Australia who were leaving their flat in Earls Court a week early. So there was this great big flat sitting empty and I went and stayed there for a few days which was great because I loathed Hounslow. If the landlords hadn't been coming to repossess the Earls Court flat I'd have very happily stayed in Earls Court a lot longer."

So this first foray up to London saw Al with his guitar actively going into clubs and searching out work as a solo performer. However, after a couple of weeks he'd returned to Canford Bottom for what turned out to be the last time. It was here that he continued to write and record.

With time on his hands Al was writing both straightforward songs and reams of nonsense verse that on occasions found themselves combined into humorous ditties such as the unrecorded "Was It Something That I Ate?" which appears in the private songbook as song 52 and is dated July 3rd 1964.

The composition is an early illustration of Al's use of irony in a love song.

WAS IT SOMETHING THAT I ATE?

Verse I

I'm trying to think back to Dinner
What was on my Plate
Was it something that I swallowed
Was it something that I ate
That made me feel like this?
It came on after your sweet kiss
They said no, they said no, they said no, no, no,
But it's love

Verse II

I've bin told that if you eat a lot
Before you go to bed
You often get a funny dream
Runnin' through your head
But it don't seem like that
It's a dream like I ain't never had

They said no, they said no, they said no, no, no,
But it's love

Chorus
Well I can't tell you just how I feel
I'm so darn crazy that it don't seem real
I'm kinda jumpy an' my head seems light
And you don't get that by eatin' so it can't be right

Verse III
I wanna know if my supper
Went straight to my head
An' if that's the reason
Why I'm bouncin' on my bed
I never felt like this
It came on after your sweet kiss
They said no, they said no, they said no, no, no,
But it's love
[END]

J.K. – "And humour continued to play a very important part in our lives as Al moved from group to group. He was always hoping that the next one would mean that he'd get to make a record. He always wanted to write a song that they would perform. The biggest change of course was that by this time he had discovered Bob Dylan. Dylan hadn't become well known yet, in fact most people in Bournemouth didn't even know how to pronounce his name correctly. Some people said *Dilan* instead of Dylan but either way his music was changing everything. However the record contracts still weren't coming for the groups that Al was with. He did make one or two private demos at this time, 7-inch, 45rpm records, of which only one copy of each exists today."

The first one of these was with The G-Men for whom Al had recently written the song "It Was Not When She Smiled", the vocal duties on the recording being taken by Dave Le Kaz. Then in August 1964 Al made another recording in Bournemouth which this time turned out to be the first of his records on which he himself actually sang. The session took place in a basement studio in Yelverton Road. The song this time was "The Sky Will Fall Down", on the reverse of which he recorded, in 3/4 time, Bob Dylan's "The Times They Are A-Changing", a song taken from Dylan's third album. The personnel on the session were quite interesting, there being three other musicians performing on the record with Al, not as a permanent group but just for that record. On drums was Lee Kerslake who later went on to become the drummer with Uriah Heep, on lead guitar was Terry Squires, who was later a member of The New Overlanders, just after the period when they had had a number one hit with the Lennon and McCartney song "Michelle", whilst the third member was Pete Ballam, the bass guitarist from Al's old group The Trappers, who later made an album himself with the psychedelic group Bram Stoker. So they all trooped into that tiny studio with Al one weekend and recorded his song "The Sky Will Fall Down", which was a short up-tempo piece in which Al predicts all manner of doom and destruction should the object of his affections desert him. The song had definite shades of '50s Dion and early '60s Brian Hyland and in musical terms at least was a million miles away from the style that Al would go on to adapt six short months later in London. Interestingly enough the handwritten label on the record bills them as *The Stewart Group*.

Al – "'The Sky Will Fall Down' was done in August 1964, upon my return from that abortive trip up to London, as was 'The Times They Are A-Changing'. One of the reasons for me doing that Bob Dylan song was that Sandi was into Bob Dylan from the very first album and it was through her that I was introduced to his music myself. From my perspective she was the source of everything hip in Bournemouth to me. She knew everything and was aloof, cool but friendly and looked exactly like Françoise Hardy. Now if you're 18 and there's this fabulous looking 21-year-old girl who knows everything about music and runs the local record shop you are bound to have a crush on her!"

THE SKY WILL FALL DOWN

The sky will fall down if you ever leave me
I'll wear a frown you know it will grieve me
Just a symbol of our departed love
Broken on the ground
The sky will fall down
The rain will fall down you know on that day
Thunder will sound if you go away
Just a symbol of our departed love
Beating on the ground
Rain will fall down

Then the night will come and until the dawn
I will stand alone lonely and forlorn

Stars will fall down with darkness descending
The roof will fall down and with night comes our ending
Just a symbol of our departed love
Broken on the ground
The sky will fall down
The rain will fall down
The sky will fall down

Much of 1964 was spent waking late, playing the card game Klubiash with Jonny and making plans for their futures. Al had always said to Jonny that he intended to try and make it in London as a guitarist in a band and have hits with them.

Al – "By now I had taken some guitar lessons off of Bob Fripp. I handed over money to him in the back room of Bev Strike's guitar shop in Westbourne and he proceeded to show me the stupidest guitar chords I'd ever seen in my life which were things probably that Fripp can play and nobody else! He'd say 'Now Al, I want you to see if you can stretch your fingers like this,' showing me a chord that was frankly impossible and when I said to him 'Fripp, I really don't think that's possible', he would reply something like, 'Well, it took me 78 hours to stretch my fingers like that!' So it was hopeless really! This all went on for a while and eventually we realised that I was never going to get the hang of it and so we gave up!"

Robert Fripp was playing in local bands The Ravens and The League of Gentlemen during these early years in Bournemouth, the lead vocalist of The Ravens being Gordon Haskell, later to join Fripp in King Crimson. From these two bands Fripp went on to join Peter and Michael Giles in Giles, Giles and Fripp. Peter and Michael Giles had been in The Dowlands and Trend Setters Ltd, their rehearsals taking place primarily at the Beacon Hotel.

Al's career seemed to have stalled somewhat Jonny recalls.

J.K. – "The strange thing is that though things slowly started to happen to some of the other people around us, it didn't happen as quickly as we thought for Al! We had led ourselves to believe, seeing the speed of everything in those days, that it not only would happen but it would happen very quickly."

The songs that Al began to write now were written of course with an eye on having them played by a band, not as a solo folk singer. They provide the missing link between The Snowballs and "The Elf" two years later. One such piece was "The Lion", song 56 in Al's book.

THE LION

Verse I

Tears and grief in a dim lit room
Not a sound to be heard
Present there yet a deep felt gloom
Wanting no uttered word
Sarah Jane, with dampened eyes
Knelt by her sister's bed
Fixed her gaze on the quite still form

Loved but dead

Verse II

Sure yet slow to abandon hope
Kneeling on bended knee
From her lips came the heartfelt words
"Lord, I beg of thee,
Bring back life to this death-cursed room
So my sister may live
And my life I will live for you
And my love I will give

Verse III

Soft but slowly the minutes passed
Soft, they passed once again
Then a little fly, once dead
Flew from the window pane
And in the room where life had gone
Creatures moved once more
Spiders rose and scurried on
From the walls and the floor

Verse IV

Then her sister moved her eyes
Slowly sat up and smiled
Sarah Jane knelt there, lost for words
Crying tears like a child
Then the rug, a lion skin
Shuddered on the floor
And with a growl it caught her up
And dragged her out of the door

Verse V

Tears and Grief in a dim lit room
Not a sound to be heard
As the once-dead sister thought
Uttering not a word
Oh, you can't make bargains with
The one who gave you breath
For you must accept that there
Is no escape from death
[End]

The next day The Beatles film, *A Hard Day's Night*, opened simultaneously in 500 American cinemas. Throughout all of this time Al was working on an occasional basis in and around Bournemouth, his final job was as an administration clerk for British Drug Houses, B.D.H. in Poole, a position that suffered from the fact that he'd arrive for work having been out most of the previous evening at a gig. Al was certainly not looking for a legitimate career and his few exam results were far from adequate should he have wanted to take up his grandfather's advice and become a chartered accountant. Most afternoons he would buy *The Echo* from Alderney Post Office, opposite the office, to check that night's gig guide. He'd travel into town by bus from Canford Bottom and then get the trolley bus around town. During this time back in Bournemouth Al joined two local groups for short periods of time. These were The Mastersounds and The Monks and appear to have been joined more or less on a half-hearted basis by Al, bored by a home town that to him now seemed even more parochial than it had before his London adventure. In The Mastersounds, for whom he played keyboards, Al found a group on the verge of a record deal and in fact he did accompany them up to the capital for a recording session but he was too new to play on it. The Monks were a Canford Bottom four-piece that featured Al, David Nixon and two others. He continued to write songs and had composed another twelve in the last three months, the most recent of which was "My Baby Was Wrong Oh

Winds of Passion Tromp Tromp Tromp" composed on 16th November.

Al had precise thoughts on what he really wanted to do – "When I was 19 I wanted to be in The Hollies, to live that life style, to get up at 11 o'clock in the morning and then go round to Top of the Pops and play my new single and then to go down to The Scotch of St James. It just seemed like such an attractive life style. I knew how it all worked but by the time I had become a singer I obviously wasn't pop star material and it was too late to have a pop hit. I feel that Wycliffe cheated me out of that. What I wanted to do was to be in the Swinging Blue Jeans or something and do the 'Hippy Hippy Shake'. I didn't miss the Procol Harum era or the Hendrix era or the Incredible String Band era or any of those other things that came later but what I missed was that initial Beatlemania 63-64 thing. I wanted to meet Cathy McGowan and all that went with it, have my picture in the *New Musical Express* and to be on *Thank Your Lucky Stars*. I wanted to hear Keith Fordyce saying 'And now all the way from Bournemouth the fabulous...' But it wasn't to be."

The worry that he would see any opportunity of a pop career pass him by unless he got himself up to London became an obsession with Al. All of his friends in Bournemouth knew that it was just a matter of time before he left for good.

Al spent the Christmas of 1964 with his family in Canford Bottom and remembers that it was a period of his life when he felt little was going right. Sandi didn't seem to be interested in him, London had all but proved to be a crushing disappointment, he wasn't in a band and had no money. But by 1965 Al had moved from Scotland to Bournemouth by way of Stratford upon Avon, a public school, *Life With The Lyons*, Duane Eddy, Lonnie Donegan, The Beatles and his own groups The G-Men and The Trappers.

However life was about to change for the better.

Al – "Writing wise things had moved along a great deal during this time. 'The Lion' had evolved into 'Child of the Bomb' and this was all to eventually take me to Bunjies coffee bar in the February of '65. This is precisely the moment when the doom and gloom of the folky vibe began to raise its head."

Neville

48 Linver Road, Parsons Green, London

Throughout all this time Al was becoming more and more in awe of Bob Dylan's songwriting. Between the Christmas holidays and the end of January Dylan had recorded "Maggie's Farm", "It's All Over Now Baby Blue", "Mr Tambourine Man" and "Subterranean Homesick Blues" for the album *Bringing It All Back Home* – songs that Al may have admired but compositions that he none the less found impossible to match when it came to his own writing. It was time to detach himself from the cosy home life of Canford Bottom and the friendships that he had made in Bournemouth and embark on his own equivalent of Dylan's move from the Mid West to New York City four years earlier.

On February 2nd 1965, the day after passing his driving test, Al left Bournemouth for good and was back in West London, staying in a small terraced house just across the road from family friends at 48 Linver Road, Fulham – an address which Al jokingly referred to at the time as the "Gateway to the South"! It was a somewhat genteel and comfortable entrée into London this time around in the mid winter of 1965 for Al.

Al – "I came up to London and Linver Road was where I lived for a while. The family that I stayed with knew my stepfather's parents who lived nearby".

The house in Linver Road, the building in the New Kings Road that had once been the sweet shop, and the church where Basil had once played the organ were all only a few minutes apart and so this seems to fit. It was here, in his bedroom, that he would compose his earliest London songs.

Al – "Although I didn't really write much at Linver Road it's quite likely that I wrote '1944' there because I didn't have that particular song when I came up to London but very soon after I arrived it was something that I remember performing around town. So yes, '1944' is quite probably a Linver Road composition and therefore my very first *London* song."

"1944" was a composition that had, both lyrically and musically, marked a major departure for Al in that it dealt with an actual event; in this case the Holocaust. It was also a song that did not in any way fit into the conventional mould of the 'pop' songs that Al had imagined performing had he been successful in his search for a gig as the guitarist in a contemporary London group performing their own original material. One such group was making very different music to that of "1944" at this time. On February 15th, for example, The Beatles were busy recording "Ticket to Ride" a couple of miles across town at Abbey Road and so the fact that Al was at least thinking about a different style of his own, at such an early stage in his time in London, shows us that he was already giving himself a 'get out' should he not join a band as a rhythm guitarist.

However, whilst still at Linver Road, Al wrote to Jonny Kremer on February 22nd telling him that he now had a job selling newspapers at W.H. Smiths in Putney High Street. The main reason for moving up to London however was to make it as a songwriter and guitarist and to further this endeavour he'd already, within weeks, made some headway. Writing in the same letter he explains that – "Larry Page, The Kinks' manager, has got one of my songs 'Never Love Again' and is offering it to a Manchester girl group for their first record along with three hundred other songs."

Looking back on this letter in 1999 Al was less naïve – "I don't think Larry Page ever even heard 'Never Love Again'. It's possible but the connection was that 'Never Love Again' sounded very similar to 'She's Not There' by the Zombies, which to be perfectly honest was the prototype for it! It was around the same period. I think the song probably kicked in – I think it had a cute little time change thing happening in it. To me it sounded like the most commercial thing I had ever written and I played it to Frank Fenter, who was a theatrical agent who had some sort of connection with Larry Page (well he claimed he knew all these people anyway) and Frank Fenter was going to see if he could get it recorded but never did. But there was a brief moment when I first got up there and met Frank and played him this when it was all very positive and jolly for a moment. It seemed like it might get recorded because it sounded like a commercial song to me. I have long since forgotten it and forgotten how to play it but at the time it sounded so good. It certainly had nothing in common with what I would soon be playing down in Bunjies, I was still writing pop songs but it was obvious, once I started work at Bunjies, that I was going to have to start writing a different kind of song from then on."

Fenter was one of the first people that Al had met in London. It came about via an advert in the *Melody Maker* that Al had answered from a group looking for a guitar player.

Al – "That same week I too had placed an advert in the same paper for 'people inspired by Bob Dylan who would like to form a band' because to my way of thinking everybody should have heard of Bob Dylan by then but very few people seemed to have done. It wasn't until that spring when he played the Festival Hall that it all happened, or even the Albert Hall I guess. Either way on the pop side a lot of people still hadn't heard of Dylan and so, ever on the lookout for work, I answered that advert for The Backwater Three and went around and played with them. It turned out, as it happened, that there were only two of them and that is why they wanted a third. However it turned out that they were playing what I understood basically to be hillbilly music in that they were playing Kentucky banjo type stuff. Totally different from what I was interested in."

So Al didn't join them but he did become a friend with the girl singer, Reina James, who turned out to be none other than the actor Sid James' daughter.

Al – "Reina was just as much a character as her famous father. And she knew a whole bunch of people and one of these turned out to be Frank Fenter, which was how I met him."

The Backwater Three, a three-piece London group on the look-out for a guitarist to give them a fuller sound, were all friends that used to meet up at the Me Pampa coffee bar in Swiss Cottage and named themselves after the song "Backwater Blues".

Reina James – "We honestly weren't very good and were forever looking for ways to improve ourselves and that's how the advert in *Melody Maker* came about. I think we had decided that we just needed a bit more sound!"

Up until that time the band had been doing gigs here and there around London, harbouring a thinly disguised ambition to be seen as contemporaries of The Settlers and Pete Seeger's Weavers. Their repertoire included the songs "Pallet On The Floor" and the Leadbelly composition "Midnight Special".

At the time that Al saw their notice none of them were writing their own original material and the impression that he got of their style from that one audition was reasonably accurate.

Reina James – "To say that we were a fully fledged bluegrass group was actually very complimentary but yes, that sort of country blues sound was what we were trying to

Soho, London April 1965: Al plays a church benefit with Simon and Garfunkel

produce and if that's how Al remembers us then I'm very pleased!"

The audition that Al was invited to attend took place at Reina's flat in Beauchamp Place, Knightsbridge, West London.

Reina James – "This really was one of the great mismatches of all time, looking back on it. There we were, doing our covers of American folk and country music and Al turns up on our doorstep in his role as the apprentice English singer songwriter! It wasn't ever really going to out work was it?"

Reina's group were at this time managed by Tony Stratton-Smith who, shortly after the abortive Al audition, put up the money for the trio to record a single that had been especially written for them; but it never got released. Reina and Al had become firm friends by this time and as a direct result of which Al was soon introduced to Stratton-Smith who a few months later would be his manager too.

Reina James – "I may very well have introduced Al to Tony one afternoon when we all met up in Soho. Tony was definitely the man with the big cigar; larger than life was an understatement! He was everybody's idea of what a manager was like, almost like something out of the movies."

Rejection was by now something that Al was getting used to but it doesn't seem to have ever caused him more than momentary disappointment. Whilst not living in the realms of blind faith in his own certainty to succeed he was clearly sure than sooner or later one of these auditions of either him or his songs would prove successful and it was that self-belief that perhaps gave him the edge over some of his contemporaries.

Al – "It quite possibly did. When you're 19 you'll try anything and very little gets you down because there's always something else just over the horizon. That's certainly how it was for me anyway. I went for auditions all over London in those first few months."

In his search for the job as an electric guitarist in a London band Al went for interviews with The Paramounts (where he was interviewed by Gary Brooker) and toyed with the notion of joining The Outlaws where Ritchie Blackmore got the job.

Writing to Jonny, in February 1965, Al talked about how Dick James was selling shares in The Beatles for seven shillings and ninepence and it's clear to see how his enthusiasm for the minutiae of the music business, chart positions, who is joining who and so on had not deserted him since Wycliffe two eventful years previously. A week before this letter was written Al had played an interesting show at a place called Studio 51 found at 10 Newport Street in Soho. Ray Sone of the Downliners Sect and some others were playing at this small club and Al, guitar to hand, had got up and performed a couple of songs. He played Dylan's "Masters Of War" and when someone in the crowd called out "pop song" he rewarded them with his own Holocaust composition "1944". So from day one in London Al was on the look out for music all across town whilst his domestic arrangements remained firmly rooted in suburban security staying with his new extended family in Fulham.

BUNJIES

In which Al learns his craft at Bunjies and Les Cousins and in 1966 releases his first single "The Elf"on CBS.

Al continued working at W.H. Smith's each morning, making the 15 minute walk from home on the edge of Parson's Green, across Putney Bridge and up the hill to the shop.

Life in London was much tougher than Al had imagined it would be. But now, if only he could have known it, he was about to enter a golden period.

One of the early groups Al auditioned for in London were The Bo Street Runners who had got their first real push when coming first on the *Ready, Steady, Win* talent contest staged over six weeks during the TV show *Ready, Steady, Go*. Al himself enjoyed some success when he auditioned for the groups The Primatifs and Simon and the Surreys, but turned down the chance of joining each of them on German tours early in 1965, electing for the moment to continue trying his luck in London.

The London music scene at this time was centred around Soho specifically but all over town clubs were springing up on a weekly basis and church halls were getting extra income moonlighting as dance halls or beat clubs. Typical of the groups you could see around March 1965 were The Bo Street Runners at the Golders Green Refectory, John Mayall's Bluesbreakers at The Crawdaddy in London Road, Croydon, Chris Farlowe, Brian Auger's Trinity and Georgie Fame at The Flamingo which was then at 33-37 Wardour Street. Nadia Cattouse, a particular favourite of Al at this time was with Martin Carthy at The Fox on Islington Green, Bert Jansch at Cecil Sharp House near Primrose Hill, whilst at Bruce Dunnett's Scots House in Cambridge Circus Owen Hand was a resident. The Scots House or more simply *The Hoose*, as it came to be known, also ran a designated "New Folksingers" session on Sunday nights whilst The New Prince at 23 Gerrard Street staged "all night folksong" on Saturday evenings. There was also a burgeoning folk scene in pubs and small clubs in the suburbs such as Folk West Four at The Emperor on Chiswick High Road, Wimbledon Folk Club on Edge Hill and The Enterprise at Chalk Farm with such performers as Davy Graham and Dorris Henderson.

Although he was "passionately involved" with Dylan's music Al couldn't see how anyone but Dylan could succeed at playing it. The folk clubs up until this time were frequented by bearded, middle-aged Scots or Irish playing rebel songs. Al had auditioned for numerous groups with mixed results, but around this time things began to get a lot easier for "folk singers", as anyone with an acoustic guitar was erroneously labelled. The established clubs in London such as The Marquee on Wardour Street, The Flamingo, or The 100 Club wouldn't give you a chance, but when Les Cousins opened in Greek Street it seemed to act as the catalyst for a whole wave of folk clubs, coffee bars, and speakeasy-style venues for the more lyrical artists.

One such coffee bar/folk club was Bunjies, at 27 Litchfield Street, a place destined to be one of the crucial venues of Al's career. The club had initially featured flamenco music but in the '50s skiffle and now folk had taken over. The likes of Tommy Steele, Terry Dene, Diz Disley, Denny Wright, Redd Sullivan and Terry Nelhams all came to play there and so by the time Lou Hart took over in 1960 it was a very successful club. With the folk boom, largely centred on Soho, in full swing he put music on every Monday and Tuesday initially and soon the club was featuring folk music every night – in fact the posters advertised music "Eight Days a Week". The entrance to Bunjies was along a small, scruffy hallway and down a narrow flight of stairs. At the bottom was a small counter with an espresso machine and behind that, a tiny kitchen. To the left was the seating area, about nine tables surrounded by low stools. On each of the tables stood an oil lamp, burning with a small flame. The overall lighting was dim and dark. Probably to hide the dirt. The walls were bare brick. At the bottom of the stairs, to the right, was another sub-cellar, down a further two or three steps. Again, it was bare brick, with a couple of wall lamps. This was the Folk Cellar, and it was filled with small wooden stools set in rows and a couple of tables and benches to one side.

Al's influences at this time were varied, when asked about these a few years later he had this to say about the R&B he'd succumbed to – "There were The Animals, The Kinks, The Pretty Things, The Rolling Stones, The Downliners Sect, John Mayall, The Graham Bond Organisation… more or less the whole British R&B scene of 1965. I was playing "Sticks and Stones" on electric piano, doing a little bit of lead guitar, but these were my immediate influences. Of course I'd listened to Bob Dylan from the word go but down in Bournemouth there had seemed to be no possible outlet for anything like that. So I had come up to London to join a group."

"When I came to town I had a Gibson Les Paul and a Vox AC30 but I didn't have an acoustic guitar; I spent about a month trying to get into various groups and I auditioned for five. Basically I suppose I must have been just about in the middle, not good and not bad, because two of the groups accepted me and they were just underneath what I wanted, and two of the groups turned me down and they were both fairly big time, and the other I think I woke up too late to audition for and so I never knew. But anyway I'd only been up in town three weeks when something happened that changed all that."

"And so it fell out I came up to London to look for fortune and fame, starry eyed in my seaside successes, and much too sure of the game" – Al writing in "Love Chronicles" four years later.

At the end of February 1965 Al walked the 50 yards down a side street off Cambridge Circus as an ex-beat group guitarist and emerged 90 minutes later as a folk singer.

Al again – "Fate helped me out that day I guess. I went down to Bunjies coffee bar as I'd arranged to meet someone there. Inside was a little folk cellar which held about 80 people and we went in and had a cup of coffee and listened to Les Bridger playing guitar. Someone then asked if anyone in the audience wanted to do a song and all of a sudden there's all this elbowing in my ribs and voices calling out 'Al can sing, he'll get up and play a song!' So I got shoved on stage much against my better judgement and performed 'The Times They Are A-Changing' with much spirit and very little finesse but to thunderous applause. There was a very healthy Dylan cult but at the same time it was quite closed in – the world at large hadn't heard of Dylan but the inmates of Bunjies were very hip to Dylan and Dylan was the *aware* underground thing to be into at the time. This was about eight weeks before that song came out as a single in the UK. I'd sung the right song in the right place at the right time and by a monster stroke of luck the club owner Lou Hart, this all sounds just like a Hollywood script but it's absolutely true, he was standing in the doorway and had witnessed all of this and as we were leaving he came up and said – 'Excuse me but are you a folk singer?'

Now I can smell a gig about three miles off so without even flinching I replied – 'Oh yes'. Lou proceeded to offer me the Friday night spot there and then and so I asked him – 'How long have I got to sing for?'

'You'll be sharing the evening with someone else but I reckon you've got to let it run for around about three hours' came the reply. And I had three songs at that moment that I could actually sing! 'So can you do it?' he asked and I said 'Oh yes'."

So Al, the folksinger without songs, was offered the residency at Bunjies Coffee Bar. The time that he would spend here, in that tiny club in the centre of London would directly affect the course of his career. The offer of the position at Bunjies allowed Al dedicate his life to music.

Al – "That was the green light, I was only making £8 a week at W.H. Smith & Sons so I just weighed it all up and went back to Putney and gave in my notice and spent the whole of the rest of the week learning the *Freewheeling* and *The Times They Are A-Changing* albums verbatim so I could return to Bunjies and sing every track off those LPs."

Eight years later, in "Post World War Two Blues", Al would refer to these days in early 1965 when he wrote – "*I came up to London when I was nineteen with a corduroy jacket and a head full of dreams*".

Initially it was on a week-to-week basis but it evolved into a residency and soon Al's repertoire was up to 26 songs. The two compères at Bunjies could not have been more diverse, Peter Bellamy singing his seafaring songs with a hand over one ear, standing there with his big voice and haughty attitude (especially towards Al) and Al himself singing his Dylan covers and a few early originals. According to Al, his performances of the Dylan songs were always in the same order as the records! He was being paid, it was not very much, just a few shillings a night.

Al – "You see I'd always written songs but the trouble was that they didn't fit into anything because I've always been hung up with the lyrics so I was writing basically R&B flavoured songs in Bournemouth in 1964 with the most absurd lyrics you've ever heard! I mean they just didn't fit it at all. I'd always tried to get into something original and the result was pure melodrama. I felt that music should break out of its bounds, it should be more than 'Hey baby with the red dress on...', I really thought it had to progress from that but I was working in a vacuum, there was no one to show me the way. Obviously the pop thing wasn't going well and I wasn't going to get into The Hollies and so I needed to do a different kind of music that would fit in with the Bunjies folk thing. 'New Ambassadors' is more or less The New Christy Minstrels, a very primitive thing but 'Nothing At All' is totally Dylan. You see I was just sort of feeling my way around this weird new folk thing."

Someone who was right there in the folk cellar at exactly the same time as Al and Bellamy was Cliff Wedgbury. On the first night that David had visited Bunjies, Al and Bellamy were sharing the bill.

Cliff Wedgbury – "As I walked into the cellar I heard Peter Bellamy singing a song from his rich traditional repertoire of sea shanties and ballads. I particularly remember the bawdy Norfolk ballad, 'The German Musician', which was hilarious and slightly risqué. He sang some songs with concertina backing, some unaccompanied and some while strumming on an old, battered guitar. He also played slow airs on a tin whistle. He looked a thin, intense young man, poorly dressed and with long, straight blond hair.

Into this traditional atmosphere strode a bright, smiling young man, full of confidence and carrying a guitar case. This was the first time I saw Al. He introduced himself to Peter, shook his hand and sat down on the stool alongside him. Peter sat on the left and Al sat on the right. I can't be certain, but I think it was quickly agreed between them that they would entertain the audience by singing three songs alternately."

Reina James – "Ah Bunjies. That was very much the place back then. I often saw Al play there. I remember that it would get so hot in there that you could run your hand down the wall and it would be soaking wet, Al would have to re-tune his guitar every ten minutes, it was very tough on the performers. I used to love him singing 'Richard Cory' and can still picture him now, swinging away down in that cellar, with his open tuning and such joy in his face."

Cliff Wedgbury again – "Al's guitar was an old rock 'n' roll type F-hole model. It sounded very tinny, but we soon saw that he played it with great talent. Mostly plectrum style in those early days, and using the bar chords of a rock rhythm guitarist. He sang mostly early Bob Dylan songs, 'Don't Think Twice', 'Hattie Carrol', 'Masters of War' and 'God on our Side'. I also remember, quite distinctly, one of his own compositions that night, 'Pretty Golden Hair', which impressed everybody. I'd never heard anyone writing songs using lyrics like 'lavatories' and 'prostitution' before, and it opened up a whole new horizon for me, in what could be written about. Peter Bellamy mocked Al's

Bunjies Folk Cellar 1965

contemporary repertoire, but in a good-humoured, leg-pulling way. Al accepted this leg-pulling with great good humour. It was obvious to all that they, in fact, had great respect for each other and their different talents."

One night a few weeks into his residency at Bunjies Al was recommended to talk to a lady called Judith Piepe who was what amounted to an 'angel' on the folk scene. He was told that he could contact her through Collets Record Shop.

Judith was born in Silesia. Her father, a Jewish Socialist Member of Parliament had fled Germany the night the Nazis had burnt down the Reichstag building in 1933. Having arrived in this country after the war from her native Austria as a Jewish refugee under the name of Sternberg she'd married and then divorced an English vicar and ended up with a council flat in Shadwell. This was the second floor house in Dellow Street that went on to be one of the key centres of the English folk scene.

Judith had been a social worker in London for three years. With the house as a base and an American friend, Caroline Culpeper, she hung out in the cafés and folk clubs of London and had taken many folk singers under her wing. Most notable of these was Paul Simon. Judith also produced a daily radio spot on the BBC broadcast between two hugely popular shows, *Housewives Choice* and *Music While You Work*. Paul had left the BBC a tape of his songs and it was decided to use some of these on the show for a few mornings. Judith wrote the commentaries between them. Each morning she introduced the song for that day. The show was called *Five To Ten* (for obvious reasons). There was always four minutes and 45 seconds of music and the announcer took up the rest of the time. Besides Paul, Al would also go on to appear on the BBC through this show.

Judith had first seen Paul perform at The Flamingo Club one night towards the end of 1964 on one of her regular forays into the folk clubs of Soho. This was the night that the headline act had failed to arrive at the Wardour Street club and Paul had got to perform a set that included "The Leaves That Are Green", "A Church Is Burning" and "The Sound Of Silence" before being joined by Art Garfunkel for "Benedictus".

Judith Piepe – "This was a very moving experience for me. I was sat there watching this young man take the audience with him to the most spiritual of places. He had them in the palm of his hand and when Artie got up there with him I just knew that I had to do all that I could to spread the word about this all. I remember it very clearly, even though it was so long ago."

Judith's campaign to get Al work was something that she by now had down to a fine art having done much the same for Paul Simon. She had become a regular visitor to the cramped and smoky offices of promoters, managers and music publishers across the West End by this time and clearly knew the business as well as anybody. Through her constant badgering both Paul and Al got work that, without her, they would never have even known existed. Between the end of 1964 and January 1965, a period when Paul was back at college in the States, Judith had worked ceaselessly on his behalf and succeeded in getting the BBC to promise him studio time on his return. This exposure played an important part in CBS advancing him the £90 to record what would soon become *The Paul Simon Songbook* at Levy's Studio in Bond Street in May of 1965.

Judith Piepe – "I was doing the best I could for Paul and Al at this time. Paul had been doing all of this a little longer than Al and so it was Al that I tended to need to help the most. Paul was getting the most bookings and so I did try my very best to give Al a hand whenever I could. He was very ambitious even then. Al was always open to any ideas that I had and was a very good student you could say."

Al – "I learned a great deal from her. I eventually went on to move out of Linver Road because I couldn't afford even £3 a week at that time so I had to find somewhere I could live for free and the obvious answer was Judith Piepe's doss house in the East End, which in those days it was, because people were sleeping all over the floor and everywhere."

Al didn't move in there straightaway however and for the time being continued to live at Linver Road. From here he would go into town looking for work and returning to try and write in the comfortable but far from stimulating environs of Parsons Green. By this time he was getting to know the people and places that made up the emerging folk scene in London. An integral part of all this was Collets bookshop.

Karl Dallas – "It was run very well for a long time by Bill Leader. It was the obvious place for people to meet at and it also staged such events as the reception for Pete Seeger when he came to Britain for the first time."

Collets had a number of branches at this time across London. Besides its record store at 70 New Oxford Street there were Chinese and Russian bookshops and the head office, the Political branch on the Charing Cross Road. The specialist Folk, Blues and Jazz record shop had originally existed as part of that shop but after two cramped years on New Oxford Street it had moved to its own premises in 1960. It was from here that for the next decade it served as the core information point for both the counter culture, with its pamphlets and marches, and the folk and blues movement, whose key and not so key players used its resources as both a shop and drop-in centre to look for gigs and catch up on the local news. It both fostered a community spirit amongst the disparate bunch of musicians that crossed its threshold and actively contributed to the renaissance of folk music in London throughout the early '60s. It was hardly surprising then that Judith Piepe was a regular visitor to the Oxford Street store. It was via Collets that she'd first met Al.

Judith – "One day when Al was in Collets, the folk record shop, someone told him that they thought that I would be able to help him with his search to get more work. So Al telephoned me and I said that he could come down and see me at Dellow House, which he did. He sang me some of his songs. It so happened that the next day I had a date with the BBC to do a recording for a Good Friday Broadcast. There wasn't any time to do any preparation at all because it was so near and I just said to Al, 'You come along with me to the radio studio and we'll do that song, 'Ides of Auschwitz', and if the producer likes it then it will go in.' Well he did like it because a short time later Al was on another of these shows. Those songs that he played me at home were his own original compositions, I wasn't interested in anything else."

This of course was a major 'leg up' for Al at this time, coming just a few short weeks after he had arrived in town from Bournemouth. It would see the initiation of a relationship that would guide him safely through that first year in London.

Al – "It meant a great deal to me and I knew it! When I first came to London my plan was definitely not to become a singer-songwriter but to be a guitar player, a hired gun session guitar player on the folk scene. Back watching TV in Bournemouth I'd seen Nadia Cattouse who had a regular folk programme. She was coloured, completely amazing and she'd sing a song each week on this show and her backing guitar player was Martin Carthy. When he left to pursue his own career there was therefore a vacancy! So basically I wanted Martin Carthy's job! I remember spending about 20 minutes on the phone talking to Nadia Cattouse trying to get her to let me be her lead guitar player but she wasn't going for that at all. Judith Piepe knew her and I think Judith gave me her telephone number but I never got to play with Nadia."

Judith would visit Al at Bunjies and he would often hang out at the house in Dellow Street in the afternoons. As an induction into the folk world of London it proved as invaluable to him as it had been for Paul Simon a few months earlier.

Al – "I remember the very first time that I met Paul that Spring. I was around at the house in Dellow Street one afternoon and we bumped into one another in the hallway just as I was going out to do something or other around town with Judith. I had no idea who he was and asked him what he did and he replied 'I suppose I write songs'. We both sat down in the kitchen, he unpacked his guitar and proceeded to play me one of his own compositions, 'Flowers Never Bend With The Rainfall'. I could see that he was really talented but I thought that the song owed a great debt to The Beatles."

When Al first met the exotic Jackson C. Frank, the American folk singer was then living on a Thames barge, which in itself was somewhat apt given the bohemian image that Jackson had cultivated for himself.

Al – "Both Jackson and I played at a folk club in Kingston upon Thames in mid-1965 and after the show we all went back to his home on the river. These were great fun times for us all. Six months earlier I'd been fed up in Bournemouth and now here I was living this totally different life and I was free!"

The Folk Club that Al remembers, The Barge, was in actual fact in Richmond. Run by Theo Johnson from an old barge moored on the Thames it had also been the place to which a young Sandy Denny had gone to sing as a floor singer whilst at Kingston Art College. Sandy was as much a devotee of Dylan as Al and on her first home demos had attempted "It Ain't Me Babe".

Judith Piepe remembers seeing Sandy there – "Both Al and Sandy were completely under the spell of Bob Dylan at that time. I first saw Sandy on the boat one evening singing 'Polly Vaughan'. She had this wonderful voice and such charisma. It was obvious to me at least that she was going to make it sooner or later. She was someone that I liked very much."

Al had first met Sandy at the house in Dellow Street. Al – "I was in the kitchen when she appeared straight from her night shift at the hospital. I asked her who she was and she just said 'Oh, I'm Jackson's girlfriend'. Now I knew that Jackson had a number of other ladies he was seeing and in fact it was a while before I regularly saw them together as an item. Another thing was that Jackson didn't like the idea at all of Sandy performing in her own right and didn't like her singing or playing the guitar. I think he managed to pin Sandy down in many ways and she was always a lot more bubbly and full of life when Jackson wasn't around. I can well remember the first song I heard her sing. The song she was doing was 'The Ballad of Hollis Brown' and it was just so clear to anyone that heard her that here was one of the great voices. I remember seeing her steam through the crowd at The Troubadour one evening and Martin Winsor yelling across the room 'Sandy Denny, you're a girl, not a tank!' but that was Sandy all over!"

The comings and goings at Judith's house in the East End provided Al with not only a whole new set of friends but also a sense of being part of a genuine music-based community. Judith's house was an integral part of Al's journey through that London folk scene.

Al had also recently started doing the rounds of the legion of small, independent music publishers in Soho, Covent Garden and Denmark Street, known universally as Tin Pan Alley. One such stop was at Lorna Music where his mission was to convince Peter Pave and Leslie Lowe that they should give him a publishing deal. Their office was truly cramped and probably hadn't changed much since Paul Simon had sat there two years before with his duffel coat hanging on the back of a chair playing through the songs he'd written to Les. Paul Simon thought very highly of Lorna Music as they'd placed his song "Carlos Domingues" with Val Doonican who'd recorded it 18 months before. They used a nice local Soho location for recording their artists – Regent Sound Studios, which was in the same street and from 1963 had been used by Andrew Oldham to produce The Rolling Stones. As Al crossed over the Charing Cross Road from Denmark Street and into Manette Street past the cafés and guitar shops and the twinkling neon sign on the side of Foyles he was mulling over what Lorna Music had said. He needed to "get some songs recorded". He had to somehow cut an acetate. And so he considered, as he walked the 50 yards down Manette Street, past St Barnabas Church and under the stone archway by the Pillars of Hercules that led to Greek Street, which of his original songs, given the chance, would be put onto the acetate? There was "Go Your Way", "Pretty Golden Hair", "Do I Love My Neighbour?" "Nothing at All", "1944 ", "Ides of Auschwitz" and several others to consider as he walked through Soho that afternoon.

Little did Al realise the chance to record a proper set of demos was just around the corner. Besides the Dave La Kaz songs and the "Dark Haired Girl" single he had recorded very few others. There had been a couple; "Swansong Of The Millionth Man" existed as a Bournemouth demo from the January of 1964 and "Child of the Bomb" had been recorded four months later. But it was the intoxicating atmosphere of Judith's house that made the biggest impression on him.

Al – "Once I started to go around to Judith's the floodgates opened and I started to write songs on almost a daily basis. It was much more of a creative environment there than I'd had anywhere before."

On March 31st Al wrote home announcing that, "Thursday is the '*A*' day", meaning that on April 15th he would be making his first ever appearance on radio during the BBC light programme show *Five To Ten*. He told Jonny that he'd be performing "…eight lines of my horrific anti-war, anti-racial hatred, anti-everything song called 'Ides of Auschwitz' which will be sung and played at the beginning and end of the talk by Judith, my Anglican church friend". He continues with "This is experimental and if successful I'll be on the programme again, perhaps regularly."

The song had been written by him on the previous Thursday but due to the length of Judith's spoken word part of the show only eight lines of "Ides of Auschwitz" were ultimately broadcast.

Al continued – "My progress around the folk clubs is encouraging. My agent is now getting me £5 a night at The Centre, see *Melody Maker* ad for 10th and 25th April." He was at last making some headway in London and continued "Bunjies continues prosperously! I'm very tied up with Judith whisking me around music publishers, producers, priests and sleazy Soho clubs!" He ends the letter by mentioning that Judith has been talking to him about performing "Pretty Golden Hair" on one of her future programmes.

On April 16th 1965 Transatlantic Records released one of the key first albums of the folk scene, *Bert Jansch*, TRA 126. The album was to influence Al more than anything anyone else put out that year except Bob Dylan. The record was a testament to the many different schools of music that Bert had allowed to influence and therein shape his music. The self-titled debut tipped its hat to the likes of Charles Mingus and Cannonball Adderley. Whilst Jimmy Giuffre's "Train And The River" was, to all intents and purposes, the song that appeared as "Casbah" in the sleeve notes. It was an impassioned and ferocious gauntlet to throw down at the feet of 1965 London and Al was as impressed as anyone else.

Al – "I went out and got myself a copy at once. It was one of those albums that almost had one of those 'Do you remember where you were the first time that you heard it?' qualities going for it. I thought it was amazing; all of us did. The guitar playing was just out of this world."

Al and Bert continued to play the same clubs around London and it must have been frustrating for Al to see Bert's album being reviewed in everything from *Folk Scene* to *Melody Maker* whilst he didn't even have management let alone a record deal. Meanwhile he did his best to get gigs around town and the most prestigious venue of all was Les Cousins. It had an intriguing history.

The premises that housed Les Cousins had changed from being the Skiffle Cellar to simply the Cellar in the late spring of 1958 when it started running two folk sessions on a Saturday and another with Steve Benbow on a Tuesday. It also became, as much of Soho had, a strip club for a short period before re-opening as Les Cousins on Friday 16th April '65. At this time its major competition was The New Prince run by Curly Goss out of premises at 23 Gerrard Street. By Saturday 15th May, by which time Al had been in London a little over three months, Les Cousins announced the first of its weekend 'All Nighters' – which would soon provide the stage (probably more than anywhere else) for Al to develop his craft. The New Prince promptly became The All Night Prince but after a few weeks of rivalry it disappeared as quickly as it had arrived and to all intents and purposes left Les Cousins with the monopoly of all night folk venues in the Capital.

Les Cousins, at 49 Greek Street, was an intoxicating and eclectic mix of lifestyles that personified all things Soho. On the top floor was an illegal gambling club-*cum*-bar, the ground floor housed the Greek Restaurant run by the Matheou family and the basement of course had its music cellar. Noel Murphy's agent, Phil Philips ran Les Cousins to start with but it was soon to the Matheou's son Andy that the responsibilities as its *de facto* manager fell. There was only one electrical socket and its capacity was 145 but its influence was immeasurable.

Over the next five years it saw appearances by Paul Simon, Donovan, John Renbourn, Sandy Denny, Cat Stevens, Anne Briggs, Alexis Korner, Arlo Guthrie, Eric Clapton, Duffy Power, Owen Hand, Diz Disley, Long John Baldry, Bob Dylan, Nick Drake, Noel Murphy, Wizz Jones, The Young Tradition, Bridget St. John, The Incredible String Band, Jackson C. Frank and Roy Harper amongst many, many others.

Al – "It was just the most magical place in the world. Andy and his parents especially were the most generous people. They would feed any of us that looked as if we hadn't had a decent meal for a while in the restaurant upstairs. They saved the lives of most of the folk fraternity at one time or another!"

Les Cousins in fact never actually promoted itself as a folk *club per se* and didn't limit itself to just folk acts but it was through them that its reputation was assured.

At the same time as all this was happening in Greek Street, Bruce Dunnet was expanding his empire under the umbrella of Associated Folk Clubs. Besides The Scots Hoose he promoted provincial folk club evenings at the Green Man in Harlow and the Blacksmith's Arms in St Albans.

This is how the late Alexis Korner remembered Les Cousins at its height – "It was a very small club. You could see everyone and everyone could see you, unless you happened to be one of the two people stuck behind a pillar. It attracted musicians who played in a variety of styles that were new and exciting. In a way, it was a training ground for many musicians. It tended to attract those players because its attitude was so much more flexible than that of the other folk clubs. It was the one club in London where you could use an amplifier and not be thrown out. Other clubs were very rigid but Les Cousins had all kinds of music – avant garde, jazz, early underground, all kinds."

Roger Hand – "Les Cousins– a lot of good things happened to do with that club, that's where everybody seemed to come from. The 'scene' was definitely centred on that club. The names that came out of there are legendary."

On the weekends the tiny cellar club at 49 Greek Street would open its doors at the foot of the stairs that led down from the pavement at 7 o'clock for a session that went on until 11. At that hour, it would be cleared of its patrons amid much moaning and some shouting in preparation for the all-nighter. This session for the all-night players would go on until 6.30 in the morning. Everyone played there. Wizz Jones was a regular.

Originally Russell Quaye's Skiffle Cellar, Les Cousins had grown up in an area of Soho rich in premises (most of them seedy and hidden) at the tops of narrow flights of stairs or down steep cellar steps. There had been the Freight Train at 44 Berwick Street, The House of Ann Widges at 9 D'Arbly Street, Le Macabre, at 23 Meard Street, The Breadbasket, at 65 Cleveland Street, The Partisan at 7 Carlisle Street and The Heaven And Hell which was around the corner from Les Cousins at 57 Old Compton Street and had been next door to the 2Is Coffee Bar. Along with the Scots House there was The Ballad And Blues Club (which was founded at The Black Horse, 6 Rathbone Place and had been started up by no less than Ewan MacColl), Bunjies and other numerous folkie hangouts such as Finchs in Goodge Street and Foley Street's King and Queen.

The Everglades at The Centre was a folk venue that was rapidly gaining a reputation at the time as an ideal location for new folk singers to learn their craft. Situated in South London's Balham High Road it put on folk evenings four times a week. Al played there again on 2nd May 1965. Interestingly enough he was using the alternative "Stuart" spelling of his name at this time for concert billing purposes.

Al sums up how he felt in May 1965 – "By 1965 I'd reached the point where I couldn't sing 'Sticks and Stones' much as I loved it. Dylan had arrived (on April 27th), and convinced me that you could sing an intelligent lyric, which was a total innovation – renovation you might say!"

On the 9th May Al attended the open air Trafalgar Square Beat and Folk Festival which featured Ian Campbell and Nadia Cattousse whose song "Port Mahon" was one of his favourite records at this time.

That same night Bob Dylan played the first of his two London shows.

In the Boxing Day 1976 issue of *The Houston Chronicle* Al looked back to this time and remembered seeing Bob Dylan at the Royal Albert Hall – "It was amazing. He was writing about all these fantastic things. There had never been anything like it before. Now, so many people write lyrics that it's taken for granted, but the first time I heard "A Hard Rain's A-Gonna Fall" I thought, this is absurd, what's it all about? Also, the standard format for concerts in those days was for somebody to employ six bands and give them all 25 minutes each and the headliner 35 minutes. That would be a show. The idea of one man standing on a stage for two hours – on his own – singing songs he'd written instead of old Chuck Berry tunes was totally radical in England at the time. So, when I saw Dylan at the Albert Hall in 1965, it amazed and convinced me. That's why I sold all my electric equipment, bought the acoustic guitar and got into the folk clubs."

Dylan's Albert Hall appearance was part of D.A. Pennebaker's documentary film *Don't Look Back* and Al vaguely recalls the filming.

Al – "I remember the cameras being there. In fact I stood next to Pennebaker 'cause I'd met Tom Wilson, Dylan's recording manager. And I remember the camera right there in front of me. Of course I didn't know what it was doing at the time. Had I stood in front of it …" he lets his voice trail off. "But you miss these opportunities. Anyway it would have been totally premature 'cause I was only about 19."

Writing back home on 9 May 1965, still at Linver Road, Al mentioned a planned trip to France in a letter dominated by personal reviews of the two new records by Bob Dylan and Bert Jansch. He calls Dylan's *Bringing It All Back Home* "probably his worst ever record with the exception of the two tracks 'Gates of Eden' and 'It's Alright Ma'!" Al dismisses the rest of the album as "boring" and suggests to Jonny Kremer that if he wanted to "be truly hip not just in Bournemouth but the rest of the country" then he should definitely check Bert out.

In the middle of May Al made that trip to Paris but then had to be financially rescued by his parents when he became ill and subsequently ran out of money following what was a somewhat haphazard search for Jean-Paul Sartre.

In travelling to Paris at this time Al was unwittingly following in the footsteps of one of his contemporaries, someone that would soon loom large in both his musical and private life. Paul Simon had made the trip from New York City to Paris exactly a year earlier and had made far better use of the experience than Al was to do now. It was during his stay there that Paul had first been introduced to the music of South America in the beguiling rhythms of Urubamba. It was here also that he first heard Los Incas play the music that he would later use as the template for his song "El Condor Pasa". Paul had busked around the Seine and at that time met David McLausland who ran the Brentwood Folk Club in Essex. It was through this chance meeting that Paul was invited to England, arriving on 11th April 1964. At his first show on the following night Paul had played the Railway Inn in Brentwood and met a secretary from Hornchurch called Kathy. This was the girl that would become his girlfriend, muse and the inspiration for some of his best loved songs including "Homeward Bound", "America" and "Kathy's Song".

By June 3rd Al was back in London and appearing once again on Judith's radio programme *Five To Ten,* this time playing a brand new song of his called "Do I Love My Neighbour?" which he'd only completed on the District Line tube train on his way from Parsons Green to Oxford Circus and the BBC studios! It was a song that he had struggled with for reasons that are easy to fathom in that it was the first occasion that the task of coming up with an original song "to order" was put before him. To Al, who was finding it hard enough to come up with an original style of his own, let alone someone else's, the discipline of composing what was in essence a "bespoke" piece of a set length was almost beyond him. It also had, in its religious theme, a lyrical content far removed from any that he was used to. The song was never recorded again

DO I LOVE MY NEIGHBOUR?
Do I love my neighbour?
Can it really be that I'd care for strangers?
Ah yes when the sun dries we'll see.
If he slips and tumbles do I really care?
Ah yes if he brings me troubles that I don't want to share.

For I'm not big enough to lend a hand,
Or I'm not wise enough to understand.

Do I love my neighbour
Like I love myself and will that love stay here?
Ah yes while he doesn't need my help.
Do I love my neighbour?
Can it really be that I care for strangers?
Ah yes when the sun dries the sea.
Do I love my neighbour like I love myself,
And will that love stay here? Ah yes while he doesn't need my help.

And must I really stand here apart to live to live
Is there no free corner of my heart to give?
So I'll love my neighbour,
For at least I see how else could I ask my neighbour to care for me?

Al even wrote to Jonny Kremer regarding this radio show saying how proud he was to have his name in *The Radio Times* that week.

Al – "When I had first come up to London Jansch hadn't even made that first LP and John Renbourn was Dorris Henderson's backing guitar player. [Roy] Harper was on the road and I met him, when he came into Bunjies one night very early on. He sang something absolutely unbelievable that went on for about ten minutes with no shape or form and he sort of swore at the audience and disappeared and I didn't see him for about another year after that! Ralph McTell was hiding away somewhere and had never performed in public – there was no British contemporary folk scene at that time."

Al continued in his letter back to Bournemouth – "Bert is justifiably the greatest folk singer at the moment. Similar to listening to Dylan three years ago", adding that "although he was better live some of the tracks are quite outstanding". Al goes on to cite "Needle of Death" as "the best song ever written in this country" saying that Bert is "the third best folk writer in the modern tradition". His full list of folk writers, in order of his estimation of their superiority was listed as follows – Bob Dylan, Paul Simon, Bert Jansch, Tom Paxton, and *Al Stewart*! He also mentions how he'd bumped into Tom Wilson, the record producer of Dylan, Baez, Peggy Seeger and Paul Simon amongst others who had seemed "quite impressed" by the songs Al had just sung. Al constantly reports on how well he'd gone down at particular clubs and isn't shy to repeat the compliments on his developing musical dexterity by those such as Tom Wilson. He felt that at last he had some momentum going in his life.

Meanwhile on June 15th 1965 the 24-year-old Dylan was in Columbia Studios in New York City to record "Like A Rolling Stone".

Al next wrote to Jonny on June 24th – "All is in preparation for the recording of my demo LP (in a studio at the BBC when Hugh Green isn't looking)." He explains that further copies of the record will be available for £3.10s" and talks about wanting their quality to be of the highest. Al suggests jokingly that Jonny should purchase "three dozen, maybe four dozen" suggesting them even as "Christmas presents"!

The Soho folk scene that Al was now part of wasn't just limited to clubs. There were folk hangout places such as the Giaconda Coffee Bar, The Star café at the bottom of Greek Street, The London Folk Music Centre at 38 Goodge Street, Gerrard Sound Studios in Gerrard Street, Harlequin Records in Berwick Street, besides the more established Bar Italia and pubs – all in Soho. People such as Jo-Ann Kelly and Simon Lawrance were playing Les Cousins as did Al himself on 10th July 1965, being billed as "*Al Stuart* – for one night only 7.30 – 11.30", Jackson C. Frank playing there a week later.

Al had by now recently moved across town to Judith's *home for strays* in the East End.

Judith – "My place was a sort of folkies' doss house. Jackson C. Frank was there but Al knew that he was about to move out and asked if he could have Jackson's room when he left and I said 'yes'. Very often when people first came to London they had little or no money and they needed a base to enable them to get themselves heard and so that was that. There was another very fine songwriter that also lived in the house called Tommy Yates, from the north of England, who was more or less destroyed by an unscrupulous record producer. The house was very small; it was a three bedroom flat. I cared a great deal for Jackson. He had done so much in such a short time."

Jackson had certainly led an eventful life. He had learnt the guitar following a truly awful fire at his elementary school that killed many of his friends. Recovering after months in hospital, he had spent the time learning to play the guitar in Cheektowaga to accompany his tenor voice. Whilst researching songs for an aborted album on the Civil War he met Elvis Presley in Memphis, saw Dylan perform at Gerdes in Greenwich Village and had been taught by the likes of Josh White Jr. and Muddy Waters.

Jackson had used the insurance money from his accident to fund a folk singing trip to London. He cut quite a dash across town, as he would pull up for a gig at Bunjies or Les Cousins in his Aston Martin sports car, girlfriend Sandy Denny in the passenger seat and acoustic guitar in the back. Al once remarked that he was the only folk singer in London that wore a three-piece suit and a bowler hat. Jackson was dogged by stage fright and by all accounts there was a haunted look about him, however once on stage he was mesmerising and had a witty line in patter. One of his most popular monologues was a long rambling story about pigeons. Jackson was truly loved by the folk fans and artists alike.

Al once commented "It was almost as if he was guilty about surviving the fire and was truly unhappy in some respects about the insurance money and the fact that he'd received the money in the first place. He seemed to want to get rid of it, to be free of it."

Judith – "Jackson didn't think that he was going to be around for very long because of his illness and so his attitude was to blow the money, have a good time and make the most of

Tony Stratton-Smith

London 1965. The busker that never busked.

things. When I met Jackson for the first time he'd just met Sandy who was still a nurse at the hospital in Kensington. I was there in the studio when Jackson made his record and when he sang the words 'send out for whisky baby' I gave Sandy a wink and she went around the corner to get him something to drink and that relaxed him a little. He wasn't used to recording and so I'd recorded him at the flat quite a bit. He used to write his songs in the kitchen because he could put his typewriter up on the kitchen table and the guitar on his lap. In the living room I hung a little cassette recorder over the back of a chair and nudged him into singing this and that. They were not good recordings because it was only a simple tape recorder but because he was relaxed a lot of it was beautiful."

Al's first few months in London were strange times by dint of the truly diverse projects that he threw himself into. Ideas, schemes and auditions that more often than not resulted in rejection or abject failure certainly forced Al to quickly mature into a more pragmatic and realistic musician than he had been in Bournemouth.

Al – "In order to be prepared for all eventualities I had held on to my F-hole jazz guitar as my acoustic but this made absolutely no sense at all because no one played them in folk clubs. Now I also had a Gibson Les Paul S.G. because I wasn't at all happy about burning all my bridges and I guess that at the back of my mind I still really wanted to join an electric guitar band. There then came a moment in the late spring of 1965 when I'd settled into Bunjies and was also tearing around London doing auditions when I came to the realisation that my F-hole just wasn't making it and so I took the big step for me of trading in my Les Paul for the famous Epiphone at Ivor Mairants shop. Now of course this meant that I *was* very much burning my bridges and couldn't join a rock band even if one that would have had me had come along anyway."

Confident in his songwriting ability, Al got himself a trial at the office of Lionel Bart.

Al – "Once there I came up with this song entitled 'Pride of a Fool' which I was absolutely convinced would be a hit for Gene Pitney and I tried very hard to sell it to Lionel Bart's publishing company! They weren't convinced about it however despite the fact that I'd spent several sessions locked away in one of their little rooms trying to come up with a pop song and in fact the highlight of my time there was when 'Unit 4 + 2' called in one day. This was the first time that I'd seen a group like this at such close quarters and so I was more impressed by that than anything else! Eventually I got booted out of Lionel Bart's offices and I don't think that Gene Pitney ever heard my song, he certainly never recorded it."

Through all this time Al was still performing at Bunjies and occasionally at other venues around town. He even started auditioning for musical shows.

Al – "I was trying very hard to get work. There was a show that was running in the West End of London, in the heart of Theatreland, called *Just A Minim* and I decided to go along and try out for it. There was a part in this revue for a folk singer who would sing a song that went something like, 'Hey daddy, won't you take me to the drive-in' amongst other songs and the guy that played him was leaving and it was his role that I was up for. I went along to the theatre with the intention to perform something humorous. The audition was just like you see in the movies with the casting director sat alone in the middle of the stalls and me up on stage lit by only the footlights performing for my life! I'd chosen some terrible old English music hall song called 'Side By Side' and the version I'd chosen was the one that John Forman had adapted, where he's married someone who keeps having bits of her body fall off! It ends with 'Her teeth and her hair, she left on the chair, side by side!' It was hardly the most sophisticated piece of musical comedy but it was a song that I'd picked up from some folk club somewhere and it was actually very funny."

So funny in fact that a few days later Al found that he'd made the final short list for the role and he was called back to the theatre for a second audition.

Al – "But unfortunately 'Side by Side' was the only theatrical song I knew and so when I got to the second audition that's what I sang for them. However it really wasn't quite as funny the second time around and I didn't get the job and therefore never appeared on the London stage in a musical!"

In letters during the summer months Al mentions the people he's now bumping into on a regular basis, such as Donovan, going on to suggest the possibility of Julian Bream playing on a cover version of "Ides of Auschwitz" – an intriguing idea that never came to fruition.

One night after Bunjies, Al got a bus down through Holborn and Cannon Street to Wapping and eventually Cable Street. As he climbed the stairs he could hear "Leaves That Are Green" coming from Paul's room. Simon had just completed what would become *The Paul Simon Songbook*, recording it in seven days at a local London studio and it was the recording's acetate spinning around on Paul's record player that he could hear. Whilst Al had been playing at Bunjies, Paul had been at The Troubadour in Earls Court, West London playing "Flowers Never Bend With The Rainfall" and "The Side Of A Hill". Paul's friend and the other half of his duo, Art Garfunkel, was due in town two days later having completed his academic duties at Columbia University and in the weeks that followed they sang together on a regular basis. The times spent at Judith's flat were spent rehearsing, talking about their plans or playing Monopoly.

There was a local all-night launderette in nearby Commercial Road where as their shirts and socks were cleaned, they would all hold impromptu shows. These were simple, happy months for Paul Simon that he's always remembered. It was during this summer that Paul and Al collaborated for the only time on a project; Jackson C. Frank's album *Blues Run The Game*.

Looking back on all of this from his home in Woodstock for the liner notes of the album when it was re-released 30 years later, Jackson still had clear memories of Al's contribution.

"Al Stewart can be heard doodling in the back on guitar. He never received proper credit for that, I'm afraid, but that's him."

Blues Run The Game was produced with advance royalties from the *Paul Simon Songbook* and despite Paul having to coax and cajole Jackson into gaining enough composure to sing his songs. "Let's check the sound level here, could you run through 'Milk and Honey' for a moment please Jackson" Paul would implore, while running the tapes surreptitiously to record one more precious track for what was to become *Blues Run The Game*. Jackson spent much of the time hiding behind the recording screens, just too terrified to come out. But with care and patience, a never-ending supply of tea and sandwiches from Artie and some luck, the album was done in a few hours. Al who was present all day in the studio, played some studied guitar on what was to become the album's fourth song "Yellow Walls". Sandy Denny would later re-record three of these songs herself – "You Never Wanted Me", "Blues Run The Game" and "Milk And Honey". The recording was critically praised to the heavens and Jackson appeared on John Peel's radio show and national TV over the next three years whilst continuing to perform. Tragically, writer's block and depression, combined with dwindling finances, led to him fleeing to Woodstock in 1969.

Many of those around Jackson theorised that he associated his money with the fire and was trying to put both behind him.

Al – "It was probably the strangest recording session I've ever been to. Even when Paul would say 'Ok we're ready', often this would be followed by two or three minutes of total silence while he [Jackson] psyched himself into singing. And then this beautiful guitar and voice would emerge. He was also totally eccentric in what he would wear. I mean one day he would be in standard folk outfit of blue jeans and whatever, and one day I saw him in a business suit and a bowler hat… He had this long, ragged yellow hair and was wearing a pinstriped suit and a bowler hat. He might even have been carrying an umbrella for all I remember. The effect was startling."

On August 5th Al wrote home with some major news of his work with Jackson.

"I am finally coming out on disc in the smallest possible way! Playing second guitar on one track of Jackson Frank's first British LP. How about that!"

He continued with the news that he "may get a gig at The Marquee" and that the jazz star Chris Barber had come up to him after one of his performances and told him "I like that talking blues that you just sang", referring to Al's version of "It's Alright Ma".

Al also now wrote to Jonny with the news that Jonny's idea of an album of cover versions of the song "House of the Rising Sun" had been rejected by none other than Art Garfunkel!

At this time Al wrote the protest song – "Who Killed Tommy McGeechie".

Al – "'Who Killed Tommy McGeechie'?, comes straight out of the Bunjies period. Tommy McGeechie was a meths drinker and he lived on a bomb-site in the east end of London and he was held together by something called the Simon Community, a social welfare centre in Cable Street that deals with meths drinkers exclusively, and Judith Piepe, apart from running a home for out-of-work folk singers, was the parish visitor of Soho and also an affiliate of the Simon Centre."

Judith – "I remember how Al came to write that song. I had the cheek to go out and talk to agents or producers on my artists' behalf. The Simon Community had several houses for tramps and meths drinkers and I took Al along to these. I felt that it would be good for them and that also it would be an interesting experience for Al. So they'd all be there just lolling about and Al would sing to them. It was evening. The trip to play for the inmates was just me and Al at Wormwood Scrubs, sometimes I would take a small group of people but the time I went with Al it was just us. He got up and played a proper little concert there, it wasn't just one song."

This was typical of the gigs that Judith would arrange for her charges. Paul and Artie had played on one such occasion in 1965 at Brixton Prison.

Like Judith, Al has clear memories of these times in London. Judith considers it a period when she was able to "make a difference" to people's lives. None the least of these was Al.

Al – "She was irrepressible! She took her little band of folk singers out and we played in some extraordinary places I can tell you. I've sung 'Tommy McGeechie' in front of meths drinkers and I've performed 'Pretty Golden Hair', a song about a homosexual boy, in a gay club in the West End. I mean I didn't know what I was doing. I was 19 and it was just like a freak show and suddenly I was surrounded by everybody in drag and they dug it like mad. I've also sung prison songs inside Wormwood Scrubs. Basically Judith used to farm out her singers in all kinds of directions to all kinds of down-and-outs. They were quite constructive years. Inside the prison were some birds caught behind some wire and Judith pointed at them and said, "Look, even the birds are in cages here."

Al looks back on the songs that he was writing in 1965 very harshly – "Most of the material I wrote in those two years was very heavily influenced by the protest movement. Much of it was idealistic, eyes shining, swords drawn, marching forward against the social evils of the day, and most of it was frighteningly adolescent and terribly written.

"The only ones that really worked were the ones that had a lot of me in them, ones that were coming from my life rather than other people's. Look, if you're 18 or 19 you can't be a meths drinker, you can write about them – and you only have to look at all the 18-19-year old would-be folk singers that are around now writing about things that have no ring of truth about them unless they come right from the source.

So my pathetic songs, which most of the early ones were, were bad, the exceptions being the ones that came from me; I suppose 'Swiss Cottage Manoeuvres', which was written about the same time and 'Samuel Oh How You Changed', were OK looking back on them."

Throughout all of this though Al still harboured thoughts of playing lead guitar in one of the many bands around town.

Al – "It wasn't exciting, in fact folk clubs were never exciting in the way that they looked. I would have settled for playing in the Dakotas any day you know. It just looked a lot more exciting somehow. I mean there was something awfully good about being a folk singer and once I got into it, like Jansch and Renbourn and then all the others who followed, it was very interesting and definitely it had its moments. The String Band playing the Albert Hall for the first time which really meant that the stuff was happening. It was amazing, but it still wasn't the same simply because I wasn't a teenager any more and it was a job and it was now taken more seriously. There wasn't the chance to be totally flippant anymore. That only happened with the initial Gerry And The Pacemakers thing that I had wanted to be part of and of course wasn't."

During these early eventful months in London Al continued to play at Bunjies and slowly but surely expanded his repertoire. Judith also put together a short TV programme for the BBC called *Outcasts And Outsiders*. In documentary style she showed the under privileged and marginalised of society, specifically the folk community of 1965 London. The other performers featured in the programme were Stephen Delft, Jackson C. Frank, Weston Gavin, Bert Jansch and Paul Simon. The producer was Kenneth Savidge.

The Bunjies faithful had been told that the footage would be used on the following Sunday's programme. Like many others, Cliff Wedgbury sat down on the night to watch it with his family. But they were in for a shock.

Cliff Wedgbury – "We had been misled! The programme was entirely devoted to drug taking in London, and the opening shots were of someone giving himself a fix of heroin in the lavatory of Piccadilly Circus tube station. The very next frame switched to Bunjies and a full view of my smiling face, sitting in the front row by Al, as he sang his way through 'Pretty Golden Hair'. When the programme was over, my late father questioned me, with a very worried expression on his face, and I had to assure him that we had been completely used and tricked by the BBC producer and film crew, and that I had never seen any drugs used at Bunjies, not even so much as an aspirin!"

Richard Thompson – "I was another person that played at Les Cousins and Bunjies at this time. In actual fact I started going to Bunjies while I was still at school to see who was playing there. This would have been 1965 and so that would almost certainly have been the first time that I saw Al perform. This was made possible by the fact that neither place was licenced and so it was relatively easy for a youngster like me to get in."

Throughout this time Judith basically looked after Al at her house in the East End. She was there when he needed advice, helped him get gigs and regularly fed him too. Life in London would have been very much harder for all of the musicians that she took under her wing had she not taken it upon herself to largely take care of things for them. She has a particular memory of Al however.

Judith Piepe – "I can still picture Al, sitting in his room through the afternoons, teaching himself songs that he'd been shown by Paul or that he was learning by listening to his records. Hour after hour he would be in there. He was determined to make something of himself and although he looked up to Paul he wasn't at all in awe of him."

It was during this time that Paul came to Al with what was a fascinating but hopeless business proposition. If Al had been able to accept it would have altered the course of both their lives.

Al – "Paul asked me one day if I would be interested in buying his entire back catalogue from him for £5000! Now seeing as this included "Sound Of Silence" it would have been a very good move on my part but at the time I had absolutely no money and I think Paul probably knew that when he asked me."

The following day Al spent much of the afternoon in and around Tin Pan Alley trying to find someone that was willing to make such an investment. Short of this allowing him to put faces to names that he had only previously heard Judith or Paul talk about it proved a fruitless search.

Al – "We just couldn't find anyone that was interested. It was all quite soul destroying in many ways. We must have visited every music publisher in town that day but we got nowhere."

Three weeks later the opportunity at last came for Al to go into the studio himself. The session would provide a unique record of how Al sounded during those first few months in London.

Al – "There was a girl called Janet Lee that I'd met at either Les Cousins, Bunjies or somewhere around Soho and she had written a song called something like 'If I Had Wings'. Wonderfully her best friend worked at the BBC and Janet wanted me to play guitar for her on this song as by this time we had become good friends. Her best friend was an assistant producer at the BBC and in those days the BBC would operate until mid-evening and then they'd basically lock the studio and everyone would go home. However her friend had the key to the studio and knew how to operate the equipment and so when they'd all gone home we sneaked into the studios to record her song. Then over the course of a couple of hours I just sat there and played everything I could think of from all the tunes that I had."

He launched into "The New Ambassadors" a song, which in its utopian themes, was not dissimilar to John Lennon's "Imagine".

"Oh I am one of the New Ambassadors,
and my country is a country of peace,
though it is just in our minds at the moment,
peace can be yours if you follow my words in good faith..."

The engineer turned off the tape, marked the sound levels and cued things up for the next song. Although it would be another eight years before he started putting his "historical" songs on record Al was writing them from this time on. "This next one is called '1944'" he said as the red light came on as the tapes rolled once more – "Oh come with me to a winter bleak when you'll hear the big guns roar..."

Within that song, we can already see many of the idiosyncracies and points of style that feature in many of Al's future songs. There are the internal rhymes, the idea of writing in the third person and giving his central character a name which forms an instant bond between listener and song plus there's the subject matter itself, the Second World War, specifically the Holocaust. There were very few people singing around London at that time about such a subject matter and it's interesting to note that the move towards historical songs on *Past, Present And Future* wasn't anything like as big a jump stylistically as it appeared at the time. It may have been very new to those fans that had grown to know Al through songs such as "Clifton In The Rain" and "Anna" but to Al it seems that it must have been a natural selection given his disenchantment by 1973 with love songs. The interest in (and shining ability to compose) historical songs was there with Al there in London in 1965. This was five years even before "Manuscript" was recorded.

The small studio where Al sat in Portland Place was steeped in history. It had been used during the '50s for news broadcasts and it was the same place that Martin Carthy had played "Scarborough Fair" on radio for the first time two years previously. It smelled of history but it was very small. Al carried on playing. Reinforcing his debt to Bert Jansch, he produced an inspired and elegant version of Jansch's "Needle of Death", so haunting that the engineer forgot to stop the tape at its bittersweet conclusion. "Needle of Death" was Bert's beautiful song about Buck Polley who had died aged 22 of an "incautious overdose" the previous year. The subject matter of the piece led many to wrongly believe that Bert himself was a heroin junkie.

The Wonderful "Anji" followed. The recorded take was heartbreaking and a worthy representation of the version he'd been doing in Bunjies for the past few months. This was of course Al's version of Bert Jansch's version of Davy Graham's song. Al had studied Bert playing it at both the Scots Hoose and Les Cousins and the version on the acetate owed as much to Bert as it did to Davy Graham. Bert had heard a tape of Graham's song, courtesy of Davy's half sister Jill Doyle, at Roy Guest's Howff in Edinburgh and had translated its magical fingering technique into something that was very much his own.

Paul Simon had sought out Davy Graham in his south London rooms to ask if he could cover it as well and so it was well known as a standard and shows Al's burgeoning confidence to take on such a tricky instrumental. Davy used the DADGAD tuning which was very strange for its day.

Al – "Paul was obsessed with 'Anji'. It seemed to me that whenever he picked up a guitar at Judith's that he would be playing that song. We all loved it and many of us were performing a version of it in our sets but Paul just seemed to play it all of the time at Dellow Street!"

Judith remembers things a little differently however.

Judith Piepe – "I know that Paul loved the song very much and of course he included a version of it on the 'Sound Of Silence' album but he was no more obsessed with it than any of the others were. I can remember him playing all sorts of songs around the flat, some of them his own but many by other people. If I came home and could hear music being played it would usually be Al or Paul."

"Go Your Way", recorded next on Al's acetate, is a relatively straightforward love song sung at a cracking pace with some equally nifty guitar work.

The recording, it should be stressed, was just Al and his guitar. No other musicians and no double-tracking. In fact, the only studio trickery used at all was a little echo here and there. All in all ten songs were recorded and a week later Al collected the acetate pressing, wrote the song titles on its label in black biro himself and was walking around town with the disc under the arm of his corduroy jacket.

Al – "And that's pretty much how I remember it being done. It was my first album I guess. I came out of the BBC with the tape under my arm feeling fantastic and proceeded to have three copies pressed up. "

One song that didn't make it onto the acetate was "Child Of The Bomb". Al remembers bursting into the plush offices of Dick James whose DJM label and music publishing had been looking after the Beatles songs in a reprise of his 1964 visit to Ember Records, announcing the fact that they just had to sign him because he was the next big thing; namely that he was a "Bomb Singer"!! When asked by a sceptical Dick James what he meant by that he replied "I write songs about bombs, about their consequences, all that sort of thing. You have to sign me!" At this point in their very brief meeting, Al produced that Bournemouth recording of "Child Of The Bomb". He was promptly shown the door and that was that. Dick James' offices at 71-75 New Oxford Street were just across the road from Collets. It was there that Al headed to console himself.

But his predilection for songs that could sustain his dubious career as a bomb singer was still in sway and there was one song on the acetate that was both superior in lyrics, being less naïve and more emotive than "Child of the Bomb" and much more in the style of the folk protest song style that he had been so exposed to by coming under the influence of those first three Bob Dylan albums. And that song was the beautiful "Nothing at All". The songs introduction is very similar to that of "Manuscript" and the melody itself runs along in a style akin to "Swiss Cottage Manoeuvres" which hadn't yet been written.

"Crashing, thrashing, my poor world goes smashing
Apart growing wilder each hour,
Nuclear stockpiles mounting like rock piles,
Sprung in steel gardens of power."

Al now became, in his own small way, a peripheral part of the London Ban the Bomb/ Civil Rights movement that was gathering pace. The Campaign for Nuclear Disarmament and the Aldermaston marches were both making huge waves through the public conscience. There were poetry readings on the subject at places like Better Books and the Royal Albert Hall and there were also seeds of an underground press starting to sprout with the *International Times* soon to appear. In May 1965 Al had watched the CND march that ended up at Trafalgar Square which was led by Donovan, Joan Baez and Tom Paxton.

GO YOUR WAY

Well go your way if go you must and with you take the gathering dust
That settled on this love affair of ours
Ah but now and then you'll think of me a glimmer in your memory
To keep it out will be beyond your power, your power.

And though you try to brush away the ties that bind and rush away
To join the new attraction to your heart
Ah but we had something deeper here and though you're gone I have no fear
There's nothing that could keep us long apart, apart

Silver Cities sounds and sights of radiance
Red or brilliance bright have dazzled down your eyes and dipped your sight
Ah but we had something more than that consistency more sure than that
Affection in itself the bride I'd like, I'd like

Behold temptations heavy ounce infatuations hollow bounce
Echoes in your mind you have no power to try
Ah but later when it's all burnt out you'll see the ashes blown about
And find it hard to understand just why, just why

So go your way if go you must and jump the hurdle of our trust
With eyes tight shut so that you may not see
You think its real but that's a scheme to lead you on a hoax or dream
And when you wake just come on back to me, back to me.

1944

Oh come with me to a winter bleak when you'll hear the big guns roar
To a time so dark as to make its mark on history's blackened door
For the summer wind had not yet come to blow away the war
And the Devil walked in Germany in 1944

By railway train there's a straggling chain of prisoners by the score
They'll go to a concentration camp till the outcome of the war
And among them there was a pretty girl who cried for she plainly saw
There's little chance for a Jewish girl in 1944.

Now Evelyn Polac was the name on the small light card she wore
And it seemed like fate had closed hopes gate and trapped her with its claw
And it seemed her tears said that sixteen years would never turn to more
She was born to die in Germany in 1944

Ah but another girl who earned her life as a German major's whore
Was watching the flock of hope lost souls from a nearby station door
And there came to her there an impulse felt too strongly to ignore
And in the gather dust she ran to the side of the girl in that queue so poor

Softly then but silently she took off the coat she wore
And put it on the dumbstruck girl who stood and gazed in awe
She said my life has yielded much now there's nothing left in store
But you are young so turn and run from 1944

As a maddened Fuhrer stamped in rage his foot upon the floor
A Jewish girl of sixteen years hid safe in a barn of straw
As the Allies bombs like needles stung in the German Eagle's claw
A heroine died in Germany in 1944.

Now nobody knows the history of her life or the name she bore
But her birth was not of noble blood and her mind was crude and raw
But you'll hear me say to my dying day that her soul was noble born
Than any heart in Germany in 1944

IDES OF AUSCHWITZ
I look old I look twisted and dying
From my sores to the lice in my hair
And the flesh round my bones is so sunken
You'd think there was just nothing there
If you guessed you might say I was sixty
And broken and filthy to see
I'm just twenty but six months in Auschwitz
Would make any of you look like me

Oh there's some that they kill on arrival
And the toughest ones last but a year
But it's only a matter of waiting
There's just one place to go to from here
And on one pale morning they will take you
To the coffin they've built for the mass
And the final act will be run down
By a curtain of cyanide gas

Oh the scraps and the dirt that they feed us
You're dog would have turned from and run
And the bruises and cuts on my body
Are only my guards' bit of fun
When I'm dead there's no one will remember
And my name won't be in history
But I pray god you don't forget Auschwitz
And the six million murdered like me.

The same evening that Al was recording the acetate found his hometown contemporary Zoot Money and his Big Roll Band playing just across Soho at The Flamingo in Wardour Street. The clientele of The Flamingo, which operated from its proverbial smoky cellar, were the epitome of mid-'60s cool. With the accent firmly rooted in jazz and R&B, it was a place where American GIs, folkies, hookers and jazz freaks could all mingle in a haze of marijuana and uppers. It would ultimately evolve by the hippy years of the mid-'60s into an equally seedy dive named The Temple. The place was more of a jazz gig than a folkies hangout but not exclusively so. Paul and Artie had sung "Benedictus" there and it was in The Flamingo that the duo had first met Judith Piepe.

There were of course by now an ever growing number of venues where Al and his fellow folkies could play. There was the Roundhouse Pub in Wardour Street and of course The King and Queen in Foley Street, which although not as influential as other folk hangouts were none the less crucial as outlets of expression for a generation of would be singer-songwriters that were coming up to London at this time to play. Another important venue was The Troubadour.

The Troubadour was situated in Earls Court three miles away from most of the other folk clubs and pubs of central London. It had been originally opened as a coffee bar in the mid-'50 by Mike Van Blumen with the Saturday evenings being given over to folk music. This wasn't the only entertainment that it offered however and on other nights there were Jazz, Poetry and Comedy on offer. But it is for its contribution to folk that The Troubadour will be remembered most fondly. Back in 1962 it had been one of the first London gigs that Bert Jansch had played, one week after a very young Bob Dylan had trod the boards in this cramped and tiny club. By this time it was being run by Jenny Barton and Anthea

Joseph and was about to embark on what is thought of as its golden era. Dylan had been in town to appear in the BBC television play, *Madhouse On Castle Street*, to be broadcast on December 30th 1962 and featuring the recorded debut of a song that he had only recently finished – "Blowing in the Wind". Dylan returned to play at The Troubadour on December 29th and January 12th. Brian Shuel took the photos of him at another gig at this time, playing at the Singers Club, which convened at the Pindar of Wakefield pub.

Ralph McTell remembers meeting Al for the first time at The Troubadour during this period – "I had heard Al's name before but the first time that we met up was there in The Troubadour. It was definitely one of the places to get a gig. Paul Simon was often there, so were Martin Carthy and Bert Jansch. Lovely atmosphere but certainly one of the worst fire traps in town!"

Thinking back over the other venues around London that both he and Al were playing in 1965 Ralph's memories are full of affection for those people and places they played together.

Ralph McTell – "There was certainly something about The Scots House, off Cambridge Circus, with its flock wallpaper and no lighting. Whatever crowd there was sat on chairs in this tiny room with no microphone and an atmosphere like a dentist's waiting room! I remember seeing Bert Jansch for the first time there but we all played it at some time or other. It was such a magical time man, it was just great. We would run into one another all over town, hear each other's songs, talk things over, there was a real buzz around this time."

Al – "When Peter Bellamy and I had this residency at Bunjies Coffee Bar in 1965 we'd start off with three songs each and then open up the stage to the floor. That's how I met Roy Harper. He walked in one day with an exercise book and a guitar and sat down and proceeded to sing these 20-minute songs at us and also to read these rambling poems about North Africa and God knows what."

Ralph McTell – "I remember Al at Bunjies very well. I also am sure I too saw Harper perform there at around this time, maybe it was the same gig that Al was at!"

Al also now first met Noel Murphy when the Irishman visited Bunjies. It would be the start of an enduring friendship.

Al – "Noel came in and played either 'McAlpines Fusiliers' or 'Rocky Road to Dublin' and went down the best of anyone that played whilst I was there, he simply tore the place apart. The crowd went absolutely wild and there were people screaming for more but he just picked up his guitar and without hanging around left. The next week he came back and did the same thing with exactly the same song! After this had happened a few times I also started to see him down at Les Cousins and when I asked him why he didn't play any different songs he replied 'I don't know any other ones!' But he went on to learn some more songs and I did a zillion shows with him."

Cliff Wedgbury – "Various other singers and musicians used to drop in to perform floor spots during the course of the night. Theo Johnson; Jackson C. Frank, with his beautiful Martin guitar; Sandy Denny who was nursing Cat Stevens, whose dad owned an Italian Restaurant around the corner; Shirley Abicair played zither; a guy named Mox played harmonica; plus a big, fat scruffy lady, in an old overcoat, headscarf and plimsolls, who had no teeth and always sang 'Danny Boy'. She was a busker who came in from the cinema and theatre queues to earn a few more shillings from us and was always bumming cigarettes. Her name was Meg. Hratch Garabedian from Armenia sang the Woody Guthrie song 'Deportees' beautifully in his sad, mournful voice… in fact he looked like a Mexican with his black drooping moustache. He played finger-style in waltz time with great competence."

Paul Simon was still regularly playing in London at this time and would still try out new material in the smallest of venues.

Cliff Wedgbury again – "I remember vividly the night Paul Simon descended the narrow stairs to Bunjies, brought down by Judith Piepe, and Al became very excited when he announced his presence to the audience. Paul came down to the folk cellar with his Guild steel-strung acoustic. He was smoking a cigarette and when he was about to begin his first song he stuck the smouldering cigarette between the strings on the machine head of his guitar. I thought that a very cool thing to do."

Paul sang for about half an hour, mostly the songs from *The Paul Simon Songbook*. To many of the Bunjies faithful he was head and shoulders above any of the other performers due to the quality of his songwriting.

Cliff Wedgbury – "He held the audience mesmerised with his fine voice, great songs and guitar technique. We watched and listened to everything in complete silence… cheering and clapping at the end of each song.

"I particularly remember 'I am a Rock' and 'A Simple Desultory Philippic' performed in open tuning with its lyric saying he'd been 'Kerouac'd'."

Al – "Those were two of the songs that everyone loved. I remember Judith often talking to me at the flat about 'being truly dedicated to something that you believe in' and citing Paul as someone who was exactly that."

Cliff Wedgbury – "Towards the end of his set in Bunjies Paul called to someone at the back of the crowded audience. 'Hey! Art! Come and sing a song.' That's when we first saw the tall and lean Art Garfunkel push through the crowd to stand at Paul's shoulder. He wore a long, light coloured raincoat and looked a bit conservatively dressed amongst the casual Bunjies crowd, but he sang some fine harmonies and their two voices won the hearts of everybody that night."

Al spent much of the summer of 1965 with Paul and Artie in London. One day they had wandered down The Strand together to Trafalgar Square when Paul decided that he would play what amounted to an impromptu show there and then.

Al – "One of the reasons for this was that Paul wanted to hear what 'Sound Of Silence' would sound like in three-part harmony and so I did my best and we sang the song to a square full of largely uninterested tourists."

The performance was cut short however when they were told to 'move on' by a passing policeman.

Al – "This of course did not go down well with any of us, least of all Paul, who made it perfectly clear that he wasn't very happy with having his music interrupted!"

Throughout all of this time Les Cousins, just across the other side of Cambridge Circus, continued to hold sway as the pre-eminent folk music venue in London. Rod Edwards has definite thoughts on how this came to pass.

Rodney Edwards – "I think also it's because they had a regular residents' thing going on down there. You knew, for instance that on a particular night you would see Bert Jansch and John Renbourn. Another night it might be Jackson or Davy Graham and so it was pretty much a cutting edge sort of place at the time. The atmosphere back then was very laid back, it was a very social thing. One night I remember very clearly is the one where Van Morrison borrowed my guitar on his first gig, he was up there on the tiny stage thrashing away on my twelve-string, and nearly broke it! There was a great flow through of people down there at this time, which was very conducive to the atmosphere. Andy would be down in the basement that was Les Cousins and his father would pop in all the time from the restaurant upstairs that was the family business."

Roger Hand – "I remember Al had spent an inordinate number of hours that August learning 'Desolation Row' by Dylan a couple of days before it came out and he played it to us the day the record came out at our flat in Warwick Road. All 13 minutes of it and then he played it at our gig that night at Les Cousins. We all got on very well together. I think it's one of those things where we all had a similar sense of humour. We came from very different backgrounds but it just worked."

Paul Simon had been at Judith's in August 1965 while Al was there in his room learning *Highway 61 Revisited* note for note. Looking into Al's room while "Tombstone Blues" was playing Paul declared it "rubbish" according to Al.

Al – "He did! Now I wasn't going to have that and so I made him sit down and listen to some more of the album. This he did. I distinctly remember playing him 'Desolation Row', in its entirety, which he liked a lot. That really did seem to get him going!"

Al remembers Paul comparing it to Ferlinghetti, someone that he hadn't heard of at the time.

Al – "I'm sure I was the first person to perform 'Desolation Row'. I got it from Collets on Thursday, the day before it came out, locked myself in a room with it for 24 hours and then on the day it came out played it in clubs all over the West End. Things like that gave me a real buzz. I was 19 and having a good time. I felt like I was bringing the news."

Reina James – "Everything about Les Cousins was wonderful. Andy was great and so were his parents. His mother used to bring him down peeled oranges, which he'd eat when he was manning the till at Les Cousins. It always used to get so cramped in there and if you got there too late then you'd end up sitting outside in the corridor under the stairs listening to all this wonderful music and then coming back upstairs, where it would almost be morning, hanging around until the first tubes started running. I used to see Sandy Denny a lot at Les Cousins and she would always give me a ticking off for wearing too much eye make-up! We were all trying to look like Julie Driscoll in those days you see – Sandy was just the loveliest woman, she really was."

Alexis Korner – "Usually, there would be two all-night players. Out of the six and a half-hours, you were expected to play for four, so if two players shared an evening, they played for two hours each. It was hard work, but most of the musicians there had played in bands, so they were used to being on stage for long hours. But the money was good and it was useful practice."

Occasionally an all-nighter would be so carried away with his music that he would go on after 6.30 in the morning and the proprietor would have to throw him out.

Alexis Korner shared the stage with Paul on many occasions as the two musicians on those Cousins all nighters. Hans Fried was another regular visitor to the club although he remembers it as being pretty squalid down there – "It was just so cramped and during the middle of the night with the floor covered by sleeping bags it could really be a bit too much."

Many people got their first break at Les Cousins.

Another of Al's fellow folkies at Les Cousins was Cat Stevens, then still known as Steve Adams, who lived above his father's restaurant, The Moulin Rouge, at 49 New Oxford Street.

Ian Anderson first met Al in Soho in the mid '60s. He is now the editor of *Folk Roots* magazine.

Ian Anderson – "All of us from the *Bristol Folk Scene* used to regularly go up to London at the weekends to all of those folk clubs around the fringes of Soho. Places like Les Cousins and The Scots Hoose. Bruce Dunnet, who ran the place, also managed the Young Tradition and is a prime example of someone who was at the centre of things and the scene was very much more interconnected in those days. Trad guys like Peter Bellamy worked with folk singers such as Al who knew and worked with more blues orientated musicians such as Mike Cooper and myself."

Ian Anderson – "The great thing about Les Cousins were the all-nighters which basically meant that it was the cheapest place to stay the night in London. After the first session ended at pub closing time the aficionados would meet in the pub across the road, The Pillars of Hercules and there was also a place that Al used to take us to called the *As You Like It Coffee House* which was this fantastic theatrical coffee house run by a bunch of gays and there was this running joke whereby the guy behind the counter would always say 'and would you all like some of my divine trifle?' So we used to all go to the As You Like It and hang out between sets at Les Cousins. We'd always leave it about an hour or more before we went back to the club so that we could make an entrance! There was this fan over the stage and wooden benches so it was pretty basic! The huge redeeming feature about the place though was that it had one, very good quality microphone. Now this was in the days when folk clubs generally didn't have PAs at all but Les Cousins had a microphone, it had this big pop shield on it and big speakers up behind you and for this reason it had a great sound."

Many people evolved a way of playing that used that microphone to get a particular sound. Techniques such as leaning into it to get the microphone onto the edge of feedback before reining it back and all sorts of tricks like that were born down there in Les Cousins.

Ralph McTell – "At this time Al and everyone else all sat hunched over their guitar. I honestly believe that the whole of that contemporary acoustic guitar singer songwriter thing came about because you could get your mouth and the guitar as close as possible to this one microphone down there. The Troubadour, Bunjies, Scots Hoose – none of them had a PA and so it was Les Cousins with one that brought about that particular style."

Richard Thompson also remembers weekends spent in Soho – "By the time I was seventeen I too was a regular at the all-nighters that Les Cousins ran each weekend. It was something that absolutely had to be done at that time. It was a rite of passage. Everyone played there."

The cosmopolitan and very tolerant society that Al encountered in Soho was totally alien to anything he'd encountered before. The gay community were central to this and welcomed straight patrons to their establishments without prejudice.

Al – "The As You Like It was run by Barry Stacey and Judith introduced me to him one day as part of her efforts to embrace anyone of an alternative lifestyle and to introduce them to one another. The first time I went there Judith tried to get me a job making sandwiches but thankfully that never came to anything. Now one of the great things about the As You Like It was this wonderful apple flan with double cream on top that Barry made and to which I became hopelessly addicted. I would go down there every night after Bunjies to this wonderful coffee bar which was always full of such interesting people."

The As You Like It also supplied the origins to one of Al's earliest songs, "Pretty Golden Hair", in so far as it took its subject matter from one of its patrons.

Al – "There was this drag queen who used to regularly be there when I visited the As You Like It called Don or rather 'Donnareena' as everyone called him and he had ginger hair and had led this terribly sad life and he did in fact kill himself in the end, years later, long after I'd written the song. So it's fair to say that the song is loosely based on Donareena. But the As You Like It was the most amazing place to be in, I remember Quentin Crisp used to be propping up the bar sometimes when I called in – it really did have buzz. I have absolutely no idea what I was doing there but visit it I regularly did over the course of many years too! No-one ever hit on me during all that time and through going in there so often and talking to the regulars I became friends with them all."

There was a true elegance to these premises which was at one with its *raison d'être* as a haven for the more theatrical gay customer; there was even an Egyptian Prince there that Al became friends with. It was exotic and it was clearly intoxicating.

It wasn't just folk music that was gaining an audience in Soho at this time.

Ian Anderson – "Jo-Ann Kelly used to do blues sessions on Sunday afternoons at Studio 51 in Great Newport Street at the same time as the all-nighters at Les Cousins and then go down the road and do Sunday nights at Bunjies. Les Cousins, Studio 51 and Bunjies were all part of the grand weekend in London for all of us. There was also another place up in Hampstead called The Witches Cauldron that wasn't much more than another coffee bar that was very much part of the scene too. Two guys who used to play at that place were Mox, the harmonica player and John Lemont, a blues guitarist."

Armed with the acetate of his songs, with the song titles written on the grey label in barely visible black pen, Al had been constantly trying to get a recording contract of some kind. He visited many offices across the capital, walked up many narrow staircases full of hope only to make the return trip a few minutes later feeling despondent and dejected.

Take a close look at the lyrics to "Bedsitter Images", which was written about these early times in Soho, to see what I mean. One of the more excessive rejections from any of the record company executives that Al visited in those months came from Louis Benjamin of Pye. All was going swell until Benjamin realised the implicit homosexuality theme of the outwardly innocent "Pretty Golden Hair". The actual words he used are lost in the ensuing 33 years but they were something very, very close to "I'm not having filth like that on my label, get out of here!" Now if, just if, he'd liked what he'd heard and signed Al, the songs on the first album would had been very different to those on *Bedsitter Images* – in fact the album wouldn't have been called *Bedsitter Images* either. Another thing – it wouldn't have had an orchestra on it.

The search for the elusive recording contract also included a visit to the offices of Shel Talmey, of Planet Records who had worked with The Who and The Kinks amongst others. Showing some interest Talmey's office held on to another acetate of Al's until his next visit. On his hopeful return to the company, with Jonny Kremer, the loaned acetate was nowhere to be seen and the situation got heated. After much shouting and complaining there was nothing to be done but to leave. That acetate, of another song, disappeared for ever.

On September 1st Al played a regular gig at The Marquee. By September he had become established as a Les Cousins regular playing at least twice a week over weekends which was where he met up with Karl Dallas, *Melody Maker*'s Folk Correspondent for the first time.

By this time Al had expanded the list of venues that he went out to play in. He continued to stay at Judith's house in Dellow Street for a while longer but at the end of the summer Artie Garfunkel had returned to the States and on 8th September Paul started out at Les Cousins on what would be his final tour as a solo artist before Simon and Garfunkel became such a hot property world-wide. Al performed at venues as diverse as strip clubs turned into folk clubs for the evening, a small room attached to the As You Like It drinking club, The Troubadour in Earls Court and Les Cousins itself. Paul was singing a set that was in essence *The Paul Simon Songbook* and which would be the basis of his upcoming "Tour of One Night Stands" around the North of England. One of the songs that he performed that night in Soho was "Blessed", written by Paul just around the corner in St Anne's Church, where he'd fled in order to escape a downpour.

On September 11th Al played live on a music show on BBC Radio for the first time when he was booked as a guest on *Folk Room* . This was followed on October 1st by a full page feature in *Folk Scene* and continuing residencies at Bunjies and Les Cousins besides other pub gigs all over town. Around this time he also almost managed to secure a record contract with the Fontana label in London.

Al – "Through all of this I continued to live at Judith's house. I had got to know Paul quite well by now and I was next door when he wrote 'Homeward Bound'. When he had finished it he came out and said 'What do you think of this?' and I didn't like it; but then he wrote 'Richard Cory' and I really flipped. I thought that was incredible. But basically it was quite a mind-expanding experience seeing songs being written like that – I mean watching Paul construct a song was very different from watching the lead guitarist in my old Bournemouth group putting together a twelve-bar with a few odd lyrics over the top. It really gave you a complete insight into how far lyric writing and music could be pushed in a fundamentally new direction. I watched, listened and did my best to put all of this into practice in the clubs around town that Judith was taking me out to perform in."

One of the new clubs that now opened up in London was the legendary Le Deuce, a folk venue that was very similar in many ways to the As You Like It – in so far as it was a sometime gay club – but on Tuesday nights it wasn't used and Judith Piepe had decided to turn it into a folk place. Le Deuce, which set up shop at 22 D'Arblay Street, opened on October 27th 1965 with a bill featuring Paul Simon, Jackson C. Frank and Sandy Denny. On November 10th Al played a gig there as compère with The Flamenco

Twins, whilst that same evening Paul Simon and Noel Murphy were playing at Les Cousins just down the road.

Al on Le Deuce – "This was great on the face of it but it was much too up-market for anything like that, it just didn't seem right. Places like Bunjies and Les Cousins were very bare and basically dives. I feel that if you are going to run a folk club then it has to be a dive but Le Deuce was just too middle class but none the less I ran this folk evening there for Judith every Tuesday for a while and we'd have people there as special guests. I played of course as did Sandy Denny and Paul Simon but after a couple of months it closed."

Paul Simon had already been very pro-active when it came to business.

Rod Edwards – "Paul was in complete control when it came to music publishing and introduced Rod and I to Lorna Music and Les Lowe. We'd been at Les Cousins for a while and one night we played "I am a Rock" and who should be sitting in the front row but Paul Simon."

Roger Hand – "I remember saying from the stage 'We're going to do one of your songs now Paul. We hope you don't mind!' It was at the time when he was just about to have a hit in the States but was still largely unknown over here. So it was that limbo period. He told us that he'd liked the way he'd heard us perform his song but not to rush into the music business and to take the time to get everything sorted out properly from day one which was typical Paul. He was very helpful and gave us a personal introduction to Les Lowe at his Denmark Street offices. And we then spent an inordinate amount of time doing demos in Southern Studios in Denmark Street and sitting by the phone waiting for the big deals that never really came from Lorna Music."

Rod and Rog would eventually go on to be managed by the same person as Al.

Soho was by now the very centre of musical life in London and on November 17th Ronnie Scott opened his famous jazz club in Frith Street.

Al was going down a storm in concert but was uncertain about whether he'd ever make the breakthrough to recording. Writing on November 18th from his new bedsitter just around the corner from Ronnie Scott's he writes – "No, I doubt if I ever will make a record; except attendance records in folk clubs which I keep breaking!"

His four or five nights a week were earning him, he wrote in the letter – "£25 to £30… incredibly, it goes up all the time and I have a sneaking feeling that it's more than most groups/pop stars recorded or not recorded!"

After what had unquestionably been a very valuable time in the East End with Judith, Al had elected to go for broke and get his own place. Looking for somewhere with a little more privacy he found the 'tiny room' on the southern reaches of Soho.

Al – "I needed to get out in the end. Judith's house was full of lunatics day and night and I basically wanted my own place. But this came at a price. Lisle Street was £4.10s a week."

Writing from this new home at 25B Lisle Street, Soho he eulogises about Paul Simon's "Blessed" which he calls "fantastic" and was something that "takes a lot of listening to like, 'Patterns'". He wrote a short critique of the *Homeward Bound* album including "Richard Cory" about which he says – "I'm speechless. The best thing outside of Dylan… Well worth the money for these alone."

He goes on to say – "On the other scene a very strange thing is happening, Bert Jansch looks like becoming a cult nationally and therefore of course really big."

Al goes on to mention that whilst regularly selling out Les Cousins, half of Bert's audience – "have adopted his style of dress and mannerisms but Bert hadn't yet become commercialised."

Lisle Street with it's darkly bohemian cast of artisans, prostitutes, pimps, shopkeepers, criminals and boarding house habitués counted Al amongst their roll of residents for a year starting in the autumn of 1965. The atmosphere in Soho was something that both fed his imagination and fuelled the creative process through which he had carved a way for himself in those first six months in town.

Al – "Something I adored about Lisle Street was how I felt like a 19th century poet amongst the *depravity* of it all. My room really did have a broken window throughout the time I was there, it had probably an inch of dirt on the lino floor and was smack bang in the middle of the red light district. To get to the bathroom you had to go up a flight of stairs and the only way to get hot water was to turn the gas on and then stand in the doorway throwing matches at it because when it did come on it came on with a bang and even then it wasn't particularly clean or even hot! However after eight years of being at boarding school you learned how to get clean under any circumstances and even though the building itself left a great deal to be desired on that front, I certainly bathed regularly and was never what you could call scruffy!"

The idea that Al delighted in during his time in Lisle Street was that this was about as far away from Wycliffe as it was possible to get and that he'd made it on his own terms.

Al – "Whilst living in this run down and decrepit place I was of course running the weekend all nighters at Les Cousins and so through the winter of 1965/1966 I never saw daylight which to me was the most truly romantic thing possible. I'd read Tolkien, Genet, Sartre and De Beauvoir until the early hours of the morning in my tiny room up above the street. I had no TV or radio and of course no telephone, so basically had no direct communication with the outside world. To be honest through all that time I don't think that I really noticed my immediate environment, that is Lisle Street, at all. Linver Road had belonged to the family that lived there, Judith's place in the East End belonged to her but Lisle Street was the first home that I ever had that definitely belonged to me, although be it ever so humble."

Besides Al there were at least half a dozen other people lodging in the building at this time on floors above and below his. Once again Al found himself as something of a *voyeur.*

Al – "It was unavoidable given the circumstances. Richard Huggett from the Hammer Horror films was in the room next to mine, there was an ex-Madam with red hair upstairs and the person who'd had my room before me was Clinton Ford who had gone on to make several hit singles for Decca – so the place was certainly choc-a-bloc full of characters and it was as if we were all occupying minor roles in some Dickensian movie. I was wonderfully happy in Lisle Street. I adored it. It was squalid but I absolutely loved it."

It was while he was living this somewhat topsy-turvy nocturnal life here that Al managed to read Tolkein's *Lord Of The Rings* three times. It would ultimately provide him with rich subject material for his first single.

For a while Al acted as compère at Les Cousins where, after introducing such people as Davy Graham, John Martyn and Paul Simon, he himself would get to sing at about 4am! By this time Paul was keeping a low profile however.

Al – "This is true. Many people never even knew that they were watching Paul Simon. I mean he was just Paul, although of course he was very good even then!"

In December 1965 Paul Simon returned to the States where "The Sound Of Silence" had become his first hit record. Back in the late autumn, Paul had been at Judith's in between the short British tour and a holiday in Copenhagen. It was during these few weeks, staying across the hall from Al, that he finished off the composition of "Homeward Bound", a song that he'd started on the platform of Widnes Railway station. The confusion over where and when this song was written seems to be settled by the logic that points to Paul initially composing the piece in Widnes and then completing it a couple of days later, writing the final definitive set of lyrics back in his room, across the hall from Al, at Judith's house in the East End.

Judith Piepe – "I will tell you exactly what happened. Paul came back from the famous *Tour Of One Night Stands* and remarked that he was really glad to be back home and said 'I've got something for you' and then he played me his new song 'Homeward Bound'. Over the next few days Paul would continue to work more on the song in his room which was just across the corridor from Al's room and it's Paul polishing up the song that he would have heard. Al would make a point of learning Paul's songs before anyone else had a chance. Once a song of Paul's got sung in Les Cousins by Al before he'd had a chance to sing it himself and Paul was not pleased. Paul thought that Al was a pushy kid, which he was. He felt the same way that a five-year-old feels about the new baby that's taking up mother's time. It would never have occurred to Al that this would have been a problem. But then a few years later Paul told me that actually he liked Al because he worked hard."

It was just as well that Al was listening so closely to Paul, because when Simon and Garfunkel had that hit in the States in late 1965 with "Sound Of Silence" they left what Al has described as both a "hole" and a "void". Al, in his mind their heir apparent, armed with such songs as "Anji", "Needle of Death", "Homeward Bound", "Richard Cory" and "Blessed" (which he was still singing in 1970 when he performed it for the BBC on Radio 1), the first three Dylan albums and a growing collection of his own, proceeded to get far more attention in the wake of Paul's departure.

Al – "Paul had left for America having played at these folk clubs all over the country and there was suddenly a gap there for me. What else was I to do? I knew most of his songs, plus a whole bunch of my own and they could have me for half of his money. So instantly I had all these gigs."

Al's first year in London ended with an all-nighter at Les Cousins on Saturday 18th December. The same evening, another of Al's contemporaries, Johnny Silvo, was playing The Troubadour in Earls Court. Al wasn't the only member of Bournemouth's beat scene to be making headway that winter. Eddie Stevens, the singer from The Master Sounds had also just released a record.

Al didn't have any particularly close friends from outside the world of folk music during that first year in London. Besides Judith Piepe and Reina James there was of course Lou Hart but no-one seems to have achieved the genuine closeness that he and Jonny had enjoyed in Bournemouth. There were friendships of course; Al remembers dating (at separate times) a couple of sisters and during the course of this going around to their flat for dinner taking his guitar with him.

Al – "These were great evenings and I got fed too which was perfect! We would all have supper and then I would sit back and serenade their mother with whatever it was I'd written that week on my Epiphone Texan. That family were the very first people to ever hear many of those early songs that year."

So Al's gentle initiation into London life continued. Now with a place of his own in Soho he could also invite people back after he's sung in the clubs.

Cliff Wedgbury – "I remember the first time I went back to Al's bedsit in Lisle Street, Soho. It was after the usual Friday night session and we pushed past some girls working the hallway and went up to his room. It was situated in a very scruffy and disreputable area of Soho. Al seemed very poor at the time. All I remember of that night and that small room was bare lino on the floor, bare windows with no curtains, his small single bed, an old gas cooker, a jar of Nescafe coffee, a tin of Marvel instant milk and the continuous flashing of neon from a strip club in the street below. That night he sang me the latest song he had composed and asked me what I thought of it. The song was 'Swiss Cottage Manoeuvres.'"

Al – "It was all very idyllic in many ways. When I was doing the all-nighters at Les Cousins I'd get up at teatime, stroll around Soho for a while, maybe meet some friends, then I'd do my stint down in the club. When we finished at seven the next morning I'd pop into the French patisserie and have a cake before walking back down the road to my room and go to bed."

From 1965 onwards it's fair to say that Les Cousins became one of Al's very favourite places to perform and he became a close friend of club regular Ian Anderson and his then girlfriend Maggie Holland. Over the years the club's residents went on to include Fred Wedlock, The Pigsty Hill Light Orchestra and the duo of Dave Mudge and Tim Clutterbuck. Al would also occasionally do duets with Tim Clutterbuck who would often act as a compère for the evening. The Mudge and Clutterbuck partnership covered many Al songs on stage there throughout the '60s themselves.

Ian Anderson – "I used to go around with Al quite a lot to keep him company on his way to gigs and he'd let me do floor spots and one of our great friends, Al Jones, would be doing exactly the same with John Renbourn. Al was very good company on those trips and I know that he did the same for others, John Martyn and Bruce Cockburn, because that's the sort of person he was and is."

In Ian Anderson Al had now found a foil, a kindred spirit that was someone with whom he could not only mull over whatever he had on his mind but who he could rely on to give him every encouragement whenever his conviction and self belief was found to be flagging.

Ian Anderson – "Well I did my best! I used to write a column in *The Western Daily Press* and one of the people that I wrote very positively about was Al. The difference between who becomes a star and who doesn't is in the end down to who is hungriest and Al was definitely hungry to become a star."

Bert Jansch called Al "somebody that seemed to be at every gig I played" and Ralph McTell commented wryly that "Al took full advantage of what opportunities were laid before him and went for it."

But it wasn't his work ethic alone that was to cement the friendship with Ian Anderson. It was something that went back to the nights at Wycliffe spent listening to Radio Luxembourg after lights out in the dormitory.

Ian Anderson – "We were both huge fans of instrumental pop records of that late '50s/early '60s period and Al could actually quote back to you the catalogue numbers of the records! I was like this too in many ways. In fact I used to keep a personal hit parade book in which I'd note down particular songs that I'd heard on Radio Luxembourg and then dutifully look up their chart positions in the *N.M.E.* and so this mutual love of all this was probably one of the main reasons why we got on so well together. People such as Al Jones and myself, by dint of our trips up to London, became in essence the talent scouts for the Bristol folk and blues scene. I well remember Al sitting in our flat in Bristol and just as an exercise writing a song in ten minutes to show Dave Mudge how it could be done. By this time Tim Clutterbuck became a complete Al Stewart clone. He had the long black corduroy jacket and he had the Epiphone Texan guitar too. Tim would learn Al's songs as soon as he heard them and performed them as part of the Mudge and Clutterbuck duo."

The song "Lowly Lo" from 1968 was written by Dave Mudge and formed part of what went on to become "Modern Times" six years later. Dave Mudge tragically died in 1998. Al would sometimes get the train down to Bristol Temple Meads Station from Paddington in the early days and on one such trip, having just seen Jacqueline Bisset in a Sunday supplement, wrote his song "Clifton in the Rain" as a memoir of that time. Along with Al on the bills at The Troubadour were Keith Christmas, Steve Tilston, The Strawbs, Graham and Anne Hemingway, Jeremy Taylor, Al Jones and Jo-Ann Kelly, most of whom he'd got to know as friends as they played in folk clubs around the country. The Troubadour was open as a folk club on weekends and there was a real sense of a folk community in and around Bristol with other venues springing up including a Bristol University Folk Club and the blues and folk record label *Village Thing* based in Royal York Crescent. There was even a club newsletter. When the folk club at The Troubadour eventually closed down The Bunch of Grapes pub in Milk Street Bristol picked up the folk mantle for the town with The Stonehouse Club and Al played there as well in 1971.

Such songs as "Old Compton Street Blues" and "Bedsitter Images" are word pictures of Al's days and nights in London during his first year away from Canford Bottom. A comparison between these songs, both lyrically and musically, with 1974's "Soho (Needless To Say)" is both dramatic and relevant to Al's development as a lyricist. It is interesting to contrast the two different viewpoints of Soho in these songs:

OLD COMPTON STREET BLUES
Oh you made it to the silver screen
And yet you're not a star
And advertising corsets didn't get
You very far

And money has its favourites and
Yours went back to them
So you modelled in a studio in Greek
St. for the rent.

SOHO (NEEDLESS TO SAY)
Rainstorm, brainstorm, faces in the maelstrom,
Huddle by the puddles in the shadows where the drains run
Hot dogs, wet clogs, clicking up the sidewalk
Disappearing into the booze shop
Rainbow queues stand down by the
News stand waiting for the late show
Pinball, sin hall, minds in free fall.
Chocolate coloured ladies making eyes through the smoke pall

Although the portrayal of Soho in the latter song is from a '70s point of view, it does serve to demonstrate the hold this famously bohemian, tatty and vibrant corner of West London retained on Al.

Cliff Wedgbury – "It was magical! One Friday night, Bunjies and the lower folk cellar completely filled with smoke! It seemed to be coming from ventilation ducts and soon it became so thick that it was difficult to see. So the whole place was evacuated in an orderly manner. Like a true Captain of the ship, Al was one of the last to leave, making sure everyone was gone from the folk cellar. We all stood out in the street, a huge crowd of people waiting for the Fire Brigade to arrive. It was a good humoured crowd including a Chinaman, standing nonchalantly in striped pyjamas, he had been fast asleep in an upstairs room. Most people drifted away and I think a few of us adjourned to a pub in nearby St. Martins Lane. The next Friday everything was back to normal and the whole incident seemed to be forgotten about."

In Soho Al often met up with Jackson C. Frank, who as mentioned, had briefly shared the Dellow Street house with Al, Sandy Denny and Simon and Garfunkel. This association had not only led to Al's first appearance on record, as 'second guitar' on Jackson's 1965 self-titled album, he also played tambourine on "Can't Get Away From You", the B-side of Jackson's single. The A-side, a different version of the LP's first track "Blues Run The Game", featured Al playing excellent guitar, an effort that earned him this glowing praise from his home town paper *The Bournemouth Echo* on February 3, 1966.

"Record fans were quick to appreciate the good guitar work and the man behind the strings was Alastair Stewart from Wimborne."

Whilst gradually gaining a following amongst provincial folk centres Al kept up the residency at Bunjies and was now being exposed to many new sounds.

Al – "This time had an enormous effect on me. I began listening to the Dubliners and the Watersons. Noel Murphy arrived at Bunjies at this time also. Some traditionalists (in the folk scene per se) were very friendly though some were very hostile to me!"

However, in spite of the comments and opinions of the establishment folk figures, Al was not unappreciative of their music. He later recorded a version of "Lyke Wake Dirge" after buying Peter Bellamy's *The Young Tradition*.

Al was also by now beginning to enjoy a respectable amount of press coverage. He had signed a contract in late 1965 with Tony Stratton-Smith's public relations agency 'Stratton Smith Music Ltd', who had offices at 31 Wardour Street in Soho and they did their best to stir up interest in Al who by virtue of his increasingly polished performances around town was now getting the occasional rave review. At one such appearance in the Ballad and Blues Club (which was at the Castle Inn in North Street, London) he was reported to have "brought the house down". Al was by now 20-years old and had been in London for just eight months. Tony Stratton-Smith also had The Merseybeats, The Koobas and various other groups on his label and didn't just run his agency. He was also the author of a novel – *The Rebel Nun*.

Al – "Tony Stratton-Smith was great but didn't ever do much for me. His attentions always seemed to be elsewhere shall we say! He was a lot of fun but as my manager, well we never seemed to get anywhere. I had a nickname for him. I would call him Stratters Platters!"

Al's appearances in London at this time were not always in tiny folk clubs however.

Cliff Wedgbury – "This is true. One of these was a Sunday lunchtime concert I attended one warm and sunny day when Al performed in the open air at St Anne's Churchyard in Wardour Street, Soho. He sang there together with Simon & Garfunkel. Paul Simon talked that day about composing "Blessed" on the organ in St Anne's Church and how he had played some rock 'n' roll to entertain those who had come to pray. Peter Bellamy and Jackson Frank were also there. I particularly remember Jackson singing "Don't Look Back" that day with great energy and feeling."

Along with the sporadic help of Tony Stratton-Smith, Al continued trying to get a record contract so that he could cover Paul Simon's "Richard Cory", a song that he'd wanted to record ever since hearing it on Paul's album.

Jonny Kremer – "Al was very big on the fact that this was a truly great song and that it could easily be a hit for him. At this time, in England at least, Paul Simon wasn't anything like as big a name as he was a year later with Art Garfunkel and so it wasn't apparent to most people that a Paul Simon song in itself would get you attention. But certainly if there was one song that could have got released as Al's first single other than 'The Elf' that was it. Ironically enough a short time later Them, featuring Van Morrison, in an attempt to continue having hit records, covered 'Richard Cory' themselves."

Tony Stratton-Smith had stirred up some interest in Al's song "The Elf" and as a result of this Al found himself on his way around to Mike Leander's home one evening. They got on very well.

Al – "I clearly remember that I went around to Mike Leander's apartment and he said 'What songs have you got then?' I played him a whole bunch of things on my acoustic

Decca Photo Shoot, 1966

David Wedgbury

David Wedgbury

Al at his room in Lisle Street

guitar and amongst them was 'The Elf' which Mike thought was pretty catchy and could be a single. He had some sort of deal at that time with Decca who in those days were still in the business of plugging songs. The record pluggers in Tin Pan Alley would sell them songs and they would then go and find people to record them."

This was where Al came in. Mike Leander had a song at that moment that he needed some help with. What happened next would go down as one of the strangest episodes in Al's career!

Al again – "They were looking for someone to sing the song 'A Pretty Girl Is Like A Melody' which at one time Ken Dodd had been due to record. Decca wanted that song although it was truly awful and Mike asked if I would be willing to sing it. He was however very hip to everything that was going on and eventually decided that we should go ahead and record four songs. This we did. We recorded 'A Pretty Girl Is Like A Melody', 'The Elf ' and a Yardbirds tune called 'Turn Into Earth' that Mike had heard through his friendship with Paul Samwell Smith. He wanted me to record that because he liked it a lot. We had this three hour session booked which allowed us to record four songs and so Mike also let me record a version of 'The Lyke Wake Dirge' which I'd turned into song called 'All'. I'd simply taken the tune to 'The Lyke Wake Dirge' and re-written it. At the time I really loved those songs but I was only 20! So it was a three-way thing between Decca wanting 'A Pretty Girl is Like A Melody', Mike Leander wanting 'Turn Into Earth' and my two songs."

Mike Leander was determined however that their recording of "A Pretty Girl Is Like A Melody" would never see the light of day. He confided the details to Al before they went into the studio for the session.

Al – "Mike was great about this. He knew that 'A Pretty Girl Is Like A Melody' was a load of rubbish and said to me – 'Don't worry. When we get into Sound Techniques I'm going to screw things up. I won't tell Decca what really happens but during the actual recording I'll ruin that song and when we take them the tapes I'll say that there was a technical fault and I don't think we can use it. But I'll have these other ones and I'll make them put out what I want!' He was great to me."

Mike Leander was true to his word and the recording of the four songs went to plan.

Al – "It all went just like he said it would and he was very definitely on my side. I have absolutely no idea about what happened to those 1966 versions of 'All' and 'A Pretty Girl Is Like A Melody' however."

Another person that has fond memories of working with Mike Leander at this time is Jimmy Page. He remembers him as a talented and generous soul.

Jimmy Page – "Yes, I did a lot of work for Mike Leander and I'm sure that he was somewhat responsible for establishing me around town. He seemed to have confidence in me and we worked together as a team very well I always thought."

Al – "Mike was certainly someone that could run a session and he was clearly absolutely committed to music and was a fan at heart."

Jimmy Page – "Mike was a splendid arranger and a real muzo. I remember that he also liked to play the drums in quite a heavy way and the later Gary Glitter things that he did were exactly how I remembered him playing back when I had first met him at Decca.

"I also remember that he had gone over to the States to record 'Up on the Roof' by The Drifters, which was quite an historic thing to do at the time I always thought."

And so it is entirely likely that it was in fact Mike Leander that called Jimmy Page down to Decca to play guitar on "Turn Into Earth" that day.

Al – "Now at this time I'd heard of Jimmy but hadn't actually met him. But I remember him walking in to the studio that day with Jeff Beck's old Telecaster quite clearly!"

Jimmy Page - "Al's quite right . And this would have been in Studio Two at Decca . Jeff had given me the Telecaster he'd played in The Yardbirds and if Al can remember me playing any kind of Fender at all then it was the Telecaster that Jeff gave me. I guess that you could call it an heirloom!"

By now Jimmy Page had an established reputation on the London music scene as a session musician and also had his own publishing company, James Page Music. And he was certainly putting his supreme talents to good use on a number of diverse projects at the time he first met Al.

Just prior to the session for "Turn Into Earth" he had been at IBC Studios where, on May 16th and 17th, where he had been working with Jeff Beck, Nicky Hopkins, John Paul Jones and Keith Moon on an arrangement of Ravel's "Bolero" that was being viewed as a possible solo single for Beck. He had previously also been the house producer at Immediate Records, co-writing songs with Jackie De Shannon and Bobby Graham for such bands as The Pretty Things. And so it was quite a coup for Al to have him play on his first single.

Jimmy Page – "Yes, I was pretty busy around this time. When I turned up for that first session with Al I was quite possibly doing around three sessions a day, five days a week."

Also present in the studio that day were Paul Samwell Smith and his girlfriend Rosemary Simon, meaning that two members of The Yardbirds were at Al's first session.

Al's memories recording "The Elf" are quite specific. Al – "Yes , I can remember bits of it! I remember that on 'The Elf' there are some backing vocalists and right at the end of the song I actually hold over one of the verses. This completely threw them because they didn't know when I was going to go into the next verse and they're still singing 'ahhh…' over the wrong chord because they didn't know when I was starting the next verse. And we only had one take!"

Mike Leander would have been well aware of Jimmy Page's interest in contemporary folk and would have played no small part in him booking him to record "Turn Into Earth".

Jimmy Page – "Yes, he knew that. You see I'd been listening to black country blues and then the whole movement that was going on in England at the time was something that I found absolutely fascinating with the likes of Bert and also of course Davy Graham. They had a sort of 'grooving' quality that I liked and I also appreciated the Arabic content that was going into Davy Graham's work.

"And I was fascinated by the way Bert Jansch played the guitar. There wasn't anyone else that I was hearing at the time that had the same musical intellect. And Bert and Davy Graham seemed to be exploring guitar far more than anyone over in the States was, excepting Dylan of course.

"I wasn't a regular around the clubs but I did go to see Jansch play quite early on at Les Cousins once. And I went purely on the strength of his first album. I remember that he didn't even have his own guitar that night. He was playing a gut strung guitar that he was making sound exactly the same as an electric, doing all of the inversions along the neck that you would expect a classical player to do and I thought 'my goodness gracious' and had a great respect for him. But sadly I never got to hear many of the others play live around this time but I was instead keeping up with what they were playing by listening to their records."

During a break in the recording Al remembers playing some guitar to Jimmy.

Al – "In the down time whilst the band were learning the chords Jimmy was showing me how to play finger harmonics and at this stage in 1966 he could play whole tunes that way. The only traditional song that I had learnt and performed was Bert Jansch's version of a piece called 'Black Waterside' and the only reason for that was because the guitar playing was fantastic. 'The Elf' happened to be in the same guitar tuning as 'Black Waterside' and I ended up playing it to Jimmy in the studio that day because he asked me to teach him it! Unfortunately he later recorded it and the name he gave it then was 'Black Mountainside', whereupon it all got very messy with writs and lawyers and suchlike. In the court case over it Led Zeppelin's manager, Peter Grant, even cited me!"

An interesting footnote to all of this is that although Al and Jimmy were enthusing about Bert Jansch's adaptation of the song, the actual riff was by Annie Briggs.

Al and Jimmy clearly got on very well that day, a fact that would directly lead to them working together again, despite that fact that by then Jimmy would be very much involved with Led Zeppelin.

And "The Elf" coupled with "Turn Into Earth" was duly released as Al's first single on August 12th 1966.

Up until this point Decca had been paying Al three percent on "The Elf" and Stratton-Smith talked him into giving one percent of that to Tony Hall to plug the song. Hall promptly got it onto the *David Frost Show* and Frost became the first person to ever play it that Friday.

Al – " I remember going into Imhoffs to buy some copies of the single and they'd sold out because it was being played on the radio and so for a couple of days I thought it was going to be a hit. But then of course it never got played again and went nowhere! I did eventually manage to buy a dozen copies."

Al had already written to Chris Owen telling him – "My record (ha, ha) is out in two weeks on Decca. I hope that you will rush out and buy 20,000,000 copies!"

Before this brief yet productive sojourn at Decca, Al was almost signed up by Pye, but as is often the case, personalities conspired to preclude this.

Al – "Yes it's absolutely true that I tried to get Tony Reeves at Pye to let me record my version of Paul's 'Richard Cory'. However the reason that I wanted to record for Pye was mainly because they were my hero Lonnie Donegan's label. It's as simple as that. I loved the song and thought that I stood a far better chance of success with one of Paul's songs that with one of my own."

The recording contract that did materialise, that with Decca, was clinched as much on the strength of "The Elf" as anything else. It is doubtful whether they would have signed him without having heard that particular song.

Al – "I'd sat in my bedsit in Lisle Street reading *Lord Of The Rings* and that book is a monster that does you in for at least a year and you walk around seeing elves everywhere! I had to do something so I wrote 'The Elf ' but I thought that it sounded too much like a singalong Mitch Miller thing at the time."

This comment is interesting as it is the first illustration of Al distancing himself from a piece of his own recorded work. It would be a theme that he would return to time and time again over the next seven years.

Al – "In almost all one's early work – and this applies to everyone from the Beatles, Hendrix, sideways, forwards, backwards, even Dylan – there's probably a great deal of enthusiasm and sincerity and very little finesse and subtlety; and that certainly applies to 'The Elf'."

The somewhat unusual subject matter was picked up by the musical press at once, though such headlines as "A Fairy Tale Folk Singer" in the review columns failed to turn it into a hit. Based on the character Legolas in Tolkein's *Lord Of The Rings*, it told the tale of a folk singer that meets an elf in a wood one night. An interview of the time included this characteristically, tongue-in-cheek response by Al – "This is of course quite impossible, as elves don't show themselves!"

Al was not averse to some earnest self-promotion for this first single (F12467). Pictures of the time show him photographed in the Branksome grounds of *The Bournemouth Times* with such Tolkeinesque artefacts as pinecones, witches broomsticks and wistful looks into the distance. Whilst in Bournemouth Al and Jonny embarked on another of their schemes in which they sought to bypass the system and go right after what they saw as the next logical rung up the ladder for Al's career. Together they went around one afternoon to the Bournemouth flat of local TV presenter Pat Sloman with a view to getting her to book Al for the evening news show *Day By Day*. She listened politely to the single but never did get Al onto the show. He did however go on to make his first appearance on national television, other than the brief sighting singing in Bunjies as part of Judith's *Outcasts And Outsiders*, performing "The Elf"on a BBC teatime children's show later that summer. If Al had taken another of his literary influences, such as Camus or Genet, the first single would have been different! "The Elf" remained in his concert repertoire for several years and the last words on it rest with its press release – "Tinkling piano, fast tempo and run-along lyrics – rather effective!"

THE ELF

I sat upon the Evening Hill
The shadows set, the night grew still
And as I sat, guitar on knee
A voice of flowers called to me

Sing, sing to me your song
Sing, for I belong to the night
In the grey morning light
I'll be gone

I turned with eyes that strained for sight
And there amid the failing light
Dimly saw a figure small
Heard a voice of magic call

Sing, sing to me your song
Sing, for I belong to the night
In the grey morning light
I'll be gone

My fumbling fingers found the chords
My trembling lips fought for the words
I stopped to ask the stranger how
He softly said, no questions now

But sing, sing to me your song
Sing, for I belong to the night

In the grey morning light
I'll be gone

Then with the magic of the elves
My fingers danced among themselves
A heart with lightness thus endowed
Formed melodies I know not how

Song, played the whole night long
Thus he danced and sang through the night
And with grey morning light
He was gone
Now whispering wind plays o'er the hill
And the evening sounds again grow still
A year or more has passed since then
Oh, he will not pass my way again

And so I sing, sing to you my song
Sing, for I belong to the night
In the grey morning light
I'll be gone

So I sing, sing to you my song
Sing, for I belong to the night
In the grey morning light
I'll be gone

Despite the release of a record at last and a growing reputation in the clubs Al was far from happy at this time. There were times when he seriously considered 'throwing in the towel' and doing something else.

Al – "Thinking about it, 1966 was probably the worst year I had in London. I had a couple of other residencies, one at Les Cousins and of course the Bunjies thing which I lived on and then there were some short-lived clubs around town that I played at but I wasn't getting any work anywhere else in the country. Even making the money to pay the rent in Lisle Street was difficult sometimes and it was all a bit dodgy back then. There was a period in the summer when Bunjies either closed down for a couple of weeks or I think I got laryngitis or something like that and I actually did go home back to Bournemouth for about a month to have a think about everything. I tried to think about what else I could do and came up with no particular answer and eventually just drifted back to London and Bunjies. I also came back to spend my 21st birthday with my parents, Jonny Kremer, his family, Terry Squires and Lee Kerslake."

Jonny Kremer – "This was on one of Al's occasional trips home to see us all and at that time he seemed far from happy to me although the get-together to celebrate his birthday was a lot of fun. I distinctly remember us all taking turns on a double bass singing Lee Dorsey's song 'Working in a Coalmine'!"

Al – "I wasn't very happy at that particular moment and was back in Bournemouth taking stock of things I guess. I was worried because at 21 you are supposed to have a job and at that time I didn't really have one. You were supposed to be working out what you want to do in life which was very easy – I knew what I wanted to do but I had found that I wasn't able to do it! So there was that sense of worry but at the same time there was a mountain of time ahead of me plus I did have faith in my music. Things were happening. The world was changing a lot too and this was the summer that psychedelia began to seep into everyone's consciousness."

1966 was an amazing year, however, for music in London. Al has on occasions mentioned that he once saw Jimi Hendrix play in a folk club. It did actually happen! The location was Les Cousins and Hendrix was there in his Humphrey Bogart Burberry coat to audition drummers for what would become The Jimi Hendrix Experience. The date was the afternoon of the 5th October 1966 and, with the various musicians still in situ by the time the club opened its doors in the evening, Hendrix stayed on.

Al – "I was there with a group of friends as I wasn't booked to play that night. Half way through the evening someone pointed out that the guitarist was playing the guitar with his teeth and so I turned around to watch him for a couple of minutes because up until then I'd had my back to the stage. So that was it really, the night I saw Jimi Hendrix play Les Cousins!"

Les Cousins and Bunjies were by now turning out to be a proving ground for an entire generation of folk artists. The intimate and relaxed atmosphere of both places allowing artists to try out new material on a knowledgeable and fanatic audience.

Richard Thompson remembers doing exactly this – "I used to play just about everything! Much of it all very predictable though I'm afraid. Everything from Leadbelly to Woodie Guthrie...on a nightly basis!"

Throughout all this time Al was mixing, on a daily basis, with an eclectic group of traditional folk singers, singer songwriters, people like Wizz Jones, who owed as much a debt to Jack Kerouac and Ramblin' Jack Elliott as they did anyone else, blues singers and people such as the wonderful Meg – Soho's legendary busking street urchin.

Al – "I never busked but I used to play with Meg. It's her that appears right at the end of the movie *Darling*. She used to play with Paul Simon and when Paul became famous she co-opted me and I used to play with her. She used to love the idea of playing to all these young kids and then having them rhapsodise about her. There's a legend that she was actually very wealthy and just acted like a street char woman because she got a kick out of it but I don't know if that's true or not. She basically liked to close a show and if I was doing a gig somewhere she'd come on for the encore and perform either 'I'll Fly Away' or 'We Shall Overcome' and the crowd would go nuts."

It was at this time that Al first met up with Robin Williamson who along with Mike Heron was part of The Incredible String Band. This would be a friendship that lasted until the present day.

Meanwhile, The Central School of Speech and Drama in Belsize Village had been one of the first places after Bunjies to book Al. It was here that he encountered Jenny Hancock, a true enigma and one whose short life would ultimately end in tragedy.

Al – "Jenny was the most extraordinary girl. I wrote 'Samuel Oh How You've Changed' for her, well it is her really. She was a truly beautiful woman in the Marianne Faithfull style. One day she was walking down the street when this record producer came up to her and said 'do you want to make a record?'. So she recorded this single for EMI. She was also very intellectual and when I asked her what name she wanted to go under she said Jenny Beckett because at the time she'd been reading Samuel Beckett. I didn't know her very well or for very long. Then she was due to do some gigs but there was a slight problem which was that she'd never sung properly before and this whole thing had come out of the blue. She also needed a guitar player and that was where I came in."

However, as far as Al is aware, she never once performed in public. To him however, Jenny had initially appeared perfectly serious about trying to become a singer in London and it was with this in mind that they started putting together a short set of songs for her to sing. But it was all to come to nothing in the end.

Al – "Eventually I think she just stayed at college. Although we did rehearse those songs. Thinking back maybe she was never really that interested in pursuing a career as a folk singer after all."

Al has a particular reason to remember Jenny Hancock that goes far beyond her immortalisation in "Samuel Oh How You've Changed".

Al – "The thing that she did say to me that stuck in my mind was 'I'm in my last incarnation and by the age of 23 I'll be perfect and there'll be no point in living any more.' Now when someone says that to you when you're 19 it makes a serious impression. She certainly looked close to perfection to me. In 1970, when I hadn't seen her for four years, I figured that it would be around about the time and I rang all of the Hancocks in the phone directory and by sheer chance got her mother on the phone."

Al asked her whether she had a daughter called Jenny that had made a record but he cannot have been prepared for what he heard next.

Al – "I asked her where Jenny was and she replied that something terrible had happened and that she was dead. Now I was just astounded because she'd done it, she really had! She'd gone off to South Africa for a while doing this and that and then she came back and committed suicide. She was the only person in my life that said anything as ludicrous as 'I'm going to be dead by 23' and then went straight out and did it. In retrospect, whether or not that meant that she was mentally unhinged or whether she actually was achieving perfection is something that I'll never know… and I've often wondered about it."

The folk club in Belsize Village where Al had first met Jenny convened in an attic space above the Embassy Theatre, somewhere that in the daytime was a location for movement classes at the school. It was also the place that Al first met another life long friend, Dave Dyke.

Dave Dyke – "I was at the Central School of Speech and Drama in Swiss Cottage at this time. I took over the Folk Club there in 1966 which was when I first met Al. He told me that he had played his very first paid gig anywhere at the club the previous year for the princely sum of £5! He talked to me all about Jenny and how he had met her there the previous year and been so smitten by her and all that she stood for. I got the impression that he had returned to our folk club out of nostalgia. You see the Central School of Speech and Drama was at this time the most fantastic place to be as it was inhabited by the most amazing women which was certainly part of its appeal to Al."

In "Love Chronicles" Al would go on to sing about "The hunting grounds of Earls Court and Swiss Cottage", referring specifically to this time.

Dave Dyke has fond memories of the very first gig that he put on there in 1966. "At my first gig I saw first hand Al's control of an audience when he dealt almost ruthlessly with any hecklers that dared to try and take him on. It was hilarious. We also got to know each other quite well because what would normally happen was that us organisers of the folk club would gather up all the money that we had managed to take on the door and spend it down at the Winchester pub after the club packed up for the evening!"

Al's behaviour did alienate some people at the time in the folk world. When he first arrived on the London scene he was quite giggly and more than a little public school, which was a million miles away from the gritty, more down-to-earth folkies like Bert or Davy Graham and this did tend to exclude him. He was different, but very much part of the scene.

Dave Dyke – "Al loved the life around the folk scene in Soho in those early days in the mid-'60s more than just about anyone else that I knew. One day we were coming out of Cousins on our way to go and see John Renbourn play somewhere like The Scots Hoose, which was just down the road, when it struck me that I was in the company of someone who seemed to be as much a part of things there as the streets themselves. He just loved it all so much."

Two people that got to know Al very well at this time were musicians Roger Hand and Rod Edwards.

Rod Edwards – "At this time Al, Rog and myself all lived for a short while in Skardu Road, Cricklewood. Rog and myself had found the place in late 1966. Later on when Al was looking for somewhere to live for a few weeks, this new flat of ours had a spare bedroom, so he came over and had a look and took it. It was above a restaurant on the corner of where Cricklewood Broadway meets Skardu Road going northbound on the A5."

But Al only stayed with them for a few weeks, being what Rod describes as "very much a city boy at heart." At this time Roy Harper was living just around the corner from them in Fordwych Road.

Rod Edwards – "We'd all return home at breakfast time after a Les Cousins all-nighter and would go to bed at about 7am whereupon the church bells directly opposite Harper's flat would start up! I can still remember him now, screaming out across the road 'Go home Quasimodo' to the bellringer in the church."

Then, at the start of 1967, Al met and fell in love with the woman that would alter the course of his life.

Al – "I met Mandi early in 1967 at the Central School of Speech and Drama where I'd gone to play as they were having a folk night. I had got up and played 'Ivich' when Mandi came up and said how much she liked it and looking wistfully at me, asked where I was next playing. So I told her that I was playing at Les Cousins and she duly came down there to see me."

This was the start of a relationship that would be at the centre of Al's life and his songs for the next four years.

FOLK DIRECTION HOME

In which Al releases *Bedsitter Images* and *Love Chronicles* before an emotional crisis pushes him to the brink of madness.

1966 had been, by Al's own admission, a bad year. Now on both a personal and professional front that was all about to change.

Al, by now 21 and a London resident for almost two years, had achieved some success in the capital while still not approaching the breakthrough needed. He now proceeded to take these matters into his own hands by approaching the seminal London management agency Folk Directions run by the truly maverick Roy Guest.

Roy Guest had a folk music pedigree that stretched back to the Edinburgh Folk Festival of 1959, where he founded The Howff Folk Club and recorded his own EP. He's also worked at New York City's Lamplight Club and had hosted the BBC's Hootenanny Show before ending up, via Cecil Sharp House, running Folk Directions. His methods, though often suspect, invariably got the job done and his gift for self promotion did no harm to the artists that he worked with.

Al – "After about nine months Tony Stratton-Smith had said to me that he really couldn't do anything else to push my career along and that I should find a folk manager. At first there was the idea that Ewan Allen, who also looked after the Ian Campbell Folk Group, might manage me and so I went to see him and played 'Samuel Oh How You've Changed', which he seemed to like well enough, but nothing ever came out of that. Now I knew that the biggest folk manager at the time was Roy Guest and so I went to see him and announced that I wanted to be the King of the English folk scene and he said 'Fine Al, just sign here!'"

Roy set to work at once and on the 25th January 1967 Roy signed a contract on behalf of Al taking him to CBS. The contract came about when the record company, seeking to sign another of Roy's acts, namely The Piccadilly Line, were told by the artful manager that if they wanted the group then they would have to sign Al as well!

Al had done his homework before going to visit Roy and as a result of the new management his out of town concert trips now became extended affairs. It provided a much needed shot in the arm for Al after the uncertainty that had dogged him throughout much of 1966. In exactly the same way that Paul Simon's return to the US a year earlier had opened up a new network of places for Al to play, Roy Guest now sent Al out to perform all over England.

Al was very aware that the arrangement had its limitations however.

Al – "It was all something of a compromise at the time. Roy had contacts at just about every folk club around the country and could get me loads of work. I knew also that he'd made those folk records of his own that hadn't got anywhere. He was going nowhere as a folkie and had therefore decided to become a manager instead. He was another of these characters who had lots of big ideas and basically no follow-through whatsoever. The downside of me getting to record those first three albums was that Roy insisted on producing them and I didn't know at the time that he'd never produced a record before in his life! He produced them largely from the pub across the road. Roy was a concert promoter more than a manager."

Julia Creasey had been given a free reign at Folk Directions from the moment that she had arrived in 1965. In the year before Al joined Folk Directions she had taken on an increasingly active role in the running of the company. Roy appears to have relied on her from the outset.

Julia Creasey – "I had turned up at Roy's flat for my interview the year before in November 1965, when Folk Directions was a spectacularly traditional concern representing people like Cyril Tawney, not quite sure of what to expect! It was obvious that he needed someone to help with the Agency side of the business because he took me on straight away."

Julia had initially been introduced to Al on one of his first visits to the office. He appeared to her to be rather uncertain and had clearly brought Mandi along that day as moral support.

Julia again – "Al had already concluded the business side of things with Roy by the time that I met him and Mandi at Roy's flat, in the lounge, that afternoon in early 1967. I already knew that I would be in charge of getting gigs for Al whilst Roy was to take control of Al's career and to be his personal manager. We used to have these 'month to a page' diaries for each of our artists and so the very first thing that I ever did for Al was to start up one of these diaries for him in order to keep track of all his gigs past and those to come."

As the diary began to fill up Julia remembers being impressed at once by Al's work ethic.

"I soon discovered something quite marvellous about Al, which was just how hard he was willing to work and the distances he was willing to drive between gigs. He was not at all worried if that meant having to zigzag all over the place. These were very important times in Al's career and it was vital that he got as much exposure up and down the country as we could find him. In fact Ralph McTell once spoke to me about Al's work ethic and how hard he worked at his craft. Once Al and I had got acquainted I literally went out around not only every folk club I knew about but also around the universities' student unions trying to get him work. The golden era of the university gigs was still five years away but even back in 1966 there was a circuit of places out there that someone such as Al could do very well at. Also, the day after he played each of these universities I'd ring up the Social Secretary to get a repeat booking!"

And so that sunny afternoon when Al had arrived with Mandi in tow, to consolidate the move from Tony Stratton-Smith's Agency to Folk Directions, Julia had been there with Roy to greet them both. She recalls a clean-cut Al with short hair, wearing one of his corduroy jackets and also that he was quite nervous, pacing the room and deferring to Mandi on the key details of the deal that they were there to discuss. Folk Directions subsequently bought out Al's contract with Tony Stratton-Smith for just £50. From here on in Al and Julia would talk each day on the phone for the next five years and she possibly knew Al as well as anyone at this time. He'd pop in each week for a cup of tea and to talk about the direction his career was going and together they shared his hopes and ideas.

Al – "The period from mid-1966 until mid-1967 had been a very tough time for me. For a start there were very few gigs besides Bunjies and Les Cousins. I was getting by but that was about it. I wasn't thinking of giving up music completely but on a purely financial level it was getting hard to cover the rent every week. The fact that I needed to borrow £100 from Mandi at this time (as mentioned in 'You Don't Even Know Me') just goes to show what dire straits I was in by then."

Hence the move to Roy Guest at the start of 1967. Meanwhile Folk Directions went from strength to strength. With such artists as the very laid-back Trevor Lucas (who went on to marry Sandy Denny), The Young Tradition, Martin Carthy and Dave Swarbrick on the agency's books, Roy Guest now set about signing what amounted to a development contract with his young duo The Piccadilly Line, namely Rod Edwards and Roger Hand. To help fund this project, or more precisely to bolster up the less than full company bank balance, Guesty secured a cash investment from the duo's parents. Unorthodox, unethical and quite possibly illegal, it was all par for the course for Roy Guest. One of the few acts of promotion that the parents' money resulted in was to end in real drama at the Folk

Directions first floor Parkway offices. Thousands of eye-catching leaflets were printed announcing the boys' appearance on the Piccadilly Line at a show to feature "free champagne and topless waitresses"! These handbills were handed out down The Kings Road in Chelsea and Carnaby Street by three sexy 17-year-old girls. The tabloid press and specifically *The News Of The World* got hold of the story, ran an incendiary piece on the forthcoming party and the next day three police vans roared up outside the carpet shop and Folk Directions' place in underground folklore was secured by a full scale police raid! The party was cancelled but the publicity surrounding the non-event achieved its aims and Rod and Roger's parents saw a tangible return on their investment. The duo had been working the fringes of the London folk scene for many months by now and had known Al for much of this time.

Rod Edwards – "We'd been visiting Les Cousins on a regular basis for quite a while and had gotten to know various people there and one afternoon we were chatting to Jackson who suggested that we thought seriously about doing a couple of our songs at his residency there and we did just that – 'Out Of My Mind' and 'Twigs' most probably. On another evening when we were playing there, I think it must have been a benefit or something like that, Al played 'Czardas' just for something different to do. We backed him on a couple of songs and played up there with our three guitars on some instrumentals because Al was a very fine technician on the guitar as well as having the ability to compose such great songs. As a result of that gig and because it went down so well we got a Tuesday

Nevern Road, West London

Neville

night residency there as the Piccadilly Line and with our new manager Roy Guest things started to get going for us."

Soon after this had all happened back in October 1966 Rod and Rog had played Al a ten-minute demo of their own original songs to see if he could help them get produced and recorded. Al considered this but decided against it. However he played them a song he'd written one day at his new flat in Nevern Road called "Primrose Lady", a composition somewhat in the style of The Byrds' "Mr Tambourine Man", and together they all went into the studio for what was the first time and recorded the song with Al himself producing it.

Rodney Edwards – "We recorded this song at a session at Kingsway Recorders De Lane Lea Studios. There was Big Jim Sullivan on guitar, Dougie Wright on drums, Herbie Flowers on bass."

Throughout all of this time Al had remained on good terms with the producer of his Decca single, Mike Leander, trying one evening to get him involved with the duo.

Roger Hand – "Al drove us all over to Mike Leander's flat and we played this song there live in front of him. But nothing much came out of that except our on-going friendship with Al. I don't know how Al really saw himself in all of this but he was very excited about the song."

With hindsight it was clearly Al trying to write a commercial song and hopefully get a hit with it but the track only ever remained as this demo. Al was the momentum behind all of this and Rod and Rog were quite happy just to go along with it.

Throughout all of this time Al's set continued to be very much full of cover versions, especially Dylan songs.

Al – "I had been writing my own songs in London for two years by now but I just loved Dylan so much and got a real buzz out of doing his stuff live. I wasn't the only one either. It seemed to me that just about all of us that were playing down in Les Cousins had at least one Dylan song in our sets."

After those shows at Les Cousins everyone would troop back to Al's new place in Nevern Road for what had become a regular card school. Musicians would also stop off there in the early hours of the morning as they drove back through West London after having done gigs around the country.

Rod Edwards – "These games were great! I remember Al would get really animated if he won and enjoyed our Wednesday nights in Earls Court a lot! There'd be people like Roy Harper and Noel Murphy who used to share our van to travel to gigs. It was quite a disparate group really, hanging out after their shows playing poker."

Meanwhile, Roy Guest worked tirelessly on behalf of Rod and Rog that year.

Rod Edwards – "When we started doing gigs with Al, Roy made some posters for us saying, "Catch the Piccadilly Line" and that's when he first got involved with him. Both Al and ourselves would do a set each at Les Cousins and we'd also work on numbers, three or four of them together, different ones for each week. They were fun things to do together more than anything else, we had a lot of fun doing them."

Al never restricted his social life in London to those venues of a folk only domain. He was a regular at UFO from day one and by his own admission "absolutely loved the place". The club used the premises of the Blarney Club in Tottenham Court Road on Friday nights. From the very outset the crowd it sought to attract were the more *avant garde* of the then London scene and in fact its original title was Night Tripper. It opened on December 30 1966. These were heady times in London and Al was present at many of the Happenings around town that now ushered in psychedelia. *The International Times* had started up in the previous October with a launch party that defined the ethos of that moment in "Swinging London". The location for the event was The Roundhouse beside Chalk Farm Station and featured not only The Soft Machine but Pink Floyd as well. Soft Machine used an amplified motorcycle as part of their act on which a guy called Dennis wearing a head-dress and gothic cape posed and revved it up. Whilst The Floyd performed their set people were given motor bike rides around the perimeter of the audience. Paul McCartney turned up dressed as an Arab, there were light projectors and enough purple hearts and French Blues to kit out the most hip of mobile pharmacies presently doing the rounds around town.

Al – "I loved UFO. People were painting their faces gold and wore long flowing robes and took lots of drugs and in fact Pink Floyd and The Soft Machine alternated as the house bands with fantastic coloured back projections and oil lamps. Although I never played at UFO I went there every week and did my best to join in the carnival atmosphere of everything."

Another band that would go on to become regulars at UFO was the legendary Fairport Convention. On Saturday 27th May 1967 they had played their first ever show at St. Michaels Church Hall in London's Golders Green Road. With Simon Nichol, Ashley Hutchings and Richard Thompson on guitar and temporary drummer Shawn Frater, the four-piece ran through a succession of covers including Love's "7 And 7 Is", "Hey Joe", the Byrds' "My Back Pages" and a number of Chuck Berry songs. In the audience of just two dozen people was Martin Lamble who would go on to replace Frater on drums from that day on. Adding Judy Dyble as a vocalist they toured the university circuit and soon became one of DJ John Peel's favourite bands through the Summer of Love. Al remembers attending several of those early shows (possibly at The Speakeasy) and slowly getting to know them around town at places like UFO throughout 1967.

Al – "They were amazing. Seeing them was just the best thing! They would usually go out and play two sets. The first would be melodic and generally quite … soft in tone whereas the second set would somewhat showcase Richard in that he would perform these amazing solos that would go on and on."

Karl Dallas – "Al and I were very probably there at the same shows that year as Fairport did indeed play at UFO. There would always be a number of different things going on there. There was this huge performance area with a theatre group in one corner, a Kenneth Anger film being projected in another area and perhaps Soft Machine playing elsewhere. But it wasn't somewhere that you went just to see one particular thing. I remember one night the club booked Procol Harum and it did become like a gig and everyone got very cross about that because UFO wasn't that kind of place. Following the whole hippy ethos it didn't have a drink license but of course drugs abounded there but it wasn't at all blatant and in fact I never saw it. But it was all quite lovely there for a while. Everyone seemed to be there. I also saw The Incredible String Band there at what must have been one of their earliest shows."

This is born out by Robin Williamson himself who, like everyone else, has distinct thoughts on UFO.

Robin Williamson – "It was one of the first places we played together in London. I remember there was this flashing light over the stairs, which meant that you couldn't see a thing as you went down the stairs. I remember Al as being very dapper but we really got to know each other down in The Cousins where between sets we'd chat about this and that and we'd sometimes run into one another around town at various clubs. In the summer of 1967 we both got offered this week-long residency at a club in Turin. It was just Al, Mike Heron and myself. When we got to perform on the first night it was wonderful because the club had sold out. But unfortunately this was because all of the tickets had been given away and our audience were what amounted to a communist rally with folk singers! In between each song throughout both of our sets this official communist shop steward would get up and explain the relevance to the communist struggle of the previous piece's lyrics! It was quite surreal!"

The situation was made more difficult as neither Robin, Mike or Al could speak any Italian. The show the next night wasn't a free gig and as such was half-empty.

Robin Williamson again – "During our week out there was a great deal of aggression directed against us because we were all seen as hippies and so truckers spat at us and threw stones too. But the geography out there was stunning and one lunchtime after we'd all been taken out to a winery country estate for something to eat I found this ruined monastery full of history books – I picked one up on pre-revolution Russia. Another day we all went out to see a 'Living Theatre' production of *Frankenstein* which was quite fantastic I remember and then it was back to Turin for that night's show. We pretty much stuck together."

It's this time in Italy that Al sings about in "Beleeka Doodle Day" written soon after their trip and recorded later that year.

Al – "It was all just as weird as Robin remembers it."

Joe Boyd – "Around the same time as UFO started, the Electric Garden started in King Street, Covent Garden. I went to the opening and it was terrible. A kind of 'hippy' environment, an attempt to be an underground place. Jay Landesman was involved. We not exactly defeated them, but we did become the place to go to. By that time it became

Middle Earth and eventually Middle Earth took over the Roundhouse when we left in October 1967."

The club was a Mecca for the underground and within weeks of its opening could boast John Peel, Donovan and Captain Beefheart besides Al as regulars.

Jo Cruikshank – "UFO was exotic, but it wasn't nearly as memorable for me as Middle Earth. Middle Earth took your breath away. It was the whole situation of it, in the middle of Covent Garden when it was Covent Garden. You'd go through these desolate, wet streets into this basement in King Street, just near the Opera House. Into this great space filled with music and incense and drugs, this great warehouse with pineapples and bananas. Light shows going. You'd go out on this wonderful surge. You'd rendezvous with people at midnight at Covent Garden Station. We had our own little universe, you'd walk in – everyone knew you."

Middle Earth was by now attracting more of a general mass patronage than the hardcore of UFO and in those terms of reference was the more successful of the two.

Al preferred UFO, but he did play at Middle Earth."

But despite his patronage, ultimately Middle Earth failed to live up to its lofty ideals. Karl Dallas goes even further in his assessment how things ultimately panned out – "In fact I feel that Middle Earth was essentially a failure. It had been financed largely by a straight-as-a-die photographer called John Adams. Now Middle Earth was much more of a venue specifically for gigs than UFO ever was."

UFO was to now serve as the lift-off point for one of Al's more adventurous projects. What happened to him goes to the very heart of all that was so unique about life in London at this time.

He had gone to the club to do nothing more than enjoy an evening out with friends but what transpired was to send his career off on a wild tangent for a few months.

Al – "It was the night that I first met Yoko Ono! One evening, during a break between bands, the club gave out one of the public service announcements that they were always making. This one was different however. They made it on behalf of a Japanese avant-garde artist who was there and wanted to make a movie and was looking for investors. This was all before she had met John Lennon. So I went and found her and liked her at once, she was unlike anyone else that I'd met up until that time in London. I asked her what the film was about and she said – 'Al, I want to make a film about people's *bottoms!*'

Yoko Ono remembers the first meeting – "He seemed a very successful songwriter; everybody there knew and treated him with respect."

Al – "Now this was 1967 and it seemed to me that if you had an entire film about people's bottoms then you were going to make money. The film was only going to cost her £1,000 to make and I happened to have the £100 she was looking for to secure a ten percent share in her movie. So being young and impressionable I gave her £100 and she gave me a signed contract to the effect that from that moment on I owned ten percent of her film *Number 4.*"

Al had never invested in someone else's work before and his sudden dive into the world of conceptual art (about which he knew practically nothing) appeared, on the surface, to be at the very least reckless. However it had very little to do with Art. He had seen in Yoko the same fire and passion that he too had felt when he had first come up to London from Bournemouth two years earlier.

Al – "I liked her immediately, that's why I wanted to be part of her film. I seem to remember that all of the people in her film had replied to a mysterious advertisement in *The Stage* and found that all they were required to do was to take their clothes off and walk on a turntable!"

Yoko – "I remember very clearly, Al was one of the very few people who invested right away in my film, without too many questions. I would like to say thank you for your confidence in my film."

Yoko would watch Al's subsequent progress and say "Good for you, Al."

The plan originally had been to show the film at the Royal Albert Hall, with the world's press in attendance, but things didn't exactly turn out like that and the film ultimately opened in London's West End. The premiere for the movie was at the less than glamorous *Jacey-Tatler Cinema* in the Charing Cross Road, on the fringes of Soho. Al took Mandi along for that first showing.

Al – "When Yoko had initially told me that the film was to be called *Bottoms* I hadn't quite understood that that was all we were going to see! I felt some genuine sadness for Yoko because the subject nature of the movie was of course sensationalised in the English press at the time and I've always felt she was totally misunderstood. It was a very brave piece of work and proved, in many ways, to be a template for many of the avant garde movies that were to follow."

The piece was in fact made in two versions and at the time Yoko explained that she hoped the film would "reveal a truth about the human race" and also "strike a blow for world peace".

The film was a montage of 365 bottoms each framed in exactly the same way for twenty seconds and ultimately the viewer finds themselves making their own comparisons between each pair. A further interesting facet of the film was its soundtrack which consisted of interviews with both those people in the work and interviews with others that are considering taking part. There was also an interview with Yoko herself in which she is able to not only elucidate on the perceived conceptual design values of *Number 4* but to remain enigmatic all at once.

Al – "During this time I was seeing Yoko two or three times a week and Mandi and I basically hung out with her. Mandi in fact became Yoko's secretary and typed out her book *Grapefruit*. Basically she also became [Yoko's child] Kyoto's babysitter back at their amazing apartment near Lords cricket ground. Everything inside had been sawn in two and painted white. It was totally fantastic, without doubt one of the most incredible places that I've ever visited. Yoko had half a bed, half a radio and half a television set. There was even half a teacup sitting on half a table with half a chair next to it. It didn't make any sense to me but was totally fabulous. I also remember that the half a bed was propped up against the wall to stop it from falling down."

Yoko – "Whenever he visited me and my then mate, Tony Cox, he passionately spoke about Bob Dylan, quoting his lyrics and telling us what a genius Bob was. I detected his genuine artistic appreciation about Bob and like that aspect of his character. We were all, you know, heart people. We were in music because we loved it. If we made money with it, I'm sure we would not have minded. But that was like some kind of side effect."

This was a time of "crossover" for the folk music scene when venues of various sizes and capacities were being used across London to showcase a growing roster of artists. Al was in the right place at the right time and was able to take full advantage of all this.

Julia Creasey – "We would even use somewhere such as the Purcell Rooms for someone who had outgrown the folk clubs around town and that actually was somewhere that we'd quite often put on a couple of artists for the evening. Not everyone liked the way that we did things however and the artists that Folk Directions represented would come and go."

Such as Rod and Rog. The eventual split between Roy Guest and The Piccadilly Line had been a gradual one.

Rod Edwards – "It was gradual but we saw it coming and in the end it was a natural enough split. At the same building in Parkway to Folk Directions was Spencer Davis' management. In fact it was the University of London entertainment agency which was run by John Miller. And gradually this agency started booking us into colleges and gradually we ended up doing less with Roy Guest and more with the Spencer Davis Management."

One example of Roy Guest's fast and loose approach to all things was how he secured

"Bedsitter Images" photo session. London 1967

the funding to record Al's first album *Bedsitter Images* and its orchestra. Having let CBS sign up Messrs Hand and Edwards on the basis that they signed up Al as well he noticed that the minutiae of the contract for Al's album included such finance "as necessary for studio musicians". This was set in place to facilitate what would normally be a drummer, bass player, maybe a keyboard player – but it wasn't specific. There was no limit to the number of musicians or expenditure on them. So Alexander Faris and The Sinfonia of London were mobilised as the studio band by Roy to the astonishment of everyone. According to Al the reason for the orchestra was probably the lingering influence of Judy Collins's *In My Life* and its use of an orchestra.

Roy Guest had sensibly waited until the London Chief Executive of CBS was out of the country before organising the recording sessions.

When Al went into the CBS studios to record *Bedsitter Images* he had all of the songs written and ready and Julia remembers Al as a very professional artist in the studio who knew exactly what sound he wanted from every instrument and as someone who was also a stickler for efficiency in the studio. He never suffered fools gladly and would get truly exasperated when someone was slow or slapdash. He was a perfectionist, Julia recalls, which would drive people mad, especially at 3am in the morning, after an eight hour session in the small studio.

For the October 1967 release of *Bedsitter Images* Al needed to consolidate his status as a performing and recording artist by staging a prestigious London concert – something more impressive than the Freedom Folk Club in Hull was clearly the order of the day. Unfortunately, manager Roy Guest decided to book one of the capital's largest and most expensive auditoriums, The Royal Festival Hall on the South Bank.

Friday November 3rd 1967 is undoubtedly forever lodged in Al's mind as a day he'd sooner forget. The result of "papering the walls with complimentary tickets" (as one paper commented) was that it cost Al, personally, £1,058. Considering all this from the comparative prosperity of 1977, Al remembered it like this –

"Another Guesty idea. One of his grand schemes. After the Royal Festival Hall, relations between me and Roy became dim to say the least, and he decided that he didn't want to be my manager, although he cannily, because he is canny, decided to keep a foot in the record making because he was getting 40 percent, which is outrageous. From here on in I only really saw Julia."

Roy's reputation was something that always preceded him. People often chose to deal with either Jim Lloyd or Julia Creasey if they could. The control over the events that he should have been running was sometimes also lacking. At the rehearsals for the Festival Hall Show there was Al, his two backing musicians, the Sinfonia of London and Arabella – who was set to dance to the music on stage that evening. As she moved across the apron of the stage, with Al and his two band members running through simple versions of the songs, the Sinfonia of London sat for much of the afternoon and waited for the call to rehearse live with Al. Eventually with only the very briefest of full rehearsals behind them they ran out of time and the grand launch of *Bedsitter Images* went largely unrehearsed. The inauspicious omens were proved right when the lead trumpet player "cracked" on the intro to the opening of the first song, "Bedsitter Images".

Julia Creasey – "Now of course it would have made far more sense for the album to be launched with a show at the Queen Elizabeth Hall next door which only held a third of the number of people of the Festival Hall. It was such a stupid idea of Roy's."

Bedsitter Images was expected to do well, but not well enough to justify such an optimistic choice of venue as The Royal Festival Hall. However, the main reason for the disastrous debt was that Al's backup was not just George Butler on drums and Jim Condon on bass but The Sinfonia of London and conductor Sandy Faris that Roy had insisted perform with Al. The sight of this 35-piece orchestra was impressive enough, but rather surreal, since Al usually played solo (35-piece orchestras being a bit much for the tiny Bunjies or Bristol Troubadour). Despite valiant efforts by Luke O'Reilly on the

24 Carrot's tour, the Sinfonia remains Al's largest backing group for a solo gig to date.

Dave Dyke – "It was quite a show too! The sections with the dancer were a little strange though. She would glide across the stage in her body stocking dancing in the most alluring way gradually getting closer and closer to Al but to me it was the one bit of the show that didn't really work; but the rest of the concert was great."

This was a major show. Tickets for the Royal Festival Hall extravaganza were priced between five and twenty-one shillings, and Folk Directions of course promoted the 8 o'clock concert. There was a large format programme on sale, the centre of which provided the Sophie Lichfield 'Highway '61' style photo.

In an article in *The Guardian* the next day Robin Denselow wrote – "Looking like an absurd parody of a pop singer, long haired, thin and twitching, he strummed his way through a collection of his own sad, tuneful, little songs. Al Stewart is being promoted too late, three years ago he would have been a *sensation*."

Karl Dallas reviewed Al's performance of "Ivich" as a song that "shines forth like a good deed in a naughty world" whilst Tony Wilson writing in *The Morning Star*, was mightily impressed declaring – 'When Al Stewart made his concert debut last night he tore off his folk tag and became a singer-songwriter. If one has to pin him down to a musical type, the choice would be the French *chansonnier* style of singer and songwriter for which there is no recognised British equivalent."

Continuing with what was both a detailed and largely positive review of the concert he selected "Swiss Cottage Manoeuvres", "Bedsitter Images" and "A Long Way Down From Stephanie" as songs that particularly benefited from the orchestral accompaniment, complimenting Al on "Ivich" and "Denise at Sixteen" for his acoustic prowess.

During the show Al swapped his acoustic for an electric guitar for a performance of Bob Dylan's "Tom Thumb's Blues" and Paul Simon's "Sparrow", a song that Tony Wilson was particularly impressed with.

He wrote – "This was the most spectacular number with Jimmy Hendrix-style guitar complete with feedback. The stage was bathed in flashing coloured lights and the dancer, Romey Young, came on and there were a few pleasant moments of musical madness."

Many of those at the show that evening in November 1967 were convinced that Al was on the brink of a real breakthrough. Certainly these included Roy Guest. The music press remained generally ambivalent however but Tony Wilson thought otherwise, writing – "The folk scene is going to lose, eventually, one of its contemporary performers, but a wider musical field will gain a very talented young artist."

As a vehicle to gain Al a wider audience, by way of the generous press coverage that he wouldn't otherwise have got, it was a huge success. The downside however was that in establishing a profile, that he never had a chance of sustaining, it ultimately resulted in more than a slight feeling of anti-climax for Al, who was back playing the London folk scene the next night.

As Noel Murphy said to Al, in the Green Room of the Royal Festival Hall, after the show – "Ah well Al, its back to Les Cousins now I suppose!"

In fact it was over to The Royal Gardens Hotel in Kensington for a private after-show party but the next night, as Noel Murphy had joked, Al was indeed back playing to the tiny crowd at Les Cousins.

One question that has puzzled many people over the years is why did Al stay so long with Roy Guest as his manager if he was so unhappy with him ?

Al – "Well it's quite simple. It was because Guesty was getting me so many gigs. I mean it wasn't something I wanted to escape from although he was taking some money from my concerts and setting some of it against the debt from the launch of *Bedsitter Images*."

Al was far from happy with the sound of the album however. He freely told anyone that would listen that he thought that the addition of the orchestra had been a monumental mistake and that the sound of it was "muddy".

Al – " I didn't really know what was wrong with him and I wasn't sophisticated enough

Sophie Lichfield/Folk Directions

Above and left: London 1967

Sophie Lichfield/Folk Directions

to know why my records sounded so bad. It didn't occur to me. Obviously it would have been nice if George Martin had wanted to produce it but we were not getting offers like that."

Julia Creasey – "I know how Al feels about the album but he knew exactly the sound that he wanted for each track. Now his ideas might not always have worked the way he envisaged but in his young head he had a clear vision of what he expected from the musicians for each of those songs. He had a great deal more input that he would have you imagine."

Talking about *Bedsitter Images* in 1972 Al had this to say – "Everything about the first record, in retrospect, I hated. The cover design I thought was terrible. I thought the Roy Guest sleeve notes were terrible, the mix was terrible… Even the songs weren't really up to the standard they should have been and more important, it had nothing to do with what I was doing live."

But talking to Julia Creasey you gain a totally different sense of what actually went on in the studio and the responsibility that not only Roy Guest and Michael Claydon but Al too should accept. The idea that Al just went along with everything that Guesty said and had no real creative input of his own is challenged by Julia.

Julia Creasey– "When a track didn't come out the way he'd hoped it was, in a way, often Al's own fault because very often it had been recorded and mixed as per his own instructions. I can picture him now, as clear as it was yesterday, up there at the desk saying 'Bring such and such up, make this louder' and so on. He was playing as big a roll in the mechanics of recording as he was in the singing itself – he was very hands-on. I was there to give him moral support in what could easily have been a very intimidating place for Al – after all he was only 21 at the time."

What is undeniable on those CBS sessions for *Bedsitter Images* was that neither Al nor Roy Guest had any proper experience of making an album before and that to christen their professional recording partnership by using an orchestra was bound to be at best problematical.

BEDSITTER IMAGES
The Subway station's closed again
Sleeps beneath its veil of rain
My footprints' broken trail behind
Steals the nightlights from my mind
The dark deserted streets stand clear
Today has lived and died in here
So I leave the chapel gloom
To find the shelter of my tiny room

But it's alright while the lights of the city shine so bright
It's all right till the last winding train fades from sight
Then alone in my room I must stay to lose or win
While these wild bedsitter images came back to hem me in

The panelled patterns on the door
Chase shivering shadows to the floor
Upon the pillow worn and thin
The memories of hopes begin
The carpet with its flowers in shreds
Expires a foot before my bed
The crack that won't return again
Advancing through my broken window pane

But it's alright while the lights of the city shine so bright
It's all right till the last winding train fades from sight
Then alone in my room I must stay to lose or win
While these wild bedsitter images came back to hem me in

The friends I've left back home all write
With laughing words that warm my sight
Saying "Tell us, how's the city life?"
I reply and say just fine
(Oh, you must be lonely)
And so you see I can't go back
Until I either win or crack
I'm standing in a one way street
The stage is set
(Oh, you know you're sad)
The story incomplete

> But it's alright while the lights of the city shine so bright
> It's all right till the last winding train fades from sight
> Then alone in my room I must stay to lose or win
> While these wild bedsitter images come back to hem me in.

And that is Al's song about living in his 'tiny room' above Soho's Lisle Street.

The 16th century songwriter John Dowland had a strong influence on Al's work at this time. "A Long Way Down From Stephanie", from the new album, owed Dowland a particular debt especially in evoking the ballad style of prose and imagery that Dowland had employed 400 years earlier. Dowland's name was of course better known in 'traditional' folk circles rather than in those of coffee bar singer-songwriters and is proof, if proof were needed, of Al's eclectic sources of referral even back then. He knew this piece by Dowland:

> Lute arise and charme the air,
> Until a thousand formes shee beare,
> Coniure them all that they repaire,
> Into the circles of his eare,
> Euer to dwell in concord there
> By this thy tunes may haue accesse
> Euen to hir spirit whose flowering trasure
> Doth sweetest Harmony expresse
> Filling all eares and hearts with pleasure
> On earth, obseruing heauenly measure
> Right well can shee Iudge and defend them,
> Doubt not of that for shee can mend them.

Family archive

Mandi

Al has always maintained an enigmatic silence on the similarities between some of his work and that of Dowland.

With his album released and the Royal Festival Hall show behind him Al had set about getting his career back on track. Roy Guest still had one more trick up his sleeve though.

Jim Lloyd – "CBS however had still not finished having their fingers burnt by the cunning of Al's manager. He somehow eventually managed to persuade CBS that the responsibility for the debacle of the Royal Festival Hall show rested with them. The basis of this was that at short notice they had put back the release date of *Bedsitter Images* and this had clearly undermined the gig's chances of success. After much to-ing and fro-ing they remarkably conceded and gave Roy Guest a cheque for £1,000. It says quite a lot for his powers of persuasion when the chips were down."

It took Al three years to pay off the £1,058. A high price to pay for obtaining that high profile.

Al's debut album was in fact reissued with some track changes a few years later.

Al – "I like to have all my words on the sleeves of LPs so one reason for the changes was that I couldn't stand the look of the thing. Later on I put a new photo on the front and new words on the back, and took off three tracks which I thought were the main offenders orchestra-wise and put on another two that were much simpler, and on the four remaining orchestral tracks I brought the voice up so that at least it was audible, and I suppose I improved the album about 300 percent but that still didn't make it a good record."

Al was still in touch with Yoko and had invited her to his Royal Festival Hall show but she and her then husband Tony Cox had been unable to make it. Al's continued friendship with Yoko was soon however to yield a great deal more than just his financial investment in her film *Bottoms Number Four.*

Al – "A great deal more indeed. I happened to own a tape recorder besides my guitar and Yoko was interested in all forms of artistic expression. She was, at that moment, looking for someone to record her singing her original compositions as demo tracks and so I got the job! Yoko always had a way of zeroing in on anyone that could be of use to her but I have to say that she was perfectly charming about it. So I set the guitar in modal D tuning, as though we were playing Indian ragas, and she would make the trip across town to my place in South Kensington and sing for hours and hours. She would often come over. One of the songs that we recorded was 'The Snow is Falling' and later on she recorded it properly and sent me a 45 of it. The music that I was thrashing away at on the guitar went on to form the basis of what would later go on to become 'Nostradamus'. So we sat there at my new basement flat in Elvaston Place doing this for quite a while."

Yoko – "I did not have a set up like Al had then. So it was great that Al recorded me. He just pushed a few buttons and said go ahead and I started singing. I was a very proud person, so I wouldn't do something like that with anyone unless I felt that we were close friends. Al may not have known that he was our only close friend at the time, but he was. We enjoyed the fact that he often dropped in to chat with us in the evenings."

Al had moved into the basement flat of 10 Elvaston Place on January 1st 1968. Having known Mandi for over eight months by that time they to all intents and purposes moved in there together.

Meanwhile, Al clearly had a rare old time being out and about in the West End with Yoko. By now he had a car in London and would sometimes drive Yoko around.

Al – "Another day when we were driving through town in my car she spotted the Aston Martin dealership. She wanted me to go in there with her and talk them into letting her saw one of their showroom cars in two but I managed to talk her out of that one! At the time I just thought that she was this slightly mad Japanese lady that was passing through my life and that would be it. She appears to have gone on to do a great deal more! Through all this Mandi and I were still going to places like Middle Earth."

By the time that Middle Earth opened in 1968 the whole vibe was changing and the atmosphere there was a lot less innocent than UFO. It was a much harder place. The people that played Middle Earth were very different too. Whereas at UFO it had been flower children bands, at Middle Earth there were groups such as Eire Apparent with power chords. It was a much darker place.

Al – "The feeling of UFO was much better than Middle Earth but it was somewhere that I still went to every week. John Peel, who was a DJ there, once introduced me at one of my solo gigs at York University as "Bob Miller and The Millermen" which remains as possibly the best introduction I've ever been given!"

It was here, at Middle Earth, that Al got to know John Anthony who would later go on to produce two albums for Al. Anthony was a DJ for a short period of time at Middle Earth.

Rod and Rog were regulars there too.

Roger Hand – "Middle Earth was the epitome of flower power. At the height of flower power in this country Middle Earth was the place to go to. As the Piccadilly Line we often did gigs there, John Peel would be sat in the corner holding court much of the time. It was completely different to somewhere like The Scots House which was really just a room above a pub with Bruce Dunnett sat behind a table by the door collecting an entrance fee."

By now Al had settled in to Elvaston Place and may very well have been as happy at this time as he ever would be in London. With Mandi there for much of the time it was far more of a home than any of his previous addresses had been.

Dave Dyke – "It was very small but also very tasteful. It was here that we first started to play Monopoly with Al. The deal was that the loser had to retire to the kitchen to make the tea. Now Al would almost always win the whole game but I remember on one occasion him losing and so having to make the tea whereupon there ensued a series of loud banging and crashings coming from the kitchen as he took it all out on the crockery! He *hated* losing at Monopoly, he really did!"

Ian Anderson – "He used to play Monopoly every time he came down to Bristol too! We often played our own version with two boards, different currencies and even an IMF fund. We'd have the TV on with the sound turned down and the record player would be playing something like a *Mothers of Invention* album. Those were the best of times."

Rod Edwards – "They were amazing times for us too! We had a residency with Al at The Marquee in Wardour Street around about this time. The folk scene had grown so much that they started putting on these folk evenings there run by a guy called Jonny G. We also went on to play on the very first Windsor Jazz and Blues Festival along with Cream, Bert Jansch, Al and Fairport Convention. Those Marquee shows came just as we had released our *Emily Small* albums and so were doing songs from each of these."

By now Al had been asked by John Martyn to produce his first album. Al considers however his production duties at that recording to have been minimal. He was certainly present in the studio but the role he played there appears very similar to the one he had carried out the previous year whilst working on his own album.

Al – "I remember well when I produced *The Tumbler* for John. We were recording it right on the cusp of mono and stereo. I presented it to Island in mono, whereupon they said 'but it's supposed to be in stereo'. So they just stamped 'stereo' on it anyway and to this day I don't think anyone has noticed! There was an engineer with me in the studio but I don't suppose my actual production called for very much because I didn't know anything about recording at the time. It was really simply a case of helping John through the process and saying 'that's great' or 'that wasn't too good, let's try it again'. I've always felt that to say I produced the album was a slight exaggeration!"

A few months after the release of *Bedsitter Images* Al brought a delicate situation to Julia's notice. The Ralph McTell song "Streets of London" which was poised on the edge of the charts was, on the surface, the same song as Al's "Samuel, Oh How You've

Changed". It seemed to be a clear case of plagiarism and Julia was all for calling in the lawyers without delay but Al's generosity shone through and he said that he'd go around and ask Ralph about it himself. When they met up Ralph said that he wasn't even aware of Al's song and couldn't possibly have used it as the basis for "Streets of London". And there the matter ended. Whatever Al thought deep down he decided to let the matter alone and Ralph retained ownership of the song.

Al – "I feel that both of those tunes are another earlier pop tune entirely that we must have both grown up subliminally hearing on the radio. I don't think that either of us wrote that song. There's something, it may be an old Brian Hyland song, that's really similar and you know everybody influences everyone else, nothing is original."

Putting the issue behind him Al now appeared on the bill of a notable London concert at the Royal Albert Hall, on February 10th 1968. At what was heralded as *Folk Festival 1968* Al was on a bill that included the Watersons (who were making their "farewell" appearance together), The Incredible String Band, Roy Harper, Dorris Henderson, and Chapter 3. His short set was well received and he returned to this famous venue on a number of occasions. This was a charity show sponsored by the Conservation Society and was typical of the politically aware and environmentally concerned concert-events that were a feature of the late '60s, early '70s in England.

On March 5 1968, Al appeared on BBC 2 TV's *Late Night Line-Up*. The subject matter of that night's show was homelessness and not dissimilar from Judith Piepe's *Outcasts And Outsiders* television broadcast of November 1966.

The song Al performed during the show was "Who Killed Tommy McGeechie" and it exists in recorded form only on this television programme. The show boasted a discussion by a panel of experts followed by Al's original masterpiece of four minutes and 58 seconds. Al also improvised a programme closing instrumental.

Throughout his first three years in London Al had not only kept in touch with Jonny Kremer.

Jerry Trehayne – "I remember visiting Al in London at this time and coming out of the Cousins with him at one or two in the morning and having a slanging match with a young prostitute hanging around the streets. I got involved in a verbal exchange and Al was saying 'Come on, we'll leave it' getting into his Triumph Spitfire and driving out to Heathrow for coffee because when you got to three, four or five in the morning it was the only place. I remember going out several times with Al in that car and we would literally go as fast as it would go! I remember driving back from London to Dorset in the Spitfire on one occasion at that time, in the middle of the night. I can also remember him doing Middle Earth, underneath Covent Garden, which again was an all-night club. We saw Soft Machine, Procol Harum and all of those psychedelic bands of that time. We also saw The Bonzo Dog Band there."

By now Al had become a regular visitor to the Bristol Troubadour in Clifton, later to be immortalised in "Clifton in the Rain".

Ian Anderson – "Ray Wilmott and his Australian wife ran The Bristol Troubadour at this time. The actual performing area was tiny. The backstage area was this very small room behind the stage where very quietly you could tune up. I lived locally until July 1968."

In January 1967 they had initiated a monthly country blues night there that had been an immediate success, so much so that after only two evenings they had found themselves with no choice but to re-locate to the Old Duke pub in Bristol city centre.

Ian Anderson – "For a year there were queues right around the block there for those evenings. After another year we'd outgrown that place and so we had to move to another pub called The Full Moon by which time the shows were in a room that could hold over 400 there in that Stokes Croft Pub. We were also reaching a much wider audience courtesy of people like John Peel"

Around this time Al regularly appeared on Peel's *Top Gear* and *Nightride* radio shows. On March 24 1968, Peel hosted Al and played the version of "Samuel, Oh, How You've Changed!" from the mono mix of the *Bedsitter Images* album. Al recited on air a whimsical "Furniture Poem" ("Don't sit there and take it like a chair/ stand up and fight like a table"), and chatted with the amiable Peel about his Bristol friends who, on their own *Saydisc* label, were producing white "blues music" by such luminaries as Mike Cooper and Ian Anderson himself. At that time *Saydisc* had out *Anderson, Jones and Jackson* and *Almost Country Blues*, both by Ian Anderson.

Al had also recently returned from visiting Paul Simon in New York, and recounted on John Peel's show how he'd flown in Simon & Garfunkel's helicopter to their gig at Cornell University before being delivered back to Greenwich Village in a Rolls Royce; "…an amazing experience, quite unique" as Al described it. When asked about future projects he announced, "Nothing at all, I'm retiring! No. I'm going to do another album eventually – as soon as I've written all the stuff for it, actually very soon as most of it is half written." So from this we learn that most of *Love Chronicles* was ready as early as the Spring of 1968. In fact, "The Ballad of Mary Foster" had been performed at the fateful Royal Festival Hall concert the previous autumn.

From a career perspective Al's trip to America had been less than successful but as a source of anecdotal material it was priceless.

Al – "When I arrived in New York City in the spring of '68 I only had two phone numbers. One was Paul Simon's, which I'd got from Judith and the other was that of Joe Boyd's brother who I stayed with that first night. After that I stayed with a girl that I'd met at a party called Enid Eidinoff. Her attitude from the outset had been that I could stay just one more night and then I would have to go. Then one day at two o'clock in the morning her telephone rang while I was watching TV. Enid had already gone to bed and she came in and looked at me and said 'Do you know Paul Simon?' and I say 'Yes' and she then said 'Oh, well he's on the phone for you!' From that moment on her attitude towards me of course totally changed. So I talked to Paul who said, 'What are you doing tomorrow?' to which I replied 'Nothing at all' and he asked me whether I wanted to be a roadie for him the next day. So I said 'Sure' and he said 'Great! I'll send a car around for you.' That next morning Enid was being very nice to me but still didn't quite believe it all, although she wanted to. Then this Rolls Royce turned up outside the door, the chauffeur rang the bell and I climbed in and waved goodbye to Enid and went off to Cornell University with Simon and Garfunkel."

Al's job that day was to carry the guitar cases, he and Paul flying out to the gig by private helicopter. This was all a long way from the time they had spent touting Paul's song catalogue around Tin Pan Alley back in 1965. As Al sat, silently reflecting on all of this, Paul spoke up.

Al – "He had just recorded 'Mrs Robinson'. Now I was nervous enough being up in this thing and Paul looks out of the window, with all of New York City beneath us and says in his own laconic way "You know if I die now I'll have my first number one hit single since 'Sound Of Silence'" and I thought 'Well what about me, if we die now I haven't had any hits!' And so later that day I went back to Enid's place and she was basically my servant from there on in. She'd taken a week off work and offered to drive me anywhere I wanted to go to. So I said 'Let's go up to Woodstock to see Jackson C. Frank' and that's exactly what we did. Jackson was living in Woodstock then with Elaine. I also tried to drum up some interest in my album while I was out there. Roy Guest had also given me the name of a guy called Cohen (Frank Zappa's manager) because Roy said that this would be a way for me to get launched in America because CBS weren't interested in putting out *Bedsitter Images* over there at that time."

Al's journey down to the New York City studio was to prove unsuccessful however.

"To say the least! I went down there to see him one day armed with a copy of the album and he said 'Why did you put an orchestra on here? I can't sell this. It's absolutely terrible. Do it with a rock band and come and see me again then.'"

Al is unsure as to whether he was serious or just trying to get rid of this English folkie that had turned up on his doorstep.

It was at a party in Brooklyn during this trip that Al had met Enid but other than that the song "In Brooklyn" is completely made up. So after this short adventure in New York, it was back home to London to see what bookings Julia had got for him.

Jonny Kremer – "Julia was great through all this. She was also a very kind and generous lady. I remember her giving me lifts across London on a number of occasions and I know that she worked very hard on Al's behalf throughout all this time. She was a lot more to him than just a manager, she genuinely cared about what he did."

Meanwhile Al and Mandi were still seeing each other. Al would often take her down to Bournemouth to meet his friends and family. Jonny Kremer remembers her as being "a very capable young woman" with a "captivating personality". There were spells when Al and Mandi didn't see each other however, Mandi describing their relationship as "off and on" at this time. Mandi was working then for *Record Retailer* at 7 Carnaby Street W1, and she and Al were visiting such places as Middle Earth, UFO and Les Cousins on a regular basis. Al, for his part, was truly happy at this time in both his professional and private life.

Al – "And it was reflected in my writing. In those days I found it very easy to write songs. I'd sit on the end of the bed with my guitar and a pen and paper and write what seemed to be quite quickly a lot of very bad songs. The lyrics and music came along at the same time."

On May 6th *Melody Maker* reported that Al had recorded The Incredible String Band's "Lover Man" along with a piano solo entitled "Sad" on the B-side of what was intended as a single. The piano track was never to see the light of day however. Another projected single discussed was the pairing of "In Brooklyn" with "Lover Man".

Mandi remembers that the first time that she heard "In Brooklyn" herself was one evening when Al performed it in Les Cousins.

When next with Peel, on the *Nightride* of May 29 1968, Al sang five of his own songs (from two different albums): "The Carmichaels", "Swiss Cottage Manoeuvres", "Scandinavian Girl" (the *Bedsitter Images* piece about a Swedish girlfriend now called "Song for Jeunne") "Samuel, Oh How You've Changed!" and "Room of Roots" (an instrumental kept in the wings until *Zero She Flies* in 1970). This Peel session was Al and guitar, no bass, no drums, and definitely no Sinfonia of London.

Al told Peel he planned to record a new album "in about three weeks time" (an optimistic prediction) and discussed the candidacy of Robert F. Kennedy for the Presidency of the United States. Incidentally, a fellow guest on the program was poet Pete Morgan, an England-born resident of Edinburgh who recited his poem "My Enemies Have Sweet Voices", which Al turned into the song of the same name for *Zero She Flies*. Morgan worked with Al on a number of concert and radio projects.

Throughout 1968, by virtue of his records, media appearances, and concerts, Al was gaining wider appreciation for his songwriting and performing abilities. He garnered praise as a lyricist, as well as a guitarist (with a style described by one mid-'60s reviewer as "firmly in the Baroque school of Jansch and Renbourn but with more melodic variation if not the same technique"). Indeed, at his shows he was playing such instrumentals as "Sonata in C", "Orange Blossom Special" and "Worksong".

A few weeks later Al returned to play on a Royal Festival Hall bill that also featured Joni Mitchell, Fairport Convention and Jackson C. Frank.

Al remained somewhat concerned throughout 1968 about the false image that his first album had given him. Talking to *Nuggets Magazine* he explained – "*Bedsitter Images* worried me all through 1968 and I was never into orchestras."

On the other hand during the 1984 acoustic tour of Europe Al remarked to Ian Anderson – "I might have been established as something the folk scene roundly detested, and I might have hated the record myself, but at least when people said 'Al Stewart' there was a reaction. The mere fact of somebody like Alex Campbell going around saying I was the worst thing since the atom bomb on Hiroshima made people aware that I was there!"

Audiences did learn he was out there, and between early 1967 and early 1969 Al went from playing for five people at Cousins to gatherings of 500 or more thanks in no small part to the work of Julia Creasey.

Al came to know just about everyone on the club and college circuits. If a researcher were to compile an A to Z of London's music scene in the late '60s, Al could probably supply all the names. Among his friends were Richard Thompson and Sandy Denny of Fairport Convention. In fact, Sandy was partly responsible for Al's fascination with songs about rain and the sea and her "Song For The Sea" was one of his favourites. Al was quite aware of his continued use of these themes and besides acknowledging a debt to Sandy, often compared this fascination to Laura Nyro's fondness for seagulls.

Al was now seeing Ian Anderson on a regular basis.

Ian Anderson – "In July 1968 I moved away to London and during this time the Wilmotts sold The Bristol Troubadour to move back to Australia. They sold it to a local night club owner called Peter Bush who put a musician called John Turner in as manager. Bush had been led to believe that the place would make lots of money but at best it only ever broke even. I was now on Julia Creasey's books as I had got to know her through Al. The college folk circuit was big business for all of us at this time and Al was certainly its biggest draw."

Sally and Mike Oldfield were now also on Julia's books at Folk Directions/NEMS but not every decision Julia made was, with hindsight, the right one. David Bowie came up the stairs one day with his first album under his arm for Julia to listen to. She didn't think it was particularly original and told him so, passing on the opportunity to manage him. So life at Julia Creasey's agency wasn't just an endless succession of old folkies!

Throughout the course of his career Al has played on some amazing bills and it was now that he played the Woburn Music Festival at Woburn Abbey. The line-up also included Jimi Hendrix, Pentangle, Donovan, Fleetwood Mac, The Taste, Geno Washington, Roy Harper, Tyrannosaurus Rex, Family and Alexis Korner.

There are three or four occasions when Fairport Convention definitely served as Al's backing band. On July 19th 1968 Al appeared along with Fairport Convention and Julie Felix on a bill at Central Hall Westminster put together by the committee of Human Rights Year.

Richard Thompson – "I do remember that we did a Roy Guest show at either The Wigmore Hall or The Central Hall Westminster around this time. John Martyn was also on the bill that night and he went out and played this song that went on for about two hours! They couldn't get him off stage! And I remember that Al was there with us that night."

Al remembers coming off stage after his own performance to find the dressing room taken over by Fairport in the midst of running through Sandy Denny's "Fotheringay" which they were wanting to include in their set. He also played a gig with them at the National Jazz and Blues Festival on Sunday August 11th performing a set that included "Swiss Cottage Manoeuvres" and "Old Compton Street Blues". Another joint performance took place, according to Al – "Sometime in 1968 or 1969 at the Marquee in Wardour Street."

Al is quite certain however where the best of those collaborations was – "We did a John Peel show together. Richard Thompson was playing some amazing guitar that time. It was an amazing show."

Al told *Southern Rag* in 1984 – "Those Fairport shows I did on Peel were all better than the versions that ended up on records. I wish I had the tapes."

On the college circuit, Fairport, Al and fellow artists played to audiences of 200 to 500, larger crowds than folk clubs could boast, and with wider musical tastes. Al was now notching two or three colleges a week, while back at The Troubadour his name was removed from the guest list and entered on the roster of residents. The Hanging Lamp Club in Richmond made a similar gesture.

On September 12th 1968 Al appeared on the BBC radio show *My Kind Of Folk*. Robert Fripp backed him.

Al – "This was the one and only occasion that Bob Fripp ever did back me on stage. We did 'In Brooklyn' which was going to be on the next album a few months later. It was always interesting to work with different musicians and as I didn't have a permanent band I asked Bob."

In fact it was not only Robert Fripp that appeared with Al on the programme, but most of the future line-up of King Crimson. Ian McDonald joined the Giles brothers, who along with Robert himself, called themselves, logically enough, *Giles, Giles and Fripp* as Al's band for this show. They actually performed five numbers in the studio which were "You Should Have Listened To Al", "Manuscript", "Old Compton Street Blues", "Room of Roots" and "In Brooklyn".

It was through Roy Guest's relationship with Joe Boyd that Al had first met up with Fairport Convention. Al and Roy had decided that the new album needed a folk rock band to back Al and Fairport were the obvious choice.

Al – "I was very pleased to have them with me there. Fairport seemed to always be available for side projects and Roy and I approached them to see if they would be interested in doing *Love Chronicles* and they said 'Yes' which was just marvellous."

So it was with added experience and greater versatility that Al went into the Sound Techniques Studios at 46a Church Street, just off Chelsea's Kings Road, to record with Fairport, the classic *Love Chronicles* album.

Julia Creasey – "Now Sound Techniques always seemed to be installing new

Folk Directions Days

Julia Creasey

Promo Shot 1967

equipment and its engineers were the best in London. It really was the place to record in at that time. I remember going there for the first time and walking in off the street and up the stairs to the first floor studio which wasn't particularly luxurious. There was basically just the sound desk and a few seats in the main area and then a kitchen/bathroom area out the back – that's really all there was. Al was the first artist from Folk Directions to use Sound Techniques and so when he was in there to record *Love Chronicles* I got my first real look inside the building."

Richard Thompson – "I almost lived at Sound Techniques at this time! I knew it very well and recorded there on many occasions."

Indeed, even as far back as their first single, "If I Had A Ribbon Bow", recorded on August 10th 1967, Fairport Convention had been recording there.

Richard Thompson again – "And I actually remember the recording session for *Love Chronicles*. I knew that Al wanted us on the record and we were happy to be there. It seemed to me to go quite well. I remember that besides the members of Fairport there was also a keyboard player with us all in the studio. There were no charts or anything like that for us to play. Al would just play each song through and then we'd do our best to fit in around him. I enjoyed it."

Fairport Convention would go on to record their best-known record, *Liege and Lief*, the following summer but by the end of the year both Tyger Hutchings and Sandy Denny would leave the band.

Richard Thompson – "Sandy knew Roy Guest of course and so by this time I too knew him quite well. I knew Julia Creasey too. Now Roy was, as everyone that was around at that time will tell you, very much the lovable rogue. He was a very nice guy but I never trusted him. Not for one moment. He was certainly one of the larger-than-life characters that you come across every now and then!"

Following the recording of *Love Chronicles*, Al and Fairport had two days rehearsal in Fulham, South London, before a couple of John Peel sessions and gigs at Windsor and the Marquee Club in London.

January '69 saw the Beatles giving their last ever live show at 3 Savile Row on the Apple building roof and the release of *Love Chronicles*, Al's new album on CBS.

With the assistance of most of Fairport Convention, *Love Chronicles* was altogether a more representative piece of Al's music than its orchestrally overblown predecessor. The songs themselves were a mixture of autobiographical dissection and the storytelling in the third person that Al still uses today. "In Brooklyn" with its use of multiple images, was the first of those deceptively simple songs for which Al is noted. The documentary value of such pieces as "Old Compton Street Blues", which he was still performing on British radio on March 24th, is no doubt equally considerable.

In the February 1969 edition of *Oz* Graham Charnock said of *Love Chronicles* – "The songs, of course, are the redeeming feature of the whole affair. They elevate it from just another pop-folk LP to a major and important one. Stewart knows better than anyone else on the scene today how to write effective narrative folk lyrics. He's remained uncomplicated where Dylan has gone off into ellipsis, and where Paul

Folk Directions

Love Chronicles Promo

Simon has floated off into whimsy and romantic fantasy, Stewart has remained with his feet in a tangible and intriguing reality: 'Maurice', said Renée, 'Why didn't you say that you'd be so late,/ The supper that I made is ruined again/ Is there anything you'd like?' 'No, nothing' he replied/ Standing by the stairs, not looking in her eyes, so stupidly Male."

Meanwhile, *The Observer, Daily Telegraph* and *New Musical Express* all gave the album good reviews.

On the album Al wrote about Old Compton Street, deep in the heart of London's Soho, a place he of course knew well. Whilst the character of the area may not be quite as bohemian today as it was then, the visitor can still walk between Greek Street, Charing Cross Road, Lisle Street, Brewer Street and Litchfield Street in a matter of minutes. Greenwich Village has often been suggested in the past as the nearest US equivalent.

"The Ballad Of Mary Foster" also has autobiographical sections, as does the third stanza of "Life and Life Only". The juxtaposition of images throughout the album can quite truthfully be seen to reflect Al's own experiences. The massively confessional "Love Chronicles" itself proved to be just as newsworthy as the use of an orchestra in 1967 had been.

Peter Oakes writing in *The People* on January 1st 1969 had this to say – "The record has not been played on the radio and the problem the BBC and their disc jockeys is facing is – should it? The BBC had this to say 'we've got lots of records to listen to before we get to this one, we can't say whether we'll play it or not'. The man at CBS who allowed the song, complete with its use of the word 'fucking' to appear in that form on the album was Derek Everett who said this at the time 'I think the word is very much in context with the lyrics. The record is not aimed at a very young audience, but at University people and colleges. If it was used in a sensational way then I would say no'. Meanwhile Kenneth Glancy, managing director of CBS, had this to say 'I've been in the States and have not heard it. We don't make it a practice to issue this sort of thing and as far as I know we have never had a record with a four-letter word. I shall be going into the whole question with the people who were in charge while I was away.'"

Al – "*Love Chronicles* was my concept from beginning to end. 1968 was my year, I chose the front cover, the back cover, I was there at the mix of all three tracks, I got Fairport Convention and Jimmy Page to play on it, and although it could have been produced a lot better it was 100 times better than the first album and it was totally sincere. I'd fallen in love which was the nitty gritty – I wrote 'Love Chronicles' for the girl that I fell in love with and it was immense; you know I'd fallen in love, the work was storming in and I was beginning to build up something quite solid, we could afford to eat and have a decent place to live.

"1968 was just the year that it all came together and *Love Chronicles* came out in January 1969. It didn't boom immediately but it sold comfortably more than the first one. The song itself … it's all written around the last segment which was 'The very first time I must confess'… right through to 'It proved to be less like fucking and more like making love' which was the line that caused people to say – 'ooh, he said a rude word'.

"But it expressed it totally perfectly. I mean up until then everything had really been bolshy in my life. I mean I'd been sent away to a school which I hated, loathed and detested and my life before that had been really pretty desperately poor. Then I got sent to public school which I loathed and stayed there until I was 17 when I contrived to get myself thrown out and after that I had four years when I was back to baked beans again, being totally unable to … I mean nothing had gone right and I can honestly say that for the first 21 years of my life nothing went right in any shape or form whatsoever, and basically you have to do something to prove that you have a reason to exist: everything I'd tried to do had fallen through and I knew that music was the last stand – I just had to succeed. Then all of a sudden I'd fallen in love and written this song and it meant

Al and Mandi, on the way from South London to Dorset. Spring 1969.

that somebody actually cared and had faith in me and she was definitely the first person who ever had faith in me and I realised I'd been playing games before that and suddenly it was real."

Lyrically *Love Chronicles* was a major step forward and was voted *Melody Maker*'s "Folk Album Of The Year" in their January 3 1970 issue. Typically enough, they mentioned in only 15 lines Jimmy Page (who played guitar by improvising, having only heard the title song once in the studio), the 18-minute duration of "Love Chronicles" and of course Al's famous use of the word "fucking". Scant information on an Album Of The Year, but welcome recognition nonetheless. The same issue awarded The Who's rock opera *Tommy* the Pop Album Of The Year mantle, whilst Miles Davis' *Filles de Kilimanaro* was voted Jazz Album of the Year.

On February 24th 1969 Al sang for his supper when he performed the song "Ivich" at Dave and Jilly Dyke's wedding reception in a house in Canfield Gardens, just off the Finchley Road.

Three weeks later, in *The Scotsman* on March 15th 1969, Alastair Clark was less than positive in an article led by the headline *Words Without Music* – "Al Stewart is one of the new singing poets of folk-pop. He emerged at the right time, has appeared in all the right places, and has attracted a lot of attention. Al Stewart is big, and I think that may be his trouble; his music can't quite keep up with his rapidly escalating image."

An opinion rendered redundant by the brilliance of "In Brooklyn"

IN BROOKLYN
"Oh I came from Pittsburgh to study astrology"
She said as she stepped on my instep
"I could show you New York with a walk between Fourth Street and Nine"
Then out of her coat taking seven harmonicas
She sat down to play on a doorstep
Saying "Come back to my place I will show you the stars and the signs"
So I followed her into the black lands
Where the window frames peel and flake
And the old Jewish face behind the lace
Peeping out trying to get to see what's cooking
Just John the Baptist in the park getting laid thinking there's no one looking
And its eighty degrees and I'm down on my knees in Brooklyn

Her house was a dusty collection of rusty
Confusion with landings and tunnels
And leaning bookcases and spaces and faces and things
Where twenty-five Puerto Ricans, Manhattan Mohicans
And Jewish-Italian pawnbrokers
Lead their theatrical lives in their rooms in the wings
While outside in the black lands
The violent day runs wild
And the black and white minstrels run through the crazy
Alleys while the cops go booking
And ruthless toothless agents sneak around when there's no-one looking
And it's eighty degrees and I'm down on my knees in Brooklyn
And oh, I'm back in the city again
You can tell by the smell of the hamburger stand in the rain

She spoke of astrology while muttering apologies
For coffee that tasted of hot dogs
I said "That's OK, mine was cold anyway, and just grand"
Then she lay on the bed while the radio fed
Us with records and adverts for cat food
And I looked at her holding my thoughts in the palm of my hand
And outside in the black lands
The evening came and went
And the bums in the street begging money for one last drink
Are hanging round the liquor stores trying to get a foot in
And the girl from Pittsburgh and I made love on a mattress with the new moon looking
And in the cool evening breeze I was down on my knees in Brooklyn

Al spoke to WMRY St Louis some years later about Jimmy Page's role on *Love Chronicles* – "Well Jimmy was always very much into acoustic music. He used to come down to listen to all the folkies. He was a big fan. So I had known him and I needed someone to play guitar on the record. Actually on all the other tracks on the album it was Fairport Convention under an assumed name, but we didn't have anyone to play lead guitar on the title track, and the title track was 18 minutes long. He comes in and I said, 'How are we going to break this up? Do you want to do it in individual bits? Take this bit, do that bit?' He said 'Ah … just play it to me.' So he listened to it once and he said 'Oh that's fine I'll just busk it!' So he just sat there and played along with it. 18 minutes of … and the song is in completely different sections and tempos and whatever. And he did a pretty good job. It was an odd session because he had this sort of great big guy carrying his guitar case for him, who I thought was a roadie and I was very offhand with this guy. I'd say 'Oh would you go and get me a cup of tea? Just sit over there and don't make any noise. ' The guy turned out to be the late Peter Grant who was Led Zeppelin's manager, an ex-professional wrestler who had a reputation for throwing people off large buildings if he didn't like them. And he was a little pussycat. I mean I didn't know who he was and I was bossing him around!"

The presence of Jimmy Page on the album represented a real coup for Al as by then he was very much involved with Led Zeppelin.

When I interviewed Jimmy for this book he spoke openly and with the same affection that had prompted him to accept that session.

Jimmy Page – "By the time that I came to record 'Love Chronicles' with Al I had already put Led Zeppelin together and in fact the first Led Zeppelin album was recorded at the end of that year. Al was a really enthusiastic guy and very interested in all of the music that was going on at the time. And I enjoyed working with somebody like that. I remember that Al mentioned to me that prior to him being a folkie he had been an electric guitarist in bands. And we made a real connection because we liked the same things. We were both passionate about our music and so it was a good pairing. When I was asked to do the 'Love Chronicles' session I said 'yes, I'd love to do it' which reflects my affection for Al."

There was one other link between 'Love Chronicles' and Led Zeppelin's first album.

Jimmy Page again – "For a while in the early days of the band I still continued doing sessions like these and in fact I financed the recording of our first album myself that way.

"And the equipment that I used on Al's session for 'Love Chronicles', both the guitar and amp, was exactly the same equipment that I used on Zeppelin's first album."

And if you listen to Jimmy Page's work on the two records you can tell it's the same guitar.

On March 19th 1969 Al hosted the BBC's *My Kind Of Folk* and performed "My Enemies Have Sweet Voices" live – a full year before it appeared on record. "My Enemies Have Sweet Voices" is the only original Al Stewart song on which he has used someone else's lyrics – in this particular case those of Pete Morgan.

Al had met Morgan, a poet of some reputation, on an earlier John Peel show when Pete had been a fellow guest, reading the poem from which Al took the lyrics for his song.

Pete Morgan again – "Al never played it back to me once he'd written out the guitar part so the very first time that I heard it was when we both appeared on Radio One together later on."

My Kind Of Folk was a radio show that featured a celebrity host who would perform live and also introduce a couple of guests. Here's the running order for that March 19th 1969 show:

Al Stewart – "Bedsitter Images" (live)
Al Stewart introduction
Al Stewart – "My Enemies Have Sweet Voices" (live)
Pete Morgan – "White Stallion" (live)
John James – "Pickles and Peppers" (live)
Pete Morgan – "Wall" (live)
Al Stewart – "Clifton in the Rain" (live)
Al Stewart – "Denise at 16" (live)
John James – If Only I" (live)
Al Stewart – "Manuscript" (live)

Al – "These shows were a lot of fun. I enjoyed talking to people on air and I could pretty much do as I chose. I remember this one primarily because of Pete but John James was a guitarist that I thought was just great and he always went down well when we did gigs together."

Al does seem particularly at ease on this show (of which a recording still exists) and uses those skills gained as the compère at Les Cousins a few years earlier to great effect. He gleaned from the ragtime guitarist John James that he'd transcribed the turn-of-the-century piece he was playing on the show himself whilst Pete Morgan spoke at length about the difference between "poetry" gigs and those at which there was a mixture of folk music and the spoken word. He continued to explain to Al how he sought to "blur the boundaries" between poetry and music. In between that first appearance together on John Peel's show and this meeting on the BBC's *My Kind Of Folk*, Al and Pete Morgan had done a number of live gigs together. "My Enemies Have Sweet Voices" wasn't the only folk song co-written by Pete at this time however.

Pete Morgan – "The folk scene was very big in Scotland and I did a number of gigs with such people as The Incredible String Band and John Martyn. The bills very often featured several different acts and I would perform a couple of sets throughout the evening."

The crossover of poetry and folk music continued at such places such as The Wick Festival of Folk and The Edinburgh Festival shows at The Traverse Theatre. Out of this came two versions of his poems recorded by The McCalmans – "Second Mariners Song" and "Loss of Two Anchors".

Pete Morgan – "Whenever we appeared on shows together it would be Al rather than I that would perform 'My Enemies Have Sweet Voices'. It seemed to stay in his set for several years after we recorded it."

Al and Mandi's relationship had now lasted over two years. In that time it is clear that it came to mean more and more to Al. It was an open relationship with them both seeing other people. On May 4th they drove to a party at John Martyn's house in Putney. Al ended up driving home a well-known girl singer that he knew and Mandi got a lift from a friend of hers who was at the party. Mandi got back to Elvaston Place before Al and there was a confrontation about who had done what in the couple of hours since they had last met. The result of the argument was that Mandi left the flat at the crack of dawn for St Pancras railway station and a train up to her brother's place in Cambridge. Things were never the same after that party.

The Sophie Lichfield cover of *Love Chronicles* that had pictured Al staring – 'intensely out into the middle distance' (*Nuggets Magazine*, February '77), had established an image of Al that had stuck in the minds of fans and critics alike. This perception of him as a romantic folkie was accurate enough but not precisely what he wanted.

Al – "It wasn't at all. In fact it killed everything stone dead. I was well and truly trapped by then. I really was."

It was now that the relationship that had been his bedrock for well over two years came to a stuttering end. Mandi, having shared Al's life since the beginning of 1967, had left him after realising that the notion of them having an open relationship was not something in reality that Al could indeed deal with after all. The split resulted in an immediate change in perspective in his life, which is there for all to see as it manifested itself dramatically in his work. There were endless newspaper articles in which Al was obviously finding it impossible not to mention her name and use their life at Elvaston Place as a metaphor for happiness and security. The songs from the next few albums make any further prying into his private life academic to say the least. The events that led to Al's split from Mandi can be precisely dated back to that party at John Martyn's Putney apartment on May 4th 1969 and Mandi's subsequent decampment the next morning to Cambridge and latterly Spain to think over her relationship with Al. She had gone out there on holiday with her parents and decided to stay on when they returned home, designing clothes for a friend's beach shop in Carvajal. Meanwhile Al was literally going out of his mind with worry over their split and his mother, Joan, remembers spending time with him at Elvaston Place because she was so worried about his health. She now took decisive action and rang Mandi's mother in Hampstead to find out where exactly Mandi was. Joan gave the address to Al who, using the money that they really had 'saved in the biscuit tin', flew out to Spain. He arrived, according to Mandi, "looking as if he had just stepped out of Les Cousins" and appearing totally distraught. He begged her to return to England and she was so worried about his state of mind that she decided to do exactly that. They had to spend time in Madrid on the way back and Al sat up in the bedroom chair all night, totally unable to sleep. On their return to London Al was so upset that Mandi remembers him "driving us back to the flat in Kensington at 100 mph". She stayed for two weeks until Al was a little more together and then she left.

Al later told Jerry Gilbert – "On July 29th 1969 the girl who caused all this up and left and this was without any shadow of doubt the biggest, most important thing which has happened and it completely destroyed me for two years.

"It came at a point when I was turning them out faster and better than at any time before in my life. 'Gethsemane Again' was the last song I wrote before the break-up and 'A Small Fruit Song' which I got in a few days before I got the letter saying she wasn't coming back. It was and still is inconceivable that I could find someone else and it becomes more inconceivable because I lived with her through all the hard times.

"And again, right back in the Spring of 1967 when we met when I had nothing she actually did go to her bank two weeks after she'd met me … take out every penny which she had which was about £100 which she'd saved up, and without knowing me she rolled up and gave me this £100 because I was thinking of quitting and going home. And she said 'Look this'll keep you going for a little bit, I want you to stay and write songs because I really think you're going to make it.'

"And apart from inspiring half the songs I probably wouldn't have been here anyway, I probably would have given up so that when she left I couldn't function, I couldn't write, couldn't sleep and was physically sick.

"I'd written the whole of *Zero She Flies* before she went. But I was in the studios recording the album and for the first time in my life music didn't matter and if it had sold a million copies it would just have been an irony. I made the record in a complete daze and threw it away almost."

It would be two years before he wrote his next song, "The News From Spain", written about his break-up from Mandi.

Dave Dyke – "When Mandi left him it was the most difficult time for Al. I remember him acting like a caged lion at Elvaston Place once she had gone. He quite clearly just did not know what he was going to do and it was just as if her departure had broken him completely and absolutely. He looked as if he had lost every ounce of spirit and it was a very sorry sight to see. He wanted to be able to forget everything that would remind him about the time that they had spent together and that was how he came to give away so many of his belongings at this time."

Back in the office in London Al grew increasingly unhappy with Roy Guest and his style of management. Attention to detail was never Roy's forte and the two would have rows on an ongoing basis. Al grew particularly unhappy with Roy Guest over the manner in which he would spend much of his time in the pub, even when he was supposed to be across the road in Sound Techniques studio producing Al's albums. Al's naturally demanding nature and Roy's laid-back approach were ill-starred in many ways from day one.

Meanwhile whilst Julia Creasey was away at this time on an extended US trip with Buffy Saint Marie, Folk Directions was bought out in a move that everyone concerned felt "came out of the blue". With showpiece concert space at a premium and with Folk Directions holding block bookings at venues all over the country they were purchased by the team of merchant bankers that controlled NEMS so that the company could have access to their theatre bookings. Vic Lewis, who was then the manager of their London office, immediately started putting US acts into these slots. At first there really wasn't very much interference by the new owners and things carried on pretty much as before at the office but this was no longer the same independent Folk Directions that Roy and Jim had developed and the two men drifted apart. They'd come a long way from the cramped space of Gloucester Avenue to this suite of offices at NEMS in Hill Street just off Berkeley Square but it was time for a change; Jim Lloyd leaving first to take up a career in the media before moving ultimately into TV and radio including *Folk On Friday* and *Folk on Two*.

Julia had by now taken on more of the day-to-day running of the company from a largely bored and disinterested Roy Guest before she too left, moving to the more pop-orientated Blackhill Enterprises in Notting Hill Gate in the Spring of 1969, taking many of her Folk Directions clients with her – free to do so because none of them, Al included, were actually under contract. Whilst at Blackhill Al was to play his only Hyde Park Free Concert. From here Julia went freelance and opened offices in South Molton Street in Mayfair, following a short spell with Joe Boyd's Witchseason Productions, with every move Al going with her, so the partnership clearly worked. Roy Guest was the last of the trio to leave NEMS, for a while running a little bookshop in a short parade of buildings in Primrose Hill. When business began to drift away he and his American wife turned it into a cheese shop – further evidence of Roy's survival instincts! This business too failed however, due in no small part to the fact that neither of them knew anything about running such a store. Then one day Roy saw an advert in the *Telegraph* for a house to let in the grounds of Chevening House in rural Kent and it was to here that he retired, living there until his death, after a long illness, in the mid-'90s.

Al and Ian Anderson had remained friends through all these moves.

Ian Anderson – "I went back to London from Bristol for another six months at this time and lived opposite Blackhill Enterprises, which at that time was run by Peter Jenner and Andrew King. Tim Hodgson was now running the club and he continued to do so up until 1971. He'd arrived as a 'man in a suit', fell in love with the place and left as a hippy! Throughout all of this time Al continued to come down and play at The Troubadour because he liked it so much. By now he was famous but still continued to come down."

When Ian returned from London for a second time he started up his own independent label with John Turner calling it Village Thing. However these were not easy times.

Ian Anderson – "I was living in a girlfriend's flat in Royal York Crescent. When The Troubadour closed the whole scene imploded. All these people like Keith Christmas, Steve Tilston, Sheena McDonald, didn't really have anywhere to play. Although The Stonehouse opened, it wasn't run by the old people and wasn't the same."

On 20th August Al again played on the John Peel radio show performing Paul Simon's composition "Sparrow" besides "My Enemies Have Sweet Voices", "Memphis Tennessee", "Clifton in the Rain", "Gethsemane Again", "Swiss Cottage Manoeuvres" and "Burbling". A week later he was back on the BBC, this time appearing on *Nightride* where he sang Bob Dylan's "I Don't Believe You", "The Ballad of Mary Foster", Paul Simon's "Blessed", "Zero She Flies", "Scandinavian Girl" and the instrumental "Ivich".

Back in March Al had hosted the edition of the *My Kind Of Folk* radio show with Pete Morgan and John James and on November 15th, James was playing Les Cousins supported by Nick Drake.

"Nick came on and sat hunched up on a stool on the tiny stage," audience member Steve Aparicio told Drake's biographer Patrick Humphries. "He played only three or four numbers before leaving the stage in some distress, when he was looked after by John Martyn. John Martyn and Al Stewart both got up and did a few songs each."

It was at this time that Al was enjoying a level of success throughout the buoyant network of clubs and universities that far outweighed his success on record. He played Warwick University so many times that people probably thought he lived there. This touring schedule kept his reputation in the public eye even though he wasn't having hits. He was making a better living from his touring than many of the so-called successful Top 30 stars of 1970.

Al told journalist Carol Sarler – "One thing I wouldn't do – I wouldn't make an appearance on *Top of the Pops*. I do anticipate having a hit record on my hands one of these days, if only because every record I bring out sells twice as many as the last one. Yet I couldn't appear on any television programme as they stand at the moment."

Al went on to give the main reasons for this: the studio audiences "jigging and trying to do the latest dances" had completely ruined James Taylor's appearance as he sang "Fire and Rain".

Al continued to spread his word-of-mouth reputation by singing in as many different places as possible.

Middle Earth North in Edinburgh was certainly different. *The Scotsman* of November 1st – "Al Stewart was sandwiched between two heavy rock groups and confronted with an audience which seemed largely unprepared for the light and shade subtleties of strummed chords from an acoustic guitar, he sat on a stool, explained patiently who he was, what he was there for, what his first song was about and then launched into 'In Brooklyn'."

Al later confessed that the gig had been "like playing in a glass jar" and that he hadn't known whether or not he'd got through to the crowd. The review of the show was very positive though.

Interviewed in *Melody Maker* on the same day by Karl Dallas Al explained his approach in a piece entitled "Stewart, becoming a citizen of the world" "I'm not ready yet, to say anything of any value of the world outside my own immediate scene. I don't want to write yet another song against the bomb or against the war in Vietnam. What does that prove? I can only write about things I really know about, and I'm in no position to set myself up as a leader. I don't even know if people need telling what to do. There was a girl at the Newport Folk Festival a few years ago, when Bob Dylan was still considered a protest singer, who shouted out to him: 'Let us kill for you, Bobby. Just tell us who to kill and we'll do it.'

"That sort of situation is dangerous. On the other hand, the world is getting so small that no one can afford to opt out. What I'm trying to work on is exactly how I opt in."

The university circuit was helping him with this. It was in this intellectual enviroment that Al was able to debate all manner of subjects both during and after his shows. He revelled in the exchange of ideas that flowed to and fro.

"I'm doing more talking than singing these days," Al told Dallas. After the show we always gather together and start arguing about everything under the sun. It helps me to get my thoughts together. In fact, one university asked me to take up residence and go to lectures and everything, which would have been great since I never got to university, but quite illegal.

"Still I'm doing a lot of studying in my own time, modern history, the Nazi war against Russia, things like that. It's not breaking through into my songs yet, but I think it may do."

On December 13th, Al was a guest on John Peel's radio show *Top Gear* where he sang "Zero She Flies "and "Burbling" before debuting the song "Electric Los Angeles Sunset", for the first time on radio.

A couple of weeks later on Boxing Day the BBC Third Programme broadcast a radio show called *Poetry And Folk* which took advantage of the revival of performance poetry that had taken place over the past two years. Broadcast from The Troubadour in Earls Court, London, it featured Al, The Strawbs, Adrian Mitchell and Brian Patten. Here Al performed "Gethsemane Again", the very last song that he had composed before the break up with Mandi.

Al spoke, at this time, about his thoughts for the future – "I'm never frightened that it might all end, no. I'd only lose money, and making money is the least thing in the world that I'm at all worried about."

It was obvious that Mandi's departure had all but marginalised the rest of his life.

The ever-resourceful Al was however still keeping a high profile going by inadvertently becoming something of a minor media celebrity. *Melody Maker* on 24th January devoted a full page to Al's thoughts on that week's new releases in its *Blind Date* section. Paul Simon had previously been invited to review songs for the same feature.

The singles provided for his perusal were diverse and of varying quality, but Al seemed to enjoy the task.

Fairport Convention's "Come All Ye" was adjudged to be "just the best record in the world". He was mightily impressed by Richie Havens' "Rocky Racoon", had no idea how Family produced their guitar sound on "Some Poor Soul", thought the Neil Young entry "Oh Lonesome Me" had no life force, and upon hearing their "Time Was", was forced to admit that he'd always wanted to play guitar with Canned Heat. Ralph McTell's "Clown" and Laura Nyro's "Luckie" obviously fared well. Her obsession with backstreets and cats were details he picked up on.

The final song put before him was "Railway Lines" by Al Jones. This being one of Al's erstwhile Monopoly victims he was diplomatic about its merits. He compared it to *Bedsitter Images* in its over-orchestration but would only call it "pleasant".

The two and a half years that Al had spent with Mandi had seen him move up from the position of an unknown folkie to being an established artist. Having now, at the end of 1969, achieved some real success there was no one at home to share it with.

Al marked time by doing nothing at all some days, which was not the best foundation upon which to record your third album. "I'd swap everything material that I possess if my girlfriend would come back to me" was typical of what he was telling the press at this time. In retrospect, it seems the attention given to Al by the press helped him through that anxious period when the new album, the universally unpopular *Zero She Flies*, was released.

Al kicked off 1970 with a nationwide tour with the Third Ear Band who were promoting their new album *Alchemy*.

In the tour programme his new album was advertised as being called *Guitar Tunes And Song Poems,* a title that was to revert back to *Zero She Flies* by the time of its release a few weeks later. The ten-concert pilgrimage with the Third Ear Band and Mudge & Clutterbuck helped to draw Al out of the exclusivity of the folk club circuit, raising him to larger venues such as The Colston Hall, Bristol; Fairfield Hall, Croydon; and The Southampton Guildhall. The tour was promoted by Blackhill Enterprises, also responsible for the celebrated Hyde Park Freak-Outs. Al had been on the bill of the September 20 1969, event (with the Edgar Broughton Band, Eclection, Quintessence, Deviants and Soft Machine) and thereby discovered his photo on the front page of the *London Evening News.*

But The Third Ear Band never graduated beyond the cult status that they occupied at this time since having started out at Jim Hayne's Arts Lab at 182 Drury Lane.

William Mann, in his review of the tour's Queen Elizabeth Hall opening night, gave Al one of his best ever reviews – "Al Stewart is a delightful singer with a shy, garrulous, nervous platform manner that may divert audiences from the captivating poetry of the words and the nicely contrived harmonies in the songs he writes for himself. A part of their charm is in their informal, quasi-unfinished features, lines that end in humming or fa-la, cadences that never happen. But there is a thoughtful idea behind every one, usually a lesson from history. Mr Stewart is a nifty, spirited guitarist, not a virtuoso but a stylist. As a songwriter he seems almost in the class of Bob Dylan ten years ago – he apologised for including a Dylan song, but it didn't dwarf his own. As a singer he is somebody to follow eagerly on his flight, already far advanced, to the stars."

However all was far from well with Al and at times he allowed it to distract him from his live performances.

Al's ongoing depression over his break-up with Mandi was all too visible at the Croydon show. *Disc* magazine described Al as "fragile-looking". "Instead of his usual rapping between songs, Stewart ran one into another – no talk at all for most of the concert. He sang 'In Brooklyn' from *Love Chronicles* and followed it with Bob Dylan's 'It's All Right Ma, I'm Only Bleeding' – sung with real potency and identification with the lyric."

This was the only cover version that he sang that night at Croydon but it was a song that Al had come to identify with so closely that he had by now made it his own. The song started off quietly, with Dylan's desperate lyrics, building up to a crescendo of guitar playing. It was a completely despairing song – as Al pointed out to the audience when introducing it.

Next he just about managed to get through "A Small Fruit Song" before finishing with "Manuscript". Despite the wild applause he was already back in the dressing room and refused to play an encore. Having performed a set that was dominated by songs written with Mandi in mind he had all but driven himself to the edge emotionally. He eventually came back out to announce to that he didn't think that he had been playing very well and for that reason would be donating his fee to Oxfam. These were dark days indeed.

This is the complete list of songs Al sang on the tour.

"Anna", "The Ballad of Mary Foster", "Bedsitter Images", "Beleeka Doodle Day", "Black Hill", "Burbling", "The Carmichaels", "Cleave To Me", "Clifton In The Rain", "Denise At 16", "Electric Los Angeles Sunset", "The Elf", "Gethsemane Again", "I Saw Her Crying" (an instrumental, later re-titled as "Once An Orange, Always An Orange", "In Brooklyn", "Ivich", "Life And Life Only", "A Long Way Down From Stephanie", "Love Chronicles", "Manuscript", "My Enemies Have Sweet Voices", "Old Compton Street Blues", "Pretty Golden Hair", "Room Of Roots", "Samuel, Oh How You've Changed!", "Scandinavian Girl", "A Small Fruit Song", "Swiss Cottage Manoeuvres", "You Should Have Listened To Al" and "Zero She Flies".

By now Al had moved across to the other side of the Cromwell Road and a flat at 39 Courtfield Road. It was a symbolic move and a clear attempt to break out of the rut in which he now found himself at the home that he had shared with Mandi.

Dave Dyke – "When he moved house to Courtfield Road he wanted to be free of anything that reminded him of his time at Elvaston Place with Mandi and that was how he came to give us his record deck I remember. Those were very much dark days indeed for him. We were very worried about Al but of course felt helpless because there had been nothing that us or anyone else could do for him during those bleak and gloomy months at the end of 1969".

In March 1970 Al spoke about his political feelings to *Music Now*.

"Sure, I could write lyrics like 'the waters of danger are flooding my mind' and all that, but what's the good of lines like that. And it's no good making sweeping generalisations while you are staring down from the stage into the eyes of 16-year-olds. If ever I do get ideas sorted out in my own mind then I might weave them into my songs; but I'm more likely to try to put them across at somewhere like the floor of the House of Commons."

It is clear from the interviews Al gave at this time that, aside from the emotions he was feeling having lost Mandi, he was already looking around for subject material other than 'love and loss' and seemed, at this time at least, to have settled on politics as both a conversation point and possible topic for future songs.

Music Now also asked Al about his recent live cover of Dylan's "It's All Right Ma, I'm Only Bleeding". "It's a good number for working off depression", Al told the magazine. "Seriously, like taking it out on the audience.

"I'm not exactly a prolific composer myself; I write about one a month but for personal reasons I haven't finished anything since last October. When the time comes round for the next album I might have to use all other people's material! There are one or two other songs which I'd consider doing on stage – Paul Simon's 'Blessed' … and Chuck Berry's 'Memphis', I've always wanted to do that. Yeah, maybe I'll do 'Memphis' … as an encore."

In fact he only ever performed those songs during radio sessions.

Interviewed over a year later in what the reporter dubbed his "gleaming kitchen" –

highly likely in that Al successfully avoided cooking for many years – he spoke again of "Manuscript" and about songwriting in general. "There's an exact truth, I was very proud of that song. 'Boots Of Spanish Leather' is a good song, so is 'The First Girl I Loved' by Robin Williamson … 'Stranger Song' by Leonard Cohen. These are exact and perfect truths … it depends on who you compare yourself with. I'm only interested in what I consider to be the best. In terms of songs other than those about love, one would have to look at 'Gates of Eden', 'It's Alright Ma', The mind boggles after that."

Asked in 1999 why there was only one "historical" song on *Zero She Flies* and no more until *Past, Present And Future* Al responded – "Well it is the Romsey connection. I had just read a book on the Mountbattens and all the Battenbergs as they used to be and it just flowed out of the book and into my song. If I hadn't just broken up with Mandi *Orange* simply wouldn't have been made the way it was. I could well have made *Past Present And Future* right then!"

Meanwhile Al's next single "Electric Los Angeles Sunset" / "My Enemies Have Sweet Voices" was released on March 6th 1970, the same day as The Beatles' *Let It Be*. It received positive reviews in the *Melody Maker*, *Disc* and the *New Musical Express*.

Zero She Flies was also the *Melody Maker*'s Folk Album of the Month.

Love Chronicles however was proving a difficult album to have released in the States.

He talked quite pointedly in a 4th April *Melody Maker* interview about the teething problems it was enduring – "The copies of *Love Chronicles* had gone out to the disc jockeys, then it was suddenly withdrawn when the heads of Columbia took offence (at the language used in the title track). This was a personal song that was written for Mandi and I'm not going to change the lyrics for anything in the world. For the past 15 months we have kept up an exchange of rude letters, cables, threats and lawsuits, and the latest thing is that the album is coming out on a small subsidiary label called Date. But I've got a lot of faith in the next album, although it's as yet unwritten. I have now recorded absolutely everything I've written and I aim to write the next album pretty fast in April as I've already got the ideas for it. I've stopped taking bookings after June and I aim to go away for three months and start playing again in October to coincide with the album's release."

However, behind the scenes, Al was far less "together" than that statement implies.

Over the previous few years Al had become good friends with the music journalist Jeremy Gilbert. The relaxed nature of the series of interviews he did with Al often portrayed Al at his most vulnerable and in many ways made uncomfortable reading.

Jeremy Gilbert introduced his April 4th interview with Al thus – "Like most musicians of similar artistic status, the daily routine of Al Stewart is physically undemanding; a comfortable apartment, no pressure of time, an afternoon of reading, thinking, playing records, writing songs, then, maybe into his MG sports car, away to a gig and back again the same night.

"But instead the last five months have found Al in a state of mental turbulence, exacerbated by the lack of physical activity to shroud it. After two and a half years of peaceful cohabitation, Al and his girl friend, Mandi (she appears on the *Love Chronicles* album sleeve) parted company back in October.

"At that moment, the prolific songwriting machine ground to a half, and as a result Al's new album *Zero She Flies* is a collection of his earlier, previously unreleased material."

"I haven't written a song since October", Al told Gibert, "and really shouldn't have gone into the studios in November, I just didn't care if I lived or died at the time and although the album isn't bad, it's very stark. As you know my songs tend to expose me quite a lot, and I apologise to any of the people who attended my bad gigs, like the Fairfield Halls.

"Actually I'm in a more hopeful state of mind now, as two weeks ago Mandi showed up on the doorstep again, and we've been seeing each other since. But I've never felt so totally and utterly defeated before, at least half the songs on the new album were written for Mandi and it got impossible to sing 'Love Chronicles' which started out as a simple statement and turned into an 18-minute long song.

"Along with dentists and photo sessions, recordings clam me up most of all as it's impossible to communicate in the studios."

The recently recorded "Manuscript", which up until the last moment Al had called "England", was a song that he considered to be superior in every way to any of his compositions up until that time. During the tour with The Third Ear Band Al told a local reporter in Southampton – "Of all the things I've written, 'Manuscript' is the best, and really captures what I'm aiming at; but that simply revolves around a trip Mandi and I made to Worthing."

Zero She Flies called upon the talents of Fotheringay's Trevor Lucas and Gerry Conway and Louis Cennamo from Renaissance. The album approached the soft rock feel that was to climax with *Modern Times*. The cover sees Al lost among the undergrowth looking more like Donovan than Donovan. On the reverse, Al is bundled in one of his famous sheepskin coats by the steps of the Regent's Park Zoo, not a million miles from Swiss Cottage. Since the title track owes much to Mervyn Peake, whose daughter Al slightly knew, it seemed only right and proper that a suitably literary set of liner notes were included on the inner part of the gatefold. The honour roll included Frank Dickens, Lord Mountbatten, Jonny Kremer and Richard Fariña (acknowledged as the originator of such liner notes). From them we also see that Al was already reading much of the material that would form part of his research for *Past, Present And Future* three years later, because he also namechecks Alexander Werth, Marshal Chuikov and Nostradamus. Sophie Lichfield, who had taken the cover photo for *Love Chronicles*, also took the photos for *Zero She Flies*, which entered the charts at number 45. That week The Beatles were at 56, Tom Jones' *Live Las Vegas* shook at 18 and *Bridge Over Troubled Water* held sway at No. 1.

Speaking to Jerry Gilbert, Al returned to the more serious aspect of his songwriting, and the harshness of the situation he now found himself in.

"The reason that I gave all the money from the Croydon gig to Oxfam was that I couldn't accept any money after that performance. I think that up until now I'd assumed that we would always be together, and I think my songs have tended to oversimplify the relationship between male and female. I'm not sure, but I think that in future my songs will bring out some of the more complicated aspects in a relationship."

Al remained pragmatic however about his position within the folk world. The split from Mandi had clearly led to him taking stock of the way that he led his life. He continued – "The way things are evolving doesn't exactly worry me, but it involves me increasingly. I regard singing in front of audiences merely as an apprenticeship, and I'm not fooling myself by making records because it leaves me a lot of time to read, think and absorb. I enjoy talking to an audience but I am a musician and I go out there to entertain. I don't want to learn anything and haven't got the brainpower for deciding what's to be done. But instead of leading purely a hedonistic life, I'd like to use my energies for the good – for the survival of this planet. I shall probably end up as part of a political conservation group, but at the moment I'm still reading and learning at a rapid rate."

This search for a more traditional and utopian existence was a theme that Al had touched on before. It was as if the void that he found himself in had wiped much of his life up until then clean away and given him a whole new perspective. He continued – "If you have any kind of capability, then you must have a responsibility. For instance in a few years time it could be better to grow a cabbage than make a record. For me, it's not a case of what I can get out of the world via Mandi, so much as what I can put into it via whatever. I try to write songs that I feel everyone can identify themselves with, but if I want to do anything for posterity, it certainly won't be in the fields of the arts, it'll be where it matters."

It is clear from these comments that the split from Mandi had crucially undermined

Al's creative drive. In fact it had almost dried up completely. So much so that he added a desperate postscript to the interview – "You see when I said I wanted to go away from July until October, well, I've really nowhere at all to go and if anyone wants one more person to make up a party or something … someone with a guitar and a sun hat … I mean I really would like to go along …"

Strange times indeed for Al. The sense of guilt at this *hedonistic* existence that he enjoyed would be a theme that he was constantly drawn back to over the new few years. Forced by the departure of Mandi to re-evaluate his motivations and future career course, his outlook was not unsurprisingly more than a little gloomy. It was a situation that he would often speculate on with his next serious girlfriend, Bena Nicolson.

BELSIZE BLUES

In which Al releases *Orange* and writes *Past, Present And Future*.
The latter album establishing historical *folk rock* as an art form.

Life, for Al, had not been easy at all for the previous few months. In the late spring of 1970 he was still, very much, feeling the effects of his split from his girlfriend and muse, Mandi.

On May 17 Al adopted the rare role of backing musician for Bridget St. John on Radio One. He also stepped forward for his own three-song set of "Zero She Flies", "A Small Fruit Song" and Paul Simon's "Blessed ".

The "News from Spain" single was at this time recorded at Trident Studios in London and was produced by Gus Dudgeon with Tony Visconti on cymbals, working as the arranger, and arriving at work each day from home on a motorbike. Jonny Kremer remembers a very hard-working atmosphere in their studio and The Tremeloes recording next door.

A month later, as a planned farewell to the London scene, he played a show at the Queen Elizabeth Hall that was beset by technical problems. Firstly, the PA system was too soft and then cut all the undertones and overtones from Al's voice making it sound like a "long distance telephone call" (according to the May 30 1970 issue of *Melody Maker*). Well, perhaps it was, and although the proposed tour of the Americas never really came to anything, it was nearly time for his sabbatical from major shows at least. Technical problems aside, a new cinematic comparison was made by one reviewer on the song "Manuscript". He commented that it was continually "...switching time levels like a *Last Year In Marianbad* style film."

He didn't know it but this was one of Al's favourite movies.

So what happened next was that Al did indeed drop out of view for a couple of months and in the spring of 1970 visited Greece for a few weeks. If the trip had been an attempt to break free from the past and write some new material it was a failure as no new songs came out of this period.

In his absence *Zero She Flies* fought it out in the folk charts with Pentangle, Fairport Convention, Carthy/Swarbrick and Judy Collins.

Music Business Weekly reported on 13th June – "Al Stewart's first album *Bedsitter Images* has been repackaged and re-released by CBS (64023). All tracks have been remixed and two new titles have been added. Said Stewart: 'I have never been happy with the mixing on the original album, and because my other two albums have all the words on the cover, I wanted to do the same with this one.'"

Record Retailer on June 20th reported – "This is Stewart's first album, originally released three years ago, but now re-released with a slight re-mixing to remove some of the more grotesque string arrangements. Since the original release, Stewart has had two other albums on the market both building him a firm reputation as one of Britain's finest folk-singers. *The First Album* has some fine tracks – especially 'Denise At 16' and 'Samuel, Oh How You've Changed' – but as a whole does not represent Stewart's present range of skills. Should sell well enough, however, to the growing number of Stewart fans who missed out on *Bedsitter Images* when it was first released."

Al surfaced back in Bournemouth during August where Gay Pirrie-Weir quite properly tackled him on why he never performed locally.

"He says there is nowhere to sing. The atmosphere is not good enough in the big halls, and he'd never fill them here, while the smaller clubs couldn't afford the fees his agents charge for him."

Al – "So I came back from Greece and it seemed that nothing much had changed.

Linda Fitzgerald-Moore

Al touring "Zero"

This was the situation. I had made three records I didn't like any of them. They weren't hits. *Love Chronicles* had become *Melody Maker* Folk Album of the Year, which was nice. They hadn't sold especially well or especially badly, then the normal stuff for English folkies. But they hadn't touched the pop world; they were something that had happened in this very small world, you know they belonged on the folk page in the *Melody Maker*. A lot of time and effort had gone into them, a lot of blood under the bridge and nothing much was coming back and I was out of contract again. The Roy Guest thing had run its course and you know I didn't have a record contract. I didn't really have a manager. I also didn't have a lot of interest in going out and singing *Zero*

Promo shot 1970

She Flies, which I didn't like in the first place. So I went to Greece and thought things over. Couldn't think of any particular thing and basically just poodled about for a while."

On his return Al turned to Julia for more gigs having decided to use concert dates as a partial catharsis for the depression that he was going through.

Al – "So I phoned Julia and said can you get me some gigs?, and I had been getting, before I went to Greece, £25 per night and then all of a sudden Julia had a fistful of offers for £75 per night, a lot of money. But I do remember when I came back I was getting three times as much as when I had left. There were gigs – like all these universities wanted me because I had been gone for a year essentially off the circuit and instead of going away people had continued to buy *Love Chronicles* and they wanted me to go and sing it."

Al even made a half-hearted attempt to join Tir Na Nog but they weren't having any of it and nothing came of a possible escape route that he had one day discussed with Ian Matthews either.

Al – "I sat down with Ian one day at a motorway service station and talked to him about me playing bass for Matthew's Southern Comfort. We were sat with our cups of tea in somewhere like the Blue Boar or Leicester Services on the M1 and he was putting the group together and I was saying 'Oh I'm not doing much, I might fancy being in a band'. We were sort of just talking it over but it didn't come to

Rehearsing at Courtfield Road 1970

anything and Mark Griffiths got that job in the end. So I went back to see Julia and she had just talked to CBS and she said that they wanted another three albums from me and would advance us £10,000. So I bought a Ferrari! Because I was just really depressed. Still thinking about Mandi…much of the time I'm afraid."

Julia Creasey – "These were not easy times for Al. I often had to cheer him up and I did my best to keep him going. He would come into the office and his mind would be a million miles away. But from a professional point of view he was totally focused once he got up on stage. He was a real trouper in that respect."

A SMALL FRUIT SONG
Said the apple to the orange:
"Oh I wanted you to come
Close to me and kiss me to the core
Then you might know me like no other orange
Has ever done before"

MANUSCRIPT
Prince Louis Battenberg is burning the Admiralty lights down low
Silently sifting through papers sealed with a crown
Admiral Lord Fisher is writing to Churchill, calling for more Dreadnoughts
The houses in Hackney are all falling down
And my grandmother sits on the beach in the days before the war
Young girl writing her diary, while time seems to pause
Watching the waves as they come one by one to die on the shore
Kissing the feet of England

Oh the lights of Saint Petersburg come on as usual
Although the air seems charged with strangeness of late, yet there's nothing to touch
And the Tsar in his great Winter Palace has called for the foreign news
An archduke was shot down in Bosnia, but nothing much
And my grandmother sits by the mirror in the days before the war
Smiling a secret smile as she goes to the door
And the young man rides off in his carriage, homeward once more
And the sun sets gently on England

Ah the day we decided to drive down to Worthing, it rained and rained
Giving us only a minute to stand by the sea
And crunching my way through the shingles, it seemed there was nothing changed
Though the jetty was maybe more scarred than I'd known it to be
And Mandi and I stood and stared at the overcast sky
Where ten years ago we had stood, my Grandfather and I
And the waves still rushed in as they had the year that he died
And it seemed that my lifetime was shrunken and lost in the tide
As it rose and fell on the side
Of England

Prince Louis Battenberg is burning the Admiralty lights

At the end of the summer Al was invited to play a rare French concert, as part of a festival staged in an aircraft hangar a few miles outside of Paris. Whilst the show was cancelled at the last moment there remains one telling element of the trip that bears inspection. Mandi was with him. And whilst their relationship no longer had the intensity of earlier times, the mere fact that they were able to spend time in one another's company allowed the split to become something that Al could, on some days at least, accept.

Back In London, with Mandi once again only occasionally around in his life, Al was left to ponder the course of his career. Thus, through the Autumn of 1970, in the flat in Courtfield Road, his first impressions began to coalesce for what would become the next

Linda Fitzgerald-Moore

Al, Wimbledon Common 1970

Linda Fitzgerald-Moore

Wimbledon Common 1970

album, *Orange*, which besides being the colour of madness was the variety of fruit that Al found to best represent the absent Mandi best.

In *Melody Maker's* Best Male Singer poll of September 19th Al came in a credible tenth behind Robert Plant and Paul Rogers. The day before this poll was published, on September 18th, another of Al's heroes, Jimi Hendrix, died in London.

Following a summer of inactivity Al gave an interview (again with *Melody Maker* and Jerry Gilbert) to spread the word about what he was up to now and for the near future. The article hit the newstands on November 7th 1970, and the accompanying photograph shows Al with slightly longer hair, open neck shirt and velvet jacket pictured sitting on the bench beside the windmill on Wimbledon Common by Linda Fitzgerald Moore. The probing article points out that – "According to the old saying, things always happen in threes.

Nothing at all has happened to Al Stewart for a long while, but suddenly he's cutting a single, embarking on a mammoth concert tour and then clearing off to America for six months – in that order."

In an informed piece that was obviously written with a great deal of understanding, Al was quoted as declaring – "So far this year things have ground to a halt since *Zero She Flies* and this will be the first deliberate single I've made for *four years*," (saying this with what Gilbert called "a kind of childish delight").

Al continued, "One of the sides is a little ditty which I quite like while the other is about six minutes long and is called 'The News From Spain.'"

Explaining the background to the song Al said this – "The emotional involvement was far too much and even a song like 'The News From Spain' – that letter from Spain … I mean I got straight on a plane and flew out to Spain to see her and asked her to marry me on the beach in Spain. She said no and the world ended – and it took a year and a half before I could have said anything about it let alone written a song about it. So the songs have to be in retrospect."

This "little ditty" that Al almost dismissed was, of course, the classic "Elvaston Place", which is just about as perfect a "memoir" about lost love as could ever be. The tempo of this song is similar to the Kinks' "Sunny Afternoon" written by someone who has much in common with Al – Ray Davies.

ELVASTON PLACE

Elvaston Place
A run-down basement in south Ken
Hiding your face
Behind the railings in the rain
Stony steps to a small grey herd
Of dustbins blinking in the sunlight
Our yesterday lives
Crouched by the fireside
In Elvaston Place
Holes in the lace-
Curtains, splintery window frames
A small furnished space
We never knew the landlord's name
Electric bar to warm your winter toes
Evening paper for the bath mat
Watching the face
Happy beside me
In Elvaston Place

The city's spreading like a stony tide across the countryside
I live alone now in London town
Cars and buses everywhere, they hide the sun and eat the air
You need a friend when it gets you down
All the money that I've ever owned
I'd give it all tomorrow
If I could lay happy beside you
In Elvaston Place

Elvaston Place
I stopped to look at you today
New whitewashed face
Behind the railings in the rain
You once held a love of mine
She changed just like the weather
The Kensington skies go on forever
In Elvaston Place

At the session for the recording of "Elvaston Place" Al Barry, an old friend from the Bournemouth days, played lead guitar. At the time of the recording Barry was playing in the group Fields, another act from Miles Copeland's stable and someone who was to soon feature prominently in Al's life.

Al was very happy with "TNFS" taking pains to point out that he considered Gus Dudgeon's production (previous recipients: Bowie and Elton John) "utterly unbelievable … the song is in my 'Beleeka Doodle Day' and 'Life And Life Only' style. It would be nice if it were a hit as this is exactly typical of where I am now, and I think it's an unmitigated gas. It's the best piece of recording I've ever done – utterly uncommercial but something I believe is good."

Music Business Weekly was brief and to the point – "Beautiful violin and cello-lined ballad, slightly mournful, with organ and guitar cutting through. A masterpiece of a production – easily the best single Stewart has ever made."

Whilst the *New Musical Express* wrote – "A sad tale of a girl who goes to Spain, then writes a *Dear John* letter to her boyfriend. He flies out to persuade her to change her mind, but she doesn't want to know. Warmly related by its composer with an absorbing backing of classically scored strings, fugal-like organ and underlying rhythm. Beautiful – but its moodiness is out of keeping with the present season."

The latest Jerry Gilbert interview that was now published announced his *24 Concerts In 5 Weeks* tour and Al had this to say in the accompanying interview – "We sent out a circular to the colleges and it turned out they all wanted me so I'm very pleased. That will take me right up until the middle of December; I shall be going home for Christmas and then in January I take myself to the States. I'm going to live in America and stay there until I get things off the ground. I don't mean a thing to anyone in the States and I'm literally going over there with no money and just a guitar, and hustle for places to stay. I've got a couple of addresses to start with … I know about four people in New York City, so I'll start there and then just work round … I shall be on everybody's doorstep."

Regarding the date of his next album, Al was unsure saying – "I've known for at least six months what the next album will be. It's going to be *The Album* if I ever write it. It's just that the things I've put down for it so far haven't been right. I've got three or four songs which are half finished and I must get those ready for the concert tour."

Since April he had at least started to compose again, and he was ready for the winter tour of the UK.

The reviews of the tour, Al's last extensive "solo" tour for twenty years were excellent. According to *Melody Maker* of November 14th, the Manchester performance of "Songs Out of Clay" was a premiere as Al had composed and memorised the song while driving to the gig! *The Kettering Leader* of December 4th compared Al for one of the first times to Leonard Cohen in a set that included "Burbling", "Room of Roots" and "Gethsemane".

In another *Melody Maker* article, from the December 19th issue, Al gave an interview to Andrew Means. The article's headline, *A New Start for Al In New York*, was an upbeat end to a not so good year.

The desperate situation that Al found himself in was twofold. He seemed unable to make the artistic breakthrough he wanted and was beginning to realise that he'd never get back with Mandi. The cathartic possibilities of a complete break with both problems must have been very tempting.

Al – "A rebirth …. yes, that's it. I am getting rid of all the material things I've got over here. I'm just taking the guitar. I just want to go over and try and conquer the United States. Five years ago I came to London totally unknown and it was very stimulating to have a challenge like that."

Al didn't even know where he was going to live in the States, but mentioned that he would welcome any helpful suggestions.

"The thing I don't want is to go over there with any kind of a name. A lot of people criticise me because I've been reasonably successful, but it isn't my fault, I came to London with nothing."

The trip to the States was clearly another attempt at running away from the corner that he had written himself into in England. Al had no real plans about how he was going to progress once he got over there, a situation that brought its own reward when he eventually made the trip. He continued – "I do things totally on inspiration and just now I have got to go and sing there and I think it will result in all sorts of things that will shake me out of the depression I've been in. I have to do it now because maybe in a couple of years I'll be too old. It's exciting. It's like going back to the roots. I think that I will have new experiences that will result in new songs."

Although he would not be seen in the UK for some time, Al was not perturbed by the thought that his popularity might suffer in this country. "The kind of people who come to see me don't come because I'm fashionable. They come because ... well, I don't know. Perhaps because they know that I'm telling them the truth. I don't particularly feel that I'm a folk singer and therefore subject to folk being in or out of popularity."

On January 1st 1971 Al formally renewed his contract with Julia. Later that same week *Melody Maker* reported that Al was playing a farewell concert at the Les Cousins Club before "heading east for continental dates and radio shows". It went on to say that Al hoped these performances would be followed by the delayed USA tour (now to include Canada), and perhaps a visit to Nairobi and Mombasa. So he left for Europe and in Holland the appearance of "Fred The Crazy Driver" is confirmed for the first time. The 100mph dash that was to be immortalised in 'Amsterdam' did in fact take place; Fred owning a racing driver school.

Isaac Guillory was also someone that Al first met during that visit to Amsterdam in the spring of 1971. After one show in Haarlem, Al went with friends to a small folk club and bar called Club Fairport where there was a longstanding tradition of jam nights.

Al – "I was cajoled into getting up on stage and ended up playing some improvised blues with someone who turned out to be Isaac. It very quickly became obvious to me that he was a great guitar player and I invited him over to England to play with me later in the year at the Cambridge Folk Festival which he eventually did and very enjoyable it was too… Isaac was an American who played in a band called The Cryan' Shames and they did a couple of albums and were quite big for a while and then broke up."

Isaac Guillory – "We played together very well. Cambridge was a real buzz for me and after that I got to know Al quite well in London. He's a sweet guy and helped me get a lot of work. I consider that the music I contributed to his live work and albums to be some of the most enjoyable periods of my life."

Throughout 1971 Al continued to perform in the UK with the American trip delayed once more. May saw him at the Walsall Doghouse and London's Drury Lane Theatre. Robin Denselow, one of the most respected journalists writing in the British arts pages, reviewed the Drury Lane show in *The Guardian* of May 17th, calling Al "professional", and pointing out that his "throwaway style" almost sought to undermine the "powerful lyrics". Regarding the same show, *Disc* magazine considered Al to be "slightly overawed" but speculated on whether there was anyone on either side of the Atlantic lyrically to touch him.

On his arrival for that Sunday evening concert Al found a good luck note left in his dressing room from someone that signed themselves as simply "Sandy". It turned out to be from Sandy Faris who was the musical director of a show that was running at the Drury Lane Theatre at that time and it was something that meant a great deal to Al.

The provincial papers were there as always and the *Slough Evening Mail* summed up Al's Drury Lane show in just one word: "immaculate".

He remained unsettled though, and during negotiations for a deal with CBS he spoke to *Sounds* on May 22nd about this desire to "fade into the background".

"I'd like to join a band if anyone wants a bass guitarist who can knock up a few lyrics

– I might have a sabbatical and go off and play with a group for a year. My immediate problem is that I'm doing more complicated things musically, but they need backing: it'll work on record but God knows what'll happen live. When I play the new things it could be that the songs won't have the same zing to start off but will when they've had backing. But the basic thing is to have the ideas – and just look what a state the music business is in at the moment."

Five days later on May 27th Al renewed his contract with CBS and on June 3rd he drove the short distance to Hampstead Heath and performed at a free festival at Kenwood House. Also on the bill were Colin Scott, Marc Ellington and Bridget St John.

Further shows at such distant points of the compass as Basildon and Plymouth demonstrate that Al was very busy at this time. The reviews indicated that many of the songs were newly written in readiness for the next album, and his Texan Epiphone, bought six years previously from Ivor Mairants Music Centre in London's West End, was clearly doing its stuff. We know this because he gave this information in response to a reader's question in the *Melody Maker* of June 26th 1971. Throughout the summer he continued gigging (a big difference from 1970) including shows at Lewisham Concert Hall, with Lindisfarne and Steeleye Span, and at Cherry Hinton Hall where on August 1st he was pictured for the first time in his career with an ice cream van! The proof of this is in the August 2nd issue of the *Cambridge Evening News*, which was reporting on the Cambridge Folk Festival where Al had appeared with Isaac.

It was now that Al upped sticks to North London when he bought and moved into a mews house in Belsize Court Garages in Belsize Park.

It was now, at a school concert he gave in Somerset, that Al met Bena Nicolson. Over the next three years Bena would provide emotional support at a time when Al needed it most and also be with him through a pivotal and magical period in his career. Having someone in his life once again wasn't an instant cure for all of Al's ills however.

Al – "So I had this mews house and I had this exotic car and you would have thought that would have done it but then the odd thing was that over the next few years, I mean it just rained money at me. I think between '71 and '74, culminating in Ian Copeland becoming my agent and charging £500 per night for me which I thought was complete insanity, I just had so much money! I basically went from about £25 per night to eventually £500 per night working four or five shows a week and all of it was cash! It was not unusual for me to toss £2,000 in cash into a drawer every week. I mean you do this for three or four months and all of a sudden you have got £10,000 in a drawer! That's a lot of money. I kept trying to put these fistfuls of money in the bank but I didn't know what to do with it all! I already had a mews house and a Ferrari, I was manically depressed about Mandi still and people continued to give me money…"

Al was only paying Julia 10 percent commission and so he started looking around for something to spend his 90 percent on. He found the answer on his doorstep.

Al – "I did the only thing that a sensible person could and I started buying extremely expensive wine! This was the local Oddbins in Belsize Village and so I started buying all the first growth Bordeaux I could lay my hands on. It was an interesting period. I just couldn't go through the money fast enough and nothing I could do could seem to put a dent in my finances. I don't buy jewellery, I did have the car and the house but there was nothing else, no material things that I wanted. I tried ordering suits from exotic Bond Street tailors and that all went wrong, they didn't do the job properly and so it was that I just couldn't get rid of it."

Richard Thompson also remembers Al spending vast amounts of money on something a little more in keeping with his craft.

Richard Thompson – "Something that I will always remember about Al is that one day he had decided that he liked Guild acoustic guitar strings so much that he should get himself a lifetime supply. And so he did just that. He went out and bought himself something like four thousand sets of them one afternoon. That's the Al I know!"

Bena

At home in Belsize Village 1971

These were strange times for Al. Earning more money than he ever had before he remained deflated and depressed, despite being on the brink of a great period of songwriting. Money had not bought him happiness.

Al again – "I began to wonder about my compatriots because half of them were making similar chunks of cash except I didn't know what they were doing with it. Harper bought a Bentley at one point which I thought was pretty wild – but it wasn't a new Bentley. I couldn't imagine what the others were doing with all this money. It couldn't have just been me. I think a lot of people in the early '70s must have been doing extremely well on the folk scene. Because there was nothing to spend it on really. There were only so many things you could eat and drink and there were only so many people you could take out to dinner every night. But it was a fascinating period. However, employing musicians put a stop to all that quite smartly."

Meanwhile Al's relationship with Bena was becoming serious, although her parents, who had nicknamed her The Camp Follower in lieu of her devotion to Al, had been against the relationship from the start.

Bena – "Absolutely, from day one. Al secretly liked my family background in the same way that he was similarly proud of his own Scottish roots. Although he didn't have a father to look up to, there's no question that had his father lived Al's would have been every bit as successful as my own father. I noticed a side to Al that wanted my father to recognise his success. My parents however never gave Al a chance and my mother even used to refer to him as 'The Rock Star'! However, my grandmother was more generous and once asked me to write out the lyrics to *Zero She Flies* for her."

Al wasn't ready then in 1971 for the New World but the time was fast approaching when the USA was ready and waiting for him. Throughout the autumn he continued to play larger halls including The Lyceum, Drury Lane and the Queen Elizabeth Hall, where on September 7th he previewed songs soon to appear on *Orange*. Before going onstage at The Lyceum in the Strand Al gave a very short interview to *The New Musical Express*. In it he went out of his way to complain about how the subject matter of many of his songs was overlooked by press and public alike.

Al – "People tend to say to me 'Oh you're the guy that sings those very personal love songs!' but that honestly only makes up about half of my material." The fact that it was the love songs exclusively that people asked him about and shouted out for at his shows was conclusive proof he suggested of that fact that "the best songs are the ones written from personal experience".

"What I try to do is write things in the truest, most concise possible way, in a way that's closest to what actually happened. I don't think I have the right to change what was.

"It's a kind of experiment in realism if you like. I've always wanted to try and break barriers. Like 'Love Chronicles' for instance. I don't think anybody had written an 18-minute love song before that.

"On the face of it I guess it would appear my personal experiences have been fairly unsuccessful. I guess I attract people with similar kinds of hang-ups to my concerts.

"I'm not sure about playing the Lyceum with electric bands. I don't have any preconceived ideas on what will happen. It could be the usual chaos when folk and rock are presented together. The last time I played there, I had Jeff Beck tuning up his guitar round the back all though my set. It didn't make things any easier."

On October 27th Al returned to the Bournemouth Winter Gardens to play his first local show in over six years. On the bill with him were Steeleye Span and Andy Roberts. Before the show Al and Jonny Kremer drove across The New Forest to the ITV Studios in Southampton in Al's new Mercedes where he performed the piece "Ivich" live on the evening news show *Day By Day*.

It was now in 1971 that Julia Creasey left Blackhill to work out of a new agency in Duke Street, Mayfair for the next three months.

Julia Creasey – "Then from Duke Street I went to work as a freelance with Joe Boyd at WitchSeason, taking Al with me, staying there until Joe was bought out by Warner Bros where upon I moved to 42 South Molton Street, still with Al."

Whilst working at Trident Studios on *Orange* that Autumn Al had, amazingly enough, been due to work with Mick Ronson playing guitar for him. However when Al asked Ronno to "play in the style of Tim Renwick" he naturally enough wasn't too keen and suggested to Al that the best person to do that was Tim himself, promptly offering Tim's phone number to Al's then producer John Anthony.

Al takes up the story:

"I had by now teamed up with John Anthony who indeed did introduce me to Tim Renwick along with Willie Wilson and the rest of Quiver. The arrival of Tim changed everything for me. I have always thought that he was the most melodic guitarist."

The album was a vast improvement over its predecessors in the level of musicianship. Lyrically, Al's boredom with the capital makes itself heard.

"All right I told you that I'm leaving London/the summer seems so long/ I've got no money to pay the rent/ I've got no place to take my songs."

This spirit of change was reflected in the early '70s music business, generally. Speaking at the time, Al told *Sounds* – "*Orange* is ... to call it a fun album is absurd because it isn't that but at the same time it doesn't labour the point, a lot of the songs have a light touch. Only 'The News From Spain' is deliberately heavy and maybe 'The Night Of The 4th Of May'. Things like 'You Don't Even Know Me' and 'I'm Falling' which come from the beginning of the relationship have quite a light feel to them.

I believe in establishing your foundations before you try and do something very complicated, and the foundation that this record has established is the kind of sound I

London, 1970

want to make on record that I never made before. I do think that the production on the first three albums is atrocious and it probably is sufficiently bad to stop people even listening to the songs and getting into them."

Al played a short series of dates after Christmas that included a show at Oxford Town Hall on Monday 31st January, driving to the gig, which was put on by the *Oxford Guitar Society* and where tickets were 60 pence each, with Bena.

A few days later, on February 7th, Al was on the BBC again with John Peel, playing "Lullaby of Birdland", "A Small Fruit Song", "I'm Falling", "My Enemies Have Sweet Voices", "Electric Los Angeles Sunset" and "Songs Out Of Clay".

The transitional album *Orange*, released in Feburary 1972, was a turning point for Al in many ways. It marked the peak of his disaffection with life in general, though it bore specific reference to his break-up with Mandi. The quartet of songs, "You Don't Even Know Me", "I'm Falling", "Night Of The Fourth Of May" and "The News From Spain" represent a successful catharsis in that regard. "Songs Out Of Clay" evokes comparison with Leonard Cohen, whilst "Amsterdam" introduces the folk-rock feel that was to later peak on *Modern Times*.

Al – "This was deliberate. I wanted to re-create a kind of group feel live and so now I had this four-piece backing group. But I would still always play a great wad of solo acoustic stuff – I mean I would never use a group right the way through but it seems to be there in the music, it does have this light rock feel to it and therefore it seemed as if it was worth having a go doing it live to see what people's reactions to it were. The lead

GREATER LONDON COUNCIL

ROYAL FESTIVAL HALL
Director: JOHN DENISON CBE
Friday 13th October at 8p.m.

AL STEWART

2 Hour Solo Concert

Management: JULIA CREASY

TICKETS: £1 80p 65p 50p

From RFH Box Office SE1
Tel. 01-928 3191

Folk Directions

Have guitar, will play anywhere

guitarist was Isaac Guillory, Tim Hinkley from Jody Grind on organ, Rob Tait from Bell and Arc on drums and Fred Gandy on bass, all of whom had been around a long time and were completely professional, completely competent, good players, good musicians. These are all like musos. But they drove me stark raving mad because none of them would ever turn up on time. As a band they didn't have a name; it was the guys I have just mentioned and they were session guys that I would hire specifically for gigs."

This experience was the main reason that Al was so anti bands when it was to become a major issue shortly after.

Al again – "I mean Hinckley would arrive three hours late and it was always a nightmare. When they did show up the first thing they would do was get stoned and then the second thing they would do was say 'we don't want to play this' then they'd have a 12-bar jam for about three hours and I couldn't get them. I just basically couldn't organise them. This was interesting because I don't think any of them took it very seriously."

Musically these musicians were straight out of the top drawer and that's where Al considers the problem lay.

"Maybe that's why they didn't treat playing with me as any big deal! Their attitude overall ranged from giving the impression that they were just along for the ride, to open hostility from a couple of them, whereby they'd deliberately turn up two or three hours late for a rehearsal and on one occasion repeated this on the night of a gig itself. They represented the most unpunctual group of musicians that I've ever encountered! Francis Monkman in fact was driven to distraction by all this and on one occasion wanted to kill one of them!"

This transitional time for Al was made all the more difficult because he felt that he was having to do so much of the work himself. Not one of the succession of band line-ups that he worked ever gave him the impression that they truly understood his music either.

Al – "So there was the Francis line up, there was the Canton Trig line up, there was the Isaac Guillory and the sort of smashed musicians line-up and there was the Home line up. And these are four different and unsuccessful attempts to get a band together! So I had these four different sets of people playing with me during this time and there might have been more too. So bands were coming and going."

Al was still on CBS in 1972 and hating it. He would go into their London offices and they wouldn't recognise him. He would tell them his name and still draw a blank. One event in particular Al remembers quite clearly. One day around about this time he had gone up to the record company to ask for a small advance of £800 to enable him to tour with a band and was kept waiting for several hours while CBS thought it over. During the course of this wait he observed them signing away £35,000 to launch the band Totem, soon to disappear without trace. He did get his £800 though.

Al found the whole process of rehearsing new backing musicians exasperating. Speaking at the time he concluded – "To get them to play in the style that I want is another matter altogether and rehearsals tend to be insane affairs – they do go off at musical tangents because they've all been in so many different musical situations before. The numbers that work best with them are old Dylan things, like we play 'Absolutely Sweet Marie' from *Blonde On Blonde* and it sounds just great."

Al composed a quartet of songs for *Orange* that focussed on his relationship with Mandi.

Al – "These four songs were my way of dealing with a situation that I hadn't, in all honesty, dealt with at all. A catharsis…. I'm not at all sure if that was my real intention or even if it worked out that way in the end."

YOU DON'T EVEN KNOW ME

All right you saw me in the International Times
You've got my picture in your book
You tell your friends not to call at weekends,
And now you wear that far-off look
All right you stole your mother's best silk sheets
And put them on my bed
And you remember all the words that I say
And now you keep them in your head

But you don't even know me
You don't even know me
You don't even know me at all

All right I told you that I'm leaving London
The summer seems so long
I've got no money to pay the rent
I've got no place to take my songs
And then you tell me I should keep on trying
You hand me an envelope
With all the money that you'd saved up
You couldn't stand to see me go

But you don't even know me
You don't even know me
You don't even know me at all

All right I took you to the Hendrix concert
On the seventh day of May
And through the summer of 1967
We were part of the seeds of change
And now you say that we can really make it
We've got nowhere to fall
And though the signs are hung in the rainy distance
You don't see them at all
But you don't even know me

You don't even know me
You don't even know me at all

But you don't even know me
You don't even know me
You don't even know me at all
You don't know me at all
You don't know me at all
All right I think that we should stay together For a while

I'M FALLING
It's Sunday afternoon and it's raining,
I'm falling
Colour sections, pastel blue, an empty church, a movie queue
And I'm falling
Watching you moving around
Taking the time
To get a proper look
It seems as though I've never really looked at you

Get up, put the kettle on, make us some tea
I'm falling
If we've got some biscuits left, please bring one for me,
I'm just falling
Spending the whole day in bed
Wasting our time
In such a gentle way
We hardly need to say a word, it's just okay

And already the sun has gone, and it's growing dark outside,
I can see your face reflected in the red electric firelight,
And our shadow is an embryo
That slowly comes to life
And as it moves across the wall
It seems to feel the fire of living
Growing stronger as it climbs
To shiver in a blaze
Across the ceiling
And the soundless crash of the sea
Fills the room with the scent of the breeze
And the waves break over
The beach of our bodies
As you reach your fingers out to me

Why don't we take the whole of next week off work,
We're falling
You can say you don't feel well, you caught a cold or something,
We're just falling
We can get out of town
Taking the time
To let it all work out
The hour glass is turning, every second counts
I'm falling
I'm falling
I'm falling
Moving around inside a dream today
Falling for you in such a special way

NIGHT OF THE 4TH OF MAY

And the days they flew by
And the leaves fell from the trees
And many times you came around
And many times you slept with me
And every time that we made love
You wrote it down in your diary
Lady of ladies
But I would always say to you
Don't ask about tomorrow
Give what you have take what you need
Your time is only now
Don't try to tie me down to promises
Live for today, today is all there is
And freedom seems to be everything to me

I took you down to a party
On the night of the 4th of May
And a strange and growing restlessness
Had hung in the air all day
The need to try and tear down
And destroy all that we'd made
Lady of ladies
You whispered in my ear and asked me
If I fancied her
You told me that he'd phoned you
When I was in America
Daring each other just to say okay
Swop for tonight, didn't I always say
That freedom seems to be everything to me

And she came and she sat down beside me
And you found an excuse to go downstairs
And she smiled and made
The kind of conversation that you do
And later on she said, "My last train has gone
Oh I wonder if you could run me home"
And I found you in the hallway and told you
That was all that I would do
Just run her home and it's through
Oh I thought you knew

But I must confess
I laid my head on her breast
And it seemed so hard
To pull it away
Her hand touched my hand
And her eyes were offering the rest
If it wasn't for you, oh I would have stayed
But I came back home through the morning
To find you lying awake
And I knew all at once what you'd done
And I heard myself say
"Why did you have to sleep with him
Anyone else
Wouldn't have mattered
Half
As much as him"

I don't want to touch you
Somehow you feel unclean
I just wish that you
Were five hundred miles away from me
Don't talk at all, don't start to cry
Just pack up your things
Lady of ladies
And though I'd always told myself
That when our time ended
I'd walk away with no regrets
And no attempts to stay
Somehow it doesn't seem to be that way
I find I'm needing every word you say
This freedom seems to be everything to me

And you went up to Cambridge
And you stayed in your brother's room
And you wrote me a letter and sent it the same afternoon
You said "I just want to hurt myself
Oh I need you so badly now"
And you told me "Without you there seems to be no horizon at all
Just no crack in the wall
No place lower to fall"

Hey don't leave me, don't leave me
The shapelessness of the dawn
Floods above and beneath me, I just can't go on"

And I had to walk right into the trap
And I had to say please come back
Though I felt all the while
My resistance slipping away
Why did I have to fall for you
Anyone else
Wouldn't have hurt me
Half
As much as you

THE NEWS FROM SPAIN
I have heard the news from Spain
Now you say you've many things yet to be learning
And you don't know if or when you'll be returning
It depends on how
Everything works out
If it can somehow
In Carvajal
And I have heard the news from Spain
Now you've found someone you don't have to be tied to
And he dried your eyes, and later lay beside you
As the simple wine
Of the flow of time
Pulled us out of rhyme
In Carvajal

Into a taxi and down to the airport
In only the clothes I was standing in
A scribbled address, a toothbrush, a passport
The money we saved in the biscuit tin

Running afraid to a strange Spanish town
Searching the sands and the shoreline ...

And I have heard the news from Spain
Now the Winter winds possess the Southern reaches
And the sea folds like a mantle on the beaches
And the crowds have gone
And I've left my song
To be killed alone
In Carvajal
In Carvajal
In Carvajal

On March 13th 1972 Al recorded an appearance on BBC TV's *Old Grey Whistle Test*, hosted by Bob Harris, to be broadcast the next day. Dressed in a Mickey Mouse shirt, Al introduced "Night of the 4th May" with a long spoken piece, delivered straight to camera, in which he mused on the subject of relationships and infidelity. He then went on to sing the most heart-wrenching version (including the one on *Orange*) of that song that exists. The next day he flew straight out of Heathrow to start a short European tour.

Bena – "Al wrote to me through that tour. On March 16th 1972 he wrote – "Dearest Fish, I played my first gig here last night, I enclose Danish press cutting for you to decipher. This is in Varde, a town of about 12,000 people and accordingly no-one speaks English too well but with true Scandinavian 'politesse' they sat through two hours of my incomprehensible songs and then clapped for more. The instrumentals go down best. Nobody has really heard of me over here but they played 'Amsterdam' on the radio the day before the concert. I expect things will pick up a bit when I reach the bigger places – Copenhagen and Stockholm."

On March 24th Al performed on *Top Gear* once again. This time he performed "A Small Fruit Song", "You Don't Even Know Me", "Old Compton Street Blues", "Zero She Flies", "Absolutely Sweet Marie" and "I'm Falling"

Two weeks later at the start of April 1972 Al hosted a special press conference during which he expanded on his motives for writing the album. He told *Beat International* – "I do try to find 'succinct' phrases – I quite like that description of my writing. I tend to be wordy to a point of fault, you see. Look, for example, at the lyrics of 'Gethsemane Again' – that is a very wordy song. I just try to get the exact phrase. On 'Electric Los Angeles Sunset', from the *Zero She Flies* album, there's a phrase: ... 'diffuse into cinerama haze

...' that was the exact phrase ... I could have looked through *Roget's Thesaurus* 3,000 times, and I still wouldn't have found anything that could have expressed my impressions more exactly. That phrase was the right phrase.

If one word is wrong, then it has to go. I must always have the exact word – and it's worth taking a little bit of time."

Al went on to single out "Manuscript" for particular attention – "It was written for myself ... totally for myself. It's a little time capsule – you could take it backwards or forwards in time by maybe 50 years, and it would still be as valid as when it was written."

He had no pretensions about his musical position saying "I play, I sing, I write because that's what I like doing." He saw himself as meeting a demand. As long as there were people there to listen, he said, then he would go and play to them.

Al had given little time to consider why his songs should seemingly be taken so close to the hearts of his audience. Was it a question of identification? He wasn't sure – "I suppose that some of my songs can be identified with", he said. "But many ... well, take a song like 'Night Of The Fourth Of May' – there's no leeway there. The song is very exact. Some of them, though, do have 'gaps' that I suppose some people do fall into."

He ended the interview by making the point that both Tolkien and Camus had been well into their careers before producing their masterpieces, ending with – "If I do write a great song, then it won't be for at least ten years. But I'm going to keep trying. It's the one thing that I really want to do."

Two weeks later, on April 26th, Al recorded two songs at the BBC for the *Johnnie Walker Lunchtime Session* for which no other details exist.

In the late spring of 1972 he once again went to Denmark for a short series of dates. The agency for the tour was *Sound* in Copenhagen and Carl Fisher worked with Al for much of the year. It was obvious to Bena that, having started to act as Al's Danish promoter, Carl was getting seriously interested in becoming Al's full time manager and she was dead against this.

Radio-wise Al continued to appear regularly on the BBC, playing "A Small Fruit Song", "I'm Falling", "Amsterdam" and Bob Dylan's "Just Like Tom Thumb Blues" on the *Pete Drummond Show* broadcast on May 18th.

Al and Bena went on a spur of the moment trip to Amsterdam in late June for just one night as a "treat for ourselves" returning the next day because Al had to drive up to the North of England to do a gig at Durham Castle.

On August 8th they went to The Lido in Venice for a two week holiday. This was a rare foreign trip for Al and Bena as Al had never been a fan of the conventional holiday. He packed his acoustic guitar for the trip and after dinner he'd play songs to everyone out in the hotel garden. This period of Al's life was one where, on the surface, he should have been very content. He was living in his elegant North London mews house, with his Ferrari parked outside and he had also belatedly overcome the writer's block that had followed Mandi's departure. By now he had also started to relax into his relationship with Bena Nicolson. He was playing for up to 1,500 people a night, which meant a lot of money, making Al up to £200 per show.

However, as Al explained in an interview in *Southern Rag* in 1984 – "It had also peaked, and what I hadn't done was break out of the cult singer/songwriter thing. I hadn't begun to get my records played on the radio, and I was still on the folk page in *Melody Maker*. I physically had to do something outside of what I was doing and the only thing I could think of was to form a band."

Throughout 1972 Al ran around London telling everyone who interviewed him that the next album wouldn't be one of love songs, it would be.... "historical". Al was at pains to explain how the only other interest he had was history. "At the back of my mind was 'Manuscript'. I thought 'Wouldn't it be lovely to have a *whole album* of 'Manuscript'. Then I wouldn't be forever the John Dowland of my age, wandering like the dong with the luminous nose, in search of his jumbly girl. It was getting out of hand!"

He told Jerry Gilbert – "I feel first of all that the best is still to come – I have to believe that otherwise I'd stop. I feel I've suddenly become a hard-liner about what I want to do. You see I've always felt that there's only one thing important to me and that's originality, and if you combine originality with simplicity than that equates to genius. I'm forced to admit, looking at the songs on the four albums that I've made, that all of them have been different but not different enough, not totally different."

Al had clearly already given some serious thought to the subject matter of the next album. This was hardly surprising as the intense nature of *Orange* had very definitely taken its toll as his friends could testify. The foundations for *Past, Present And Future*, his breakthrough album, were clearly being laid at this time. He spoke of recording an album that would be "radically different from anything I've done which makes it the most exciting thing ever from my point of view".

To the casual observer of his career this was a complete departure from his work to date. He continued – "You see I've always been fascinated by history in terms of people's lives, the way they lived, what they did with their lives, how they lived against the pressures of their day and their age, and I think I can make songs three-dimensional where up until now they've been two-dimensional: you had the words and you had the music. Almost like a book which is one-dimensional and writers like Leonard Cohen add music and make it two-dimensional, and I want to add the time element and make it three-dimensional."

He then sought to justify, anticipating the flak that would come his way, his own candidacy for the job – "I don't think anyone can do it better than me because nobody's got my background. All that time when I was left on my own I did nothing but read history books and I really do know the 20th century."

The details of this future project that he shared with Gilbert are fascinating especially when set against how the project actually finished up.

"I want to do a concept album using each track as a different decade of the 20th century – and that gives you eight separate decades of this century. I want to call it something like *Pieces Of The 20th Century* because they are just little fragments that are left on the trail… Little glimpses of the 20th century, only not on a huge scale, just from individual small lives of people like Somerset Maugham with his *Three Fat Ladies Of Verona* in 1934 – it's a period piece, it's perfect, it's exact.

"This will never be in the foreground, but that gives you a whole sense of pace. I want to live in all those decades and bring them to life, rub the dust off them and make them real and this will probably freak CBS out because they won't understand it.

"You see I've stopped thinking about hype and I believe that the only way I could be successful and the only way I want to be successful is if I did something so good it had to be successful. I'm going to take something that I really know and have a long look at it, and I'm going to turn out maybe eight songs that for me are going to be the best ones I've ever written."

This underscores the fact that Al was making a deliberate attempt at making a successful album. In later interviews he has suggested that he did not expect the album to sell very well but this was clearly his plan all along.

Carl Fisher, who up until now, had been acting as Al's *de facto* tour manager on just his occasional Danish dates, now took to spending a great deal of time with Al in the UK, something that would come to cause some friction in the Belsize household of Al and Bena.

The conflict that was in play between Bena and Carl Fisher was in stark contrast to the affection that she felt for another member of their circle; Francis Monkman of Curved Air.

Bena – "Francis would come around to the house every day for lunch. In many ways he had a truly calming influence on Al and I in that he was a very spiritual guy. When it came to *Past, Present And Future* he was also a great help musically because of his classical training. Al couldn't read music and so when it came to recording it was a bit of a problem because he'd have to get someone else to write out his scores for him. Although he had a wonderful ear for what instrument would sound good where. I can still picture him back in the studio for *PP&F* doing exactly that."

Al continued to compose songs throughout the Autumn for what was a planned return to the studio in the month before Christmas. On October 8th Al sang on the BBC's *Sounds On Sunday* performing "Amsterdam", "I'm Falling", "Clifton in the Rain", "Electric Los Angeles Sunset", "A Small Fruit Song" and a version of a work in progress piece, "Nostradamus". This shows just how long Al sometimes worked on his compositions. He'd performed a prototype of the song in question, which would appear on his next album, as far back as January 1970 at London's Queen Elizabeth Hall but here he was still tinkering with it.

It's clear that the work needed in preparing the songs for the next album was taking its toll on Al. He may very well have enjoyed the research but the effort needed to turn it into finished songs was a discipline new to him. He may very well have joked in years to come that he "just put the words of Nostrodamus into a song" but that was not quite how it appeared to those around him at this time. However Al and Bena enjoyed a very comfortable lifestyle at home in North London with musician friends popping in, writing songs, going to movies and out to dinner.

But this all came at a price. The combination of Al entering what became an almost manic period of inspired writing along with his uncertainty about commitment often left Bena feeling isolated. Another factor was Carl Fisher, who had by now moved in to their guest room as a lodger. Ultimately Al interceded and Carl returned to Copenhagen in mid November.

The following day Al went to Gloucester for a week, returning in time for a gig in Liverpool on 16th and on November 20th he went to the States.

Bena – "These were difficult times and it was, I suppose, like the Mandi situation in that if you had a relationship with Al he still had to be free, but that didn't apply to me of course! Whilst Al was away I got so low that I caught pneumonia and pleurisy because I wasn't looking after myself."

On December 17th Al went into the studio to record *Past Present And Future* and on the same day wrote "Post World War Two Blues".

Al's mews house, The Belsize Tavern, the local greengrocer, Oddbins and Conrad's Bistro (with the smaller Witches Cauldron in the basement) were all within about 50 yards of one another in that area of the village. A little further down the street was the local café and just beyond that around the bend was Dave and Jilly Dyke's house and so in many ways Al had all his creature comforts close at hand.

Jilly Dyke – "Oddbins was in fact the most tiny of places. I remember that it had all these baskets of wine bottles scattered around the shop floor and it was a revelation to us all when we discovered that they had all these obscure wines. It has to be said that that particular branch was exceptional and all of a sudden it became somewhere where Al would begin to spend a great deal of time! We all thought that we lived up in this little North London backwater where nothing much happened and then suddenly there was this wonderful little shop literally on our doorstep."

Al would still perform occasionally at secret gigs with friends where he could try out his new material for the first time in a low-key way.

Dave Dyke – "Al and I would sometimes perform together as a duo at my gigs. Now at these I would just introduce him as my accompanist but the audience would pretty soon rumble who he was and he would do some songs of his own, which suited everyone just fine."

Bena again – "The first gig that I had seen after we'd met, was at Drury Lane, when I realised that he had quite an audience and there he was just sat on the stool on his own in the middle of the stage. This was a million miles away from the shows for *PP&F* with the band, a huge PA and the back-projection of those Russian tanks behind them all. All of this success hadn't, I would say, gone to his head because he was just as arrogant, single-minded and self-possessed when he'd been playing the folk clubs and university circuit as when he was playing these vast gigs in 1973! Obviously he had to be a bit more careful and began to get a little more nervous and did start creating more of a build-up before the gig with various little routines."

It was now, in the winter of 1972 that Al first met Abi Kremer who was destined to play an important role in his life from here on in. She first saw Al at University College London.

Abi – "I was taken along to this show of Al's, never having even heard of him before, which was absolutely wonderful! So much so that a short while later I received *Zero She Flies* from my parents as a 16th birthday present. I must have somehow anticipated how much this day would come to mean to me because I burst into tears during the evening for what appeared to be no reason at all. It was definitely fate that I should meet Al at this time."

And so it would prove to be when Abi eventually met and married Jonny Kremer.

Dave Dyke – "At this time sometimes those evenings at the bistro went on into the wee small hours. I remember one evening downstairs at The Witches Cauldron with Al, Tim Renwick and Francis Monkman that ended up with an impromptu jam session. It was that night that the Australian parody of 'Roads To Moscow' was born when the evening had basically degenerated into a bit of a shambles. It turned into 'Roads to Adelaide'."

Living with Al, Bena was able to see first hand the gradual process whereby Al did the research for what would become *Past, Present And Future*. It wasn't quite the studious days spent at the Imperial War Museum that some would imagine!

Bena again – "It most certainly was not! Al would always watch documentaries on WW2 throughout our relationship and it was clearly not something that he'd just taken up as an interest for the album. Certainly he'd always be reading history books at home and I think that he had a genuine interest in history. Al wasn't really into material possessions and that included books so the house wasn't full of books, we just had what we had recently bought. As far as I know he didn't belong to a library. He'd just go into town and buy books as and when. I never got the impression that Al had consciously elected to change his style and write about history and it appeared to me, right there at the time, that it was just a subject that he had a great interest in."

Bena – "Regarding 'Nostradamus', I was with Al when we visited Erika Cheetham at her house. The composition of 'Old Admirals' I remember very well, especially the line 'sands run through the hour glass each day more rapidly'. 'Soho, Needless To Say' also was one both for the amazing lyrics and the fast guitar work that I can remember clearly, I remember Al being especially proud of that one too when he finished it at the house. These were fun times you know for us all."

1973 kicked off with another short series of dates for Al in Denmark. These shows, which included a gig in Aarhus on March 28th, continued to feature tracks from *Orange* ("Electric Los Angeles Sunset", "I'm Falling" and "Amsterdam") and cover versions of Chuck Berry's "Memphis Tennessee" and Bob Dylan's "One Too Many Mornings".

In the early spring of 1973 Al toured the East Coast of America with no record company support. He had been under the mistaken impression that *Orange* had been released there. It hadn't. It was proving impossible to get going in the States.

Upon his return he was a guest on John Peel's *Top Gear*, performing "Electric Los Angeles Sunset", "Once An Orange Always An Orange", "Post World War Two Blues" and also "Nostradamus". He then embarked on a short British tour that included a gig at the Central London Polytechnic.

It was here that he had one of the seminal meetings of minds of his career.

Between his two solo sets, backstage at the Poly, he first met the enigmatic Luke

all pics: Jill Furmanovsky

Al singing "Roads To Moscow", 1973.

O'Reilly. Luke was there to record the gig for his company *Radio Concerts International*.

Julia Creasey had already given Al notice that by 1974 she wanted to give up management. Luke's arrival at Al's London show could not therefore have been timelier.

Luke – "I think that the gig at Central London Polytechnic Canteen was at 7 or 8 o'clock, something like that and I must have come back to the theatre about 7 or 7.30, just in time to put in a nice appearance and I'm coming around the one-way system there and I see this long line of people which is surprising to say the least because I'm not even outside the front of the building yet, I'm still down the side. I see that the line is mostly good looking girls with pale faces and long hair, not exactly hippyish but certainly the style of the time and I thought to myself 'wow, this is cool, I wonder who this is for?' and so I drive around the front and they're all going into this Al Stewart gig! So I continue around the back, say 'hello' to the technician, walk into the building and the place is already packed."

In the two months that he had been in England up to that point, Luke had seen nothing like this and it made a lasting impression on him.

Luke – "A lasting impression indeed. People were usually reserved in the UK compared to the US and here I was and I couldn't even move around in the hall. I had to go all of the way around the building to get to the backstage area. So showtime comes and as I'm walking around the back as does Miles (Luke had a business partnership with Miles Copeland at this time) and then this guy with a beat-up old Ephiphone Texan, this skinny little runt walks on stage, sits on a stool and captures the audience in the palm of his hand like nothing I'd ever seen in my life! With most artists you're embarrassed when they speak between songs. The overwhelming majority can only manage 'How ya' doin' London?' and to be honest you just wish that they'd shut up, but with Al that night in London he was a total entertainer, I just couldn't believe it. And as I said, Miles came in a couple of songs into Al's set and as Al finished a particular song the audience went crazy and then quietened to listen to Al's next song intro. At that moment Miles turns to me and says 'Hey, not bad huh?' and there and then about two dozen rows of the audience turn around to us and go 'shhhh …!'"

Luke was even more impressed with Al than Miles that first evening. At this time it was still early days in the relationship between the two.

Luke – "Miles had never even heard of Al Stewart before then, having travelled from Beirut to Birmingham, Alabama and University, arriving ultimately in London. I'd met Miles because when I'd been working in Philadelphia as a disc jockey I'd played a lot of Wishbone Ash who were one of Miles' acts and we'd all hung out together at gigs."

Back in London a few months later, teaching dry ski-slope skiing at Lords Cricket Ground, Luke had rung up Wishbone Ash's office and had re-established the relationship with Miles that led to the two working on Radio Concerts International projects together.

Luke again – "Halfway through the gig Al had a break and I ran around to see if there was anything I could get him, I think he was drinking cherry brandy at the time, then he goes back in to do the second half of his show. At the end of the concert we sat down and started talking and we find out straight away that we have a great deal in common. I told him that I couldn't believe why someone of his quality doesn't have their records out in America and his reply was that 'If you can get my records released in America you can manage me!' So that's quite literally how it started. I then went back to America. You see I wanted to be a star's manager and Al wanted to be a star."

That last line is something that Luke told people for years to come about that very first meeting with Al. Up until that time Luke hadn't really, if the truth be told, decided what it was he wanted to do.

Luke – "Al and I just sat around in the bar that night and discovered that we both had a lot in common which was something that hadn't happened when I'd met artists previously. I actually liked this guy, he had something to say, we'd come from very similar backgrounds. My father had died when I was one, we both had the same social history, we'd each been to boarding school and so I was somewhat sympathetic to him. I liked his music. But I didn't leave the building that night thinking 'I'm going to manage Al Stewart' and I didn't because it was somewhat left up in the air because I was due to go to America to tour-manage Miles' group The Climax Blues Band and I said to Al 'I'll take your album out with me and we'll see what we can do with it'."

So Luke took the album along with him to the States but couldn't at first get anyone to listen to the recording. It is important to note here that he had only the bare bones of an agreement with Al at this time and was in every respect being driven by pure instinct.

Luke – "But I had this friend, Alan Mason, who had been FM promotions man for A&M and when he'd been out in Philadelphia I'd met him one day when he'd come by the radio station WMMR. More than most promotions men, he was very good. He got you interested and because we all liked him so much we used to play his bands as much as we could on the air. We used to actually think, 'Oh, let's play one of Alan's bands'. So I met up with Alan whilst I was out there with The Climax Blues Band and he was just about to begin negotiations with this tape company GRT who had bought Chess Records."

GRT had been the tape duplication company for ABC Records. They had however been forced to diversify when, with the cost of mass tape duplication machines falling, it looked very much like their clients ABC would soon be doing the job for themselves.

Luke again – "Chess at the time were being run by Marvin Schlacter and Stan Hoffman and essentially what had happened was that this company GRT had gone out and got some advice from an independent consultancy which told them that if they didn't do something within two years then they would be out of business because their only income was from licences to tape copy for ABC records. Now ABC at the time was quite big and in two years they were not expected to renew the contract because machines were now cheap and it would be worth their while to go out and invest in their own to do the job themselves. So this modern American company had gone out and bought Chess Records which was struggling to match its glory days of the '50s. They had the Chess catalogue and they had their own contemporary label called Janus that had acts such as Ray Stevens (of 'The Streak' fame). But these were two old music business guys who were used to just selling singles. You know: 'when you make a few bucks off a single, add to your house because they can't take that off you!' And so they had been bought out by GRT who proceeded to open an LA office for Janus Records, hiring Alan Mason as their head of A&R."

With a new label to sign bands to, Alan Mason was in the right place at the right time to help Luke out with his new venture. It only took a couple of meetings and a deal was struck. Luke had conjured a record deal for Al out of nowhere.

Luke – "And they signed us! We did this deal, we couldn't get much money so I did a deal where I think they gave us a $20,000 advance and about another $20,000 tour support. Whatever they didn't spend on us in tour support had to come back to us in cash. Now this had the advantage that we owed 50 per cent of that to CBS, so when we got the release from them it gave Al and myself $10,000 to split, which we did. Now this had all happened over that summer when I'd come out with The Climax Blues Band in May 1973 and met with Alan Mason."

Meanwhile, oblivious to all this good news, Al was away on a short Dutch tour.

Alan Mason and Ed De Joy had met when they were both working for A&M Records. When Stan Hoffman offered Ed a position on the West Coast with Chess Janus, he took Alan with him.

The motivation behind Ed De Joy bringing Alan Mason with him out to Los Angeles was to tap into his promotion and A&R skills that would enable them to find and hopefully break some new acts for their new employers. This was a great and fortuitous move for Alan Mason who was in fact unemployed at the time having already quit A&M. He had forged a strong friendship with Ed De Joy, besides a successful working relationship. Two Baltimore guys moving out west to save a record company – who could resist?

Ed De Joy – "This was all absolutely wonderful of course as it was Alan Mason that first turned me on to Al Stewart. It's as simple as that."

Ed De Joy had wanted to get away from promotions and into signing artists for a long time. The main enticement for him to go and work for Chess Janus was Stan Hoffman who had been the general manager of the record distributor that Ed had worked for when he first started out in the music business back in Baltimore.

Ed De Joy – "The idea was that they very much wanted to build up his pop division because it had somewhat lost its way. Alan had already talked to me about signing Al Stewart and once won over, I spoke to Stan and Marvin about him too! I remember being very impressed by the rough mixes of what was to become *Past, Present And Future* that Luke brought for us to hear in 1973. So I did some research about his back catalogue because at this time he was really signed to Columbia Records. But we managed to get a release for the USA and Canada and signed a very simple deal for just one album with future options."

Back in England these would turn out to be the last days of the Al and Julia partnership and as such it was proving difficult for both of them.

It was at this time that Luke now returned from the States. True to his word he had already achieved more in a few short weeks that anyone had before. However the initial greeting that he received from Al took him by surprise.

Luke – "I came back to England and called Al up and he said 'Don't ever go away that long without calling me again!' to which I replied, ' Well you knew where I was going and anyway I have some good news. I think I've got an American release for you, it's not the best label in the world, it's the smallest possibly, but it's a release.'"

While Luke had been away in the States Al had been putting the finishing touches to *Past, Present And Future* and so he now invited Luke over to the house in Belsize Village to talk over a number of points. This would prove to be a key meeting for them both.

Luke – "Al had a number of things on his mind that day. He said, 'Look, I've got what I think is my best album ever. I've supposedly got a tour set up with the Derek Block Agency and I've got some problems.' Derek Block had just rung up and said that there was a chance he was going to cancel the tour because Julia was never in her office on a Monday and he felt that she was only working part time."

The prospect of the tour being cancelled was a source of genuine concern to Al. It is important to take stock here of where exactly he stood at that particular moment. With four albums behind him and a career that had, in his own words "plateaued", it was vital that he gave *Past, Present And Future* his very best shot. For Derek Block to carry out his threat and cancel the tour would have presented Al with real problems that he could do without. The time was right for Luke to formally approach Julia Creasey about the plans that he and Al had been discussing.

Luke – "So I went to see Julia and she very generously backed down because she presumably could see that we were going pretty high power on all of this. Actually there were discussions to make her a part of it but ultimately it wasn't appropriate and Al and Julia parted company but on the very best of terms."

Julia now formally handed over the reins to Luke during an amicable meeting at her office. She had worked very hard on Al's behalf over the previous seven years and the legacy of the decent and caring manner in which she did that job was a seamless passing of the torch now to Luke.

The bravado that Luke had shown in his offer to manage Al several months before was somewhat at odds however with the way that he was really feeling the night that he went up to Al's house in Belsize Park to discuss the nuts and bolts of his future involvement with Al.

Luke – "It was a million miles away from how I was actually feeling on my way up there. When I arrived Al was there with Bena and Dave Dyke. They all ate this wonderful beef stroganoff that Bena had prepared for dinner but I was too nervous to eat anything at this stage! We hadn't actually agreed for sure how we were going to work with one another and so I was pretty much on tenterhooks that night!"

So much so in fact, that Luke wasn't to finally make up his mind for another couple of days. When he did say yes he and Al went out for a walk, and during that afternoon Al made a point of telling Luke that the one thing he valued above all others in a relationship was loyalty. It was a simple enough request and saw the genesis of what would become Kinetic, the company that Luke would form to handle Al and Al alone; at least that was the idea back then.

Bena Nicolson remembers that first meeting clearly – "At the end of that evening when I first met Luke and we all had dinner together, Al had asked me what I thought of it all and I told him that I thought it was just fantastic. In Luke Al had found someone that was very centred with a tremendous amount of energy and drive and that was exactly what Al needed. We'd often talked about the situation with CBS in America and his frustration that nobody over there would allow him a look-in. Even on his trips over there they'd make half-hearted promises to him, patronising him really and then nothing would happen and here at last was someone that really looked like they could do something for him over there. Al had this persona that he'd created and was very single minded about what he was going to do with his life. I think that he created this persona back at Wycliffe and the reason that it was created was that he was a bit of an outcast, he didn't have the same amount of money as the other boys at the school, he wanted to play the guitar and that had been declared 'immoral', he was skinny, he didn't like games and it was very tough. But unfortunately this persona was not very user-friendly to other people. Luke's arrival definitely helped with all of this."

These were clearly testing times for Al as he came to terms with the transition from being under the care and protection of the mild-mannered Julia to that of the less restrained Luke.

When Luke arrived on the scene one of the biggest hurdles Al had to overcome was that he wasn't used to have things arranged for him. He also had to come to terms with the fact that he wouldn't always be in on the planning stages of things.

Bena – "Luke was always having to say – 'Al, I'm your manager. Trust me. This is what you're paying me for. Don't tie my hands and stop me from doing my job.' Al had got himself into this almost laid-back attitude to his career and suddenly here was Luke planning things and he had this busy schedule that meant he was going to have to get out of bed and get on the road and work and work. With the arrival of Luke he immediately had a great deal more work which was exactly what he needed to give him a leg up in his career. Those last years with Julia were a very sleepy period and she wasn't pushing him enough."

Luke – "Before WMMR I was at one of the Ivy League colleges, Dartmouth in the North East, and I got there quite frankly because I was an Olympic skier. Although they don't have sports scholarships in the Ivy League they gave me one because when I went in for my interview I was wearing my Olympic tie and a blazer with a Gold Olympic badge on with the British Flag from the British Snow Ski team. They took me on immediately. I'd been in the '68 Olympic team in Grenoble and at college I'd always thought radio was fun."

Luke had listened to Radio City in London, which would broadcast from the Thames Estuary. They used to have a *5 By 4 Club* at 4 o'clock every evening on which they'd play music by the Beatles and Rolling Stones that Luke loved.

Luke – "So I'm here at college in Dartmouth talking to this guy one day after class and he says 'Sorry, I've got to go to read the news on the radio!' and I said 'Wow, you can do that sort of thing here?' And he replies 'Yes. It's student owned and run!'"

However when Luke went down to the station he found it to be very conservative, bound up in playing '50s and '60s oldies.

Luke – "I wanted to be a DJ but they wouldn't give me a show; they kept giving me overnights. In the Fall of 1970 I came back early to Dartmouth from summer vacation, the college radio station had been on the air all Summer with a skeleton staff and when I asked if I could do some shows for them they said 'Yes'. I just played what I wanted and one evening I was on the air and unbeknown to me all of the student directors of this radio station were downstairs when I gave out the station's telephone number on air rather than the studio's number."

With the switchboard downstairs jammed those directors rushed upstairs to Luke and offered him the job on the spot! Luke continued there and then a few months later read an article on a radio station in Philadelphia that was doing really well. He started thinking about a move.

Luke – "My girlfriend lived down there and so I thought that I'd send them a tape, not expecting to get an answer, but I was working there within a month. So I was still at university writing my thesis. At 9 o'clock when the library opened I'd be there at the front door, would stay there till 4 o'clock in the evening, then I'd go to work at WMMR. It was here that a fellow DJ – Michael Tierson, introduced me to Al's music."

Luke soon grew tired of being stuck in the studio, which led to him taking that sabbatical teaching skiing back in England on the Lords dry ski-slope.

Upon his return from his trip to America with The Climax Blues Band Luke went around to Miles Copeland's offices in North London to get his thoughts on what he had negotiated for Al with Janus. It was a time that he needed the help and clear advice of Miles more than ever. He also needed an office.

Luke – "That's true! So I got back from getting this deal with Alan Mason and went to Miles and said 'I might be an artist's manager, I've got a client here and I think he's great, will you help?' This was because I wasn't really in the business and if you're going to be in the business you need some help. Whilst I didn't exactly need monetary support I certainly needed somewhere to hang my hat. Previously it had been me that had introduced Miles to The Climax Blues Band, he'd got to manage them and then he'd hired me to look after them for the first couple of months of their life with him. So I had had some experience and we're now in July 1973 and Al wants me to manage him and he gives me the tape of *Past Present And Future*. I'm staying at Miles' place just around the corner from Abbey Road Studios at the time and I took the tape back there and played it and realised how good it was. It was different, it had a unique sound and the tunes were great and so I got back to Al, we agreed a deal and I started to work things out."

The first thing that Luke did was to schedule a meeting with CBS in London.

Luke again – "Now that was a can of worms if ever I'd seen one! But I didn't really care because I was 24 years of age and I didn't understand the meaning of 'No?' I thought Al Stewart was a hit and if you happened not to agree with me then you just had no taste whatsoever! Now I wouldn't be as arrogant as that today but I was at the time and it just became my thing."

Luke now set about holding a series of business meetings with the same executives that had previously dealt with Julia Creasey. The contrast between the mild-mannered Julia and Luke, in the first days of his representation of Al, must have taken their breath away.

Luke – "At the first of these I was dragged in by one of the business affairs people who said 'Well if you're the new manager then you'd better come down to see us and we'll have a talk'. So he gets me in and then starts lecturing me about money and how they weren't prepared to be treated the way that they'd been treated by Al on the last album and I said 'Well, what exactly do you mean?' to which they replied 'On the last album we agreed to pay so much and Al would run up that bill and then we'd have to pay more and we're spending more on production than we're getting back in sales so how the hell are we expected to make any money?'"

By now in the conversation Luke, running purely on instinct as usual, had elected to up the ante and go for the jugular.

Luke – "So I replied, which was something far-reaching for me to say to them in my first conversation with them, 'Look you guys make more in your back pockets long before you account to the artist for a penny and you know it. By the time the artist has broken even you guys are rich!' So he was somewhat taken aback by that and I then said 'On the other hand I'm surprised that he only spent £12,000' or whatever it was on the album because 'it's worth every penny and I'm frankly surprised he didn't spend more because it's going to be a huge album.' The guy there at CBS said 'What do you mean? The last album only sold 14,000 copies, as did the one before' and he showed me all of the figures to prove his point and I said 'Sure, but they weren't as good as this one.' He went on and on with 'But even with *Love Chronicles* we only just came into profit' to which I replied 'Well, as I said, they weren't as good as this one!'".

Luke then dropped the bombshell news that he had a US record company willing and able to put out *Past, Present And Future*. He asked the CBS executives to sign a release there and then allowing this to happen.

Luke again – "At which point they went all topsy turvy because that was something that they hadn't seen coming! But we got the release from them."

Through all of this time Abi Kremer had continued to go to Al's shows

Abi Kremer – "Throughout all this time I was completing my 'A'-levels at South Hampstead High School for Girls, which was, although of course I didn't know it at the time, just around the corner from where Al lived. It was now that I started taking people to Al's gigs myself. I would buy the *Melody Maker*, see where Al was playing and then go out and get tickets! The first of these was at St Mary's College in Hampstead in the early Summer of 1973 where I spoke to Al for the first time during the interval of his gig. A short while later I was walking through Belsize Village, on my way back from doing some voluntary work for an organisation called Task Force at an old lady's house in Fitzroy Avenue when I literally bumped into Al by the entrance to his mews. It was really lovely because he remembered me from the gig and invited me in for a cup of coffee. I remember that I'd just returned from a short trip to the Middle East and we had a long chat whilst we pored over the maps that I had with me."

Al proceeded to invite Abi out for dinner the following week to meet his friend (and Abi's future husband) Jonny Kremer. The invitation wasn't quite as simple as that however.

Abi once again – "The only stipulation was that I was also to bring along a friend that was to look like Barbarella as a blind date for him! This I tried to do but in the end I turned up on my own for the date. Needless to say we all had a lovely evening, I mean Jonny and I ended up getting married which just goes to show how right Al was about all this! One thing in particular that I remember about that first meeting with Jonny at Al's house was that Al played The Incredible String Band's 'The First Girl I Loved' to us which was wonderful."

This was very much a time of transition in Al's life too. In Luke he had found someone who was determined to move things up a gear and make changes that, initially at least, Al would have trouble coming to terms with. The very fact that these changes were largely forced upon him continued to occasionally undermine Al's total faith in the new direction his life had recently taken and of course he could have had no idea that he was about to enter one of the key periods of his career.

BAND ON THE RUN

In which Al writes his masterpiece Modern Times and the breakthrough album Year Of The Cat.
He moves to Los Angeles.

Now, with Luke onboard things really got moving. It was September 1973 and Luke had been working hard on the tour's preparation for over a month. It had been a period in which he had taken himself on a crash course in artist management too.

Luke – "I'm in charge now and we go out on the tour for which most of the dates had already been booked by Julia Creasey. At the time I was sharing an apartment with Miles' brother Ian at 87A Reddington Road where a lot of hard partying and good times were had by all! So Ian had been very busy every day with hundreds of acts that he'd book out for 50 bucks or whatever and I was sharing this place with him whilst he was working flat out and I was sat around feeling frustrated. Ian would get back to the flat in the evening and I would start in saying 'Well this is all great but what about Al?' Now this is how we started out and I managed to convince Al that I was right in my opinion that if he wanted to get anywhere with all of this then we were going to have to put a band together because the album that he had was too good to be played on just an acoustic guitar."

If Al had hoped that the timely arrival of Luke would somehow preclude the need for him to ever worry about touring with a band again then he was very wrong. The tour kicked off however with solo gigs in Cardiff and Aberystwyth Universities on October 11th and 12th before a concert in Southampton on the 13th.

Luke – "I was still living with Ian as Al, even when he was touring, couldn't give me enough to keep me occupied 24 hours a day and so I started hassling Ian for work and I managed to persuade Al that we should at least try having a band. Now he didn't want to do this really because he said he'd tried it and had found that working with other musicians was fraught with problems and that he'd found it difficult to say the least and as experience proved I ended up agreeing with him!"

Meanwhile *PP&F* had been released. The level of support that Al at once received from Janus was far in excess of anything he had experienced before with his British record company. Al played 35 shows on that tour including gigs in Ireland and concerts at The Brighton Dome, Newcastle City Hall and three performances in Bristol where he was still as popular as ever.

Al – "I now played a show at Manchester Free Trade Hall with Canton Trig on November 26th and that was the first time I met Alan Mason. He flew over from America just to see us. Things seemed to be happening at last. I could see, even then, that perhaps I had at last turned a corner with regard to having some sort of a career in the States."

Al had not anticipated any substantial commercial success with *PP&F* but it instantly became his best-selling work up to that point. "Nostradamus" and "Roads To Moscow" became his most requested songs and it gave his public profile a shot in the arm when it needed it most. "A quantum leap" was Al's appraisal of its achievements. It opened the doors that took him from the colleges to the concert halls in 1973.

He had seemingly invented historical folk-rock overnight and at 28 was at last a star.

As was his good friend Sandy Denny. On September 3rd 1973 Al went down to The Howff in Primrose Hill to see Sandy perform a one-off solo show at Roy Guest's club. It was over a year since he had last seen Sandy and what he saw just before she was due to go on stage shocked him.

Al – "It had been a while since I had seen her perform and I was shocked by her stage fright before the show. She was totally paranoid about going out and singing. She didn't want to go out there at all and she'd never been like that with Fairport and so it came as a shock for me to see her that shaky. It was upsetting. However once she got out there she was her normal magical self, just as if what I had seen before the gig had never happened."

The music press that Al had courted so adroitly during his tenure as Bedsitterland's favourite son were now beating a path to the door of a member of the "musical literati" and his casual mentions of Camus, Sartre or Peake made him a unique interviewee. The column inches he now generated were vast. People began to listen to what he had to say.

Throughout these interviews and reviews Al's made the point on a number of occasions that the highest compliment that you could bestow upon the new album would be to say that it had a '60s feel. He spoke to the *New Musical Express* first of all.

Al – "But I don't know whether the teenagers of today will be able to relate to it all. I haven't a clue. Actually, of all the albums I've made and of all the songs that I've written, this is the one that I'm least worried about whether people relate to it or not, because it's from beginning to end something I'd always told you I was going to do, and I've done it, right?."

Besides "Old Admirals", which from the outset appeared to be Al's favourite track on the new album, he was often picking out "Terminal Eyes" for special attention.

Al – "The similarity to 'I Am the Walrus' was deliberate. I took the Walrus, he could've been anyone with long hair at UFO, anyone with a gold face or whatever and I've symbolised him as being the symbol of the Woodstock dream. My longhaired Walrus who went out and penned these songs. This is a serious song if you read the lyrics of it and it is the suicide song of the Walrus, hence the tempo and the rhythm and the feel of it."

The song was a million light years away from those on *Orange* and Al was very proud of his work.

The entire album was "serious". He dabbled in surrealism with "Post World War Two Blues". He called it his "photo-montage song", as it brings rock 'n' roll stars and politicians of his time together in a piece that sets out to be biographical. The songs on the album were also all contemporary, whether they were about a World War I Admiral, the massacre by Hitler of a Nazi leader and 2000 of his storm troopers in 1934, or the German drive into Russia in 1941. The only song that was exactly what it seemed to be about was "Roads to Moscow", for which Al read a reputed 40 books!

The *Future* part of the album was provided courtesy of Erika Cheetham. Her book on Nostradamus and her close collaboration with Al on the track were invaluable. In fact, it was Ms Cheetham's notes for her book that Al worked from, and this research was exhaustive. Did he really believe that a 16th century Frenchman knew about the EEC and that Israel was going to defeat the Arabs? "My impression is that it's fairly amazing", he said. "I think it's very possible" he told Karl Dallas.

CBS, now slightly more interested in Al's career than before, proceeded to host a bizarre lunch to announce the launch of *Past, Present And Future*.

Jerry Gilbert – "It was all very strange! While the assorted hacks tucked into their Italian fare Al stood at the head of the table explaining, track by track, the background, meaning and references to each song individually!"

Karl Dallas initially found the new role of Al as Professor difficult to accept and was someone who was yet to be won over.

Karl Dallas – "This was all new to me and I had known Al for a long time by now you must remember. Up until this point I'd always thought of Al as a very talented singer-songwriter who was basically writing very uninteresting songs. This changed for me when Al wrote and recorded *Past, Present And Future*."

And he wasn't alone. This was the album that broke Al on US FM radio courtesy of

"Roads To Moscow" and initiated a series of American Tours whose scope would, up until now, have been wholly unrealistic to undertake.

Luke – "We got crazy reports that that song was No. 1 in such and such a state" he told *Nuggets Magazine* in 1977.

Upon its release Al spoke to journalist, John Beattie about the new album and the single from it, which was "Terminal Eyes". In a piece in which he continued the deconstruction of the song's sources and inspiration, something that he had initiated at the album's launch, his debt to John Lennon was freely acknowledged.

Al – "I've taken the Walrus as a mythical figure to represent the movement of popular music in the late '60s. I'm basically involved in imagination which is the soul of creation and to me, this was quite an important time of original and good thinking … a lot of these people went on to drugs and failed to fulfil their potential and I saw the Walrus symbol as a movement to committing suicide. It's like the movement went into a high, lost its roots and withered."

It took someone of considerable character to stick to his guns with something he had faith in because the musical trends of the time had well and truly stacked the cards against him. Alice Cooper was hanging himself nightly across the world, Bowie was changing from Ziggy to Aladdin on a million bedroom walls, whilst historical folk-rock's First Sea Lord had charted a course that was totally at odds with what in 1973 was considered commercial. The album was apparently therefore something that could be only expected to, at best, sustain his hard-earned cult following in the UK.

Abi Kremer – "It was a fantastic album to see performed live, Al's delivery of the songs at those shows being very true to the versions on the album. And throughout all of this time I would go down to Bournemouth to visit Jonny and Al would often come along with me. These were lovely times and I can still remember many of the things that Al and I would talk about as we travelled down to Hampshire. It was a chance for each of us to learn much about the other and those trips formed the basis of why we're all still such close friends today."

These are Al's own notes on the album:

"'Old Admirals', that's my favourite on the album. I'd read an early two-volume biography about Admiral Sir John Fisher, titled *The Life Of Lord Fisher*, and the song traces his story.

He was Britain's First Sea Lord, the man most instrumental in bringing the Dreadnoughts prior to World War I and therefore responsible for the modern British Navy. He resigned in 1915 during World War I after a dispute with [Winston] Churchill, then First Lord of the Admiralty, over how the Admiralty was being run.

The story's poignancy comes in after Fisher's resignation. He knew more about the British Navy than anyone did. He was very headstrong, and no doubt suffered through his enforced retirement realising that he could have prosecuted the war more successfully than his successors. But he was never called back into service.

The line in the song – 'Old Admirals that feel the wind and never put to sea': I had this image that whenever a breeze lifted and blew across his veranda, Lord Fisher would be standing there looking out over the sea, wishing he were on deck once again. He was an exceptionally interesting guy and probably at least 20 years ahead of his time.

Warren Harding on the other hand was about 20 years behind. On the surface, it may sound odd to hear steel drums in a song about Harding, but keep in mind what he spent most of his time doing – boozing and gambling and hanging out with the press until all hours of the morning.

Harding certainly wasn't very much into the serious business of governing. Corruption was rampant during his administration. He probably would've been happier running a bar. His slogan may have been 'A Return to Normalcy', but the country got anything but with him. Harding was a man P.J. O'Rourke would call a 'Republican Party animal'. So this isn't a complex song, but the juxtaposition of the story and music was great fun.

Kim Dyer researched the facts behind the song for 'Chronicles' – 'Warren Harding was the 29th president of the United States. He was inaugurated on March 4, 1921.

Harding's administration was riddled with scandals. The conduct of several of his cabinet members brought considerable criticism against the president and the Republican Party.

The 'Teapot Dome Affair' was perhaps the most important scandal of Harding's administration. After jurisdiction over naval oil reserves was transferred to the Department of the Interior, Secretary Albert B. Fall leased Teapot Dome to oil interests in exchange for a bribe. He eventually spent time in a federal prison because of his actions. The incident also resulted in the resignation of Secretary of the Navy Edwin N. Denby, who had consented to the transfer of the reserves.

Attorney General Daugherty was charged with receiving payments from prohibition violators, and was forced to resign by Calvin Coolidge (Harding's successor).

Harding's wife, Florence Kling de Wolfe, was a powerful and controlling influence. A woman of wealth and influence, many believed that she forged Harding's political career. Their marriage was a stormy one, and Harding had several affairs. These included fathering a child by Nan Britton, a woman 30 years his junior.

In the summer of 1923 Harding was visiting Alaska when he received a coded message from Washington. The contents so distressed him that he collapsed. Corruption within his administration was far worse then he had thought, and he planned an immediate return to Washington. When he reached San Francisco, however, he became gravely ill.

Harding died on August 2, 1923. The official cause of death was listed as a stroke. Some doctors felt that a more likely cause was a heart attack. Some people believed that Harding's wife had finally become fed up with his affairs, and poisoned him because the scandal was coming to the surface. The fact that Mrs Harding refused to allow an autopsy, and would not permit a death mask to be made, gave fuel to these rumours.'

Al – "'Soho (Needless To Say)' is about the mid-1960s, during my early days, when I spent a while living and playing in Soho. I was doing Bunjie's Coffee Bar from 7 to 10 on a Friday night, then running to play the all-nighter at Les Cousins from midnight to 6 in the morning, and again on Saturday from midnight to 7. So there was a period when I rarely saw daylight during the winter.

In the song there's a kaleidoscope of crazy people who were around Soho at the time. 'Going nowhere with nowhere to go' – much of the time it did feel that way. But the mid-'60s has been fascinating.

Soho is something of a throwback to the style of my first four albums, in the sense that it's not an historic epic. I just thought it was written a lot better than the earlier songs. It has precedents in, shall we say, 'Old Compton Street Blues', but is a lot better written. Four years earlier, I'd never have been able to write, 'Rainstorm, brainstorm, faces in the maelstrom/huddled by the puddles in the shadows where the drains run'.

'The Last Day Of June 1934' – I'm comparing the peacefulness and frivolity of England and Europe with the rearmament of Germany after World War I. June 30 1934 was one of the history's longest, darkest nights. The elimination of Ernst Roehm (as a potential adversary) basically gave Hitler free rein to do what he wanted in Germany. And to a lesser extent, the song's about the execution of Gregor Strasser, another of Hitler's chief rivals within the Nazi party, on the same night (leaving Hitler in total control).

'Post World War Two Blues' – since it came after Don McLean's 'American Pie' and has B.J. Cole's steel guitar on it, this was called 'English Pie' by some wags in England. Others have referred to it as a 'Country Blues for British Baby Boomers'.

There are tons of people in here, some of whom may be familiar to Americans, some not. There's Bevan, the Welsh Labour leader who brought in the National Health Service. *Life With The Lyons* was a popular radio show. There's Churchill and Lord

Mountbatten and (Prime Minister Harold) Macmillan. There's the Suez Canal, Buddy Holly, *TW3* (*That Was The Week That Was* starring David Frost), and the scandalous Christine Keeler. 'Ramona' and 'Desolation Row' were Bob Dylan songs – he was obviously a big early influence. And on it goes.

By the way, 'Post World War Two Blues' is the only song I've ever written in my sleep. I woke up about 7 o'clock one morning with the chorus in my head. I'd actually been singing it in my sleep. So I got up, wrote the chorus down, went back to bed, and wrote the rest of it later that morning.

'Roads to Moscow' – The idea had been bowling around in my head for something like four years. I'd been reading an endless series of Russian history books. General Guderian turns up in one line in this – I read his biography, Panzer Leader. Amazing book. I'd read William Shirer, Alexander Werth's *History of Russia At War, 1941-45*, Solzhenitsyn, Koestler, Chukovskaya … just endless. The influence of all of them is in there somewhere, but probably more Solzhenitsyn than anything else. Being packed off to the Siberian labour camp – most of that comes from *One Day In The Life of Ivan Denisovitch*.

The song is more specifically about Hitler double-crossing his ally Stalin and invading Russia on June 22 1941. Volumes have been written about this, but the Germans were supposed to have attacked on May 15. Had they not got distracted on another front, in Greece, history might've turned out far differently. When the Germans turned around and headed for Moscow in October, they ended up caught by winter, and freezing in the snow. They didn't stand a chance. By Christmas, the Russians had stopped the Germans, and even pushed them back.

There are different sections to the song's arrangement because I wanted the song to ebb and flow, for dramatic effect. Pete Berryman actually calls this one my 'Cecil B. DeMille thing'.

The rather abrupt cross-fade at the beginning wasn't John Anthony's fault. For some reason, he wasn't there when I was mixing this. We had two different introductions and I wanted to use both, so I went from one to the other in a cross-fade which, in retrospect, I didn't do very well.

'Terminal Eyes' – My Beatles thing, circa 1972. But this is my rewrite of Lennon's 'I Am The Walrus' – stream-of-consciousness nonsense with some fun words.

'Nostradamus' – The seed was planted as far back as September or October 1969, when I read a magazine article on Nostradamus, the 16th century prophet and seer, by Erika Cheetham. It was very well written, and caught my imagination."

Al elected to go and find out as much information as he could from Ms Cheetham and this had all by now turned into something of a campaign for him. Up until this point in time he had relied on his own experiences and that perceived role of '"voyeur" to inform his songs. Even "Manuscript" had been viewed from the perspective of his grandmother with a coda featuring Mandi. But now he was using a more clearly defined set of research notes that were not his own. To go for broke and attempt to legitimise his writing in this way was a brave thing indeed.

Al – "Through the magazine, I was fortunate enough to get hold of Erika a few years later. She was then working on her first book, *The Prophecies of Nostradamus* [1973]. She's since written two others *The Further Prophecies Of Nostradamus* (1985) and *The Final Prophecies Of Nostradamus* (1989). When I went round to her place, Erika had her notes spread all over a table. I asked her to tell me what Nostradamus' most interesting predictions were, then I put them into the song, so it pretty much follows the storyline of her first book. She also was kind enough to write a note for the record sleeve."

Al has always remained ambivalent about the *merits* of the Nostrodamus prophecies:

"I must say, though, that I've always been, and still am, completely noncommittal about the whole Nostradamus thing. I neither believe nor disbelieve. I have no idea if any of it is true, or if it's all wishful thinking. I've never known. But I do know that, at the very least, it made a terrific idea for a song. 'Nostradamus' has indeed caused its share of consternation over the years. One Nostradamus freak thought I'd reincarnated him from the dead. Another person wrote me a very nice letter saying that he'd been deaf for years, but that halfway through the guitar solo, his hearing had come back. All manner of strange manifestations happen when I play it. But as I said, I'm still completely noncommittal about the whole thing."

Al did a great deal more than just writing the song and then turning up in the studio to sing it.

Al – "Most of the guitars on this track were done by yours truly, even the backward-guitar seagull sounds. In those early days, I was playing 'It's Alright Ma (I'm Only Bleeding)' by Bob Dylan. For the central section of 'Nostradamus' – the instrumental passage – I took the middle section of 'It's Alright Ma' and turned it into an epic."

The album he made was his first true 'record' rather than just a collection of songs.

In an interview with his friend Karl Dallas, in *Melody Maker*'s November 10th issue, he spoke about his thoughts on the '60s – "I'm without a shadow of a doubt a Sixties person adrift in the Seventies,' he said, recalling the Melly aphorism. "My loyalties belong to the Sixties almost entirely, you know."

He sat there reminiscing about the '60s, not caring one little bit whether the teenage folkies who've nourished their sexual fantasies on "Love Chronicles" will be able to relate to a song like "Old Admirals" which is about the creator of the modern ironclad Royal Navy, or even to the whole spirit of his newest album which is purest '60s, punk rock to psychedelic.

"That would be the highest compliment you could pay me," he said, "to say this new album's got a '60s feel. But I don't know whether the teenagers of today will be able to relate to it at all. I haven't a clue."

Karl Dallas went to the Roundhouse show at Chalk Farm on November 4th and was largely unimpressed saying that – "Essentially, very little has changed. The concert was a sell-out, predictably, and there were the small predictable crowd of groupies hammering on the doors of London's Roundhouse trying to get some non-existent seats, though most of them were male.

He came on, cocky and sassy as ever, still very much the young Soho lad with the flash guitar, jumping up and down on his stool like a puppet, hooked on amphetamines, his mop head bent low during the solos, his head thrown back until it was almost off mike for the upper cadences of his vocal melodies ... the influence of Dylan looms large as ever in his tumbling jumble of images."

The ongoing problem of whether or not to perform with a band was continuing to cause Al problems however.

Al – "We had screwed round with all sorts of little bandlets before this period of time and I did a whole tour [Autumn 1973] with Canton Trig. Canton Trig was Ian Hunt on acoustic guitar, Graham Smith on harmonica and he would later resurface on 'Flying Sorcery' and various other things. Canton Trig was a Bristol-based outfit and I did a fair number of gigs with them. But they were still fairly acoustic-based. They were playing with me and they were a backing band. I think there were three of them and it was very acoustic. They weren't like an electric band."

Canton Trig would in fact join Al on stage for an ensemble "Roads to Moscow" each night. It was the first step along the road to have Al working with a band.

Luke – "I had realised already that the notion of Al working with a group was going to take time and so this, in essence, was the start of a gradual process for us. It wouldn't be an immediate *Al goes electric!*"

That would have to wait until the following spring.

Jerry Gilbert wrote in the November 24th issue of *Sounds* – "Al has very little idea of what nature his next album will be 'But I do know in my mind very clearly what another album will be although I'm not sure if it'll be the next. I must get one done by

March 31st to complete my contract with CBS so it'll probably be a collection of songs ... but I do have this idea for a 3D love song based on Kafka's *Metamorphosis*.""

This project, ambitious even by Al's standards, never saw the light of day.

Jeremy Gilbert again – "Al realises that apart from his lyrical complexities he is also coming up with more musical ideas, although that old faithful minor key is still pretty prevalent. As he says – 'I think I'll be writing better when I'm 40 – I might write a book and I'd like to do some film scores. I think I could write surrealist things but in my own life I'm going through such a totally existentialist period that I'm relying on the historical thing as something that has its own strength. I mean at the moment, providing I write something like "Old Admirals" well, then that comes under fire and not me.""

He went to great length to explain his left over from the '60s feeling: "I think of all the people that grew up in the Cousins era. I'm the only one that's retained that Cousins feel because I'm still living in 1968."

So the ultimately unfulfilled dreams of composing a soundtrack and writing a novel can be traced back as far as 1973. It remains something that Al regrets not having had the opportunity to have done.

He explained some of his writing methods to Fred Dellar in the *NME* of November 3rd when he confided that he had "adopted the deceptively simple method of quoting exactly what was written in the books I've studied. Nostradamus had predicted the Great Fire and Plague of 1665-6 with the words 'Fire and plague shall come to London in the year of 6 and 20's 3' and I've used this exact phrase to rhyme with 'An emperor in France shall rise and Pay Nay Loron his name shall be' which is only an inversion of what Nostradamus originally said."

Charles Shaar Murray however filed a damning review in the *New Musical Express* – "Al Stewart has always been a sitting target for any evil-minded cynic with a mind to take pot shots at sensitive young singer-songwriters. His new album, sad to say, is unlikely to ease the situation; the scope of its ambition and the audacity of its concept are matched only by its inability to realise its intention."

Karl Dallas however, gave the album a glowing review – "He's done it! I always knew the lad had it in him, once he could drag his attention away from that interesting area a few inches below his navel, and he's done it, producing an exciting, outgoing, upbeat album that is fit for adults to listen to. As a concept, it sounds strictly a no-no, a series of historical sketches each covering one decade of the 20th century. The first one's about Admiral Fisher who created the Dreadnoughts of the World War I navy, then there's Warren Harding, the last American president to be impeached, a look at Soho in the sixties, pre-war Europe with the Nazis beginning to show their teeth and nobody noticing, the world after the war from 1945 to the death of Hendrix, the German invasion of Russia and Stalin's prison camps afterwards, the death of flower-power, concluding with his already well-known song on the prophecies of Nostradamus."

Dallas, usually so guarded in his praise of Al, was clearly impressed by this new work. He saved the best for last though:

Karl Dallas – "But if you've heard and loved 'Manuscript', his first attempt at this sort of thing, you'll realise that it doesn't have to sound as dull as it seems. It is not merely the power of the songs that grab at you; it is not even the backing musicians (who are basically Quiver with the addition of assorted superstars like Dave Swarbrick, Isaac Guillory, and Rick Wakeman). This is also the best, and the least over-produced album Al has had in his recording career. Al, you just made yourself a masterpiece."

Fair praise indeed from someone that had been casting a very critical eye over Al's work from his first days in Soho.

Krysia Kristianne sang the amazing backing vocals on *Past, Present And Future*. She would go on to play a key part in Al's career for the next decade. Al had first heard her play in The Natural Acoustic Band in 1972.

Past, Present And Future had been largely written at home in Belsize Park. The house would be Al's last in England. Together with Bena it was gradually decorated in a style that was very much '70s London. Once in through the front door from the mews there was a small hall and then the ground floor living area with its brown cord 'L' shaped couch, shelves of records and a huge brown leather swivel chair in front of the television. Across the room to the left just past the entrance to the kitchen (with its saucepans inhabited by spiders; Al never cooked) was the piano and next to that was an open plan staircase leading up to the first floor with its three bedrooms and a further staircase leading up to the roof garden and its view of Belsize Village. Throughout the house were copious supplies of peppermint Aero, Crunchie bars and on top of the piano a huge jar of mint humbugs. Meals would invariably be from one of the many local restaurants, Le Chateaubriand which was his favourite, the place next door called Conrad's Bistro which would later prove to be the inspiration for *24 Carrots*: Mondo Sinistro or Abbots in St Johns Wood where Jonny and Abi had their first meal. There was a pub just across the road, The Belsize Tavern and local Indian and Chinese takeaways both of which saw a great deal of Al over the years. Five minutes away on Haverstock Hill was the small deli-café Hill House to which Al would walk for breakfast on a regular basis. The area was very much village London and Al was to keep his house here for seven years, far longer than he'd spent in all of his other London homes put together and it was here that many of his very best songs were composed and played to an audience for the first time. "Roads To Moscow", "Nostradamus", "Not the One", and "Flying Sorcery" were all written in Belsize Court Garages.

SOHO (NEEDLESS TO SAY)
Rainstorm, brainstorm, faces in the maelstrom
Huddle by the puddles in the shadows where the drains run
Hot dogs, wet clogs clicking up the sidewalk
Disappearing into the booze shop
Rainbow queues stand down by the news-stand, waiting for the late show
Pinball, sin hall, minds in free fall
Chocolate-coloured ladies making eyes through the smoke-pall
Soho (needless to say)
I'm alone on your streets on a Friday evening
I've been here all of the day
I'm going nowhere with nowhere to go

Football supporters taking the waters
They're looking round for the twilight daughters
Non-stop strip club pornographic bookshop
Come into the back and take your time and have a good look
Old man laughs with flowers in his hair
Newspaper headline "Middle East Deadline"
Jazz musicians are down on the breadline
Soho (needless to say)
I'm alone on your streets on a Friday evening
I've been here all of the day
I'm going nowhere with nowhere to go

Soho feeds the needs and hides the deeds, the mind that bleeds
Disenchanted, downstream in the night
Soho hears the lies, the twisted cries, the lonely sighs
Till she seems lost in dreams
The sun goes down on a neon eon
Though you'd have a job explaining it to Richard Coeur de Lion
Animation, bar conversation, anticipation, disinclination
Poor old wino turns with dust in his eyes
Begs for the dregs from the bottom of the kegs, man
You've never seen a lady lay down and spread her legs like

Soho (needless to say)
I'm alone on your streets on a Friday evening
I've been here all of the day
I'm going nowhere with nowhere to go

Soho (needless to say)
I'm alone on your streets, or am I dreaming
I've been here all of the day
I'm going nowhere with nowhere to go

There now followed a very important date in Al's evolution as a folk rock performer. Luke had been trying to get Al to use a backing band for months and with the next gig things began to take shape. The key event was a show in North London that featured most, if not all, of the BTM roster of artists. BTM being Miles Copeland's *British Talent Management*.

Luke – "Now I got a gig for Al at the Alexandra Palace in North London for Saturday 22nd December 1973 and on it were mostly Miles' acts. There was Wishbone Ash, Vinegar Joe, Renaissance and Al and it was called 'Christmas At The Palace'. I'd told Al all about Miles at our very first meeting, I'd told him that I wasn't big enough to do what I wanted for him at that time, perhaps I would be in one or two years but at that time I needed someone else's office to work out of and he said 'I don't care where you go or what you do as along as your finger is on the trigger'. Anyway I persuaded Al that maybe he should have a band and he said that maybe he'd give it a go after Christmas, which was a start, so I started putting in some dates for January and February. One interesting fact is that although Al was selling out almost all of his shows he was only getting up to £150 a night and so this was something that I now went to work on. It was necessary because we had all of the tour dates up until Christmas like this on those Derek Block dates and there was just no profit."

The show in North London was one of the key events in the promotion of *Past, Present And Future*. It also provided Luke with an opportunity to try out some fresh ideas.

Luke – "We came to this date at Alexandra Palace and I asked Annie Haslam of

Renaissance, along with Miles' secretary at the time, to sing back-up at the show. I also found this guy Dave Freeman, the originator of the string synthesiser. He had built his own box and we got it from him and we asked Francis Monkman to play synthesiser with Norman Watt Roy from Glencoe on bass. So we proceeded to play this one-off gig. However, because everyone said that they didn't have time to set up the stage for a band for Al, we only got to do two or three songs as this ensemble but it all went off very well – the audience were very receptive. It was a satisfying experience for us."

Luke earnestly believed that working with a band was the way forward for Al and this in fact marked the time when a series of bands came to work with him. After the show and over the Christmas break in London Luke tried to convince Al of the benefits of such an enterprise.

Luke – "Eventually Al and I reached a compromise when I spelt it out and said 'Your highest paying gig on this last winter tour was £150?' Al says 'Correct' and then I suggested something that I had had in mind for a while. 'Supposing I guarantee you £150 in your pocket, in your contract, for every show you do and you then let me keep the remainder. From this I'll hire a band and pay all the expenses and if I have to dip into my own commission then so be it.' To which Al replied that we had a deal. So right after Christmas in January 1974 we booked ourselves the first tour with a band!"

But they had no band! A series of rehearsals now followed, with varying degrees of success, featuring a succession of groups including on one occasion Elton John's Band. These were tough early times for Al and Luke. At one audition in a small room, hired by the hour, Luke had unloaded the equipment himself and then had a sound engineer set it all up. After a spell in the pub down the street the group wandered in announcing "You just play away Al and we'll busk along behind you."

Luke – "Quite frankly that rehearsal lasted about ten minutes and I asked them all to leave! But we managed to put a band together eventually."

That band would in fact come to be partly drawn from Francis' friends in Curved Air. There was Isaac Guillory, Florian Pilkington Miksa and Pete Zorn who were joined by Annie Haslam for their radio debut on a John Peel session broadcast on January 10th 1974 where they played "Post World War Two Blues", "Soho, Needless to Say" and "Roads To Moscow".

Florian also came to the band's rescue when they needed a rehearsal space. He lived in some style inside a Barnes mansion and it was there that Al's makeshift band rehearsed for the tour. Gigs were now booked including Nottingham on January 12th, Reading University on January 19th and further London shows at both Kingston Polytechnic and The Roundhouse at Chalk Farm."

Abi Kremer – "That London gig is one that I will always particularly remember with affection because it was there that he dedicated 'I'm Falling' to Jonny and I."

There was a surprise in store for Al when the show came to York's Theatre Royal on this tour. Introducing "My Enemies Have Sweet Voices" he announced: "Here's a song that I wrote by writing a very simple song on just the bass guitar string to a wonderful poem by the Scottish poet Pete Morgan. I don't know what he's doing these days, probably driving a bus somewhere!"

Little did he expect Pete's voice to call back from the darkness of the theatre's balcony with "Oh no I'm not!", thus re-introducing two friends to one another after a break of over three years.

Throughout this time there wasn't always sufficient work with Al to occupy Luke on a daily basis and so he would sometimes go out as the tour manager for other bands from Miles' BTM stable.

Luke – "This was all part of my crash course in management! I thought that the work with other bands was great and figured that if I went out on tour with a group such as Renaissance then I could make my mistakes with them and would then know what to do when I went out on tour with Al!"

And so Luke became BTM's *de-facto* in-house tour manager for a while. However when working for Al, now with a band to support on the road, the fee was to rise from the £150 it had been throughout the previous two years, in speedy increments.

Luke – "Now this honestly was one of the funniest things that I've ever seen in my life! What happened was that we did a couple of day's solo up north to get some money together because I needed cash and then we booked some more shows. Ian had got us a couple of nights where we got good money, to provide our road fund, so I had gone out and got us a band. I'd then turn up in the evening at home and I'd say to Ian 'You know that £250 we're getting at wherever it was? Well I can't do anything for £250 now, I'm going to need £350'. So Ian would ring up and tell these guys that the gig they'd previously booked for £250 was now £350 and then I got some more expenses and with one thing and another we jumped the price to £500."

What no one up until now had realised was that the ticket price for one of Al's shows was something that his fans would quite happily pay much more for than they had up until then been paying.

Luke – "Ian was now actually calling people back and telling them 'You know the £350 gig – sorry it's now gone up to £500!'. And it turned out that if they charged as much as they did for Al as they did for everyone else and Al had a band then they'd make four times as much anyway. They'd been packing the place out at 50 pence and hadn't realised that they could pack it out for £2 and we did just that. We took over and said 'Right, now we're a rock band!' Al didn't like it very much and he was quite right because we did have troubles from the musicians and crew, no end of trouble on a daily basis. We had some very well-known musicians who were well respected people and quite frankly their behaviour was sub par but they didn't get very far with me, they thought that they could walk all over Al and so I'd just get on their case!"

Conrad's Bistro had by now become Al and Luke's *de facto* office and most of the business decisions concerning Al were now made there. As the restaurant emptied after lunchtime they would stay on and talk into the afternoon about what they should do next.

Luke – "This was great because I was only paying myself £40 a week! Al and I would meet up once or twice a week at Conrad's where for £5 you could get a couple of steaks and also half a bottle of wine!"

There were also occasions, when money was really tight, when Al offered Luke all the proceeds from a gig just to tide him over.

Luke – "But my ego wouldn't let me accept it. I would have loved to get my hands on £300. I could have got out of debt and paid the phone bill but I was just too embarrassed to accept."

Living in Belsize Village, Al had a number of fellow musicians as neighbours. One of these was Richard Thompson.

"I used to see Al quite often at this time. Not just at places like Les Cousins but socially too. We knew lots of the same people and of course worked together every so often. I also got to know Luke quite well. Al is great company and it was always good to catch up."

Al's band had by now grown to feature Pat Donaldson from Eclection, Francis Monkman, Florian Pilkington, Gerry Conway and Jean Jacques Roussel.

Donaldson, Donahue and Conway had also all come together in Sandy Denny's acclaimed but ill fated Fotheringay and so the credentials of this new band of Al's could not have been higher.

But Al continued to have real misgivings about working with a band, whilst at the same time craving American FM radio play. He now prepared to go out and have a serious crack at the States.

Luke – "So we went out to America, Al flying there on April 30th. It's now the Spring of 1974 and *Past Present And Future* has been out since that January. We did lots of press and all the things you have to do. Now I was having some problems because he

Al touring "Past, Present And Future" with l-r: Jean Roussel, Gerry Conway, Pat Donaldson and Simon Nicol. 1974

didn't want us to take a band out to America and neither did Miles, because he said it would all cost too much. Ian backed Miles, although he knew better, despite me telling everyone that if you go to America without a band you die a death and that Al was far too good to suffer that fate and that a band would make him sound fabulous, just like he did on the album."

However on this moot point Luke got outvoted by the other three and Al played those American dates as a solo act.

Luke – "For the first and last time! After that we didn't have votes. We did some dates and Al was having a tough time playing with the likes of Hot Tuna in New Jersey and in Providence Rhode Island. These were gigs that I'd managed to secure by very simply sitting on those agents' desks for sometimes hours at a time and eventually by having me physically there in the room the promoter would get us gigs because that was the only way they could get rid of me!"

It is quite possible that the only person who could have managed to get Al bookings in and around New York City at this time was Luke. Had it been left to Miles, the momentum that Luke now conjured out of nowhere, would have achieved far less.

Luke again – "Things don't always work out as well as we had hoped though and at those dates Al didn't go down too well. He then played The Bottom Line and it didn't get any better. To say he was greeted with vast indifference would be true enough. We were on the bill with Alan Price who had the number one US hit 'Lucky Man' out at the time and the audience were there that night to see him and not Al."

It was a strange night all around. The New York City audience had paid little attention to Al during his set and in so far as it being a showcase for the new album it proved to be largely a waste of time. That wasn't the only thing to come out of the evening however. Mandi had shown up for the start of the show but something happened

Al & Luke at the Cambridge Folk Festival

and she wasn't there at the end. Luke describes the day as "cathartic".

Luke – "So at the end of the evening Al comes up to me and says – 'OK Luke, maybe you're right, let's give a band a go,' because I had pointed out that things at that moment in time were a *farce* and that if only we'd had a band then we could have forced it down their throats. I felt that this was the only way forward."

Before this could come to pass they had to honour the rest of their contract by playing some further dates in the North West supporting the comedian George Carlin, Luke not wanting to incur the wrath of the agency by pulling out of a tour.

Whilst they were still going through the motions on this dismal East Coast trip Luke had set about putting his masterplan into prompt action. At this point everything that Luke knew about the UK music business had come courtesy of the offices of BTM and so it was there that he went for help. By now though, Al was once again telling his manager that he had reservations about the whole issue of being backed by a band, but it was too late!

Luke – "Too late indeed! I had already telephoned Miles from the States and it just so happened that Home had broken up at that very point in time and he had four members of the band sans vocalist just sitting around. Then Al and I fly back to England, we have one week there and I'd had arguments with everybody but to Miles' eternal credit he made Home available to us just like that and for that reason I shall always be grateful to him. There might never have been another US album but for that. Working for Al was all new to the guys in Home but it was a way of going to America for a while. In 1974 if you asked a bunch of kids if they wanted to tour the States for six weeks you wouldn't get the answer 'No', especially when your band's just broken up, you've got a new manager and you want to go on with it. So they were quite happy to come along."

So Al and Luke returned to the UK in order to rehearse with Home for a week before flying back out to America with them. This was a difficult time in their relationship. The transition that Al was seeking to make, with Luke's guidance, from British folkie to American FM favourite had barely started and here they were returning home with their tails between their legs and far more uncertainty than they had left with just a few weeks earlier. However a corner had been turned and it was with new impetus that Luke went to see Home as soon as he got back to London.

Luke – "I also gave them a pile of Al's albums and told them to memorise them! And by now we'd gone out and bought a bloody Mellotron! I'd secured an advance from the record label and with it had bought this thing for about £1,000. Now at the time this was an absolute fortune but I thought it was the right thing to do because I wanted people to hear what was on the record and if we turned up able to reproduce that live for them then things would be a lot different in Al's world. So we went out and did that tour but it ended in a big down."

Al – "In many ways, yes, this is true. The very first thing that I remember is the Mellotron being dropped on the tarmac at the airport and never working from that moment on! There were some other problems on that tour and it was difficult for all of us. We tried so hard to get something going but it seemed that everything was against us sometimes, it really did."

These shows on the East Coast were compromised by the fact that Al was sick for some of the period.

Luke – "We were due to finish with a few shows on the East Coast in Boston. Unfortunately though the first night was a weak night which was not good news as the record company were in the audience. Then Al got ill. Now he was genuinely sick, he'd got a cold, was sniffling and he couldn't play the next night. We had been looking towards having a good weekend but, so far, Al had only played just that Thursday night. Now for some reason hotels in Boston were far more expensive than anywhere else in America at this time. Whereas we'd been paying $20 a hotel room everywhere else, here in Boston rooms were about four times that and at the time that was a fortune and I didn't have the money to pay the bill! Although the record company were obligated in our contract to pay us these were, you must remember, old school record company guys and they'd come all of the way up to Boston and Al had got sick and they weren't that impressed. The fact that Al was genuinely ill didn't seem to matter and had nothing to do with the world of reality."

So for a couple of days Luke shuffled to and fro between Boston and New York trying to get the funds together to pay the ever increasing hotel bill.

Luke – "Everyone else was just hanging around at the hotel. We had two or three days there hoping that if we maybe had to cancel just the one show then perhaps Al would be well for the others. And we all kept hanging on at the hotel, hoping against hope to play a show because we had the record company people coming in again."

But unfortunately Al didn't get well enough to sing. They did finally escape the hotel though.

Back in London Luke set about retaining Home for some further dates through the early summer whilst he and Al used the short respite from the band shows to ponder their next move over a series of lunches at their "office", Conrad's Bistro. Al also took the opportunity to help out Abi.

Abi – "Al was proving to be the most wonderful of friends to me at this time. I was having a fair amount of conflict in my life due to the fact that I wanted to go to Art College, which was not what my family wanted me to do. But he was a rock to me because he said that I should do exactly what I wanted and make such decisions based on what I wanted to do and not what anyone else thought – which was exactly what I wanted to hear. He was very sensitive and thoughtful."

Al's next shows were part of a short European tour kicking off on June 1st. Back home ten days later he went out and bought a new piano on June 12th, the one that much of *Modern Times* and *Year Of The Cat* would be composed on. That evening at tea time Sandy Denny came around to try it out, spending a couple of hours singing standards and accompanying herself on the piano.

On June 27th Al recorded a BBC Radio *In Concert* at the Golders Green Hippodrome with Krysia and Home. Then a few days later he played The Howff, in London's Camden Town, with the same line-up. Isaac Guillory opened that show which was recorded for American radio.

John Beattie in *Record Mirror* on July 20th reviewed Al's London show – "The set was almost entirely devoted to the singer's last album, *Past, Present And Future* and the songs included 'Old Admirals', 'Roads to Moscow' where he was joined by three female

CBS

CBS promo

backing vocalists and 'Terminal Eyes', his last single taken from the album. Monkman's fluent keyboard work was definitely an asset as it draws the audience away from thinking that the songs could have been performed as a purely folk-type basis and William and Cook looked particularly relaxed in their respective roles even although they have been working with Stewart in the States.

"We even had his version of 'All Along the Watchtower' to snigger over but even that was commendably done with Wishbone's Andy Powell, Mick Stubbs (formerly with Home) and Isaac Guillory all joining in for a jam session."

Beattie went on to comment that Al's confidence had doubled since he went to the States and that the time Al was about to spend in the studio would "...prove valuable breathing space for his ego to cool down as well."

Karl Dallas, someone who had himself in the past, taken issue with Al's ego, was a regular visitor to The Howff:

"For a while Roy Guest's London Howff was the most wonderful place. I remember seeing Sandy Denny play a beautiful set there. Fotheringay played there too."

Al, Miles and Ian were not the only ones unsure about the musical direction that Al seemed to be taking at that time. Dave Dyke also felt that the addition of a band was largely unnecessary.

Dave Dyke – "It may well have been the right thing to do at the time but I personally never felt that Al needed a band behind him on any of those tours. I'm sure that Luke was sure that it was all a good idea and that it all made sound sense but Al on his own was always more than able to hold an audience in the palm of his hand. I know that Al very often felt the same way too."

That was of course to ignore the seminal element in Luke's use of a band for Al that was for him to be able to faithfully reproduce the sound on stage that he had on album. The use of electric guitar specifically on albums from now on was key to securing that all-important FM airplay. To many, used to seeing Al at folk clubs and universities in the UK, this was tantamount to heresy.

Luke – "We had played The Howff as a special concert to let everyone know that things were a little different now. We did that venue because it was small. Roy Guest, the owner, would let us do whatever we wanted and we didn't have to worry about selling it out. It was a showcase to demonstrate to the record company how things were changing."

The show at The Howff may not have been perfect but it was very clearly a step along the way in Al's evolution under Luke's guidance. This was also the night that Al first met Marion Driscoll, who would be his partner on the rollercoaster ride that would ultimately lead to the house in Bel Air.

Abi Kremer – "Jonny and I were there that night. It really was a great gig and it was one of those times when just about everyone turned up. I remember it was one of the first times that I met Miles and Ian Copeland. Luke, of course, Jonny and I had met many, many times before. Luke was always great to us both and in fact he use to refer to Jonny, Al and himself as 'The Three Musketeers!' After the show we all went around to a party at Ian Copeland's house in Reddington Road."

These were times when Jonny and Abi were seeing a great deal of Al. Abi, who remembers Al as "…invariably wearing velvet; either bottle green or burgundy" had herself always lived in London up until then but on July 14th 1974 she and Jonny got married and set up home together in Bournemouth. Al was best man at their wedding.

Abi once again – "This was hilarious because not only did he refer to me as Abi throughout his entire best man's speech, thus confusing my entire family who up until that moment had only known me as Gail but he proceeded to adopt the self same ironic tone as that which he was used to employing at his own gigs! It was very much one of the

London 1974

promo shoot

funniest parts of our day!"

Two weeks later on July 29th Al appeared, backed by Home, on Bob Harris's BBC Radio One show where he sang "Terminal Eyes" and "Post World War Two Blues".

The following month he made a solo visit to London's Capital Radio and sparred live with DJ Sarah Ward for an hour and played some of the new songs on his acoustic in the studio.

The 1974 US tour had clearly scarred Al and he reflected on its implications to Fred Dellar later that week – "I went over in March 1974 and did a month's solo work – which was not a very good idea. The first concert I did with ELO started late, and the audience had three hours to booze and get smashed out of their minds. By eleven the promoter was so terrified he just refused to go out and announce me – so I got pushed out unannounced in front of all these heathens… I don't exactly blame them, but there were all these 16-year-olds booing and shouting, and I defy anyone in the world to make an impression in those circumstances. …America doesn't work like England – over there you have to fight very hard to get people to listen to you, whereas over here people will listen, and then it's just a matter of how good you are… I don't know if the mixture of Home and me was the right one – but for America it was perfect because if the audience made a noise then Home could make a louder one – and that worked. Not that the result was as tasteful as I would have liked."

"Stormy Night", "A Sense of Déjà Vu" and "Swallow Wind" were all recorded at this time over a two-day session well before the recording of *Modern Times*. The musicians were exceptional. There was Simon Nicol, Richard Thompson played guitar on "Stormy Night" and "A Sense of Déjà Vu" whilst Francis Monkman, who by this time was with the group Sky (along with John Williams and Herbie Flowers), played on "Swallow Wind" as did Andy Powell. Al would go on to perform "A Sense of Déjà Vu" live with Francis during the English band gigs later in 1974.

Jonny Kremer – "These tracks were all laid down during evening sessions at Morgan Studios in Willesden, North London which Abi and I went along to. Luke was very keen on 'Swallow Wind' that night and it's appearance on Al's next single was very much at his behest I suspect."

Luke – "I liked it because I thought it was a great song that Al well and truly nailed in the studio that night. It was one of those studio sessions that we had booked just to keep us on our toes and to see what we could do with the new material that Al was writing at the time."

In fact what had happened was that Luke had persuaded Al that it would be no bad thing if he were to show willing with regard to recording what was clearly single material for CBS. It would also bolster the image of Al as a "happening act" that Luke had worked so hard on.

But, like all of the others before it, "Swallow Wind" failed to chart. It is, however, a real gem of a record.

SWALLOW WIND

Look out, look out, Phoenix cried
My time must be at hand
I'm feeling cold and I don't know why
The ground moves where I stand
All the lies she gave to me
In words that twist and bend

Now the only place for me is down in the Swallow Wind

Far off and long ago
She came when I was young
A silver moon shining in her eyes
And strange the song she sang

All so easy I trusted her
I thought she was my friend

Now the only place for me is down in the Swallow Wind

And I don't really know what to tell you now
It's something I just can't control
I thought you wanted to take my love
Now you want my soul
Last time I saw her
She was standing in the sand
The ashen moon was in her hair
And a cross was in her hand
I'm sailing alone she cried
Though I can't believe I sinned

Now the only place for me is down in the Swallow Wind

Al started to record *Modern Times* in August 1974 at Abbey Road Studios. A short tour followed including – Sussex University (Oct 11th), Birmingham University (18th), Bristol Polytechnic (19th), Liverpool University (23rd), Brunel University (25th) and Loughborough University (26th)

Al was profiled in *Melody Maker* in their November 2nd issue.

In the long piece he pointed out how he had reacted to the criticism of the previous albums when he had recorded *Past, Present And Future*, which had promptly turned out to be his best selling record so far. That criticism had been directed at Al's continued use of his own love life as the subject of his songs.

In a piece entitled *Allegorical, Allusive, Metaphorical* he explained it like this – "To a certain extent, you're caught between two lines of fire. Maybe wrongly, but certainly when you first start writing songs you want to get at an exact truth as I said in 'Songs Out Of Clay'. But maybe writing it down as an exact truth isn't the exact truth for the people listening to it. Whereas if you write a song like this, it's possibly an exact truth for any number of people."

Considering the new album, Al pointed out the similarities between one of its key tracks and a song from *Past, Present And Future*.

"'The Dark And The Rolling Sea' is a relationship song turned into a metaphor in the same way that 'Old Admirals' was a metaphor really, like growing old and becoming unwanted. This one is like, Right you think you're the cat's whiskers and you're going to go off and leave me like somewhere out there in the middle of the ocean you're going to come unstuck. Essentially, that's all it's saying. It's that kind of a song. I think it's very malicious, it's sweetly malicious, but it's certainly a malicious song."

He then played one of the few tracks on the album that had allowed him to cut loose musically, "Carol", which would go on to become one of his most performed songs in the next few years. At this stage he was still considering changing its title so that it wouldn't get confused with the Paul Anka rocker. The genesis of the song had come from the US tour that he had completed earlier that year with Home.

Al – "As much as anything else I got the idea from a girl that Home picked up in Max's in New York City, one with orange hair, who was really zonked, permanently, roaming about the hotel. She kept on coming out of a different room every morning. 'White rose face, orphan clothes, embroidered jeans and silver chains,' – those lines are specific and yet non-specific to me.

"She was one of those really groovy groupies. It's really very much of a Max's Kansas City song, bittersweet.

"'I think it's time for running for cover. You're everyone's and nobody's lover.' as the song says.

"It's not an experience of my own, of course. I didn't experience that one as it happens. I thought too many other people had…"

The next song discussed was "Apple Cider Re-Constitution", Al's fantasy about a couple making love on an abandoned railway station, with rusting steam engines by the side of the platforms. Here too he sought to make a comparison between a new song and one of his earlier compositions saying – "'Carol' and 'Apple Cider Re-Constitution' are what you might call the lighter tracks on the album, by virtue of the fact they're up-tempo stompers. 'Apple Cider' has a clear similarity to 'Love Chronicles' in its mood. What I'm talking about is atmosphere, youthful optimism –'And the rails go on for ever…' I like things going on forever. It's my intrinsically conservative nature. The song is so unlike *Past Present And Future*, say, in its feel."

Al continued to discuss the album, making the point that Kurt Vonnegut (whose book *The Sirens Of Titan* had been used as both title and theme for one of the other tracks on *Modern Times*), was far more relevant to him than "Nostradamus" had been the previous year.

Al – "Vonnegut attracts me far more as a philosophy, but it is not diametrically opposed, because the final *dénouement* of *The Sirens Of Titan* is that the entire course of our civilisation for the past 50,000 years has been predetermined by the Tralfamadorians in order to carry a message from one side of the Universe to the other, which I would have thought puts it exactly in line with Nostradamus!"

Al also played them a song inspired by The Band, "Willie The King", which in fact never made it on to *Modern Times* when the album came out. The failure of the track to make the final cut can have come of no great surprise to *Melody Maker* who described the demo that they heard at Al's that evening as being "indescribable… a made-up story about a retired late 19th century American gambler. He's sitting at the bar and he's recalling his earlier life. More musical, I'd say than lyrical."

Another track that was recorded by Al and the band in the studio at Abbey Road but never properly finished was "Belsize Blues". Whilst basically a bar room honky tonk with shades of the song "Next Time" it was, however, worked on on at least two sessions. The lyrics are the most interesting facet of the song as they are strongly biographical, name checking much of Al's neighbourhood of that time throughout a tale in which he uses a flood as his chosen thematic device. In essence Al was employing the flood as the same kind of "theatrical backdrop" that he had used the 20th century for two years earlier on *Past, Present And Future* and would go on to use on several of his subsequent albums. "Belsize Blues" uses the flood as a backdrop for a series of character sketches in a similar way to that with which Bob Dylan used the earthquake in "Black Diamond Bay", also written at this time. "Belsize Blues" remained unreleased until it came out as a bonus track in 2001 on EMI.

Another song, destined to be acknowledged as one of Al's classic recordings, was still in its infancy when the interview took place. Al was clearly having problems with the composition of the song's lyrics and the theme of the piece would in fact face major renovation that Autumn. This is what Al said at the time – "Then there's another one called 'The Man With the Pipe'. It's a song that I've done a lot of rewrites on and I'll have to do a lot more rewrites yet again. It's one of those songs that I'm round but I haven't got right. It's a surrealistic thing, based on the Magritte painting. I don't know what it's about, but I will quote you the first few lines:

"'It was the kind of grey November day that washes away reflections in the eyes of hotel porters. And the lattice wooden benches by the sea contains no travellers or Irish lady authors.' It's me being prosaic…"

This, of course, became the haunting and elegant "Not the One".

"And then there is 'Modern Times'", Al continued "based on the Chaplin film. What usually happens is, like on the last album, the long one is the last one to get written when you've done everything else. So I am in fact sifting around now for a song under the title of 'Modern Times' though it may not be called that. But I've got the feel of it. 'Modern Times' is an ambiguity, because the phrase itself is an old phrase and yet it seems to refer to now, thought it doesn't. Again, a time ambiguity. It's at the same stage that 'Roads to Moscow' was before I actually came to terms with it. But the author reserves the right to change all these titles round and leave any of them off the record that he wishes and write any new ones he wishes before they come out. These are some ideas. What happens is that you record an awful lot and then you try and push it into shape when you've got enough things down."

With the prospect of Al performing major tours with a band now a certainty it was time for Luke to find a capable and reliable deputy. It was at this moment that he met up with Nigel Lendon.

Luke – "We wouldn't have been able to do things the way we did without him, he was quite simply the rock on which our whole touring based itself. He was this young roadie whom we had met when we'd done this tour with Nichol and Marsh in England through the winter of 1974. They were signed to CBS, like ourselves at the time, and CBS had offered to give us a full-page ad for Al's tour if we'd take Nichol and Marsh out with us as support. They also supplied the transport and pa."

Al – "You need good people around you. Nigel was a huge help to us at a time when everything had just gone up a gear and we needed to be much more professional on the road."

The next job was to find a producer for the new album.

Luke – "When we were looking for studios and a producer to record *Modern Times* I first asked John Anthony but he wasn't interested because Al can be a little prickly in the studio and he turned us down."

They spoke to other people including Geoff Emerick at EMI but he said that he couldn't do it but that they might try Alan Parsons whose claim to fame at the time was producing the group Pilot and that he'd been the engineer on part of the Beatles' *White Album*.

Luke – "Somehow or other it got around to us considering Alan Parsons for the job as producer and he and Al met and got on well together, both being bright, both ex-public school boys with similar senses of humour and it looked like it could work."

It was Seamus Ewans, who ran The Howff in Hampstead and someone Al had known for years, that in fact introduced him to Alan Parsons. It was at The Howff that Al and Alan met up on several occasions prior to the autumn recording of *Modern Times* to discuss both the direction that they saw the album taking and their own work practices.

Alan Parsons – "Seamus was very well connected in folk circles and I had met him at Abbey Road Studios where he had a technician's job and I believe he was a partner in The Howff actually. I'd already been given a few of Al's earlier albums to listen to and I remember telling Al how I'd thought that 'Terminal Eyes' should have been a hit. I myself had given him a copy of Cockney Rebel's *Psychomodo* as an example of my work and that was that really."

There was only minimal contact between the Stewart and Parsons camps in between this first face-to-face meeting and the recording sessions themselves. Luke later met with Alan to find a period when they were all free to record *Modern Times* but that was about the only course of action instigated by either party, prior to going into Abbey Road.

Alan Parsons – "This album came very early on in my role as a producer and I wasn't sure what musicians we would need to record it with and so ultimately it became a mixture of people that I'd worked with previously and others such as Isaac Guillory that Al knew."

Al didn't give Alan Parsons a tape of demos for him to hear before they met up in the studio (probably because they didn't exist in any recorded form) and so the first time Alan got to hear them was at Abbey Road itself. This makes the fact that the album was largely recorded over a three week period all the more remarkable.

Alan Parsons' ability to forge an immediate relationship of mutual respect between himself and those musicians was essential to the success of the recording process due to the absence of specific music parts for the musicians.

Alan Parsons – "Al would play the song through for the musicians who would make notes about key changes or where a bridge would come for example but that was about that in as far as any set musical parts went.

"To put down the backing track for each of Al's songs we'd record at the very least bass, drums and keyboard; over this Al would hum a rough guide vocal. He was certainly very responsive to my suggestions and respectful of me in my role as his producer."

Luke – "Now *Modern Times* isn't my favourite album. It was made under a new regime, my first time there on an Al Stewart project and I was in there every day because of studio costs and we weren't going to over-run on production costs if I had anything to do with it. At this time quite frankly I feel that Al had a little too much pressure on him to change his style and deliver the goods and in fact that was the quickest album that we made together, being produced between mid-Summer and Christmas at Abbey Road studios with Al, as usual, working in the evenings."

Luke's involvement in Al's affairs, far more expansive than Julia's or Roy's had ever been, also included the selection of songs.

Luke again – "The way that the album was put together was like this. Al would write the basic tunes at home and then play them to me and I'd say 'Yes' to one 'No' to the next and so on. I had an ear for what could be a hit in America and Al really wanted to crack the United States and so far those early tours hadn't been particularly pleasant."

The album was made under a lot of pressure, the abiding feeling of the time was that they needed to get it out and to get things moving. Now in its own way this was probably their best course of action. That first American tour together had been a very difficult time.

Luke – "If Al hadn't been a strong individual he could have just given up the whole idea of having a band there and then but although he was depressed he had come back the next morning and said 'OK we'll do it your way.' I admired that as it took a great deal of strength but it still took a long while before things began to turn around. This was the time that we had one of the world's two greatest guitarists with us, Tim Renwick, the other being Richard Thompson. It was Al who first pointed Tim out to me and ever since I first heard him I thought he was wonderful and at this time he was with The Sutherland Brothers and Quiver who I handled briefly while Tim and Peter Wood played with us. I had heard that The Sutherland Brothers and Quiver were maybe about to split up and Ian Copeland, to his eternal credit, said "Well, let's go and get them" and we jumped in the car and did precisely that."

For once Luke took something of a back seat at this meeting as Ian swung into commando action and did most of the talking. The importance of this day is highlighted by the fact that within a year, of course, Peter Wood went on to co-write "Year Of The Cat" with Al.

To supplement the existing road crew Luke had taken on two additional people to take care of Al's stage needs – one to mix sound and the other to oversee the stage requirements. These were two semi-legendary *Roadies For Hire*, Pete and Rik respectively, who were seconded from The Groundhogs.

Nigel Lendon – "The three of us looked after the tour's equipment and sound and I guess it must have gone quite well because at the end of the tour Luke took me to one side and asked me straight out whether I wanted to work for Al. I was flattered of course but I told him that I wasn't interested because I'd worked very hard at forging a relationship with Ken and Pete and wanted to stay around and honour the commitment I'd made to them. I explained to Luke about how it was a simple question of loyalty that it wouldn't be right for me just to walk away from that."

From that moment on Luke's interest in managing Nichol and Marsh faded very quickly and on a business level the final deals in which both sides were jointly under the care and protection of Luke can be dated to the end of that British tour. However at the same time things were not too rosy between CBS and Ken and Pete. Neither their album or its single had troubled the charts and without any full time management in place to take care of things the situation became, over a short period of time, one where something had to give.

Nigel Lendon – "We lost our momentum with Nichol and Marsh really and although at the outset it wasn't a situation that had 'The End' written in capital letters all over it, one thing led to another and when one day several months later Luke contacted me again out of the blue with the same offer over a lunch we had, I listened to him this time and came on board. Luke said that there was 'x' amount of money that he could start paying me and that although I didn't need to work for him at all for the time being I needed to stay available and on call. He also told me that I should be prepared to move to the States."

This confers respectability on the notion that from the very earliest times of Luke's management of Al he intended for the move to the States to happen and for it to come about at the earliest opportunity.

Nigel Lendon – "I was certain that Luke and Al were going to be successful and this financial commitment that Luke was making to me was something that I was very excited about it. We got on very well together. Luke had very powerful and clear ideas and was looking for someone that he could delegate to with confidence and that person turned out to be me."

In January 1975, Al met Peter White for the very first time. It was a meeting as important as any in his career. Both Al and Luke agree that, although the issue of whether Al really needed a band may very well have already been settled by this time, Peter's arrival certainly vindicated Luke's faith in searching for key musicians. This is Peter's story.

Peter White – "Sometime in 1974 I went to Hitchin Technical College to see a band play and that band turned out to be Principal Edwards. I had in fact seen them play before when they were Principal Edwards' Magic Theatre. They'd been favourites of John Peel and one night they had come to play in Letchworth. And were they psychedelic! They had dancers, weird lighting, the blob show, strobes and multi-coloured costumes and it truly made an impression on me – but at that time I was still at school."

By the time he saw them this second time in 1974 they'd slimmed down to just six people. Having left school in 1973, Peter had worked in a soup factory for a short time and also performed at a Cornish holiday centre playing cover versions like "Tie A Yellow Ribbon". That ended at the end of the summer and by September Peter found himself facing a dilemma.

Peter White – "I thought to myself what was I going to do with my life? I certainly didn't want to go back to work and I started looking through things like the *Melody Maker* and one day I saw this big ad, about 2 inches square that said 'name band with record contract seeks keyboard player'. So I called them up from a pay phone and it was only then that I realised that it was the same group that I'd seen playing live only a week earlier. I went down to London on the train and met them at this rehearsal room that they had in Hendon and even as I walked up towards the door I felt terrified because I was just a 20-year old kid and I was pretty sure that they would want someone with more experience."

However Peter's worries were very soon forgotten as he launched into a few Keith Emerson licks on the piano and suitably impressed the other band members of Principal Edwards that were present. Peter was not the only person up for the job though of course and as he played there were others sitting outside waiting their turn to be called in.

Peter White – "They all looked better qualified than me and much more experienced and I wasn't at all sure that I'd get the job."

Peter had given the band his neighbour's telephone number, because there was no phone at home in Letchworth and a few days later the band left a message there that they wanted to see him again. So Peter journeyed down to the band's flat in West Kilburn where he was told that he'd got the job.

Peter White – "I was over the moon and told them that I had nothing going on whatsoever and could start at once. This was very, very exciting for me and it got better."

The bonus was that not only did Peter have a job now but also along with his new status of keyboard player with Principal Edwards came accommodation in London! The group had just fired the percussionist, David Jones, whose position (albeit as keyboard player) Peter was filling and along with Jones' place in the band went his old room in the house in West Kilburn!

Peter White – "And so here I was living in London, which had always been my dream and I could give people a telephone number to contact me that began with '01' – 01 969 6751 – I can still remember the phone number to this day!"

The tradition at this time with such eclectic, art school bands as Principal Edwards was to spend a lot of time getting to know each other on many levels. To help establish a rapport such as this – it was almost *de rigeur* to get out of London to "get your head together" – and Peter's new-found cohorts back in the Autumn of 1974 were no exception.

Peter White – "We therefore got it together in the countryside. We went down to Devon with all of our equipment. I took my Hammond L100 electric organ which was something I had had to get because it was the keyboard that Keith Emerson had. It was the organ that he used to put the knives into and throw around which was easy because it was a smaller model than the B3. It had cost a small fortune and my mother had signed a hire purchase agreement for it because it was about £500. So we all trooped down to this little farmhouse in Devon where we managed to record about ten songs that the other guys in the band had written. I wasn't writing anything myself at the time. Root Cartwright was the main writer, Nick Pallet was the singer and Geoff Nichols was on drums".

And so by November 1974 they were all back in Kilburn with a bunch of new songs on tape that they took to their manager, the legendary Miles Copeland, who duly listened to the recording of the Devon sessions in his office.

Peter White – "And so he goes through all the songs and says 'Well, you know, I don't really hear anything that I want to hear and I'm afraid it's over!'. And so that was it. The band broke up literally overnight and it was all over – *just like that!*"

BTM had been very much involved in the group and Copeland's decision to pull the plug on Principal Edwards as a BTM act was sufficiently catastrophic to preclude them functioning in any capacity as that group, and so there was no option but to split. That dramatic day had also included a peripheral introduction for Peter into the world of someone that would be a leading player in his professional life for the next eight years. That was Luke O'Reilly.

Peter White – "That day I remember seeing this other really loud and brusque individual prowling around with floppy hair and a very forceful manner and that of course was Luke. It was all a bit 'big time' up there in those BTM offices. Very much 'do this, send that, go there, take that call, I don't have time for all this – bang bang' very much high octane stuff."

Peter also met Nick Blackburn who was BTM's lawyer in London at that time and these were obviously very dark and dismal days for Peter. He'd seen what, for all he knew, was perhaps his only chance at a professional career in music, blow up in his face before the band had even played a gig with him.

Peter elected to stay on in the room, paying £4 a week rent, hoping that his fortunes would take a turn for the better. It was during these lean times that Peter became a good friend with Joe Reed who had played bass in a Principal Edwards line-up that had preceded the final one that included Peter. They decided to form a band together along with Nick Pallet and Geoff Nichols. This is the point where Peter started composing songs in earnest for the first time. He booked a rehearsal room in Letchworth and the band were all going to live at Peter's mother's house – much to her surprise! This had all taken place in the weeks surrounding Christmas 1974 and then in the first week of January 1975 Peter received a telephone call from the brusque, loud and intimidating figure that had been there at the BTM meeting a month earlier – namely Luke O'Reilly.

Peter White – "Luke comes on the phone and says 'Are you interested in coming to play for Al Stewart?' And he gives me this address in St John's Wood, which turns out to be Miles Copeland's place. So off I go and it's this marvellous big house in St Johns Wood. Immediately after my phone conversation with Luke a taxi cab had arrived at the house in Bradiston Road, with an advance copy of *Modern Times* from which I'd learnt 'Carol', 'Dark And The Rolling Sea' and 'Apple Cider' over the few days preceding my arrival at the audition for the job with Al at Miles' house in Marlborough Road. There at the audition were both Luke and Al, no other keyboard players this time, just me – along with Mark Griffiths and Roger Swallow out of Al's group."

This then was the first time that Al played music together with Peter – in the basement studio of Miles Copeland's house in North London in January 1975. Al played guitar and sang, Mark Griffiths and Roger Swallow played bass and drums respectively and Peter played the Fender Rhodes keyboard that was set up there as they launched into the tunes that Peter had taught himself over the previous 48 hours from the copy of *Modern Times*. At the end of the short session Luke, who wasn't in the room for the run through, came in and took Al outside.

Peter White – "Obviously they were outside discussing whether or not I'd got the job! Then Al came back in and said 'Well that's fine then, let's all go over to the pub'. To which I replied 'Do I have the job then, could someone explain to me what's happening?' and Al says 'Well of course, yes, as far as I'm concerned you've got the job!' So we go across to the pub whereupon I made a terrific *faux pas* because in listening to his music I had developed an opinion about it and I told him that I considered it to be middle-of-the-road, which was completely the wrong thing for me to say to him. What I was trying to say was that it wasn't heavy rock and it wasn't folk but I didn't explain myself very well and if I could take it back now I would. Another thing that Al said to me in the pub was that every band sooner or later breaks up but that had never happened to him because he wasn't a band!"

Al – "It was clear to us all from day one that Peter would fit in very well with the line-up that we had then. *Modern Times* was an album that we really wanted to perform well on tour and so it was crucial that we found someone that could do the job. That person was Peter."

That day in the rehearsal studio wasn't the first time that Peter had seen Al play. He had seen him on a bill that included Richard and Linda Thompson in Stevenage a few years previously and also at the infamous Wheeley Festival that featured Stone The Crows, The Groundhogs, King Crimson, Rod Stewart, Family and T. Rex.

Peter White – "In between all of these heavy and loud groups along comes Al, who I guess had been put on the line-up to fill in the gap with an acoustic set whilst a set change was taking place at about 1a.m. I seem to remember him performing 'Love Chronicles' and it was great and I was a real fan."

A short period of band rehearsals then followed Peter's audition before their very first show together at Edinburgh's Usher Hall.

Upon the release of *Modern Times* on February 14th 1975 Al explained that there would be no return in the foreseeable future to the intensely personal love songs that proceeded *Past, Present And Future*. Not that Al had abandoned the obsession that inspired so many of his earlier works: it was to appear on the new album in the track "The Dark And The Rolling Sea". However, in direct contrast to the very specific "date, time and place" references of his old songs, the new work was allegorical, allusive-metaphorical. That track, like so many on the album has stood the test of time and is still an occasional member of the composer's performance repertoire.

Al talked to the *Melody Maker* late at night after a recording session for *Modern Times* about this abrupt change of style.

Al – "There's a limit to the amount that one can take out of too precise a thing. To a certain extent you're caught between two lines of fire? Maybe wrongly, but certainly when you first start writing songs you want to get an exact truth as I said in 'Songs Out Of Clay'. I'm sure I'll perform 'Bedsitter Images' again one day, just to fool everyone. I'm sure I will. It'd be a good number to do with the band apart from anything else."

Having come to the conclusion that in the UK he was typecast as just a folkie, Al determined to consolidate his success in the US by realising a folk-rock sound in response to the American taste for a strong rhythm section, and a vibrant lead guitar. Alan Parsons' production and Tim Renwick's guitar answered the need. Luke had got Al out of his CBS deal in the US and onto the Janus label, which had a permanent staff of just ten who worked very hard on the new album, and it proved to be a hit.

Alan Parsons – "It would be fair to say that Luke was certainly a presence at those *Modern Times* recording sessions! Looking back, I can't recall him interfering in my job as producer on the album, and to be perfectly honest I found him very positive when I came to picking singles for instance."

This is not to say, of course, that Al was not his own man in the studio and Alan Parsons' memories of the recording of *Modern Times* are worth attention here.

Alan Parsons – "I'm sure I'm not the first person to say that Al didn't particularly relish going into a recording studio. However, once he was actually there he became the driving force behind that session. His vocals were always something that needed special attention due to the very pronounced 's' he has. I was possibly one of the first producers, this was 1974 remember, using a 'de-esser' prototype machine. It was very new at the time and was a simple 'plug in and go' type box, which just had one knob on it and was wonderful for the time. However, the difficulty was that if you recorded a track to tape and overdid the 's' reduction element then you couldn't get it back! Al would sing the song through a couple of times on tape and then we'd go through re-recording certain phrases and punching them into the master version. Al was as diligent as anyone else that I've worked with at this; we'd play a track back and would mark the lines that we

Eric J. Reinbott

thought were good and conversely those that we weren't so sure about also. More often than not Al would take a tape home to Belsize Park and would return the next day with the news that musically it was fine but he had now changed the lyric!"

This was something that, since John Anthony's time, each of Al's producers had had to come to terms with as a regular occurrence.

Al – "It's the way that I write, what more can I say? I feel that lyrics are the most important part of my songs and very often they change during the course of recording an album. I know that it causes problems but I like to try and get a song as close to what I set out to say with it in the first place as possible. Often this takes a few drafts."

Alan Parsons – "This was always very frustrating because we'd all spend hours on what would, on the Tuesday night, be seen as a finished track by everyone only to be informed on Wednesday evening by Al that he'd re-written it and it was time to start the lead vocals and obviously on occasions the backing vocals again!"

Modern Times was totally different both lyrically and musically to *Past, Present And Future* and, musically, owed a great debt to the arrangement and production style of Parsons.

Alan Parsons – "Al was quite clearly looking to escape from the role of 'Folksinger' and I was given quite a free rein, musically at least, to make good the transition. He told me that he wanted a more expansive and grand production than he'd achieved previously even though the previous album had had tracks like 'Roads to Moscow' which were a step up from his earlier work. I think we achieved this."

One fact that is often overlooked is just how new Alan Parsons was to production at this time. In *Modern Times* he was taking on a project that would call on all of his skills.

Alan Parsons – "It's interesting that on 'Apple Cider Re-Constitution' it marked one of the very rare occasions when I scored an arrangement for a quartet which at the time terrified me because I'd never written for real musicians before! I had to draw on my limited schoolboy knowledge of notation and just about struggled though it, conducting them personally at Abbey Road in the end. In fact, once *Modern Times* had been released, I came to wish that we'd had a full orchestra on those three songs on side two ('Apple Cider Re-Constitution', 'The Dark And The Rolling Sea' and 'Modern Times'). Of all of the songs on that album that we did I've always felt that 'The Dark And The Rolling Sea' was the standout track, it's got a genuine sense of grandeur."

Al's voice was one of the key factors that determined the duration of a session.

Alan Parsons – "There were of course good throat days and bad throat days. Sometimes Al would give up after only a few lines because he wasn't sure of his ability to carry a song".

Al was still drawing on events and places from his past in seemingly unconnected songs.

Al – "It's something that I have always done. In fact the true origin of 'Apple Cider Re-Constitution' was the local train station at my childhood home at Wilmcote. It had been closed down and seemed to my young eyes to be overgrown and abandoned and when 20 years later I came to write the song, it was Wilmcote that I had in mind. Likewise 'Timeless Skies' refers specifically to the very same place."

Another track, "What's Going On?", was also loosely based on fact. It is about Michael De Barre, from *Detective*.

Interestingly enough, for the song "Modern Times", Al had the title (which was inspired by the Chaplin film and a misunderstanding by Al of Jean Paul Sartre's wartime newspaper's name) but up until the last moment did not have the song written.

Al – "One of the later sets of lyrics to be written but I think that it was worth it in the end! Like many of my songs it appears to be about a real person but it's really not. I'm always being asked about that song! I can remember writing it at home and thinking to myself that it was a very simple story that did seem to be real. But it's not. All made up I'm afraid."

All three songs on side two featured melodies that were not, to varying degrees, strictly Al originals. "The Dark And The Rolling Sea" was based on an Irish ballad, "The Maid Of County Down", "Apple Cider Re-Constitution" bore more than a passing similarity to Dylan's "Absolutely Sweet Marie" whilst of course the title track had a melody and lyric co-written by Al's friend Dave Mudge.

The album cover featured Dave Gilmour's wife and Jimmy Page's Cord, astride which Al was photographed for ads to promote the tour which travelled from Edinburgh's Usher Hall to London's Victoria Palace via such towns and venues as Newcastle City Hall, Warwick University, Leeds Town Hall (on February 14th, Valentines Day 1975 and the album's release day) and the New Theatre, Oxford. Tickets were priced at around £1 per show! Brinsley Schwarz, old friends of course, were the support group. Besides Peter White, the band performing with Al featured ex-Southern Comfort members Roger Swallow and Mark Griffiths.

Meanwhile, throughout all of this, Miles Copeland's direct involvement with Al was slight and therefore Alan Parsons would almost always deal with Luke on business matters.

Alan Parsons – "Miles' involvement through BTM didn't really impart itself into the recording side of Al's career. Certainly he never came to any recording session with Al, be it in London or Los Angeles. I seem to remember having a meeting with him once at his office but that was about it."

Alan Parsons' involvement with Al was formalised via Kinetic Productions which Luke had set up specifically to oversee and administer Al's work. Parsons take on all this, albeit with the benefit of hindsight, is damning.

Alan Parsons – "This situation was to ultimately turn out to be a real problem in later years for me. I wish that my arrangement had been with the record company, things would have been a lot easier to control. If there's ever any one piece of advice that I'd offer to an artist, it would be for them to never work for a production company if that situation can be avoided. Basically, I made *Year Of The Cat* for which I was given an advance, and then I had to wait until '95 before I received anything else except for the advance for *Time Passages*. The blame for this however doesn't rest with Al, I will say that".

It was an arrangement that would go on to cause major problems for Kinetic. Luke recalls that Eric Wolfsan (Alan Parsons' manager), who had previously worked for CBS, refused to do the deal directly with them. Luke remembers Al signing a piece of paper, requested by Wolfsan, in which Arista were required to pay Alan Parsons directly; something that for some reason never in fact happened. Luke agrees that, with hindsight, the routing of everything through Kinetic was a mistake all round.

Luke – "I honestly believe that. Production houses were the fashion of the time but they turned out to be bad for everyone. I've never set up another one since!"

NOT THE ONE
It's the kind of grey November day that washes away reflections
In the eyes of hotel porters
And the latticed wooden benches by the sea contain no travellers
Or Irish lady authors
And the girl in the raincoat walks the lanes of Brighton
With her collar turned against the wind
And hovers in the doorways of second-hand bookshops
Among the dust and fading print
And you're not the one she's thinking of
And you're not the one she really wants
Just a point along the line she's leaving from

She goes into a café, orders tea, looks at the menu
But there's nothing really on it
And the place is as deserted as a plaza in a heat wave
And the cloth has jam upon it

But the girl in the raincoat doesn't stop to count the tealeaves
Or turn to see the mists around the sun
For the winter's unfolding around her
And it's time for moving on
And you're not the one she's thinking of
And you're not the one she really wants
Just a station on the line she's leaving from
And so you sit there in the middle of the carpet
With her suitcases around you
And it comes to you she journeyed to the centre of your life
But she never really found you
Just another girl in a raincoat
Who shared the passing of the days
And you're glad of the warmth that she gave you
And you hardly need to say
That she's not the one you're thinking of
No she's not the one you really want
Just a point along the line you're leaving from

And BTM told *Melody Maker* in their February 15th issue – "His British tour, which began in Edinburgh this week, is scheduled to finish at London's Victoria Palace on March 2. Eight days later Stewart begins an American tour with Leo Sayer and Prelude."

John Anderson reported in *Sounds* on February 22nd – "Stewart's backing band on the British tour features ex-Matthews Southern Comfort members Roger Swallow (drums) and Mark Griffiths (bass), together with keyboards player, Peter White. A new Stewart album, *Modern Times* will be released later this month to coincide with the tour."

During the accompanying tour the press were invited to his Usher Hall show. The *N.M.E.* reported "There have to be better ways of setting out on a world tour than going to Edinburgh on the first night and filling only 800 of the Usher Hall's 2,500 seats. But Al Stewart wasn't downhearted. He's more into student audiences and a lot of the local intelligentsia were up the road at Clouds, paying their respects to Stackridge. Al walked on to the stage laughing – the only way when one has a touch of glandular fever. Like he had. His bass player, too, Mark Griffiths.

"All things considered, the music wasn't bad at all ... if one was obliged to consider, too, that this was the first time Stewart had played with this band. He had rehearsed for 'only a few days' with Griffiths, lead guitar Ken Nicol (a stand-in from Easy Street), Peter White (keyboards) and Roger Swallow (drums). Griffiths, by the ways is a 'founder member' of the new band and recently played this hall with David Essex."

While the British tour was taking place Luke was busy putting the finishing touches to the band's imminent trip to America.

This came up in a John Gibson profile of Al in *Melody Maker* at the end of the month – "A man's got to do what a man's got to do, meaning that when Al Stewart opened his British tour (in fact it's a far-flung safari that will end in America) with glandular fever at the Usher Hall, Edinburgh, there was no going back. As his business associate Luke O'Reilly said backstage, where the dreaded fever had caught bass guitarist Mark Griffiths: 'We've invested a quarter of a million dollars to get this show on the road and take it to America, so naturally Al had second thoughts about calling off tonight.'"

The British Press was still largely hostile to the notion of Al with a band however.

John Gibson again – "In a programme built largely round extracts from his new album *Modern Times* there was nothing to whack 'Old Admirals' from the preceding *Past Present And Future* collection. If I've got to be lumbered with something that can be very loosely described as a sea shanty, I'd prefer to hear it like this.

"Midway through the set the band walked off leaving Stewart alone with his acoustic guitar. The point where the lyrical content of his writing and his ability as a guitar player came over loud and clear."

Melody Maker profiled Al on March 1st in a piece that continued the theme of Al's attempts at achieving a wider recognition in the States.

"Stewart admits to being slightly hurt that he's never received the acclaim in this country he feels he has earned, and now appears to be getting in the States. So it's an easy enough decision for him to make to concentrate fully on America. At the end of his current British tour, commitments in the States take him through to the end of the year and if all goes well he'll have settled in and there'll be no question of coming back then."

This was a time of reflection for Al. Success in America had come to mean everything to him and now, just a week away from flying out there on a crucial tour, he took stock about his roots.

He was featured in a major article in the *Daily Express* – "One of the most attractive features about American audiences to him is that they don't hold so many preconceived notions about his work. In Britain he definitely feels he's been hampered by the folk image. True, he did come up with the folk revival when London clubs were at their strongest, but before then he was playing in beat groups in Bournemouth, so his roots lie in rock also.

"He says he loved the whole folk club period, however, and regards his survival in the wake of overwhelming retirements and undignified withdrawals as proof of his sincerity.

"'The ones that survive are the ones that are truly committed to their work, and as each year has gone by they've not fallen back but have actually pushed a little bit further. I have great faith in the word amateur in the sense of lover. I'm not really sure that I'll ever be very professional on stage because in a sense I'm an amateur in the Renaissance sense.'

"Fired with the enthusiasm of an American big-seller Stewart holds grand ambitions for the future. He describes himself as an immature person not yet ready to tackle half the ideas in his head but he talks of forming an idyllic folk-rock band, and later turning to writing as his main outlet. He has prepared a substantial amount of material for a 'surrealist' novel and he can see himself in the future as a novelist.

"'Everything I do at the moment is a process of learning. I haven't even reached the first space of what I've done after ten years. And yet everything has been stored away. The whole of life can only be seen in a direction as a journey. I don't think there is an arrival point. I don't expect ever to make it. It's how you make the journey and whether you can sustain improvement."

The final gig of the UK *Modern Times* tour was reviewed in the *New Musical Express* that hit the news stands on March 8th – "Al Stewart said goodbye to his London audience Sunday night with a polished and self-assured, but unaffecting set.

"It was as if, having made the decision to concentrate on his ambitions for America, Stewart's involvement on this last British gig was somewhat remote.

"The band is a tricky proposition for Al. While removing him from his unwanted 'folkie' image and providing a professional backing, the band treatment in some cases – 'Old Admirals' particularly – either trivialised or submerged his lyrics, leaving the impression of just one more good but unspectacular rock band.

"On his own for a few acoustic numbers Stewart's strong, clear voice and intelligent work was more impressive, especially on the unusual 'Roads To Moscow'.

"This is not to say that 'Al Stewart has sold out because he's gone electric', because the last numbers with the band, 'The Dark And The Rolling Sea' and 'Modern Times' were high points."

Whilst *Melody Maker*, reviewed the farewell show thus, also on March 8th – "In truth, it wasn't quite the *Grand Farewell* everyone seemed intent on manufacturing. In the end it came right with a rousing reception and an outstanding solo version of 'Post World War Two Blues' but prior there had been moments of doubt and uncertainty. Stewart never has been the most professional of performers and Victoria Palace revealed more than a few rough edges, although he gave a brilliant performance – but a question mark must be raised over the band behind him."

Doubts about Al and his band were also expressed when *Melody Maker* reviewed *Modern Times* on March 15th – "Al Stewart has constantly shown the symptoms of a frustrated rock 'n' roller. There have been frequent and often not very successful attempts to get a boogie band behind him, and Stewart's approach has been that of a man who longs to front a gutsy band. Previous efforts in this direction have lacked credibility because of the emphasis and self-importance attached to his lyrics, and because he has appeared to want an instant and total transformation involving some heavy musicians instead of letting things run a natural and gradual course."

With *Modern Times* though, *Melody Maker* felt that Al had probably made a move in the right direction. In the past they had devoted many column inches to this debate but now it appeared Al and Luke's faith in a band had been vindicated at last.

Melody Maker again – "On this album, there's been a sensible compromise which in terms of a progression to rock, make it reasonably successful. The songs are generally lighter and more suited to an up-tempo treatment, while the accompanying band supply the extra body without getting too carried away. As a deliberate and wisely cautious step in a heavier direction, it's fine – you can tap your foot and hum along, appreciate a couple of outstanding guitar solos without it ever getting too hairy. Yet, I'm sure a lot of Stewart devotees will be disappointed."

Peter White – "And lo and behold at the end of the British tour Al announces that we're all off to America! This was when I met Steve Chapman for the first time. On the first date we opened for Leo Sayer and Steve was his drummer."

Al – Steve of course had been sharing that apartment with Tim Renwick and Peter Wood and Charlie Harrison all of whom I worked with. So yes it was all very incestuous!"

Peter – "We also played on a bill in Milwaukee with Billy Joel and Sha Na Na at which time I went straight out and bought myself my first Les Paul guitar. Then, one day when I was holding that Gibson Les Paul, I bumped into Jimmy Page at the Hyatt House Hotel in Hollywood!"

During this first tour Peter was strictly the keyboard player with Tim Renwick on guitar and Peter Wood piano.

Peter White – "I played the Fender Rhodes, Hammond B3 and a string synthesiser besides a little mini moog. At this time of course I wasn't playing any guitar at all, having been hired as the keyboard player."

Not only had these been Peter's very first gigs in America with Al, it was Nigel Lendon's first time working for him anywhere! His experience, as what amounted to Tour Manager (although no job resumé was ever written down) was testimony from day one of the complete faith that Luke had in Nigel's abilities to cope with any eventuality and to leave him to it. It was a heady brief.

Nigel Lendon – "All I was given was an air ticket and a brief to fly over to Philadelphia in advance to sort everything out! I was sitting on the plane flying across the Atlantic thinking 'This is great, of course it is, but what exactly have I let myself in for here?!' On my arrival at the Holiday Inn the very first thing I did was to get in touch with the company that were providing the sound system for the gig in a couple of nights time. The guy with them invited me down to the Arena where they were doing a Gladys Night And The Pips show, with a not dissimilar sound desk to what we'd be presented with for Al's show. So that's what I did. It was then up to me to basically arrange everything, I eventually discovered, which was …well it was an interesting challenge for sure! This was also the first time that I met Steve Chapman."

Steve Chapman – "I had had a band with Chris Stainton, who was Joe Cocker's partner. The other members were Les Nichol on guitar and Charlie Harrison on bass. We got hired to back Leo Sayer throughout his US tour of March and April 1975. This included doing The Midnight Special in Los Angeles and a week at The Bottom Line in New York City where Hall and Oates were our opening act."

Randall Armor

Tim Renwick is a very quiet and modest person. He is also someone that rarely gives interviews. He made an exception however in 2002 and agreed to share a few memories of the work he's done with Al.

Tim Renwick – "I'd heard of Al long before Quiver first came to work with him and of course I played on *Orange* in the early seventies and I enjoyed that. He was someone that always seemed to know what he wanted in the studio and this is a great help to a musician like myself. When I played on the Alan Parsons albums there seemed to be a lot more time spent in the studio and those three albums are unique in many ways. They're a genuine trilogy and have their own sound. I'm quite an instinctive player and I enjoyed recording *Modern Times* especially. People often ask me about the playing on that. I think that the long songs especially mean a great deal to the fans. There were a few complications concerning The Sutherland Brothers and Quiver at this time and Al was always very generous to me. I remember playing some American dates with Al and his band just after *Modern Times* had come out but unfortunately I haven't played that many actual shows with Al which is a pity. He's a very talented individual. We should have played more shows together…"

On the first night of the tour where Al was co-headlining with Leo Sayer at The Academy Of Music, the opinion of all the band members is that they got a great response.

Luke – "But I was disappointed as it was somewhat frigid and I'd hoped that we were going to do better than that because we had this great band. The problem turned out to be the venue that was so formal that people were a little intimidated because at that time rock 'n' roll was still played in clubs and seedy cinemas. So going into a beautiful venue like that was unusual, so that wasn't ideal; but then we stopped off in Milwaukee and did a couple of gigs where we were supporting Billy Joel. Then he pulled out on a gig so we were stuck in the mid-west. We then flew out to the West Coast with the band and to be honest it was always a hand to mouth existence at that time."

Touring with a band and only the bare minimum of financial support was of course a situation that Al was used to by now. Luke had a remedy for this however.

Luke again – "I'd made a commitment that we were going to have a band and that was the way the cookie was going to crumble. So before the tour we'd done some solo gigs in England to get a road float. Anytime we needed a road float I'd book a couple of solo dates, we'd get £500 of which Al would get £150 per show and I'd get £700 over the two gigs to put into the band. So I had a float to pursue my dream and Al had the security of £150 a night at least and it was an arrangement that suited everyone."

On this trip, possibly for the first time on a foreign tour, Al was surrounded by a crew that was up to the task. In the band he had his best musicians to date.

Nigel Lendon – "It was a very fast learning curve for all of us on that first American tour. Now, of course, much of the material was drawn from the new album on which Tim Renwick had featured so prominently and Al made no secret of the fact that he considered Tim Renwick to be the best guitar player in the world bar none. Those dates that we played with Tim with us in the band were very memorable for me because, not only was I getting to grips with working for Al and Luke but I was also being introduced to Al's music, night after night on this American tour. It wasn't all plain sailing though…"

Al – "Well everything in those days was chaos, I mean it had been chaos all the way through, if you look back. I mean basically you know the first album was a nightmare, the second one I had a cold on one of the tracks, then the catastrophe of *Zero She Flies* and the mistake of all those horrible love songs on *Orange*. *Past Present And Future* was a turn up for the books, but then you know all the sort of horrible things that were going on around that period of time. And then with *Modern Times* we arrived and all the amplifiers blew up on the second night of the show at the Paramount Theatre, Portland."

Luke – "Yes they did! We get to the West Coast to do the Portland show and the room's got about 1,200 people in it. Although the gig hadn't gone spectacularly well I thought it was OK and I walk backstage and Al comes up to me immediately and says that this is wrong, that's wrong, the monitors are no good, all that sort of thing. What happened was that the band had spoken to Al, and I so I take it and I march off down to the promoter."

This was a genuine turning point in that tour as it was, in many ways, Luke's reputation and integrity at stake here as the notion of having a band (and hence all that equipment) was largely his. He went to work.

Luke – "I start yelling and screaming saying that 'We've got to have this done this way!' and so on and so forth and 'I know you guys are nice guys but you can't put me in this position again'. The promoter promised that he'd have everything sorted out by the next day and in my innocence I walked away and felt that I'd got everything sorted out satisfactorily and that the next night's gig would be great. One thing I'd always said to Al was that whenever we started to make money he'd see a difference but until that time arrives he should just ignore all of the hassles. I told him long before that night in Seattle that 'if I couldn't get the best lights we'd get the second best, if I can't get this we'll do that' and that's just the way it is until you make money for people. I said 'once you start making money for people and we go into a profit-making situation I guarantee you that things will change'. I quoted that many times on the tour."

And so the following day everyone travelled the short distance to the next show which was in Seattle. As soon as Luke arrived it was obvious to him that things had indeed changed for the better.

Luke – "They had changed completely! We arrived at The Paramount in Seattle and went backstage and found everything there was totally perfect! I stood there thinking that we only had a deli-tray the night before in Portland with some dried up pieces of cheese and some sodas and now we had champagne on ice, seafood on ice. I thought well, how clever I was and I remember leaning out of the window and I could see this huge crowd queued all of the way round the building and I wondered if perhaps the great treatment we were getting from the promoter was due to the profit-making situation rather than my heated words the previous night."

In fact Luke went on to become close personal friends with John and Ivy, the promoters. His optimism that night regarding the ticket sales was well placed.

Luke – "I asked someone at the theatre how well we were doing on tickets and they say that things are going pretty well and I decide that we'll go on first that night because I don't want a loud band to go in front of Al and deafen people's ears. So we've got the record company up from Los Angeles in town for the show, we've got every DJ in town there as well and all of this is very positive. And I walk out on stage to introduce Al and I still get shivers down my back when I think back on this. What comes back from that audience was just amazing and I knew then back in 1975 that I was right. I can't really describe what happened but it was one of those defining moments, right up there with that first evening at The Canteen at The Central London Polytechnic when I'd first see what Al's charisma could do to an audience. That audience crawled all over me and I was just introducing Al! It was something electric and was something that I'd never felt before."

Luke is certain that he knows where that reaction had come from.

"The love of that audience that night in Seattle had come from airplay on K20K. Al and I had come up the time before with George Carlin and had bothered to go around the radio stations, although Al at the time was wanting to get back to England. Here we were now and guess what was the most played song for the previous year behind 'Layla' and 'Stairway To Heaven'. It was 'Roads To Moscow'. It was totally amazing to discover this although I have to say that the tour was a pain in the butt. One of the other pieces of icing on the cake was that the promoters were John and Ivy Baeur and they were in big with ICM and the very next morning they were on the phone to us about how great all this was. After our set we had a party, the other band were still rocking away upstairs, the audience had mostly left and they'd obviously all been there to see Al and it was one of the more exciting moments in my life. From the first note of the very first song to the encore the audience went mad and Al could do no wrong. It was a response like no other that I've ever heard, it was a 3,000-seater theatre that could have taken off."

Not every night was like this though. Al had quite a hard time on this tour with the new equipment!

Al – "Luke had had specially designed a PA cabinet so that I could play my acoustic guitar through it. These great big white boxes were custom built. But the whole back line went half way through the set. Everything was dead. They not only blew up but they blew up everything else up on stage. It was like a chain reaction. All these things were like going out one after the other. Total disaster. I remember being upstairs in the dressing room and half the band wanted to go home. It was just so amateurish and I think Tim Renwick was almost on a plane at that point back to England and Luke was screaming and I of course just was despairing. Peter Wood was probably hiding! You just felt that it was total madness. I don't even know who built these things but they were just wretched. They weighed three tons, you couldn't put them on and off aeroplanes because they would cost a fortune to move around and when you did finally set them up they didn't work. We had all these big boxes and then on the Home tour we shipped the

Modern Times Tour. Spring 1975.

mellotron over also, no one could lift this thing. It was horrible."

In fact they used *three* Mellotrons on the tour.

Al – "All of which broke! They cost a fortune and they kept breaking down, nobody could make them work. Plus the van broke down all the time!. The early days of touring to me were just everything breaking. I mean nothing ever worked. I mean it is like you plug something in and there was an explosion, it was like fireworks night every night. You never knew what to expect and we could not make anything work on that tour. We couldn't seem to make equipment work; it wasn't until at least around the time of *Year Of The Cat* that anything started to work properly. We never did sort it out; it went on and on."

The frustration that Al felt with the stage equipment was, to a large extent, justified – given that it was a facet of his live performance that had dogged him since he toured *Orange* in England for the first time. He was of the opinion that whenever he allowed himself to be talked into some new piece of stage hardware, be it an instrument or part of the amplification, then it would invariably literally blow up in their faces.

Al – "Basically from around about 1971 when I first started putting bands together, to deep into 1975, there was a four year stretch where I am playing with any number of musicians and on not one occasion do I remember things working properly. Part of it was the equipment of the day, it just didn't work very well anyway. I mean I would even go and see other bands and their stuff would break down all the time. Audiences in those days were just used to standing around while people repaired things. But ours broke down more than any one else's. Eventually we had a string synthesiser and that didn't work either! I would stand hopelessly on the stage listening to feedback and distortion and explosions and it just happened night after night. It wasn't fun working with a band but Luke was determined that that was what we should do. Nigel Lendon was so nice. He was forever running around trying to fix all this rubbish. Horrible things that we were carting around all of which weighed a ton and none of which worked properly."

This being Peter's first overseas tour with Al, he had been naturally anxious to fit in. Towards the end of this first leg Al and Luke discussed the situation of him staying on, regardless of whether or not Peter Wood returned for the second leg, and just before they flew home Al took the initiative.

Peter White – "At the very end of those first US dates when we got to O'Hare airport in Chicago I remember something that happened as if it were yesterday. Al took me to one side and said how grateful he'd been to me and how also he felt I'd been the most enthusiastic band member and had always played my best, day in day out and how he truly appreciated it. Now this coming at this time was something that meant a lot to me".

Luke – "Peter had had to put up with an *awful* lot on that trip and he dealt with it all with the utmost maturity throughout. He worked harder than anyone despite everything that was going on around him. I really liked Peter."

There was then a short break in the tour before Al flew back to the States on the midday flight from Heathrow on 4th June for the second leg that would include the gig at Kent State University where "Year Of The Cat" was born. Peter Wood *did* in fact play that second part of the tour.

Luke – "This of course wasn't part of the plan! Back in England for a couple of weeks in May I had been working on getting The Sutherland and Quiver a record deal. One day we were all in Miles' office about to have a meeting about their careers when Peter Wood stood up and announced that he was quitting the band! So he joined us which of course didn't make me too popular with the band members he'd left behind!"

Peter White – "I guess the logical thing would have been for Luke to have fired me at this point because having two keyboard players wasn't really necessary but perhaps they weren't sure about how long Peter Wood was going to be around for. Al and Luke both liked me and I was kept on. This was despite the fact that Peter Wood and Tim Renwick had decided to formally leave The Sutherland Brothers and Quiver and Peter Wood did actually decamp to America whereupon he joined Natural Gas, whom he played with besides gigging with Al. Through all of this I was aware of the fact that Peter Wood really didn't like me, which was no doubt based on the fact that I was a keyboard player and possibly a threat to him. I could not understand this because compared to me he was a veteran of the music business, but he always made it very clear that he did not want anything to do with me and basically threw out all of these bad vibes towards me whenever we were around one another. So I just kept out of his way as best I could."

Nigel Lendon – "Luke took a far more pragmatic stance on this. I'm sure he realised that ultimately Peter White was going to be around for the long run and tolerated this simmering tension as something that he could keep the lid on."

Luke – "He was young, enthusiastic and a great musician even at that early stage. He was just the right sort of guy. These were early days and we were still bringing him along and the rest of us really liked him because I always stick up for the underdog. I was determined that things were going to run my way and I wasn't going to be dictated to ever again by a band, it just didn't seem worthwhile.

"By this mid tour break *Modern Times* had got to number 28 in *Cashbox* and number 30 in *Billboard* and we'd done a lot of radio and therein given the impression that there was quite a buzz going on and things were going well."

For the second part of the tour Snowy White replaced Tim Renwick on guitar. Luke had seen Snowy play his Gibson Les Paul at a gig at The Marquee Club in London and earmarked him as a possible guitarist in the band a while before. And so it was with yet another line-up Al prepared to consolidate the early success of *Modern Times*, touring the Deep South, including Austin, Texas, with Queen.

The band then returned to the UK and Peter divided his time between the family home in Hertfordshire and the flat in West Kilburn. Back at base, the other remaining members of Principal Edwards were not enjoying any success at all in their individual quests for work within bands.

Meanwhile Al embarked on a musical departure. The hours spent working at Trident on *Orange*, in the studio next door to where Bowie was at the same time recording *Ziggy Stardust*, influenced Al in many ways. He was the first to admit an admiration for Bowie's use of language and expressed a genuine affection for his music in the most charming and direct way – he now wrote a Bowie song. It was a piece that used many of the oblique calling cards of style that remain Bowie's hallmark. The sense of isolation, a melody based around simple rhythm piano, even the vocal phrasing and double tracking of his own voice in two octaves were total copies of Bowie. The result was the mysterious "Dangerzone". Mysterious, because it gives no clue lyrically as to how the singer of the song found himself in such a situation, whilst musically it is unlike any Al song before or since. Lyrically it's a lost Spiders From Mars song *circa* 1972, but musically it's absolutely *The Bewlay Brothers* meets a slowed down *Rebel Rebel*. There are even maracas on it. Written and demoed in the summer of 1975 it's Al's Bowie homage.

DANGERZONE
Nothing but a target on my chest
Is getting me worried
Nothing but the water rising round my ears
Slow and unhurried

I was in the Dangerzone
I was all alone no one around
I was in the Dangerzone
I was all alone
No help to be found
Suddenly I saw you standing there
My hopes were growing
Will you get me out of here?

But you just kept going
I was in the Dangerzone
I was all alone no one around
I was in the Dangerzone

I was all alone
No help to be found

It was also the first Al recording that Peter White ever appeared on. He plays piano on it.

Now, in late June 1975, Tom Bonetti of Janus entered the fray. He told Luke that in order for Janus to fund the recording of the next album, something that CBS had done for *PP&F* and *Modern Times*, Kinetic would have to agree to an extension to their existing agreement with Janus. Luke felt that the timing for this was less that perfect. Although the sales of *Modern Times* had been good (it had been a top 30 album in the States), they had not been amazing and he felt that he and Al were not therefore in the strongest bargaining position at that time. However the situation was resolved when CBS returned the masters of the albums *Bedsitter Images*, *Love Chronicles* and *Zero She Flies* to Al because their contract on them had expired. These were then given to Janus instead of a contract extension and secured the small advance that was sent straight to Abbey Road to cover the start of the new album's recording.

The summer of 1975 now saw the first work at Abbey Road Studios on what was to become the *Year Of The Cat* album with Alan Parsons once again as producer. Meanwhile, the tension between the two Peters continued.

Peter White – "This is what actually happened on that first day at Abbey Road. Al came in and said 'Look, Peter Wood is here today so why don't you play some acoustic guitar? We could do with some finger-style guitar work here. Could you help out on that?' To which I replied 'Sure, but I haven't got a guitar here.' So Al unpacked his Guild guitar and I played that acoustic guitar on the track on the first day of those sessions at Abbey Road. So all was well and good but the next day, before the second evening session, Al rang me up and said that he'd got some bad news for me. This was that Peter Wood had made it obvious that he'd like it if I weren't around in the studio at the same time as him! Now this somewhat flattered me because I was really just this nobody and here I was freaking out this quite famous piano player in Al's band."

This situation continued throughout the recording of the album and the two Peters managed to avoid each other completely. Much of this time Peter spent hanging out with Marion up at the house in Belsize Village.

Peter White – "I just waited there playing the piano and wondering what all of the fuss was about!"

This strange situation continued for much of that stage of the Abbey Road recording sessions. It would remain unresolved for the next 15 years.

Peter White – "In fact I wasn't really there for most of the making of the album. Then one day Al called up and said that he had this song called 'On The Border' for which Tim Renwick had already done an acoustic guitar piece that wasn't exactly what Al had been looking for and would I have a go at doing a Spanish guitar solo. To which I replied 'that would be great' but I did not have a Spanish guitar!

"So he got me a guitar and up until this time I knew very little about the song, I knew it was F-sharp-minor and that was about it, although I had heard the track played. So what I did at home was that I recorded myself strumming in that key on a tape recorder and then playing on top of it working out all of these little solo sections. From there I went into the studio and Alan Parsons said for me to initially record one track with me playing all the way through, whereupon we do that and he asks me to do it again but this time not to do anything until Al sings the words 'On The Border', which at the time I thought was a terrible mistake because I'd thought that the acoustic guitar should be there from the very start. But of course he was absolutely right and it had much more effect his way. So that was my second day in the studio, recording 'On The Border'."

Peter had thus managed to make an immediate impression on those sessions by dint of his musical dexterity and so establishing himself as one of Al's right hand men in the studio. He also by now had got to know Luke a little better.

Nigel Lendon – "In these early days of Luke's association with Al, I felt that it was actually very Luke-dominated in so far as business decisions were concerned. Luke's word was law and whatever Luke thought, they did."

For Peter White these were amazing times: less than a year before he had been looking into the abyss that had followed the break-up of Principal Edwards.

Peter White – "I loved my time at Abbey Road and throughout it all I would spend hour after hour up in the control room there whenever I got the chance. It was totally fascinating to me to be in there watching how a record got made. I remember Alan Parsons saying I was free to go home once and I asked him if it was OK for me to stay and just hang out watching it all. I learned a lot."

The origin of the music for the title track came out of a US gig on the *Modern Times* tour in the summer of 1975. As such it was something of a unique song for Al. Up until now almost all of his songs had been written by Al at home on the guitar with him composing the lyrics later on. With the song "Year Of The Cat" though, the song's genesis was very different.

Luke – "Al had been moaning at me for a while saying 'Why can't we get consistent musicians?' and I replied that 'You've either got to have a hit and pay them a lot of money for publishing or you're going to have to write songs with them because that will keep them around.' At the sound check for a gig that Spring at Kent State University they started up this riff and I stood there thinking 'God I like this!' and so I ran up to Al saying 'That riff, that riff Al, I love that riff' and he replied 'Yes, that's Peter Wood's riff' and it was something that the whole band had been playing along with. So after the sound check Al walks over to Peter Wood in the dressing room and says 'You know what, we really should do something on that tune together sometime.'"

And that's how the song "Year Of The Cat" was born.

Luke – "Now on the album before this, *Modern Times*, I'd been quite strict with Al on the studio costs although it was with his agreement. I didn't have the authority to say you'll do it this way or that way. This is how we worked on *Modern Times*. We did two tracks a night. Al would spend an hour and a half teaching the group the song and then they'd record the track and we'd record two songs a night like this for a week and then the rest was overdubs. These backing tracks were all completed within ten days! But with *Year Of The Cat* we had a rehearsal period before we did all of the backing tracks, including the one that became 'Year Of The Cat' which at the time was called 'Foot Of The Stage', which had an embryonic set of lyrics that were never completed."

For Nigel Lendon the gig at Kent State is one that remains with him to this day.

Nigel – "Playing there in 1975 was a very sobering experience coming as it did so soon after the student shootings. I remember vividly going outside onto the Campus to take a look around and I know several others in the group did the same thing on the afternoon between that sound check and the show later than night. We walked around for quite a while actually…"

Luke was continuing to exert a great deal of influence, far more so than any of Al's previous managers had ever done up until that time. The success that Al had enjoyed under his care and control over the last two years was proof enough that their relationship worked and worked very well.

Luke – "At the time what I was saying to Al was that you've been crossing all of your i's and dotting all of your t's. The songs about you and Mandi were all fine, very well and legitimate at the time but you're going to have to write in the third person in order to interest more people so that more people can become familiar with and identify with your music. He'd already successfully written his lyrics in the third person on *Past, Present And Future* and I wanted to try and stop it from going back to songs in the first person such as those on the first four albums. I had this dream and vision of what we needed to do to be successful and I wanted Al to be aware of certain things."

Luke had by now put some real backbone into Al's management in order to expedite this 'dream' and 'vision'. He had Marion on his side too.

Luke – "With all of my bands I've always said come to America and listen to radio and you'll understand. Marion was saying the same thing too. She was saying 'Listen to Luke, these songs of yours should be available to everyone'. So Al made a conscious effort to do this on *Modern Times* and by *Year Of The Cat* things had eased up a bit because he was feeling a little bit easier with the new genre and whether he liked it or not he'd played 80 or 90 dates with a band thrashing behind him and I don't care what anyone says, that always improves things and you cannot play that many gigs with a band and *not* have it influence you in some way."

There now followed a nine month hiatus in the middle of the recording of the album. There were several explanations for this.

Luke – "Quite frankly, Alan Parsons wasn't available all of the time and he wasn't willing to produce the album until Al had finished the lyrics and Al, as usual, wanted to finish the lyrics as he was riding in the cab to the studio, just like he'd done so many times before! We had done all of the backing tracks and when Al got lazy about writing those lyrics I certainly wasn't going to push him like the previous time because we were a little disappointed with *Modern Times* and all realised that it had been a little too rushed."

A few weeks later, in the late November of 1975, Al was offered a break from recording in the form of some shows at The Tower Theatre, Philadelphia and at Madison

Square Garden in New York with Renaissance. He jumped at the chance.

Luke – "I then got back to the American promoter to say that we weren't willing to go all that way to do just four dates and so he booked us some more and we ended up playing a dozen shows. The reason that I think Al wanted to go over to do those shows at that time was that it would mean he wouldn't have to come up with the album lyrics for the time being. Either way, we now lost some of our momentum and the process of doing the album somewhat petered out for a while."

Al decided to use different musicians for this short series of American dates. He retained Peter White however.

Peter White – "So it looked like I was a proper member of the band! The album had been due to be finished and released by Christmas to be followed by an American East Coast tour but it was still nowhere near completion by Autumn 1975 when Miles offered us those East Coast dates. Al decided that he wanted a different band for them and so we held auditions in an abandoned church hall in London which involved Byzantium, and out of this Al decided that he'd hire Charlie Harrison and Steve Chapman."

Steve Chapman was ultimately destined to be one of the most influential people in Al's career. Born in North London in November 1949, his career in music had included work with The Fables, Pandemonium and Juniors Eyes. He'd also worked for music publishers Shotton and Co. and Essex Music, rising through the ranks there from office boy to promotion work, via a stint as librarian. Destined to manage the careers of, among others, both Al and Peter, this was to serve him well 20 years down the line! The band that flew out to Philadelphia were Charlie Harrison, Snowy White, Peter White, Peter Wood and Steve Chapman.

Marion accompanied Al on the trip and even went onto appear on stage at one of the gigs as "Slender Splendour", wearing a multi-coloured wig!

Whilst they were in the US they took a short break at the funky Gramercy Park Hotel at the bottom of Lexington Avenue in New York City. The purpose of the extended trip was also to keep Al occupied and, from Luke's perspective, to expose him to US radio on an increasing basis so that it would seep into his writing more and more.

Al and Luke may very well have made some key personnel appointments in Nigel and Peter but finances continued to restrict them in 1975.

Nigel – "With those band tours of America it was, in many respects, back to basics. The band would fly but of course the equipment had to be driven, with the roadies and myself taking turns at the driving – grabbing some sleep along the way in the truck. Those early days really were very hard work."

With *Modern Times* doing well it was obvious that the role played by Alan Parsons had been a key factor in its success. The actual selection of songs and where they appeared on the album, in particular the three song suite on side two, was a subject of much debate by fans and press alike. In reality the songs had basically chosen themselves however.

Al– "I have a plan! Over the years people have constantly asked about the sequencing on my albums, specifically *Modern Times* and how the running order was selected. There's no great mystery to it however. What I do is write down all of the song titles and then all of the keys that they're in and I then make an effort not to have songs next to each other that are in the same key. That's all there is to it."

When *Modern Times* came out in the UK it sold significantly more than any of Al's previous albums had and so Janus picked up the option to release it in the States.

Ed De Joy – "On the first East Coast tour for *Past, Present And Future* I didn't meet up with Al; that came on the next tour but through all of this Alan Mason was the contact between Janus and Al. Alan had also established a good relationship with Luke. It was clear to me, when I had got to know both Al and Luke, that Al had absolute trust in Luke which with hindsight was maybe a mistake."

Despite any misgivings he may have harboured over the nature of Luke's involvement, Ed De Joy couldn't fail but be impressed by the facts when it came to seeing Al in concert at this time.

Ed De Joy – "When Al started to play sizeable venues in places such as Seattle and Philadelphia I was blown away. Philadelphia was a similar town to Baltimore with a black rock 'n' roll sound happening and not, I would have thought, a liking for Al's style of folk music – so when he found that he could fill such places as The Tower Theatre then that was amazing! It had nothing whatsoever to do with the musical culture of those two markets and everything to do with the dynamic of Al's music. It made a major impact. Janus probably sold 50 per cent of their copies of *Past, Present And Future* in those two markets. The first time I saw Al perform live was in a small club in Philadelphia and although his music wasn't a style that was my particular favourite I found the performance mesmerising – as did the rest of the audience."

From this time on Luke was working on his own in the role of supporting Al.

Luke – "We finished that short American tour but Miles and I had recently fallen out and would no longer work together. BTM was Miles' company but Al was signed to Kinetic and Kinetic assigned some rights to BTM. So Al's contracts were always with Kinetic. The other acts' contracts were all with BTM. Al's were with me and I had a deal with BTM so Al was never really a BTM act.

"So we've finished the US dates and it's largely a question of 'When can we catch up with Alan Parsons?' We would in fact have to wait another six months."

Ever on the lookout for some interesting press coverage Luke eventually came up with his own angle on their enforced sojourn in the States. It was not a new trick, Al himself had talked about it in the past but now the time seemed just right for them go for broke.

Luke – "So this is when we pulled the 'Al leaving England' thing. I had been saying to Al that 'the only way we were going to break the British market was by going and breaking America and then returning here and I guarantee then you'd sell out'. To be honest, when I said that to Al I had no idea that it would in fact do as well as it did back in Britain. I had a good idea that it might but I was spouting beliefs rather than certainties! We'd done this tour back in the UK with Brinsley Schwarz, nobody had made any money, we'd got about 1,000 people or so in when we played the big halls but nobody was that interested and much of the press was very anti-Al. Somehow Al had upset some journalist's ego who wrote under the name of Captain Kool who was always writing things like 'Al Stewart is arrogant' and 'Al Stewart zzzzzz ...' and I thought well, we don't have to put up with all this nonsense, Al, so let's go somewhere where they don't know us and where they'll accept us for what we are now, not the fact that you're someone who was folkie of the year in 1969 and is a has-been, because I don't think that at all."

At this time CBS weren't prepared to pay more than $30,000 for the album and one of the unsuccessful pitches made was to Richard Branson at his Virgin Records offices in Notting Hill, London.

Luke – "As I recall the conversation, Richard was very nice but he said that it wasn't really his sort of music. I do recall that we made a very good presentation right across the desk from him but at this time he didn't have any pop acts and hadn't got wise by then. He told us 'It's good stuff but doesn't quite fit in with us, so no thank you' and that was that! Al and I were somewhat disappointed because we both really thought that Virgin Records would have been a good move for us."

Up until this time CBS had financed the recording of the albums that Janus then picked up to release in the US. Without CBS, Al and Luke now needed someone to finance the recording of the new album. Janus came up with the money.

Ed De Joy – "The deal that Janus had with Kinetic was that Luke had been due to deliver a finished album and upon delivery we would pay him a set fee that would be deductible against royalties. Once the recording of *Year Of The Cat* had started to drag on Luke informed me that the costs they were incurring were substantially more and that Janus would need to put up money in advance. Now we were the obvious people for him to come to for money and I had had no problem with that, but the methods that he used were all unnecessary and hard to relate to. I would have given them the money anyway because Janus needed the album and Alan had heard some of the material that would be on it and said how great it was. So I advanced Kinetic an additional $60,000 over and above what I was committed to paying. At a GRT event that he came to Al was so nice to everyone, he even went around those company offices in Sunnyvale thanking people for all of their hard work. Once we had the album we realised that it was the one we'd been waiting for and we all had a meeting at which we all agreed to give it 100 per cent effort."

Ultimately, on March 24th 1976, a contract was signed in London between Kinetic and RCA for the UK.

Luke – "We went to RCA when Peter Bailey, who had been the first record company executive to call me in a few years earlier at CBS, signed us for a $35,000 cash advance plus a very good royalty rate."

Al flew out to the States in March 1976 for a month's break to primarily get what Luke called a "quick fix of LA". All was far from hunky dory however upon their arrival on the West Coast. Luke had asked Janus to provide them with a suitable hotel for their visit, the bill for which would be taken out of future royalties. However when Al and Luke arrived they found that they'd been booked into a cheap $20 a night hotel by the record company. So they jumped back into their car and drove on up Sunset and booked themselves into The Hyatt, otherwise known as The Riot House, for their stay. Whilst they were there Al played on the Strip and they also looked into long term accommodation for them both, it always having been Luke's intention to return to live in the USA. When Al flew back from the sunshine of the West Coast he was met by one of England's hottest summers on record, a fact that certainly influenced the lyrics that he now sat down to write in Belsize Village. That English summer of 1976 would prove to be the catalyst for some of his most upbeat lyrics ever. He returned home to London that April, writing them for the next four months.

It was now clear to everyone that they would need to relocate to LA in order to complete the recording of *Year Of The Cat*. This was due, in the main, to Alan Parsons' continued involvement in an album by Ambrosia that had kept him in Los Angeles throughout much of mid-1976. This latest trip by Al and Luke to LA would occupy a month of that summer. Luke's thinking was that if he and Al literally showed up on Alan Parsons' doorstep in LA then they stood a much better chance of getting the job done. This soon proved to be the case.

Al – "This all seemed fine at the time. It had felt natural to allow *YOTC* to evolve at its own pace rather than rushing things. I honestly believe that."

Throughout his career Al has written several features and essays for specialist wine magazines. The first of these appeared now in the June 1976 issue of *Crawdaddy* in a piece headed *Wines And Lovers – Taste Treats.*

Al – "I had been asked once before and never quite found the time but now seemed as good an opportunity as any to write something about wine. Now this I found so much easier than the novel which was just locked inside my head and not getting on to the written page at all. But that *Crawdaddy* article was a breeze compared to all that."

In writing this initial piece of non-fiction, Al also got his name across to a legion of people that up until then didn't have a clue who he was. With the article written he packed his bags and left England for ever.

Luke – "So we flew from London to LA on July 16th 1976 and once there we at last hooked up with Alan Parsons. We were of course still having to do all this on our credit cards and for this reason I initially stayed at the old Tropicana Hotel on Santa Monica Boulevard, not giving anyone my telephone number there because I was too embarrassed to admit where I was living! Meanwhile Al stayed at the Sunset Marquis."

Nigel Lendon – "So Al, Luke and myself were at last out in LA and we all knew that something big was about to happen. You could just feel it! We were certain, as we boarded that flight out of Heathrow, that this was the case and that therefore we wouldn't be coming home for a long, long time. We were right!"

Luke – "And by the end of August the album was finished! We duly delivered it and I said to Al that I thought that it was absolutely fantastic but that it was a shame that there wasn't a hit single on it! Anyway I was rushing around doing this and that, taking the cover artwork in, checking this and checking that because we really loved the cover which was after all very different to our previous ones."

Al and Luke had again used Storm Thorgerson and Hypgnosis because of their connection with Miles. The same team had previously done the covers for the American version of *Past, Present And Future* and *Modern Times*.

Luke – "With the art copy for *Year Of The Cat* they brought us what was almost the finished artwork and I said to them that I needed a logo and so I said 'I want that' pointing to the strongest, most masculine image I could see in the design."

Luke requested that the *cat* image be in the corner of the cover in black and white, deciding also that it would be their logo for the upcoming US tour. He flew around LA making all the necessary arrangements that Summer for the concerts to take place.

Luke – "I can always remember the day that it was time to book the first date. The album had just come out and Al had agreed that we could book the first show so now I could go out and rent a car for the tour! This meant of course that I'd be able to drive something that wouldn't break down on the way to the office every day which was a major plus I can tell you."

With the album completed, Al had moved out of his hotel and into a small apartment at 1010 North Hammond Terrace, just off of the western end of Sunset Strip. It would be his home for the next year. Luke now moved into a "shack behind the house" at 123 Ocean Park Boulevard in Santa Monica. It was 20 yards from the beach and just a few doors down from Alan Mason.

Luke felt that now they were really making progress; "I had cable TV, a car and was here to stay!"

Steve Chapman rang Luke in LA at this time to let him know that he was available for work.

Steve Chapman – "The upshot of this was that I got hired, although Charlie Harrison unfortunately didn't. Robin Lamble got the gig on bass in Charlie's place. Luke told me that I'd recognise him because he'd be carrying a violin when we met up at Heathrow airport and that was exactly right. We flew out to Los Angeles, got picked up and taken to The Tropicana Hotel, checked in and went straight to a rehearsal. Mark Goldenberg was there playing guitar by this time. He'd been in a Chicago group called The Eddie Boy Band that had just broken up and had got the gig with Al through the Musicians Contact Service. Robin of course had been in Byzantium."

Al – "With Robin we found someone who could do lots of different things and do them very well. He was great. It made all of the difference when we could actually perform a song such as 'Broadway Hotel' the way that it was on the record. I also like to have some sense of things continuing with people that I work with and I had of course worked with Robin's brother when Fairport played with me years before in England."

Robin Lamble – "Byzantium were a band that I formed with three buddies from school in 1972. We had all been at University College School in London. We were very lucky and got a record deal with A&M within a year and went on to make two albums over the next two years which we recorded at Trident Studios where of course Al had done lots of work. Just prior to the break up of Byzantium we'd opened for Al at Hilall House, a Jewish Foundation venue in London, in 1974. Now Al obviously knew who I was because of my brother but our meeting at this gig was in fact the first time we'd ever met. It was a couple of years later when Al and Luke were casting around for band members for that American tour that my name came up. The main reason I had been considered was that Al remembered that I'd played violin at that Byzantium gig. Luke called me up out of the blue and said 'Do you want to go to America as part of Al Stewart's band?' In between the gig and this offer from Luke there had been another time when I almost got to play with Al."

This was the series of auditions, held 18 months previously, at Miles' London house that resulted in Peter White joining the band in February 1975. Byzantium had collectively been invited to audition for the US section of that tour. This would have been a lifeline for Robin's band at that time but it was not to be.

Robin Lamble – "So we got copies of the albums and went away and rehearsed about half a dozen songs before doing an audition at a church hall where Curved Air used to rehearse. It was at this audition that I first met Peter White. We didn't get the gig. So a year later I took this call from Luke and to be perfectly honest I accepted because I didn't really have anything else going on. His very first words to me were 'Would you like to go to America?' and my initial reply was 'Well, not really!' But I did go! I flew out economy class to Los Angeles with Steve Chapman. Robin Gee and his rental car met us at the airport whereupon we get driven directly to rehearsal at the SIR Studios on Sunset Boulevard. Peter Wood, Peter Robinson and Peter White were all already there along with Mark Goldenberg. We only had ten days to put the show together and so it was a rush job. Peter Robinson couldn't do the first few dates of the tour and so Peter Wood was going to do those with us."

Phil Kenzie had played the sax solo on "Year Of The Cat". Well known as a respected session musician, his work had enriched recordings by The Beatles, Bowie and many other top-flight artists. "Jet" by Wings was one of his. However the solo on "Year Of The Cat" was performed on an alto sax that didn't even belong to him!

Phil Kenzie – "I had never played alto, other than to look at one, hold one, and blow on it for a few seconds. I'd never played one on a record in my life. The session was at Abbey Road. I'd been pretty successful and was making enough to buy a house. In fact, that very day we had been out house hunting, finding the house we eventually bought. We went around to see some friends – one was another horn player – and tell them about our good fortune in finding this house at last. The horn player said he had some good fortune too. He said there was a sax player who died in the '30s, and his widow was so distraught that she took his alto, which was brand new, and hid it under the bed for years, and never let anybody touch it. Finally she decided to part with it and my friend acquired it. I took a look at it."

It was a classic silver-scrolled Selmer Balanced Action 20,000 Series, very much sought after and rumoured to have been made from WWI cannon shells.

Phil Kenzie – "I said I wouldn't mind having a play on it, and he said I could borrow it. That night the call came. As I'm sitting watching the TV, Alan says 'I've got this session I want you to do'. So I'm thumbing through the diary, saying 'Oh, when?' He says, 'Now.' Mentally, I'm going 'Damn', because I'm dreaming of this house, I'm looking at a movie, and I don't want to move. I said, 'Where are you?' and he said 'Abbey Road'. That's only five minutes away but I was so reluctant and said 'I'll see you in an hour'. So I went around the corner and went in and all there was was Alan in a darkened studio. A beautiful track with all violins, but no vocal yet. Al was behind the newspaper in the corner, kind of hiding. I said 'Hi', the newspaper came down and he said 'Oh, how do you do?' I looked around the newspaper and replied that I was just fine. I put the tenor down and Alan said, 'You know something, this would sound really good on alto'. I said, 'You're really lucky, because I just happen to have one with me.' That's how it happened."

Luke has fond memories of the session that evening. He was convinced from the start that the addition of Kenzie's sax would transform the song.

Luke – "Thinking back about the saxophone on 'Year Of The Cat' the actual mechanics of it were quite simple. Phil Kenzie came in, listened to the backing track once maybe twice, played his piece and that was that. Of course as soon as we had a *hit* the manager of every artist that recorded on the album came up to me and said that it was their idea! But as I told them all at the time 'There's more to it than that guys!'"

Phil Kenzie – "I actually did that solo in 20 minutes, it was two passes. They had played the whole song and came to this section, that acoustic guitar, and I thought, 'What's happening, it's a guitar solo?' Of course the guitar ends, and they said, 'Right here, we need something'. I took one pass, and he said just one more. We did the end section and he said to me to just keep blowing out to the end of the song. That was it. Alan's usual accolade for everything is 'I think that'll do'. The newspaper came down again and Al said, 'Yes, I think that's very good'. I had my cheque and I was out the door!"

Alan Parsons – "The very mention of a saxophone was enough to make the hackles on Al's back rise. He just did not like saxophones! However once it was recorded and obviously fitted so well he said, using his favourite phrase – "So be it" and the rest, as they say…"

This session at Abbey Road would have long standing implications for Al's career. With the addition of the alto sax, to what would become his signature song, Alan Parsons had inadvertently redefined what would pass as Al's *sound* for the next five years.

Al may very well have come to hate the sound of a sax on his recordings but in the case of "Year Of The Cat" it was in fact the piano that Alan Parsons felt was recorded poorly. He considers that it was recorded too thin in the final mix of the track.

Asked at this time about their choice of Alan Parsons as producer, Al had this to say – "Well I met him in a club in London. I was looking for a new producer, because John Anthony, who had done me for the two albums before, was more into rock 'n' roll – he did Ace's "How Long" and this sort of thing, and Queen and a few other things. His interest lay in bands, and I wanted another producer. Alan had worked at Abbey Road Studios; he engineered *Dark Side Of The Moon* and was extremely impressive. I was particularly looking to find a producer who could give a clean sound because I think rock essentially should be cleanly produced. I listened to something he had just done, which happened to be a Cockney Rebel LP, and he listened to *Past Present And Future* which I had just done; and we thought we'd give it a go and did *Modern Times*, which was a learning album – and then *Year Of The Cat* which I think is a lot better. I think he's a very good producer indeed."

Al, speaking at the time about his relationship with record companies – "Columbia is no kind of label anyone would want to be on, unless they're a heavy-metal band. All I can tell you is that in six years I was with Columbia, they never even answered my letters. I'd phone them up, and they'd always be out. We'd go over, and people would be out of the office, even when I'd come 3,000 miles just to see them – and they wouldn't release any of my records. But it could just be that they didn't like me because they must have been working on something. It's a huge building and I know that there were guys in that building, and I know that they were working on something. I know what they weren't working on, because it was me!

"Janus is the total opposite. Every time I go in there, all I hear is me, and people running around doing Al Stewart things. It's the absolute opposite end of the scale."

The treatment that Al had endured on Columbia had been an ongoing irritant to him for several years. He continued – "I don't want to sound as if I feel too hard about it; it's all in the past now. I'm sure that they were good for Paul Simon and Blood, Sweat, and Tears and Chicago and Janis Joplin, but all I know about Clive Davis (Columbia President at the time) is that I'd wait six months for an answer to a letter, and I'd never get it, and eventually a secretary would send me something in the way of, 'We'll try to get around to your request as soon as possible'. I've got a collection of his rejection slips at home. I'm sure he did what he said for all those people. All I can tell you is that I have the other point of view. I'm the English artist that for five years sent Clive Davis every album I made, and had every one of them thrown into the wastepaperbasket and probably not even listened to."

This was of course with the exception of *Love Chronicles* which, having taken 18 months to negotiate a deal for, had come out on Epic and then disappeared that same week. The head of Epic had been replaced the week the album came out and within two weeks the new head of Epic had deleted it and so *Love Chronicles* was consigned to the bargain bins.

Al – "My history with Columbia from 1967 to 1973 is my letters to them, all filed somewhere and their eventual, very tardy, rather nondescript, completely-avoiding-the-point replies... 'Dear Al, we're really excited about your new album; I believe the person who sweeps the floor is going to listen to it next month!'. I had a six-year contract with them, and I had to fulfil it. Even in England they weren't much better; all they were interested in was David Essex. I've never heard a word from them; the last communication I had with them was in 1972 – that's when they turned down *Orange* which was my fourth album and the fourth one in a row they'd turned down. At that point I gave up, and took it to Janus. Then, of course they immediately started demanding percentages – 'Now that you're on another label we're interested, and we'd like this much...'

When Janus Records opened up they were originally in the 9000 building before moving to a location next to The Olde Worlde Restaurant on Sunset Boulevard, just across the street from Tower Records. Janus' parent company, GRT, a recording tape business, were in Sunnyvale near to San Jose in Northern California.

Ed De Joy – "But things didn't really work out as planned. GRT had realised that the best way of coping with the downswing in the tape business would be to own their own masters, hence the diversification into making music and acquiring Chess Janus. The plan was right but they screwed it up. The harder we all worked at Janus the less successful GRT was. All of the money that was being generated by Al for Janus was being used to develop and support other businesses within the GRT group rather than doing the smart thing and re-investing it back into the record division that was making the money in the first place."

"I had many meetings with GRT about all of this. I felt that the future for Janus was in several artists' hands but primarily Al Stewart's. What we were able to offer artists was a small boutique label where you were very important to all nine employees at Janus. We did everything that we ever told anyone we were going to do and gained a reputation for that. People liked us for that. For instance if I called up Music Plus and said that I needed space in their window to promote *Modern Times* I'd get it – even though they realised that it wasn't going to compete with the new Fleetwood Mac album or whatever."

Nonetheless, the relationship between Luke and Ed was at best problematic and very often simply uncomfortable. Luke cites as an example the particular difficulty he had in obtaining additional funding, in the form of an advance against royalties, for those extended *Year Of The Cat* Abbey Road sessions. Ed, for his part, claims that Luke was just plain difficult to work with.

Ed De Joy – "From day one however I realised that I couldn't trust Luke and found him to be volatile. This was a terribly difficult thing to relate to in a positive manner but I had to because he was the person that controlled Al and the access that Janus had to him. Al's complete faith in his manager was not unusual amongst other artists that I worked with. Artists do not, as a rule, want to get involved in the hows or whys of getting things done and in that regard Al was no different to anyone else. Luke was the one that was there to manage. But dealing with Luke on a day-to-day basis was a nightmare. I was never 100 percent sure of where I stood at any time. He could be as charming as anyone you could ever wish to meet and then be vicious moments later. The luckiest day of his life was when he met Al Stewart. He was always issuing threats and intimidating people also: 'if you don't do this then we'll be moving on' – that sort of thing. The success that came his and Al's way was just too big for him to handle and because he didn't know how to deal with it he made enemies. Al and Alan Mason had a very special relationship and Alan would have spent at least half of his time at Janus going over Al-related projects. This closeness between the two was something I know that Luke didn't like."

Luke's response to that echoes the conviction that personifies the way that he always saw things.

Luke – "If I had just sat back and waited for Ed to do things then the album would never have got made. It's as simple as that. My loyalties were to Al and Al alone."

The themes of many songs on what would become *Year Of The Cat* changed many times over the year that it took to record, as Al tired of lyrics and then changed them, often before they were even demoed in their original form. One such example was "One Stage Before". The song started out as an observation piece about someone coming home from the war to find that their family had changed. This set of finished lyrics were completely discarded for another set written in a totally surreal style about how it felt to be lost in a forest and these were themselves thrown away in favour of the version that made the album. So there in one song we have three of Al's most favoured themes that crop up over and over again in his songwriting, namely the use of war as metaphor, Mervyn Peake/Edward Lear fantasy and finally that of Time itself. Some songs also had last minute changes of title. "Broadway Hotel" had originally been "Chelsea Hotel" and as such can be judged one of Al's true "New York City" songs.

In "Midas Shadow" there was one of those very rare occasions when Al completed a finished vocal in just the one take.

US Tour Poster

Alan Parsons – "Very rare indeed! Al wasn't at all convinced; in fact he just didn't believe that he'd supplied a perfect vocal to that song in just one run-through. He took the tape home with him saying 'This is most irregular! It's never happened before.' In fact that song did stay largely as that one tape. When he sang the vocal I had the tape running but he'd thought he was just doing the run-through in preparation for the recording proper."

Thus using the same trick that Paul Simon had used in order to coax the best out of Jackson Frank back in 1965.

Peter White – "That's the way to do it of course. It's such a good idea to tape absolutely everything from the run-through. I remember with 'On The Border' the final mix includes several sections from the run-through when I wasn't sure about whether the tape was running."

With *Year Of The Cat* now recorded Al was asked to travel up to Canada to perform at a showcase gig arranged primarily for industry staff. Put together as a "Thank you" for everyone at Janus' hard work on various Al projects over the previous three years it was to evolve by the end of the evening into something of a seminal gig for everyone.

Luke – "So we've finished the album by September '76, Janus is getting it ready for release and we go up to Canada because they're having a GRT Canada Convention up there. The time comes in our set for 'Year Of The Cat' and we start playing the recording and come to the saxophone part and everyone in the room jumps up and cheers. These, you must remember, are old record company people from ABC distributors, one of the main independent distributors at the time and who had been around for quite a while and so it was another affirmation of our belief in *Year Of The Cat*."

By this time Al and Luke had developed relationships with radio stations around the country on trips financed on their own credit cards. Al visited radio shows this way in Toronto, Montreal, Vancouver and on to Seattle and Portland. The album had only cost them $75,000 to make. But money was tight and when the tour kicked off at the start of October it was, for financial reasons, minus a sax player.

Luke – "This was the sensible thing to do because 'Year Of The Cat' wasn't the most popular song on the tour although we were finishing off the set with it. People were pleased enough to hear it but that was about it."

After a short period of rehearsals with the new band, the month-long first leg of that US tour had opened on October 21st at The Roxy on Sunset Strip. Elektra Asylum's Steve Ferguson opened for Al.

Harvey Kubernik reviewed the first show – "Los Angeles: The queue at the Roxy for Al Stewart's four shows was the longest since Bruce Springsteen's last year. Many people take Al Stewart for granted. His last album, *Modern Times*, was in the US Top 20 without massive airplay or hype, an almost unheard-of feat. There's always been the stupid comparison here between Stewart and Cat Stevens, but Stewart's recordings are more sophisticated and intelligent, if less well known. He is finally breaking across the United States, however, and by the end of the year he will be one of the most important performers/writers of 1976 in the States."

By this time Luke and Al had been together for three-and-a-half years and Luke had gained a reputation for himself as thorough, shrewd and tough.

Two days into the tour he found himself profiled in the October 23rd 1976 issue of *Cashbox*. In it he gave this informed and illuminating insight into life with Al. At that moment of course no one realised quite how successful the new album would become. As an indicator of just how far Al and Luke had come in their three years together the article is priceless.

Luke was direct and to the point as always. "'The turning point came when Al put a band together; up until then we didn't have one. American audiences weren't very receptive to him playing solo. On the first tour we played The Bottom Line, without a band, and the shows didn't go over very well. A band was formed and now you can hear the different layers of sound that are on the records. A regular nucleus of musicians came about; they are not a permanent band. Each member comes on tour, or records with Al, depending on his working situation."

The first Al Stewart American tours didn't come off without a hitch. There were times when they spent days sitting in the New York Holiday Inn, just trying to get concert dates. More recently, they've been able to turn down dates. A year ago November, Stewart played the Tower Theatre in Philadelphia for a week to sold out audiences, for over 12,500.

The two most recent LPs *Modern Times* and *Year Of The Cat* have sold fairly well, helping to further enlarge the Stewart audience, O'Reilly told *Cash Box*, "At the time of the first American release LPs were costing more in production than they could ever hope to recoup.

"Inflation was a real demon. Bands are also expensive. You have to pay $15,000 a week to keep a band on the road. Three years ago, you could spend $10,000 and do a six-week tour. Now it costs $5-7,000 a night. Al wants to play for as many people as possible. So we're prepared to pay to make the tour successful. Janus Records have advanced us the money. They recognise the fact that Al can make it now but he needs the extra push."

"Stewart is 31 now and it seems his career, to some degree, is just beginning. He is interested in recording a film soundtrack. This should be no great transition, since his songwriting contains strong and vivid images. Most of his lyrics are in story form. For the current show, during the song 'Roads to Moscow', 42 slides will be shown. The song is concerned with the German occupation of Moscow. Slides from German and Russian films will be used."

O'Reilly discussed the tour in more detail. "We had to get a new keyboard player. The one we had was experiencing visa problems. The ICM agency is handling the tour. The equipment on stage, not counting the amps, cost over $35,000. I've been offered to manage other groups, but I've recognised that I probably couldn't handle more than one right now. Al and I have learned to work on limited objectives. And he's more than intellectually capable of knowing what's going on with his management. We sometimes discuss matters over a bottle of wine. We're not afraid to yell at one another, if it becomes necessary. If it's a large problem, then we have two bottles. I respect Al a lot. He would like to be a star. And I would like to be a star's manager. I enjoy the creative side of my work. Sometimes I offer different ideas for a show or in the recording studio. The discipline I also find to be stimulating. You have to work on a day-to-day basis, monitoring everything. If you pay attention to detail, the big things will take care of

Jill Furmanovsky

themselves. A manager's main task is to advise and encourage his client. Al's career is a combined project for the both of us.'"

Luke had good reason to be hopeful for the new album's chances.

Luke – "I was very excited about the reaction the album could expect because typical of this was the way the engineer that did the duplication work on the backing tracks reacted when I called to pick them up in July 1976 from Abbey Road to take them to Los Angeles, when he said that he thought they were great. Now this was an engineer at Abbey Road who gets to hear everything and so it was little things like that that meant a lot to us and I remember getting on the plane to the States and feeling pretty buoyed up about things."

On November 8th Al and the band played The Bottom Line in New York City. This date is important because Mandi came to the show. It was the first time that they had met in a very long time. They travelled to the show together.

Here are Al's original thoughts on the album, track by track – "'Lord Grenville' – This is actually one of my 'Old Admirals'/'The Dark And The Rolling Sea' songs. Lord Grenville was a British mariner in the 16th century who attacked 53 Spanish galleons very unwisely and got sunk for his troubles in a ship called the Revenge. What this song was about was that most of Europe, including England, is in the grip of computer politics. And England's reaction to things is generally 'what is everybody else doing? We'll go between these two points of view' which is really no point of view at all. I'm not saying we should bring back crazy people to run the country – just that a little craziness, imagination, if you will, would not be amiss. So when I'm saying 'I never thought that we would come to find/Ourselves upon these rocks again,' it's really England I'm talking about.

'On The Border' – Another song about the decline and fall of the British Empire. This one is about the civilian being on the front line of duty. And that first bit about 'smuggling guns and arms across the Spanish border' is really a bit of Basque separatism. Actually, it's the idea of everyone standing on the border when the border is right there at everybody's feet. I suppose you could say that it's about disruption closing in on the world and the individual's ability to influence it.

'Midas Shadow' – is about money. The line that says it all for this song is really indecipherable to Americans. It's the one that says 'Conquistador in search of gold – For all the jackdaw reasons'. I didn't know it when I wrote the song that Americans don't know what a jackdaw is. Well, the jackdaw is a bird in British fairytale mythology that is supposed to steal gold rings and bright tiny objects, anything that sparkles, and then puts them in its nest. What it relates to is, say, a businessman who makes money, lots of it, as a reflex action, as an intuitive thing – just as you would draw a breath. Such a person would have a Midas Shadow. 'When your well runs dry – You'll want to know the reason' – that person, if the money ran out or he stopped making it, would want to know why, because he always assumed it would be there. That is the Midas Shadow.

"'Sand In Your Shoes' – This I have nothing to say about at all except that when I make an album, I try to write one short song with a nice tune in an effort to get played on AM radio. And it never works. This is really a bit of a hodgepodge lyrically. It's supposed to sound like a 1966 Bob Dylan track, although it probably doesn't.

"'If It Doesn't Come Naturally, Leave It' – I like this one. That's a nice little sub-Springsteen song. I'd much rather this one be the single. And it's much more fun to do on stage. Interesting how it came about. I was writing this song here, 'Year Of The Cat'. I had spent a whole day on it and nothing was coming to me, sitting in this hotel room in New York. Then, just like that, I wrote 'Nothing that's forced can ever be right. If it doesn't come naturally, leave it'. Which was exactly how I felt. So I wrote that line and went out to a movie. When I came back, I looked at it again and said 'Ah-ha that sounds like a good title for a song'. I sat down and finished the whole thing right there. You always need a good up-tempo number on an album and so this is my rock number for it.

"'Flying Sorcery' – This is just pure English folk-rock. It's pre-me, really – folk-rock without any other musical influences. I like it, and I like a lot of the lines in it, what with all the flying and aviation images."

The writing of lyrics, generally regarded as being Al's strong point, could still prove to be a stumbling block for him. "Flying Sorcery" provides ample evidence of his obsession with language and rhyme.

Al – "I spent a couple of days thinking about how on earth I could get the word aileron into the song. I remember that once I decided it was going to be about aeroplanes, I wanted to get aileron into it and after two days gave up because I couldn't get the stupid word in. That sort of thing has always held up my songs."

With specific regard to "Flying Sorcery" it was not only the song lyrics that were subject to change. The title of the composition had originally been "A Perfect Immelman Turn" – an Immelman being a flying manoeuvre from that bi-plane era and a phrase pulled from a book on WWI aviation that Al had bought to help him compose the song.

"'Broadway Hotel' – is a song about people who live in hotel rooms because I spend a lot of time in hotel rooms. It's a song about trying to understand people who live in hotel rooms, people who are rich and can afford houses but prefer to live in a hotel room. That's like living with no past, nothing tangible you can attach them to. The song also has a desk clerk, rather a laconic one, at that, and I think he's quite funny.

"'One Stage Before' – That one I'm not really sure about except that it seems to be about reincarnation. 'And some of you are harmonies to the notes I play' – that's the idea of the karass in Kurt Vonnegut's *Cat's Cradle*. You are all going to be in harmony with each other while 'others talk in secret keys' means that whatever you say to them, they will all hear it slightly differently. This is really about being on stage, other stages, in past lifetimes. Like if you are playing on stage in Philadelphia for 3,000 people, they are actually 3,000 people all reincarnated that you saw in the Colisseum in Rome. It's all mass reincarnation – for what reason I have no idea.

"'Year Of The Cat' – This one has a certain insistence, especially the line '…in the year of the cat'. When I wrote it, that's all I had, that one line. I then had to build it up from there, which was very difficult. As for the meaning of it, last year was the Year Of The Cat in Vietnamese astrology, and last year was when I started writing it. Finally, it ended up about a guy on a coach party to North Africa, on one of these buses with a one-way ticket. He stops in a town, Casablanca or whatever, and he finds this girl, who must be a California girl because she wanders about and talks about 'years of cats' and things. So he spends the night at her place and when he wakes up, the bus is gone and he's stranded. If you miss the bus, that's it. He just figures, 'well, this isn't really the way I'd planned my life, but I might as well stick around and make the best of it: it's just another interesting point in my development as a person'… I thought this could have been the single, but at 6:40, it's too long and I don't see how you can really edit it. You can take out the long intro and fade, but the instrumental section in the middle is the best part.

"Musically, I think it's the best album I've ever made. Lyrically, I could have fixed up a line here and there. There are some odd ones, like the chorus in 'Sand In Your Shoes'. But with each album, I try to put right those mistakes I made on the one before. This does not necessarily make each one better, but I just learn with each thing each time.

"We were recording on and off for about a year, August 1975 to August 1976. And there were some big gaps in there. In a way, you gain a lot by doing it that way, because we would lay down backing tracks and let them sit for three months while we did something else. And in those three months, you pretty much figure out what should be there, what with that long to think about it.

"Usually you make a record and a year later, you think, ah, I should have had this here and that there. But if you take a year to make it, you pretty much end up with all the right things in all the right places."

The original storyline of "Year Of The Cat" however was about someone very different from the guy who missed the bus back home from Morocco.

Al – "It was a completely different song. You would have to be English to know of him but there was a very famous comedian in the '50s and '60s called Tony Hancock. He was this legendary cult figure. And it became fairly obvious to the press, if not to the public, that the man was having a nervous breakdown. He'd been the most popular comedian in the country with his partner Sid James and when he decided to go solo he proceeded to have even greater success with such BBC series as *Hancock's Half Hour* but then it all started to go wrong in the most terrible way for him."

Hancock was finding it hard to match his earlier successes and was in the midst of an emotional downward spiral. Dogged by bad reviews, haunted by self-doubt and compromised by a litany of addictions he now decided to return to the stage with a one-man show.

Al – "And I *saw* him when he came to Bournemouth to do that show and he was obviously in a really bad way, anyone could see that. I must have still been a teenager at this time."

Al isn't strictly correct here. He had been back in Bournemouth for his 21st birthday in September '66 and it was during Tony Hancock's week-long residency at the Bournemouth Winter Gardens at this time that Al had gone along to see him. Hancock was there from September 5th to try out new material for an upcoming short season at London's Royal Festival Hall. However a combination of depression, nerves about the new show and the fact that his estranged wife was in Bournemouth attempting to forge a reconciliation between the two of them turned the Winter Gardens booking into a nightmare for the comedian. It is well documented that he appeared upset throughout the week and would ramble and fluff his lines on a regular basis. He was supposed to stick to the new material but instead reverted night after night to old routines and would invariably wander to the very apron of the stage and address the audience directly. It was this tragic performance that Al witnessed. It is hardly suprising that it affected him so deeply that he was able to draw on it for the lyrics to "Foot of the Stage" a decade later.

Al – "He came on stage and he said 'I don't want to be here. I'm just totally pissed off with my life. I'm a complete loser, this is stupid. I don't know why I don't just end it all right here.' And they all laughed, because this was the character that he played … he played this sort of down-and-out character. And I looked at him and I thought 'Oh my god! He means it. This is for real. This is not put-on. He absolutely means it.' About halfway through the audience got bored and some of them started to leave. And he was basically just saying what an awful life he was living. Well a couple of months after that he went to Australia and committed suicide. [Hancock actually committed suicide on June 25th 1968.] I really had the vibe that he really was going to do it. And he did. That's how I came to write the song 'Your Tears Fall Down Like Rain At The Foot Of The Stage'. That was the original, and that was how it was going to be, but it was a double whammy. First of all, no one in America knew Tony Hancock and secondly it seemed to be taking advantage of a tragedy in the man's life which I didn't want to do. So I rewrote it."

Al supplied a further alternative version to his producer of the genesis of the lyric that turned "Foot of the Stage" into "Year Of The Cat".

Alan Parsons – "I asked Al what it was about when I first read the lyric and he explained to me that it was written about the year in which 'The Cat', by Jimmy Smith, the jazz rock organist, had been a hit. That's what I've always believed it to be about, he seemed perfectly serious to me when he explained it back then at the time."

Perhaps a case of Al having some fun at his producer's expense! Either way "Foot Of

The Stage" evolved into "Year Of The Cat".

Proof, if proof were needed, that Janus had *lucked in* with Al who had by now become their most valuable asset. To consolidate this high profile Al had a radio liaison person on tour with him from that day on. It did the trick.

Al's fame was by now international and transcended both the mainstream and the music press in Europe and America. *The Toronto Star* reviewed his Canadian show on its front page saying – "Stewart came on like a cross between Lou Reed and The Dave Clark Five with a delivery derived from Dylan".

It could almost have been a Kinetic press release!

FLYING SORCERY

With your photographs of Kitty Hawk
And the biplanes on your wall
You were always Amy Johnson
From the time that you were small
No schoolroom kept you grounded
While your thoughts could get away
You were taking off in Tiger Moths
Your wings against the brush-strokes of the day
Are you there?
On the tarmac with the winter in your hair
By the empty hangar doors you stop and stare
Leave the oil-drums behind you, they won't care
Oh, are you there?

Oh, you wrapped me up in a leather coat
And you took me for a ride
We were drifting with the tail wind
When the runway came in sight
The clouds came up to gather us
And the cockpit turned to white
When I looked the sky was empty
I suppose you never saw the landing-lights
Are you there?
In your jacket with the grease-stain and the tear
Caught up in the slipstream of a dare
The compass roads will guide you anywhere,
Oh, are you there?
The sun comes up on Icarus as the night-birds sail away
And lights the maps and diagrams
That Leonardo makes
You can see Faith, Hope and Charity
As they bank above the fields
You can join the flying circus
You can touch the morning air against your wheels
Are you there?
Do you have a thought for me that you can share?
Oh I never thought you'd take me unawares
Just call me if you ever need repairs
Oh, are you there?

It was now November 1976 and England, about to change forever with the advent of Punk, was to be Al's next port of call. The grey winter skies that greeted Al and Luke as they motored down the M4 from Heathrow Airport into London were in stark contrast to the bright blue ones that they had left behind just three months earlier. It wasn't the only change that awaited them.

Luke – "We came back and played a British tour which was completely sold out. It was only just over a year since our last dates there and it was basically a college tour. *Year Of The Cat* had done well in the UK and was continuing to do so."

In England Al appeared with his band on BBC TV's *Old Grey Whistle Test* on November 30th performing "Year Of The Cat".

Phil Kenzie – "This was the next time that I saw Al. They were doing the show and Luke called me up in London. I went down to do it and Luke said that the record was going quite well for them. I kind of had to relearn the sax part because I couldn't remember what I had played on the record. I hadn't a clue! I said, 'Oh, there's the vocal, that's what it's all about.'"

Harvey Kubernik spoke to Al in LA just before he left to play the British dates – "Al who plays London's New Victoria Theatre on December 2, is now enjoying greater success in America.

"'At the moment,' he says, 'the West Coast particularly seems to be a stronghold. More things are happening now than they ever did in England. That has a lot to do with the image I had in England. I was thought of as a folk singer. No one ever wrote about *selling out* folk clubs. I did, but consequently you didn't read about it.'

The manner in which Al was treated by the British press during his trip back bears some consideration at this point. Whilst it still (as ever) seemed necessary for Al's perceived desertion of his *folk roots* to anchor most UK reviews, the momentum that he was presently riding in the US was something that no one (least of all those journalists that had previously dismissed the notion of him achieving breakthrough success in the US) could now avoid. His thoughts on, well just about anything really, were indulged like never before over a series of London interviews he now gave. A point not lost on Al – "Something had changed and I honestly think that it was down to me delivering what I said I would! At this stage the new album hadn't done anything like it was going to anywhere but it was becoming clear to me, to Luke and of course everyone at Janus, that this was quite possibly going to do it! And I feel that people in England were looking at what was happening in the US and realising too that it was about to happen. It was a period of being absolutely on the brink of something life changing and it was more than a little surreal being back in London talking about it as it was actually happening over in America."

Al gave an insight into stage technique to *Melody Maker* at this time – "'I like Bowie a lot, and went to see him at Wembley. [Al had been to the May 1976 shows on Bowie's *Station To Station* tour where he appeared in a set straight out of the German Expressionists as *The Thin White Duke.*] I don't know if he influenced me, combining the little theatre with the music. The back projection cost about £3,000. We could have bought a whole set of string synthesisers for that. It was all Luke's idea.

"The slides are historically accurate. The show starts off electric and dips down to an acoustic segment and back up to electric again. 'Roads to Moscow' is getting a tremendous response every time we do it.'"

Melody Maker deemed *Year Of The Cat* Stewart's most accessible album.

"Alan Parsons cleaned up the production totally" Al told them..

"'This album has a very thick sound where something like *Love Chronicles* had a very thin sound. *Love Chronicles* still sounds fine on a set-down record player, but that's the way it was made.

"Musically though, there is nothing I can do to change the Al Stewart identity. What the Al Stewart identity hinges and depends on is my peculiar approach of using literature and history as backdrops in my songs.

"As long as I continue to do that, that will be my identity, much more than whether I use saxophones on record.'"

The British tour included Reading, Bristol, Birmingham and London.

Back in the UK for Al's tour was Nigel Lendon who explained recently how he mixed the sound at those *Year Of The Cat* shows at the end of 1976.

Nigel Lendon – "Al's vocal always had to be out front and then around that we building up an 'Alan Parsons' sound where all the elements are there in layers. There is a layer of sound that was interwoven with multi-instrumentation. We had two keyboards, three guitars, bass, all sorts of things and it was therefore quite a complex mix but then out of that we created dynamics to stop it being flat."

Whilst in London in December 1976 Al had given an interview, in the proverbial restaurant, to Bob Edmunds of the *New Musical Express*. It would appear on January 6th – "Only two albums from the British folk scene have ever got in to the American Top 30", Al told Edmunds.

"Out of Steeleye Span, Incredible String Band, Pentangle, Fairport Convention, Roy Harper, Ralph McTell, John Martyn, Michael Chapman – you know the list – only two albums have ever made it. They're *Modern Times* and *Year Of The Cat* – both by me.

"I don't know if I should make quotes like that," Al conceded. "It's the sort of thing that really alienates me from the rest of the world, I'm sure.

"It's work, it's work, it's work" he said "with crusading fervour". "If I was a manager, I could make successes out of the people I mentioned if they would do what I have done. But so many of them are so well known in Britain and make so much money, they're not prepared to do that.

"I know for a fact that Ralph [McTell] was invited to go to the States, to start playing for $50 a night in clubs, and he was earning £1,000 a night here. He just couldn't see it. I think he thought you could do it by records but you can't."

The last point that Al made assumed that Ralph, like Al, really did want to crack the States in the first place. At home in the UK Ralph McTell had a fan base that was quite possibly as great as Al's but the number of places that he could perform in was much greater at the time. He was not perceived as having abandoned his folk roots and could sell out venues the length and breadth of the country throughout the year. Al, with a band in tow, had far fewer places to play and could not have continued playing shows in the UK as often as Ralph. He would have gone bust in a couple of months. So in many ways the entire scenario of Ralph not being a success in the States because he wouldn't listen to Al, who was enjoying more and more success there, was a red herring.

The *NME* continued – "After five years on the road in America and two chart albums, he says he's '150,000 down', but confidently expects that things won't stay that way too long."

"I was prepared to go at huge loss into the dross end in America and support all sorts of unlikely people. You have to take all the shit for a start.

"For example, being third on the bill to Sha Na Na in Milwaukee, or supporting Queen in San Antonio, Texas. With the Queen audience. I just did what I did and 10,000 people hated it but 50 liked it and went out and bought the record. So I've got a foothold in San Antonio, Texas. They immediately invited us back at ten times the fee.

"I once supported Hot Tuna, and the first three rows were totally out of their brains on Quaaludes. They yelled 'boogie!' all the way through my entire set. Not only that, they were so smashed that when Hot Tuna came on, they yelled 'boogie' at them as well. Once you've faced a few of those, you've learnt a lot.'"

It was almost as if Al was a man on a mission. Having tried and failed on a number of occasions to achieve success in the States his perspective on it all had to be taken seriously once he started to make major inroads into the American market himself. Up until this point all of his theories on how to get on in the USA could be discounted as merely that. Now he felt vindicated. And he let everyone know it too!

Al had always been at pains to deny that his music was "intellectual", something that had dogged him for the past six years, since the days of "Manuscript". He told Bob Edmunds – "My songs are like *kindergarten rhymes* when compared to Mervyn Peake. I got the same buzz the first time from *Lord Of The Rings* that I did from *Bringing It All Back Home*. In the '70s, I got the same buzz from *Court And Spark* and *Nashville* and

Kinetic

'YOTC' logo, 1976

Ragtime by E.L. Doctorow. It's a physical sensation. I don't consider myself an intellectual. People into the same things as me aren't intellectuals."

Al could be more than a little prickly when asked just how accessible he felt that his music was to anyone at this time and became defensive when accused of sometimes talking down to people. He often told interviewers that he was convinced that popular taste was very often underestimated.

He then told the *NME* on January 6th.

"There's the fact that people choose not to give vast portions of the British public access to three-quarters of the movies, nine-tenths of the books, and 60 percent of the records that could be available, on the grounds that they'd be too obscure.

"Those are exactly the grounds on which John Lennon's books weren't published in the States for four years. Every American record company and most of the British ones turned down *Tubular Bells* until one saw its worth. Those are the sorts of gross miscalculations that are made.

"On the other hand, other people see me, with great justification, as a low point of popular taste, but I think it is fatal, as well as demeaning in the extreme, to talk down to somebody. If anyone does talk down, the audience is really quick to spot it. Be it *Coronation Street* or Joni Mitchell, there has to be a recognisable involvement by the artist."

Al's obsession with figures never deserted him and that December in London he was thousands of miles away from where he hoped his fortune was being made. Even back home, after an evening out on the town with a journalist, he found the prospect of finding out just how well his "Year Of The Cat' single was faring in the charts over there irresistible. The visit back to the chic address in Belsize Village, catching Al excitedly on the brink of finally being able to leave all of this behind, was duly written up in the *NME* after Christmas.

"A sign outside warns: 'This is a private mews'. Inside, everything is '60s good taste. Teak panelling, pampas grass scatter cushions, an antique settee, a print of a *Punch* cartoon, massive Tannoy speakers dispensing Joni Mitchell.

"If there are mothballs about, they are well hidden, but the fact is that Al Stewart now spends most of his time in America. No matter how much at ease he may seem in London, this is no more than a 12-day promotion visit. Bigger fortunes are at stake across the Atlantic, and bigger houses than those in a London mews.

Business is Al's first concern across the threshold. A call to America reveals that the single, the album's title track is at 83 with a bullet in *Cashbox*. 98 in *Billboard*. The album is at 38 in *Record World*, 27 in *Billboard*. There is AM play in Houston, Texas, 35,000 albums have been sold in this week alone, taking *Year Of The Cat* to 290,000 or thereabouts. Al is understandably exultant."

The prospect of him finally managing to get out of debt was by now a real possibility. It was with this in mind that he set about completing the UK dates and returning to the States and his first Christmas in Los Angeles. Those British shows included a show at the New Victoria Theatre, the night after the Sex Pistols' legendary appearance with Bill Grundy on TV in London.

John Hayward reviewed the New Victoria show: "London's New Victoria Theatre was packed to bursting point last Thursday night, despite strong competition from Kiki Dee at the Albert Hall, for a concert from Al Stewart and his band – part of a major UK tour promoting his new RCA album *Year Of The Cat*, and his first dates here for eighteen months.

"Stewart, a slight and stooping figure, made his name in the early part of the decade playing wordy, introspective songs that appealed to lonely young women in bedsitterland. In those days he played acoustic guitar and used a string section on album. On Thursday he was backed by a tasteful electric band, which had the effect of adding more power to the music, with its interesting melodies providing plenty of opportunity for keyboard or guitar solos."

The band now returned to the States to play ten extra dates before Christmas. These included shows in Houston and Detroit.

Al – "So it's now very nearly Christmas 1976, we'd finished the tour and the album is selling at the rate of 100,000 copies a week. It had gone up the charts slowly. The single had dipped once and then gone back up the charts in the States. Things seemed to be going OK."

Robin Lamble remembers very clearly the change in pace that took place that Christmas – "Now this tour had been my first time ever in America and it was all new to me. I didn't even know how the money worked! The first leg of the tour had been in reality quite short, lasting for just two months. Most of the band then went home for Christmas and whilst there Luke called up to say that we all had to get back to Los Angeles by January 2nd because everything had suddenly got real and the *Year Of The Cat* album was racing up the charts. This came as something of a surprise because when that initial two month tour had come to an end there had only been the very slightest suggestion that there would be more work and I'd returned home thinking 'ah well, that's that'.

Finding himself feted in England, with *Year Of The Cat* flying up the US charts, Al could have been forgiven for thinking that things couldn't get much better.

They were just about to.

CITY OF ANGELS

In which Al lives the life of a King in Hollywood and signs a million-dollar recording deal with Arista.

It had been quite a year. If Al had known, the previous Christmas, that it was to take this long to get the new album released he would have been a worried man. But now everything was about to get very exciting indeed.

Back home in Los Angeles, after the hectic events of the previous six months, Al set about getting ready for Christmas. Marion, having stayed behind in London at the end of the tour, was due to fly in to Los Angeles on Christmas Day.

Al – "Simply the most wonderful time. That's what it was. It was Christmas Eve and *Billboard* had frozen their charts over the Holiday period. I think *Year Of The Cat* was then at number 21 because it didn't all really explode until January. It had already done much better than *Modern Times* and it was obvious that we were on a roll and we were going to do better but none of us knew just how well! We had album success and the single was beginning to get stations although it hadn't yet got the major ones. It was all looking awfully good, I had my apartment in Los Angeles and I was living with Marion."

That afternoon Al found himself driving through Beverly Hills.

"I wanted to have a fabulous bottle of wine for Christmas because after a year like 1976 that was what I wanted more than anything. Someone had told me about a place called *The Beverly Hills Wine Merchant* and so off I went but I got there just as they were closing at about 5 to 6. Inside there was a man there in a brown stockman's coat with a broom in one hand that looked like the janitor and he asked me what I wanted. I replied that I was looking for some good wine, a great Bordeaux maybe and on hearing this he somewhat reluctantly let me into his shop. He then said 'What do you want?' and I told him that I would really like some *Chateau Margaux* (which was a good thing to say especially to the person I was saying it to). It was 1976 and I told him that I normally bought the '66, which was a wine I was drinking a lot of at the time. I then said 'But you know, it is Christmas Eve and I would like to try the 1961! That is if you don't have the *Palmer* '61, which is meant to be a better wine. But then again if you had a 1953…"

Things were getting out of hand here and Al soon realised that he had happened upon someone that not only shared his love of wine but also his sense of humour. He had in fact been talking to the owner of the shop. His name was Dennis Overstreet.

Al – "Dennis told me that he had the 1953 *Margaux* but had I tried the '45? I was looking at this guy and I thought 'Wait a minute!'. Standing there holding a broom, I think he is there to sweep up and he is looking at me, I have long hair and a velvet jacket and now you would think nothing of someone knowing about wine but back then it was something that people did not widely know about. I am standing there and it is obvious that he thinks I have come to rob the place and I think that he is the janitor. So I say, I am now taking a shot totally in the dark, 'The '45 yes but what about the '28?' And he says 'I don't know about the '28 but of course you know the real one is the 1900!' I had heard that the best Bordeaux of the Century was the 1900 *Margaux* but of course I had never tasted the thing and then I said 'Yes, well if you can't get the 1870!' Then he said 'Well who are you?' And I said 'Well who are you?' and he replied 'I own the joint!'. And that was that, I ended up buying the 1953 *Margaux* and the 1961 *Palmer* and those were the two favourite red *Bordeaux* at the time and I took them home."

Dennis Overstreet – "It was plain to me on a personal level that Al was a genuine enthusiast with incredible energy when it came to his interest in wine, about which I would suggest he was passionate. He'd come in late on Christmas Eve and I didn't have a clue who this guy was. I may have heard *Year Of The Cat* on the radio in the car but I certainly made no connection when he told me his name."

Al was in such a state of elation after that first visit to Dennis' shop that he managed to largely forget much of what he had gone out for that day.

Al – "I had wanted to get smoked salmon and a turkey, we just wanted to get something to have with this fabulous wine. So I went out and I don't know how I did it but I got salmon that wasn't smoked, it was cold, it looked like smoked salmon, but it wasn't and it was horrible, but this is absolutely mind boggling – I managed to buy a smoked turkey! I got it completely reversed. I don't know how I did it – I was in a hurry! It was awful and the smoked salmon didn't taste like anything. It was like eating lard and both of these were inedible things but, well, we had these fabulous wines, we had a completely inedible Christmas dinner and I had to go out and buy cookies. We had the best wine in the world and the worst food that Christmas."

Marion had flown into LA from London on Christmas Day to join Al and Luke. That first Christmas in Hammond Terrace was by no means spent in the lap of luxury however. The dining table was an upturned industrial power wire reel set, the wicker chairs were meant for a patio, there was a couch, coffee table, floor lamp, a double bed and that was it!

Luke – "*Year Of The Cat* had already gone gold and we were sitting there at the end of 1976 flat broke."

Throughout all this time everyone was still very much making up the plot as they went along. A good example of this is the role of a sax player at the early shows.

Ed De Joy again – "When Al sold out the Santa Monica Civic Auditorium just after *Year Of The Cat* broke he didn't want a saxophone. I spoke to Luke on a number of occasions and said that he could not play that song in Los Angeles and *not* have a saxophone. So I paid for the sax player! (In fact it was of course funded as an advance against future royalties.) When the guy walked out on stage for his first solo on 'Year Of The Cat' the place went nuts and Al had a grin on his face from ear to ear."

Luke – "The truth is I felt that we couldn't afford a sax player at that time! We were all basking in this all really and just thinking 'wow' and so a little while later I decided to go for broke and I called up Phil Kenzie and he came out and joined us for some of those dates."

Steve Chapman has a clear memory of how this all happened.

"Once the tour got started it became obvious that we needed a sax player and so a friend of Mark Goldenberg's came out with us at the start of '77 to play on a few dates. He'd had quite a wacky history having been William Shatner's tour manager but after a few dates Luke decided that it would be best to fly out Phil Kenzie and that's what we did. I'd originally flown out for just three weeks work but stayed for several months."

This just goes to show how much everyone had underestimated the potential of the single and the part that the sax could play in Al's true arrival on American FM radio. A few weeks into the New Year, Phil Kenzie got the call.

Phil Kenzie – "It must have been late January 1977. There was a call from Luke and he was all excited as the record had taken off. He was saying, 'You've got to come over right now because the tour's already started!' So I flew over to New York with Ian Copeland and then into Denver; full of adrenaline, I went to walk on stage with Al to play the song and I couldn't breathe!

"I was jet-lagged and there was no oxygen in the air. In fact, Al opened his mouth for about his third song and turned green. They had to have oxygen on the side of the stage.

"We staggered forward, basically a bunch of limey English guys, trying to survive with no oxygen!

"The moment we landed in New York, Luke was full of celebration and he had got this big silver limo. We were in the back with champagne and he's playing with the radio and he finds 'Year Of The Cat' and I remember saying 'Luke you'd better enjoy this, it's the only time it happens.' 'Don't say that, we're going to have more hits' Luke replied. 'Yes, but there's only one first time, one first hit.' I told him."

Luke – "Ah yes, the limo into Manhattan. I remember it as if it were yesterday…"

Meanwhile Ed De Joy's hard work was about, at the eleventh hour, to pay off spectacularly.

Ed De Joy – "When we released *Year Of The Cat* we were a small company with limited capital but enough to do a good job. We committed every dollar that we had to Al Stewart. If that album hadn't been successful then we would have been out of business in 1977! I invited two guys who were in independent promotions work out to my house and I played them *Year Of The Cat* and they went absolutely nuts about it. They were happy for me and also for Janus and to be honest they worked that single for no money. Now a while later we had stalled on the single at a chart position somewhere in the mid-30s. We needed the RKO Radio organisation on board but we just could not get them to add Al Stewart. One day I came home from the office absolutely depressed because I felt that we'd blown the record. If we were going to get no higher than the mid-30s then the album would sell 250,000 copies, which was a nice move from *Modern Times* but disappointing bearing in mind how far I felt that we'd come."

A friend of Ed's, John Leader, was the afternoon drive disc jockey on KHJ. He had called Ed's wife that day and told her to make sure that she had the radio on at 6 in the evening.

Ed – "He wouldn't say why but was insistent that we should do that. So I arrive home and I'm sitting down at the dinner table talking to my wife about how we'd failed to get the ads we were looking for and how we would probably now start losing radio stations that had been playing 'Year Of The Cat '. This was a very sad moment because I knew that it was a better record than that. My wife had tuned the radio in and it was on when we sat down which was something that we never did, but she wouldn't really say why she had it on at the dinner table."

Then just after 6 o'clock John Leader's voice came on and he announced that he had the privilege of being the first person to play a new song that had just been added to the station's play list.

Ed – "He continues by saying that he considers it to be a certain hit and through all of this I wasn't caring very much because I wasn't thinking that it could have anything to do with Janus at all. And then he introduces 'Year Of The Cat'. I started to cry. I really did. From that moment on all the resistance was gone and it got added to play lists everywhere. At once the orders started coming in like never before and it was phenomenal. Stores that were ordering maybe 100 copies before were suddenly demanding 1,000 and it became at once one of the defining records of the '70s for me."

Al was profiled in the Boxing Day edition of the *The Houston Chronicle* – "Stewart didn't know it when he was in town last week for his first Houston concert, but *The Year Of The Cat* had already achieved gold record status, according to a spokesperson for his record company, Janus Records. The gold record – signifying a healthy 500,000 units sold – needs only the Record Industry Association of America's certification to make it official. And Janus was holding back the good news from Stewart until the company's Christmas party. Such are the ways of in-house record company politics – the artist is always the last to know."

Peter White – "With regard to the band Al specifically wanted an American rhythm section because he thought that they were the best in the world and it would fall to me to be the glue and the musical director and generally oversee the rehearsing and those auditions. But after all this we decided to stay with Steve Chapman as our choice."

Peter Robinson joined the band at that time also. Peter had been in Shawn Philips band when they played with Al and Peter on those dates in North and South Dakota together back in 1975.

Peter White – "In fact if you take a look at the film *Fargo* those are all places that we played on a college tour opening for Shawn Philips! So we'd got to know Peter Robinson and now, a year later, recruited him to play piano. During the set I'd come out from behind my keyboards for just one song, 'On The Border', sit on a stool and play Spanish guitar." The US edit of "Year Of The Cat" caused a few problems however.

Luke – "The edit they put out of the single in the States was a horrible edit I thought and Al himself did the English edit which was much better and fine and natural. However it was a hit in the US so what do I know!"

Peter White – "Edit or no edit when we first realised that we had a hit on our hands my first reaction was that it was scary! I was still thinking that I was just this young kid from Letchworth, I don't really know what I'm doing and all of a sudden we're selling out 3,000 seaters every night across America. I also remember Al saying to me 'you know what, now that I've achieved a little success I'm never going to let go of it like everyone else does, I'm going to make sure that I hang on to it, you see.'"

Al continued to play gigs through the early spring of 1977. These dates included the prestigious Avery Fisher Hall in New York City. The venue had been unsure about Al's ability to do well there and so Luke offered to buy back from them, at full price, any tickets that they were left with. In actual fact the date sold out in just two hours!

Then Al suddenly cancelled the rest of the tour in the middle of February with a month of sold-out dates still remaining. To do such a drastic thing, when he was at the peak of his popularity, was not something that has ever been adequately explained. Whilst it is true that he was suffering from problems with his throat, he was also feeling somewhat jaded by the experiences of the previous six months. It remains a situation that Al has largely elected to keep silent about ever since.

He was well enough on Monday March 7th 1977 to be inducted into the *Compagnon de Bordeaux* in a ceremony at Michael's Pub on 211 East 55th Street New York City. The reason for this, the publicity handout trumpeted, was "In recognition of his efforts in making the wines of Bordeaux better known to Young Americans". The ceremony, by invitation only, was attended by various record and wine industry staff from the West Coast. At the event Al was quoted as saying "Wine absolutely helps me write my songs!" It quite probably did!

Dennis Overstreet – "Luke virtually chaperoned Al around in those days. In fact it was so much so that you could say that Luke saw himself as Al's shadow. It was really like that! Luke would make it his job to know about all aspects of Al's business. Whatever Al took an interest in Luke would follow and develop a similar interest likewise. I saw it happen time after time."

With regard to Al's specialist knowledge of wine, Dennis sees it as something of a more pragmatic interest on Luke's behalf.

"It gave Luke the ability to be able to converse with Al, on a similar level, about something that Al was passionate about."

Quite probably the strangest incident in Al's career had taken place shortly before and was duly reported in *Rolling Stone* in its March 10th 1977 issue – "A 22-year-old man, identified as a student at the University of Montreal, rushed toward Al Stewart on stage during the sound check before a January 21st show at Western Washington State College in Bellingham. Jacques Duchesneau cried that he was Lord Grenville (a character in a Stewart song), that he wanted to avenge Stewart for resurrecting Grenville from the dead, and according to one campus security officer, that he wanted to kill Stewart. Duchesneau was pinned down by roadies before he could get to Stewart. At his trial five days later, Duchesneau said that he was merely trying to show Stewart some poems. He was sentenced to five days in jail and a $50 fine."

"I just saw this figure charging and bellowing something" Al recollected. "He got on the stage but Robin's bass was in the way so he had to sort of try and poke that out of the way and I think it kind of bashed him in the ear or something and by the time he had managed to fight his way past the lead guitarist Lendon had him round the waist and that

Jonny and Abi visit Al during the last days of him being on Janus

Al & Jonny, Janus Records 1977

Al & Abi, Hammond Terrace 1977   *Alan Mason, Al & Jonny, LA 1977*

was about the end of it! But he was saying, and this is the salient point, that he *was* Lord Grenville and I had reincarnated him from the dead, which you know you can put down to whatever drug he was taking at the time probably."

Those dates that Al had cancelled earlier in the spring were rebooked for the start of

April. But the impetus had been lost and they were only half full whereas they had originally all sold out. Financially this was very bad news as Kinetic were also having to pick up the bills along the way for all of the money that the promoters had laid out for the earlier cancelled gigs. However not all was doom and gloom and it was now that Jonny and Abi arrived in Los Angeles to see how Al was faring with this new life.

Al had promised to fly them over if the new album sold over a million copies and so they now got to see all of the places that Al had been telling them about in LA. Al put them up in some style at The Sunset Marquis on Sunset.

The Early Years compilation of tracks from the first three albums was now released by Janus in the US and RCA in England on March 10th.

And so with Al's back catalogue now belatedly getting a legitimate US release and the new record continuing to do well, Luke arranged some extra promotion for the album's title track. Luke – "I had gone to Midem (to Al's considerable chagrin, he was working at the time) and whilst I was there I met two guys from Holland and I spent the whole evening chatting to them saying 'Look how big this is out here' and out of this came the video of 'Year Of The Cat' which was filmed by the Dutch TV Show *Top Pop* at the RCA studios in New York City."

This was one of the more "rock star" like days of Al's career. The band flew to JFK, got the helicopter to the top of the Pan Am building in Manhattan, and then took the elevator down to the street where they walked across to the studio.

To many this may have all seemed a very long way from Al's life in London but Abi Kremer had noticed some similarities

Abi Kremer – "Al's place on Hammond Terrace was similar in many ways to his house in Belsize Village. It had a huge lounge and an amazing square sofa with a large coffee table in the middle. It also had the obligatory pinball machine of course, which was very American we thought! When we visited him, Marion was there in residence, knitting something for one of Alan Parsons' young children I remember! Jonny also celebrated his 30th birthday whilst we were out there."

Nigel Lendon – "I was there too! In the early days I shared Luke's apartment which was in the very same block as Al. Money was scarce and it just made sense for everyone. Looking back, there was a real family atmosphere about all of it at that time."

Al was performing the song "The Dark And The Rolling Sea" from *Modern Times* that featured an accordion, and during his shows this was a song that he particularly loved playing. It was Peter Wood that played the accordion in the early days but when Woodentop left the band Al asked Peter White whether he could play the accordion in his place.

Peter White – "I told him that I could play a little. When I was a kid we'd had this pretty average accordion at home which I played a little but that was it. The main stumbling block however was that I didn't own an accordion now! This wasn't a problem though because Marion had one that she'd inherited but couldn't play! She very kindly lent it to me and that's how I started to play accordion on stage, the famous red one that I played for many, many, years. I bought it in the end for about $500 because it was worth a lot of money by that time. I love the sound of the accordion, I've used it on Basia's and Al's recordings over the years."

Meanwhile, on the face of it, Al was doing very well. For facts and figures a profile of him that now appeared in the US press makes interesting reading.

On April 2nd Al spoke to *Billboard* – "'When the album came out nobody expected it to make such gains. The initial shipment on the LP was only 70,000 copies. But then for *Past Present And Future*, my first on Chess/Janus, it was only 6,000 copies shipped.

"By the time the single 'Year Of The Cat' came out, the album had already sold 450,000 copies. So the single was icing on the cake."

Al continued to talk about the second part of the 1977 tour that was about to kick off. These were the dates that had been rearranged following the cancellation of gigs at the start of the year.

Al – "I think that I will be able to keep the band I have now. We are beginning a six-week tour in Miami on April 4th. For the most part we will be playing 3,000 seater halls.

"So far we have always lost money touring. I employ 24 people on the road, with some of them getting percentages. It costs $5,000 a day to run the band on tour.

"We accumulated such debts touring that what the success of the record has done is get us out of hock!"

Al did have a plan should *Year Of The Cat* not have been a hit however.

Al – "If *YOTC* had been a flop it would have been very difficult for me to continue living in America as there wouldn't have been any gigs! I guess that's not completely accurate as *Modern Times* had done quite well but in so far as me having then been able in 1976 to live off Sunset Boulevard and have had this amazing life, no, it wouldn't have happened the way it did. It would, I hope, have happened one day but it couldn't have happened then. I would have just returned to England and tried to get a hit with the next one."

Steve Chapman – "But with the record a success we all flew back out to the States when Al had recovered and rehearsed for about a week at the Coconut Grove in Miami which was a lot of fun. At the end of that tour I'd saved a little money and decided to stay out here in the States for a while. I played with a number of other local bands and then at the beginning of December 1977 Charlie and I started working with Poco, staying until the middle of 1984."

One of the unique facets of Al's concerts had always been the use of storytelling and monologue during his performance. This he dates from observing the early gigs of Paul Simon around the folk clubs of England circa 1965.

Al – "With many of my more obscure stories I'm entertaining myself as much as anything else and usually it works out OK in the end. However once on the *Year Of The*

Philadelphia 1977

Cat tour in Pittsburgh, I introduced a song with the line 'This next one is about the Swingle Singers trapped down a mineshaft!'. Unfortunately this reduced our keyboard player, Peter Robinson, to hysterics and he fell off his stool, hit his head on the keys of the synthesiser and sent this loud boom out through the auditorium that reverberated around for what seemed like an eternity which then sent me into hysterics myself. The band weren't sure what to do so they started playing the song and I basically laughed my way through the first verse of what was supposed to be 'Broadway Hotel'. Now through all this the audience weren't laughing at all but I was and basically only managed to sing about a verse and a half of the entire song! They clapped politely and I can only presume that they thought that this was part of our act! The next song up was 'Roads to Moscow' which terrified me because I just couldn't see myself getting through it, but somehow I did, but it was one of the hardest things I've ever had to do. So the moral of this tale is that sometimes these introductions can go wrong! It's my version of stand-up comedy and it's been part of my act since Bunjies."

The regular support act on the Spring 1977 tour was Wendy Waldman and her band. Joan Armatrading also opened for Al. Peter White would go on to work with them both. Through the Spring of 1977 Peter would go down to the Janus Records offices and hang out with Ed De Joy, Alan Mason and the other staff there on a regular basis. Nigel would often join him.

By the *Year Of The Cat* US tour dates of 1977 Nigel Lendon had come to play a more important role in coping with the logistics of being on the road.

Nigel Lendon – "Luke would ask me to quote for how much it would cost to do say a particular 12-date tour of the East Coast. I'd go away, do the sums and come up with $18,000 to which Luke would demand it be brought in for $11,500 and would then compromise at around $16,000 by us both giving up particular parts of the budget – saving on a hotel here, an extra roadie there and so on. I went from being a sound engineer to being the Production Manager."

Luke had by now also discovered a simple means of kick-starting each tour's finances.

Luke – "There was a venue in Phoenix, Arizona where I could make a fortune in three or four days, called The Celebrity Theatre. $20,000 at the beginning of the tour as road float and $20,000 at the end of the tour for us. When we first came over here I discovered Phoenix as a market. We didn't need to take our own sound and lights so we used to fly out to Phoenix at each end of our tour for three or four days to this theatre in the round and we'd always sell out and it would help with the kitty."

To an outsider everything would have seemed perfectly in order with Al's career at this time in March 1977. However beneath the surface Luke had become increasingly disenchanted with his American record company.

It was at this time that Al and Luke left Janus. It was the result of a situation that had been brewing for a while with neither of them in reality facing up to the situation. There was however a great deal of sentiment involved in the parting of the ways. After all it was Janus that had given Al the chance to release his records in the US when no one else was interested, four years previously.

Luke – "Al was getting increasingly concerned because these guys were seemingly being cheap and an artist only gets one chance in their career. We were due an account statement now for the period up until Christmas 1976, which failed to arrive, and I also didn't think that his relationship with Alan Mason was one of complete trust at this time either. There were occasions when Al had felt it was very hard to get a straight answer out of Alan on key issues."

Things now began to move apace. When the royalty statements eventually arrived at the end of March they claimed to show that Kinetic were still in debt to Janus. However Luke knew that the *Year Of The Cat* album alone had already grossed $4,000,000 for the record company. Before the second part of the tour he had looked closely at the

Al Stewart

Al Stewart

Cashbox

The Folk Rock God

paperwork and realised there was a pick-up renewal date for Al's contract with Janus that had been due around the middle of January.

Luke again – "I didn't say anything at all until after the pick-up date and then I went and spoke to the record company. I went in and said, 'You realise that there was an option pick up, did you pick it up?' and they told me 'Sure, we must have done' and I thought to myself that if that's the case then they must have done. So we get to the end of the tour and Janus are really being mean with us and claiming that they only owe us $100,000 in *Year Of The Cat* royalties."

The album had by then shifted over 1.5 million records and it was clear to Luke that something was wrong. Luke also suspected that Janus hadn't actually picked up the option as Ed De Joy had claimed. But for now he kept all of this to himself.

Luke – "I said to them that I didn't care what our expenses were but that they owed us more than $100,000, but we took that money temporarily. Now in fact they *had* missed the pick-up date but they'd told me that they'd made it! So we get back off the tour and I'm having problems financially over the whole thing and I don't like the answers I'm getting. I'm also having to deal with this guy at GRT called Tom Bonetti who wasn't in the music business at all. He never had been."

What happened next, as Luke and Ed drove north one day from Santa Monica, would have dire repercussions for them all. Set against the background of Al's ongoing huge success the logic of Janus seems baffling.

Luke – "So I started negotiating in good faith one day with Ed De Joy, Janus President, as we're driving out to Malibu. I've got a $3,000 Volkswagen and Al's driving the cheapest water-cooled Porsche you could get so we weren't living that well considering the success we'd achieved and at this point Janus were trying to do a deal whereby they gave us just $350,000 an album! Ed then said something that got my blood going. He said 'That's all you need' and at that point as far as I was concerned Janus were history. It's as simple as that. You don't tell me what we need and at that point I knew that I wanted out and in a way it was another one of those defining moments. I can clearly remember him saying it and my reaction of 'Don't you dare tell me how much we need. Who do you think you are? This is a partnership, we're not slaves.' So I was very, very angry. We got back and Tom Bonetti tried to reduce the deal further a week later. He just rang up and said that they wouldn't pay $350,000!"

The new reduced deal that Al and Luke were offered was for just $250,000.

Luke was shocked at the action of Tom Bonetti and now pretended to go on holiday whilst, in essence, he started calling around at once to locate the best lawyer to represent Kinetic.

Luke – "Now I of course have to go and speak to Al and I expected to have to persuade him that this was simply necessary despite any misplaced feelings of loyalty that he may have because loyalty is dollars at this point and that he would be living until he was hopefully very old and that we wanted him to have money at that time and that it wasn't right that people should steal it. And I was prepared for this big long chat with Al but all I had to do was to open my mouth to say 'I want us to leave Janus' and he said 'Good, I wondered when you were going to come round and say that'. So I went out and got us a lawyer."

Having decided not to go with Alan Grubman, whom they had been with up until then, Luke met with several of the major law companies all of whom knew exactly who he was, of course, the moment he mentioned Al's name.

Luke – "The advice I was getting was all saying that when anyone makes the pick-up of a million-selling act they will send you pieces of paper to sign and they basically told me not to fret. They were certain that if Janus hadn't sent me pieces of paper to sign then they hadn't picked up that option."

One feature of all this that Luke found difficult was Ed's desire to separate his own actions from those of Tom Bonetti. As Luke says, "I had to deal with both of these guys!" Everyone blamed everybody else!

Ed De Joy – "We did indeed have an option that was due to be exercised in the Spring of 1977. Luke O'Reilly not only had no idea about it not being exercised, he had no idea about there being an option full stop and neither did I."

This is not quite the same version of events that Ed gave in his court deposition at the time.

Ed De Joy again – "GRT were responsible for doing all of the legal work involved and they should have had on their calendar the option dates for all of our artists. They neglected to do that and at this stage Luke didn't realise it either. The ongoing negotiations that Luke was having with Tom Bonetti were not going well and he was just looking for a way to cash in on Al. So he got some attorney in San Francisco to go over the books. And lo and behold there was no letter from GRT taking up the option. So Luke flies back down to Los Angeles and we meet up and he says 'Eddie, we don't want to leave Janus. You've all been really good to Al and I and we've got to work this out but I'm not going to deal with Tom Bonetti any more.' And so Luke and I hammered out a deal between the two of us which was to advance him $250,000 which was a lot of money plus we agreed to increase the advance that Janus would make on each album delivered to us by Kinetic on behalf of Al."

This is not the figure of course that Luke remembers. Ed De Joy considers that this was the very best deal that they could offer Luke and that they shook hands on the deal.

Ed De Joy – "Behind my back though, at the same time, he was making deals elsewhere. I knew nothing about the move to Arista though until after the ink was dry on the page. When I discovered this I was absolutely devastated. GRT's position was that as we had negotiated with Luke and had agreed terms for an extension to our contract then we had plans for a countersuit. I had taken him at his word, which proved to be a mistake. A formal contract was being drawn up but it never of course got signed."

Luke – "Not strictly true. Yes, Ed and I certainly did shake on a deal. It was that time that we were riding in his brand new pale green Cadillac that he'd been bought by Janus with some of the proceeds that we had earned for them by being on the road for the previous nine months! We'd been paid next to nothing and Ed was driving around in this fancy car and so I wasn't in the best of moods to start with. We had toured that album so hard for them. It's easy for a record company to telephone Iowa in mid-winter, you just see how much harder it is to actually get there with a band! But Ed and I shook hands on the advance of $350,000 per album that day in his Cadillac. Tom Bonetti then called me to knock it down to just that $250,000! So quite simply we left them."

Ed De Joy – "When I found out I went nuts. I went nuts at Tom Bonetti and everyone up there. I pointed out that whereas it was our responsibility to find the artist and develop them, his responsibility was only to make sure that we keep them. As simple as that. If GRT had been on the case we could have kept Al Stewart and they made a foolish mistake. It was certainly one of the worst things to happen to me in my life to get that phone call about the missed option. There are triggers that you set up to inform you about options that are due in five, ten, fifteen days or whatever. We could even have taken up the option at a far earlier date and thinking about it the perfect time would have been immediately after *Year Of The Cat* was released and not the following spring by which time it was a smash."

Why Janus failed to even belatedly take up the option on Al's contract, even after they were alerted to the fact that the pick-up date had come and gone, remains a mystery to all concerned.

The fact that the Janus profits from *YOTC* had largely been used to prop up GRT rather than being reinvested in the record company had done little of course to bolster Luke and Al's continued confidence in them as their long-term record company. There was also the fact that, due to their size, Janus couldn't always guarantee having sufficient albums in the stores to satisfy demand. This was a problem that they could only have dreamed of when they had signed Al four years earlier.

Luke had already swung into action with a plan to find Al a new record company whose credentials matched Al's perceived needs. This was a very different situation from 1973 when he signed with the only company willing to take a chance on Al, the now sad and beleaguered Janus.

Luke – "It's quite simple in reality. My loyalties were to Al and no one else. Now, record company-wise we didn't want to go to Columbia because it was too big and I wasn't sure that we'd see eye to eye with Walter Yetnikoff who was in charge over there at the time. We had a number of very good offers including one from Warner Brothers. But I've got a feeling that Al wanted to gain revenge over Clive Davis because Clive had been the executive at Columbia that had blocked the release of *Love Chronicles* years before and I think that Al got off on the fact that it was now going to cost Clive a lot of money to get Al back. I think that appealed to Al! I'd got my lawyers to call the head of every label in the country and they gave them my phone number and everybody called up and gave us a spiel and I then selected the top three or four and went to Al with them. So he, as I expected, said that it was basically up to me. This was a very different situation to the one of a year before when we'd been looking around for someone to put out *Year Of The Cat.* People were chasing after *us* this time! So anyway we go with Arista for a large advance of a million dollars and three cases of fine wines. One thing that I've always regretted, and I knew it was going on at the time but I couldn't get any sense out of anybody, was why we were leaving Janus but not getting paid a million bucks for royalties and what my lawyers told me was this. They said that Janus were going under and that I shouldn't add mayhem to mischief because if I tried to get the money out of them then they may go bankrupt and that may happen before we get the records in which case they may get sold to anyone on the open market and then we wouldn't get a penny."

By the time a year later when Luke went up to sign the final deal there were only a few people left in the Janus office. A couple of them asked him whether it was really correct that they had lost Al for the sake of a simple $100,000, a fact that Luke could do little else than acknowledge as being true.

Al is quite clear on one thing – "We were just out of the door. If they had treated us better and not tried to rob us blind I think that we might have negotiated for another contact. But that didn't happen."

Luke and Nigel Lendon now took a short break in Hawaii.

Once the decision to change record companies was made however things moved on apace through the summer of 1977.

Clive Davis had been a major player in the music business for twenty years when he signed Al to Arista. Having joined Columbia Records as an attorney in 1960 he was appointed Vice President and General Manager of CBS Records in 1966, and, in 1967, was named President of the company. It was Davis that had personally signed Janis Joplin's Big Brother and The Holding Company to Columbia. Following that he was directly responsible for signing many key rock artists, among them Blood, Sweat & Tears, Santana, Loggins & Messina, Laura Nyro, Billy Joel and Bruce Springsteen. Besides developing the rock roster, Davis also built up the label's catalogue in many other fields of recorded music, such as R&B, country, jazz and middle-of-the-road. Davis left Columbia in May, 1973 and, after writing his best-selling book, *Clive: Inside The Record Business,* he had founded with Columbia Pictures, *Arista Records* in the autumn of 1974. So the company that Al was joining was still, at that time, relatively new.

The agreement between Kinetic and Arista was signed on August 24th 1977 and the official announcement was made soon after by a proud Clive Davis at the record company's 1977 San Diego convention.

"It is with enormous pride that we welcome Al Stewart", he announced. "He is a brilliant artist who combines intellect and sense of words with keen musical vision. Literate, aware and surpassingly talented, Al Stewart is a major voice for our time."

It would be fair to say that being Al Stewart was quite a good thing to be at this time. He was enjoying both critical and commercial success all over the world, he was living a life of some style in a city that he had come to have genuine affection for, he had new friends and a new record company to pay for everything. If Al could have taken a polaroid of a single moment and held it up as a template for the rest of his life he could have picked any day that summer.

Record World had news of trouble however. In a piece filed from Los Angeles by Sam Sutherland on 16th October that was entitled 'Stewart Sues Janus/GRT' it reported: "In the opening round of what is looming as a probable court battle over singer/ songwriter Al Stewart's recent signing with Arista Records, Kinetic Productions Ltd., which manages the platinum album artist, has filed suit in Superior Court here seeking declaratory relief from GRT Inc., which owns Janus Records, Stewart's label since 1974.

"Kinetic's complaint, filed on September 14th, seeks a court determination on Stewart's freedom to negotiate with other labels based on the plaintiff's assertion that the original Janus contract had expired at the end of its initial three-year term on January 14th 1977. According to the Kinetic complaint, Stewart had pacted with Janus for three albums, with that label receiving options on three additional albums; that option, the complaint continued, 'was exercisable by GRT only upon 60 days request in writing during the term of The (original) Contract. GRT never made such request and has never exercised said option.'

"GRT's position, however, contests the Kinetic complaint, with counsel for the defence John Greenfield having requested depositions from key Kinetic and Arista principals on September 19th. Stewart, Kinetic principal and manager Luke O'Reilly, and an unnamed custodian of records for Kinetic were to give depositions last week, while Arista lawyers Allen Grubman and Bert Padell and executive VP Elliot Goldman are scheduled to give their statements Tuesday (11th) in New York.

"Also requested from Kinetic by the defence were 'any and all documents including but not limited to correspondence, notes, memoranda, appointment books, desk calendars and diaries' which pertained to the original Janus contract, a May 9th 1975 ongoing communications between Janus/GRT and Stewart/Kinetic and communications between Arista executive, Stewart, Kinetic and their legal counsel regarding Stewart's pact with Arista.'

"In Sunnyvale, California, official comment from GRT verified that Janus/GRT would contest Kinetic's claim and the newly signed Arista contract. Jim Levy told *Record World* – 'It is our contention that Al Stewart owes us additional product and it is presumably Arista and Kinetic Production's contention that they are free of us ... it's not going to be resolved until it gets into court.'

"While declining to comment in detail on GRT's specific counter-charges to the Kinetic action, Levy went on to say that the defence would raise a number of points aimed at blocking the Kinetic action and Al's new agreement with Arista. He continued – 'The fact is that the lawsuit was instituted by Kinetic Productions, not by us, which shows you how much confidence they have in their ability to operate freely.'

"With depositions for the defence still being collected at that time, no trial date had yet been set, nor had any countersuit been filed by GRT."

Ed De Joy – "Ultimately we were denied our injunction to delay *Time Passages* and to be honest I never believed we would get it anyway. When we applied for all of Kinetic's diaries and notebooks as part of the deposition it was in order to try and find some reference to all of our negotiations with Luke."

Al acted in a surprisingly detached manner throughout all this, especially considering it was his money!

Al – "I don't remember being that worried at the time, in fact I really don't think I even bothered to meet any lawyers throughout – I left all that to Luke. However, at that point in time we had just had the smash hit with *Year Of The Cat* and Luke was at the top of his game and he appeared to know what he was doing. It never dawned on me who was paying for the lawyers or even if there were lawyers."

Nigel Lendon remembers clearly the moment that things peaked. The scene was played out inside a Beverley Hills bank one Summer's afternoon in 1977.

Nigel Lendon – "To me this will always be the day that Luke and I deposited the Arista cheque for a million dollars in the Kinetic Bank account at Wells Fargo, Beverley Hills. When, like Al had, you've gone from Belsize Park to Bel Air and have been working towards this exact moment for ten years it's bound to be a time when you sit back and take stock of everything."

The bank's first floor entertainment division, at the junction of Camden and Little Santa Monica, was only generally used by the Kinetic office for the collection of an office float on a Friday afternoon. Luke had earlier signed the deal with Arista in San Diego where he had picked up the cheque.

Luke – "So I grabbed Nigel and we jumped into Al's Mercedes and drove down to the bank. This was a such a special day for all of us and something that we'd been aiming at for years and Nigel and I felt vindicated! The secretary at the bank, who had helped me get my first US credit card back in 1976, got half way through completing the deposit slip before she noticed what it was for. Moment's later Nigel and I are led into this big room by the President of the bank, the drinks cabinet comes out and it was just fantastic! I too will always remember that day ... and yes I guess it was the peak of everything."

In many ways Al and Arista looked at what the cheque represented in totally different ways. Arista saw it as an investment in Al's future whilst Al saw it as a reward for his past. To draw a line in the sand therefore and call it a turning point in Al's career would actually be to *underestimate* a tricky situation that was unfolding quite clearly in front of Arista's eyes.

Al wanted to take his foot off the gas now that he had banked their advance in Wells Fargo.

Much of the pressure applied on the Al camp by the million dollars would, from now on, be fielded by Luke. He realised that it was largely up to him to reverse the reality that pointed towards a loss of momentum at the critical hour in a career where the logical course of action would have been to "go for it" with a shift up in gear. It was a task that he would ultimately fail in but not before a very protracted and emotionally draining fall from grace.

Nigel Lendon – "Although everyone was, on the surface, very upbeat about everything there were a whole slew of relationship issues which everyone was addressing in their own way."

The human cost of having come this far now began to impart itself into the day to day running of the Kinetic machine and whilst the wheels hadn't exactly come off at this time there was a palpable sense of the fact that the adventure had peaked and from here on in it would be more of a slog.

Luke – "Now of course once you've been paid an advance of a million dollars you can't just do what you want and Al had to come up with a new album which had to be written quite quickly but he didn't turn down the million dollars did he? But yes, I do regret now that we didn't take a little more time with *Time Passages* but it's hard to see looking back how we could have done it any differently."

The week after they had paid the cheque into the bank Luke realised just how much things had changed when he was forced to pay far more than he had anticipated for the services of one of the key musicians that he wanted to play on the new album. In this respect their success counted against them. Then there were the legal bills for the various lawsuits which would cost Kinetic $300,000 over the next few months. Luke now sees this as the point where "the fun was over" for him.

The licensing of the tracks for *The Early Years* back in the Spring had brought to a head an issue that had been brewing for a while. Luke had long suspected that there was a potential problem with regard to Al's publishing in the UK, something that for financial reasons he had been unable to pursue. Now he could do something about it.

Luke – "I had discovered that Roy Guest had sold Gwyneth Music, who handled Al's publishing. Before I came on the scene he'd sold it quietly to Dick James' company DJM before Al had even realised it was up for grabs. We only found this out now. Through Gwyneth, DJM should have been paying Al 50 percent of any publishing royalties that they collected but due to Dick James sub-publishing to himself Al had only been getting half of this which was completely wrong."

There had been a precedent for such a case. In the British High Court a judgement had been previously reached in a case between the writer Macaulay and his publisher Schroeder. The decision the judge arrived at was that Macaulay couldn't have anything back from the past but he would receive more from here on in. After Kinetic had paid over $60,000 in legal fees Dick James agreed to settle on the terms of that Macaulay-Schroeder ruling.

The million-dollar advance was not simply loose change in Al's pockets however. Legal and business fees to Brian Rohan and Bert Padell cost $100,000. The litigation bill from Mitchell, Silberberg and Knupp swallowed up $250,000 whilst the recording of the new album took another $190,000. Once the remaining $460,000 had 40 percent US tax taken out of it Al was left with only $276,000 out of which he had to pay Luke and find money to live on.

The initial agreement with Arista was for three albums over four years with an option held by the record company for a further two albums over the succeeding three years and so they were clearly making a long term commitment to Al at that stage.

The minimum advance for each album was $400,000, which was just as well because by now Al had become quite the social animal around LA. Typical of the parties he was invited to was a reception at Le Dome on Sunset Boulevard in late May 1978 for Patti Smith where Al mingled with the likes of Ray Bradbury, Phil Spector,

Michael Lippman and Bernie Taupin. Then of course there were all the new friends he was making courtesy of Dennis Overstreet. Al's life had changed dramatically over the last 18 months.

During each of the short breaks in the *YOTC* tour Peter would return to England for a month or so before getting the plane back out to America for the next leg of the tour. *Time Passages* was started back at Abbey Road studios exactly two years after *YOTC*. Al and Peter wrote the title track at the Hammond Terrace apartment.

Peter White – "I'd played the riff to Al on the piano during the *YOTC* tour and Al had picked up on it and said how much he liked it and that when we all finished the tour that he and I should write a song around it which is how I came to be sitting there with Al, with myself playing the piano and Al coming out with a word here and there and much of the melody. The reason that this was the only song on that album written like that was primarily because I was only just starting to write songs at that time; those were early days for me."

However with regard to other joint compositions Al could be far more precise with his ideas.

Peter White – "With regard to 'End Of The Day', Al's brief to me was to specifically write a song that was similar to 'Wind Cries Mary' by Jimi Hendrix and so I borrowed the key and rhythm but the actual song is completely different. Al took this and adapted a melody for his vocal. The actual construction of a song in the studio was like this. Al would come into the studio with a very rough demo of either clunky piano or him strumming a guitar which we'd all listen to and put in our own ideas about how it could be made better. Then we'd all play it through a few times and Alan Parsons would offer up his ideas and the whole thing gradually evolved in the studio where I guess the atmosphere was something of a melting pot. Al was there all of the time for this album too."

By now of course Peter had got himself noticed by much of the LA music community. Whereas the occasional session for someone else had always been something that he would strive to fit in around his Al commitments, the offer of a full time job with another band was something that he was suddenly forced to give some serious thought to.

Peter White – "Just before we started recording *Time Passages* I went for an audition with Joan Armatrading to play keyboards. I got offered the gig and so I went back and told Al who wasn't keen at all and explained to me how the instrumental that eventually became the actual song *Time Passages* was high on his list of songs to be recorded. So that was enough for me and I rang Joan Armatrading's manager and turned it down."

Peter felt that his future was with Al because he was also involved in the writing and arranging of the songs. That was the closest he ever came to leaving for many years.

In the three years that Peter had been working with Al he had gone from keyboard player to *de facto* band leader and now, it appeared, co-composer of future platinum selling records. And so it was probably not that difficult a decisionfor Peter which, given the timing of it, was just as well for Al. Another personal tie was unravelling at this time however.

On 17th December 1977 Marion, who had been with Al since the Howff gig in the summer of 1974, left him and moved in with Luke at his new house on Ridgemont. Al and Marion's once serious relationship had slowly evolved into one of just friendship and at the same time she had grown closer to Luke. It was a logical next step for Marion and Luke to be together. It was all very amicable. So amicable in fact that the three of them travelled together to Arista's third birthday party the next day in New York City! At the party Al bumped into Mandi, seeing her several times over the next few days. They got on better than they had in years and from that time on kept in touch.

Peter White – "It was very strange for me to see Marion with Luke because I'd known her up until now to be with Al and so at first it was something new for us all."

It seems to be a situation that evolved at its own pace over a long period of time. Certainly it was never acrimonious and in Luke, Marion had found someone to turn to.

On December 31st Luke threw a New Year's Eve party at his new house. Al went as a Circus Ringmaster.

Soon after this, Peter remembers Al getting more and more into partying at The Rainbow Bar and Grill which was, after all, just up the road from his apartment on Hammond Terrace. Peter, at this time, was living literally round the corner on Harratt Street but seeing more of Krysia and Robin Lamble than Al and with them he started doing gigs which featured Krysia as the lead singer, which was part of the reason for her being in Los Angeles anyway, Luke having promised to make her a star if she moved out to LA. to live. Together they played such places as The Troubadour with her original compositions providing much of their repertoire at this time.

Peter White – "Al called me in December 1977 whilst I was back home at Letchworth for Christmas and suggested that I fly over to Los Angeles straight after the holidays because he had a spot on the Merv Griffin show and also it was time to do some more work on the album. We did the TV show and then end up at Davlin Studios on Lancashome Boulevard where we recorded 'Valentina Way' and did lots of odds and ends. Things like adding Phil Kenzie on saxophone for the track 'Song On The Radio' were all done there at Davlin in Studio City at the start of 1978."

At this time Al had just bought the house on Roscomarre Road in Bel Air but wasn't yet living there as he was having some improvements done and asked Peter (who was staying with friends in Los Angeles at this point, as he didn't have his own place in town) whether or not he might like to house-sit whilst the work was being done.

Peter White – "I stayed there for a while but moved out because it was very isolated and quite lonely and although I did have a rental car at the time to get out and about in I didn't stay there very long."

Krysia – "Like Peter I too lived there for a while when it was still just empty rooms. I felt that the building had a weird vibe and so I decided to counter this by setting down incense candles in the four corners of each room. However I failed to appreciate that I should have put something down under each burner and when I got up in the morning there was a burn mark under each one. The carpet in every room had a hole now in each corner."

This is the reality of a story that Al told everyone for years; the tale of how Krysia came to very nearly raze 'Roscomarre' to the ground!

Chris Desmond was the engineer on what was to become *Time Passages*.

Chris Desmond – "My relationship with Alan Parsons was very, very productive. At this stage this was the first time I had ever met him and of course he was already legendary not only in my eyes but in everyone else's for the work he had done with the Beatles and Pink Floyd. Recently he had been working with friends of Al's in a group called Ambrosia. So basically my memory of those sessions was that it took me a while to get used to the dynamic because Al was tough, he was very contrary and he made it so difficult for everybody and everything to work. I mean that aside from everything else because I love him and he is a very, very dear friend."

However, in working now with Al, Chris was forced to accept the manner in which he wrote his songs. It was something that he found both difficult and frustrating at first.

Chris again – "Al's process is basically that he is great when it comes to putting down backing tracks but then he has to go away and struggle for an eternity with the lyrics. Unfortunately with Al, while they are gestating in his brain he looks like he isn't really doing anything. It looks like he is doing nothing and isn't really bothered and has perhaps lost the plot. This couldn't be farther from the truth. He is very spontaneous about how he puts things together and he has a natural gift for juxtaposing images. He has got an almost *Lewis Carroll* kind of whimsy but it's all mixed with this geo-political sensibility that he has got mixed with his real romantic streak."

The pressures brought about by having a million dollar advance do not appear, at this time, to have affected the way that Al and Luke did things though.

Luke – "It still took us a year to get that album out and at that time the interest on that million dollars to Arista would have been over $100,000. Recording *Time Passages* we did the same as we did with *Year Of The Cat* – using both Abbey Road and Los Angeles. But this time I didn't feel it necessary to spend quite as much time physically there in the studio as I had done previously because I had faith in everyone not needing me to be there to push them on."

Chris Desmond – "During *Time Passages* we would start in the evening 7ish, as that was Al's time and perhaps sometimes we would start a little earlier and we would do some preparatory work. Particularly during the vocals we would work for only an hour, because the big problem was that he would lose his voice. I think the stakes had been raised with the earlier albums previously, but his pattern seemed to be that particularly during the time that he had to do vocals he would get himself focused with whatever lyric he was working with and come in and work for an hour or so then go and have dinner and then he would come back and work on some more vocals into the early hours of the morning. Overdub and overdub."

Al's social life was eclectic and varied. He did however have his "local".

Luke – "The 'Rainbow Bar and Grill' was a rock and roll restaurant and they loved Al up there because he'd go in for dinner every night and although he was a big star it didn't matter where they put him and yet these drunk, quaaluded-out people would come in and demand this and that but they loved Al because of the way he behaved. Sometimes he'd go in on his own if Marion wasn't over and if I wasn't around. The people that worked for us were our friends and we all used to hang out together and Al was Mr Sunset Strip, I couldn't keep up with him."

Al – "I had moved to Hollywood which is the greatest place in the world. I discovered the Rainbow, I discovered Los Angeles girls, I had waited 30 years to get somewhere sensible and finally there I was, you know. I should have been there when I was 21 but got there when I was 31 and there was no way I wanted to be in a recording studio! I was completely diverted in the best possible way. I would think if I could, in a more perfect universe, I would have just stopped time and lived in the Rainbow for the rest of my life. It was the beginning and end of the most perfect existence imaginable. It is the only time that I have been truly happy in my life. It is exactly the epitome of what I thought would be the most wonderful thing. It was all those nights at the Scotch of St James (where I waited outside and even Jonny Kremer could get in and I couldn't) all put into perspective with one almighty atomic blast and there it was. I was in the Rainbow Bar and Grill, I had a record in the top 10 and every girl in the place wanted to come and sit on my lap.

"You have no idea what that is like, after 15 years of not getting it. Of course I didn't want to go and make a follow up record and I had to be dragged kicking and screaming into the recording studio. I wouldn't have cared at that point if I had never made another album. I would have probably come out after about 15 years and said 'OK am I supposed to be a pop star?' But no, I didn't want to do it. A more serious answer is that the *Year Of The Cat* tour went on for seven months because they kept adding gigs all the time."

The success of "Year Of The Cat" meant that millions of record collections all over the world now included one of Al's albums. As Jimmy Page mentioned when I interviewed him for this book – "There were so many chicks that I met in America that had 'Year Of The Cat'! That record had obviously made a dent and was much respected."

The idea of Jimmy Page constantly coming face to face with Al's album as Led Zeppelin laid waste to the known world is truly something to behold.

Despite this success, Peter White remembers everyone having their feet on the ground at that moment.

Peter – "Everything at this time was fine. So was Luke. The madness didn't start until the next year!"

The litigious atmosphere that had pervaded the previous 18 months was still in full swing though as the Autumn approached.

On 16th September *Record World* carried the following report – "Janus Records has been denied an injunction that would have blocked the release of former Janus artist Al Stewart's first album for Arista Records, *RW* has learned.

"Janus sought to delay the release of Stewart's *Time Passages* until such time as litigation between Arista and Janus was resolved. Janus' motion for an injunction, filed earlier this year, was denied at a hearing that took place in Los Angeles on September 1st."

This then was the sad litigious end to Al's relationship with Janus. The fact that the recordings of those Janus albums had only ever been leased to them now of course acted in Al's favour.

Ed De Joy – "After we lost the court case we were allowed to continue manufacturing *Past Present And Future*, *Modern Times* and *Year Of The Cat* for a short period of time and after this those rights reverted to Kinetic. So we never owned the masters."

The release of his first Arista album was a period in which Al and Luke not only had the full support of a major record company but its major league Boss too. The September 23rd issue of *Billboard* carried an occasional feature entitled *A Day in the Life* within its pages. That week's issue featured Clive Davis as its subject and on the day he was shadowed by *Billboard* Luke was occupying much of his time.

"Arista's President Packs In Every Moment With Meetings and Music While Scurrying Around LA.

"At 1.30pm Davis meets with Luke O'Reilly, manager of Al Stewart, whose first Arista album, *Time Passages* was just released, nearly two years after his Janus breakthrough LP, *Year Of The Cat.*

"Also at the meeting are Howard Smith and Lou Meisinger, O'Reilly's attorneys. During the conference, which goes on for nearly two hours, the four men pore over the wording of a lawsuit against Janus.

"This is a task for which Davis is well qualified, having graduated from law school in 1956 and having served as Columbia's general attorney from 1960 until he became the label's administrative vice president in 1965.

"The first part of the suit deals with the way the public in many cases will associate the absence of produce over an extended period of time with failure.

"The attorneys note that if they can cite specific examples where this has happened, it may help their case. Davis thinks for a moment and then gives two examples from his Columbia years: 'Sly and Laura Nyro – when they tried to get back after prolonged absences they couldn't'.

"The second argument in the suit deals with the way individual folk artists have fallen out of vogue due to mercurial public tastes. Again Davis is called upon to cite an example; again he pulls one from his CBS years – Donovan, who is also on Arista now.

"As O'Reilly leaves, he urges Davis to call Stewart. 'He'd really appreciate it,' O'Reilly implores, becoming one of several managers during the day who endeavours to spark a personal contact between Davis and their clients.

"Davis becomes visibly upset when he learns that an Arista employee has called Stewart at home, rather than following protocol and going through O'Reilly.

"'She has no right to call artists at home,' he says. 'You deal with managers, especially with major stars: you never deal with artists directly. In the same way you don't call Barry Manilow himself, you don't call Al Stewart. Managers get threatened by that. She should apologise to him. She was being zealous without understanding.'"

Al had thus somehow blundered into the paranoid and self-serving world of LA rock 'n' roll ethics. Back in the relative sanity of the British press the new album was earning him some of the best reviews of his career.

On September 30th 1978, *Record Mirror* in England gave the first Arista album this five-star review – "*Time Passages* is irrefutable proof that Al Stewart is one of Britain's foremost song-writing talents. Over the last decade he has progressed from being a competent folk artist into a musician with total finesse and allusive subtlety, now in the same league as Paul Simon. [High praise indeed.]

"Like a painter, he creates images, using lyrics as his oil colours. Ever present is a pervasive atmosphere such as enhances *Time Passages*. Al's obsession with time, and his deeply considered ideas about it, are highly relevant to the album. Whereas on *Year Of The Cat* there was, for instance, a distinct Bogartian mood, now the concepts move across time with the ingenuity of H.G. Wells."

Meanwhile Warren Kurtz in the October 26th issue of *Scene* offered equally fulsome praise: "After two years, Al Stewart follows the success of *Year Of The Cat* with *Time Passages*, one of the finest albums of 1978.

"His compositions remain in the same genre as selections on *Past, Present And Future*, *Modern Times* and *Year Of The Cat*. The new creation is closest in overall sound to the latter.

"Perhaps the main similarity between the two albums is the title tune on each. 'Time Passages', the album's first single, features the same sax, acoustic guitar, piano and orchestrated production that made 'Year Of The Cat' Stewart's most popular single.

The album's quieter moments capture the feel of Donovan in the mid-'60s. Both Donovan and Al Stewart have similar geographical and musical backgrounds so the comparison is not without cause. Especially on 'Almost Lucy' Stewart captures the style of mid-'60s folk-rock with a bit of a Spanish guitar flavour, musically hinting at accomplishments of Simon and Garfunkel."

Al was confirmed as being very much at the top of his game. The one moment in his career when universal critical acclaim coincided with staggering record sales was now.

Al and his mother in Bel Air

Optical Illusion

In which Al embarks on a World Tour and writes the classic 24 Carrots album.

The next few months were full of incident in that the new album got attention from day one, unlike *Year Of The Cat* which took a while to get noticed. It had taken a long time to record however.

Some songs of course didn't make it onto the album *Time Passages*.

Peter White – "I remember specifically the song 'Life In A Bottle' which I thought was a great song when Al played it in the studio during those sessions. Alan Parsons leaned back in his chair and thought for a moment before pronouncing – 'Well Al – it's not one of your better works!'

"Al accepted this though happily enough and we moved onto working on something else."

"Tonton Macoute" was another case in point of a lost song from *Time Passages*. This got as far as being recorded at Larrabee Studios in Los Angeles as a demo and through the summer of 1977 Al was playing it in concert but again it was given the thumbs down by Alan Parsons once the actual album's studio sessions kicked off. One song that did survive the Larrabee in concert/actual album route was "Palace Of Versailles", a song that endured a series of re-writes in the months leading up to its actual recording.

Throughout the middle of 1978 Al recruited some new members for the band and planned to hold lengthy auditions in Los Angeles. Mark Goldenberg had left and the band needed a lead guitar player. Adam Yurman joined the band for the *Time Passages* tour.

Songwriting, or more specifically lyric writing, was continuing to cause Al some problems. Writing the lyrics for "Song On The Radio" he was searching for a woman's name to use in the verse and ultimately used two women, one from the early 20th century and the other a more contemporary figure, combining their two names together for the purposes of the song. Lillie Langtry and Paloma Picasso becoming *Lillie Paloma*, Paloma having been chosen by Pablo Picasso as the name of his daughter as it was Spanish for "dove". The song "Timeless Skies" went through a lengthy genesis being demoed as both "Warm Californian Night" and "Warmth Of A Summer's Night" at various stages in its evolution. The early versions included references to both the Hollywood sign and St. Stephen's day and it was recorded at the same session as "Song On The Radio" as were "Tonton Macoute" and "Life in a Bottle". Al would invariably only have the bare bones of a chord structure for one of his new compositions when he played it to the band for the first time and improvisation on their behalf was very much the order of the day at that time. On other occasions he would demo it at home on the piano and turn up at the studio with a home taping.

Robin Lamble – "That album was largely written with everybody chipping in their own individual ideas whilst we were putting the first demos together. My first studio time with Al was when we started working on *Time Passages* at Abbey Road Studios in London. Alan Parsons didn't really think I could cut it as a musician and I almost didn't make it onto the record but all of the other band members stuck up for me, which I truly appreciated, and I got to play on it. One thing that he wanted me to do was completely change the way that I played the bass because he didn't like me playing with my fingers and so I played with a pick. It was a very tense situation straight away for me there in the studio in London and I honestly thought that I was for the chopping block. But in the end I played on the whole of the album. So I played on the demos for *Time Passages* at a little studio on Santa Monica Boulevard and then on the actual recording starting off at Abbey Road. I also had a hand in those sax parts on 'Song On The Radio' and 'Time Passages' itself. We'd be sat around in the studio with Phil Kenzie just trying to come up with ideas for what he should play and on a number of occasions I made suggestions for parts."

Pat Gallagher reviewed Al's gig at The Palace Theatre on September 29th – "Al Stewart is a singularly successful musician. He has struck popularity far beyond cult status with a song style that is literate, faintly intellectual, and suffused with romanticism. A lot of groups have flopped over the years pushing' PhD rock', but if you think Al Stewart's stuff is too far out of the mainstream of rock music, you should have been there Sunday night.

"The English singer charmed, entertained, stimulated and rocked a full house at the Palace with a selection of old and new songs, mostly drawn from the *Year Of The Cat* album and the new one, *Time Passages*. Seven musicians enabled Stewart to reproduce his album versions faithfully and with verve. His more familiar work holds up very well on replaying and his new pieces like 'Song On The Radio' tend to grab the listener right away."

In actual fact this was a song that Al had never particularly liked and he was already uncertain about having it out as a single. Gallagher, on the other hand, was impressed with the way that the show was put together.

"The show moved along without any dead points, expect for a too-long intermission mid-way in Stewart's act. However, there was no break following a brief opening set by Krysia Kristianne, a young woman who sings backup for Stewart live and on record. She offered several English folk songs done in a style similar to Fairport Convention and the Incredible String Band.

"Stewart opened with the brooding 'On The Border', and proceeded through 'Broadway Hotel', 'If It Doesn't Come Naturally' and 'Time Passages'. The second half of the show concentrated on Stewart's psychological/historical narratives: 'Life In Dark Water', 'Sirens Of Titan', 'The Palace Of Versailles' and the epic 'Roads to Moscow'. The last was movingly – even hauntingly accompanied by two-tone slides depicting scenes of Hitler's invasion of Russia."

The concert introduction to "Year Of The Cat" had by this time evolved into an improvised piece that gave a clue as to one of its original sources. It was just one of many examples of Al's tongue-in-cheek take on performing, where a wistfulness and sense of fun were always paramount.

Pat Gallagher again – "Stewart has a sense of humour, too. He teased the audience by prefacing the anxiously awaited 'Year Of The Cat' with a long winding piano solo by his pianist that included a hinting passage of 'As Time Goes By' from the movie *Casablanca*. And, when the band returned for the first of two encores following 'Year Of The Cat' it was with a slinky bit of the 'Pink Panther Theme' complete with a pink panther doll. Touches like that keep Al Stewart from falling into the 'high art' trap that proved the fatal flaw of groups like Procol Harum and Renaissance. The new album and this strong live show permanently raise Al Stewart above the level of cult figure. Yet, happily, his continued aesthetic appeal should serve to keep the adoring hordes of pop fans at a distance."

Al's ongoing love of the electric guitar and the flamboyance of electric guitar players was demonstrated very clearly to Adam Yurman right after the first night of the *Time Passages* tour in Phoenix.

Adam Yurman – "I'd had a real good time that first night and was worried that perhaps I had maybe overstepped the mark by my running up to the edge of the stage, right by the monitors, for my solos, doing my best impression of Pete Townshend. I confided my worries to Peter who said not to worry but Al must have overheard us because a little while later he said that he liked his guitar players to be demonstrative. So that was a green light to me as you can imagine."

LIFE IN DARK WATER

Oh come away from the day, here I stay
Living on the bottom of the sea
Down metal snake corridors steely grey
Engines hum for nobody but me
No sound comes from the sea above me
No messages crackle through the radio leads
They'll never know, never no never
How strange life in dark water can be

Oh mariners spare a thought when you pass
Those who live the submarine life
Far in the deep sonar eyes never sleep
Hiding like a shadow in the night
Jet planes nose through the clouds above me
They look for radar traces of me to see
They'll never know, never no never
How strange life in dark water can be

Wonder what the stars look like
Coming out tonight
Tell my girl she must be strong
She sits and waits all night long
Just looking for a better day
She'll have to find another way to go

No memory, tell me what's wrong with me
Why am I alone here with no rest
And now the name of the ship's not the same
How long has it been "Marie Celeste?"
Now there's nobody from the crew left
Five hundred years supply of food just for me
They'll never know, never no never
How strange life in dark water can be

In the middle of the tour Phil Kenzie left to play with Rod Stewart, a situation that Luke had anticipated, Rod having been at one of Al's Roxy shows a few weeks earlier. Brian Savage, who Bill Ashton knew from Aspen, replaced him on saxophone.

Out on tour the album flew into the charts and almost at once was number 28 in *Billboard*, 27 in *Cashbox* and also in the *Record World* charts. Throughout October they played Music Hall, Houston; Pershing Auditorium, Lincoln; Northrup Auditorium, Minneapolis; Performing Arts Centre, Milwaukee; Ford Theatre, Detroit; Riviera Theatre, Chicago; Music Hall, Cincinnati; Palace Theatre, Cleveland and Mosque, Pittsburgh. The new band members were Robert Alpert on keyboards, Adam Yurman on lead guitar, Harry Edward Stinson on drums and Krysia Kristianne on background vocals. In its very first week it was the album "most added" to the radio station play lists canvassed by *Record World*, *Cashbox* and *Goodphone* and one week later achieved the same with *Billboard*. This was very much the big time now.

Krysia – "I played on the British leg of the *Year Of The Cat* tour and then Luke rang me and said 'Why don't you come to the States to see what it's like for a few months?', he also offered to manage me. In England when I opened for Al I was playing guitar and singing but for the *Time Passages* shows I was using a couple of members of the band *Shot In The Dark*. I had come over as a separate entity to them all and then Luke was saying 'Well you're here, why don't you play this tambourine, maybe you could play this keyboard part?' All of this happened very naturally." And so she was in.

Krysia had only been in LA for three days when she promised herself that this was where she was going to make her home.

"Everything was put in place for me by Luke and Kinetic. They found me a place to live and generally looked after me. The situation progressed from one where I was just opening shows for Al on his tour to where I was being worked into the band. Now at the time I was completely unaware of the review coverage that my performances at the shows were getting. Moving to America in itself was amazing enough."

Krysia had already started to write songs with fellow band member Robin Lamble. Theirs was a partnership that was soon to transcend the bounds of a purely professional relationship.

Krysia – "I also worked occasionally with Peter on little writing projects. You see I'd been doing this stuff for years on my own anyway and had a great deal of experience of writing with other people from my time six years earlier with the Natural Acoustic Band. Back in those early days in Scotland we were not only all very young but were also musically unskilled. Although I didn't write anything down as actual notes I could read music."

Shot In The Dark were not always called that. Originally they were going to be called Flying Sorcery. Nigel Lendon was in a perfect position to observe what was going on with regard to the band and specifically with regard to Luke's support for Krysia in those early days.

Nigel Lendon – "I can see how Krysia was led to believe that there was more for her in America and that a greater interest in her career would be taken by Kinetic than actually transpired in the end. Whether this was because Luke found priorities elsewhere or if it was because he was simply unable to find work for her I don't know. I've always felt too that there was a conflict in characters there and that Krysia found it very difficult to work with Luke."

The two year hiatus between *Year Of The Cat* and *Time Passages* was definitely too long however. Press comment on this was evident in many papers – Dennis Hunt wrote this in *Los Angeles Times* – "Artists prize momentum. Having it means getting lots of exposure, because of a hit record and a thriving tour. It is especially crucial to new artists or those who have been struggling for years.

"Right now A Taste Of Honey has momentum and so do Teddy Pendergrass, Foreigner, Dolly Parton and the Bee Gees. Then there are those unfortunate artists who had momentum and lost it. Scottish singer-songwriter Al Stewart is one of those. An artist maintains momentum by rapidly following success with another. The cardinal sin, which Stewart committed, is allowing your career to cool off.

"In the first half of last year Stewart was in demand. Because of his first hit album, *Year Of The Cat*, and his first hit single, the album's title song, a six-week tour was stretched to seven months. To maintain momentum, Stewart would have had to come up with another album four or five months after the tour ended in August. But Stewart has been tardy. That follow-up album, *Time Passages* has just been released by his new label, Arista, exactly two years after *Year Of The Cat* came out."

To which Al replied – "I don't worry about momentum. It takes care of itself. If you put out a quality record, it will sell. If you're a talented performer, people will come to see you perform… quality will carry the day." They both had a point.

Part of the delay in *Time Passages* getting made was Al's exhaustion from the previous tour and part merely stemmed from his ongoing casual attitude to momentum.

Al – "I felt no pressure to get a record out. I feel no obligation to fill up the world with records, I just put them out when they're ready."

Switching from tiny Janus Records to bigger Arista wasn't particularly time-consuming. Eager to capitalise on the momentum established by *Year Of The Cat*, Arista expected an album much earlier but they decided to let the album take its long course.

In 1985 Peter White reflected – "It may have seemed to the world that we were taking forever writing that album but we didn't actually write together, the only time was 'Time Passages' itself when we sat around the piano. This chord or that chord, let's try that or let's try this, or he left me alone and said 'You play around with it'. Usually I'll make a tape of it at home and give it to him and then he'll work with it and change it a bit and play it back to me and I'll work with it. It goes back and forth. He'll always make the lyric fit the music, that's how he's always done it. He'll find a way. To him the music is always the starting point, which is funny considering he's a lyricist. Often I come up with the purely musical parts. For example, on 'Time Passages' all the parts where he's singing were his musical ideas, all the in-between parts were my ideas. In that song, it's very delineated. In 'End Of The Day', for instance, that was my melody. He was very loath to sing that, he said it sounded more like an instrumental. In the end he wound up singing it and it was great. He did change the middle eight. If you notice, the guitar plays one middle eight then it's soloing and he sings a different middle eight. He couldn't sing mine so he made up another one."

"End Of The Day" has remained one of Al's favourite songs and the recorded version is something that he "wouldn't change in any way whatsoever, the whole song seems perfectly in place on the album to me," he said ten years after its release.

Out on tour, the set list was able to include much of *Time Passages* for the first time, things were going reasonably well.

The LA show from October 4th was reviewed in the *Daily Variety Hollywood* a couple of days later on October 6th – "'Actually, this song means absolutely nothing if you've grown up in Los Angeles', Al Stewart opined, in just one of a string of similar intros he made for his songs Wednesday night at the Santa Monica Civic Auditorium.

"It wasn't that he meant to be condescending; and a near-capacity crowd didn't appear to take it as such. But Stewart, a literate man who cares very much about the precise impact of his carefully chosen words, wanted to help his American fans understand that they were faced with a lyrical complexity and importance which is rare in today's music.

"Principal problem is more than the fact that Stewart is very much the Englisher and his audience Wednesday night was not, although that certainly creeps into it.

"More specifically, Stewart, for all his rock success via the platinum-selling *Year Of The Cat* LP in 1976, is creating music from within the context of the English folk music tradition, with all its love of myth and legend and sense of history, and, in many cases, this is alien turf for contemporary music aficionados in this country."

With Krysia, now billed as Krysia Kristianne, opening for Al out on tour she too was getting good notices. The two performances that particularly got rave reviews, night after night, were of the songs "A Leaf Must Fall" and "This Life, That Life I'm Really Not Sure".

However, Krysia's solo career never really lifted off: "I came out here initially essentially as a solo artist" Krysia explained in 1999, "and was borrowing Peter and Robin as and when. Luke was working behind the scenes to try and get me a record contract and he was reasonably successful in this in as far as record company people would come and see my little shows from time to time. The main reason that I moved out to Los Angeles was so that Luke could manage me as an individual. I was a totally separate entity to Al. I'm sure that there are many things that happened behind the scenes that I will never know about. One thing that I did discover much later was that there was at least one record company that were very interested in me as a solo act but I didn't get to find out about this until much later on. Now as to the reasons and machinations for me not knowing about it at the time well I can only guess, but I was certainly not told this important news at the time."

Luke makes the valid point that he made sure that all the important bills in Krysia's life in the US were taken care of by Kinetic. The fact that she was able to continue living in the States, with no record release, points to the fact that they did indeed look after her. It seems illogical to suggest that Kinetic would therefore have passed on the chance of her ever getting a deal of her own.

Certainly Luke was already working flat out on the growing success and ever more pronounced profile of Al at this time. He obviously cared very much about Krysia and had lobbied continuously for her to take a chance and come out to America in order to find true success and fulfilment as an artist.

Luke – "We had this little rehearsal studio down on Ventura Boulevard and Al had suggested that I should manage Krysia because she was the best thing since Edith Piaf. So I started doing just that and on that first British tour for *Time Passages* she opened for us. Now 'Al Stewart plus another' … isn't going to pull any more of a crowd than just Al Stewart and I didn't want to have other people mucking about with our stage set up. So I persuaded the guys in the band to go on stage with her and to help out with a song here and there but I had to reassure them that it wouldn't take the place of Al because they *were* concerned about that."

Whilst it's easy to come up with several conspiracy theories as to why he wouldn't want Krysia to become successful in her own right – the implicit demise thereafter of *Shot In The Dark*, the loss of the female presence on stage with Al and at the same time the responsibility of another 'solo' charge, maybe the suggestion that Luke was never really serious about Krysia having a solo career in the first place, these are all largely disproved by the eyewitness testimonies of Robin and Peter that show how hard for a couple of years Luke was seen at close quarters to be working on breaking Krysia in the States. Perhaps in the end it was just bad luck visiting itself on the criminally underrated Krysia rather than a smoking gun with Luke's fingerprints all over it left smouldering on his desk at Kinetic.

Al – "It's a mystery to me why Krysia never quite achieved all the things that we had hoped for her. A lot of time was spent on looking for projects that she could work on I remember. But yes, I did suggest to Luke that she come out to be with us in Los Angeles."

Krysia – "I thought that I'd arrived over here with a bunch of, what I considered to be, fairly esoteric accessible songs but perhaps I wasn't what the industry at that time was looking for. Those decisions made on my behalf were made for 'business' and not 'artistic' reasons. Those early tours, whereby it changed from me opening solo to playing with Peter and Robin and then the expanded group that became *Shot In The Dark* were a natural progression personal-wise because I enjoyed being part of a band more than performing solo. I was coming from a very naïve and not very complicated place about that development from solo artist to band member."

Luke – "The *Was Krysia had?* topic is, I fully understand, a good angle. I have to say that my response to all of it is – *No she most definitely was not*. She had her career within the band, enough money to afford to live in America and run a car and all of those things. In the end she didn't quite make it with her solo career for a number of reasons."

Meanwhile the various band members had to work hard at the multitude of roles they were being called upon to play. They were performing with two artists that had subtle yet important differences in their styles as Adam noted.

Adam Yurman – "It was sometimes very difficult in the early days on that *Time Passages* tour where as the opening act we were basically Krysia's band. Now there I did have to be careful. After all, the last thing you want to hear in the middle of a Celtic folk song is a short blast of Jimi Hendrix!"

On October 31st David Fricke, writing in *Circus*, interviewed Al – "There's more pressure on you," he explains with a charming but slightly nervous smile, "to create if you've had no success because then you become paranoid, especially if you've made six albums without a hit. Then if you do have a hit record, if anything, it's a relaxation."

This was proof, once again, that Al saw success as an opportunity to gently take his foot off the gas. This easy-going attitude was a blessing however when it came to not getting distracted by the various writs that were flying around.

Fricke noted that – "He also seems rather unconcerned about a recent flurry of lawsuits with the GRT Corporation, parent company for his old label Janus, which threatened to delay the new album indefinitely. Stewart says crisply that 'it was our opinion that the contract was over; it was theirs that it wasn't.' Al's manager Luke O'Reilly says he has no complaint with Janus, only GRT with whom he differed over 'their commitment to a major artist like Al Stewart' and whom he says 'don't care whether they're selling baked beans or songs.' (A GRT spokesman replied that, while he understood Luke's 'emotional complaint' as a manager looking out for his artist, 'I don't think he can say we didn't put everything behind *Year Of The Cat* and the results speak for themselves.')

"Whatever the legal complications, *Time Passages* makes clear that, unlike some of his contemporaries, Al Stewart is not dealing in baked beans. Highlighted by a glistening instrumental blend of guitars, strings and keyboards mixed by Alan Parsons, the album is a tribute to technical perfection, for which Parsons holds himself partially responsible. 'I've developed more of a perfectionist attitude in my work and it's possibly rubbed off on people like Al. We seem to spend more and more time on the little details.'"

Speaking to *Stars and Stripes* December 5th issue Al spoke in depth about his relationship with Alan Parsons – "We balance each other" he said. "He's interested in sound and I'm interested in words. I think we approach records from a different angle and we meet somewhere in the middle." Commenting tellingly, "my sound did need improving".

The issue of just how good a record *Time Passages* was, was taken up by Don Shewey of *Rolling Stone* when he reviewed the album on November 30th. – "Time has always been Al Stewart's favourite subject. It's in the titles of his albums – *Past Present And Future, Modern Times, Year Of The Cat* – and it's in his songs, in the form of reminiscence, history, prophecy. What Stewart says about time is often commonplace (*Time runs through your fingers/You never hold it till it's gone*), but what he implies is more arresting. The cover of *Time Passages* features a view of the desert, interrupted by a sort of warp into which a mobile home is vanishing. The title track uses this idea of a warp to describe 'time passages' into which people disappear and from which – sometimes – they unexpectedly return. 'Life In Dark Water' eerily projects such a warp into the future: a submarine crewman, daydreaming of his girl back home, suddenly finds himself inexplicably alone on board with a 500-year supply of food.

"Something like that warp – call it a sleight of hand that's his best trait – permeates Stewart's song-writing: somewhere there'll be a verse that introduces a startling ambiguity into an otherwise ordinary narrative. He also tackles *Big Themes*, an admirable show of thoughtfulness for a pop composer whose thoughts are at times insubstantial. 'A Man For All Seasons' for instance, simply strings together existentialist clichés, while 'The Palace Of Versailles' lazily restates previous Stewart history lessons. But romantic fantasy and resignation commingle intriguingly on 'End Of The Day' and 'Almost Lucy' depicts a prototypic dumb beauty who untypically smartens up."

The spectre of still, after all this time, being in debt hung over Al and Luke as they embarked on the European leg of the tour in Germany, Al admitted to journalist Dan Warfield – "Al Stewart is still running in the red. But he says he hopes to sell enough copies of his latest album – 1.2 million or so – to get him out of debt for the first time in 10 years. *Time Passages* with a hit single pushing it along, ought to do that well, perhaps a little better. In an interview, over dinner on his opening night in Europe at the Offenbach Stadthalle near Frankfurt, the Scottish-born singer-songwriter chuckled as he discussed the uncertainties and contradictions of his trade.

"'In the past, when I was coming out with my acoustic guitar, I sometimes managed to clear 100 quid in an evening', he said nibbling at a set meal of steak and French-fries. 'Now, what with lawyers' bills and tax and everything else, the break-even point on this album is about 1.2 million copies.'

"Tours helps boost the costs. His current 28-member globe-trekking expedition is expected to show a net loss of about £250,000 between Sept 1st and Dec 31st said Luke

O'Reilly, Stewart's manager.

"'Not bad,' quipped the star, 'working for 15 years and breaking even.'"

The 1978 European tour started on Monday 27th November at the Stadthalle in Offenbach and continued through Munich, Essen, Hamburg, a taping of the popular "in concert" television show *Musikladen*, then further shows at The Hague and then Amsterdam before arriving in England to play at the Brighton Dome on 7th December. They performed shows at many of the venues that Al had played through the first part of the decade. There were shows at The Hippodrome in Bristol, The New Theatre in Oxford and the Manchester Apollo before the solitary Scottish date at The Odeon in Edinburgh. After this was a show at the Birmingham Odeon before three triumphant nights at The Hammersmith Odeon, the first time that Al had ever played there.

Before the first date he went out to lunch with *Melody Maker's* Colin Irwin, who a few days later had a feature length article published under the title "Time is on the Artist's Side". It would once again give Al's sense of fun a free rein in a national magazine.

Neville

O D E O N   HAMMERSMITH Tel. 01-748-4081
Manager: Philip Leivers

Harvey Goldsmith Entertainments presents
AL STEWART plus support
EVENING 8-0 p.m.
Saturday, Dec. 16th, 1978
STALLS
£3·00
BLOCK
23   A23
NO TICKET EXCHANGED NOR MONEY REFUNDED
This portion to be retained   No re-admission

"I identify completely with *The Dong With The Luminous Nose*," Al told a clearly amused Irwin.

"I understand him. I understand how he was feeling. I understand the total waste of his life, the sense of loss, the sense of waste. It's fantastic. When people write 'Oh baby I love you, if you left me I'd be blue...' *The Dong With The Luminous Nose* is light years beyond that, though it was written a century ago.

"I do like the idea of fantasy and surrealism. Lewis Carroll ... Mervyn Peake ... Edward Lear. Carroll and Lear used to do exceptionally well creating fantasy characters which had some of the attributes of the human being. I think this could be done with music. It could take five years to get together but it could be enormously evocative.

"Yes ... I wouldn't mind being the *Edward Lear of Rock*."

The fact that Al still felt able to identify with the work of Lear may very well have kept him sane over the previous 18 months. In having such a perfect foil for all the trials and tribulations of moving to Arista, he had been able to easily absent himself from much of the nitty gritty that imbued the lawsuits.

Irwin asked Al if he ever worried about appearing pretentious?

"Of course, of course ..." Al laughed. "I'm the easiest target in the world for that. Calling me pretentious is rather like saying Black Sabbath are too loud. But pretentious is when you say or do things just for effect, but I'm actually excited by all of this. I don't talk about things that I don't personally find exciting, relevant and important. I'll continue to do these things and if they appear pretentious, they appear pretentious. Why do I want to infect people with Jean-Paul Sartre and Thomas More and Lord Fisher and Edward Lear and Lord Grenville, why am I doing this, for Christ's sake, if these things aren't relevant to me?"

The article not only succeeded in pinpointing many of Al's more eccentric traits. In so far as Al ever actually having had an agenda it was almost laid bare on a number of occasions that day. As was so often to be the case in interviews conducted around 1978, he comes across as being almost mortally vulnerable.

Al also explained to Irwin his jurnalistic approach to issue-raising: "I have a distrust of artists who make strong personal commentaries. Especially political statements. I'm not convinced I've met anyone who knew enough to make a strong comment. I think it necessary that artists should be slightly naïve, that's where the creation comes from.

Very often you write things because you don't understand or know. The excitement is in exploring. Therefore any statement of what you believe is difficult. If you ever came to believe in anything totally you're no longer an artist, you're a bigot.

"You can raise issues. You can comment but I don't think you can ram dogma down anybody's throat. It depends. Cato for example, felt it was the job of the artist to comment on society. Aristotle thought it was necessary just to raise the issues for debate in open forum."

The piece may have caught Al at his most whimsical but it also showed how passionately he still cared about many of the books that he had read when he was a child. It was as if, for Al, he could inhabit those worlds whenever the mood took him and that it was his own means of escape to lose himself in them at will. He appeared to use them as a shield.

Back in the real world Bill Ashton was now taken onto the Kinetic payroll as Al's personal tour manager. He had attended Dartmouth College where he had been Luke's best friend.

Luke – "I wanted to hire Bill for a number of reasons – his temperament was great, he played a musical instrument and he had a knowledge of computers. So we computerised ourselves and even as far back as 1978 we were carrying Apple IIs around with us on tour in huge flight cases for printing itineraries out while we had dinner!"

There had already been a succession of previous tour managers that had worked for Kinetic, none of whom had been completely on top of things. In fact Nigel Lendon had been the only member of the touring party to have stayed the course.

Luke – "I was sick and tired of hiring people who would soon not only prove to be not up to the job but who would then try and tell me how to run the band. Bill Ashton was my Nigel Lendon on the band side of things."

Al spent Christmas '78 at home in Wimborne with his parents, returning to Los Angeles on January 29th.

"Tonton Macoute", written for *Time Passages* but never used, was sometimes performed live on the tour.

TONTON MACOUTE

Come on to Haiti, you don't need a treaty
Papa Doc will do you ok
Tonton in the sun – he's polishing his gun
You'd better just stay out of his way

If you turn a critical eye, he'll drill you through the middle and cry
It's just Tonton
It's just Tonton
It's just Tonton Macoute
Idi Amin Dada slowly going gaga
Some say it's the yaya decay
Country's going broker – but Idi he's a joker
You'd better just stay out of his way

Anything you say that's not right, you're floating in the river at night
It's just Tonton
It's just Tonton
It's just Tonton Macoute

Papa had the voodoo to bring you down and cool you
Idi learned the lesson OK
From Neo to Stalin, Froward to Mussolini
They've always had to have it their way

But you can't make political pie, with such a hypocritical lie
It's just Tonton
It's just Tonton
It's just Tonton
It's just Tonton Macoute
It's just Tonton Macoute

Randall Armor

During the *Time Passages* tour it became obvious that, with so many musicians and crew on board, it was no longer possible for Nigel Lendon to do everything. He by now had responsibility for much more than just mixing Al's sound each night and ultimately it was the latter task that had to go and someone else was hired in to deal with the duties on the sound board.

Nigel Lendon – "This was very strange to me initially because for as long as I'd been with Al it had been me that was behind the desk. We always tried to put on the very best show we could, given the financial constraints of the budget and the major constraint was getting everything into just one trailer because as soon as you move up the scale to two vehicles your costs start to escalate dramatically. That was therefore one of the governing factors that dictated the level of production we would go to."

With money less tight the logical next step for Al was to somehow invest in the wine trade. Along with his new best friend from the Beverly Hills Wine Merchant he set about finding a venture that would enable him, now at the peak of his popularity, to mix business and pleasure.

Dennis Overstreet – "Al now had money in his pocket and we set about finding something fun to do. Luke of course was involved too and was out tracking down antique furniture and the like. Now I put together a small select group of investors that included the rock group Boston and Keith Richard from the Rolling Stones along with Al and myself and we set out to buy a vineyard! Now there was a guy called Charles See, of See's Candies, who had this vine along with about 200 acres. On the property was this amazing house along with what amounted to a menagerie. He'd collected all of these species of wild birds and the whole place was just amazing. The actual price tag was around $2.5 million, which in those days was a lot of money, but which when split between all of us really wasn't such a risk considering what we were getting!"

One day Dennis, Al and Luke flew up from LA to see the estate, which was in the Napa Valley in Northern California. Such a trip to Napa must have delighted Al and he was undoubtedly in high spirits that day. What followed was therefore entirely predictable.

Dennis Overstreet – "We drove into the estate through these huge ornamental gates and had a personal meeting with the owner. He shows us around and is going on about his collection of birds which he is clearly very proud of when Al turns around and in his own idiosyncratic way says 'Well I don't really like birds you know but if we're going to own this property we'd better grind some peppercorns for them as soon as we can.' The owner stopped dead in his tracks and gave Luke and I this amazing mystified look as if to say 'Just who exactly is this lunatic I've got looking around my property?'"

The sale to Dennis' esoteric band of musicians never went through.

When the *Time Passages* tour passed through Philadelphia, *Crawdaddy* magazine ran one of the most incisive and detailed profiles of Al to date and put it in their February 1979 issue. It stumbled across Al at a pivotal moment in a pivotal tour and, though the themes discussed echoed the Colin Irwin *Melody Maker* piece, *Crawdaddy*'s article in many ways managed to get closer to him than almost any other late '70s piece did.

Firstly they caught him pre-show.

"Upstairs, Al Stewart slumps on a couch in his dressing room. He is skinny, but not like a rock star – more like a Dickens character. His wrists trail out of his shirt cuffs like wet socks, and the circumference of his ankles, which peek out from under short, high-waisted pants, suggest a Bob Cratchit before the beneficence of Ebenezer Scrooge put meat on his table. Stewart is the star of tonight's show, with a hit single and a new album (both called *Time Passages*) comfortably settled in the Top 20. But he presents a remarkably retiring figure. He does not so much *inhabit* his chair as he becomes a part of the upholstery pattern.

"Stewart looks melancholy; I hasten to change the subject. Since he is a voracious reader of nonsense verse, I mention the name of a writer he likes, Mervyn Peake. Stewart grows expansive, citing snatches of Peake he particularly enjoys. Then a melancholy crosses his face, as if he just remembered something sad.

"'Have you ever heard Edward Lear's poem *The Dong With The Luminous Nose*?' he inquires, then begins to recite:

'Long years ago,
The Dong was happy and gay
Till he fell in love with a Jumbly Girl
Who came to these shores one day ...
For day and night, he was always there
By the side of the Jumbly girl so fair,
With her sky-blue hands and her sea-green hair
Till the morning came of that hateful day
When the Jumblies sailed in their sieve away
And the Dong was left on the cruel shore
Gazing – gazing for ever more.
And since that day, he wanders till ...
'For ever I'll seek by lake and shore
Till I find my Jumbly Girl once more!'

"'But, you see, he'll never find her,' Stewart explains, a little agitated. 'He's searching on the shore, and the Jumblies are at sea, so the Dong's search is hopeless.'

"Stewart slumps even further into his seat. 'That poem scared me when I read it ten years ago, and it scares me today. Some things are just too intense to even contemplate.'"

There was a sense of anti-climax and loss pervading this latest glimpse of Al on the road.

After Al had been called back for three encores that night the magazine tracked him
backstage at the end of the evening, where their solemn characterisation of him as a
vulnerable and somewhat lost figure was played out against all the noise and bustle of a
dressing room quickly filling with strangers.

"The artist is dancing on air when he finally makes it back to the dressing room. 'I
think it really went well tonight … I think it really did,' he says to no one in particular.
Then he crashes onto the couch, exhausted. With his eyes closed gently, and his arms
folded on his chest, he looks like a child who's fallen asleep during a bedtime story.

"Ten minutes later, the dressing room is wall-to-wall people: disc jockeys, press, old

'Time Passages' promo

friends, hangers-on – and a bevy of
buxom 17-year-old girls.'"

Most of whom Al had never met
before and would in all likelihood never
see again. If he had appeared somewhat
lost at sea in the *Crawdaddy* profile then
it was something that Al had chosen to
do. In electing to absent himself from the
realities of the tour by seeking solace in
the fantasy of Peake and Lear he was
merely repeating his actions of 20 years
before when, trapped at Wycliffe, he
retreated into the realms of nonsense
verse and in so doing discovered an
outlet for his own creative genius.

After the tour Krysia played a dozen
solo gigs under Luke's management in
the UK. Nigel Lendon remembers
picking Krysia up at Kings Cross Station
in London after she'd made the trip
down from Edinburgh, Scotland.

Nigel Lendon

Nigel Lendon – "I remember doing some dates with Krysia at universities around this
time. We'd put short mini tours together and throw her guitar and an amp into the back
of a Volkswagen estate and off we'd go. This was Krysia on her own, without a band."

Meanwhile, back in the US, these were bad times for Janus.

Ed De Joy – "GRT were going under anyway and they dragged Janus down with
them. The fact that Al left Janus, terrible as it was, didn't directly precipitate its demise.
One example of GRT's crazy use of money was that they took income from the record
division, that should have been re-invested back, and bought a ski hill called Mountain
High with the money! They didn't however have a snowmaking machine and when it
didn't snow the situation became a disaster!"

In the end GRT sold off Chess Records and as a result of this Camel would join Arista
along with Al.

Ed De Joy – "The day in April 1979 we had to close Janus Records was a very sad
day for me. We were an artist-related company and I honestly believe that the artists that
were signed to us genuinely loved working with us because it was a really free-spirited
operation. They were good people and I was proud to be associated with them. We did
something against all of the odds and Al Stewart was our guide. Hopefully we had
something to do with Al's evolution as an artist by way of the creative freedom we gave
him. Once we'd lost Al it really took the heart out of everyone."

Luke – "Now up until this time we'd both been living in Hammond Street, renting
places in the same building. He'd moved in September 1976 and I took a place in the
floor below him in the December. Something I remember about this time was how
generous and nice he was to me. I wasn't really looking to buy a house at this time
because I didn't think I could afford one because I didn't know what was going to
happen in two or three years from there and I was extremely nervous. Then one day Al
calls up and said 'I've found the house for you' and it was only the second one I'd looked
at. I went and looked at it and thought that it was wonderful and Al encouraged me to
buy it and my business manager said 'go ahead'."

Al had continued living in his apartment on Hammond Terrace until recently whilst
his new home up in the hills through the Bel Air West Gate was being extensively
remodelled.

These were busy times for Al. On February 7th 1979 the Venetian *avant-garde*

Promotion Company wrote to Luke with a firm proposal for a Summer tour including Rome's Teatro Temda, Viareggio, Rimini's Altromondo Club, Portofino's Covonordest and The Muretto in Venice. The tour never took place though.

The *Musikladen* TV show, that Al had recorded before Christmas in Bremen, was broadcast for the first time in Germany on February 17th and a couple of days later there was an enquiry from a Japanese promoter that would result in Al playing Japan that summer.

Offers were now coming in from all over the world, though Al declined an invite to play his first Australian show.

Throughout 1979 Luke was, as ever, on the lookout for other people to manage besides Al, under the umbrella of Kinetic. His partner in this quest to find one such group in the UK was none other than Jonny Kremer.

Jonny – "Yes, for a short while Luke and I were business partners. That year one of John Peel's favourite tracks had been 'Language School', by a local Bournemouth band that I knew called *Tours*. Both Al and Luke loved this song and so it was decided that I would approach them with a view to Luke and I managing them!" Unfortunately Tours were dropped by Virgin after just one single and proceeded to split up.

Al in Japan, 1979. "I was a Rock Star at those shows"

Luke

Al, Mandi and tour group in Japan, 1979

Back in the States that July, *Variety* reported that *Year Of The Cat* held the dubious honour of being the only platinum-selling record on the now defunct Janus label.

It was now in the summer of 1979 that Al recorded one of the strangest and most beautiful songs of his career. Accompanied by a small group of friends including Dave Dyke and Mimi Fariña he went into the studio to record "Lyke Wake Dirge", the same song that he had re-written as "All" for the sessions back in 1966 that had produced "The Elf".

Dave Dyke – "Tom Gans was there too. Mimi Fariña was both Richard Fariña's widow and the sister of Joan Baez. We separated into two groups at the session and I got to stand next to Mimi and sing which was a real thrill. I couldn't read music and she was helping me get to grips with what I was supposed to be doing there that day!"

"Lyke Wake Dirge" was a song that had been recorded by The Young Tradition and was something that Al had always thought would work well with a rock arrangement. Mimi Fariña's involvement had followed Al playing at her San Francisco *Bread and Roses Festival* in 1977.

Al – "A festival that I well remember! Joni Mitchell was also on the bill and for some reason she was dressed as General Eisenhower when I spoke to her. It was just so hip. She really did look just like she was straight out of World War Two! But that's how I came to record that song."

"Lyke Wake Dirge", based on a traditional 15th century ballad, remains unreleased.

From July 18th until August 1st 1979 Al toured Japan for the first time. He and Mandi were back in touch again by now, a situation that led to Luke suggesting to Al one evening that she came on the tour with them as their publicist, an idea that Al accepted with alacrity. It was during this trip that the format of Al's shows was to change once again. The concerts would open with a 20-minute set from *Shot In The Dark*, then Al would walk on and join them for 40 minutes before a 10-minute interval. Then everyone would troop back on stage for a second set of a full hour's music. This was quite a show and successful enough a format to be retained for the *24 Carrots* tour of 1980.

Adam Yurman – "Japan was a lot of fun. During that tour the fans were wild. These girls outside the shows would rock the limos from side to side; it really felt like we were rock stars!"

Al – "Japan to me was complete madness! I know for a fact that they had no idea of what I was saying let alone singing about. But it was all very rock 'n' roll and in its own way all very glamorous too, lots of trips to gardens and palaces."

After Japan Nigel Lendon's involvement with Al started to decline. On the way back from the trip he spent some time on Hawaii in order to re-charge his batteries.

By now Al's social circle had grown to include Alice Cooper who he had got to know through the attorney Michael Lippman. One evening Al was backstage at Alice's LA Forum show, watching the proceedings on a video screen when Alice, oblivious to the fact that Al was there at all, introduced his keyboard player to the 18,000 fans as an "Al Stewart lookalike"!

Al – "And this was what it was like for me. It was this amazing, surreal, wonderful existence. I was living in Bel Air, writing my folk-rock songs and hanging out with people like Alice every evening!"

Life in Hollywood, 1980

It could get even more surreal. Al had first met Alice when he had attended his birthday party in Hollywood. Upon leaving the party's venue, Le Dome on Sunset Strip, Al was snapped by one of the waiting paparazzi that he slightly knew. This did not go down well with the person that was coming out of the restaurant behind Al. That shadowy figure was none other than Phil Spector who proceeded to chase Al down the street, shouting all the way, until a couple of bodyguards caught up with him and physically dragged him away. As Al commented in 1979 – "All true, every word of it and once again only in Hollywood!"

Across town Robin and the rest of the band had been hard at work all this time on another project of their own.

Robin Lamble – "We'd gone out and recorded a whole bunch of Krysia demos. It was at this time that she had to change her name, because up until that time no one was able to spell or say it properly. At this time everything was focussed on her. We performed a number of showcase gigs with her in order to get her a foothold in the industry. Krysia was doing a set during this period that was part cover versions and part her own original material. Financially speaking, Kinetic couldn't afford to keep the band on a retainer when Al wasn't touring. This was one of the original reasons for us getting our own identity."

This was also a way in which the band could keep busy and therefore stay together as a unit.

Robin – "Peter had some songs at this time that Al didn't look like he was going to be using, 'White Man's Boogie' for example, so we started out with those. That particular song was a shuffle originally and we turned it into 'All My Life is a Dream'. Once we got into the studio Al might not have been there that much in his role as co-producer but he certainly played his part in the songwriting department. He re-wrote some of my material too. 'Playing with Lightning' was a case in point. It was called 'Doing the Right Thing' when I wrote it but I didn't have a hook for it. Al came in and re-wrote part of it and also suggested that title so it was a real joint effort. Krysia and I were sharing an apartment at this time on Beechwood Drive and it was often to there that Peter would come if there was any writing as a group to be done for *Shot In The Dark*. We had a piano there and we'd sit in the lounge thrashing out ideas. We took the making of our album very seriously and I was very pleased with the results."

For the production duties on what was to become *24 Carrots* Luke turned first of all to Alan Parsons.

Alan Parsons – "I was in fact asked to produce a fourth album for Al even though I had been telling people that I didn't want to oversee any outside projects for a while. I turned it down because I felt that three albums with the same producer was enough for anyone. By then you've become somewhat stale and find it hard to reproduce the enthusiasm you once had."

Luke – "We're due to go in and record *24 Carrots* and Al is ticked off with Alan Parsons who was not always available and Alan is saying that he's not sure that he wants to work with Al and his management were saying that Al didn't want to work with Alan which just wasn't true! The record company is coming down on me because they've just given Al a million dollars advance on the condition that it was Alan Parsons that produced Al's next album. He had already been paid to do it so it was all a bit up in the air. Chris Desmond, who came to produce the album, was an engineer at Davlen Studios in the Valley, Los Angeles that was a studio we liked and it had been where we'd finished the recording of both *Year Of The Cat* and *Time Passages*. For whatever reason we decided not to use Alan Parsons but to get Chris Desmond instead because Al had said 'Look Luke. Alan Parsons was really only an engineer when we used him for the first time on *Modern Times*' and that *was* pretty much irrefutable logic."

Chris Desmond – "My impression of Alan Parsons' state of mind at the end of *Time Passages* was that he needed a break. I know that he was expensive but then he was a world-famous and hugely respected producer and *should* have been expensive. I believe Luke told me that the money had been an issue as far as he and Al were concerned but the other thing was that they were both unhappy with the amount of bass on the album. I don't know to what extent Luke, to be honest, was part of this but I know that Al was very, very unhappy and it was passed to me through Luke that with the sound of *Time Passages* they felt that the bottom end was too light. Music was changing at that point, funk was omnipresent and there were the Eagles doing the *Long Run* and you had these huge kick drums, everything in there was these huge kick drums pushing a lot of air on the bottom of the records and the flat bottom end. One of the glories of Alan's technique is that everything is there, beautifully balanced but he does not fill the audio spectrum with kick drum and bass because as soon as you do that on a technical level it reduces the scope. One of Alan's great gifts is to use reverbs and delays to create these sound-scopes."

Back in June, before the trip to Japan, some work had in fact already been started on the new album at Black Orpheus Studios.

But this album would not prove to be anything like as easy to record as the preceding trio of Alan Parsons-produced records had been. And so Al, to whom recording had never been his favourite pastime anyway, came up with a novel means by which to make the most out of the studio time ahead.

Luke – "One day we walked outside of this place on Ventura Boulevard, just Al and I, and he reminded me that he didn't like to work every day and so why didn't we make an album with the band at the same time. Al and I had encouraged the band to make good use of their spare time and the band were writing their own songs and were for ever saying 'If you give us a place to play we'll play all day!'"

Nigel Lendon – "We were in Black Orpheus for just a while though. We did up the rehearsal studio. Now it just so happened that there was a recording studio in another part of that same building that we tried to work in but it just wasn't up to it."

Chris Desmond agrees that the situation had been far from ideal. "We went into this horrible little room, there was a studio; it has not been there for years now but it was on Ventura Boulevard and there is now a post-production studio there called Screen Music. It didn't look like anything at that point and basically there were just two small studios. There was one studio in front and behind it there was this tiny little studio where we were packing this huge band into this one tiny room. I think 'Midnight Rocks' was initially recorded there in demo form and a few other backing tracks.

"Al was trying to get a harder edge to his music at this time. He wanted the album that would come out of this to have much more of that hard edge than *Time Passages* so there was a lot more rock and roll going on both in Al's head and in the studio. Everything was becoming much more guitar-driven. 'Paint by Numbers' was also one of the first numbers to come along that we laid down in demo form there and also, although it is not a rocker, 'Optical Illusion' was around in those early days as well. The studio though was a disaster. We came out of it after just one night and I was so frustrated that I couldn't make this work. First of all I was having technical problems and there were just too many musicians in this one tiny room."

This was a situation that called for immediate action and so the band relocated to Davlen Studios.

"'Running Man' was the first track that we recorded properly" Desmond continues. "We were also trying to get the right drummer for the right tune. We hired Jeff Karl who was perfect for that because he was the shuffle king and he played high hats like nobody else. We cut the demo stuff with Jeff and he was playing drums at this point along with Mark Sanders who was a very fine drummer and I was happy with everything that he did. Al was on the fence a lot of a time through this, not sure which way he wanted to push things."

Certainly the manner that this album was put together was fundamentally different to the way in which the trio of Alan Parsons records had been made. Al's own involvement wasn't as full on as it had been in the past despite the fact that he was credited as co-producer.

Chris Desmond – "There were usually some guide vocals, some lah lahs and some bits of melody floating around. Robin Lamble did a lot of the singing. He did a lot of the words for this album, which would involve him covering for Al's parts during the initial recording. He would learn the melody, he would sing the melody in everybody's headsets while the track was going down, to get everybody going if Al hadn't laid down a track. That really helped things along. Also at the same time as this of course we were cutting *Shot In The Dark*'s album."

Peter White was by now having serious reservations about the direction that things had gone in.

Peter – "Throughout the recording process of *24 Carrots* Alan Parsons was sorely missed, because none of us really knew what we were doing. I was learning there and then how to make records. Luke was convinced that, due to the advent of Punk Rock that everything had to be 'fast and loud' but of course, in retrospect, it's obvious that it was a mistake to record it this way. I listen to the album now and there are so many instances of a guitar solo starting out on an electric guitar where an acoustic or 12-string would have been so much better. We missed Alan's sense of judgement and his timing on *24 Carrots*. His restraint was also something that we could really have done with at that time. Being a musician I knew how to play, but not when to play, and on *24 Carrots* there was none of that guidance. It was basically just a 'free for all'."

The lack of discipline at the sessions goes part of the way to explain how they came to drag on for so long.

Alan Parsons – "If there's one thing I do as a producer it is to make decisions. Many people tend to fill the tape up with stuff and then sort it all out at the end but that's something that I was never happy with. Working that way, you just end up with too many choices. In fact I've always looked upon mixing as a formality."

In the studio conflict between Adam Yurman and Chris Desmond at times slowed things down.

Adam Yurman – "I think that Chris Desmond probably found me very difficult to work with. Chris was this new producer with very high production values and in many ways he was a perfectionist. Whereas I was this new guitar player who was coming in with very clear ideas of what he should sound like, whereas Chris was expecting a session musician who would do what he was told. With hindsight I think that I spent too much time moaning at him about my guitar sound and I quite probably took up more of his time than I had any right to. I was very neurotic about my 'sound' and as such set myself up for a great deal of ribbing especially from Peter during the recording of that album. A lot of the time it worked out just fine though; I remember doing that guitar solo on 'Constantinople' in just one take one day when Al was in the studio beaming, things like that tend to stick in your brain. 'Pandora' on *Indian Summer* a year later was another case of one take being all that was required."

Chris Desmond – "Al wasn't there every day although he was the producer. He figured out what he wanted or needed and when he needed to be there and I think he was there for most of the tracking. The tracking for both albums was done simultaneously. We did *Shot In The Dark*'s album and *24 Carrots* simultaneously on alternate days."

There was already some record company interest in Peter at this time. Luke and Al were both very aware of this although it didn't, at that time, come to anything other than the odd tentative enquiry.

Chris Desmond again – "He was obviously very much present and accounted for on *24 Carrots* and when we did *Indian Summer* a little later on there were numerous discussions with record company executives about Peter. I mean I was hanging out with the guys from Arista and there were all these other people coming specifically with an interest in watching Peter and possibly signing him, even at this stage whilst we were playing the Roxy back in 1981. So there was a certain amount of subtext involved in it because he did have enough of a track record. It was really hard for Peter and I raising those two albums. We had to finish the band's album in order to get a record deal for them, we had to finish Al's album to satisfy Arista and the tour schedules etc."

A pivotal moment for *24 Carrots* came when Luke delivered a mix of "Midnight Rocks" which was going to be the single, to Arista. They at once despatched Richard Palmeesie, Clive Davis's right hand man, down to the studio. There were a number of changes to it that he was looking for.

Chris Desmond again – "He pulled me aside and said basically, 'Well if you can convince Al to cut that song down a little bit, knock out the sax solo at the end and do this to it, then reconfigure it this way we will be happy and we will be very grateful as well.' At the same time I had Al digging in his heels and Luke who, if he had heard the conversation, would have slammed me up against the wall. That was a crucial moment because Arista was not thrilled with 'Midnight Rocks' as a single. It came out as a single but they were not on board 100 percent."

Chris feels that the association between Clive Davis and Al was doomed from the outset. He considers it a classic case of two very strong personalities meeting head on.

Chris Desmond – "Clive has this kind of imperial way of going about dealing with artists and it was a real match when he met Al. I don't think they should have ever wound up working together."

In fact by the time Al came to record "Midnight Rocks" it had already turned into something of a saga. It had been a long time in the writing.

Luke

Luke

Peter White – "I was sitting in my apartment in LA and I came up with the guitar riff for 'Midnight Rocks'. There's an interesting story to this song. I wrote a whole big epic song around this riff, and we rehearsed it forever. Al said 'That's great, yeah,' but what I didn't realise was that he liked the guitar riff, he didn't like anything else. I had written this bridge which was 32 bars long. It was so complicated! Then he came to me one night, we were in Davlen, the studio in North Hollywood where we recorded most of *24 Carrots* and mixed *Year Of The Cat* and *Time Passages* – he came up to me and said 'I've rewritten your song, I hope you like it!' He played to me what is now 'Midnight Rocks'. It really taught me something. He cut through all the bull and took the important

Shot In The Dark

parts. In the bridge, 'Oh you know, you know it's easy,' that was his idea on top of my guitar riff. Originally I had the vocal with the guitar riff, he put it in between. You can start off with the raw material for a song and see it go off in so many different directions. The raw materials are still there. We could probably rewrite any one of these songs 100 different ways."

Many people felt somewhat alienated by the sessions for the new album. Certainly many longstanding relationships were put under the spotlight. Others felt surplus to requirements.

Nigel Lendon – "To be honest my role during the recording of *24 Carrots* was that of the person who went out and got the burgers at lunch time! Everything just seemed to be taking forever."

Krysia – "*Shot In The Dark*'s studio work there wasn't totally spontaneous. We had a list of songs, that we'd written over the previous couple of years, that we worked our way through during those sessions. It was something that we really thought was going to go somewhere."

At this time the band still didn't have a record deal. That wouldn't come about until after Christmas. In the studio Luke spent time helping the band out, just like he was doing for Al on his album.

Krysia – "Creatively too Luke was very helpful to all of us. I always thought that he had very good taste. He had a very finely tuned ear for picking up on stuff. The basic truth was that he was a very creative person and it made it a whole lot easier to pick up on his inconsistencies. Once the album came out I certainly don't remember us all getting treated any differently with better hotel rooms or anything like that at all really. It was enough that we had our own lives and an identity not only as Al's backing band."

Krysia remembers how Peter and Al would split the workload between them at this time. Al's work ethic, that Chris Desmond found so hard to fathom at first, was not something that Krysia found that surprising.

Krysia – "Peter, as band leader, would get everyone together so that we could get much of the basic work done before Al would show up mid-afternoon in the studio. Now I know that he's very committed as a creative artist but he projects this image of disinterest to such an extent that he almost believes it himself. I feel that Al wears a mask for much of the time because he doesn't want to reveal himself and who can blame him?"

Al – "There was definitely more pressure for this album. Now whether or not this was solely because we were missing Alan Parsons I'm just not sure. I doubt it. Things are never that simple. We needed to do well with that album, that was something that we did know!"

Many of the songs that were written at this time, some in the studio and others at home, appear to have been interchangeable between Al and *Shot In The Dark*. One such example was "Constantinople" which was a song that Peter had composed with a view to *Shot In The Dark* having it on their album.

Peter White – "That was the plan anyway. It was swapped for 'All My Life' which was originally written for Al. In fact there is a version of Al singing a whole alternate set of lyrics to 'All My Life' which we recorded. I can still hear Al singing it now… 'Nancy came back to amazing acclaim… give me more of the same'. He actually wrote that chorus but I think we forgot to credit him."

However, without Parsons' firm hand, the sessions dragged on for six months.

A great deal had changed in the five years that Peter had been with Al. *Modern Times* had been recorded in a few weeks and they toured in a van. Now they couldn't even get out of the studio.

Peter White – "Rightly or wrongly Luke had been determined to use all of the band on this album and saw it certainly in terms of a means by which he would propel *Shot In The Dark* to stardom. So there we all were at Davlen Studios (Luke was in Europe) and one day I decided that we'd work on a *Shot In The Dark* song whereas actually Luke's idea had been that we were due to work on an Al song that day. When he found out Luke flipped totally and made out that Al was livid but I'm not at all sure about this and certainly never heard it from Al myself.

"So there was all this paranoia everywhere. It wasn't helped by a worry that Al's sound wasn't maybe going to be popular any more what with the advent of Punk and everything and so a decision was reached to give everything a harder edge and therefore a more contemporary sound. Songs like 'Mondo Sinistro', and 'Running Man'. The '70s were obviously over. But listening back to songs like 'Mondo Sinistro' I realise that we could have done things differently and perhaps if Alan Parsons had been there we might well have done. That song would have been great if it had been played on a 12-string acoustic guitar. Al's involvement on *24 Carrots* as producer was minimal. On a day-to-day basis it was Chris Desmond and I at the controls. But it wasn't enough to save the album and it didn't do anything like as well as we'd hoped and proved to be the beginning of the end of Al's huge success. I realised this at the end of the recording of it, I felt we'd lost our way a little. The role of a producer that had produced before would have included hand picking different musicians for each song rather than using just the band as its core but none of us had really produced an album before (Al's role on John Martyn's *The Tumbler* was minimal) and that was, as I see it, the main problem."

At this point Kinetic moved its office up-market when the lease expired on their existing offices at the junction of Laurel and Kingswood on Laurel Canyon Boulevard in LA. The original reason for acquiring such substantial offices as the new ones at 8055 Selma Avenue was to place Al's money into a long term investment that could not be frittered away. It was certainly impressive, being just off of the eastern side of Sunset Boulevard and only a few hundred yards from the old Janus Records offices and the place that was in many ways the operation's true HQ – The Olde World Restaurant.

Luke – "It cost us $210,000 and it was a way of giving Al a diversified portfolio. It was an old family house, overlooking Schwab's, that had been built in the 1920s. Upstairs there were three bedrooms, a kitchen, a dining room, three front rooms and a little conservatory. Whilst downstairs we had a room that we used to store tapes, a bedroom and another large spare room – so it was pretty impressive. Outside there was even a three-car garage and I have to say that it was a beautiful building."

One of the standout songs on the album was "Merlin's Time". The opening guitar riff was not strictly speaking originally written for the album. Peter White had written the basic tune on the piano when he was 16.

Peter – "I played it like a Gregorian chant, in parallel fifths, with a bass drone. It sounded almost like a Red Indian war chant. Somewhere along the way I had transferred it to the guitar and I happened to play it to Al one night when we were in the studio. He said 'Oh, that's nice and I've got part of another song that would fit that.' He played his bit, I played mine, and that's how that worked."

MERLIN'S TIME
And I think of you now
As a dream that I had long ago
In a kingdom lost to time
In the forest of evening
The archer is bending a bow
And I see you bring him bread and wine

Down the legions of years
The invaders have taken this land
And bent you to their will
And the memories fade of the ancients
And all that they had
Though the magic lingers round you still

Oh who would walk the stony roads
Of Merlin's time
And keep the watch along the borderline
An who would hear the legends passed
In song and rhyme
Upon the shepherd pipes of Merlin's time

OPTICAL ILLUSION
In my darkest hour just before the dawn
There's no sound from the empty street
But sleep won't seem to come to me
All your words in my head
Linger on and on
They've come to steal my time away
Till the night is gone
I must be losing my shine
Like an old dusty Burgundy wine
In a cellar cool and damp
Dull beneath a yellow lamp
No one turning the key
To come and get me today
The more I think about You now
The more I'm feeling that way
I see you there, everywhere
Optical illusions
Telephone, let it ring
I don't want intrusions in my life
I know tomorrow I'll find
There's nothing here at all
Just some trick your mind'll play
With shadows on the wall
I see you here, feel you near
Optical illusions
Nothing real that I feel
Just some confusion of my time
In my darkest hour, when all the blinds were drawn
You're just some mirage I saw
Just before the dawn

Peter White – "Luke started to get manic and by the recording of *24 Carrots* realised how much he'd bitten off in trying to make two albums at the same time. So that didn't help the situation of course! There was all that expense of making the *Shot In The Dark* album and *24 Carrots* both simultaneously. There was also the running of the Kinetic building which he'd bought and I think that everything was getting really overwhelming for him."

Luke – "Well it all sounds very dramatic doesn't it! Maybe I did overreact on occasions but I was only trying to protect the band. I was in a better position than anyone to have an accurate overview of what was going on and these were worrying times. It was my job to do something."

And certainly no one else could have done half of what Luke did anyway. His instincts were almost always proved right and his loyalty was beyond question. There was equal pressure on both him and Al. And Peter, with his new-found responsibilities, was himself keenly aware of the implications should the new album fail. He suffered as much as anyone.

Peter again – "I actually became ill for quite a while when the stress of it all started to catch up with me and it was as much as I could do to even drag myself into the studio because it just wasn't going as well and as easy as those previous albums before *24 Carrots*."

Through all of this however there remained a genuine sense of affection and mutual respect amongst the band members. Through 1979 and 1980 Peter shared a house with Nigel Lendon on Barham Boulevard and in 1980 got his first place on his own on Dickens Street off Ventura."

Luke – "It was at this time, once *24 Carrots* was recorded, that we did the wine tours with Dennis Overstreet. The first single had got quite high up in the charts and by that time I'd realised that it was cheaper for us to play smaller venues, taking a smaller crew because actually we weren't making any money from touring anyway and it was just a case of us trying to keep up with the Jones's. The death of any band was the 3,000-seater because you couldn't get enough money out of such a venue to cover your expenses of getting in there in the first place. At the time there weren't these outdoor sheds. Al would quite simply have been saved by the outdoor sheds because with those venues you get between 5,000 and 7,000 seats underneath the covers and then a great lawn built up in a hill behind it where you can get about another 10,000 people."

But at the time of the *24 Carrots* tour these weren't built everywhere and in fact there were only about half a dozen of them spread across the whole country.

Luke – "In America you want to work as often as you can and the trucks have got to get from place to place and if you're going down south for instance to Texas it takes you a couple of days to get there and a couple of days to get back and we were losing money. So I decided to have a shorter tour of just the main cities and we couldn't afford to play the south. Dennis Overstreet had just written a book and he arranged for Bollinger to provide the champagne and we used this to go to all of the radio stations to back up the release of *24 Carrots* in the south and all I had to do was fund Al and I at a few hotels for a few weeks as Dennis was paying his own way."

Al – "The tour was great fun. One of the most amazing things that I saw on that tour was when Marvin Overton (a major wine collector from Texas) arrived for dinner one evening with a magnum of '52 Bordeaux. He had done something that I had never seen before. He had decanted the wine, put it back into its bottle and then inflated a balloon inside it to stop any air getting to the wine. This was the sort of thing that was going on all throughout that tour and I learnt a lot!"

This new mode of touring thus gave Al a tour of the southern states with an original and media-friendly reason to come into town. It was such a success that they repeated the itinerary a short while later.

Luke again – "We came back later and did a much shorter tour where we brought our own 12-foot truck, put everything inside and just did small venues."

It was a solution that made sound business sense. With *24 Carrots* not doing as well as had been expected, Arista stopped spending money on promotion and so the logic of a more cost effective tour would have been hard for Al and Luke to ignore.

Dennis Overstreet – "I had a book out at the time and to be honest it seemed to be a lot of fun to take Al along with me on my tour promoting it. I was already set to go out and do it anyway and it was in fact Luke that made that initial suggestion that we link their tour for *24 Carrots* along with my book tour. It seemed to me to be a perfect match and so I arranged for someone to help underwrite it for us and that someone was Bollinger. The tour started out at the Universal Amphitheatre here in Los Angeles. Bollinger sent along some very rare champagne that they knew Al especially would rave about on our subsequent tour of radio stations."

But here, once again, Al found it impossible to stay *on message* and upon tasting the product at the launch party announced to everyone present that he hated it. He hated the sponsor's product! It's hard not to believe that he was perfectly aware of the chaos that his comments were bound to cause and it took some masterly work by Dennis and Luke to turn the situation around.

The trick to making the tour a success was to go from radio station to radio station presenting Al as the folk-rock singing connoisseur of fine wines and to do it in original way with a new twist each day so that it sounded fresh and credible (and so that Al, Dennis and Luke didn't get bored). Al's rite of passage from Belsize Village to Bel Air as a devotee of wine would be described in terms of the vintages he had drunk along the way, some *24 Carrots* songs would get airplay and Dennis would delve into *Wine Secrets* and spin some tales – at least that was the plan.

Dennis Overstreet – "It may well have been the plan but right from the outset it was obvious to me that Al was in no mood to toe the company line and follow the script which made it very difficult for me. He was totally honest and if he didn't like a particular wine he would say so! One time were in a place called the *Pyrenees* in Denver, Colorado and doing an interview in a wine cellar. During the course of the show Al spots some insecticide in bottles, decides we are in a museum of waxworks and the show goes off at a tangent and never recovers. That was typical of the tour. You just never knew what Al was going to come out with next – he absolutely refused to be constrained or restricted in any way."

That is not to say that Al's involvement in the co-venture was ever considered to be in doubt. Indeed both Al and Dennis remember these times with some affection. And the fact that these trips made, financially, a lot of sense made Luke sleep easier at night.

Throughout this time the rest of the band stayed safely back in Los Angeles. As a means of getting the word out about the new album though this unusual tour was something of a success.

The profile of Al's wine guru Dennis had been growing steadily over the years – not least due to his regular appearances on TV as the most in demand "wine expert" on shows such as *Good Morning Los Angeles* and *The Dinah Shore Show*. Al appeared with him on an edition of the *Mike Douglas Show*, recorded in LA and shown nationally in September 1980 where he sang and also performed a blindfolded tasting on the show live. His unpredictable remarks and unwillingness to stick to the script on the Champagne Tour did however knock on the head a projected appearance with Dennis on the *Johnny Carson Show* that Dennis did on his own. During the course of his very close friendship with Al, Dennis was party to a great deal of arm twisting by people who for a variety of reasons sought to gain influence over his friend. In many ways Dennis acted as a buffer to protect Al. Luke usually took much of the day-to-day responsibility away from Al, making most business decisions for him and when he wasn't personally around it logically enough fell to Dennis to step into those shoes.

Wine continued to be a passion of Al's. In 1985, during the round of press interviews for the *Russians And Americans* album, Al was asked what he would do if he weren't a musician. This was his answer – "Something that would pay my wine bills. I collect wine, which is fairly well known and so the obvious answer is that I could run a wine store, but I prefer to keep wine as a hobby. I see what happened to me with music. As soon as music became a job, I had to work at it, whereas while it was something I did in the garden shed at home it was much easier because if I didn't want to do it, I didn't do it."

A concerted effort was now made to get press coverage for Al that focused as much on his love of wine as it did his musical credentials.

The November 16th edition of *Valley News* carried one such piece entitled – "They're starry eyed about Wine…"

"Finally, there is rock star Al Stewart, a well-established wine expert. When Stewart sees and hears numbers, he almost always translates them into vintages, thinking to himself, 'Ah, 1961 was a great year, 1977 wasn't. I probably had my first good wine in 1971. That is when I bought Calon-Segur 1961 in a wine shop just down the street from me. It cost me about $10, which was relatively expensive back then. Thereafter, once or twice a week for about a year, I worked my way through the 1961 vintage. By the middle of 1972 I was hooked.

"'My interest in wine began as a curiosity but it soon became an obsession for a while. Now it is more of a hobby. I no longer drive 50 miles to find one example of a label I didn't have.'

"Al requested it be put into his contract that he would be given a bonus of three cases of wine (La Tache 1966, Chateau Palmer 1961, and Petrus 1961) if he finished his first album for Arista on time. His request was granted.

"When he did Arista happily ordered the wines for him. But what they did not know was that each one of those wines cost somewhere between $400 and $500 a bottle. And there are 12 bottles to a case."

That same month, during an evening at the home of Burgess Meredith, Al was given the honorary title of Les Maitres Conseils M.C. en Gastronomie Francaise/Maitres Conseils en Vins De France. Once again the evening was duly reported in the Los Angeles press. *Valley News* carried an ironic quote by Al – "In part that means a *Master Counsellor of French wine*" explains Al. "You get a certificate and you get a hat and robe. You can keep the certificate but you have to give the hat and robe back!"

The US tour to support the album was a mixture of small clubs and much larger venues. It had kicked off on September 8th with a West Coast leg that included San Diego State, The Old Waldorf in San Francisco, The Mesa Amphitheatre in Phoenix and two nights at The Universal Amphitheatre in Los Angeles.

David Fricke in *Rolling Stone* on November 12th – "On *24 Carrots*, Stewart – with his fine band, *Shot In The Dark* – presents himself as a jack-of-all-trades and, surprisingly, makes it work. Though his fragile, whispery voice isn't ideal for high-volume rock and roll, he does a credible imitation of lounge lizard Bryan Ferry in the Roxy Music-like raver, 'Mondo Sinistro'. He also manages to hold his own against the cranked-up, neo-heavy-metal guitars of 'Paint By Numbers' whose central riff bears a suspicious resemblance to the one in Blue Oyster Cult's '(Don't Fear) the Reaper'.

At the conclusion of the US dates in late November Al was met in New York City by Patrick Humphries who interviewed him for the December 6th edition of *Melody Maker* that preceded the UK dates – "Al now lives in Los Angeles, and talked of being able to get your phone fixed the same afternoon as you choke on the smog, confessed he did miss the cricket, but at least he can get Twinings tea in LA. As a self-confessed *Child of the Sixties*, I wondered if Stewart felt there would ever be a return to those golden days of protest song and optimism?

"'I don't see it coming back. It had to do with a period of innocence in American history. I mean, we are talking about American based folk-rock – my influences were The Byrds, Dylan, Simon and Garfunkel – it was the last innocence really, the Peace Corps, the Freedom Riders...'

"It was almost as if the shootings at Kent State in 1970 – tragically, quite literally – sounded the death knell for the alternative culture, and led to Nixon getting elected in 1972 on the biggest ever-popular vote. Which brings us, eventually, to President Elect Reagan, a fact that Stewart agreed would have been 'Unthinkable' in the mid-'60s."

This was Al at his most reflective. It is interesting to note that he very often refers to the late '50s and early '60s as 'halcyon' times. He went on to mention that he considered that the decline in idealism was closely tied to economic reality dating back to Macmillan's 'Never had it so good' years. In so doing he was pontificating in much the same way that he had back in the *Music Now* interview for *Zero She Flies* ten years earlier. This may of just been coincidence, or perhaps it was an understandable route to return to with a British journalist but it is interesting none the less that Al's mind so often rewinds to the early '60s.

He told Humphries – "It did look as though there was a continual upward trend in the quality of people's lives. Now when somebody works – and however hard they work – it doesn't appear they're going to be any better off, all of a sudden they become different kinds of people. They're not looking for idealism, they're looking for survival. Therefore the music reflects anger, disenchantment and a reflection to grab what you think is yours rather than reflecting optimism, hope and sharing.

"I believe these things are tied to the relative affluence of the society in which they exist."

Al also talked about the novel, "very much in the style of Mervyn Peake" that he intended to knuckle down and start in the new year. This project, which he had already been mentioning in interviews for a number of years, would never see the light of day.

After the US dates, Al and the band played three nights at the Hammersmith Odeon. These shows were broadcast, in an edited form, on London's Capital FM radio the following January. In the middle of Al's residency at the Hammersmith Odeon, John

Lennon was shot dead outside the Dakota building in New York City. A few hours earlier, 5,000 miles away in London, Al's final song on stage had been a surprise encore performance of The Beatles 'Day Tripper', almost certainly making him the last person ever to perform a Fab Four song on stage in London in Lennon's lifetime.

Al also appeared in London as a guest on Capital Radio along with Toyah Wilcox (later to marry Robert Fripp) and Muhammad Ali.

Once they all returned to the States Luke succeeded in getting *Shot In The Dark* their own deal with Robert Stigwood's RSO label.

Chris Desmond – "I think the tour helped because on a number of occasions record company executives came down and watched *Shot In The Dark* open for Al. And in fact this was specifically why they would open up shows for him, it allowed prospective record companies to see them as their own entity, not just as Al's backing band."

Emotions were still running high with regard to whether or not *24 Carrots* had done as well as they had all hoped it would. There was a slight feeling of dissatisfaction on Al's behalf with the finished product and he started telling friends that the *Shot In The Dark* album sounded a lot better than his own record. Al's album was also lacking an obvious single.

Al – "I should have done more with 'Murmansk Run/Ellis Island'! In performance, where they were performed as completely separate songs in 1979, they were much stronger and in fact the lyrics themselves had been revised for the bridge of 'Ellis Island' by the time the album was recorded later on in 1980."

The Spring of 1981 saw the release of the *Shot In The Dark* album. However it wasn't out for long.

After three weeks, the single released to promote the album had already made number 71 on the charts but then a week later RSO collapsed. There cannot, of course, ever be

Randall Armor

a good time for such a thing to happen but for *Shot In The Dark* to have this happen to them right then must have been heartbreaking. If the record had never been released by RSO at all, then it would have had a chance of being picked up by another label. The fact that it had come out though (and therein already sold copies) would now act against them. In many ways this was a turning point for everyone.

Robin Lamble – "RSO going bust didn't come completely out of the dark for us. We knew that it was a possibility but it was the only deal that we had and so we ran with it. When they went belly-up we decided to tough it out with Al's van and equipment and went out playing gigs in the LA area. We played places like The Blue Lagoon on Lincoln Boulevard in Marina Del Rey where we had a Tuesday residency. Through all of this time we had very little money. Whenever we needed to pay bills we'd be forced to go cap in hand to Luke or Al and plead our case. In the end, when everything was falling apart, we were all told to simply go out and get jobs! We were never paid a retainer."

Luke – "I went up to New York City as soon as I heard the news and spent a week there trying to persuade Robert Sherwood at Polygram to do something but they'd fired everyone and RSO had just become a label of Polygram's. I tried every record company in the country but no one wanted it because it had been already released by RSO. The entire situation was a huge disappointment for us all."

In fact Luke put $10,000 of his own money into trying to get another label interested in taking on the album and the band. But it was hopeless. Al took Luke out to dinner in LA one evening and told him that he thought Luke was thinking with his heart and not his head about the whole situation, an event that Luke remembers as something of a wake up call in his relationship with Al.

Luke – "It made me realise that unless I was very careful I was going to have real problems here."

Not that this came as any great surprise to Luke, the disappointing sales of *24 Carrots* and the failure of RSO having proved ample excuse for everyone in Kinetic to take stock. No one was immune.

These were sobering times for everyone concerned.

Peter White – "I remember thinking that all the dreams that I'd had about stardom and being in a big band were all coming to nothing and by the time the end of 1981 approached I was thinking 'Now what?!' I'd always thought through all of this that things would turn around and Al and I would write a great song again together like before."

But deep down they all knew that things had peaked.

However, in a profile by Roberta Metz, Al seemed to be in good spirits.

"At first sight I was struck by a lean, pleasant looking guy, dressed casually in cords and a cotton shirt, bereft of pretensions" Metz wrote. "He spoke cordially about the changes in his life since his hit album *Year Of The Cat.*

"'Rock and roll, crime and sport seemed the only quick way of breaking out of your environment and achieving success. Crime was too dodgy, and I wasn't designed for sport, so it meant music.' Stewart claims."

The Al being profiled here in New York City was a very different person to the one that *Crawdaddy* had caught, looking like a character out of some Charles Dickens novel, just two years earlier in Philadelphia. It was as if all of the worry had abated and he was able to be far more pragmatic about his life. There was certainly little trace here of the melancholy that had defined that earlier piece. His lifestyle, hedonistic though it was, is described in a very matter of fact way.

"An insomniac, he never goes to bed before 4 a.m. and stays up the night watching old movies. He wakes at noon, plays pinball, breakfasts, receives and makes phone calls and takes care of business at hand. His hedonism is tempered by repentance. 'If I take a beautiful woman out to dinner, share a good bottle of wine, then romp around in the sheets for four hours, next day I might read a few pages of Solzhenitsyn.' Taking a quick breath, he makes an analogy: 'You can't go to the bank and constantly withdraw; occasionally you have to put something in.'

"Al Stewart claims he is one of the unsung master pinballers and changes his machines every few years because they get too predictable. His present one is called *Time Warp*. When he scores half-a-million he is certain the day is his; 50,000 makes him put off all major decisions until tomorrow. He admits to being a sensualist and loves good food. 'If I go a week without an Indian curry, I start going into withdrawal.'"

Very much a picture of contented and pampered bliss. But only half the truth. And as Al himself would later admit, the cracks were starting to show. In the circumstances (and with the benefit of hindsight) what happened next was therefore somewhat predictable. Because it was now, with Al clearly in need of regaining the flagging interest of his record company, that the fatally flawed decision was made to deliver a live album to Arista.

ON THE BRIDGE OF THE TITANIC

In which Al releases *Indian Summer*, loses his manager and his deal with Arista, before recording *Russians And Americans*.

24 Carrots, having not been quite the success that everyone had hoped for, needed to be followed up by a new album much quicker than the two year gap that had divided it from the previous one, *Time Passages*. This, in many ways, was to prove impossible as the events of the next few months testified.

But to record a live album now seemed to make a good deal of sense. The fact that *Shot In The Dark* was Al's band both for studio and live work meant that what Al would, in essence, be delivering to Arista was a *live* 'Greatest Hits'. Confronted by such compelling logic, Luke picked up the phone one day and booked The Roxy.

The Roxy Theatre was one of the pre-eminent music venues in Los Angeles at that time and had been selected as much for its place as a landmark in the musical folklore of LA as for its dubious acoustics And so to drop a ten-piece string section into the room, so cramped already that they had to be accommodated behind plexiglass on the balcony, was always going to be prlematical.

There was ultimately no expense spared on the recording of the Roxy shows. The strings were overseen by David Campbell, one of the most in demand string arrangers in town and a man who had worked with Bob Dylan, the Rolling Stones and Neil Diamond. He'd also played viola on Marvin Gaye's "Let's Get It On". Campbell already had a son by the time *Indian Summer* was recorded. Taking his mothers' name the boy was to go on to great things of his own in the '90s and is still a major star today. His name is Beck. It's strange to picture Campbell coming home from another evening at The Roxy trying to get the sound of the (ultimately un-used) string section just right for Al and Luke, telling the young Beck all about his day!

Al – "Those shows at the Roxy in Los Angeles were in many ways a great deal of fun. But we did try and do far too much with them. That string section took forever to get right but in the end I think that the concerts themselves were very good shows. We were doing new material and it was all very experimental in a way."

Chris Desmond – "We were actually recording at the Roxy for two days, performing four shows. They were proper concerts that people paid to attend and we recorded using this 24-track mobile studio. We were going to have to go and mix, I wasn't going to go live with a two-track mix for final release. There were some things that got done again, in fact many of the tracks got done again. 'Riyadh' was specifically designed for live performance because Al wrote that as one of the things specifically for the live side of the album. It was a sort of 'Let's create a kind of suite, tie these things together and do these thing over here and split the song into different sections' sort of performance. And it worked out beautifully, it was great fun, and I think it stands out as one of the definitive tracks on the album. So anyway the recordings were finished and the tapes were shipped off to Arista."

Not before some major surgery however on them. This would go on to take both time and money, neither of which Al had at the time. It would also create a situation that would do lasting harm to his relationship with Luke.

Chris Desmond – "We had to redo many of the vocals in the studio because we had those technical problems and we also found we had to re-do the strings because the performance at the Roxy had been far too much for that one room and sound-wise it just couldn't handle the band and the string section. Some of the live vocal stuff was used

but certain things had to be fixed up and replaced again and so a string section was brought in and we had to recreate the vibe of the Roxy in a studio in order for us to successfully finish the album. This was quite an experience, it was a huge room, we had everyone in there, and lots of friends, music business people, everyone we could think of and it sounded wonderful. We did this at Evergreen. From my point of view it was magic. It wasn't like we were creating total fraud in trying to replicate, it was just that we needed to recreate some of the transactions and so that is why we did it this way. So basically the *Indian Summer* live sections were partially recorded at the *Roxy Theatre* and partially recorded several weeks later at Evergreen studios."

The recording of the studio tracks for the album were much easier to complete than the live sessions had been. "Indian Summer" itself was recorded in a single take. Clive Davis now ventured down to the studio to see how things were progressing. This was one of the very rare times that Clive was to visit the studio during any recording that Al made for Arista.

Al – "He had his job to do and we had ours. It was difficult at times for all of us I feel. He wanted our records to do well for Arista and so, naturally enough, had opinions about lots of things. I had liked *24 Carrots* much more than *Time Passages* but *Time Passages* had sold so many more copies than the new album had. So it was a delicate situation that we were all skirting around for a while there!"

Chris Desmond again – "The day Clive Davis came in to the studio he had probably just come from his bungalow at the Beverley Hills Hotel. He curled himself into the chair in the control room, threw his leg up and proceeded to pontificate, before he had heard a word from us, about how Ricky Lee Jones' career would have been so much better if she had only had a hit single on her second record. It was a lovely record but she just didn't have the wherewithal or the whatever and so on and so forth. And this is what you are being faced with when you are dealing with Clive. He would listen to several of the tunes rather politely and said 'well basically I don't hear a single'. He sat through the stuff but obviously was not hearing what he wanted. I won't say he left abruptly but he went without lingering too long. Within a few days word filtered back from New York that he had loved the live stuff but wasn't too sure at all about the studio tracks but they had to put it out. Arista were contractually bound to release the album and so they did."

Throughout all of this the band members all did their best to make sure that the recording, overrunning though it was, remained fun for everyone. Key to this was Robin Lamble.

Robin – "When it came to doing the re-recording of 'Indian Summer' I turned up with a couple of huge Union Jacks, amongst other things, in an effort to try and brighten up the atmosphere because the whole concept of having to go in and re-do this supposed *Live* album was a bit of a strange situation for us all. I wore a velvet jester's outfit and a hat with a feather in it and marched onstage with the flags on poles. They were then draped across the back of the stage." This is par for the course for the wonderful Mr Lamble.

Al considers the re recording of the live album to have been "…interesting!"

Nigel Lendon – "The re-recording of the Roxy sessions at Evergreen Studios in Burbank were great. The room was quite sizeable into which we set up a little stage area with just a couple of monitors, so it most certainly wasn't a big production. Although Al and *Shot In The Dark* played live at Evergreen it was very much a controlled live situation."

Luke – "The idea to do a live album was, with hindsight, a mistake but our advisors didn't seem to think it was so wrong to have three sides of live material and one side of new studio tracks which we aimed to finish quickly."

The album was essentially an attempt to get some money in the bank for Al but already there were signs of disappointment in the Arista camp concerning Al's recent record sales.

The responsibility that presently rested on Al's shoulders should not be underestimated here. From a creative perspective alone the problems of the previous year cannot have made life easy for him. And yet to those around him, he appeared as contented and good-humoured as ever. But even with Luke acting as the buffer that allowed Al to concentrate on his music, there were still days when he felt that things were slipping away. The irony of the fact that on *24 Carrots* he felt that he'd written some of the best songs of his career was not lost on him.

These were difficult times for Al, a fact that Luke was very much aware of. The momentum that had been achieved up to *Year Of The Cat* had only just been maintained with its follow-up, *Time Passages*, but following the poor sales of *24 Carrots* they very much had to come up with the goods this time. Following the Roxy shows in April the studio tracks took from June until August. This was far longer than had been expected.

Al – "These were new songs that I felt were very strong. I wanted to get them right because the live sides of the album hadn't exactly turned out the way that we had hoped. So I made sure that they came out how I wanted them too. I know that they took a long time!"

And of course Al has a point. He wanted the studio tracks to be as perfect as possible. And ultimately it was his own money that was being spent on them. Luke was free to counsel Al on the implications of all this (that was his job after all) but in truth it was something that Al probably already knew.

Luke – "Those studio tracks just cost us too much money, they were really good performances but took too long. I was there in the studio and I had thought that we were going to be there for a week and we were there for a few months and so it didn't work out the way that I had intended or hoped. The idea originally was to make a record as cheaply as possible, as well as we could, but as inexpensively as we could, and let's make some money. At the time we felt that the easiest way to get some hits back onto the radio would be through this live album, it just turned out that we were a year or two *late* for a live album."

Luke still to this day has strong emotions attached to the whole issue of Kinetic's (and therein Al's) finances pertaining to this period, citing decisions that with the benefit of hindsight he wishes they had made quite differently.

Luke – "It's all very well to take a million dollar advance as I said but that obviously put Al under a lot of pressure. I still feel a little rotten because Al was owed a million dollars by Janus Records that he never got, he never saw it and he was due it. We had a weak album in *24 Carrots* and then he came back with this live album. Now, with hindsight, we should have said 'to hell with recording a live recording' and to have come back with a stronger studio album. *24 Carrots* was an album that we had hoped would sell 750,000, budgeted for 500,000, but it only sold 250,000 initially."

Put like that it's easy to see why Luke was so concerned. A rare moment of comic relief in all of this came in the selection of a title for the album. His sense of irony once again to the fore, and in keeping with the ongoing vegetable theme *of 24 Carrots,* Al had originally wanted to call the new record *A Turnip For The Books* – visualising its cover as a pile of books with a turnip on top. Remarkably enough this was not a concept that Arista thought appropriate, electing instead for the safer bet of *Indian Summer.*

DELIA'S GONE
Delia's gone
And the days they run so slow
Here in the islands
Delia's gone
It's the only thing you know
Here in the silence
Fine rain combs the sand
The first breath of winter across the land
Try but you won't understand
How she could slip right through your hands, Delia's gone

Delia's friends no longer come to call
What can they say now
Delia's pictures are hanging on the wall
You can't look away now
Dream figures with moons for eyes
Stare from under an alien sky
Seem to watch as you pass them by
If they should know, they won't say why, Delia's gone

Delia's gone like a darkening of the sky
A change in the weather
Delia's gone like a moment out of time
Maybe forever
Lines of coffee cups on parade
Soldiers for keeping the night away
Soon, too soon, you'll be moving out
There's nothing here to hold you now
Delia's gone

The idea of sticking to budgets at this time was clearly an emotive subject. Other issues, simmering below the surface, clearly made communication between Al and Luke difficult for much of the time. Al was still exasperated 20 years later.

Al – "Basically I didn't start to think about budgets terribly much until Arista reneged on the deal and all of a sudden we couldn't have Arista money. I was generally aware of budgets and numbers but they weren't real. Part of the reason they weren't real was because I would ask Luke how we were doing and he would say we are doing great, about 'half a million dollars', and I could ask him the very next day and he would say 'we are a quarter of a million dollars in debt'. I wouldn't see how it was possible that we had spent three-quarters of a million dollars in 24 hours! He was so incredibly vague about numbers. I never knew where we were. Because I had nothing to go on I couldn't worry about what budgets were because I didn't know what the budget was in the first place! It was only later on, when Luke had gone, that I had to sort through the ruins and I discovered where everything was and basically put it all back together again. But by that stage I don't think I paid a lot of attention and I think in a way it was unfathomable because you would never get a straight answer. What is the budget? Well the budget could be $400,000 but that wasn't the budget because you had forgotten that various people, business managers, and agents were always taking percentages. So that wasn't the real budget and so the actual budget might be $200,000 and even that wasn't the real budget as a producer's fee had to come out of that etc. It never stopped, so there seemed no way at getting at any numbers and I like numbers and I tried to get to the bottom of it all at the time but it never got me anywhere!"

All of which paints a somewhat unflattering picture of Luke's grasp of things at this point. And to simply go along with the suggestion that, as a result of the past eighteen months' problems, Luke was now starting to lose the plot, seems a bit too simplistic.

Such considerations aside, Al was still writing. More often than not such songs were worked out on his piano at home in Bel Air. He would sit and play the songs that he'd always played; 50's rock 'n' roll, school hymns, improvisations based on his own work and sometimes, on a good day, something new would grow out of it.

In 1981 Al heard news of a film project that featured the 1978 John Irving novel *The World According To Garp* which he had read during the *Time Passages* US tour. He then proceeded to put a set of lyrics on the themes of the book to a tune that had been left over from the *24 Carrots* sessions two years earlier. The book itself would have appealed to Al on both a conscious and subconscious level. The story kicks off by outlining one woman's own personal feminist movement. Soon afterwards the novel blossoms into a dissertation on the outrageous life of her bastard son. The story mixes comedy and tragedy, enabling the reader to identify with and champion Garp. There were a number of parallels between the novel and Al's own life. In *The World According To Garp* Garp's mother is a nurse who has a relationship with a pilot. The pilot, Garp's father, dies before he is born, thus echoing very closely Al and Joan's own circumstances. The song itself rocks along at a pace similar to "Running Man" with a tune that's a mixture of "Constantinople" and "Valentina Way". It wasn't taken up for the film though and there is no clear evidence that it was ever actually submitted to the producers as a viable song for the soundtrack. In the end, Lennon and McCartney's "When I'm 64" played over the credits.

GARP

It's a restless world and the hands take hold as your eyes watch out for a fall
Then you end up flat on the landing mat as you try to fathom it all
Any sudden move could out manoeuvre the plans you made at the start
But hopes and schemes are ghosts and dreams in the world according to Garp

I was born one day under skies of grey and called New England my home
And the single name that my mother gave was all I had of my own
I was taught the rules of Steering school though they all fell short of the mark
But these things never meant too much in the world according to Garp

Bonkie grows older the nights they get colder
The lights burn low in the nurses home
And the days won't wait
You can't make them slow
See how they go
See how they go
See how they go
See how they go

It's a restless world and the lips are curled as the hands coming reaching your way
But the writer's pen simply moves again and puts it down on the page
On any stretch of road the undertoad could be waiting there in the dark
But all these things are what life brings to the world according to Garp
All these things are how it seems in the world according to Garp
In the world according to Garp
In the world according to Garp

Al was by now in need of a break and Dennis came up with the idea that they take a trip to France (and specifically to Chateau Pontet-Canet) at the end of the summer. Al didn't have to be asked twice.

Al – "The right trip at the right time as far as I was concerned! From the day it was first suggested I was excited about it. *Indian Summer* had taken a while but we'd finished it now and so off we went to France."

In the period between finishing *Indian Summer* and flying to Europe with Al and Dennis at the start of September, Luke spoke to the various members of *Shot In The Dark* in order to clarify for everyone the serious position that they were now in.

Luke – "I basically had to tell them that with their salaries for the new album that was it and that there was no more money left. I felt bad about this but what I told them was the truth and as far as I was concerned that was it and it was over."

Having already bought *Shot In The Dark*'s publishing from them, advancing the band "around $50,000 overall", Luke now prepared to fly out to Europe with a sense that at least everyone now understood the reality of the situation before them.

Al spent the early part of September in London and Wimborne, celebrating his 36th birthday with his family and Luke. Three days later, on Tuesday 8th, he flew out of Heathrow to Paris and by Friday 11th was in Bordeaux at Chateau Pontet-Canet with Alexis Lichine.

Al Stewart

Al Stewart

Dennis Overstreet , Baron Philippe de Rothschild and Al.

Dennis explains what they were all travelling out to France for that September.

Dennis Overstreet – "Every two years a different Chateau gets to 'bring in' the vintage and there is a tradition of inviting a celebrity to do this and so I suggest Al's name to Albert. I flew in from LA and met Al at the Chateau when he flew in from London. Now after a couple of days of madness, the time for the ceremony arrived and of course Al wanted to do it in his own way and he wanted to make his speech totally in French! This he did and I have to say he did it very well."

Al – "I was actually very nervous about it of course but I think that I just about got through it OK in the end. Then one afternoon, after about seven different wines, lunch was still going on at four in the afternoon and I had headed back to the house to have a lie down. I was just coming up to the front door step when I saw this old man wearing wellington boots and an anorak coming towards me and as he got closer I realised that this was none other than Baron Philippe de Rothschild! I then waited until he was beside me before greeting him with 'Bonjour Monsieur Le Baron'! A little later that afternoon Dennis came pounding down the drive of the house to get me and we got our photo taken with him."

The purpose of having someone such as Al at the ceremony was to use the cachet of their celebrity as a lucky omen for the new vintage. And so the invitation for Al to be involved at that time was entirely appropriate. Dennis had, of course, been key to all of this.

Dennis Overstreet – "I love wine. Wine was my life but up until this time I'd never had a disciple, but now with Al that's exactly what I had. He was just so fantastically enthusiastic. I would introduce him to a new wine and it would be – 'yes, we should now go out and experience all of these vintages, the power is with us!' And we would drink wonderful wines. There was a surreal feeling to this however, while I was staying at Al's house once. Al, as everyone knows, kept absolutely no food in the house and we would very often be sat by the pool drinking the most amazing wine with a late supper that consisted of tinned mushroom soup and potato crisps!"

When Luke got back to LA from France he was feeling rested and happy but soon came down to earth with a bump when confronted by the Kinetic issues that he had been able to put behind him for the last couple of weeks. The situation with *Shot In The Dark*

Chateau Pontet-Canet, September 1981

was difficult for Luke to deal with as the band had been with Al for so long. There was trouble ahead.

The new album lacked an obvious single and so Luke next suggested to Al that it would perhaps be a good idea if he were to go into the studio for a day or so each month to work on new single material that Arista could consider. Al balked at this, claiming that Luke didn't understand him any more and further damage was done to their relationship. To add oil to the fire, *Indian Summer* was released a couple of weeks later and basically disappeared without trace, and shortly after that David Greenwald stopped working for Al after a disagreement over the promotion of the new album. So all was by no means sweetness and light in Kinetic's office at this time.

But life went on and throughout all of this it had remained Luke's avowed intention to recruit other artists to Kinetic's ranks. Then one evening in the spring of 1981 he discovered Angie Wilby singing a Patsy Cline number in a London pub. Within a few short months Luke had brought her over to LA and put her on the Kinetic payroll in exchange for her initially doing receptionist duties in the office.

Luke – "Angie had the most amazing voice and looked great on stage. She was also an unbelievable Country singer and I saw her as a revenue maker for us all."

The plan was that by working in the Kinetic office Angie could get to know many of the industry people, find her footing in LA and so gravitate up to doing shows herself. But it all took a while to get going and she began to feel neglected.

Angie Wilby – "I moved to LA and into the apartment below the office on Selma, ironically kicking Nigel (Lendon) out of there in the process! But it was a little confusing for me and looking back on it I was being naive. After a while nothing much seemed to be happening with regard to my own career but I just assumed that Luke was busy with Al's album and that eventually it would be my turn."

Angie's turn duly came at the end of the year when she started working with Peter White in preparation for a November appearance at the Blah Blah Cafe.

Peter White – "Angie did work very hard to prepare for the gig. Luke had got her to move out to LA, which she had done at once and it all looked rosy for a while there. And I can still remember rehearsing for the show, where we tried out a great number of songs."

Some of the new pieces they went over during this period were songs by Billy Thermol, who had previously written for Linda Ronstadt among others. Luke had been interested in managing him and so Peter now made use of the demo tape of Thermol's songs in his search for original material for Angie to perform at the debut.

Angie: "And so Peter took me under his wing, which was just what I needed. He was just great through all of this. It all led to me indeed playing at the Blah Blah Cafe, where I opened for Jude Johnston and *Shot In The Dark*."

And so it appeared that the tide had turned and Angie was on her way. The show had been a success, she was happy and soon after was invited to spend Christmas with *Shot In The Dark* who were travelling up to Aspen to play a series of shows.

However, the genesis of this trip was not all that it would seem.

Throughout the autumn of 1981 relations between Al and Luke had not improved and they had seen little of one another. Luke had by now advanced more of his own money to the band, in the form of personal loans, as they hadn't worked with Al for almost six months, and it was in order to give himself a break from all of this that Luke now announced the trip to Aspen.

Luke – "In actual fact what had happened was that I had decided to go up to Aspen skiing for a couple of weeks that Christmas. When the band found out they asked me if they could come too and play some shows up there. Now this wasn't such a bad idea as over Christmas the entire music industry went to Aspen and it was a pretty good place for them to go and get noticed. So I put that short series of shows together. I saw it really as one last chance for them."

Luke

Aspen, December 1981. Angie on lead vocals

The season of *Shot In The Dark* shows in Aspen were to be the last gigs ever to involve both Al and Luke. Pitched to the band members as a *Shot In The Dark* can't lose situation, a mixture of vacation and concerts everyone travelled up to Colorado with high hopes. Meanwhile, Al stayed at home for Christmas in Bel Air, blissfully unaware that he was already billed in Aspen as being the *Special Guest Star* at the Continental Hotel at the end of the month. He would only discover this news himself upon his arrival at the resort on New Year's Eve.

The various people that made up the party that visited Aspen all have slightly different recollections of what actually happened there.

Peter White – "It was a fun little place that we actually played in, there were seats set up in front of this little stage at one end of the bar and we played pretty much every night for a couple of weeks. Besides us playing our own *Shot In The Dark* songs, Angie, who had also worked up a set of cover versions of her own, would come out and we would back her on Shirelles' songs and the like before doing an hour's worth of our own material."

Meanwhile Krysia had had to confront the possibly delicate situation of having Angie performing with the band. Their styles were very different of course and it was this that in many ways diffused much of any potential conflict between them.

Krysia – "Angie was a nice, sweet and uncomplicated person. She chose very different material to what I was doing and certainly sang it in a totally different way to me! My own solo material was pretty esoteric and metaphysical whereas Angie was singing cover versions of modern pop! Certainly she believed that Luke was grooming her for stardom. What she clearly needed was the help of a producer or someone to give her guidance because at this stage it was an aspect of her career conspicuous by its absence! She herself was not a writer, certainly not like the guys in *Shot In The Dark* were, and she would have needed someone to help her with that side. The whole trip was a wonderful black comedy. It really was! Angie and I stayed in a house up there owned by Bill Ashton and we got on just fine."

Both Angie and Krysia remember these times with some affection despite the way that things sometimes worked out.

Angie Wilby – "Like everyone else I got sacked once by Luke! I had to wake him up one morning for some reason and I just could not rouse him. So he sacked me and I stayed sacked for three days!" Boring, their lives were not.

Krysia – "So we then discovered from Luke that Al was really coming up to see us in Aspen and was bringing his girlfriend Lori with him for the weekend. We were all thinking that there would be fireworks because we knew that Al didn't have a clue about the subterfuge afoot that had preceded his arrival. I also remember having a conversation with Bill Ashton about how we could pull out of the show. For what it was worth, I dug my heels in and said that it was not a problem of *Shot In The Dark*'s making and that we would be getting up on stage to do the show no matter what!"

Meanwhile, Al remained back home in Bel Air, still unaware of everything that was going on in Aspen.

Robin Lamble – "We had had a small amount of rehearsal with Angie before we all went up to Aspen. The motivation behind all of this was quite complex because I'd got the impression that Luke was looking to replace Krysia with Angie in *Shot In The Dark*. Luke and Krysia's professional relationship had deteriorated quite badly by this time. The evening would kick off with an announcement that said 'Ladies and Gentlemen – Miss Angie Wilby' and Angie would walk on followed by the rest of us. Her set was mostly cover versions and we all had a great deal of fun doing it."

Angie's songs that she performed in Aspen included "Dancing in the Street", Kate Bush's "The Man with the Child in his Eyes" and *Shot In The Dark*'s own song "Landing Lights".

Robin Lamble – "There would then be an interval after which we'd come on as *Shot In The Dark* with Krysia. Angie would join us for a couple of these numbers too. We were all primed about Al coming up and originally I think it was going to be for three nights. I was very unsure about the whole thing and I remember making it perfectly clear to Luke that all of this was his responsibility. It was his gig. When Al arrived and everything became clear about how the event had been staged it did look quite bad in the dressing room for a while. There was a little uncertainty about the evening actually taking place but it was jam-packed out there and Al did play."

Peter White – "We all thought that Al was going to play for three nights but that's not the way that it turned out because when Al arrived he discovered that what was supposed to be just a guest appearance had in reality been advertised as '*Al Stewart – featuring Shot In The Dark*' for that New Year's Eve and Al wasn't happy at all with Luke when he saw this, because quite simply he'd wanted it to be *Shot In The Dark*'s big chance, our gig not his."

Angie Wilby – "There was a horrible atmosphere surrounding that show and at the time I didn't understand why, but now looking back on it it's clear that Al arrived expecting the trip to be one thing and once he got there it was another. I walked past a room backstage just before the gig and heard Al say quite distinctly – 'Well I just think it's some person's excuse for a skiing holiday!', which showed what he thought about all the pretence."

Luke – "The notion that the only reason for those *Shot In The Dark* dates in Aspen was to get Al to play up there himself is laughable. It really is! We were already up there when Al called me from his home saying that he and Lori were all alone down in Los Angeles and could they come up and join us for a few days? I told him that if he wanted to come up then that would be great and that if he could also perhaps play with the band for 20 minutes each night then that would be even better and that it would help us all.

He said that he would come up and agreed to play with the band at the hotel. I had pointed out to him that the whole reason for the trip in the first place was to try and keep his band alive and he realised this *before* he flew on up to Aspen."

This explanation does seem logical enough. Luke had invested a further $10,000, virtually the only money he had, in the band's Christmas Aspen trip. When Al arrived however he was greeted by a stream of complaints from band members in what was basically an outpouring of six months-worth of frustration over their lack of work and money.

Luke – "By this time the band all realised that their career with Al was fast coming to an end and it was this dissatisfaction with the situation that they found themselves in that I think fed the resentment that manifested itself in the way that they all acted up there in Aspen. I'm sure that they all believe that their recollections are perfectly honest and correct but all I can say is what possible reason could there be for me to put up my own money for a series of dates in Aspen other than to try and help get them noticed? I certainly wasn't ever likely to make a cent out of those shows – but *they* all got paid! Having agreed to do the shows up there I just couldn't understand why they all acted the way they did by going and moaning at Al."

In fact, to this day, Luke considers that bringing the band to America and putting them on a salary, paying their medical insurance and supporting them in all manner of ways for several years was the major strain on his relationship with Al and that, had he not done it, hiring musicians instead on an "as and when" basis, then things with Al may well have lasted longer and been even more successful than they turned out to be.

That was the only show that Al played in Aspen. He cancelled his involvement in the remaining dates the next morning, citing a cold and sore throat, at which point Luke packed up and flew on back home to LA ahead of everyone else that same day. By the time that the band members had driven back to LA a few days into the New Year they found that Kinetic, the company that they had all been part of since joining up with Al, had shut up shop and to all intents and purposes no longer existed. Deeply hurt by his treatment in Aspen and pushed financially to the brink by the diminished returns from the company he had created nine years earlier, Luke had returned to LA and closed the company down. He had all the phone lines disconnected, surrendered the relevant credit cards, made his staff redundant and hung a sign on the door that made it perfectly clear to anyone that came by that it was all over.

Six years earlier everyone had such high hopes and a keen sense of expectation that was fuelled by their ever-increasing record sales and the firm belief that major success in America was well within their grasp. They had all had their ups and downs but to see it come to this was upsetting for every one of them.

Angie Wilby – "By the time a couple of days later that Nigel and I got back to Los Angeles, the Kinetic office had been closed down and I was homeless! Everything had changed and obviously something quite major had happened between Luke and Al. Luke explained to me how he'd already rented out the upstairs part of the building and how in fact he'd moved himself down to where I'd been living and so that was it. No job at Kinetic, no home, no career. So I did the sensible thing and moved in with Nigel!"

In spite of Angie's recollections, no-one really believed that it really was all over at the time. Out of them all, Luke probably believed it more than anyone else did but even he now admits that in those first few weeks of 1982 his resolve to simply shut everything down was put to the test.

But Kinetic did stay closed and never represented Al again.

Throughout the first few months of 1982 Al and Luke continued to have the occasional meeting over dinner in LA, during which Al would invariably open up the topic of Luke's general unhappiness with their present working relationship. Luke freely acknowledges that he was miserable at this time. Things ultimately came to a head one evening over a dinner at Chianti between Al, Luke, Lori and two executives from Wells

Fargo Bank when Al and Luke had a very public falling out. It was an incident that forced Luke to take stock of all that had happened, the difficulties in managing both Al and *Shot In The Dark* and his own motivation for being part of it all and after a night of soul searching he called Al's business manager, Barbara Sherry, the next morning to say that it was all over. And as it turned out it really was.

Luke – "When we split up Al kept the house that we'd bought for the Kinetic Offices at the junction of Crescent Heights and Selma. We had had money and we didn't want it to be wasted and to us bricks and mortar were more reliable than a business, and actually there had been talk of us investing in a restaurant at one time. So we bought the office but when we split Al got it because it was in his name and because he wanted to get rid of it at once, and as at that time property prices had fallen he made a loss. If you panic and sell at the bottom of a market you've got to expect a loss. If he'd rented the house out and waited, he'd have got everything back and more. When we'd bought it I didn't just go out with Al's cheque book. All the advice we took said that it was a good idea to buy the house. The intention had been not to spend all our advances on touring by the time of *24 Carrots* and to make some money instead but that's not quite how it turned out."

And so with no Al production work on the table, Chris Desmond set about working on tracks for the band.

Chris Desmond – "The swansong for my involvement with Al and the band came around this time when we were attempting to put demos together with for what would have been the second *Shot In The Dark* album. We did demos for this and they were really lovely songs. We did them at a place called Universal Studios which was a demo session place down in Hollywood. This was a while after we had finished *Indian Summer* and I remember Richard Tompkins was hanging around. It was a real tragedy that they didn't get to release that work. Everything would have been so different if that album had stayed out in the stores longer."

Chris Desmond wasn't the only person that thought that the album stood a chance. At the time of its release it had got some excellent reviews and attracted much media interest.

Chris Desmond – "I also discovered over the following years that the *Shot In The Dark* album had been very well thought of in the recording music community in Los Angeles. It did make a wave, which is nice. But anyway we did these demos for what would have been their second album and unfortunately the label said 'no they didn't like it' and that was the end of it."

The end of the business relationship between Al and Luke also had obvious implications for the band.

Krysia – "As soon as things fell apart with Al and Luke things also fell apart between Al and us, insofar as him having us as his band. We kept going as *Shot In The Dark* but from there on in we did everything for ourselves. Naturally enough he had to scale down things and only retain the parts that he really needed and I was a superfluous part of his band anyway and that was that. Peter called in Jude Johnston to do some work. She was a piano player and singer and would open shows for them and would then do what I used to do on stage with Al and Peter. With regard to the scaling down of things generally, there was obviously a great deal of sorting out to do between Al and Luke that was going to take time. It was a very messy period."

Through all of this though, Al's record company had seemed happy enough with him. Although his record sales for Clive Davis had failed, since 1978, to live up to everyone's expectations, Al was far from being *persona non grata* at Arista. This is borne out by Luke's observations of what, from a business perspective, was happening concerning Al and his relationship with the record company.

Luke – "Despite the fact that neither *24 Carrots* or *Indian Summer* had been hits, there had been no talk whatsoever of Al leaving Arista at the time. Now this was hardly surprising because that just wasn't the way that a record company works. It was a guaranteed contract and there was just no way that they would ever have walked away from their association with Al.

"Arista seemed to be seeing everything in its true perspective at this time and it was after all a 'live' album that hadn't worked and so they were never ever going to drop Al on the basis of that, and that's how I left everything when Al and I split up that March."

The split with Luke didn't however stop Al from recording demos in LA for a prospective Arista studio album throughout the late Spring of 1982 with musicians mostly drawn from *Shot In The Dark*.

A couple of months into the new year Dennis Overstreet telephoned Luke and invited him up to Roscomarre for dinner with him and Al. There was a specific reason for the call, they needed Luke's help.

The atmosphere between Al and Arista had however now grown very tense. In the '30s, with the Hollywood studio system in full swing, this is what would happen to a star under contract when one of their movies failed at the box office. The studio executives would team them up with a writer, in a cabin at the back of the lot, and basically leave them there until the star realised that until they offered to reduce the terms of their contract they wouldn't be offered another movie.

Luke – "Well that is exactly what Arista now did to Al. They kept asking him to re-record tracks knowing that he was having to use dwindling resources in order to do this and that he would therefore be forced to look for a way out. They had him up against a wall. When I got there Al asked me to sign a document that, in effect, was the legal piece of paper that would release Arista from all their obligations to him. He explained that without my signature he'd be forced to go back to England and just be a folkie again."

The choice, as Al saw it, was simple. He could stay with Arista and quite possibly not have anything released for a number of years or he could surrender the contract and take his chances elsewhere. There may very well have been an obligation for Clive Davis to release anything, technically up to standard, that Al presented Arista with, but they knew that he lacked the finances to prove this in court. Luke felt that he *should* do this. Al wasn't so sure. Despite the fact that they no longer enjoyed a relationship of any kind Luke was almost protective in the advice that he now gave Al.

"Al's contract with Arista in fact stated that whatever we gave them they had to accept. I told him that I thought that for him to give up on Arista would be absolutely the wrong thing to do and that the advice he had been given was completely wrong in every way. My lawyer agreed with me when I went over it with him a couple of days later. If he had gone to court with it there is no doubt that he would have won. But there was the cost of mounting that case to be considered. I told him that the advice that he had been given by his lawyer, John Espidal, was not something that I thought he should act on and that it would be the wrong thing for him to do."

But Al was adamant that he wanted Luke to sign the release and eventually, against his better judgement, Luke gave in and signed it. Clive Davis and Arista did however stay on the sidelines as Al's *de facto* record company through the rest of that year, 1982.

John Espidal now stepped into the breach and took over the reigns of Al's faltering career. He became Al's manager in the spring of that year, joining that short roster of people who had represented Al since Tony Stratton-Smith 16 years earlier.

Brian Rohan had been Al's lawyer at the time that the contract with Arista had been formalised back in 1977 and indeed it was he that had negotiated that multi-album deal. Great at seeing through the big "contract signing" aspects of his brief, he had however been released from the day-to-day charge of Al's affairs when they proved to be reliant on someone with different day-to-day skills than the ones that he was bringing to the post. There now arose, with the surrender of the ongoing contract with Arista, a situation that was ultimately to result in the final nail in the coffin of Luke's association with Al. Rohan was now to claim that he was still due a share of the proceeds from albums that Al had only recently, with the help of Luke's signature, freed Arista from any obligation to release. If ever there was a "cat among the pigeons" moment in Al's career in the 1980s then this was surely it!

The case ultimately ended up in court.

Luke – "Now I knew that we'd fired him but the core of his case was that John Espidal had never actually done this at all. The judge went on to be very critical of me in her summing up and decision, saying that I hadn't actually fired Rohan and that I had instead given the job to somebody else! This I felt very bad about as Rohan had in fact himself fired my previous lawyer. He'd told me that that was how it was done, it was 'don't you do it, I will, it's my job'. So when we took on John Espidal, I did what Rohan had told me – I asked one lawyer to fire the other. But Espidal never did that and the result of that was that we had to pay Rohan several hundred thousand dollars."

In the court case that Al and Luke lost, the judge found in Rohan's favour. It was to prove the sad, last throw of the dice in the business relationship between Al and Luke; Luke surrendering Kinetic's rights to Al's career in order to fund his own share of the settlement to Rohan and thus formally ending their partnership.

Al and Luke never worked together again.

Al now proceeded to scale down his touring commitments in the most dramatic way possible. He stopped touring completely. It marked a deliberate return, in many ways, to how things were back in the days of Julia Creasey, when Al had just himself to worry about. He was clearing the decks.

Al – "The reason for this was that Luke told me categorically that it was impossible to tour due to the amount of money we were losing out on the road which was in no small part due to the number of people and the ridiculous amount of equipment that we were carrying around with us".

Thus with big, high-profile touring no longer an option, Al somewhat disappeared from the public's consciousness for a couple of years.

The situation where Luke had pretty much taken all of the decisions in Al's life had left him in a dangerously vulnerable position once Luke had left his side, and in many respects he had to fend for himself for the first time since Soho in 1965. On a level of daily practicalities Al had never been particularly resourceful and a Christmas story that Dennis Overstreet relates is a good example of this.

Dennis Overstreet – "Al decided one Christmas time, when we were both at a low ebb, that to cheer ourselves up we should get a Christmas tree. So we went out and got one and split the decoration chores between us. I said that I'd do the Christmas decorations if Al would do the lights. So I spent many hours putting all the decorations on the tree and it did look really great. I went to bed at about 4 a.m. and at 8 a.m. there's someone at the front door. So I climb out of bed, open the front door and there are these two guys stood there. After a short discussion I established that they were electricians and was on the point of directing them to the control box, presuming there was some problem that I didn't know about, when they told me that they'd been called out to put up the Christmas lights! This was total rock and roll madness – where you hire two guys to hang Christmas lights at $150 an hour!"

The irony of all this was not lost on Al. It was not as if his friends were afraid to point out the somewhat odd thought processes that he would so often embark upon. This was simply because they loved him for it. It went beyond loyalty.

Meanwhile, on the concert front, things remained moribund.

Peter White – "You can say that! In fact through the whole of 1982 Al didn't do a single concert as both his record deal with Arista and personal management by Luke were in limbo."

Luke had always been very encouraging to Peter about his abilities and it was Luke that had suggested to him that he learn more about composing music and attend an orchestration course. This he did through 1982, taking an evening course at UCLA where he met up with Dave Camp for the first time. Things were very tough for Peter, who at this time was surviving on his royalty cheques for "Time Passages" that came to him from BMI.

Peter White again – "I was basically just living off of my savings except for occasional session work. Al started retreating at this stage, just staying up there at Roscomarre and not doing anything very much at all. I'd go up to Al's house from time to time with the idea of us recording some songs. I would take with me some songs for us to work on and that we would do for a while but there certainly wasn't any serious work going on because Al wasn't interested in doing anything very much"

Whether this was a malaise or disillusionment born out of the sense of loss fostered by both Luke and Arista disappearing in quick succession, or whether it was an unwillingness to work hard to recapture some lost ground in his career, nobody knows but for whatever reasons, Al seemed apathetic and listless.

Peter White – "By this time I'd gone out and bought my own four-track cassette player-recorder in order to do my own demos and I was also starting to get together with other people to do work occasionally for them too. Then out of the blue one day Al said 'You know Peter, we should put a band together and do some shows – besides which we need to meet some girls.' Now left over from the Kinetic days was a white truck that Al remembered we still had and we set up some gigs and went straight out and played them, discovering en-route that touring could be fun again!"

Meanwhile the other band members had by now been forced to accept the situation for what it was. There would never be a return to the lifestyle of the late '70s for any of them.

Robin Lamble – "I went up to Al's house in Bel Air in 1982 to basically try and find out exactly what was going on. I needed to know whether or not we had a band still or perhaps if I should now go back to England. Things had got that bad. Luke seemed to be around less and less and all of us in *Shot In The Dark* had spoken separately to Al about the situation. We were all a bit rudderless without Luke. But then when Luke got fired by Al it became very clear that that was it and he wasn't going to be around any more. I was getting along by doing sessions for people like Silent Partner and Michael On Fire."

Having left the band, Krysia still kept in touch with Al – "I cared about him a great deal. Al's stuff had always been beautifully tight and it remained so after I'd left the band. I remember the first time that I saw him and the band perform after I had left and I came away thinking 'god, these guys are great'."

It was now that Al started to work with the producer Mike Flicker. They had first met several years previously in 1976 when Flicker was producing the group Heart, the band attending one of the early Universal Amphitheatre *Year Of The Cat* dates. Al then met them in 1979 at Robert Stigwood's party for the *Sergeant Pepper* movie and it was at one of their LA shows, a short while later, that he also came to meet Paul Getty Junior. The meeting has a special place in Al's memory. Getty went on to mention to Al that he had a race horse that had been named after one of Al's songs, that horse being *Midas Shadow*.

Mike Flicker: "I knew Al's music before this time of course but after seeing him perform at those shows it put the idea in my mind that I would certainly like at some stage to work with him, given the chance. There was a real magic between Al and the audience at those LA shows."

It was around this time that Mike, who was then running the label Mushroom Records, first encountered Clive Davis who went on to license Heart to a world-wide deal with Arista following protracted negotiations with Mike Flicker and the group. It was several years later that Davis suggested to Mike, at a meeting in New York City, that it would be a useful exercise for both of them if Mike were to do some production work for Arista. Mike was free to do this because by this time he was an independent producer. And so it was, that every few months demo tapes would wing their way from Clive Davis and Arista to Mike along with roster lists of the artists that were on Arista that may at some time in the near future need some production work done on their behalf. After this had been going on for almost a year Al's name appeared on one of these lists and Mike circled it adding a side note to the effect that he had always admired Al's records and would like to work with him, before duly returning it to Davis. Whereupon another long silence ensued before Trudi Green (Mike's girlfriend and manager who was looking for a project for him to work on) spoke to the attorney that was Al's *de facto* manager following Luke's departure who, in turn, spoke to Al's accountant Barbara Sherry, and between them they pushed Mike's name to the top of the list of possible producers.

Mike Flicker – "Clive hadn't been at all happy with the tracks which Al had, up until this time, been sending him. However the situation was quite clear in that contractually Arista were obliged to let Al put out another album. And so Clive said that we could start to record a few tracks, with me as his approved producer."

In fact when the process of Al and Mike working together started off, there was no firm proposal from Arista to commission an album from them and these soon progressed to become uniquely stressful times in Al's career. Certainly in private he was the first to admit that to all intents and purposes things had obviously plateaued since the highs of 1979. Al was finding song writing increasingly difficult, due not only to the many distractions that LA had to offer but also because of a severe case of writer's block that at this time was making the composition of new material equally as problematic as the post-Mandi hiatus a decade earlier. This, naturally enough, didn't exactly fill Clive Davis with confidence.

Mike Flicker – "I'd already had some knowledge of the situation at the time between Al and Clive as I'd been involved in the process of listening to demos that many people, including Al, would send in for Clive's opinion. In many ways Clive was baffled by the way that Al worked and one of the reasons that I was brought in was to try and make some sense of everything."

In fact some of Al's demos for what would become *Russians And Americans* went on to basically become the finished masters themselves with only the bare minimum of extra work being put into them.

Throughout all of this Peter White, being the only member of *Shot In The Dark* to have carried on working with Al on anything like a full time basis, found himself in the unique position to act as the bridge between the old and the new. His even-tempered and thoughtful approach to this transitional phase was one of the key factors in the next album getting finished at all. He was of course continuing to write material himself. One of the first pieces to be worked on was in fact "Rumours Of War".

Peter White – "'Rumours Of War' was one of those early things that we did. I went up to Al's house one evening and played him a tape of what was my original demo. The way it starts off is exactly the same as it is now, up to the verse. He had the music for a verse of a song he had written before, that was already called 'Rumours Of War'. It was sort of Dylan-like. He said 'If I change this into 4/4 it will probably fit with your bass line,' so we tried that and it worked! The trumpet thing remained the same too."

Mike Flicker – "The starting point for work on what was to become *Russians And Americans* was a pile of half-written songs, many of them with only a vague suggestion of a lyric which would arrive in the studio as one of Peter's programmed backing tracks or an Al piano track with occasional pieces of melody or the odd word sung over the top of them by Al."

The album made full use of three different studios selected by Mike. These were Cherokee Studios in Hollywood, Orca Studios in Encino and Kendun in Burbank.

Mike Flicker again – "We used Cherokee because it was a very large room to record in and so when a track needed lots of players we'd go there and so each location was used as and when, dependent on what we needed for that song."

Throughout all of this Clive Davis would be sending Mike Flicker songs (which were basically ridiculous pop tunes) for Al to cover, which were totally inappropriate and go some way to substantiate the case that Davis never understood either Al or his work ethic from day one.

Mike Flicker – "An example of this is that the only track that Clive sort of liked at all was '1, 2, 3' which was a cover version! The fact that this was Al's idea and not Clive's of course is somewhat ironic."

Throughout all this time, however, Clive Davis remained clearly disaffected with Al's work. He didn't understand the convoluted way in which Al put an album together and little by little he lost faith in him. Eventually things came to a head with only half of the new record completed.

Mike Flicker – "Arista said that from their perspective things didn't seem to be working out for either party and so an agreement was reached whereby they gave Al a certain financial consideration that allowed him to complete the album without them having to release it."

The overall project took just over a year from beginning to end, starting in the middle of 1982. But of course this by no means meant that they were in the studio every day. Ultimately, when Mike Flicker was forced to decide between continuing his association with Clive Davis or finishing the album with Al, he chose Al. This then, in essence, was the end of Al and Arista's six year relationship.

Once the Arista arrangement had come to an end Al, Mike and Peter all sat down together and elected to continue the album the way they'd begun and to try and pick up a new label to put it out once it was finished rather than shopping around with a batch of demos. Mike Flicker was free from any record company restraint to produce Al's album and in order to get the very best out of Al, Mike turned, not surprisingly, to Peter White.

Mike Flicker – "It seemed the sensible thing to do! Once we had an idea that Peter and I both liked then he would take it over to Al and if he liked it then things would start to happen. Peter would be very much involved in the arrangements and orchestrations and as someone who could fire Al up. He was an 'igniter' you might say."

The process of lyric writing by Al is an element of his recording that has proved very difficult for many of his producers to deal with and it's something that Mike Flicker has put into some perspective over the years.

Mike Flicker – "Al has got this mode of writing that has been very successful for him over the years and he sees no need to change it. He has this motif that he's created, I don't know how it happened, perhaps that in itself was an accident, but anyway he has this motif that dictates how he composes. He needs to be inspired and then he has to have this last minute pressure to come up with the words and it will not happen before that time, which was certainly something that drove Clive Davis totally crazy because he'd get demos that were only partially completed and then he'd call me up and say 'what's this song about?' and I would have to say that I had no idea!"

Dennis Overstreet saw a great deal of Al around this time. As such he is in a better position than most to put Al's actions into some form of perspective. He has some interesting things to say about how his friend lived at this time.

Dennis Overstreet – "Al did not, does not, and quite possibly never has, lived in the same world as the rest of us. It's very easy to get sucked into this *Alice In Wonderland* world that he's lived in forever it seems. He's inhabited this private world for as long as I've known him and probably for years before that. If you're close to him for a while you end up seeing things his way. It's a character devoid of scepticism or cynicism and one that takes anything said to him at its word."

This does paint a somewhat isolated picture of Al.

The album was certainly one of the hardest that he had found to write, especially when he was obliged to come up with a single.

Al – "Yes, I found that very hard. Basically singles I find incredibly hard to write. 'The One That Got Away', I wrote maybe 12 to 15 verses for and actually it was in essence three different songs. It was called 'In Red Square' and then it became 'Secret Affair' for some of the time. For *Russians And Americans* I have an exercise book full of just two songs that I worked on, being 'Lori, Don't Go ...' and 'The One That Got Away'. The others were very much easier to write out."

Mike Flicker – "On one of those occasions when we all sat down with one another to talk about the direction that the project should take I pointed out that when I had seen Al and Peter live it was something that the fans were almost hypnotised by and it was that feeling that I wanted to capture on record; the atmosphere of what came to be known as 'the live duo'."

During breaks in the making of *Russians And Americans*, Peter and Al had continued to gig both as the duo and with other band members, in an exercise that served to both pay some bills and keep all the musicians fresh. And through all this Luke still continued to be, theoretically at least, involved as Al's manager. However on a day-to-day basis he certainly was not around at all. Mike Flicker's business dealings continued to be done through Al's attorney at the time. Trudi Green had come to be the person who was now in charge in an intermediate capacity as Al's personal manager and business affairs continued to be handled through the offices of Barbara Sherry, as they still are today. Many studios were used for little bits here and there and besides Yamaha and Kendun studios the original Record Plant studio was used but mysteriously left off the album credits.

In 1985 Al explained the reasons for the three year hiatus in between *Indian Summer* and *Russians And Americans.*

Al – "The gap is unexplainable to anyone who isn't in the music business because it would occur to most people that it doesn't take two years to get out of a contract with Arista, but the fact of the matter is that it does, simply because Clive Davis doesn't give you a yes or a no. He says 'I don't like these songs, go and record some others and send them to me when you've recorded them'. So you spend six months doing it, then he does the same thing again. This can go on for a long time, until you finally call a halt and say to him, 'Are you ever going to like anything I write?' and he says 'No', in which case you have to begin the negotiation of getting with someone else. It takes an extraordinary amount of time. I think we did it reasonably quickly!"

RCA sent an executive over to meet with Al and pick out a UK single. He didn't like "The One That Got Away" or "Gypsy And The Rose" but thought that an instrumental he heard was a possible UK single. This gave Al just ten days to come up with a lyric for what became "Lori Don't Go Right Now".

Al – "The American album is the album that more or less I had in mind, though it underwent some changes because there were several songs on the original tape sent to Arista which Clive spat out and didn't like, which, over the course of the year that it took to arrive at the final shape of the thing, got left off in the final event simply because I wrote some more which I liked better. The ones that didn't make it on that one might make it on the next one. They're all lurking around somewhere."

And so the spring of 1984 saw the release of the first non-Luke album in over a decade, the criminally underrated *Russians And Americans*.

ACCIDENT ON 3RD STREET
Linda was killed last Saturday about fifteen blocks from where she lives
In a car crash, people gathered around the graveside friends and relatives dressed in black
Preacher mumblin' how she's bound to go to Heaven
The service started at half-past ten, it was all over by eleven
They say it's God's to give, and God's to take away,
But why He happened to pick Linda on a Saturday night, no one could say.
Maybe it's just one of those things
One of those things
They found the guy who did it, he had the lobotomy and the chicken eyes,
And he gazed around the courtroom with a kind of vague surprise

Reminded me of one of those Vikings with the long-handled swords
The kind of guy even Joan Baez would not feel non-violent towards
Said he wasn't looking, maybe he had had a bit too much
It was dark, it was raining, he didn't see the light or some such
It was just one of those things,
One of those things.

I asked my local guru about the situation and he gave me this reply
While pointing a bony finger up into the general direction of the sky:
"Get on with your own life, it is not ours to reason why"
Said he used to worry about it once when he was young
Now he doesn't even bother to try
He left me with a feeling that what he said was basically sound
Like a black hole in space, or philosophy, useless but profound
Just one of those things,
One of those things.

Tonight I'm gonna take myself down to my local cafe
Gonna get smashed out of my mind, gonna waste myself away
Gonna drink and drink and sink into that dark abyss
I wanna be just like that Viking, I wanna know if ignorance is truly bliss.
Linda's in the cold ground, won't see her anymore
Somewhere out on the highway tonight, the drunken engines roar
It's just one of those things,
One of those things.

Oh, just one of those things.

THE CANDIDATE

Inside the lonely building
Sits the candidate
His speech is typed and ready
The hundred-dollar plates
Sit on deserted tables
Beneath fluorescent light
But no one comes to hear him
No cheers disturb the night
So where are all the voters?
Where the voter's wives?
They've all gone to the movies
Trying to understand their lives.
The candidate is slipping
Into some dream of old
Not noticing around him
A thousand rubber chickens going cold

Peter White – "So the album was finally completed and then in 1984 Al got an offer to play Europe, which he hadn't done for four years but the offer was for a duo, not a band. Maybe that was the case or perhaps it was the money we were being offered wasn't enough to tour with a band, I'm not absolutely sure, perhaps that was it. Either way it had always been something that we'd talked about doing and we decided to give it a go and set off for Europe."

There had been a gap of almost four years between the shows at the Hammersmith Odeon and the next British date, which was at the tiny *Yesterdays* folk club in Bristol. This gig and the one the next night at The Maltings in Farnham, Surrey were to be used as warm up performances by Al for a show that Britain hadn't seen before, namely the duet with Peter White. The previous time that Al had sung in Europe without a band had

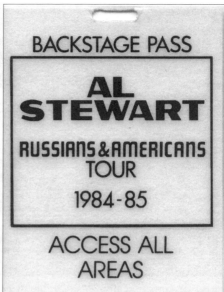

'Russians And American' European tour, 1984

been in Denmark during 1973 promoting *Past, Present And Future* in the early days of his partnership with Luke O'Reilly. Sitting on a couple of wooden stools in the intimate atmosphere of that Bristol Folk Club, Al rolled back the years to perform "Accident on 3rd Street", "The Gypsy And The Rose", "Rumours Of War" and "Café Society" from the new album *Russians And Americans*. Old favourites included "The Dark And The Rolling Sea", "Old Admirals", "Broadway Hotel" and "Time Passages" with Al on his various Ovation acoustic guitars and Peter on guitar, keyboards and accordion. These were also the first shows that the song "Bear Farmers Of Birnam" was performed at.

Two shows were booked for London's Royal Albert Hall but the first of these was cancelled on the afternoon of the gig itself because of Al going down with flu. The rehearsals for the concert, which was to feature special guest appearances by acoustic bass player Danny Thompson, Tim Renwick on electric guitar and Peter's brother Danny White on keyboards were in full swing on the day of the gig when word of the definite cancellation came through at 4.30, catching everyone by surprise because those that knew about Al's cold had presumed that he'd be able to do the show.

This left just the next evening's performance which was able to go ahead as planned, Al having recovered and travelled from the Berkeley Square Marriott, arriving at the gig with his mother.

The show itself went very well and the encore performance of "Bear Farmers Of Birnam" was given a surreal twist when a couple of sound engineer Jonathan Saville's friends in bear costumes danced on the stage. From here the short tour moved onto Paris and The Eldorado Theatre on Rue de Strasbourg. Al was feeling very relaxed about his first French show in 14 years and talked happily to a few fans that had managed to sneak into the soundcheck.

He even sat down at the piano and played "Not the One" as a request that afternoon. Peter White's mother, Gilberte, was there to see her son's first show ever in France and RCA gave Al a special celebration dinner afterwards. After the meal Al was out on the streets looking for a cab and not having much luck. So he elected to take some drastic action and was reckless to say the least. He flagged down a passing car, offered them a bundle of money to drive him back to the Paris Hilton and was promptly kidnapped. The

Michel Mazzoleni

Michel Mazzoleni

'Russians And American' European tour, 1984

occupants of the car took his wallet and Al, in desperation, kicked out a window and unlocked the passenger door of the car before running off. He had recovered sufficiently to fly with Peter up to Amsterdam the following afternoon for a gig in Utrecht. Back in London a few days later, Peter was in Soho Studios to work on Matt Bianco tracks with Danny and Basia including the classic "Half A Minute".

Somehow then, Al and Peter had managed to surprise themselves and claw back the bare bones of a live act. After a period in which Peter had begun to question the very logic of them continuing to work together, that short European tour was to herald in a true renaissance of Al as a performing artist.

CASINO YEARS

In which Al forms another band but releases just a couple of studio albums in a decade. His live album, recorded with Peter, is however a classic. Al also marries.

After a period of much uncertainty things seemed to be looking up for Al and Peter. They built upon this in the next few months, having returned to the USA both well satisfied with the European tour. Once again, it seemed that a momentum had been kick-started.

Peter White – "Whenever my mind goes back to that time a smile comes to my face because that was the beginning of it being fun again for me. I felt fully involved with the music again because, quite simply, I was the band. We came up with the figure of $1,000 dollars a week salary for me whilst we were touring and that figure in fact stayed the same for at least the next five years! As soon as we got back from that short European series of gigs in May 1984, Al said that it had been so much fun that we should really do some more, which was something that I naturally enough jumped at."

Suddenly then Al was in need of a band once again. Dave Camp was one of the first to be recruited.

Dave Camp – "Now at this time I got a call from Al's ex-sax player, Kaz Macino. He had an opportunity to go on the road with Sheena Easton and needed someone to cover him for his shows with Al. So when Kaz called I immediately phoned Peter White. I had known Peter from doing sessions for classes at UCLA, where students hired studio

Neville

Warwick University, 1985

bands to play their charts and make demos. That's where Peter met Ken Schmidt too. I have been playing clarinet and flute on those demos, so Peter never knew I played sax, and was surprised when I called. I carried around a tape for a couple of weeks to learn the solos, and then went up to audition for Al. The songs I played were 'Year Of The Cat', 'Time Passages', and 'Running Man'. It was up at Al's house with Peter on the piano. I remember having this uncompromising attitude, thinking I didn't have to impress anybody by dressing up, that how I played should be all that mattered. Well, Al liked my playing, but afterwards he told Peter he wasn't sure if I'd look all right with the band. Peter said, 'Yeah, he'll be fine. I'll take care of it.' So, somewhat more decently attired I went out with them.

"In the first couple of shows I was gratified by standing ovations, but no one told me if I had found a regular place with the band. I knew they were playing a month's tour of the US so I had to go to Peter and ask him if I was coming too. He said, 'Oh yes. Sorry, we didn't tell you!'"

Al had no real management at this time. Peter suggested an associate of his named John Ratz, whom he had met whilst working with local Los Angeles bands over the previous eighteen months, as a suitable candidate for tour manager. One of Ratz' artists at that time was a young guitar player, Steve Rekker, who Ratz volunteered as a van driver, roadie and occasional guitar player and so the duo became a four-piece. It was now the summer of 1984. Dates started coming in thick and fast and one night Peter suggested to Steve Rekker that he join them on stage for a song and gradually he was worked into the band on a full time basis and they turned the next year into a time of playing gigs. Al performed more shows that year than they had in the previous four years added together.

Peter White – "It was great because we were all helping each other out, setting up the stage, tearing it down afterwards and it felt so great to be back doing that again after so long."

These are the times that Al would belatedly come to call the "Casino Years".

The band was augmented further, soon after this, by the return of Steve Chapman who had originally joined to play percussion on just a few dates. At Peter's suggestion he also started playing drums despite his initial worry about this infringing on another role that he had taken on, that of being their tour manager.

Robin Lamble – "Now at this time in 1984 things were not going too well for me to be honest! Then Juice Newton's tour manager, who I knew from way back, called me up and said that she was looking for a tour manager and also a bass player. So I did an audition and eventually got the gig and stayed with her for 18 months, playing big places because she was hot then. We also opened for Alabama on a lot of those dates."

Peter White – "It was now that we started playing Tahoe and Reno. I loved playing those shows – to me it was just like a holiday. In the summer of 1985 I'd moved into Fulcher Avenue and set up a home studio in the garage and Al would come over quite regularly and we would write songs together, which we'd record there and then as demos on an eight-track tape recorder that I'd set up."

Al spoke to Vinyl Exchange in Canada for their June 1985 issue.

Al – "Basically the album was recorded about a year before it was released and the label change required lawyers talking to each other which is never done quickly in America. Lawyers make a $100 to $150 an hour so it is therefore in their interest to discuss anything and everything at lengths normal human beings would find totally impossible to understand, in this case something like a year before they arrive at the self-same conclusion that they would have arrived at in the first afternoon if they'd been in a hurry. So we had to sit around and let these teams of lawyers run up huge sums of money so they could take their sons skiing and buy BMWs, and in the meantime we had this record and it came out about a year behind when it was supposed to. Because it took so long there are two different tracks on the American record. 'The One That Got Away' was replaced on the UK pressing by a song called 'Lori Don't Go Right Now' which is pretty terrible, you don't want to know anything about it. It was something the English record company wanted for a single, and there's a nice folky song called 'The Gypsy And The Rose' in the place of 'Night Meeting', but I must say that the American album is much better than the English one."

He was asked whether he had anything prepared for a follow-up since the album had taken so long to be released.

Al – "No, *Russians And Americans* was a one-off deal. It became obvious that it was not a commercial record and would not be released on a major label so here it is on Passport. And by chance it was the last album I had to make for RCA in England which leaves me totally out of contract at this point in time and I really haven't given the matter much thought."

Al may not have been on the lookout for a new deal but certainly his management were. It was something of a necessity in fact. He himself was pessimistic about getting a deal with a major.

Al – "People in my position such as Richard Thompson who just signed with Polygram, but prior to that had done about ten albums for small labels, plus the McGarrigles and Leonard Cohen and Ralph McTell are finding themselves in the similar position that major labels are now concentrating on heavy metal and dance music. Singer-songwriters are not particularly what they're looking for, so I think if I make another record it would probably be for a small label, but at this point in time I don't know who and I haven't written any of the songs, although I have probably got a whole album's worth of tunes in my head. When I get off this tour I think the first thing I'll do is sit down and try to put some lyrics to them and take it from there."

Al was asked at the time about the low profile of the release of the new album compared to his previous Arista and Janus albums.

Al – "That's because it's on Passport records and they don't have a publicity department. I think people hear by word of mouth, and it has sold reasonably well around the world, so at least it's a better record than the last. So when you look at the career as a whole, I seem to jump from album to album from being or trying to be commercial to being very uncommercial, so it gives a somewhat scattered image. It isn't a consistent image in the way that you can say Richard Thompson is always Richard Thompson. I've been both very poppy and very unpoppy. 'Song On The Radio' and 'Roads To Moscow' have nothing in common with each other."

Steve Chapman was now working harder than ever behind the scenes and Al himself had been reunited with someone from back in the BTM days of the mid 1970's.

Steve Chapman – "Al by now was back with Ian Copeland's Frontier Booking International (FBI) having been with various agents since we had previously worked together. I was initially asked to come on board as tour manager and would play percussion on three or four songs. My role on the British tour in 1985 was one of looking after Al whilst we had Chris Coates as the general tour manager. I would go on to become Al's manager in 1987. Up until then I wasn't involved in Al's personal or legal affairs. The tape of songs we got together featured 'How Does It Happen?', 'In The Dark', 'Where Are They Now', 'Licence To Steal' and 'Electric Air' which had come out of the many sessions in Peter's garage. It was put together in association with Greg Harrison who was Al's attorney at the time and between us we both looked around for labels. Geffen were very interested as well as Enigma. Gary Gersh, who at that time was A&R at Geffen, really liked those demos which I felt were very strong. He was good friends with Joe Chiccarelli and what Gary wanted to do was to get some money together to allow Al to go into the studio with Joe to cut a few tracks in order to gauge just what sort of record they would be able to make as a team. So at this moment in time there was no commitment to a deal but certainly there was a possibility of taking things further. However in the meantime Enigma really were very positive in their desire to get Al to make a record and that was where ultimately Al felt most comfortable in going."

Another abandoned song from this period was "Open Window". It was demoed but remains unreleased.

Meanwhile, the combination of the downward turn that his career had latterly taken and the lack of a consistent and stabilising relationship in his private life resulted in Al suffering a personal crisis that ultimately manifested itself as a severe lack of self-esteem for him. The solitary existence, that was so often his lot at Roscomarre, now provided ample opportunity for him to use alcohol as an escape from whatever demons that passing 40, with his career in the doldrums, had stirred up.

Peter White – "This was a bad time. It really was. Al got into a gin and tonic phase in the mid-'80s at gigs. In fact it may even have been on the rider at the shows! Al would start drinking before the show and then there would be a time towards the end of the show where I'd play a song and when Al returned he'd be much the worse for wear having had a large drink in the dressing room. Once, at a gig in Alberquerque, he lost his way a little during the set. He announced to the audience that we were going to perform 'Café Society' and I was forced to point out to him that in fact we'd just played it."

It would get worse. There was another show around this time in Denver when Al played an open air food festival where he was booked to play two sets. In between them he had been drinking and as a result was almost incoherent.

Peter White – "It was terrible. I was counting off the songs so that he'd stop rambling on to the crowd. After that show in Denver was the only occasion that I ever got really mad with Al. I shouted at him and told him how I'd been embarrassed to be on the same stage as him in that condition and that he'd better shape up or I wouldn't have anything more to do with him. A couple of days later Steve Chapman and I together went up to the house on Roscomarre and confronted him about his drinking. He was very contrite about all of this and ended up saying – 'Well I guess what you're telling me is that the '70s are over!'"

Peter and Steve were by no means the only people who felt concerned for Al during this time.

Al – "Now of course this tends to make me look and sound like a somewhat sad and tragic figure. But in reality this wasn't how I was feeling at all. I think that I was actually feeling quite happy with life, albeit in my own strange kind of way. To me it seemed a very nice life. I would open a bottle of wine and delve into one of my history books and get completely lost for hours on end until I would go to bed at about 4 a.m. Looking back I was completely happy, I really was."

Al spoke about the songs under consideration for the next album to *Chronicles* in early 1988. As usual things were by no means certain, given that the release of the record was still several months away.

Al – "The first song was called 'Mondo Groovo', then 'Electric Air' and now 'Bad Reputation'. Don't count on it ending there either. The better Peter White's basic riffs are, the harder I find it to write words to them. This version is based on the English movie *Mona Lisa* that I saw twice and loved. It'll probably make it on to the album in some shape or form. The bass line reminds me vaguely of the 'Peter Gunn' theme, a fave rave. Next is 'How Does It Happen?' Apparently it doesn't. At least not to most people who've heard it. I think it helps if you were a Jane Wiedlin fan. Next is 'License To Steal'. The USA has 690,000 lawyers and the numbers are growing. It was Charles Dickens I think who said something like, 'They feed human misery, for it feeds them.' *Plus ça change*. Having had dealings with a few rather unsavoury ones, I use this straightforward rocker as a form of therapy. Basically it calls for some form of limited nuclear action against them!"

In fact "License to Steal" was a thinly based satire of Al's own experiences the previous year and the positioning that had happened once Luke had gone. It also became one of the standout songs that he performed live. As did "Josephine Baker".

Al again – "I'm particularly fond of 'Josephine Baker'. I saw her in a PBS documentary on black female entertainers, going back to the turn of the century. Even

Randall Armor

in the company of the other greats, Josephine stole the show the way the Rolling Stones did every time they appeared on *Ready, Steady Go*. I'd like to record this; the verses seem fine, but I haven't got the chorus right yet. Time will tell. Then there's 'Where Are They Now', a song about doomed love and its aftermath set to a string of military metaphors. Sounds fun? Well surprise! This is my personal favourite of the new songs, and will not only be on the next album but I wouldn't do the album without it."

Al made the point in another interview at the time that, when writing the piece, he was thinking about 'my first girlfriend', referring to Mandi and how he could now 'chat quite casually on the phone to that person'. He had in fact been back in touch with Mandi since 1976 and she had accompanied Al on that 1979 Japan tour as his publicist.

In the *Chronicles* interview from 1988 Al expanded on many of the themes that *Last Days Of The Century* had touched on. Whilst sounding very happy with the music, much of it as usual supplied by Peter, he was largely non-committal about the lyrical content.

Al – "Peter White wrote the music, and it has a lovely, lilting, acoustic feel, and some unexpected chord changes. I wish they all came out like this. I think 'In The Dark' should really be called *The Prince And Princess of Wales Visit An Unnamed African Country, While My Love-life Disintegrates!* Charles and Di are in the background on TV while I'm berating some poor female in my living room. All very odd. And even stranger, a country and western chorus slipped in there while I wasn't looking. I was probably out watering the geese!

"'Fields Of France' is a short song about a World War I French pilot, and the girl he never came back to. Interesting tune. I like this one; completely uncommercial and very me (I think). 'Ghostly Horses' is a Steve Rekker guitar piece that I added some words to, rather in the style of 'End Of The Day'. Ostensibly about the Old West in the late 19th century, but it will mean whatever you want it to – some songs just do that."

Al wasn't quite as ambivalent about everything he'd written recently however. It is interesting to note that the song that he was most enthusiastic about was the title with the most obvious historical credentials. He often seemed more comfortable discussing something based on fact that one of his 'made up' songs. This time was no exception.

"'Helen Of Troy' is another new song. It all started with the wedding of Peleus and Thetis, and that nasty golden apple. I can't think why the French named their capital city after Paris. Helen may or may not have existed. Ditto the Wooden Horse. But some of the characters did, which makes it a point where history and mythology collide. In retrospect, I should have written about Cassandra; much more interesting. Maybe next time. Then there's 'Last Days Of The Century'. A galloping Peter White bass riff, and a zoomy Al Stewart chorus. What else could you ask for? Words? Ah, yes, well … let's call this a work in progress. The music

At home, Bel Air, July 1988

sounds wonderful – let's hope inspiration strikes and produces the right lyrics. 'Night Rolls In' is another new song. I know this is good because a music biz lawyer called it boring. Slow, melodic and moody; Peter White likes this best of the songs that are purely written by me. So do I. It sounds like it should be the last track on side one. 'Mixed Blessing' is the last one. I don't suppose this jazzy little piece will see the light of day."

It did. The song went on to surface on the rarities CD *Seemed Like A Good Idea At The Time* a decade later.

In the spring of 1988 Al met the woman he would eventually marry.

Al – "Kris and I met at one of my shows in Reno, Nevada and started living together at this time. I was 42 by then which is of course the meaning of *Life The Universe And Everything*! Up until that point I had had four major relationships, none of which had quite lasted three years. However with Kris, things just seemed to get better and better and a couple of years later we decided that this was it and we would get married."

In June of 1988, when he and Kris had been seeing each other for a few months, Al spoke about performing old songs on stage – "Some of them have got far enough away so that I may look back and think that while the recordings were genuinely dreadful, maybe they can be done better now. I don't want to start something off here, but the song

'Last Days Of The Century', first USA gig, July 1988

that's been banging around in my mind, the one that I think would make a tremendous sort of full-tilt folk-rock bang-blast number is, of all things, 'Gethsemane Again'.

"Just the other day I was imagining it in a setting of organ, drums and bass, hammering away, in a big folk-rock thing. There are no immediate plans to go back and record any that way, but it's quite possible that I may dig some of the stuff out and learn it with the band. Gradually we've been lengthening the list of songs we do; we're up to 46 or something, from about 15 when we put the band together, so there's no reason to go back and explore some of those. I have done 'You Should Have Listened To Al' and 'Bedsitter Images' so something might come up."

In July, 1988 Al had released *Last Days Of The Century* on Enigma. For the title track he had eventually drawn on the themes of Barbara Tuchman's *A Distant Mirror: The Calamitous 14th Century*. Choosing, as usual, to take an elliptical viewpoint on things he had disposed of almost all reference to *A Distant Mirror* by the time he finalised the lyrics to the album's title track.

Al – "Great book, great book. It really got me thinking although it was more the spirit of the narrative than anything else that informed the song. Like many of the things that I've written I guess ..."

In the book Tuchman writes with a sweeping narrative of the cataclysmic 14th century, when the energies of medieval Europe were devoted to fighting internecine wars and warding off the Plague. Whilst there were those thinkers of that age that chose to interpret those disasters as simply divine punishment for mortal wrongs, others elected to view them as God-given portals to the realms of the fiscal riches that they could otherwise only dream of. It is one of these, the French nobleman Enguerrand de Courcy that features prominently throughout Tuchman's opus. She takes the spellbound reader through the Hundred Years War, the collapse of the medieval church and a litany of like minded events that had Al hooked when he read the re-issue of *A Distant Mirror* in LA in the Autumn of 1987.

The album featured the last song that Al wrote about Mandi; "Where are they Now?".

WHERE ARE THEY NOW?

I sent my crack divisions through the early morning mist
When they fell on your positions you were powerless to resist
Encircling and probing for the weakness in your line
By night you were surrounded; your territory mine
I called for your surrender; this you swore you would not do
So I stormed the very fortress you thought could shelter you
I held you then upon your knees and turned to give my thanks
To the regiments assembled in their ranks
Where are they now?
Where are they now?
I raised you to your feet, with your hand inside my own
We set off upon a journey, each together, each alone
In the days that followed, oh, our lives did overlap
I learned the contours of your body like the roads upon a map
You sweetened every evening, I savoured every day
Just when I was certain it would always be this way
You slipped beyond the reach of my outstretched fingertips
With all the kisses we'd placed upon your lips

Where are they now?
Where are they now?

Oh, close. You're close
Someone, come shine a light
Oh, near. So near
But just out of sight

I went in search of alchemy to resurrect the dead
Sent my spies to fathom out the secrets in your head
They said they heard your laughter
Spinning through the summer night
In the company of strangers
And your eyes were wild and bright
Though I grew reclusive and my days became withdrawn
I held the banner of our love, now tattered and forlorn
And swore that it would one day fly above us once again
To do this, I had my reasons then

Where are they now?
Where are they now?

Close. You're close
Once again, come shine a light
Oh near. So near
But just out of sight

Perhaps there are some passions that are tempered by the years
You reach accommodation, the intensity recedes
Some of this occurred to me the time I saw you last
Your face familiar in a way. Your voice out of the past
Every gamut of emotion shared from tenderness to rage
Fell away between us in the turning of that page
It seemed like only yesterday we swore that we'd be true
Two innocents believing that they knew

Where are they now?
Where are they now?

Neville

Last ever band photo shoot, Hollywood 1988

Al next gave his fans an insight into the new album *Last Days Of The Century* through an interview with David Dasch. In the eight months since his last interview with *The Chronicles*, the album had been completed and his thoughts on many of the songs had changed completely.

Al – "The title track was, as a lot of these things are, a Peter White riff. He tends to give me these cassettes with nine or whatever different tunes on them. Something like that will jump out at me. It was very slow when I first heard it, and I thought we should speed it up. The middle eight was mine, so it was one of those things in which Peter

Neville

Steve Chapman, 1988

wrote a chunk and I wrote a chunk. As to what it's about – only two people of all those who have heard it have even asked me what it's about. My mother asked me about what was shining down, and I said it's a spaceship landing or nuclear annihilation or the Age of Enlightenment. She liked the Age of Enlightenment. It's one of those things like 'Year Of The Cat' for which, if asked for 100 different explanations, I'll give 100 different answers – it sings very easily, with words like 'Chinatown'. There were lots of other lyrics to it. I had one line that I liked that went 'The sun sits unblinking as a Pharaoh', but the Pharaoh disappeared. I had a whole pile of different verses.

"I took out the line 'You like late shows, old movie stars and Dutch beer' and turned it into 'I still get the shakes when you get this near' because it seemed too specific. The rest of the lyrics weren't as focused as that. It was either that, or Chiccarelli said it didn't sing very well, or maybe both."

"Real And Unreal" had taken a long time to write and even longer to record. Like many of Al's songs it owed a debt to the '60s, something that he conceded in the interview.

Al – "With the track 'Real And Unreal', we have something that reminds me of 'For The Benefit Of Mr Kite', especially if you take away the New Orleans trumpet. It's sort of The Beatles visiting New Orleans, the best of two worlds, to me, and is one of my favourite tracks on the album. It's probably the best-produced track on the record. Lyrically, that part where she's walking downtown and you have all those images, the umbrella and so forth, that seems to recall something of the flavour of 'Good Morning, Good Morning'. In fact, I had an image of John Lennon singing 'She's just an ordinary girl'.

"'The King Of Portugal' was the last tune that Peter wrote, we were already in the studio a long time. I didn't have any lyrics whatsoever, I liked the tune, and Vinnie Colaiuta was the perfect drummer to do that sort of rhythm – so we thought we'd just put down a backing track and see. I found the riff to be hypnotic, I like the chord progression, and I'd never done anything in that tempo."

One of the quickest sets of lyrics written for the new album had been for "Red Toupée". It would go on to become one of Al's most popular songs in concert and its genesis was, once again, a session at Peter's garage studio in North Hollywood.

Al – "I was round at Peter White's demo studio and he had this really catchy riff. He doesn't write many in major keys so I thought we better grab this. As he was mumbling something about what the tune was called, an aeroplane flew by, and I thought what he said was 'Red Toupée'. I told him to put a backing track down and in the three minutes it took him, I wrote most of these lyrics. Sometimes I write lyrics very quickly, making them up as I go along, just so I don't lose the tune. I was rhyming the first things that came into my mind, so I wasn't being whimsical. I have no idea where the fishing boat came from. We played the demo to Chiccarelli and he loved it. I told him I'd go write the lyrics and he said something like 'What are you talking about? These *are* the lyrics.' He insisted 'I love it, I love it!' I had wanted to call it 'Pink Café'. I like the idea of using the girls and Robin Lamble to echo me. I had to make up a story as to what it was about. I decided it took place in the year 2005 and Henry Cisneros, now the mayor of San Antonio, is then the President. The ozone has got markedly worse and everyone's hair has fallen out, which gives way to a fashion fad for brightly coloured toupées. Everyone has them in different colours, this character happens to be wearing his red one. Another consequence of the greenhouse effect is that the jellyfish on the West Coast of America have grown to about 600 yards across, and they eat everything that's put out to sea, including atomic submarines. So it's an act of great bravery to set off in a fishing boat for Catalina Island.

"The guy falls through a time warp back into 1988 and arrives in his red toupée, which becomes a shock to all these people with hair. For the first time in his life he's actually ahead of his time – by an entire generation. It made him feel important so he went around doing cartwheels in shopping malls. This is the story I made out of the song, after writing the song. Also appearing at the very end is my buzzword for the album – I always try to fit a buzzword onto every album – which was 'cormorant'. I had written it into 'Don't Panic' in one of the sets of lyrics I didn't use. We were coming down to the wire and still no cormorant, so I thought I'd have one just fly by. But the moment of pure magic in that song, which wasn't planned, came when I was laying down my vocal after the background vocals had already been done. I said 'A cormorant flew by' and it just happened that it sounds as if the background voices complete the sentence by singing 'In a red toupée'."

And so it is clear from this that Al's rare talent for the surreal had not deserted him through those uncertain mid-80's years. The involvement on the album of Tori Amos, then largely unknown, made its recording all the more memorable for some of those involved.

Robin Lamble – "I would agree that the vocals were pretty interesting on *Last Days Of The Century*. Tori and I shared a microphone on 'Red Toupée' to do harmony vocals. Now when she sang she was very, very intense with full on eye contact all of the time."

Al had met Tori Amos through the producer of *Last Days Of The Century*, Joe Chiccarelli, who had produced her first album called *Why Kan't Tori Read?*

Al – "She was doing a vocal and we went into this room and at this moment in time I had no idea that she could play the piano and she just sat down and proceeded to play in the most amazing way. I was completely astounded because I'd genuinely never heard anyone play like that before or since! I said to her 'This is quite wonderful. You should write me a song.' That's exactly what she did too a little while later."

The song that Tori eventually delivered to Al became "Charlotte Corday". It would go on to be included on *Famous Last Words*.

It was by no means plain sailing all the way during the recording of the album however. There was a personality clash every bit as disruptive as the one between Peter White and Peter Wood during the recording of *Year Of The Cat* over a decade earlier.

Peter White – "During the making of *Last Days of the Century* Al and Joe Chiccarelli had such a bad falling out that they wouldn't be in the studio at the same time! For a while I had to keep the peace. Whenever Al came in Joe would leave and I'd continue working with Al and then when Al left Joe would come back! If you think that I had a problem with Joe then Al had a far worse one and vowed never to work with him again!"

Al – "I will say that recording *Last Days Of The Century* was most certainly not one of the most enjoyable times of my life. There was a great deal of conflict and yes, it did get in the way of things for a while. We all seemed to be under a lot of pressure but that wasn't new and so I guess it was just down to the usual clash of personalities. Ultimately I think that we made quite a good record though."

Indeed this was very much a watershed album for Peter White.

Peter White – "That album was completely different from how I'd thought it would be and how I'd intended it to go. It was a lot different. Much of it I really liked but there was also much of it that I didn't care for. By the time the album was recorded and released I'd managed to emotionally distance myself from it to the point where I decided that it was Al's record and Joe Chiccarelli's production and that's obviously what they wanted it to sound like and so be it. It was a huge disappointment to me because ever since 1984, when *Russians And Americans* was released, I'd spent a lot of time and effort writing and arranging songs in a form that allowed them to be presented to a record company and after all those were the songs that did get him the deal with Enigma. Songs like 'Electric Air' for instance were, in my opinion, far superior to what they turned into ultimately on *Last Days Of The Century*."

Peter was to use this bad experience to his advantage eventually however. In many ways he had been restricted in his musical development by the schedule that Al worked to and he now set about making some changes.

Peter – "By the time all that was over I'd learnt a big lesson which was that I was really just a sideman and if I ever wanted to be more than that then I was going to have to make my own album my own way. By this time *The Wave* had started up as a radio station and I was introduced to all of this acoustic music, including Acoustic Alchemy, and I realised that that was exactly the sort of thing that I should be doing and so I gradually started working towards doing an album of my own. Up until this time almost every song I'd written in my home studio had been composed with Al in mind because it had never occurred to me that there would be a market for instrumental music. I had written songs with Amber Delano and through that expanded my horizon, but it wasn't until 1988 that I made the break and concentrated on my own project. Even though I was still playing with Al and enjoyed playing with Al I realised that I had to do something for myself. There could easily have been another period of three or four years when Al wasn't working. What was I to do? I'd seen the writing on the wall."

Much of the summer of 1988 was taken up by the band touring the US, where they played a series of festivals, followed by gigs in Britain. The three week British tour that started in October included gigs in Cambridge, Glasgow, Reading and Kentish Town in London where Al played at The Town and Country Club on November 5th. He also appeared on the BBC where they broadcast a recording of Al and Peter performing "Antarctica" at a London Dominion sound check.

In 1989 Al was thinking forward to the next album and trying to come up with a theme for it. At this stage no one realised that it would be another four years before the record would come out. The imminent demise of their record company Enigma was not apparent to Al or Steve Chapman. The idea for the next album that Al liked the best was to explore the theme of 20th century women and to this end came up with a title, *It Must Be Love*, but no songs were ever demoed for this purpose. There was also the intention, again fated never to come to fruition, of putting out a retrospective box set on Enigma.

Speaking at the time this is what Al had to say – "This is the year when my old records revert to me. We're in negotiations as to where they will go. If they wind up on Enigma we might see a special Al Stewart boxed set collection, with some rarities, hits, maybe things like 'Willie The King'."

The same situation applied to Europe where RCA were at this time coming to the end of their ownership of Al's masters. The album *Russians And Americans* wasn't a part of all of this though, a situation that would lead to Al commenting wryly, "No-one knows who owns that album!"

Seeking to clarify all of this he continued – "*Bedsitter Images, Love Chronicles* and *Zero She Flies* were bought up by RCA from CBS so that covers that. *Past Present And Future, Modern Times* and *Year Of The Cat* went through Janus in the US and that all went to Arista. What happened here, you will be quick to note, is that *Orange* slipped through the net, so at the moment we're not sure what will happen to *Orange*. It's all being sorted out."

That first album of the Enigma deal would ultimately turn out to be Al's solitary release for the label. On this occasion though it was due to reasons that were all well beyond his control.

Steve Chapman – "Enigma was basically Bill and Wesley Hine and Bill especially was a long-term Al Stewart fan. Enigma had a distribution deal with Capitol/EMI and part of that deal was that Capitol was able to cherry-pick one or two acts a year and one of these was Poison. Following hard on the heels of Poison was the hard rock band Stryper and around about this time they found themselves in a position to make Al such a good offer – it was a five album deal. *Last Days Of The Century* came out in August 1988. However Enigma eventually over-extended themselves and it all came tumbling down a couple of years later and this was our only album with them in the end."

Meanwhile Al was accumulating songs, not all of them his own.

The tape of demos that Tori Amos eventually delivered to Al had included three other songs besides "Charlotte Corday". Interestingly none of these were ever released as a finished composition by either of them. They were "Ten Cents", "Dreaming" and "Ballad Number 2".

Al's memories of Kris and him entertaining Tori up at their house in Bel Air are vivid.

Al – "These were highly charged evenings! Tori would come up to our house and go over to the piano, where she would perform entire mini-concerts on the spot for Kris and I. These performances were theatrical in that Tori poured her heart into the songs she was playing, even though it was just Kris and I sitting there in front of her in the house. It would be just the three of us."

Here is the original set of lyrics that Al wrote for his guide vocal to Tori's tune, "Charlotte Corday".

Look out for the dangers on the road tonight
Look out while you're waiting at the traffic light
Driving through the slanting rain don't change your point of view
Things will trickle through your brain, they're so brand new
Just like Charlotte Corday
I can see you there behind the driving wheel
With your absent mind and with those nerves of steel
Skidding round a corner do you stop to think you're way
Is there anything to say today
Just like Charlotte Corday
Stars in the window see them shining bright
Anywhere everywhere what do I know
Stars in the window see them shining for anyone else anyone else
You can find a lost and found well out amongst the grey
You can look to see yourself then slip away
Just like Charlotte Corday
Stars in the window see them shining bright
Anywhere everywhere what do you know
Stars in the window see them shining for anyone else anyone else
Be sure there's danger on the road tonight
So keep a watch when you are at the traffic light
Driving through the slanting rain you may just slip away
Keep your hand upon the rain, that's all I'll say
Fading to grey
Things you never could say
You let them all slip away
They'll be back some day
Just like Charlotte Corday

This then presents us with a very different song from the one to grace *Famous Last Words* two and a half years later. In many ways it's a formula Al song, the sort of lyric that he could knock off in his sleep and in this demo form it provides little more than novelty value to the more completist Al fans. Its dark meandering narrative has parallels with "Warm Californian Night" and "Timeless Skies". All of these original demos have almost stream-of-consciousness lyrics about LA, but by the finished song we're in Europe with a completely new set of characters. Al would eventually lift a verse from one of his earlier songs, "In The Dark", to complete the much revised version of "Charlotte Corday" that would go on to appear on *Famous Last Words*.

At the same time as "Charlotte Corday" was demoed, Al recorded another Peter White tune. This became "4 Of A Kind". It was one of his black humour, surreal songs similar in some ways to "Necromancer" and "Real And Unreal". The lyric ushers in musings on Eastern Europe and Orson Welles, ending with a "Strawberry Fields Forever"-style meeting with a gnome. It is ironic, in the style of "Red Toupée" and the never to be demoed "Life After Death".

LIFE AFTER DEATH
The rockets came down with a hell of a bang
Vaporised my torso
It was like fireworks only more so
The men from space took away my remains
Far beyond the solar system
I was in no shape to resist them
They placed my parts in a vacuum jar
I must confess it was fine.
They fed warm tea to the bits of me
Freeze dried, powdered wine.
I found my world in a blown up girl
Our atoms gently mingle
When we rub them close, they tingle

Al flew to England in the summer of 1989 for the Cambridge Folk Festival. On the warm up dates, with the regular band at Worthing and Cardiff, he premiered a couple of old songs that he'd re-learnt especially for the tour. He performed a wonderful and exuberant "In Brooklyn" at the Worthing show and then at St David's Hall in Cardiff he sang "Manuscript", playing acoustic guitar backed by Peter on keyboards. He hadn't performed that since 1973. Playing sets at Cambridge on the Saturday night and Sunday afternoon he totally mesmerised the crowd with a set that included "Nostradamus", "Sand In Your Shoes" and "Roads To Moscow". Roy Harper was in the wings watching every note of the Sunday show, after which Ralph McTell got together with Al in his trailer to shoot footage for a documentary of his that was never released. Together they sang a song, written by Ralph about Alex Campbell, one of their contemporaries, who had recently died.

In the early Autumn Al and Peter were going through a particularly productive period centred on Peter's garage studio in North Hollywood. On October 16th 1989 they recorded a stripped-down and staggeringly elegant demo version of "Coldest Winter" there.

However things at Enigma had not been going well that year.

Steve Chapman – "Not well at all! Early in 1989 Enigma had gone into a joint venture with Capitol/EMI whereby Capitol/EMI bought half of Enigma. At this time Enigma really beefed up their staff, bringing in a new general manager, new head of marketing and a new head of promotions too – a very experienced team that had been around a long time. So they moved to a big new building and started signing acts like Devo and David Cassidy. However none of the product that they released really took off and the upshot of this was that after about a year things certainly began to get a little tight at Enigma financially. At this time Al started to record again with Joe Chiccarelli in spite of his vow never to work with the producer again, and although he didn't have an album's worth of songs, we figured that it would be a good idea to go in and record what we had. The idea was that once we'd recorded about half an album's worth of material we'd take a break and Al would go back and write the other songs. At this time we were also hooking Al up with various other writing partners."

The lost demos from the Joe Chiccarelli sessions for what was intended to have been the second album for Enigma had included "Don't Forget Me", "Necromancer", "Coldest Winter In Memory" and "Charlotte Corday". It was felt that Al needed to keep

Al and Kris in Dorset twenty five years after Al left there for London

the momentum going with his recording hence him going back into the studio in 1989.

A few months later Al told *Chronicles* the results of the negotiations over his back catalogue.

Al – "We just gave Arista a five year extension, so everything they used to own they still own, which as far as I know is everything for America. I doubt whether they have plans to put out anything apart from the CDs of *Year Of The Cat*, *Time Passages* and *The Best Of* which are currently out. They have 1,200 CDs of *Past Present And Future* and asked if we wanted them. They were zoning it out. The status of that is unknown."

EMI had won the race for the English rights, bidding far in excess of the other companies that were in the frame and eventually putting out *Bedsitter Images*, *Love Chronicles* and *Zero She Flies* as the 1993 double retrospective *To Whom It May Concern*.

Through all of this Peter had continued to give the idea of his own solo career serious consideration. During the making of *Last Days Of The Century* Steve Chapman had suggested to Peter that he made an album and also offered to be his manager. Peter had made a demo tape of three songs – "Romance Dance", "Moonlight Montreal" and "Danny Bianco" which Peter and Steve took around to various record companies without any real success. A worrying state of affairs that continued into 1990 until Cliff Goroff, who Peter had met through Basia, offered to make some introductions on Peter's behalf and put him together with Chase Music – a small label operating out of Glendale and immediately it came out Peter was touring with Basia, during whose set he had a solo spot each night playing "If Only For You."

One novel idea for a song that was now discussed was the possible updating of "Year Of The Cat: and for that express purpose Al turned to the person that he had co-written it with, Peter Wood.

Steve Chapman – "Back at the time of the work for the never-to-be-released second album on Enigma, Al and Peter Wood came up with "Katu", as in *Cat 2* , but that song was never really completed and just existed as a rough backing track. It was similar to *Year Of The Cat*, in that it was a piano-based song split into distinct sections, and ultimately the idea had been to add a saxophone to it. There were a couple of sets of lyrics written by Al but he never came up with anything he was happy with."

Still on Enigma, Al continued to write songs at home in Bel Air whilst 30 minutes across town in North Hollywood Peter would be doing just the same in the garage studio beside his house. And that's exactly what it was. For many years Peter had no choice but to park his car at the front of his house as inside the garage a home studio with all of his guitars and keyboards took shape. New songs being worked on at this time were "She Follows Her Own Rules" and "Betty Boop" (not to be confused with the track with a similar name on *Between The Wars*), both of which were Peter's songs whilst Al had "Thinking Of Her", "Dark Side", "Kiribati", "Life After Death", "Choose The Moment" and a country and western parody called "Remove Your Footwear".

Two other songs, written and demoed by Al and Peter at the same time as "Necromancer" were "Fantasy" and "She Told You Then"; neither of these making either *Famous Last Words* or any future Al album. Although the lyrics in both pieces were honed only up to this demo level both songs had developed their own individual personalities and in that sense were complete opposites. "Fantasy", whilst not remotely encroaching on the boundaries of plagiarism is very similar both in music and lyrics to Queen's "I'm Going Slightly Mad". One of Al's wistful and dreamy songs, it would have been far more suited to *Russians And Americans* than *Famous Last Words* and would have acted as a bridge between "Pandora" from 1981 and 1988's "Red Toupée". "She Told You Then" relates one of Al's *end of an affair* compositions that like "Fantasy" continued a theme, the continuum comprising of such songs as "The News From Spain", "Rocks In The Ocean" and "Lori, Don't Go Right Now". Its brooding narrator, mulling over the break-up of what was clearly a difficult relationship, manages to sound both menacing and helpless at the same time. The song echoes "Mixed

Blessing" in its atmospheric production and very definitely "Café Society" in its band arrangements.

DARK SIDE

Lately I'm becoming aware of your dark side
The private demons hiding there in your dark side
Your mood swings and you rush to turn them loose
But you hurt yourself more than anyone else
With your dark side

There's a promise lost behind your dark side
And a secret no one wants to find in your dark side
Why try to drive the world away
'Cos you can't give and the world can't live
With your dark side

I know that you say to yourself
"This is time to be changing"
Ah but there is no easy way, oh no
There's a pattern here that's plain to see in your dark side
Repeats itself endlessly in your dark side

Your mood swings and you rush to turn them loose
But you hurt yourself more than anyone else
With your dark side
Your dark side

KIRIBATI

There's a place I know in the southern ocean
Where we both could go if we had the notion
You could hold a pearl white shell in your hand
You could dip your toes in silvery sand
Out in Kiribati would you like to party?
Out in Kiribati the living is slow
Maybe we'll never go home

Oh the sun shines bright and the days grow longer
You would feel all right like the Queen of Tonga
You could see the coral out in the blue
You won't have to take your socks or your shoes
To Kiribati would you like to party?
Out in Kiribati the living is slow
Maybe we'll never go home

You can hold that pearl white shell in your hand
While you dip your toes in silvery sand
Out in Kiribati would you like to party
Out in Kiribati where living is slow
Maybe we'll never go home
Stay in Kiribati
Out in Kiribati the living is slow
Maybe you'll never go home

None of these pieces ever made an album due to the collapse of Enigma, which meant that Al never got to go into the studio with the songs. They were very nearly recorded however. A date, July 29th 1990, had been booked for rehearsals to start and it was everyone's intention to go into the studio in early August.

Now something happened that caught Peter very much by surprise.

Peter White – "Al called and said that Peter Wood really wanted me to play guitar on a song. I was really surprised because the only time we'd played together since the early '70s was whilst we were making *Last Days Of The Century* and even then we had only spoken briefly to one another. But for this recording, a hip-hop version of "Soho", I actually went to his apartment in New York for the session and I remember that it kind of broke the ice. Peter shook my hand and thanked me very much for doing it which was very nice because it meant that we were friends again after so long. He was later to play on *Famous Last Words* which was the last time I saw him."

Throughout this time Al had been writing with other people besides Peter White and Tori Amos. With Jim Creegan (who had been in Family, Cockney Rebel and Rod Stewart's band) he'd recently completed "Another Lonely Night", he had written a set of lyrics to an Essra Mohawk riff which he'd been sent and had also half completed the words to an Andrew Gold tune. Along with Peter Wood he'd completed "Sailing Into The Future" and "Japanese Garden" and with Peter White had worked on "Beat Of The World" and "I Told You So". He was clearly searching for inspiration and finding things very difficult at the same time.

With those songs alone there was enough material for an album but none of them were ever released in any official form. "Night Rolls In" and "Necromancer", both still several years away from their release on 1993's *Famous Last Words*, had also each been finished as compositions by this time, the summer of 1990. Al now worked briefly with Windows, recording both "French Laundry" and "Blue September", performing the latter just once, in the late summer, at one of their shows.

Al – "'Blue September' was a Skipper Wise tune to which I elected to write some somewhat obscure lyrics. It's about the mass migration of much of the East German population through Czechoslovakia and Austria into West Germany at a time when it was obvious to me that Honecker was losing control and slipping into unreality. In the song I was trying to get inside his head and to imagine what he was thinking and as all of this was going on. I called it 'Blue September', because that's *exactly* what it had become for him."

This next song was one of those co-written by Al and Tori Amos. Tori was still a year away from re-locating to West London and the writing of "Little Earthquakes" when she gave a number of tunes to Al for him to cast his eyes over in the summer of 1990. It was recorded for possible inclusion on what would have been Al's second CD for Enigma and so never made it onto an official release.

TEN CENTS

Like an echo in a
Like an echo in a well
When rain is falling
Like the ocean in a
Like the ocean in a shell
You hear her calling

You can't say she didn't
You can't say she didn't try
Oh she did you know she did
But now she's gone you don't know why
Now she's gone you don't know why
Don't know why
Don't know why
Don't know why
You can't hold on to tomorrow, she won't hold on to today
She'll be a hard act to follow, 10 cents and she's on her way
On her way

Like the ghost of summer
Like the ghost of summer flies
From false embraces
So you know there'll come a
So you know where'll come a time
She'll leave no traces
Free and easy is her
Free and easy is her way
Oh it is you know it is
Well you will ask but she won't
You will ask but she won't say
She won't say
She won't say
She won't say

You can't hold on to tomorrow, She won't hold on to today
She'll be a hard act to follow, 10 cents and she's on her way
Don't know why
Don't know why
Don't know why
Don't know why

She can't hold on to tomorrow, You won't hold on to today
She'll be a hard act to follow, 10 cents and she's on her way
You can't hold on to tomorrow, She won't hold on to today
She'll be a hard act to follow, 10 cents and she's on her way
She'll be a hard act to follow
10 cents and she's on her way
On her way
10 cents and she's on her way
10 cents and she's on her way

Another song that Al had now been working on for a couple of years was "The Coldest Winter In Memory". Based in part on a book about Dunwich, the small East Anglian port that fell into the sea in 1709, it also deals with the decision of Charles XII of Sweden to invade Russia at a time when the sea had actually frozen off the coast of France. Performed live at Santa Cruz previously it had been subjected to several re-writes caused by the song getting "melodramatic" in Al's words. The final version is a fantastic song that ultimately turned up on *Seemed Like A Good Idea At The Time* six years later.

Al – "'Coldest Winter' is a song that I am very pleased with but at the time it was written and recorded it got somewhat overlooked. This was for two reasons. Firstly, we didn't get to release a second album on Enigma, which is where it would have appeared and also because to perform it live it really needed an electric guitar and Peter and I were an acoustic duo!"

The list of songs that Al had collected and in many cases demoed for his next album had by this time reached over 30. But when it comes to writing songs with other people nothing is ever easy. Enter Michelle Shocked.

Al – "There's another lost song from this time. During the last days of Enigma Michelle Shocked played me a song that I thought was really good. After three months I'd written a set of lyrics and went into the studio with Peter White. I kept the title 'No Sign of Rain'. We duly sent her the demo, thinking she'd think it was good. Immediately a panic ensued. Her manager came on the line to Steve Chapman and said 'We've got a problem here! We didn't hear from you and Michelle has done her version of it and she wants to record it for her next album.' So I couldn't use it!"

Michelle Shocked included a version of "No Sign of Rain" on her 1996 album *Kind Hearted Woman*. The last track on that album, it featured largely different lyrics to the original.

Neville

Michael Fagrey, Steve Chapman and Harry Morton

In the April 23rd 1991 issue of the *London Evening Standard* Al contributed this short and ironic article on the ideal qualities a desert island should offer up should he ever become shipwrecked. It's difficult to discern fact from fiction in what Al relates abut it certainly all makes for an entertaining read. "Should my island benefit from volcanic springs it will remind me of the time a San Diego multi-millionaire invited me to dinner at his home – it had more marble than all of Italy. We drank nine different vintages of Montrachet from crystal goblets and ate off gold plates. After dinner our host invited us all to play naked games in his Jacuzzi. I politely declined and asked for a glass of brandy. In these incredible surroundings he gave me a bottle of cheap Greek liqueur and a plastic cup. My host had totally forgotten to cater for more conventional after-dinner enjoyment.

"However judging by the shrieks from the Jacuzzi the other guests were enjoying the balmy Californian evening. My passion for fine wine started in the early '70s. At the time I had just finished three albums for CBS, which gave me a £10,000 advance to work on another three; before or since I have never had so much immediate money. With the CBS proceeds I bought a house, a Ferrari and lots and lots of wine. In 1977 I signed to Arista Records and in my contract I negotiated that I should receive three cases of wine as a bonus. Arista thought this would cost $300 but I had asked for 1961 Chateau Petrus, 1966 La Tache and 1961 Château Palmer. It ended up costing Arista $7,500 and I still have one bottle of the Petrus left. The collection has now grown to more than 2,500 bottles, which I keep in my Los Angeles home. Most good restaurants in LA will let you bring your own wine and I always decant mine at home. I give some to the maître d' and the chef and the food and service usually improve dramatically. One special night four of us were sharing a magnum of Chateau Cheval Blanc 1961 – a definite favourite – and I dispatched a glass to the kitchen. This is a wine guaranteed to brighten any meal, but my steak that night was something special. And what did the chef think of the wine? Nothing, as it turned out; he wasn't drinking that night. But it seemed a shame to waste it so he had cooked my steak in it."

Al concluded his confessional about his more extreme dining experiences with this report of a wine tasting he had once attended that took a bizarre turn.

"A few years ago I attended a wine tasting in San Francisco of every Chateau Mouton Rothschild vintage from 1945 to 1977. Faced with the prospect of drinking so much wine we sat down to a dinner prepared by a former chef to the Kennedy family. The start was a dish of pigeon's entrails followed by casserole of sea urchins – totally inedible – and we were all getting slowly inebriated! I told the waiter that I belonged to a special religious sect and would only eat bread and cheese. In the end we all feasted on Camembert and Brie, washed down by the greatest wines of the century. As I can't count on having a decent chef on the island, I hope to have at least a case or two of Mouton Rothschild 1945, which should render even the most mundane meal of coconut and breadfruit palatable."

Now in the late spring of 1991 Al undertook a major British tour and for the first time since 1973 it was solo. With ex-Fairport and Plainsong singer-songwriter Ian Matthews opening for him, they travelled the length of England playing shows at venues including Glasgow, Wolverhampton, Hereford, Poole, Leeds, Norwich, Newcastle, Hayes and London's Mean Fiddler. On the way down to Hereford and afternoon tea with his Aunt Hazel one Sunday afternoon he finished off "Rest In Peace" in the back of the car and it joined the other new songs, namely "Angel Of Mercy" and "Trains" on the set list. Isaac Guillory came by and played at the Newcastle show and then came London's Royal Festival Hall and the appearance of Tori Amos with Al. Tori had been sent over to London by her record company to seek inspiration and to write some new songs. Al and Kris knew this of course, and got in touch with her at her flat in London's Brompton Road. So whilst Al was away on the tour, Kris and Tori spent time together and Tori agreed to sing and play piano for Al at the Royal Festival Hall show. After an hour's rehearsal in a side room at the auditorium Tori was ready and came on for a slightly slower than usual version of "Year Of The Cat". After the show there was a backstage party where apart from Al's parents, Jonny and Abi, Harry and Carol and Bena, were Tori's very proud mother and father – there to see their daughter's first ever appearance on stage outside of America. Al used a pseudonym for Tori when introducing her as, strictly speaking, her visa precluded

Randall Armor

her from performing in public and so for one night only she became a Russian Princess! She had little idea just how successful she would shortly become when she told me that night – "Well I'm up there in my little London flat working away at writing my songs. This is just so great that I'm playing somewhere like this and it was very nice of Al to ask me. As you saw we've only had a short rehearsal backstage but I think it's going to be all right. 'Year Of The Cat' is such an unusual song, I hope that I do OK!"

The tour also threw up an interesting nod of recognition by Al back to those nonsense poems in the Wycliffe School exercise books exactly 30 years previously. On an almost nightly basis he would walk back onto the stage for the encore with a small sheaf of papers in his hands and read a poem. There were four that he read at various times on the tour, all of them blending an eclectic take on history with Al/Lear/Vonnegut whimsy. One of these was about a chance meeting between *Sadducee and Pharisee Beside the Sea of Galilee* and they were uniformly well received.

At the end of the tour Al and Kris got married in the ancient parish church at Chalbury. They had a traditional service in front of about 70 close friends and family followed by a reception in the local village hall, at the end of the lane that ran past both Al's parents' house and the church itself. Guests included both sets of parents, Al's Aunt Hazel, Jonny, Abi, their son Daniel, Monty Kremer and his wife Blanche, Jerry Trehayne, Harry and Carol, Tori Amos and Robert Fripp.

Meanwhile back in California, Peter had been able to concentrate exclusively on his own projects for the past six weeks.

Peter White – "And through all this time I was busy working on my second album and was very excited about it. It was as if I'd discovered this whole new life."

Peter was still happy enough to work with Al if he was free. In July they toured Japan, playing Tokyo, Osaka, Kyoto and Yokohama, with Michael Fagrey acting as tour manager and also recording each show onto DAT for a possible live album.

Steve Chapman – "It was just too cumbersome to take all of the recording equipment to Japan and so the one track on *Rhymes In Rooms* that originated from there was simply recorded live straight onto the DAT. *Rhymes In Rooms* was funded by EMI UK who then

Al and Kris at their Wedding Reception, 1991

*Joan and Basil at home on the morning
of Al's Wedding, 1991*

*Al and Robert Fripp
at the Wedding, 1991*

Al, Jonny and Jerry at Al's Wedding, Dorset 1991

owned the rights for the album for the world excluding North America. We then did a deal with the label Mesa Blue Moon for the States on which we got a cash advance. With an artist as established as Al he has to march to his own drum and my role with him is that when he wants to do something then I put the elements in place to enable it to happen. I certainly can't get Al to do anything he doesn't want to. By the time of the making of *Rhymes In Rooms* it had become clear that Peter had established his own career and wouldn't be with Al for the rest of his life. There was such a dynamic between the two of them on stage and that album was a way of documenting it. I always felt that it was a very cool record and it ultimately became an unplugged greatest hits album."

The album was well received and would go on to sell very well. The conclusion of its recording allowed Peter to return to his own solo work.

Peter – "Once *Excusez-Moi* was finished I put a band together and played my first big show at The Casino on Catalina Island in the autumn. Emotionally, I really didn't feel that I needed Al as my sole means of support."

But they continued to work together. Back to work in Peter's North Hollywood garage studio after Christmas Al recorded demos of "I Swam" and "It's A Girl Thing", both of which were destined to end up as unreleased tracks. These were recorded on Peter's four-track with a view to going on what would become *Famous Last Words*. "It's A Girl Thing" rattles along with a melody that has strong similarities to "Runaround Sue" with a regulatory sax solo for the middle eight. Other than that the piece itself is harmless enough but is ultimately just a poor cousin of "Candy Came Back".

Steve Chapman – "It wasn't until Al had enough songs together for another album that I went out and got those deals with Mesa Blue Moon in the States and Permanent for the rest of the world. Those two record companies funded the recording of the album between each other. The tie up with Ross Hogarth was through myself. I'd known Ross for quite a while. He'd done a lot of producing and engineering and his strong points as an engineer and Peter White's strong musicality were well suited."

It had been five years since Al had last released a studio album. After such a long hiatus Peter White had been looking forward to playing on it. That's not how things turned out though.

Peter White – "Ross Hogarth was someone who had worked with John Mellencamp as an engineer. He'd also worked with Larry Carlton. He was a good guy and we got on well together. Steve Chapman suggested it, as Ross was more of an engineer and I was more of a musician. We recorded it at Clearlake Studios which was very close to the house on Fulcher where I was living. The one big problem that I had was that I hurt my hand halfway through the recording process and couldn't play but luckily I was able to carry on working as an arranger and producer until my hand got better. I played most of my parts on the album on the last day of recording and after that my fingers really were very sore!"

Al – "Peter, not being able to play the guitar, spent a very long time producing the album instead! I think that his guitar work was missed, by the way. I didn't play guitar at all though, which was a pity!"

Peter – "One thing I regret is that Al didn't play any guitar himself on the album because I insisted on playing it all and it came back to bite me later when a few people complained about me usurping Al's position! Our shot at being commercial on that album was 'Don't Forget Me' – but it never really happened! There had been a big push on that album to return to guitar based songs. When it had been started a year earlier with Joe Chiccarelli as producer, I had only been invited in to play on one song, 'Coldest Winter In Memory'."

That song turned out to be the stand-out track from those sessions. Peter's guitar work on it is stunning.

In April 1993 Al spoke at length about the track "Trains" from the upcoming *Famous Last Words* album. The song would go on to become one of his most popular compositions of the decade.

Al – "'Trains' is a track that I've got to find a way to arrange properly but that one is basically written. It's a historical epic. It basically traces the history of the railway system. And I think what it's about – in as far as it's about any one thing – is how you can take something that has no moral status: it's neither good nor bad. In this case, the railway system, which was in the first place a method of transportation, gradually became a method of military invasion. They were laid out along military lines and eventually were used to transport the Jews to the concentration camps. So, various German rulers gradually and systematically perverted the idea of the railway system. I watched *Shoah* all the way through. The final scene, with the train that goes on and on, was probably the direct inspiration for it. I thought *Shoah* was a brilliant film."

But the sources that Al drew on to write "Trains" were not restricted to the movie. As was so often the case it was partly autobiographical. This was deliberate.

Al – "The song is insidious in that it gradually builds on you. It actually begins with my boyhood. 'Trains' is a long song, one of my mega-historical things. I began it rather like "Love Chronicles". The first couple of verses are about me, travelling first of all to school on trains and then travelling to London and Bournemouth. Then I dip back into the 19th century,

AL STEWART

to examine the construction of the railway system, and whether or not it was designed for transportation, and if (and how) it was used by the military. Then we get into the First World War, and I have this picture in August of 1914 of soldiers waving and laughing on their way to all these terrible places. We have a completely different musical section that goes through the inter-war period, and then I pick up with trains going to the concentration camps. Then I get out of it completely, and deal with childhood games (I had a book called *Thomas The Tank Engine*). In the last couple of verses we come entirely up to date; in fact, I'm riding on the Amtrak from New York to Philadelphia. It's long and roundabout, four or five different time zones, and several different countries. A mechanical object is neither good nor bad. It's good when it's used correctly, and bad when used badly. Having initially become interested in the subject while watching *Shoah*, I decided to set the song in different times and different moods to use trains in. Trains could be taking you to Auschwitz or taking you to visit your mother – the train is neutral. The object is not responsible for the action."

TRAINS

In the sapling years of the post war world
In an English market town
I do believe we travelled in schoolboy blue
The cap upon the crown
Books on knee
Our faces pressed against the dusty railway carriage panes
As all our lives went rolling on the clicking wheels of trains

The school years passed like eternity
And at last were left behind
And it seemed the city was calling me
To see what I might find
Almost grown, I stood before horizons made of dreams
I think I stole a kiss or two while rolling on the clicking wheels of trains

Trains
All our lives were a whistle stop affair
No ties or chains
Throwing words like fireworks in the air
Not much remains
A photograph in your memory
Through the coloured lens of time
All our lives were just a smudge of smoke against the sky

The silver rails spread far and wide
Through the nineteenth century
Some straight and true, some serpentine
From the cities to the sea
And out of sight
Of those who rode in style there worked the military mind
On through the night to plot and chart the twisting paths of trains

On the day they buried Jean Juares
World War One broke free
Like an angry river overflowing
Its banks impatiently
While mile on mile
The soldiers filled the railway stations arteries and veins
I see them now go laughing on the clicking wheels of trains
Trains
Rolling off to the front
Across the narrow Russian gauge
Weeks turn into months

314

And the enthusiasm wanes
Sacrifices in seas of mud, and still you don't know why
All their lives are just a puff of smoke against the sky
Then came surrender, then came the peace
Then revolution out of the east
Then came the crash, then came the tears
Then came the thirties, the nightmare years
Then came the same thing over again
Mad as the moon
That watches over the plain
Oh, driven insane

But oh what kind of trains are these
That I never saw before
Snatching up the refugees
From the ghettoes of the war
To stand confused
With all their worldly goods, beneath the watching guard's disdain
As young and old go rolling on the clicking wheels of trains
And the driver only does this job
With vodka in his coat
And he turns around and he makes a sign
With his hand across his throat
For days on end
Through sun and snow, the destination still remains the same
For those who ride with death above the clicking wheels of trains

Trains
What became of the innocence
They had in childhood games
Painted red or blue
When I was young they all had names
Who'll remember the ones who only rode in them to die
All their lives are just a smudge of smoke against the sky

Now forty years have come and gone
And I'm far away from there
And I ride the Amtrak from New York City
To Philadelphia
And there's a man to bring you food and drink
And sometimes passengers exchange
A smile or two rolling on the humming wheels of trains

But I can't tell you if it's them
Or if it's only me
But I believe when they look outside
They don't see what I see
Over there
Beyond the trees it seems that I can just make out the stained
Fields of Poland calling out to all the passing trains

Trains
I suppose that there's nothing
In this life remains the same
Everything is governed
By the losses and the gains
Still sometimes I get caught up in the past I can't say why
All our lives are just a smudge of smoke
Or just a breath of wind against the sky

The autumn of 1993 also saw Peter's third appearance at the Catalina Jazz Festival and the second time as headliner in the splendid art deco Casino. It was at shows such as these, with their high profile and huge media interest that Peter cut a swathe through the ranks of other artists and rose to the top of the tree that grew into Smooth Jazz.

Released in England on John Lennard's Permanent Records, *Famous Last Words* was recorded at O'Henry Studios in Burbank California and Clearlake Audio in North Hollywood. The producer was Ross Hogarth. The musicians were Peter White, Peter Wood, Tim Landers, Denny Fongheiser, Ross Hogarth, Todd Sharp, Charlie Bisharat, Robin Lamble, Ed Tree, Louis Conte, Dave Boruff, Daryl S., Alan Mathews, Neal Morse, Eric Williams and, playing tuba on "Hipposong", Freebo.

The cover shoot took place in the library of Richard Riordan, the mayor of Los Angeles.

Al – "He won his election while we were talking about the cover, and we'd already decided that we wanted to shoot it in a library. In LA, because all the film companies know that Disney can spend $25,000 for a day's shooting and won't even notice it in the budget, the big libraries don't care if its Warner Brothers or Al Stewart, they're going to charge the same. So we were looking around for something that was free. I pointed out that I wasn't a voter because I'm English but many of the people who work at Mesa/Blue Moon were voters, and that a newly elected Mayor might want to get people on his side! He said 'yes' and we ended up being there for eight hours The picture on the front was taken upstairs but the picture on the inside, on the back of the booklet, was taken downstairs. He says he has about 40,000 books".

At the start of 1994 Al played what turned out to be his last British dates for several years with Peter White. The short tour included shows at venues in Clapham, Northampton and Cheltenham. Whilst in London he also spent an afternoon arranged by the Red Herring TV production company for Scottish Television. The purpose of this time was to film Al, Wizz Jones and Bert Jansch roaming around Soho from one old haunt to the next, ending up at Bunjies where Al and Bert performed "Blues Run The Game". The programme, entitled *Acoustic Routes*, was centred around the career of Bert Jansch and was shown on the BBC the next year. Once Al had finished filming in Soho he joined Peter and played live on the Nicky Campbell radio show on BBC Radio One.

Peter's own third album *Promenade* would be released later in the summer but meanwhile, although they didn't realise it at the time, he and Al had just played their last ever tour together.

FLANEUR

In which Al meets Laurence Juber and records "Between the Wars", ending the 20th Century touring solo once again.

Back home with Kris in Los Angeles Al was faced with a problem that had been brewing for quite a while. His own work schedule had been, when compared to Peter White's, relatively light for the past few years. Workaholic that he was, Peter had managed to fit in his own three albums and gigs around work with Al on *Last Days Of The Century*, *Rhymes In Rooms*, *Famous Last Words* and Al's own sporadic gigging. But now in the spring of 1994 there were some shows in the mountains that it didn't look like Peter could make and Al started asking people to recommend someone that could fill in for Peter on what was probably a temporary basis. Enter ex-Wings guitarist Laurence Juber.

LJ – "I was introduced to Al by James Jensen, who runs Acoustic Music Records USA, who felt that my background in UK pop and folk would be compatible with Al's style. Peter White was unavailable for some spring 1994 shows, so I suggested to Steve Chapman that I might jump in and try out for the gig. We did some shows in Colorado that went well and it seemed that there might be some chemistry between us.

"Subsequently, I invited Al round to my studio to record a demo of a nascent 'Night Train To Munich' which ended up very similar to the final album version. Demos of 'Lindy' and 'Sampan' quickly followed which met with approval by Mesa and the go-ahead to produce an album was given. Credit must be given to Steve Chapman for his persuasion of the 'powers that be' to give me the producer's reins."

In fact, had it not been for the work of Steve Chapman, it is quite possible that Al would have been without a recording contract for a lot longer. Al and Laurence had clear ideas about what they wanted to achieve with the album. The basic game plan was to have an acoustic guitar-based album that could be adequately performed live as a duo.

LJ – "Not only an expedience of promotional logistics, but also a creative choice. To have Al do what he does best, namely to play guitar and sing was essential. My strong early memories of Al at The Fishmongers Arms in Wood Green, North London in the late '60s singing 'Love Chronicles' with simply an Epiphone acoustic for accompaniment came into play here. Also a consistent historical focus seemed appropriate for the 'Munich' and 'Lindy' type of subject matter."

Al's dislike of the recording process was tempered by the use of LJ's home studio for much of these sessions. It was an arrangement that would prove to suit Al very well and in time produced some of his best music in over twenty years.

LJ – "However we found that with the two of us working together in my home studio the process was fairly painless. A rhythm was established where the writing and recording processes blended together. I think this kept a quality of freshness and spontaneity about the album. Another twist was that Al mostly writes on piano rather than guitar so part of the development of the arrangements involved transferring the songs to the guitar and avoiding some of the potential guitaristic clichés."

Al – "Laurence did all of this very well and we got on with everything at once. It was a pleasure making that album whereas some of the more recent ones had not been so. I knew at once that I'd made the right decision from the first day in the studio. The songs flowed out immediately and we were a team!"

LJ – "The basic recordings were mostly done with Al sitting and playing guitar while I played and ran the equipment. The usual game plan was to complete the arrangement of each song and then immediately put it on 24-track analogue tape with a click track and time code so that it could be synchronised to the computer. Once the guitars felt right, then a quick and dirty bass and percussion track would be added along with a guide vocal. Al would then leave me to finish off the arrangement in my own time and gave me ample room to experiment with different guitars and microphones to provide some sonic variety. We did have one session with Tim Landers playing bass along with us, which produced the tracks 'Life Between The Wars' and 'Black Danube'. However logistically it was quicker to work with fewer people in what is a fairly small workspace. James Hutchinson [Bonnie Raitt] overdubbed on various bass guitars both acoustic and electric. We found that acoustic upright bass seemed to take up too much space, so Tim's Kramer acoustic bass guitar and Hutch's Washburn are the common bass sounds for the album. The exceptions being 'Age Of Rhythm' and 'League Of Notions' which I played finger-style bass on a Jerry Jones' 6-string electric bass guitar."

Percussion and light drums were added later. Studio percussionist Steve Forman, whose credits are too numerous to mention, would come by with various instruments both exotic and mundane and add some groove and colour. Bruce Gary [the Knack, Jack Bruce] and Jim Keltner [Travelling Wilburys, Ry Cooder etc.] provided tasteful drum fills.

LJ – "Andrew Powell was gracious enough to perform on synths a string arrangement for 'Laughing Into 1939'. We might have used a real string orchestra but we liked the personality of his performance and it seemed more in keeping with the underlying philosophy, not to mention a whole lot less expensive! Suzie Katayama [Prince, The Chieftains etc] added cello which gave the appropriate soloistic string ambience. Her other forte, accordion, was useful for the East European flavours of 'Joe The Georgian' and 'The Black Danube'."

Marin County 1996
Hope Juber, Violet Stewart and Laurence Juber

Neville

Al and Dennis Overstreet, Los Angeles 1995

Al spoke to *Chronicles* at the time about some of the tracks.

"I love 'Night Train To Munich'. I was actually quite a big Django fan from when I was about 15. It was updating my record collection to CD format, coming across a boxed Django set, and finding I was playing it more often than I expected, that proved the initial inspiration.

"From all of that, the riff to 'Night Train To Munich' must have come into my head, and when I started working with Laurence it turned out that he liked Django too. So we sat down and turned it into a song. So the starting point for the track was Django Reinhardt, and the fiddle player was someone who could play in the direction of Stephane Grappelli. We found the oldest player we could lay our hands on, who's actually 70, and, since the album is set between 1918 and 1939, he was there in the period. Lyrically it owes a debt to the British film director Carol Reed. He had a penchant for setting his black and white thrillers on trains and there were always spies chasing each other up and down corridors."

For "The Age Of Rhythm" Al was very influenced by the 1994 Alan Rudolph movie *Mrs Parker And The Vicious Circle*. In the film Dorothy Parker looks back to the wild 1920s days of the *Algonquin Table* in New York City.

Al – "I thought Jennifer Jason Leigh was wonderful in it. I thought the film was good, but the song really isn't based on it. The first line says 'Today I feel like Dorothy Parker', *not* 'I am Dorothy Parker'. 'Today I have the critical eye…' – which she surely did have. It is set during Prohibition and the speakeasy time, and so the scenes that ensue would certainly be those with which Dorothy Parker would have been familiar – but it's a simile rather than a metaphor. It's very much influenced musically by LJ's tune 'Rules of the Road'. 'The Black Danube' I spent some more time on. I kept playing it all the time on the piano, I thought it was a really pretty tune. It was actually a piano piece that was played on guitar.

"There's bit of 'Midnight In Moscow' by Kenny Ball in there too! What I was actually trying to get at here was a blend of two very, very early musical influences, both of which I was very fond of when I was about 15. One was Django Reinhardt – again, and the other was The Shadows – and 'The Black Danube' is just the sort of thing the Shadows would have played on electric guitars. I had in mind, what would happen if you took a Shadows tune and had it played by Django Reinhardt. Conversely, what would happen if you had a Django Reinhardt tune played by the Shadows on acoustic guitars. In both cases, it would sound pretty much like 'The Black Danube'."

Al had read the memoirs of David Niven and had also appeared on a chat show with the Hollywood legend back in 1980. He now used one of the characters from those books as the central figure for a song on the new album. He told David Dasch at the time – "I took the 'Marion The Chatelaine' title out of *The Moon's A Balloon* and *Bring On The Empty Horses*. David Niven called her that because she was the host at Hearst's amazing castle. She had to entertain all these people who came lumbering through there all the time. I don't think she ever fell out of love with Hearst, but she became very disillusioned with his organisation. As the years rolled by she became much worse for wear for lots and lots of gin. The most amazing thing about Marion Davies is that when Hearst died, his family and the administrators of the estate managed to prevent her from going to the funeral, after she had spent 32 years with him."

The song has remained a staple of Al's concert set list ever since.

MARION THE CHATELAINE

When the great collector found her
She was just a girl
She rang a chord inside him
And he stole her to the centre of his world
Many wished they could be in her shoes
But she surely did know how to have the blues

He tried to make a star of her
She never did know why
And though she could have told him
There were some things that his money couldn't buy
She never knew a way to refuse
But she surely did know how to have the blues
They say tomorrow's such a long, long time
They say tomorrow never comes
Whatever happened to this dream of mine
Count the days as they run
He built himself a castle
On a hill above a bay
Where Marion the Chatelaine
Charmed every single one who came to stay
Some never knew, while others read the clues
That she surely did know how to have the blues

They say tomorrow's such a long, long time
They say tomorrow never comes
Whatever happened to this dream of mine
Count the days as they run

When all the parties ended
In the castle on the hill
The paintings and the statues stood alone
And all the corridors grew still
She got caught between the shadows and the booze
And she surely did know how to have the blues

LIFE BETWEEN THE WARS

Paul Gervaise picks up the Herald
And sees the face of Zelda Fitzgerald
She's part of the scene
Of life between the wars

The tropic sun is sticky and warm
And it bakes the head of Somerset Maugham
Who is writing a scene
Of life between the wars

You're waiting by the hotdog stand
In the onion air
As the ball flies through the park

Violet and Vita run
Through the streets of Paris
Their laughter floating through the dark
A fog that fell is swallowing London
Coco Chanel came back with a suntan
To brighten the scene
Of life between the wars

There will be a pint of milk
And a Hovis loaf
At the end of every street
You can hear a silver band on the radio
And it makes the grocer tap his feet

The King is leaving Buckingham Palace
It's all too cold
He'd rather have Wallis
They're part of the scene
Of life between the wars

Al was offered the opportunity to play the Glastonbury Festival in 1995 and flew into England with Laurence to play not only that show but also others at the Union Chapel in Islington and Folkestone. This performance at Glastonbury reunited Al briefly with Martin Carthy and it marked the European debut of him performing a They Might Be Giants song along with the new pieces from *Between The Wars* such as "Night Train To Munich", "Marion The Chatelaine" and "Joe The Georgian".

The end of the year saw Al, Kris and their young daughter Violet preparing to move house. Al had lived at the same address in Roscomarre Drive since before recording *Time Passages*. The seclusion atop its tree-lined canyon was perfect for a bachelor but, as Violet grew, the small fence between the swimming pool and the mountainside began to look less and less of an obstacle to her curiosity. The house was about to go on the market when Luke's wife, acting in her capacity as an estate agent, asked Al to let her show a couple, for whom the house would be perfect, around one afternoon. Walking from room to room they came across the den with its huge record collection and a complete set of Al Stewart albums on the shelves. Upon being told the reason for this they had a stiff drink, confessed to being lifelong Al fans and offered the full market price on the spot! So the Stewart family had to find a new home at once or jeopardise the sale. Kris had vaguely started looking at homes in the Bay Area of Northern California and after another trip a house was found in San Rafael that Al at once labelled "The money pit".

At this point, the compilation CD of out-takes, *Seemed Like A Good Idea At The Time*, was released.

Al – "It was a period of taking stock I guess. We moved house and for the first time in 20 years I didn't live in LA anymore. That was a sobering experience I can tell you! During those years in Bel Air we'd accumulated all of these demos and oddities that people were forever asking to get hold of and so we had a clear out! We just pressed up a thousand of them. That's how 'Coldest Winter In Memory' finally got to be heard."

And what a wonderful song it is!

THE COLDEST WINTER IN MEMORY
The coldest winter in memory was 1709
The sea froze off the coast of France all along the Neptune line
By the lost town of Dunwich the shore was washed away
They say you hear the church bells still as they toll beneath the waves

Come all you earthly princes, wheresoever you may be
From the Sun King in the court of France to the Tsar in Muscovy
Take heed of Charles of Sweden, the Lion of the North,
On the cracked earth of summer with his army he goes forth

Guardian angels wherever you may be, reach down and keep my soul for me

I was there amongst that number, I heard the trumpets strain
I saw the host of banners spread across the Polish plain
Those who stood against us, they soon were swept away
They may have the numbers but it's Charles shall have the day

We cut our way through forests, crossed on frozen streams
They fell away before us like a murmur in a dream
And they burned the land around us as snow was closing in
And the arms of winter took us as we fired against the wind

Guardian angels wherever you may be, reach down and keep my soul for me

Through all the courts of Europe there's a rumour from the East
The kings have come to battle and it's Charles who's known defeat
They'll shake their heads in wonder at how this came to be
But it's nights without a shelter that have made an end for me

Now Charles is fled to Turkey, left his men afar
And they'll be marched through Moscow now as prisoners of the Tsar
And had I but known last summer what I now understand
I'd have never set my foot inside this bleak and bitter land

Guardian angels wherever you may be, reach down and keep my soul for me

The coldest winter in memory was 1709
The sea froze off the coast of France all along the Neptune line
By the lost town of Dunwich the shore was washed away
They say you hear the church bells still as they toll beneath the waves

At the end of January Al flew to London and on to Amsterdam for an 11-date Dutch tour. In the previous two decades he'd only played a handful of dates in the whole of Europe, so this looked set to be something special. And so it was. With the promoter Mojo Enterprises taking good care of things Al was in great spirits for the whole tour. EMI Holland now put out a special compilation CD entitled *An Acoustic Evening With Al Stewart* and although frozen throughout, the relatively small size of the country made travel through the ice and snow quite an easy affair for the tour mini-bus.

Al – "It was a lot of fun. In the past going to Europe had always been a lottery. But Laurence and I had a great time on that tour and we played most of the songs from 'Between The Wars' at some time or other over there."

During the course of the tour Al and Laurence did two TV shows and two radio shows, one of which was with a small orchestra and featured a version of "Laughing into 1939". Laurence also found time to host three guitar clinics booked for him by Taylor Guitars.

The pace of life in San Rafael was, naturally enough, much slower than that in Los Angeles. Al was now doing fewer gigs than ever before and gradually began to assimilate himself into the life of a new father in semi-retirement with the fresh circle of friends that the parenthood and re-location had provided him with. He was the first to admit that being a *dad* didn't come that easily to him and Al undoubtedly found it difficult not only adapting to the new responsibility but also coping with the strains that

Al with Petrus des Bois

Al in Bordeaux

it came to place on life at home. He did however quickly make a number of new friends in the Bay Area as Violet started school and he gradually developed an extended network of contacts in the wine trade there. But he continued to feel isolated and missed Los Angeles as much as ever.

Later that year Al, Kris and Violet joined Dennis Overstreet on an extended trip to Bordeaux, during which time they visited Chateau Valandraud, Chateau Margaux and Chateau Petrus.

He toured England, this time with local San Rafael guitarist Paul Robinson, in the Winter of '97, an annual tour that had now turned into a tradition. The only new song, albeit one that he had been working on for a while, to come out of the trip was "Curtain".

CURTAIN

I once had a girl in London
She told me a lie
It took me so long to discover
I never knew why
She used to live by the river
In the Spring she let her hair grow long
Pulled forward 'til her face was gone
Curtain drawn

She told me her life was a nightmare
When she was a child
Her parents would always be fighting
They let her run wild
She ran away to the river
In the summer when the days grew long
In this place where nothing's wrong
Curtain gone

And so one day unexpectedly I came
Into this world that she made for herself
She liked to play and I think that she made
Some kind of effort to push me away
Wouldn't you always say
That the more that you're pushed away
The more that you try to stay?
I too was drawn to the river
In the autumn when the leaves turned brown
Something in her turned around
Curtain down

And so one day unexpectedly she said
It's over it's over it's over you know
And you must leave and leave right away
I thought I told you a long time ago
I've got someone back home
I thought you'd never know
You stayed too long that's all
Curtain falls

I once had a girl in London
She told me a lie
It took me so long to discover
I never knew why

1998 was an even quieter year in the States and once again the major concert dates were in the UK. The tour kicked off with a short season at London's Café Royal on Regent Street. Here he joined up once again with Andrew Powell for a set that included "Peter On The White Sea", a song that Andrew had worked on for the *Famous Last Words* album in 1993. The solo acoustic dates that followed included a gig at The Lemon Tree in Aberdeen, Al's first Scottish show in seven years. For the final concert, at Croydon's Ashcroft Theatre, Peter White came on as a special guest for the second half of the show. Andrew Powell also played that night making it the only time they ever all three played on the same stage together.

Now in the spring of 1999 Al felt ready to take the first tentative steps towards recording new material. Working at Paul Robinson's home studio they laid down half a dozen guitar instrumentals with the working title, *Music Of The Vines*, Al even contributing electric guitar at some of the sessions. But that was as far as those recordings went, none of them being turned into finished songs. Al next flew to London for a solo British tour that occupied much of that November. Kicking off in Exeter and continuing up and down the country from The Whitley Bay Dome to The London Astoria, the tour finished at Sheffield City Hall where he played what would be his last gig of the 20th Century a few weeks before Christmas.

Meanwhile plans were already in hand for Al to go into the studio for the first time in five years.

The intention would be to release an album in the late summer of 2000 but nothing is ever quite that simple.

SECOND VINTAGE

In which Al records an album about wine for a label that
immediately goes bankrupt.
He tours more than he has in 25 years.

Five years after *Between The Wars* had brought together Al and Laurence Juber, they reunited at Laurence's home studio to record what would become *Down In The Cellar*. It
would be released on Miramar; the Seattle-based record label with Russ Martin at its
helm. Everything was suddenly looking very good for Al.

Russ Martin – "I had been a long time fan of Al's and back in the 1980s I was
working for Capitol Records who distributed the Enigma label and so through that I got
to meet both Al and Steve Chapman. Following this I worked for Precision Sound who
distributed a number of record labels upon one of which was Peter White and so through
that I renewed my association with Steve in his capacity as Peter and Al's Manager.
Then in the summer of 1999 we meet for coffee here in Seattle and ended up discussing
the possibility of maybe Al recording an album for Miramar. I suggested to Steve that Al
could perhaps marry together *Wine and Music* and that, if he was to do that, then maybe
we would have a deal."

They did have a deal and Russ proved to be one of the most capable people that Al had
worked with. The album was written and recorded the next year between January and
June. With the new work due for release on October 17th, I talked to Al at his home on
June 26th, the day the finished master of *Down In The Cellar* arrived there via Fed Ex.

Al – "Russ Martin from Miramar wanted us to do an album and at some stage, very
early in the proceedings, it was decided that it would be an album all about wine. But
whether it was his idea or whether it was my idea I'm not sure. I think there was an idea
to do a wine album going back even before that. But I don't really know how it solidified
into that as a concept.

"I think Laurence was always going to be the producer. I think that I mentioned to

*Al, Peter and Laurence Juber, Studio City, California 2000. Al is calling out, "Go and
find us a van Neville and we'll do the Tour right now!"*

Neville

Writing 'Down In The Cellar' at home in California

him there was a possibility that there was a record label interested in funding a new album and at that point I think he said that he'd like to be involved.

"We did the demos in his house and then went on to do the tracks at Capitol. But until I walked into his home studio he hadn't heard any of the songs at all. I walked in there and sat down at his electronic keyboard and then banged around on the piano I think mostly. This was in the middle of January. The first set of demos I've got have the date of January 26th 2000.

"There were something like 16 tunes and out of those there were some that didn't make it. There were about four or five of those. There's a new song about William McKinley that I like and if I do another album it might go on that. Then there was also another long slow piano tune, that didn't make it, that went on to become 'Pictures In The Wine'. That was on and off it a number of times and in the end didn't make it. And there was a kind of Nirvana-type thing that I loved which we demoed also. It is basically very much like 'Smells Like Teen Spirit'. But it had no reference whatsoever to this record as it was not about wine, it was a blasting rock 'n' roll thing and I absolutely adored it. However everyone agreed that it didn't belong on this particular record. Then there are a couple of other things too. So, of the initial bunch of songs that I took down, we dumped four or five of them straightaway. 'The Night That The Band Got The Wine' was a last minute addition as it was the very last thing I wrote and so it wasn't there until the last moment. It certainly wasn't on the original demos. 'Waiting For Margaux' was originally called 'Miami Miami'. The understanding is that when I think up tunes I always give them silly names and I very often write silly-sounding lyrics and they end up on an album like *Seemed Like A Good Idea At The Time* and people think that they're the ultimate sets of lyrics and they're really not! They're just things that I use to count syllables with. So if I need seven syllables I might say 'She went up to the dustbins' or something similar but you're not to take this as meaning that I'm making some statement about dustbins because I'm really just counting syllables.

"'Down In The Cellars' seems to be everyone's favourite at the moment. It's actually quite short. It is about the firm of Jean-Louis Chave that's been in the Rhone Valley since around 1481. I think the cellar dates back to then. It is the oldest father-to-son winemaking operation in the Rhone Valley. 519 years is quite a long time! Their cellars are just how you would imagine. There must be at least 26 generations of Chaves who've been wandering around, down there in the cellars blending their wines and trying to make Hermitage as well as they possibly can. And I often wonder whether any of the more recent Chaves have thought back about their own ancestors from centuries before, creeping about down there in the darkness. When I say 'lives are written here pages on pages, ages on ages just disappear', it's just how it all seemed to me. It just seems to me that the ghosts of those 26 generations of Chaves are still wandering around down in the cellars.

"It was actually incredibly easy to write. I was thinking of French nursery rhymes. The tune of this particular song is probably the simplest yet at the same time the most melodic on the album. It's just a very simple, very melodic thing. And sometimes those are the best. When I first wrote it on the piano, I almost left it off the record, because I thought it was too simple. It just goes to show. I did think at first that it didn't have enough chord changes in it but everyone seems to like it a lot at the moment.

"Now, just as with 'Night Train To Munich', or a least a major chunk of 'Night Train To Munich' the version on the album is in fact the demo. This is, I've learned, one of the amazing ways in which Laurence works. Whenever you do demos with Laurence you've got to do them *perfectly* because if they're good he just never goes back and re-does them. He just moves on. Laurence just moves ahead like a steam train and he doesn't look back! If it sounds good you're onto the next song and in the case of ' Down In The Cellars' the only thing that's different from the demos is I put a new vocal on it. Otherwise this *is* the demo. Peter will do things until they're perfect but Laurence's approach is just to attempt to play them perfectly the first time. Very often Peter won't play them perfectly the first time or at least he doesn't think so. It's just a difference in personalities, I guess."

Sitting across from Al, at his kitchen table, listening to him compare the methods of Laurence and Peter, was an illuminating way to spend the morning.

"'Franklin's Table' was actually provisionally called 'Rupert Brooke'. I don't think it was really about Rupert Brooke but it was a sort of desperation song in which a female protagonist was saying ... 'there is a part of me that is forever broken'. Of course Rupert Brooke had also written that there was some part of a foreign field that was forever England. So it had that Rupert Brooke echo to it. And I never really got through to writing all the words to it when it was 'Rupert Brooke'. And then right before we did it, and partly because I couldn't find a wine reference to it as 'Rupert Brooke', I re wrote the song and it ended up being about Ben Franklin, simply because Thomas Jefferson, who was even more into wine than I am, used to share his wines with Ben Franklin. So I could have written about Thomas Jefferson, but the idea behind this song is that it is sung from the point of view of one of his neighbours who goes around every now and then to Ben Franklin's place and doesn't understand a whole lot about world affairs and even less about all these inventions, but he really likes the wine and the food! He's quite content to sit at Ben Franklin's table and listen to them all rambling on as long as he can dig into the roast beef and pour the claret down his throat. So it comes from a totally unexpected angle I think.

"'House of Clocks' began life as a total Dire Straits tune! I was playing electric guitar very much in the Mark Knopfler style, very upbeat like 'Sultans of Swing'. I kept running into the same problem with it which was that there were so many guitar notes that I didn't have any room to put the words in. I mean the guitar was just all over everything. I'll say this for Miramar, they stayed out of the way a lot and let me get on with it. But I occasionally got little bits of feedback, especially from Steve Chapman, saying that this really ought to be acoustic. This was a wine album! I got this terrible feeling that maybe what they wanted was like a new age flute album and I was discouraged from plastering screaming lead guitar all over it! I personally disagree. I think wine lovers appreciate loud music just as much as they do soft music. However, in the interests of making everyone happy, we eventually turned this into an acoustic tune and we basically halved the number of notes. Now in terms of what all the clocks are about, I really don't know, apart from the fact that in England I've got this Victorian grandfather clock that I've been trying to get shipped over here for about the last ten years but don't seem to be able to do it. I think I was becoming nostalgic for my clock back in England. 'I grew up in a house of clocks', well I did.

"You also have to realise that this was a *record record* in many ways in the sense that it was the fastest album I've ever done. I went from a blank slate in January to a finished master in June and I never work that fast. Basically I was asked if I could make an album about wine and I smiled and said 'Yes, I can do that'. Then I thought 'Can I do this?' I then started writing it. The most extraordinary thing from my work point of view is that I wrote all the lyrics in about ten days. Kris was going to England to see my mother as I had discovered that I just couldn't write with Violet and Daisy watching *Sesame Street* in the background. *Big Bird* just has to start singing and there would be just no way! I know all these silly songs now!"

TASTING HISTORY

Stephanie's father came here from Alsace
He bought a grey Victorian house
Filled with coloured glass
He kept his old wine bottles
In a cellar down below
On Friday nights, he takes some out
And stands them in a row
And all that he said
All of us there were tasting history

Those perfume-laden liquids
Whatever they might be
He dispensed them like a chemist
From the sixteenth century
Then leaned back in his armchair
With understated glee
While we tripped upon our tongues
To trace their ancestry
And all that he said
All of us there were tasting history
And all through the night
In glass-filtered light, tasting history

Stephanie went to Egypt
To an excavation site
And works beneath the Pharaoh's moon
Deep into the night
Her Dad still opens Chambertin
As the candle burns away
It was the favourite of Napoleon
That's what he liked to say
And all that he said
All of us there were tasting history
And all through the night
In glass-filtered light, tasting history

DOWN IN THE CELLARS

Down in the cellars of Jean-Louis Chave
All the shadows are leaving
Bottles lying asleep in the caves

You'll see history breathing

From Cote-Rote down to Hermitage
The vines are trellised in evening
In the cellars of Jean-Louis Chave
You'll see history breathing

Generations go slipping away now
What can you say now, five hundred years
Lives are written here
Pages on pages, ages on ages
Just disappear

From Cote-Rote down to Hermitage
The vines are trellised in evening
In the cellars of Jean-Louis Chave
You'll see history breathing

Al – "I know that I may appear to have a work ethic of sorts but I really don't. I'm just not that prolific. But with 'Down In The Cellar' it at least proved that I could be whenever I had to meet a deadline. If push came to shove I think that I could make two albums a year but I just don't think like that."

The release of this CD in the States was delayed however due to the closure of Miramar by its parent company Unipix. In fact it was EMI who were the first to release it anywhere when they put it out a couple of days before Al started a massive 20-date UK tour on Valentine's Day 2001.

The album got some of Al's best reviews in years. *The Guardian* called it "Typically well researched … a vintage performance" and *Q Magazine* gave it three stars.

Visiting such regular venues as The Brook in Southampton and The Stables in Milton

David Washington

Al on stage in England, 2001

Keynes plus new ones such as London's Jazz Cafe, Al produced a set that was his most ambitious in a decade. Playing songs on the tour that varied from Elvis Costello's "London's Brilliant Parade" to "Rocks In The Ocean" and a nightly encore of "The Elf", Al was at his most relaxed in years and started making plans to return for even more shows in the Autumn.

During the trip Al was asked to come up with a selection of his favourite songs for BBC Radio Wales. Some of his choices were predictable whilst others were not. This is the complete list of songs that he handed to them.

REBEL ROUSER – DUANE EDDY
GRAND COULEE DAM – LONNIE DONEGAN
THE NIGHT THEY DROVE OLD DIXIE DOWN – THE BAND
THE STRANGER SONG – LEONARD COHEN
BIRDHOUSE IN YOUR SOUL – THEY MIGHT BE GIANTS
JACOB MARLEY'S CHAIN – AIMEE MANN
NEW AMSTERDAM – ELVIS COSTELLO
THE TIMES THEY ARE A CHANGING – BOB DYLAN
CAN'T EXPLAIN – THE WHO
LIFE ON MARS – DAVID BOWIE
GOD ONLY KNOWS – THE BEACH BOYS
JEANIE WITH THE LIGHT BROWN LAMP – THE SHADOWS

For many of the dates Al was accompanied by the bass player Doug Mann who had flown over for the second half of the tour with Al's friends David and Mary Liskin. This made for somewhat of a party atmosphere on the trip, with diversions to country hotels and castles en route. For the tour's final throw of the dice however, Jonny Kremer put together an amazing show in a tiny room in Bournemouth, at which Al was joined by The Europa String Choir and his old friend Geoff Westwood from The Trappers. Together they played "Walk Don't Run" for the first time in almost 40 years in front of an

*Al, playing the piano at his parents' house
in Dorset, Spring 2001*

audience that boasted what amounted to an A to Z of the Bournemouth Beat Scene from the time that The Trappers had *last* performed together.

The notion that he would still be in the music business by the time that he reached his 50s was not something that Al had seriously considered whilst living in Los Angeles. However with the album *Down In The Cellar* he at least approached what he had anticipated doing with his middle years.

He had told *Melody Maker* in 1977 – "My ultimate ambition is to have a little vineyard somewhere. If fortune smiled I could see myself at 50, lurching amongst the vines … It's the sort of renaissance view of art – writing a novel, making a record now and then, making a few bottles of wine. It's a sensationally hedonistic view of the possibilities of life."

He was asked about his perception of identity.

"I'm an internationalist, I've lived in England. The only way to continue to grow is to continually place yourself in different environments. I mean, I won't be in Los Angeles forever. Even Los Angeles won't be in Los Angeles forever."

For the time being, an album *about* wine rather than *owning* a vineyard *or* having back his old life in LA, was going to have to do.

GRACE CATHEDRAL

With *Down In The Cellar* now finally released and a highly successful UK tour promoting it behind him, Al returned to the States and a series of concerts in the late Spring that were as diverse as ever. That June he opened for America in Red Bank New Jersey and two days later played with Ambrosia at The Wolf Den in The Mohegan Sun in Connecticut. Playing with Ambrosia, as he often did, was proving to be something that Al felt was working out well. As he commented on the drive from Manhattan to Connecticut for the show that Saturday afternoon – "It might seem odd to some people that I would enjoy shows like this but I have to tell you that I do. I get to play three songs, usually 'Time Passages', 'On The Border' and 'Year Of The Cat', with a band of great musicians who I don't have to put up in hotel rooms or fly around the country. I'm then off stage at at thoroughly civilized time and can go and have dinner. If you ask me it's paradise!" And whilst this attitude could be easily perceived as reflecting a certain disdain for the evening's performance, the reality could not be further from the truth.

Al's performances with Ambrosia, part of a show in which a series of artists would each perform their hits using Ambrosia as the *de facto* 'house band', were invariably the highlight of the evening; Gary Wright's rendition of "Dream Weaver" being the only performance that got anything close to the ovation Al's three songs would each night. That Al was returning to the less than perfect situation of not having any of his albums available in American record stores was a situation that, for the moment, he was content to accept with a wry "Well it's par for the course" when pressed about it by a reporter in New York. "These things take a while to sort out at the best of times" he continued. "I'm at the end of a long line of people that are tangled up in the Miramar situation. It could take years." No one, least of all Al, had any idea just how accurate that last comment would turn out to be.

Out on the road Al also continued to perform with Dave Nachmanoff, more often than not at local Californian shows. On August 11th they played together at the Freight & Salvage in Berkeley, playing a set of standards augmented by the three tracks from *Down In The Cellar* that Al had come to enjoy playing on stage the most, namely, "House Of Clocks", "The Night The Band Got The Wine" and "Waiting For Margaux", which would invariably be the second encore number.

Due to the success of the UK tour at the start of the year Al, now being looked after in the UK by Pete Smith, had agreed to undertake a second British tour starting on September 13th in Bury. This would be the first time since 1974 that he had toured more than once in the same year in his home country but with Miramar now a full year into bankruptcy (and the situation showing no sign of being resolved just yet) there was clear logic in doing shows in territories that EMI held sway in. And the UK was the obvious choice.

Al flew back, as he always did, a few days before the start of the tour to try and beat the jetlag of the transatlantic trip. On his first morning back at his parents' house in Dorset he was due to do an interview with the BBC when the events of September 11th changed everything.

It was thus a somewhat restrained tour party that mustered in the lobby of The Holland Park Hilton just two days later on the morning of the first show. The occupants of the tour bus included Teddy Thompson, who would be opening for Al this time around. Son of

Richard and Linda and still smarting from being recently dropped by his record company, Teddy would prove to be the perfect person to have along at such a time. His dry sardonic wit and tales of life as a struggling artist amongst among his more famous friends in LA would soon brighten up many a journey as we travelled up and down the UK for the next three weeks.

To misquote Al – "The first show was very nearly the last show..." when the first date on the tour, at Bury's Metropolitan Arts Centre, was beset by a series of technical problems straight out of *Spinal Tap*. It all boiled down to there not being anyone on hand at the venue to run the mixing desk and the resulting sound, both through Al's onstage monitors and in the house was awful. It was a mess in fact. For much of the show.

And by the time the tour played the Huntington Halls in Worcester a couple of days later, Al had turned the occasion into a song, in a piece entitled "Feedback and Ribena", the appearance of Ribena in the title being a wry reference to the wine that had been provided in the dressing room. He played it just the once, more as a dare than anything else, in front of an audience that evening in Worcester that included his Aunt Hazel and Uncle John.

By now things had begun to settle down a bit on the tour and Teddy was proving to be quite the hit each night, playing songs from his Joe Henry-produced CD of the previous year. One of these in particular, "Wake Up",was routinely getting a reception that would bring the house down.

And Teddy was now instrumental in setting the stage for a notable date in England's Folk Rock history when his mother, the legendary Linda Thompson, came down to see the fourth date of the tour in Hayes on Tuesday 18th. Sixteen years earlier, Linda had made a dramatic and sudden exit from a folk world she had helped to create when, as a result of both her divorce from husband Richard and a rare and debilitating anxiety-based illness called hysterical dysphonia, she had gone in to self-imposed exile. An exile that many now assumed was permanent. She had all but slipped off the radar except for occasional appearances with The Royal National Theatre. But Linda had recently been recording with Edward Haber, chief recording engineer for WNYC, the New York outlet for National Public Radio and the man responsible for *Dreams Fly Away*, the 1996 retrospective of her work. It was therefore hardly surprising that, with Teddy using her Chelsea home as his base for Al's tour, she would listen to his tales of life on the road and in them see herself. And so, at around 8.30 that Tuesday evening, towards the end of Teddy's set, Linda Thompson walked out on to the stage to perform three songs with her son, so ending her exile in as dramatic a manner as it had begun.

The tour meanwhile continued to make its way around the country, playing to good sized audiences and clearly consolidating the success of the February tour. Liverpool was a case in point. A few months earlier Al had sold out the town's Neptune Theatre, a situation made all the more crazy by the fact that up until then he hadn't even been offered a Liverpool gig in almost thirty years. This time around local promoter Henry Chesterton booked Al in to the Pacific Arts Centre, just across the River Mersey in Birkenhead. And sold it out.

There were two more gigs on this tour that stood out for quite different reasons. The first of these had as much to do with its surroundings as anything else. EMI, having recently reissued *Year Of The Cat* with extended liner notes and two bonus tracks (a live "On The Border" from 1979 and an out-take from *Modern Times*, "Belsize Blues"), hosted a showcase gig for Al in the very same Abbey Road studio that the album had been recorded in twenty-six years earlier. Hosted by Mike Heatley, the evening featured what was, in essence, an edited version of the tour in that both Teddy and Al each performed short sets to an invited audience of friends, family, press, musicians that played on the album and EMI staff. It was the first time that many of these people had seen one another in years, some since the actual recording sessions themselves, and the evening proved a notable marker on an eventful tour.

And then on Friday 28th Tim Renwick joined Al on stage in Exeter for what was only the second time in twenty years as together they performed majestic versions of "Apple Cider Reconstitution", "Year Of The Cat" and "Carol". After this there were more concerts including shows in Reading, Swindon and London's Queen Elizabeth Hall, before the British leg wound up in High Wycombe on Monday 8th October. There was then a short European side trip to do some foreign press and three shows. These were in Mainz on the 11th, Brussels on the 12th and Utrecht on the 14th, after which Al flew back to San Francisco for a short break before a show in St Louis on October 28th.

So he was definitely doing all that he could to promote *Down In The Cellar*, despite the fact that there was still no sign of the Miramar bankruptcy being resolved. And it had now been over a year.

In the period leading up to the British tour Al and one of his new Marin friends had set in motion the plans for what would become one of Al's most anticipated shows in recent years. The show was 'Al Stewart Live At Grace Cathedral' and Al's good friend was Louis Weiner.

Louis had worked at Grace Cathedral since January of 2001 and had initially got to know Al through meeting Kris through the school run. And, just like Al, he had led a life in which playing music had been pivotal.

Louis – "When I was first starting out I had a regular solo gig at Straw Hat Pizza in Marin playing songs by Gordon Lightfoot and people like that. I also played at The Lark Creek Inn on weekends for two years, playing five hours a night!"

He was also part of a duo. "Back in 1973 I also played with my friend Paul Haas. We wrote songs together and played at places such as The Lion's Share in San Rafael and The Sleeping Lady Cafe in Fairfax, Marin having hung on to its hippy roots a little longer than much of the world!"

As a duo they played around town and even made the trip to Hollywood and auditioned for legendary producer John Rhys at the famous Rocking Chair Music studios. However, ultimately Louis decided to devote himself to classical music and achieved great success in this. Within two years he was part of the Music School in Princeton and singing in the choir at Carnegie Hall. A by-product of Louis' re-commitment to the classics was that he gave up the guitar. Completely. Louis – "I most certainly did. I put my guitar away and didn't really play it again for almost twenty years!"

But he never completely forgot the days when he had, by his own account, "worn out the Bert Jansch album *Rosemary Lane*", and so one afternoon he contacted Al with a plan.

"I got bold and basically just called him up on the phone and asked him if he'd consider playing in a Cathedral?" To which Al replied that he would play "anywhere I was asked to" and so Louis proceeded to explain how the nature of the venue was such that it demanded something a little more substantial than just Al and his guitar. Out of this grew the bare bones of an agreement and after a short period (but without at this time any special rehearsal) one, and then two, shows were pencilled in for Al to play at Grace Cathedral in the heart of San Francisco on November 18th and 19th. There were of course many logistical problems in producing a show like this but even so there was only one partial run-through before the first night! On the one occasion when Al came down to the Cathedral he remained to be convinced if this was all really possible. They ran through bits of songs, stopping constantly to fine tune this and that.

Louis – "In truth he was initially very sceptical about whether or not this was something that on the night would all work out OK. I think that he grew in confidence as we ran through a few songs with the organist but I'm not sure that he was absolutely certain that all would be well as he arrived for the first show."

These concerts became the centrepiece of what amounted to an Al Stewart Convention in the city arranged by the ASML and Kim Dyer and they were a huge success, both performances selling out. They were also filmed and as result of this the *Grace Cathedral* DVD was later released.

Grace Cathedral 2001

The shows kicked off with a perfectly-judged introduction by Louis followed by a set that included "Antarctica", "On The Border", "Old Admirals" and "Roads To Moscow". The Grace Cathedral shows also featured Doug Mann and Dave Nachmanoff. Dave had by now begun to establish himself as Al's *de facto* onstage partner but the genesis of his arrival on the scene can be traced directly back to Al's 1984 European tour and beyond. Dave had talked his way backstage at the Royal Albert Hall show and told Peter that if ever they needed another guitar player that he was their man! He knew all of Al's songs and he was available!

A full decade passed until one night in late '93 when Al and Peter were performing together at 'The Great American Music Hall' in San Francisco and Dave got the chance of jamming with Peter after the gig. At that moment in time Peter's solo career was about to really get going and his commitments to Al were proving difficult to fit in. Peter was therefore on the look out for someone to step in to his shoes. The day after the San Francisco show he called Steve Chapman and within a couple of days Dave was auditioning in Al's house in Bel Air!

It would be fair to say that Al almost certainly had some misgivings about the events that day. Peter had been with Al for almost twenty years. Up until the time that Peter first arrived on the scene in 1975 Al had been struggling to find a group whose members could cut it both in the studio and on stage. And for the very first time, the musicians selected to go out on the 'Modern Times' tour, had been a group that were up to that task. Peter's arrival turning out to be a pivotal moment for both him and Al, as his apprenticeship through the Kinetic and Arista years would produce a band leader uniquely qualified to steady their ship through the uncertain waters of the 80's and 90's.

To Al, with his last album *Famous Last Words* having not been the easiest CD to either record or find distribution for, the spectre of Peter heading off into the sunset at that particular moment must have given him genuine cause for concern.

Dave – "Al showed us into the living room and gestured to a couple of Ovation guitars, one of which I picked up and off we went. Not very much chat and certainly nothing by way of discussion as to what we should play or even what would be a good key to play in. None of that at all. It was a question of diving in and hoping for the best in many ways."

As it turned out Laurence Juber got the gig of course, but Dave was now on the radar at least. Over the next few years Dave got to step up and play the occasional show with Al at places like Sacramento, Modesto, Berkeley and Mount Shasta. He would sometimes pop up as a special guest and play violin or accordion on specific songs and then on other occasions he would play the whole show. And little by little Al came to realise that, in Dave, he had someone that he could depend on, much as he had been able to rely on Peter for the period of *Modern Times* to *Famous Last Words*.

And so it was no surprise that Dave was asked to be part of the Grace Cathedral evening.

SOMEWHERE IN ENGLAND

2002 continued in much the same vein as the year before with Al doing short runs of shows in the US. At the end of February he did a short East Coast tour, performing in New York City (where he played The Bottom Line in Greenwich Village with John Wesley Harding), Northampton and Philadelphia.

By now it had been a year since *Down In The Cellar* had been released in the UK on EMI. Steve Chapman – "2001 had of course seen Al doing two British tours and they had both played to good audiences and of course the new record was available there, unlike the US. And EMI were quite pleased, as they would be! So the decision was made for Al to go over and do his third UK Tour in fifteen months."

Chris Jagger was the support act and a tour of sixteen dates was booked, opening at the Newcastle Opera House on May 22nd and playing a diverse selection of venues such as The Lowry Theatre in Manchester, Liverpool's Neptune Theatre and The Anvil in Basingstoke. There was also a three show mini-tour of Ireland, ending at Dublin's historic Olympia Theatre on 11th June.

The day before that show, walking through Dublin en route to a matinee showing of the movie *Almost Famous*, Al spoke about being on the road. "It's a bit like a military campaign to me. All of this moving camp every couple of days. Most of the time on tour is just hanging around, waiting in airports or sitting on the bus and the show itself is when I'm happiest. This is all very nice though. I mean who wouldn't like to be walking through Dublin on a sunny Spring afternoon like today, going to the movies, maybe having some lunch if we can find somewhere. But I don't like the travelling itself. Bob Dylan seems too though…The Never Ending Tour is not for me but trips like this are fun."

On his return to the US, there were more shows on the East Coast including gigs in Rhode Island and Massachusetts where, during dinner at The Blackthorne Tavern he came up with a surreal set list of cover versions he said he'd one day like to do. Al described this enigmatic roster of his favourite songs as "My version of *Pin Ups*" after the classic 1973 album of covers that David Bowie had released in the wake of retiring Ziggy Stardust.

The songs Al picked included Lonnie Donegan's "My Old Man's a Dustman", Bowie's "Life On Mars" and Led Zeppelin's "Communication Breakdown". Rounding off the list was that day's obligatory Dylan cover "Like A Rolling Stone."

Throughout the trip Al had been reading *Stoned*, Andrew Loog Oldham's classy memoir of the 60's, a book which would prove to be the catalyst for a major new song the following year. It's interesting to note what he said about the book as he was reading it – "I love this book. I mean, how couldn't I? He knew everybody it seems. It's maybe the best book about swinging London that I've ever read. It breathes the 60's…and I should know because I was on the fringes of lots of this stuff. It's one of those books that you don't want to end."

The short East Coast trip ended with a huge free show in the middle of Boston, where Al opened for Don McLean. It was during this short series of concerts that Al announced that he would be doing a major tour of The Netherlands that October, along much the same lines as his 1996 trip there with LJ to promote *Between The Wars* and once again playing in Arts Centres. This would be his fourth trip to Europe in under two years.

The trip opened in Papendrecht on October 3rd and continued on through such places

Randall Armor

Boston 2002

Peter de Bock

Netherlands Autumn 2002

as Groningen, Breda, Lelystad and Cuijk, ending up in Drachten on October 23rd, having played thirteen shows. "Arnold Layne" was the tour's nominated cover version and local resident Iain Matthews came along and played at the Venray show on October 22nd.

So all in all it had been a very busy year for Al on stage but there was still no news of the situation with Miramar being resolved and Al's CDs continued to be largely unavailable in the US. Al's take on all of this remained as pragmatic as ever but towards the end of his trip to Europe he spoke about the effect it had on his songwriting. "I have ideas for songs all of the time and some of these stay in my head and then sometimes I'll have a tune that seems to fit and I'll work on it at the piano or on the guitar. But I don't collect finished songs on a weekly basis in the way that, say, Elvis Costello seems to. I'm much better at working to a deadline and finishing the lyrics in the studio. And for that reason there are very few songs that have slipped through the net and not made it on to an album. And Miramar going bust certainly hasn't helped this creative process. It could be another five years before I have a US record label that would release them anyway."

And with that Al flew back home to California for Christmas.

2003 started with more American gigs. Al played in St Louis on 16th January, Milwaukee on the 17th and Chicago on 18th January. Meanwhile up in the Pacific Northwest, Ron Scott, an importer of vanilla by day and a concert promoter by night, had taken a chance by putting on some local Al gigs and had booked Portland's Aladdin Theater for 31st January and Seattle's Tractor Tavern for the day after. These shows proved to be the first of many that Ron would promote for Al and the support that they received confirmed that Al was still as big as ever up there. Spurred on by what had always, way back to the Year Of The Cat Tour, been a fanatical fan base there, Al came up with a very different set list for the Seattle gig, including "Life In Dark Water" and "You Should Have Listened To Al" in the show.

There then followed more Californian shows before, in mid-June, Al headed out to Nashville to record his long-awaited Country and Western album. Well, not quite! In reality he flew south to play what became two very different shows in Tennessee. On Saturday 14th June he played the Chattanooga Riverfest with Ambrosia and got to sing "Get Back" with Billy Preston on keyboards as an encore.

The show a couple of nights later was a totally different affair, being in the legendary (but tiny) Bluebird Cafe, situated in the Green Hills neighbourhood of downtown Nashville. This show was particularly noteworthy because Phil Kenzie turned up with his sax and joined Al for spellbinding performances of "Year Of The Cat" and "Time Passages". This was the first time that they had played together on stage since 1977.

The next major date in Al's calendar was July 26th when he was booked to play The Calgary Folk Festival. Just before he flew up to Canada he received, by Fedex, the contract for a new American deal with Warners; all outstanding Miramar issues having now been resolved and the Warner offer being the best offer that Steve Chapman had received. The terms of the deal were that Warners got to lease the rights to all of Al's albums for a five-year period and this of course meant that for the first time in over three years his records would again be available in US record stores. He signed this not insignificant contract in the kitchen of his house in Marin over breakfast a couple of days before the Calgary show.

The Warner offer was only for his back catalogue though. And Al had been saying for the past three years that he wasn't even going to think about writing songs for a new album until the Miramar situation had been sorted out. There were, at most, four ideas for compositions that he had worked on in varying degrees but that was it. No stack of demos secretly recorded at Laurence's studio, no notebooks full of thirty verse songs on enigmatic characters from the footnotes of obscure biographical journals. In essence Al had done exactly what he said he would do. He had just waited out time until the attorneys at Miramar had got around to dealing with the portfolio of assets that included his contract with the company that they had closed down in 2000. But now that he was free from

Miramar he was also free to find a home for his next album; an album for which he had few, if any, songs.

On this tricky but unavoidable subject Al had this to say on the afternoon of the day that he'd signed the Warner contract.

Al – "The fact that I don't have a batch of songs all ready to be recorded doesn't mean that I don't have ideas for songs! I wrote much of the last album in a week and if needs be I could do the same again." On the subject of whether or not these "ideas" had a common theme he said "In many ways that restricts your options. *Past, Present and Future* obviously had a theme. That being the 20th century. And the last two records (*Between The Wars* and *Down In The Cellar*) did to a lesser extent but I'm not sure that I want to do that this time. But who knows? I could write three or four songs that, on the surface, have a central theme and the mould could be set. I just don't know. Ask me at Christmas."

Calgary proved to be a lot of fun and Al performed a well-judged set of hits along with a superb version of "In Brooklyn" to the thousands of fans enjoying the Calgary sunshine that Saturday afternoon. Ani Di Franco was also on the bill and she sat on the edge of the stage for all of Al's set paying close attention throughout.

By this time Dave Nachmanoff was performing with Al on a proper, paid basis whenever Al played gigs in California and Al was continuing to perform all out-of-state shows solo.

Dave – "Things were going just great and I felt that we had built up something of a rapport with one another that worked very well on stage. Then in the summer of 2003 a friend of mine in Texas mentioned to me that it would be a nice idea if I could somehow play with Al at his upcoming shows in Houston, where he was playing two nights at the Mucky Duck and also in Austin, where Al was booked to appear at the legendary Cactus Cafe."

And so Dave took this as his cue to suggest to Al that perhaps the time was right for 'out-of-state' gigs to be considered as shows at which they could perform together. Al said "Yes".

By now Dave did indeed have quite an act going with Al and the show that they played that Saturday night in Austin had sold out weeks before they even arrived in the town. One of the highlights of the show was by now an extended "Running Man" that would routinely bring the house down. "Coldest Winter In Memory" now invariably made the set list and the diversity of those two pieces shows the growing confidence that Dave had in his own performance and that, in turn, Al also had in Dave.

The success of this first 'out-of-state' trip resulted in Al asking Dave to accompany him on a short run of East Coast dates at the end of September. These included shows in South Easton Mass, Piermont and New York City's Bottom Line. At the New York show Al was introduced on stage by old friend Carol Miller, in her capacity as a leading disc jockey on Sirius Radio. Towards the end of the show John Wesley Harding joined Al and Dave for twenty amazing minutes as they performed "I Don't Believe You", "The Dark and the Rolling Sea" and "You Should Have Listened To Al". As he fairly bounded off stage at the end of the set Al remarked, to no one in particular "Ladies and Gentlemen...that was Folk Rock at its best!"

Al's shows with Dave may well have been getting better and better but their live gigs remained the only time that they ever really got together and played though. Dave – "Because there are no real periods of rehearsal or joint practice. No sitting around jamming or working on new ideas in the afternoons. It is all based around the actual gig. It's quite true that often the first time that I have ever seen Al play a particular song is when he decides to do it at a show and I have to work out what tuning it's in, where he's putting the capo and all of those things during the intro! But it is all part of what an Al Stewart show is. I realised that very early on."

And even writing a song together would not be quite as easy as you would imagine.

Neville

Dave – "My way and Al's of writing a song are polar opposites. I almost always start with a topic and lyrics whereas Al will almost always start with a piece of music and, as far as I can see, has no particular idea of what the song will be about until he starts to write the words."

But they have written one song together, "The Loyalist", recorded in the summer of 2000.

Dave – "The topic of 'Loyalist' was one that had intrigued me since I first heard the story, but it was difficult to put it into a song of any sort of manageable length. I came to Al with a long draft and explained the story – then we sat at his kitchen table, having tossed out the draft, and we noodled on the guitars. He came up with the opening riff, and made up some version of the first four lines. I kept going and wrote the next four. We messed around with that for a while and he sent me off to construct more verses. Several months later I returned with a draft and he helped me rewrite it. Sometime after that, I added the bridge. Most of the song was recorded in New Jersey, and the tape was flown to California where Al added his part (which he wrote in the studio). Then we mixed it in New Jersey. I love playing it live, as it feels like being "part of" an Al Stewart song – and yet, because it's about my wife's ancestor, it's also very personal to me. Playing it in front of an Al Stewart audience is usually great, because they come expecting to hear folk-rock historical ballads, and generally like that kind of song. It has gotten a good response from other audiences too though, and is a way of introducing my fans to Al's music I guess."

That summer also saw the initial discussions between Al, Steve Chapman and Henry Nash for Henry to maybe facilitate the recording of Al's next album. One key factor in all of this was when Laurence Juber would be available to produce it but by December a schedule, Laurence's availability and a deal would all be agreed.

The East Coast trip that September also included shows at The Blackthorn Tavern in South Easton and the legendary Caffe Lena in Saratoga Springs. Then on September 26th Al played a solo gig at the Sylvia Theater in York, South Carolina, this being one of several solo trips to the East Coast that year. He played shows in Sellersville and Reading

AL STEWART

PA just a few weeks later in mid-October. But there were still no new songs in the set. He had tried out a piece entitled "Dark Side Of The Street" a few times but freely admitted that the song may not be in the running by the time that the new album came to be recorded (he was right). One bit of positive news on the horizon regarding all of this was that early January had by now been pencilled in for recording sessions in LA, once again with Laurence Juber as producer.

That November Al sat down at home to go through the final photographs that were under consideration for the "Life In Pictures" book project that now had a new working title of *Lights...Camera...Folk Rock!* Many of the pictures were family snapshots and as such were unique and so the decision was taken to have a mobile studio set up in the dining room and a local photographer duly came up to the house and scanned the images in one weekend.

These included the complete *Love Chronicles* session that Al had as colour transparencies, black and white school photos of his first band and pictures of his trips to France. These turned out to be some of the key images in the finished book and as such were a real find.

As soon as the New Year arrived Al drove down to Laurence's The Sign Of The Scorpion studio to start work on their third album together, recording the first track (a demo of "Somewhere in England 1915") on January 6th. The recording process would follow something of their standard routine in that Al would spend a week based in LA, recording in the afternoons, before returning to San Rafael to write either new material or to polish up the lyrics to existing demos. Then he'd drive back down to work some more. And all of the time he was doing gigs and trying these new songs out on audiences. A case in point was when he took a break from the initial recording sessions to play at McCabes Guitar Shop in Santa Monica on January 11th, where he performed "Dark Side Of The Street" which he had just demoed.

Towards the end of the month Al headed up to the Pacific Northwest for some more

Al and Laurence. February 2004

shows promoted by Ron Scott booked for January 23rd and 24th. The night before the first gig at the Aladdin Theater, Al attended a special wine tasting that had been arranged in his honour at Vigne, on Portland's 10th Avenue. So impressed was he by their cellar that the next night he told the audience at his Aladdin show that Vigne was somewhere that they had to visit!

The Portland show itself was one of Al's best shows in years which was hardly surprising as it had so much going for it. Al had indeed spent much of the time since the previous summer thinking about new songs, just as he had promised – remember his "Ask me at Christmas" response when pressed on this very topic six months earlier. And so on the flight up to Portland he duly had two new songs to perform. Two songs that, as he would soon inform the audience, were still very much "works in progress" and that had "actual gaps where I make up the words as I go along" but, as Al said in the dressing room just before he walked out on to the stage, "This makes it all the more interesting both for me and the people out there. It will give tonight's show an edge anyway. Maybe they'll hate them both! But my audience like obscure songs and if these are anything then they are obscure. I bet that no one has ever even mentioned Oriole Records before in a song here…ever!"

That last comment of Al's was directed at a song which was then called "Somewhere In England 1958". And it was an epic. The premise of the piece being that in 1958 British music had changed overnight with the release of "Move It" by Cliff Richard and the Drifters (as the Shadows were then known), a song so radical that it at once spelt doom for the hordes of homegrown cabaret singers that had, up until 1958, not only been covering the latest American hits but had also been taking these tacky remakes high up the UK Charts. Al's song chronicled the wave of British bands that appeared as a result of Hank Marvin's opening guitar intro and along the way made ironic and knowing reference to Oriole, a record label that was forever an also-ran in the general scheme of things and was, by that token, perfect material for one of Al's songs. And it rocked!

That evening's set was eclectic even by Al's standards. The second song was "Helen and Cassandra" and after a few pieces from *Down In The Cellar* he spent several minutes setting up his first new song of the evening, "Somewhere in England 1958", which Al confided was "beyond weird in terms of what I normally do…" to a, by then, hushed Aladdin audience. He then played an almost flawless thirteen minute version of the song. And they went wild. Al seemed a little taken aback that such a song would have gone down quite that well and then someone called up from the stalls "It's a keeper Al!" He was grinning from ear to ear as he introduced the next song; the very different "Somewhere in England 1915". These two new additions to the Set List could not have been more different. This second work in progress took the sense of optimism that we all feel 'in the beginning' and how that emotion is pre-destined to be diminished to some extent, as its central theme. Being an Al Stewart song it was set within the confines of a dream that kicked off on a railway platform straight out of *Brief Encounter* and continued via the WW1 War Poets to the present day.

It is worth noting that these two songs, both of which were still very much in their infancy in so far as being 'road tested' before an audience, would change very little between this show and their release eighteen months later.

Next up Al played "Immelman Turn", his tale of the daredevil wing walkers that had toured the US between the wars. And although he had performed this song before, it was still new to most of the Portland audience. So that made three new songs in a row. Then he went straight in to "Nostrodamus" and "Running Man" and introduced "Year of the Cat" with a surreal tale of how, in a previous life, he had been a Courtier at the Court of Henry VIII and how he'd subsequently moved in with "Katherine of Oregon", when Henry VIII had left her; a situation made all the more perfect by the fact that she had taken with her all of Henry's manuscripts and sheet music for his compositions including… "Year of the Cat".

"Katherine of Oregon", at this point in time little more than an excuse for a pun, would in fact end up taking centre stage amongst Al's new songs a year later. He came back on for encores of "Runaway" and "Optical Illusion" and that was it. If the remainder of 2004 was going to be anything like this then the new album, if there was going to be a new album, was already shaping up nicely.

The next day, Saturday, started with a lunchtime drive from Portland up to Seattle and a show at the Tractor Tavern, another place that Al knew well and another sold-out show that tonight included performances of "The Dark and the Rolling Sea", "Mondo Sinistro" and "Old Admirals", besides the two new songs that he had introduced to his set list the night before in Portland. And so that was very much the way of his shows at the start of 2004.

Al was very upbeat about how things were going and clearly the pairing of him and LJ remained a very efficient and productive thing. "I work as well with Laurence as any other producer I've known. If I want to re-record a vocal he sets things up before I've even walked across to the microphone. If I mention one day that it would be interesting to hear some electric guitar on a certain track then it's magically there on a CD at my home the next day. Laurence is everything in the studio. He really is."

There were already clear differences between this and previous albums they'd worked on though. Laurence had this to say – "It became obvious quite early in the process that this would not be as piano-driven as *Down In The Cellar*. In fact, I was happy to find that there was plenty of room for electric guitar, as well as the usual acoustic stuff. It was also clear that Al was highly motivated and, as a result, the project progressed quite rapidly. That is, at least, from a creative perspective. There were some long gaps in the early scheduling to accommodate our respective tour schedules."

Gaps or no gaps, things continued apace and not just in the studio. Henry and wife Sue formed nash2music and in February they had a formal contract with Al to finance the album. Up until this time there had been a real chance that "Coldest Winter In Memory" would be re-recorded for the album. However it was by now clear that Al had more than enough new songs to fill a CD and so the idea was now dropped.

Lyric revision in Los Angeles. Summer 2004

On February 13th Al played a special hometown benefit concert for the local Coleman Elementary School in San Rafael at the Marin Showcase Theatre. The event sold out, due in no small part to the advance work of Kris, working in her capacity as President of the school's PTA.

And a few days later Al was back in Los Angeles recording tracks including "Mona Lisa Talking" with LJ and also finding the time to play another show at the Coach House in San Juan Capistrano and so he was certainly busy. By late February Laurence had completed demos of "Immelman Turn", "Beacon Street", "Anniversary", "Somewhere in England 1915", "Grace Cathedral", "Somewhere in England 1958", "Mona Lisa Talking", "Sovay", "Out In The Snow", "Mr Lear", "Dark Side Of The Street" and an (as yet untitled) LJ instrumental. Laurence again – "This production project seemed to have a nice smooth rhythm right from the start. Technically, this is the first of Al's records to be recorded and mixed digitally from start to finish, which improved the logistics of the process – no more rooms full of 2" recording tape and time spent waiting for machines to rewind!"

That March Al played further gigs at BB King's Club in New York City (where he opened for Jim Capaldi), the Towne Crier in Pawling New York, Northampton's Iron Horse and at the Dennis Flyer Memorial Theater in Blackwood, New Jersey.

It had by now been two years since Al had played a concert in the UK, a situation partly caused by the fact that he had completed three major British tours in the sixteen months between February 2001 and May 2002 and with no new CD to promote a 2003 tour had seemed a somewhat risky proposition. But the Asgard Agency had offered Al a series of dates for May 2004 and this eventually grew in to a sixteen date tour that stretched from Southampton to Glasgow, kicking off with a date at Aylesbury Civic Centre on May 5th. Dave joined Al for the tour. By the second night in Ebbw Vale Al was informing the audience that throughout the tour he was trying to write "a new song every day" and although this was, sensibly enough, downgraded to something a little more realistic by the time he reached Scotland on the first Sunday, the trip was still jam-packed with new songs, many still very much open to revision. "Class of '58" was being re-written on a daily basis throughout the entire trip and Al was not averse to making good use of Google in order to inform certain elements of the new songs! It is a matter of record that for much of the afternoon of Sunday 9th May Al sat in front of a hotel computer checking and re-checking that his use of "victrolas" (as in "Class of '58") and "naugahyde" (in the, as then, simply entitled "Gina") was appropriate.

Glasgow also marked the debut of "Rainbarrel", when Al and Dave played it half way through their set. As Al quite truthfully informed the audience, "the lyrics had just been written in the van and the tune at the soundcheck" and indeed the guitar riff was so new that it took them a little while to remember it up on stage. However this early version of "Rainbarrel", just like the early versions of "Somewhere in England 1958" and "Somewhere in England 1915" would turn out to be very similar to the version that would go on to appear on the new album.

Yet after the concert Al still remained to be convinced about "Rainbarrel", saying "I think that it went pretty well but I might alter the tune. A tune that I love! It has an Eastern European feel that I think sits very well with the lyrics. But those lyrics…I think that I might have to play around with those too and so we will see. Not an easy song to play either, as we found out!"

The following day was free and so the tour party embarked on a very British 'day out' in Edinburgh to meet up with Al's old friend Maggie Holland. There was also a vague plan to visit the "Travels with Edward Lear" exhibition of watercolours at the National Gallery of Scotland as Al was presently working on a song about Lear, one of his earliest influences. And so after lunch with Maggie in Edinburgh, everyone trooped up to the National Gallery, only to find that the Lear exhibition had closed a few weeks earlier. However after some arm twisting by tour manager Chris Runciman, the gallery promised a private view of their Lear archives if the party came back in half an hour. And that is how Al came to find himself sitting at a desk, deep in the bowels of his homeland's National Gallery, surrounded by the very sketch books and water colours that would later appear in "Mr Lear".

Neville Judd

Neville Judd

Neville Judd

Neville Judd

Neville Judd

There were shows in major venues in Liverpool, Manchester and London that were all virtual sell-outs and through all of the these Al was experimenting with all of the new songs and it was during this time that "Somewhere in England 1958" became "Class of '58", along the way being revised to feature a completely different mid-section that documented the reality of being on the road. The song had become a pivotal element of the album that looked all set to take its title from the track.

The UK trip also included one of the more surprising side trips of this (or any) recent tour, when on 26th May, en route from Worcester to Milton Keynes, the tour van made a detour into the town of Stonehouse and for the first time in over thirty years Al revisited his old school, Wycliffe College. That is the Wycliffe College of "Love Chronicles" fame, a place that Al had called both "a prison" and "part of my life that I didn't enjoy at all" in various interviews over the years.

But Wycliffe had also been the proving ground for something every bit as positive in Al's life as the school's rules had proved restrictive. And that was his love of Skiffle; as manifested in Al's involvement with The Snowballs and The Sunbeams, his very first groups, at the school forty years earlier. The idea for the excursion to Wycliffe had come from Al himself the previous evening but by the time the van was driving through the town centre the next afternoon he wasn't quite so sure that this was such good idea.

First stop was the record store where he'd bought his first single. The fact that it was now a hairdresser's did nothing to diminish the broad smile on Al's face as he looked in through the window.

From here he walked down to his old school house and then the chapel, where he posed for a few photographs. Al was by now on the very perimiter of the school grounds and so there was nothing else for it but to drive in through the gates. And this was when the day took on a surreal nature that, with hindsight, was entirely appropriate. Wycliffe's headmaster, who was passing through the school's reception office, announced that he himself would be very happy to give an ex-pupil a tour of his school.

His curiousity had already been piqued by the news that the ex-pupil in question was "on tour" and so the moment Al walked in he asked his name. And that is how Al discovered that the present day head of Wycliffe College, a place that had banned his first guitar on the basis that it was "an immoral instrument", owned three of his albums and up until that day had had no idea that Al had ever attended his school!

Henry and Sue caught up with the tour in London. Henry was keeping a journal of sorts, documenting the making of the album. He was clearly impressed by the evolution of "Class Of '58". He wrote – "In the case of 'Class of '58' things have changed much more dramatically – Al has re-written the entire second half of the song (that's about 7 minutes of re-write!). Several new melody sections have been added and the ending is now much more dramatic (although a few great humorous lines from the original version have been lost...) This goes down well at the QEH."

At this moment in time the working title of the CD was *Mona Lisa Talking* and the CD cover itself had by now taken on a life of its own and was all set to feature Al in a café scene, surrounded by characters from 50's and 60's rock 'n' roll. Jonny Kremer drew up a list of likely candidates and the plan was to have them all grouped together (*à la* Hopper's *Nighthawks At The Diner*.) Those up for consideration included Joe Meek, Andrew Oldham, Christine Keeler, Tony Newley, Françoise Hardy, Mary Quant and Bournemouth's finest, The Dowland Brothers.

The tour ended with a show at The Bloomsbury Theatre on June 1st after which Al returned to the US and alternated occasional shows that summer with further recording at Laurence's studio. "Gina" and "Rainbarrel", songs that hadn't even been written when Al was last in LA, were duly recorded within a month of the British tour ending. Once this was done Laurence went into Capitol Studio B on July 6th to turn the songs that he and Al had recorded since January into actual album tracks and final mixing was completed on August 26th.

Early design for the new CD cover

Things had progressed to such a point that a playback of selected tracks was arranged at LJ's studio. Steve Chapman attended, as did Ron Moss. Henry and June Nash also joined Al and Laurence to hear what were, at that time, seen as some of the tracks that would be making up the new album. Over lunch before the playback Henry made a final pitch for *Mona Lisa Talking* to be the album's title but *Class of '58* won out in the end, the track having latterly grown into such a defining force on the album.

Back home in Marin a few days later Al now set about assembling the running order, using his long standing method of aiming to avoid having sequential tracks in the same key. The process thus involved him darting between a notebook containing the evolving track list and his piano, where he would double check that there were indeed no two songs of the same key following one another. The double check was necessary because sometimes the key of a song would alter between the demo and the final studio version being cut. The running order took just a morning to complete.

Al – "And that we thought was that. The plan had been to get the album to EMI by early September and we'd done it. I was happy with the songs and especially "Class of '58" which, despite all of the rewrites, still had real spirit." But that wasn't it. Laurence had produced the final master and it had been duly sent over to EMI in London but a few days later Steve heard back from them and there was a problem. Whilst Laurence, a man rarely daunted by anything, would ultimately come to describe what happened as merely a "curve ball", it seemed serious enough at the time.

Henry's journal again for the beginning of September – "We are hit by a bombshell. EMI like the album but hate "Class of '58"! They don't want to take it in its present form – they are concerned that the track is too esoteric and the record may do poorly if everyone focuses on this as the cornerstone of the album. This is made more ironic by the fact that apparently it was a comment by EMI that gave Al the idea for the song in the first place!"

Henry's initial reaction was, understandably, one of acute disappointment and this led to him looking into the viability of independent distribution. However, Al and Steve had been here before and so wiser counsel prevailed and this unexpected news from London was soon being viewed postively as an opportunity to perhaps feature more songs on the album. But an album with a title that would now need changing!

But first Al and Laurence tried a quick fix on the track that was causing such concern at EMI. Henry's journal again – "Al & Laurence try out a new shortened version of the song – which turns a 14-minute 'Rock 'n' Roll Chronicles' into a good four-minute rock song. It sounds good as a song in itself, although has a totally different feel to the original.

Steve sends this to EMI to get their reaction – they like it, but now the album is too short (since we just lost 10 minutes)!! Al and I meet for lunch to talk about progress, discussion focuses on a new title for the album (*Just Yesterday* is Al's current favourite) and different cover. We come up with the idea of using the classic Christine Keeler 'chair shot'."

And so all of a sudden everything was up in the air and Laurence's success in delivering the project on time to EMI had been for nothing. And so it was no surprise to find Al in a somewhat relective mood, backstage at a gig in Paramus New Jersey at the end of September, as he kicked around the various options now on the table as he viewed them.

"I understand EMI's concerns. I just wish that this had occurred to us all a little earlier. And of course everyone is now asking me what I'm going to do now and the simple answer is I haven't a clue. Of course this could be the chance for "Coldest Winter" to dash in and save the day but of course that's another epic. So I don't think so. Maybe I'll write some new songs. I've been thinking about that just today in fact."

Up until now Al had been sitting, arms crossed, at the piano in an otherwise spartan dressing room as he considered all of this and he now turned towards the keyboard and started to improvise a medley of songs from the new album before stopping abruptly, asking no one in particular "What would the Dowland Brothers do in a situation like this ?" to which Dave Nachmanoff, who had been only been half listening as he tuned his guitar, replied "Dowland Brothers…who are they?" Al replied without missing a beat "Oh just a band I knew back in Bournemouth. I bet they've got some songs. I wonder what they're doing next week?" At which point he got up and started to write out that evening's set list. "I think I'll play 'Egyptian Couch' tonight" he said, "I haven't played that live yet." And so it was that if you came to see Al at this time you would witness a show still very much finding its feet after a year of transition but all the more compelling for it.

Meanwhile Steve Chapman and Henry met up in London a couple of weeks later for a special meeting with Mike Heatley from EMI to plan the way forward in the wake of them having accepted the new, slimmed-down *Class of '58*. It was agreed that a couple more songs were definitely needed and at this stage "Dark Side of the Street" was once again considered as a possible contender, although it only existed in demo form and would therefore need re-recording. It was also here that plans were first discussed for

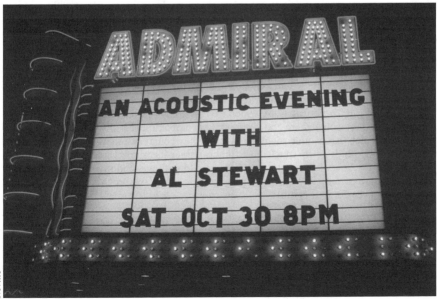

Neville

events surrounding Al's 60th birthday, now less than a year away.

There remained (and by now it was mid-October) the nagging issue of the album's US release and the simple fact that no label had yet made an offer. This was a subject that would come to occupy more of Steve's time than he had anticipated. Through all of this, Skyline, the booking agency run by Bruce Houghton, had been increasingly successful in securing Al concerts in Arts Centers, presumably on the basis that an audience raised on "Year of the Cat" would far rather now attend shows in the more comfortable settings that such venues could offer as opposed to those provided by any number of more down-at-heel venues on Main Street. To that end Al played a rare "showcase gig" for promoters in Bellevue Washington at the end of October and followed it with a show in Grant's Pass, Oregon at the town's Rogue Theater where he played "Midas Shadow" live for the first time in over twenty years.

He followed this with a rare trip down to the Southern States for a weekend of shows, kicking off with a concert in Duluth. On November 5th he played the latest Arts Center gig that Skyline had got him, at The Opera House in Newberry, South Carolina. From the outset Al was keenly aware that, for whatever reason, the audience that night were more than usually receptive to the stories he was telling between songs, listening in abject silence before bursting into spontaneous applause at the end of each of these spoken word interludes. And so little by little, as the show progressed, these usually brief anecdotes were expanded and embellished by Al to such an extent that the set list became all but abandoned and the evening ended up evenly divided between conversation and song. So much so that as his encore he simply told the full story of the day he met The Beatles. And it went down a storm. If there was ever a moment when the idea of Al touring a one man show of stories about his eventful life turned from fantasy to reality, then this was it.

The next day it was all that he could talk about. "I always said that I was just a stand up comic" he said, only half joking en route to that night's show in York. "And I think I'd pay to hear someone talk about knowing Paul Simon before he was famous or about getting Jimmy Page to play on their first record or hanging out at The Roxy with The Bangles. And then there's Fairport and Yoko of course! Maybe I could do this…" And so perhaps *Rolling Stone*'s crowning of him as "The Alistair Cooke of Rock" a quarter of a century earlier hadn't been wide of the mark at all. But for now the prospect of a new career in a new town rested solely with Al and his thoughts as he gazed out of the window and the car sped north through the Carolinas.

At Thanksgiving Al sat down at home in Marin, with a CD of the tracks he and Laurence had completed so far, a set of neatly typed lyrics and a cup of tea to discuss the album as he then saw it.

Al – "At the moment we still don't have a label to release it in the US. It looks like being either Appleseed or Artemis though. I think that we looked at eight or nine labels that specialised in folk singer songwriters. But if you look carefully at what they release, a great deal of it is 'Americana', by which I mean it is blues-based guitar, usually with a harmonica in there somewhere and a minimal accompaniment beneath that nasal Dylan/Springsteen voice that is quite rough in so far as they sound like they've been sleeping in a truck for a month. It's very much music that can trace its origins directly back to Woody Guthrie. But my voice has absolutely nothing to do with this and my musical influences are English pop of the 1960's and so trying to sell one of my records to a label such as Rounder is never going to work!"

In truth this search for a US label had taken much longer than anyone had expected and with EMI now planning a Spring release the need to find the album a US home was now paramount in everyone's thoughts. Everyone except for Al that is.

"I'm not worried. It will come out somewhere I'm sure. I spend more time thinking about what I'm going to have for lunch than the search for a label."

Which was something of a conundrum as Al was clearly very happy with the tracks that he and Laurence had recorded over the previous ten months, a fact clearly

Neville

Portland, Oregon 2004

Neville

York, South Carolina 2004

demonstrated by the manner in which he now discussed those songs.

Al – "Immelman Turn" was perhaps the first song written for the album. My tale about daredevils in the 1920's where, as I keep reminding everyone, I finally got the word 'aileron' into a song. It took me almost thirty years but I got there in the end! It has the sense of Fairport's 'Matty Groves' to it I always thought. But the oldest piece of actual music on the album is probably 'Beacon Street' which was for the longest time just a piano instrumental that I'd been trying to find a home for. I thought that it would have worked as background music in a movie but when that didn't happen I wrote these lyrics for it. 'Class of '58', which was of course originally 'Somewhere In England 1958' is now very different to how I originally wrote it. 'I've got a flip-side co-write, my name's right there', that said it all to me. But EMI then famously said that the original sounded like the Baron Knights…which I took as a compliment because I always liked the Baron Knights! But anyway, EMI didn't like it."

There is a good deal of irony in all of this. The Baron Knights were a British musical comedy group that recorded tongue-in-cheek parodies of 60's pop hits for Columbia Records, enjoying considerable chart success themselves along the way and even appearing on the bill at Beatles' Christmas shows as a result. To that end they probably had more in common with Peter Sellers than British Pop and so it is easy to see why Al would take it as something of a compliment to be compared with them while EMI would be thinking just the opposite!

Al also drew comparisons between this and an earlier song of his from 1968. "In a way it was like 'Love Chronicles' all over again, in so far as both songs had strong partisan support but many other people thought that they were both just too long! And if there is one thing that I've learned it is to never become too partisan about your songs!"

But while in public he put a positive shine on all of this it was clear that, had EMI not turned down the full length version of the song, he would have been perfectly happy to have it sat there centrestage on the new CD. The mere fact that the edited version no longer made any mention of Oriole Records (home to The Sputniks and Rory Storm and the Hurricanes) was sufficient to diminish it in Al's eyes.

"But then again I think that Laurence did a great job with the edit and I love the 'Red guitar, red guitar' refrain and so it's not all doom and gloom!"

As usual there were tracks on the album that were open to interpretation in different ways. There was "Out in the Snow", dubbed "'The Optical Illusion' of the record" by Al and featuring one of the album's best lines – "The exhalation of an Arctic God" and also "Anniversary", two songs rarely performed in public but among Al's personal favourites nonetheless. And on the subject of lyric writing Al was unusually candid as he sat there in the kitchen of his home in Marin taking stock of this latest collection of songs that he was about to release.

"The music still usually comes first, either as a fragment of a tune in my head or something that I've been playing around at on the piano. And for that reason the music often takes up the lion's share of the time. The new record has become much more of a guitar album than *Down In The Cellar* ever was but much of this album was in fact still written on the piano because it's sometimes easier to work that way. If I'm telling a story with lyrics then I tend to write just as fast as my pen can move across the sheet of paper. And sometimes I only stop because I physically have to because my hand is tired."

He spoke about "Rainbarrel" mentioning that it was loosely based on the Atom Egoyan movie *Ararat* and how he had "taken liberties with the storyline" as result of which it had become "one of those songs of mine that have taken on a life of their own. Musically it is very different to the pieces I write on the piano which all tend to be slower and more melodic. It is similar to 'Class of '58' in that respect."

Al then expanded on one of recurring themes of "A Beach Full of Shells", his character studies of 60's icons. "The song 'Class of '58' is full of them of course and in many ways 'Gina in the King's Road' is its companion piece.

"'Gina in the King's Road, in a raincoat shimmering white.
Hands thrust in her pockets like Julie Christie might!'
"It's the land of Carol White, *Poor Cow* and *Room at the Top*. 'Don't you cast aspertions at my naugahide affair' And ultimately this song became very much the 'Carol' of the album. I wanted something bright and zingy and to me that was the King's Road in 1968."

Humour, as ever, was centre stage on the new album. Sometimes it was somewhat black, as in Al's mention of A&R in the full version of "Class of '58" whilst other times it was ironic, as in the strategic placement of Oriole in the same song. But occasionally it provided the source material itself, specifically with "Mr Lear."

Al – "I grew up with Edward Lear. He was and remains a constant presence and something of an inspiration. And I don't quite know why it has taken me so long to write a song about him. As you know I was writing virtual eulogies to him back in school at Wycliffe." The song's lyrics are largely taken from the writings of Lear himself, including a passage from his *Incidents in the Life of my Uncle Arly*. To which Al added a few important events from Lear's life, such as his painting trip to Egypt. When asked about the influence of Lear on his own compositions Al commented "Yes, I can see his hand on some of the songs I've written but as to why I've written this song now I just

Daniel Coston

Daniel Coston

Neville

don't know."

However the motivation for the piece was something that Al was more sure about. "I wanted to convey the sense of joy that he had in life. I hope that comes through." But in reality Lear's life was often solitary and sad, something that Al touches on in the last verse -

When I was an old man I had a cat named Foss
Now he's gone, I wander on
With this unquenchable sense of loss

But the song almost had a different ending. Al "A very different ending! Originally I had written -

'He's walking away with the tip of a small top hat'
and in many ways I like that ending better…"

"Mr Lear" was the single new song that kept its place in Al's concerts throughout the making of the album. "Immelman Turn", "Somewhere in England 1958" and "Rain Barrel" would all come and go but Al's homage to Lear remained one of the first songs that made the set list each night through 2004.

"Egyptian Couch", which had originally been an instrumental called "Grace Cathedral", was described by Al as "just the standard Al Stewart track about steam ships and Chinese curses" while "Mona Lisa Talking" was something that he thought would have made a good follow up to "Year of the Cat" in the days when mid-tempo ballads got radio play. "Somewhere in England 1915" had remained intact since Al had first performed it a year earlier, which is interesting when the theme of the song is considered; a theme that would ultimately repeat itself throughout much of the new album. And it was unquestionably one of reflection and taking stock.

Al – "The song is about how everything is easier at the beginning. With all of the great endeavours of our lives we start them in one frame of mind and end them in another. It doesn't matter what it is, it can be a love affair, a war or what you do with your life. We start all of these things with a great deal of optimism but ultimately our feelings are very often tinged with regret." But even then, in his song of shifting time zones and haunting images Al can't resist an ironic twist and drops in a middle section where he looks down to find that a girl, someone that he'd "left long ago" is not, as he surely would have hoped, currently lost in the pages of *King Lear* but is instead reading *Twelfth Night*!

SOMEWHERE IN ENGLAND 1915
On the platform of an old railway station I enter a dream
And the couple is saying goodbye through the noise and the steam
But it's just *Brief Encounter*,
My mind is trying to rerun
And I wait for the poignant finale but the dream has moved on
And the train has turned into a ship which is sailing away
And the platform is a beach full of shells on the wintery gray
And the girl on the beach is an English Prime Minister's daughter
And she watches the ship disappear at the edge of the water
And the pain in her heart feels like it will be never-ending
And everyone feels this way in the beginning
And she watches the ship disappear for the length of a sigh
And the maker of rhymes on the deck who is going to die
In the corner of some foreign field that will make him so famous
As a light temporarily shines to illumine his pages
Then the scene has changed once again: now it's moonlight on wire
And the night is disturbed by sudden volcano of fire
And a skull and a trench gazes up open-mouthed at the moon
And the poets are now Wilfred Owen and Siegfried Sassoon
And nobody talks anymore about losing or winning
And everyone feels that way in the beginning
And I'm up in the air looking down at a girl on a bed

She is lying asleep on her side with a book at her head
It's someone who left long ago
Was it something I said?
And I hope that she's reading King Lear but it's Twelfth Night Instead
Now the girl and the train and the beach and the ship are all gone
And the calendar upon the wall says it's ninety years'on
I go out to the yard where the newspaper waits
There's a man on the cover we all know,
Defying the fates
And he seems very sure as he offers up his opinion
And everyone feels this way in the beginning
So if you feel that the pain in your heart will be never-ending
Well everyone feels that way in the beginning

The run up to Christmas saw Al playing more Californian gigs with Dave Nachmanoff including a show at McCabes in Santa Monica at which Robin Lamble guested on a couple of numbers. He then set about giving some proper thought to the content of a special performance that had been booked for New Year's Eve at Bryn Mawr, a show that was being billed as an "Evening of Music and Wine". The original plan had been somewhat ambitious in that Al would match songs with wines throughout the evening and take time out between each course to talk about what everyone was drinking and hearing. However by December 31st this had evolved into something that made a lot more sense and the evening was a mixture of fine wine and rarely performed songs, including the first ever performance of a new compostion "Katherine of Oregon".

By January 13th Al was back in LA at Laurence's studio to record "Katherine of Oregon" and "Royal Courtship", two very different songs but pieces that, once set against the others on the (still untitled) new album, would result in a record no longer compromised by a single track in the way that the original version, featuring the unedited "Class of '58", had been.

Al – "And I think that in the end we did have a better record due to EMI's intervention. Having, I thought, just finished a year of writing and recording back in August, there was no way that I would have written those two songs without the need, suddenly, for new material. As it turned out I like those two very much indeed." And Laurence agreed, saying that the late additions of those two songs "served to 'finish' the album with a broader narrative that suits the final title."

It took Al just two days to record the tracks and by January 14th they were done. Two weeks later Al looked back at the now completed album and specifically the two new tracks.

Al – "These are two completely different pieces. 'A Royal Courtship', my song about a King looking for a Queen, is really an exercise in language, in this case that of the Royal Court of the early 19th century. But at the time I wrote down those first words 'I sent my major domo to your emanuensis' I had no idea what they meant and so the line just sat there for a while. Then as I was actually writing the song I began to feel sorry for him and so by the time it was completed it had become quite a plaintive piece of writing and at that stage it had a different title." That original title was "A Royal Lament", something that Al soon changed to "A Royal Courtship" on the premise that this more accurately reflected the song's theme. Al had used the music of Leonard Cohen's "Suzanne" as a reference point for the lyric writing and indeed both compositions are in a similar metre.

It was first performed live in Fairfield on January 28th, Al introducing it as "My song about the protocols a King must follow in his search for a wife. Because a King can't just call up some distant Princess and ask her out to a movie can he?"

Finally Al turned to "Katherine of Oregon". By the time that he came to write this song most of the album was already completed and so it's interesting to note that he chooses to reaffirm one of the album's most enduring themes, that of reflection and taking stock, so deliberately here.

Al – "The song is about growing old and as such is self-explanatory. It came to me as a series of images, such as the line that mentions a garage full of nicknacks which is based on my stepfather's hobby of collecting old radio parts and others such as the verse about me wearing 'clothes with their colours all clashing', which is very much me I'm afraid! And when I'm old I can think of nothing better than to buy a jukebox and fill it up with all of my old Lonnie Donegan singles. I would be in heaven. I've always said that Lonnie Donegan was responsible for about fifty per cent of what I do and so for me to grow old

Neville

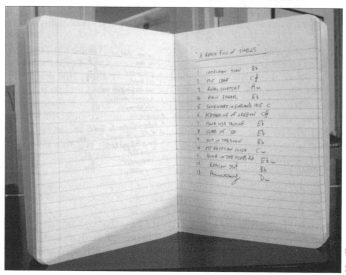

Neville

listening to all of those old songs is entirely appropriate!"

For Al, someone so well schooled in the use of metaphor, to now write such a simple and straightforward song about himself can only have been deliberate. And so "Katherine of Oregon" came at the conclusion of a year in which Al had not only recorded "Class of '58" and "Gina in the Kings Road" (two pieces with their origins firmly rooted in his memory of starting out in 60's London) but also "Somewhere in England 1915", a song built around the optimism that we all feel 'in the beginning'. A fact that escaped no one, least of all Al.

So how ultimately does Al now see himself? He has always delighted in using nouns to describe the characters that inhabit his songs. Such as 1970's "Zero She Flies" – "She's a swallow, a willow, a cello, a pillow, a bow and also a physician".

But in February 1979 he was asked to turn the tables on himself. The two objects he chose were both comic and surreal.

Al – "I think, first of all, a *cake*, because of Mervyn Peake's wonderful poem *The Frivolous Cake*. I've always thought cakes conveyed a sort of happy innocence, and sadness. Not just because they get eaten, but because it's a very straightforward thing, being a cake. I would also have to choose a *hatstand*. Among all one's furniture, a hatstand is very noble. It has a great sympathy for the human race, also a great benevolence. It spends its life supporting a variety of outrageous objects, some of them not too clean, some of them not too dry."

The author of that piece, over 20 years ago, felt that had Al not fallen into the music business he might have become a noted author of children's books or a slightly dotty stamp collector.

Al was then asked whether the creative mind flirted dangerously with madness?

Al – "Well yes, it does. But that doesn't mean you have to go mad to be creative. I have enough trouble keeping my mind on reality without *encouraging* it to go any further!"

And keeping his mind on reality was never something that Al was particularly interested in doing anyway. Remember, it was perhaps his closest friend in America, Dennis Overstreet, who told us how he felt that Al lived day to day in some kind of parallel universe, baffled by much of the modern world but forever curious none the less.

If that's the case, then the writer of "Old Admirals", "Optical Illusion" and "Roads To Moscow" really is *The Edward Lear of Rock*.

COPYRIGHT OF LYRICS

Lyrics quoted in this book by the kind permission of –

THE ELF
Al Stewart
Stratton-Smith Music
1966

BEDSITTER IMAGES
Al Stewart
Gwyneth Music Ltd.
1967

OLD COMPTON STREET BLUES
Al Stewart
Gwyneth Music
1969

IN BROOKLYN
Al Stewart
Gwyneth Music
1969

ELVASTON PLACE
Al Stewart
Gwyneth Music
1970

SMALL FRUIT SONG
Al Stewart
Gwyneth Music
1970

MANUSCRIPT
Al Stewart
Gwyneth Music
1970

THE NEWS FROM SPAIN
Al Stewart
Gwyneth Music
1970

YOU DON'T EVEN KNOW ME
Al Stewart
Gwyneth Music
1972

I'M FALLING
Al Stewart
Gwyneth Music
1972

NIGHT OF 4th MAY
Al Stewart
Gwyneth Music
1972

SWALLOW WIND
Al Stewart
Gwyneth Music
1973

NOT THE ONE
Al Stewart
Gwyneth Music
1975

FLYING SORCERY
Al Stewart
Gwyneth Music
Dick James Music Inc. BMI
1976

END OF THE DAY
Al Stewart & Peter White
Frabjous Music/Approximate Music/Lobster Music
1978

LIFE IN DARK WATER
Al Stewart
Frabjou Music/Approximate Music
1978

OPTICAL ILLUSION
Al Stewart
Heath Levy Music Co. Ltd.
Frabjous Music/Approximate Music
1980

MERLIN'S TIME
Al Stewart & Peter White
Frabjous Music/Approximate Music/Lobster Music BMI
1980

SOHO (Needless to Say)
Al Stewart
Frabjous Music/Approximate Music
Dick James Music BMI
1981

DELIA'S GONE
Al Stewart
Frabjous Music/Approximate Music
1981

ACCIDENT ON 3RD STREET
Al Stewart
Frabjous Music/Approximate Music
1984

CANDIDATE
Al Stewart
Frabjous Music/Approximate Music
1984

TRAINS
Al Stewart
Frabjous Music BMI
1995

MARION THE CHATELAINE
Al Stewart
Frabjous Music BMI
1995

LIFE BETWEEN THE WARS
Al Stewart
Frabjous Music BMI
1995

COLDEST WINTER IN MEMORY
Al Stewart
Frabjous Music BMI
1996

WHERE ARE THEY NOW
Al Stewart & Peter White
Frabjous Music/Lobster Music
1996

TASTING HISTORY
Al Stewart & Laurence Juber
Frabjous Music BMI/Juber Music
2001

DOWN IN THE CELLARS
Al Stewart
Frabjous Music, BMI
2001

GINA IN THE KINGS ROAD
Al Stewart
Frabjous Music, BMI
2005

SOMEWHERE IN ENGLAND 1915
Al Stewart
Frabjous Music, BMI
2005

The copyright of unreleased songs vests in the songs' author.

SOURCES

This official biography has been written with the direct assistance of Al, his friends and family. As such, the majority of the source material has been gathered through extensive interviews with those people. To them I remain eternally grateful. I have also been given access to Al's complete cuttings library and for this I owe Steve Chapman a huge debt. The sources quoted from there are acknowledged in the text. I also used the National Libraries in both London and New York City.

Finally I would also like to thank my parents, James and Betty Judd, for all of their help and support as this book set out on the long journey from a note book full of vague ideas to what you now have in your hands.

Neville Judd. London. 2005.

INDEX

AL STEWART
a life in pictures
By Neville Judd

ISBN 1-900924-90-0
Luxury paperback with jacket flaps
224 pages of photos including
16 pages of full colour photos 310mm X 227mm £25.00

This is a collection of photographs, most never seen before, from both the public and private life of Al Stewart. From Al's earliest days in post-World War Two Scotland, his pop bands in '60s Bournemouth and his early Soho Coffee House days and life as a folk legend in Swinging London, through to his success in Hollywood and beyond, this book is there with him, every step of the way.

Ashley Hutchings: The Guvnor and the Rise of Folk Rock – Fairport Convention, Steeleye Span and the Albion Band
By Geoff Wall and Brian Hinton
As founder of Fairport Convention and Steeleye Span, Ashley Hutchings is the pivotal figure in the history of folk rock. This book draws on hundreds of hours of interviews with Hutchings and other folk rock artists and paints a vivid picture of the scene that also produced Sandy Denny, Richard Thompson, Nick Drake, John Martyn and Al Stewart.
Paperback   ISBN 1-900924-32-3   256pp   234 X 156mm
UK £14.99   US $19.95

Brian Jones: Who Killed Christopher Robin-The Truth behind the Murder of a Rolling Stone
By Terry Rawlings
The basis for Stephen Wooley's new feature film The Wild and Wycked World of Brian Jones due in cinemas August 2005, this first ever paperback of an out-of-print classic includes new photos of the movie set, new evidence and a deathbed confession. In 1969, The Rolling Stones' founder Brian Jones was found dead in the swimming pool of his home, Cotchford Farm, AA Milne's former residence. Through exhaustive research, Terry Rawlings has amassed evidence contradicting the official Accidental Death verdict and in this book he names Jones' murderer. While Brian was initially the Stones' leader and creative driving force, by the mid-60s, his drink and drug intake began to spiral out of control and his resulting unreliability led to rifts within the band; Brian left the Stones in 1969. Three weeks later the 27-year-old rock star was found dead in his swimming pool – a verdict of misadventure was recorded. Terry Rawlings has interviewed in depth those who were present during Brian's last days and with the benefit of a deathbed confession he has solved the mystery of the tragic premature death of a Rolling Stone in this highly gripping page-turner.
Paperback   ISBN 1-900924-81-1   288pp   234 X 156mm   8 b/w photos
UK £14.99   US $19.95

True Faith: An Armchair Guide to New Order
By Dave Thompson
The first ever book to focus on the music of New Order, one of the key rock groups of the 1980s. Formed from the ashes of Joy Division after their ill-fated singer Ian Curtis hanged himself, few could have predicted that New Order would become one of the seminal groups of the 80s, making a series of albums that would compare well with anything Joy Division had produced, and embracing club culture a good ten years before most of their contemporaries. From the bestselling 12-inch single 'Blue Monday' to later hits like 'Bizarre Love Triangle' (featured in the *Trainspotting* movie) and their spectacular world cup song 'World In Motion' the band have continued making innovative, critically revered records such as their 2001 hit 'Crystal' that have also enjoyed massive commercial success. This book is the first to treat New Order's musical career as a separate achievement, rather than a postscript to Joy Division's and the first to analyse in-depth what makes their music so great. New Order release their eighth studio album in 2005: *Waiting For The Sirens' Call*.
   "Not only is this exhaustingly thorough … it's actually interesting as well… Fascinatingly comprehensive, this will be ambrosia for fans of New Order and contains enough juice to keep even the most lax fan occupied." NME
Paperback   ISBN 1-900924-94-3   256pp   234 X 156mm   8pp b/w photos
UK £12.99   US $19.95

Music in Dreamland: The Story of Be Bop Deluxe and Bill Nelson
By Paul Sutton-Reeves
Authorised biography of the flamboyant guitarist, singer and songwriter Bill Nelson, whose glam rock theatrics are revered and remembered by industry fans such as David Sylvian. The late John Peel was also a big fan. Be Bop Deluxe came to prominence during the 70s through a combination of rock theatrics and Nelson's fancy guitar work, moving from glam rock to new wave, via their art rock masterwork, *Sunburst Finish*. After Nelson split the band, he formed the acclaimed but short-lived Red Noise, with whom he recorded the new wave classic, Sound On Sound before embarking on a solo career. *Music In Dreamland* draws on hours of new interviews with Bill Nelson and other members of the band, as well as admirers such as Stone Roses' producer John Leckie, Steve Harley and Reeves Gabrel. Cover artwork especially designed by Bill Nelson himself.
Paperback   ISBN 1-900924-04-8   384pp   234 X 156mm   16pp b/w photos
UK £16.99   US $25.00

Belle and Sebastian: Just A Modern Rock Story
By Paul Whitelaw
First ever biography of the ultimate reclusive cult band – drawing on extensive interviews with band members. Formed in 1996, this enigmatic Glasgow band has risen to become one of Britain's most respected groups. For years, Belle and Sebastian were shrouded in mystery – the 8-piece ensemble led by singer-songwriter Stuart Murdoch refused interviews and the band scarcely toured. Their early singles though built them a strong and committed cult following. Their debut mail-order only album Tigermilk sold out within a month of its release and the follow-up, If You're Feeling Sinister, with its Nick Drake-influenced melodies and dark, quirky lyrics, found favour in alternative circles as far afield as San Francisco, Japan, South America and especially France. Oddly, for a band that sings about kinky sex and S&M, Stuart Murdoch lived above a church hall, sings in a choir and reads the bible. Such idiosyncratic contradictions are rife in this fascinating and

curious tale. This is not only the first biography ever written on the band, but the most official that might ever hit the market. The band has agreed to participate in the project and to give the author extended interviews, paraphernalia and both personal and publicity still photos. Stuart Murdoch himself has agreed to design artwork for the cover. Paul Whitelaw is an arts writer from Glasgow who has met and interviewed Belle and Sebastian on several occasions and he was the first journalist to champion the band in print.

Paperback   ISBN 1-900924-98-6   288pp   234 X 156mm   16pp b/w photos
UK £14.99

Rush: Chemistry – The Definitive Biography
By Jon Collins
The first truly in-depth biography of one of the most enduring and successful cult bands in rock.
Acclaimed Marillion biographer Collins draws on hundreds of hours of new interviews to tell the full story of the enduring Canadian trio who are one of the most successful cult groups in the world. From early days in Canada to platinum albums, stadium shows and the world's stage, taking in tragedy, triumphs and a wealth of great music, this is the meticulous and definitive study of one of rock's great enigmas. Against a background of media disinterest and a refusal to bow to mainstream industry marketing pressure, their success was by no means guaranteed. Only the determined efforts and downright stamina of the band members and those around them were sufficient to counter the wall of silence their originality encountered.

Hardback   ISBN 1-900924-85-4   320pp   234 X 156mm   16pp b/w photos
UK £20.00   US $30.00

Kicking Against The Pricks: An Armchair Guide to Nick Cave
By Amy Hanson
Complete career retrospective of one of the most important singer-songwriters of the last twenty-five years. Nick Cave is the only artist to emerge from the post-punk era whose music and career can truly be compared with legends such as Bob Dylan or Van Morrison, with a string of acclaimed albums including *Junkyard* (Birthday Party), *Tender Prey*, *The Boatman's Call* and his most recent epic, *Abattoir Blues/The Lyre of Orpheus*. Cave left Australia to become part of a maelstrom unleashed to awestruck London audiences in the late 70s: the Birthday Party. Miraculously, Cave survived that band's excesses and formed the Bad Seeds, challenging his audience and the Godfather-of-Goth tag: as a bluesman with a gun in one hand, a Bible in the other; a vamp-ish torch singer with echoes of Vegas-era Elvis and a sensitive writer of love songs. *Kicking Against The Pricks* chronicles in depth these diverse personalities and the musical landscapes that Cave has inhabited, with a penetrating commentary on all his themes and influences. Cave's memorable collaborations and forays into other media are covered too: duets with Kylie Minogue, PJ Harvey and Shane MacGowan, the acclaimed novel *And The Ass Saw The Angel*, film appearances such as in Wim Wenders' *Wings of Desire*, and his stint as Meltdown 2000 curator. Ultimately, it reveals Cave as the compelling and always-relevant musical force he is.

Paperback   ISBN 1-900924-96-X   256pp   234 X 156mm   16pp b/w photos
UK £14.99   US $19.95

In Between Days: An Armchair Guide to The Cure
By Dave Thompson
The Cure's complete career, chronicled for the first time. The Cure are one of the most respected and well-loved of rock's survivors, traceable right back to punk's fabled 'Bromley Contingent'. The band's labyrinthine story has at its centre the enigmatic, charismatic frontman Robert Smith, forever shuffling personnel, themes and styles to make enduring music without losing an iota of credibility. In Between Days is the first book to make sense of a uniquely versatile band who are far more than the Goth band, documenting their development from the new wave attack of 1979's *Boys Don't Cry*, the existential rock of *Seventeen Seconds*, the near-religious angst of *Faith*, the joyous pop of *Wish*, the dark beauty of *Disintegration* – right up to the majesty of *Bloodflowers* and 2004's The Cure, consecutive 21st century masterpieces. *In Between Days* also singles Robert Smith's brilliant interweaving literary influences from Mervyn Peake and Coleridge to Albert Camus and Jean Cocteau. Album-by-album, track-by-track study of the extraordinarily popular and enduring post-punks behind hits such as 'Love Cats' and 'In Between Days'.

Paperback   ISBN 1-905139-00-4   256pp   234 X 156mm   16pp b/w photos
UK £14.99   US $19.95

From the Velvets to the Voidoids
By Clinton Heylin
Exhaustively researched and packed with insights to give a detailed and all-encompassing perspective of American punk rock's 60s roots through to the arrival of new wave – this is the definitive story. Long overdue, fully revised and updated edition of the definitive account of the rise of US punk and the 'new wave' movement, led by acts such as Richard Hell, Television, The Ramones, Blondie and Talking Heads. Also includes more obscure acts of the era, as well as legendary venues like CBGB's and Max's Kansas City. This was originally published by Penguin in the early 90s. Clinton Heylin is the acclaimed author of a number of books including highly regarded biographies of Bob Dylan, Van Morrison and Orson Welles.

'No other book or account succeeded so well in accurately bringing the period to life.' Richard Hell

'This is a great story, and before Heylin no one saw it whole.' Greil Marcus

Paperback   ISBN 1-905139-04-7   288pp   234 X 156mm   16pp b/w photos
UK £14.99

On The Road With Bob Dylan
By Larry Sloman
In 1975, as Bob Dylan emerged from 8 years of seclusion, he dreamed of putting together a travelling music show that would trek across the country like a psychedelic carnival. The dream became a reality, and *On The Road With Bob Dylan* is the ultimate behind-the-scenes look at what happened. When Dylan and the Rolling Thunder Revue took to the streets of America, Larry 'Ratso' Sloman was with them every step of the way.
'The *War and Peace* of Rock and Roll.' Bob Dylan
Paperback   ISBN 1-900924-51-X   288pp   198 X129mm
UK £12.99

I'm With The Band: Confessions of a Groupie
By Pamela Des Barres
Long overdue return to print for the ultimate story of sex, drugs and rock 'n' roll – the definitive groupie memoir from the ultimate groupie. From the day she peeked at Paul McCartney through the windows of a Bel Air mansion, Pamela was hooked. Graduating high school, she headed for the sunset strip and rock and roll. Over the next ten years, she dallied with Mick Jagger, turned down a date with Elvis Presley, had affairs with Keith Moon, Noel Redding and Jim Morrison, and travelled with Led Zeppelin as Jimmy Page's girlfriend – he had 'dark chilling powers' and kept whips in his suitcase. She hung out with Cynthia Plastercaster, formed the all-girl group the GTOs, and was best friends with Robert Plant, Gram Parsons, Ray Davies and Frank Zappa.
'Ah, those were the days, and this is still one of the most likeable and sparky first-hand accounts.'   ****Q
'Pamela's mixture of hippy enlightenment and teenage lust is terrific.' *The Guardian*
Paperback   ISBN 1-900924-61-7   320pp   198 X 129mm   16pp b/w photos
UK £9.99

Wheels Out of Gear: 2-Tone, The Specials and a World on Fire
By Dave Thompson
Fascinating study of the 2-Tone ska revival of the late 70s and early 80s that plots the sounds of the remarkably successful scene against a backdrop of a Britain beset by unemployment, racial tension and large scale rioting. Taking its roots from Jamaican ska, rock steady and reggae, the 2-Tone sound was honed into a modern urban multi-racial mix by bands such as The Specials and The Selecter. Coming on the back of punk, 2-Tone was remarkably successful. The Beat and The Selecter also enjoyed strings of chart hits and groups born out of the same era such as Madness and UB40 forged their early success. 'Thompson recounts the rise of The Specials, Madness, The Selecter, The Beat et al with a tangible passion and also sets the music in the political and social context of those strange and disturbing times...a fine book that is as much social history as musical biography.' *Uncut* *** Top 30 Books for 2004
Paperback   ISBN 1-900924-84-6   256pp   234 X 156mm   16pp b/w photos
UK £12.99   US $19.95

Electric Pioneer: An Armchair Guide to Gary Numa
By Paul Goodwin
The first ever book to concentrate on the music of Gary Numan, 80s icon turned cult hero – adored and reviled in equal measures with a foreword from the pioneer himself. From selling 10 million records in 2 years, both with Tubeway Army ('Are Friends Electric?') and solo ('Cars' et al), to more low key and idiosyncratic releases through subsequent decades, Gary Numan has built up an impressive body of work and retained a hugely devoted cult following. *Electric Pioneer* is the first ever guide to his recorded output, documenting every single and album and featuring sections on his live shows, memorabilia and DVD releases.
'Nothing will alter the fact that I think he has written a couple of the finest things in British pop music.' David Bowie
'Gary Numan is a man who deserves respect for his songwriting and dedication to electronic music... Sometimes it takes a real fan to do it properly and I'm glad this one did.' *DJ Magazine*
Paperback ISBN   1-900924-95-1   288pp   234 X 156mm   16pp b/w photos
UK £14.99   US $19.95

Sex Pistols: Only Anarchists are Pretty
By Mick O'Shea
What *Backbeat* was to The Beatles, *Only Anarchists Are Pretty* is to The Sex Pistols! Drawing both on years of research and creative conjecture, this book, written as a novel, portrays the early years of the Sex Pistols. Giving a fictionalised fly-on-the-wall account of the arguments, in-jokes, gigs, pub sessions and creative tension, it documents their day-to-day life – chaos, rancour and a strange innocence. Before singles like 'Anarchy In The UK' and 'God Save The Queen', tabloid outrage and the recruitment of Sid Vicious, back in the years 1974-1976, the band were a bunch of rock 'n' roll obsessed street urchins and petty crooks, hanging around Malcolm McLaren's shop Sex [*Only Anarchists* takes its name from one of McLaren's shirt slogans] listening to his war stories of managing The New York Dolls; arguing, fighting, and forming a band to relieve the boredom.
'The idea alone is genius...an antidote to the self-important toss that is generally written about punk rock...*Only Anarchists Are Pretty* is unexcelled.' **** *Classic Rock*
'Engaging...true or not, this is the real story of the Sex Pistols.' ****Uncut*
Paperback   ISBN 1-900924-93-5   256pp   234 X 156mm
UK £12.99   US $19.95

Psychedelic Furs: Beautiful Chaos
By Dave Thompson
Rise and fall of glamorous post-punk pioneers best known for US hit 'Pretty in Pink.' The Psychedelic Furs were the ultimate post-punk band – combining singer Richard Butler's hoarse rasping vocals, reminiscent of Johnny Rotten, with the Bowie-esque glamour of his angular cheek bones, and a blistering futuristic wall of sound that merged distorted guitars with saxophone and synths. When John Hughes wrote a movie based on their early single 'Pretty in Pink' the Furs hit the big time in the US with a re-recorded, though inferior, version of the song. The now-leather jacketed Butler and co became MTV darlings and appeared poised to join U2 and Simple Minds in the premier league. Then just as quickly, they withdrew behind their shades. Recently reformed and playing energising live shows in the US, the Furs are one of the few 1980s rock bands to have survived with their mystery and integrity intact.

'Charts in an engaging and sardonic manner the rise and fall of the Psychedelic Furs...a loving portrait of a ramshackle bunch of visionaries that is well-written and informative...' *** *Classic Rock*
Paperback	ISBN 1-900924-47-1	256pp	234 X 156mm	b/w illustrated throughout
UK £14.99	US $19.95			

Bob Dylan: Like The Night (Revisited)
By CP Lee
Fully revised and updated edition of the hugely acclaimed document of Dylan's pivotal 1966 show at the Manchester Free Trade Hall. Documenting the most legendary concert and tour in rock history, this is a riveting eyewitness account of the controversial concert where fans called Dylan Judas for turning his back on folk music in favour of rock 'n' roll. Having been out of print for a number of years, this new edition covers the release of the official album and the resulting controversy over the emergence of the Judas accuser, as well as featuring additional previously unseen photographs.

'A terrific tome that gets up close to its subject and breathes new life into it... For any fan of Dylan this is quite simply essential.' *Time Out*
Paperback	ISBN 1-900924-33-1	224pp	198 X 129mm	b/w illustrated throughout
UK £9.99	US $17.95			

Steve Marriott: All Too Beautiful
By Paolo Hewitt and John Hellier
Definitive account of the Small Faces and Humble Pie main man: Mods, clothes, hit records, drugs, booze, mafia, bankruptcy, schizophrenia, classic rock 'n' roll, premature death and one of the great, great voices! Following his childhood debut as a street urchin in the original stage production of Oliver! Marriott became the world mod icon and prime mover behind 60s chart-toppers, The Small Faces, who scored a string of top ten singles including the classics 'All Or Nothing' and 'Tin Soldier'. They lived together in millionaire style at their chic Pimlico home, travelled by limousine, dated models and actresses and frequented London's most fashionable clubs. In 1968 Marriott and his band mates released a number one classic album *Ogden's Nut Gone Flake* and the world beckoned. But it was with Humble Pie, formed with Peter Frampton, that Steve and his blistering rock 'n' blues guitar playing achieved legendary status in the USA. After years in seclusion, Marriott's plans for a comeback in 1991 were tragically cut short when he died in a house fire. He continues to be a key influence for generations of musicians from Paul Weller to Oasis and Blur.

'Revealing...sympathetic, long overdue.' *****Uncut*
Hardback	ISBN 1-900924-44-7	288pp	234 X 156mm	8pp b/w photos
UK £20.00	US $29.95			

This Is a Modern Life
Compiled by Enamel Verguren
Pictorial and anecdotal documentation of the 1980s London Mod scene.
Lavishly illustrated guide to the mod revival that was sparked by the 1979 release of *Quadrophenia*. *This Is a Modern Life* concentrates on the 1980s, but takes in 20 years of a Mod life in London and throughout the world, from 1979 to 1999, with interviews of people and faces who were directly involved, loads of flyers, posters and a considerable amount of great photos.

'Good stuff ... A nice nostalgic book full of flyers, pics and colourful stories.' *Loaded*
Paperback	ISBN 1-900924-77-3	224pp	264 X 180mm	b/w illustrated throughout
UK £14.99	US $19.95			

Everybody Dance
Chic and the Politics of Disco
By Daryl Easlea
The life and times of one of the key partnerships in musical history who were best known as the quintessential disco band Chic. Led by Black Panther activist Nile Rodgers and family man Bernard Edwards, Chic released or produced a string of era-defining records: 'Le Freak', 'Good Times', 'We Are Family', 'Lost In Music'. When disco collapsed, so did Chic's popularity. However, Rodgers and Edwards individually produced some of the great pop dance records of the 80s, working with Bowie, Robert Palmer, Madonna and ABC among many others until Edwards's tragic death after a Chic reunion gig in Japan in 1996. *Everybody Dance* puts the rise and fall of the emblematic disco duo at the heart of a changing landscape, taking in socio-political and cultural events such as the Civil Rights struggle, the Black Panthers and the US oil crisis. There are drugs, bankruptcy, up-tight artists, fights, and Muppets but, most importantly an in-

depth appraisal of a group whose legacy remains hugely underrated.

'Daryl Easlea's triumphant *Everybody Dance* is the scholarly reappraisal the "black Roxy Music" deserve.' *Time Out*

'A lovingly crafted account of how Nile Rodgers and Bernard Edwards lovingly crafted some of the most sophisticated music of all time.' **** *The Observer*

| Paperback | ISBN 1-900924-56-0 | 288pp | 234 X 156mm | b/w illustrated throughout |
| UK £14.00 | US $19.95 | | | |

ISIS: A Bob Dylan Anthology
Edited by Derek Barker
Second outing for the acclaimed anthology, oral biography, reference book and listening guide from the ultimate Dylan experts. *ISIS* is the bestselling, longest lasting, most highly acclaimed Dylan fanzine. This fully revised and expanded edition of the ultimate Dylan anthology draws on unpublished interviews, further rare photos and research by the *ISIS* team together with the best articles culled from the pages of the definitive Bob magazine.

'This book is worth any Dylan specialist's money.' Ian MacDonald **** *Uncut*

| Paperback | ISBN 1-900924-82-X | 352pp | 198 X 129mm | 16pp b/w photos |
| UK £9.99 | US $17.95 | | | |

Smashing Pumpkins, Tales Of A Scorched Earth
By Amy Hanson
Initially contemporaries of Nirvana and Pearl Jam, Billy Corgan's Smashing Pumpkins outgrew and outlived the grunge scene with hugely acclaimed commercial triumphs like *Siamese Dream*, which legitimised heavy metal, and number one album *Mellon Collie and The Infinite Sadness*. Drugs, the death of a band member and other problems led to the band's final demise. Seattle-based Hanson followed the band for years and this is the first in-depth biography of their rise and fall.

'Extremely well-written – a thrilling and captivating read.' *Classic Rock*

| Paperback | ISBN 1-900924-68-4 | 256pp | 234 X 156mm | 8pp b/w photos |
| UK £12.99 | US $18.95 | | | |

Got A Revolution: The Turbulent Flight of Jefferson Airplane
By Jeff Tamarkin
Acclaimed music journalist Jeff Tamarkin chronicles the band's long, convoluted history – they were on the scene before the Grateful Dead, Janis Joplin, or Santana. Rendered in crisp, engaging prose and informed by scores of insider interviews with former band members, friends, lovers, crew members and fellow musicians this is their fascinating full-length story.

'This book brings it all back: the music by turns powerful and puzzling; the dysfunctional family-as-rock band!' *Rolling Stone*

| Paperback | ISBN 1-900924-78-1 | 408pp | 234 X 156mm | 8pp b/w photos |
| UK £14.99 | US No rights | | | |

Love: Behind the Scenes – on the Pegasus Carousel with the Legendary Rock Group Love
By Michael Stuart-Ware
Their masterpiece Forever Changes still regularly appears in critics' polls. Yet the band never truly fulfilled their potential and broke through to the LA premier league inhabited by Crosby, Stills and Nash and The Doors. Michael Stuart-Ware, Love's drummer, shares his inside perspective on the band's recording and performing career and tells how drugs and egos thwarted the potential of one of the great groups of the burgeoning psychedelic era. As one fellow band member tells him: 'There wasn't any love in that group. It had nothing whatsoever to do with love. It was all about hate. That should have been the name of the band.'

| Paperback | ISBN 1-900924-59-5 | 256pp | 234 X 156mm | |
| UK £14.00 | US $19.95 | | | |

The Fall: A User's Guide
By Dave Thompson
Album-by-album, track-by-track guide to the extensive, highly idiosyncratic 25-year oeuvre of one of rock's most enduring cult acts.

| Paperback | ISBN 1-900924-57-9 | 256pp | 234 X 156mm | b/w illustrated throughout |
| UK £12.99 | US $19.95 | | | |

Be Glad: An Incredible String Band Compendium
Edited by Adrian Whittaker
The ISB pioneered an eclectic, 'world music' approach on 60's albums like *The Hangman's Beautiful Daughter* – Paul McCartney's favourite album of 1967! – taking in experiments with theatre, film and lifestyles along the way and even inspiring Led Zeppelin. Featuring interviews with all the ISB key players, as well as a wealth of background information, reminiscence, critical evaluations and arcane trivia, this is a book that will delight any reader with more than a passing interest in the ISB.

| Paperback | ISBN 1-900924-64-1 | 288pp | 234 X 156mm | b/w illustrated throughout |
| UK £14.99 | US $19.95 | | | |

In Search of The La's – A Secret Liverpool
By Matthew Macefield
With timeless single 'There She Goes', Lee Mavers' La's briefly overtook The Stone Roses as the great hopes for British guitar rock and paved the way for Britpop. However, since 1991, The La's have been silent, while rumours of studio-perfectionism, madness and drug addiction have abounded. The author sets out to discover the truth behind Mavers' lost decade and subsequently gets drawn into the musical underground of a secret Liverpool before finally gaining a revelatory audience with Mavers himself.
Paperback   ISBN 1-900924-63-3   192pp   234 X 156mm   8pp b/w photos
UK £10.99   US $17.95

The Clash: The Return of the Last Gang in Town (revised)
By Marcus Gray
A revised edition of the exhaustively researched, definitive biography of the rock band whose instantly memorable hits 'London Calling,' 'Should I Stay or Should I Go' and 'Rock the Casbah' made them the greatest rock 'n' roll band of the post-60s era. The book vividly evokes the mid-70s environment out of which punk flourished, as the author traces their progress from pubs and punk clubs to US stadiums and the Top Ten. This edition is further updated to cover the band's recent induction into the Rock 'n' Roll Hall of Fame, band members' post-Clash careers and the tragic death of iconic frontman Joe Strummer.
   'Revised edition of the superb band biography. Gray masterfully deconstructs the Clash's self-mythology. A fascinating, fiery read.' **** Q
Paperback   ISBN 1-900924-62-5   448pp   234X 156mm   8pp b/w photos
UK £14.99

Surf's Up: The Beach Boys on Record 1961-1981
By Brad Elliott
A detailed chronicle of the group's extensive recording history replete with a 385-entry chronological discography, an extensive discussion of unreleased material including studio outtakes and radio and television appearances and over 100 photographs
Paperback   ISBN 1-900924-79-X   512pp   234 X 156mm   16pp b/w photos
UK £25.00

Get Back: The Beatles' Let It Be Disaster
By Doug Suply and Ray Shweighardt
A singularly candid look at the greatest band in history at their ultimate moment of crisis. It puts the reader in the studio as John cedes power to Yoko; Paul struggles to keep things afloat, Ringo shrugs and George quits the band.
   'One of the most poignant Beatles books ever.' Mojo
Paperback   ISBN 1-900924-83-8   352pp   198 X 129mm
UK £9.99

Hit Men: Powerbrokers and Fast Money Inside The Music Business
By Fredric Dannen
Hit Men **exposes the seamy and sleazy dealings of America's glitziest record companies:** payola, corruption, drugs, Mafia involvement and excess.
   'The best book ever written on the business side of the music industry... Unreservedly recommended.' Music Week
Paperback   ISBN 1-900924-54-4   416pp   234 X 156mm
UK £14.99

The Big Wheel
By Bruce Thomas
Thomas was bassist with Elvis Costello and The Attractions at the height of the band's success. Though names are never mentioned, *The Big Wheel* paints a vivid and hilarious picture of exactly what it is like touring the world with Costello and co, sharing your life 24 hours a day with a moody egotistical singer, a crazed drummer and a host of hangers-on. Originally published by Viking in 1990, Costello sacked Thomas for writing it.
   'Laugh-out loud tales pepper the pages...conveys a wit that readers of Motley Crue's The Dirt will find hard to fathom.' Q ****
Paperback   ISBN 1-900924-53-6   192pp   235 X 156mm
UK £10.99

Pink Floyd: A Saucerful of Secrets
By Nicholas Schaffner
From the psychedelic explorations of the Syd Barrett-era to 70s superstardom with *Dark Side of the Moon*, and on to the triumph of *The Wall*, before internecine strife tore the group apart, Schaffner's definitive history also covers the improbable return of Pink Floyd without Roger Waters, and the hugely successful *Momentary Lapse of Reason* album and tour.
   'Schaffner succeeds ...this remains all but definitive.' Q****
Paperback   ISBN 1-900924-52-8   352pp   235 X 156mm   8pp b/w photos
UK £14.99

Waiting for the Man: The Story of Drugs and Popular Music
By Harry Shapiro
Fully revised edition of the classic story of two intertwining billion dollar industries. From marijuana and early jazz, through acid-rock, speed-fuelled punk, to crack-driven rap and ecstasy and the Dance Generation, this is the definitive history of drugs and pop.

'Wise and witty.' *The Guardian*

Paperback   ISBN 1-900924-58-7   304pp   198 X 129mm
UK £10.99   US $18.95

The Buzzcocks: Harmony in My Head – Steve Diggle's Rock 'n' Roll Odyssey
By Terry Rawlings and Steve Diggle
First-hand account of the punk wars from guitarist and one half of the songwriting duo that gave the world three chord punk-pop classics like 'Ever Fallen In Love' and 'Promises'. Diggle dishes the dirt on punk contemporaries like The Sex Pistols, The Clash and The Jam, as well as sharing poignant memories of his friendship with Kurt Cobain, on whose last ever tour, The Buzzcocks were the support act.

'As a first hand account from the punk front lines, it's invaluable, but it works best as a straightforward sex, drugs and rock 'n' roll memoir.'**** *Uncut*

Paperback   ISBN 1-900924-37-4   304pp   235 X 156mm
UK £14.99   US $19.95

The Dark Reign of Gothic Rock: In The Reptile House with The Sisters of Mercy, Bauhaus and The Cure
By Dave Thompson
From Joy Division to Nine Inch Nails and from Siouxsie and the Banshees to Marilyn Manson, gothic rock has endured as the cult of choice for the disaffected and the alienated. During the mid-80s it was the underground alternative to the glossy throwaway pop of the day. The author traces the rise of 80s and 90s goth from influences such as Hammer House of Horror movies and schlock novels, through post-punk into the full blown drama of Bauhaus, The Cure and the Sisters of Mercy.

Paperback   ISBN 1-900924-48-X   288pp   235 X 156mm   8pp b/w photos
UK £14.99   US $19.95

Back to the Beach: A Brian Wilson and the Beach Boys Reader
Edited by Kingsley Abbott
Revised and expanded edition of the Beach Boys compendium *Mojo* **magazine deemed an 'essential purchase.'** This collection includes all of the best articles, interviews and reviews from the Beach Boys' four decades of music, including definitive pieces by Timothy White, Nick Kent and David Leaf. New material reflects on the tragic death of Carl Wilson and documents the rejuvenated Brian's return to the boards.

'Riveting!' **** Q

Paperback   ISBN 1-900924-46-3   288pp   235 X 156mm
UK £14.00   US $18.95

Serge Gainsbourg: A Fistful of Gitanes
By Sylvie Simmons
Rock press legend Simmons' hugely acclaimed biography of the French genius tells the story of the classy, sleazy, sexy, funny, hard-drinking, chain-smoking Gallic icon who invented French pop and inspired a new generation of louche wannabes.

'I would recommend *A Fistful of Gitanes* [as summer reading] which is a highly entertaining biography of the French singer-songwriter and all-round scallywag.' JG Ballard

Paperback   ISBN 1-900924-40-4   288pp   198 X 129mm
UK £9.99

Blues: The British Connection
By Bob Brunning
Former Fleetwood Mac member Bob Brunning's classic account of the impact of blues in Britain, from its beginnings as the underground music of 50s teenagers like Mick Jagger, Keith Richards and Eric Clapton, to the explosion in the 60s, right through to the vibrant scene of the present day.

'An invaluable reference book and an engaging personal memoir.' Charles Shaar Murray

Paperback   ISBN 1-900924-41-2   288pp   198 X 129mm
UK £14.99   US $19.95

King Crimson: In The Court of King Crimson
By Sid Smith
King Crimson's 1969 masterpiece *In The Court Of The Crimson King*, **was a huge US chart hit.** The band followed it with further albums of consistently challenging, distinctive and innovative music. Drawing on hours of new interviews, and encouraged by Crimson supremo Robert Fripp, the author traces the band's turbulent history year by year, track by track.

Paperback   ISBN 1-900924-26-9   288pp   234 X 156mm   b/w Illustrated throughout
UK £14.99   US $19.95

A Journey Through America with the Rolling Stones
By Robert Greenfield
Featuring a new foreword by Ian Rankin. This is the definitive account of The Stones' legendary '72 tour.
'The Stones on tour in '72 twist and burn through their own myth: from debauched outsiders to the first hints of the corporate business – the lip-smacking chaos between the Stones fan being stabbed by a Hell's Angel at Altamont and the fan owning a Stones credit card.' Paul Morley #2 essential holiday rock reading list, *The Observer*

Paperback	ISBN 1-900924-24-2	256pp	198 X 129mm	
UK £9.99	US $17.95			

BACKLIST

Title	ISBN	pp	UK	US
The Nice: Hang On To A Dream By Martyn Hanson	1900924439	256pp	£13.99	$19.95
Marc Bolan and T Rex: A Chronology By Cliff McLenahan	1900924420	256pp	£13.99	$19.95
Razor Edge: Bob Dylan and The Never-ending Tour By Andrew Muir	1900924137	256pp	£12.99	$18.95
Calling Out Around the World: A Motown Reader Edited by Kingsley Abbott	1900924145	256pp	£13.99	$18.95
I've Been Everywhere: A Johnny Cash Chronicle By Peter Lewry	1900924226	256pp	£14.99	$18.95
Sandy Denny: No More Sad Refrains By Clinton Heylin	1900924358	288pp	£13.99	$18.95
Animal Tracks: The Story of The Animals By Sean Egan	1900924188	256pp	£12.99	$18.95
Like a Bullet of Light: The Films of Bob Dylan By CP Lee	1900924064	224pp	£12.99	$ n/a
Rock's Wild Things: The Troggs Files By Alan Clayson and J Ryan	1900924196	224pp	£12.99	$ n/a
Dylan's Daemon Lover By Clinton Heylin	1900924153	192pp	£12.00	$ n/a
XTC: Song Stories By XTC and Neville Farmer	190092403X	352pp	£12.99	$ n/a
Born in the USA: Bruce Springsteen By Jim Cullen	190092405-6	320pp	£9.99	$ n/a
Bob Dylan By Anthony Scaduto	1900924234	320pp	£10.99	$17.95

Firefly Publishing: An Association between Helter Skelter and SAF

The Nirvana Recording Sessions
By Rob Jovanovic
Drawing on years of research, and interviews with many who worked with the band, the author has documented details of every Nirvana recording, from early rehearsals, to the *In Utero* sessions. A fascinating account of the creative process of one of the great bands.
'Manna from heaven for the completists ... A painstakingly exhaustive catalogue of every track at every session.... The author's determination to concentrate purely on the music is admirable... If you're planning to invest in the box set, this will make an excellent companion piece.' Kerrang

Hardback	ISBN 0-946719-60-8	224pp	234 X 156mm	b/w illustrated throughout
UK £20.00	US $30.00			

Thin Lizzy: Soldiers of Fortune
By Alan Byrne
Led by Dublin-born Phil Lynott, Thin Lizzy forged a brand of carefully crafted pop, mixed with hard-edged rock panache. This, coupled with their hard drinking, ladykilling, rock'n'roll reputation, made them one of the most successful musical exports from Ireland throughout the seventies. Lynott himself was an interesting character; a hopeless romantic, he was raised by his mother following the disappearance of his father, his six-foot plus wiry frame and the label of 'the only black man in Dublin' ensured that he stood out from the crowd. Alan Byrne has spent the last five years carefully researching this book – he has interviewed more than 100 people, from Lynott's mother Philomena, through band members Brian Robertson, Scott Gorham and Brian Downey, as well as collaborators who worked with them over the years.
'Respectful but vibrant account of Lynott's rambunctious life.' **** *Uncut*

Hardback	ISBN 0-946719-57-8	224pp	234 X 156mm	8pp b/w photos
UK £20.00	US $30.00			

Prince: Dancemusicsexromance
By Per Nilsen
Chronicles in-depth the Purple one's hugely prolific first decade, when he transformed the state of black music and, with tracks as diverse as 'When Doves Cry', 'Purple Rain' and 'Sign of the Times' established himself as the first music icon of the 80s.

Paperback	ISBN 0-946719-64-0	352pp	198 X 129mm	8pp b/w photos
UK £9.99	US $14.95			

U2: The Complete Encyclopedia (Fully revised and updated)
By Mark Chatterton
Definitive compendium of facts, anecdotes and insights about the biggest band in the world.

Paperback	ISBN 0-946719-63-2	320pp	246 X 174mm	b/w illustrated throughout
UK £16.99	US $24.95			

The Music of George Harrison: While My Guitar Gently Weeps
By Simon Leng
Santana biographer Leng takes a studied, track by track, look at both Harrison's contribution to The Beatles, and the solo work that started with the release in 1970 of his epic masterpiece *All Things Must Pass*. 'Here Comes The Sun', 'Something' – which Sinatra covered and saw as the perfect love song – 'All Things Must Pass' and 'While My Guitar Gently Weeps' are just a few of Harrison's classic songs.

Hardback	ISBN 0-946719-50-0	256pp	234 X 156mm	8pp b/w photos
UK £20.00	US $26.00			

The Pretty Things: Growing Old Disgracefully				
	0946719454	224pp	£20.00	$30.00
By Alan Lakey				
The Sensational Alex Harvey	0946719470	224pp	£20.00	$30.00
By John Neil Murno				
Poison Heart: Surviving The Ramones	0946719489	224pp	£9.99	$ n/a
By Dee Dee Ramone and Veronica Kofman	(Sold, USA, Brazil)			
To Hell and Back with Catatonia	0946719365	224pp	£12.99	$18.95
By Brian Wright				
Soul Sacrifice: The Santana Story	0946719292	224pp	£12.99	$18.95
By Simon Leng	Rights available (Sold, Germany, Poland, Spain, Italy)			
Opening The Musical Box: A Genesis Chronicle				
	0946719306	224pp	£12.99	$18.95
By Alan Hewitt				
Blowin' Free: Thirty Years Of Wishbone Ash				
	0946719330	224pp	£12.99	$18.95
By Gary Carter and Mark Chatterton				
Minstrels in the Gallery: A History of Jethro Tull				
	0946719225	224pp	£12.99	$18.95
By David Rees	Rights sold (Germany, Czech Republic)			

www.helterskelterbooks.com

Email: info@helterskelterbooks.com